American Foreign Relations

VOLUME 2

A History · Since 1895

BRIEF EDITION

Thomas G. Paterson

J. Garry Clifford

Shane J. Maddock

Deborah Kisatsky

Kenneth J. Hagan

HOUGHTON MIFFLIN COMPANY

Boston   New York

Publisher: *Charles Hartford*
Senior Sponsoring Editor: *Sally Constable*
Senior Development Editor: *Jeffrey Greene*
Project Editor: *Kerry Doyle*
Senior Marketing Manager: *Sandra McGuire*
Manufacturing Coordinator: *Priscilla Manchester*

Cover art: William H. Johnson (1901–1970), *Historical Scene WWII (China After WWII),* ca. 1945. © Smithsonian American Art Museum, Washington, D.C./ Art Resource, N.Y.

Printed in the U.S.A.

Library of Congress Control Number: 2005930482

ISBN: 0-618-38222-4

2 3 4 5 6 7 8 9-CRS-09 08

for

Colin Graham Paterson

Carol Davidge

Vera Low Hagan

Emily Rose Maddock

About the Authors

Thomas G. Paterson, professor emeritus of history at the University of Connecticut, graduated from the University of New Hampshire (B.A., 1963) and the University of California, Berkeley (Ph.D., 1968). He has written *Soviet-American Confrontation* (1973), *Meeting the Communist Threat* (1988), *On Every Front* (1992), *Contesting Castro* (1994), *America Ascendant* (with J. Garry Clifford, 1995), and *A People and a Nation* (with Mary Beth Norton et al., 2001). Tom has also edited *Cold War Critics* (1971), *Kennedy's Quest for Victory* (1989), *Imperial Surge* (with Stephen G. Rabe, 1992), *The Origins of the Cold War* (with Robert McMahon, 1999), *Explaining the History of American Foreign Relations* (with Michael J. Hogan, 2004), and *Major Problems in American Foreign Relations* (with Dennis Merrill, 2005). With Bruce Jentleson, he served as senior editor for the *Encyclopedia of American Foreign Relations* (1997). A microfilm edition of *The United States and Castro's Cuba, 1950s–1970s: The Paterson Collection* appeared in 1999. He has served on the editorial boards of the *Journal of American History* and *Diplomatic History.* Recipient of a Guggenheim fellowship, he has directed National Endowment for the Humanities Summer Seminars for College Teachers. He is a past president of the Society for Historians of American Foreign Relations. In 2000 the New England History Teachers Association awarded him the Kidger prize for excellence in teaching and mentoring. Besides visits to many American campuses, Tom has lectured in Canada, China, Colombia, Cuba, New Zealand, Puerto Rico, Russia, and Venezuela.

J. Garry Clifford teaches at the University of Connecticut, where he is a professor of political science and director of its graduate program. Born in Massachusetts, he earned his B.A. from Williams College (1964) and his Ph.D. in history from Indiana University. He has also taught at the University of Tennessee and Dartmouth College and has taught in two National Endowment for the Humanities seminars for high school teachers at the Franklin D. Roosevelt Library. For his book *The Citizen Soldiers* (1972), he won the Frederick Jackson Turner Award of the Organization of American Historians. With Norman Cousins, he has edited *Memoirs of a Man: Grenville Clark* (1975), and with Samuel R. Spencer, Jr., he has written *The First Peacetime Draft* (1986). He also co-authored *America Ascendant* (with Thomas G. Paterson) in 1995. Garry's essays have appeared in Gordon Martel, ed., *American Foreign Relations Reconsidered* (1994), Michael J. Hogan and Thomas G. Paterson, eds., *Explaining the History of American Foreign Relations* (1991 and 2004), Arnold A. Offner and Theodore A. Wilson, eds., *Victory in Europe, 1945* (2000), and in the *Journal of American History, Review of Politics, Mid-America, American Neptune,* and *Diplomatic History.* Garry has served on the editorial board of *Diplomatic History* as well as on the editorial board of the Modern War Series of the University Press of Kansas. He frequently participates in American professional conferences and has also lectured in Russia and Northern Ireland.

Shane J. Maddock is associate professor of history at Stonehill College in Easton, Massachusetts, where he also serves on the faculty of the Martin Institute for Law and Society. Born in North Dakota, he earned his B.A. from Michigan State University (1989) and his

Ph.D. from the University of Connecticut (1997). He has also taught at the U.S. Coast Guard Academy. Shane has edited *The Nuclear Age* (2001) and has published in the *Journal of American History, International History Review, Pacific Historical Review, Presidential Studies Quarterly, Mid-America, Journal of Military History, American Jewish History, Canadian Journal of Latin American and Caribbean Studies, History in Dispute,* and *The Encyclopedia of U.S. Foreign Relations.* He has received fellowships from the Institute for the Study of World Politics, the U.S. Arms Control and Disarmament Agency, and the Hoover, Truman, Eisenhower, Kennedy, and Johnson presidential libraries. Shane has presented lectures and papers on his main research interests—U.S. nuclear nonproliferation policy and the intersection of popular culture and foreign relations. He is currently working on a book titled *The Nth Country Conundrum: The American and Soviet Quest to Halt the Spread of Nuclear Weapons, 1945–1970.*

Deborah Kisatsky is assistant professor of history at Assumption College in Worcester, Massachusetts. Born in Pennsylvania, she earned both her B.A. (1990) and her Ph.D. (2001) from the University of Connecticut. Deborah is the recipient of numerous awards and fellowships: the 1998–1999 Alexander von Humboldt Foundation Bundeskanzler (Federal Chancellor's) Scholarship for research in Germany, where she also served as a Junior Fellow of the Center for European Integration Studies, University of Bonn; the Myrna F. and Stuart L. Bernath Dissertation Grants of the Society for Historians of American Foreign Relations (1996 and 1999); a Franklin D. Roosevelt Library Lubin-Winant Fellowship (1996); and a Harry S. Truman Institute Research Grant (1996). She has published in *Intelligence and National Security, The Historian, Presidential Studies Quarterly,* and *The Journal of Interdisciplinary History,* as well as in the *Encyclopedia of U.S. Foreign Relations.* Deborah's book *The United States and the European Right, 1954–1955* was published by Ohio State University Press in fall 2005.

Kenneth J. Hagan is an adjunct professor on the faculty of the U.S. Naval War College, Monterey Program, and professor emeritus of history and museum director at the U.S. Naval Academy, Annapolis. He previously taught at Claremont McKenna College, Kansas State University, and the U.S. Army Command and General Staff College. A native of California, he received his B.A. and M.A. from the University of California, Berkeley (1958, 1964) and his Ph.D. from the Claremont Graduate School (1970). Ken is the author of *This People's Navy: The Making of American Sea Power* (1991), a comprehensive history of American naval strategy and policy since the Revolution, and *American Gunboat Diplomacy and the Old Navy, 1877–1889* (1973). His scholarship also includes two edited collections of original essays: *In Peace and War: Interpretations of American Naval History, 1775–1984* (1984) and *Against All Enemies: Interpretations of American Military History from Colonial Times to the Present* (1986). He frequently contributes articles to the journal *Naval History* and lectures annually at the Canadian Forces College in Toronto. Besides regularly participating in panels at conferences in the United States, he has given papers on the history of naval strategy in Sweden, Greece, Turkey, France, and Spain. A retired captain in the naval reserve, he served on active duty with the Pacific Fleet from 1958 to 1963 and currently advises the Naval ROTC college program on its history curriculum.

Contents

12 *Imperial America: The United States and the World
Since 1989*   **313**

Maps and Graphs

Preface

Since the first edition of *American Foreign Relations: A History* was published in the 1970s, a generation of teachers and students has used this textbook in college courses through six revised editions, the last of which appeared in 2005. Because the text is too long for many instructors, we have written an abridged version of *American Foreign Relations,* cutting the length by more than one-fourth. As colleagues and students have suggested, a briefer text allows instructors to assign more collateral reading. In preparing this abridgement, we have retained the basic narrative structure, chapter sequence, broad chronological and geographic coverage, and interpretive themes of the longer edition. Because we have deleted all endnotes in this brief edition, readers might wish to consult the 6th edition for the sources of quotations.

Cataclysmic events of the past few years have rekindled interest in the history of America's foreign relations. The triumphal ending of the Cold War fifteen years ago did not, as some have argued, signal the end of history. Nor has the passing of America's "greatest generation" of World War II heroes reduced history to nostalgic memories. Consider some recent headlines—shocking photographs of American military personnel inflicting torture and humiliation on Iraqi prisoners in Abu Ghraib prison near Baghdad, serious debates on the limits of dissent and whether terrorist enemies should be protected by the Geneva Convention, the reelection of President George W. Bush after a heated electoral campaign in which the Vietnam War records of both candidates became the focus of partisan debates, the death of Yasir Arafat and a possible new opportunity for peace between Palestinians and Israelis, the reorganization of America's intelligence agencies under a new director of national intelligence, ongoing concern about weapons of mass destruction, including possible "dirty" bombs from terrorists and putative nuclear threats from Iran and North Korea, continued complaints about America's behavior as a "hyperpower" despite efforts to repair rifts with allies, increased alarm over environmental decline and fast-spreading diseases such as AIDS, and finally a graphic demonstration of American humanitarianism as U.S. naval task forces airlifted food, expertise, and funds to tsunami victims in the Indian Ocean region in early 2005, followed by more extensive relief efforts personally led by former presidents Bill Clinton and George H. W. Bush. Indeed, much of what has happened since September 11, 2001, has riveted attention on America's global travails and how and why they came to be. *American Foreign Relations* seeks to introduce students to this complex history.

In this abridged edition we engage influential approaches and interpretations, especially those articulated by younger scholars. We seek to explain foreign relations in the broadest manner as the many ways that peoples, organizations, states, and systems interact—economic, cultural, strategic, environmental, political, and more. Our text emphasizes the theme of expansionism, explaining its many manifestations. We also show that on almost every issue in the history of American foreign relations, alternative voices unfailingly sounded among and against official policymakers. Americans have always debated their place in the world, their wars, their overseas commitments, and the status of their principles and power, and they have always debated the people of other nations about the spread of U.S. influence. We try to capture with vivid description and quotation the drama of the many debates.

A historical overview such as this one necessarily draws on the copious work of scholars in the United States and abroad. Their expertise informs this book throughout and helps lend it the authority instructors and students expect. Our "Further Reading" sections are one way to thank them for their books, articles, and conference papers. We have also appreciated their recommendations for text revisions and their suggestions for teaching the courses for which this book is intended. We thank them, too, for challenging us to consider the many different approaches and theories that have commanded attention in this field, including world systems, corporatism, dependency, culture, psychology and personality, medical biography, lessons from the past ("thinking in time"), bureaucratic politics, public opinion, executive-legislative competition, gender, national security and power, impact on recipients of foreign aid, the natural environment, and ideology. This book also presents the findings of our own ongoing archival research and writing as we discover and rediscover the past.

The traditional topics of diplomacy, war, economic intercourse, and politics remain central to our presentation of the foreign-relations story. We also discuss the cultural dimensions of foreign relations: race-based and gender-based images of other peoples that condition the decisionmaking environment; how the "reel" world of films reflects cultural myths and captures public perceptions of international events; the proliferation abroad of American mass culture (such as rock and roll and sports); the foreign responses to "Americanization"; travel and tourism that help create a pool of knowledge about foreign places that promotes an expansionist consciousness; and cultural transfer through "public diplomacy"—the presentation of a positive image of the United States abroad through, for example, propaganda, radio and television, and trade fairs. We especially stress the self-conscious expansion of American "empire" from its westward displacement of Native Americans in the eighteenth and nineteenth centuries to its overseas incarnations in the twentieth and twenty-first centuries. Issues that spring from human interaction with the natural environment and the international conferences convened to deal with damage to the environment also receive attention, as does the linkage between the civil rights movement and American foreign relations with the Third World in the 1940s through the 1960s. New scholarship prompted by anniversaries—such as the Louisiana Purchase and Lewis and Clark expedition, the Spanish-American-Cuban-Filipino War, victory in World War II, the Cuban Missile Crisis, and the Vietnam War, among others—have enabled us to bring fresh insights to these important events.

Equally important, with the Cold War International History Project providing scholars with a treasure trove of declassified documents from foreign archives (Russian, East German, Cuban, and Chinese among them), we offer fresh insights into Joseph Stalin's goals and tactics during and after World War II, the origins of the Korean War, Sino-American relations, Cuban policy toward Africa, the Soviet invasion of Afghanistan, the failure of détente in the 1970s, and the end of the Cold War in

1989–1991. Similarly, recently declassified U.S. government documents made available via "electronic briefing books" from the National Security Archive have added nuance to our coverage, for example, of the India–Pakistan War of 1971 and the Indonesian invasion of East Timor in 1976, as well as new evidence regarding Washington's Cold War initiatives toward the Soviet Union, the People's Republic of China, and Fidel Castro's Cuba. The declassification, duplication, and public release of presidential audiotapes from the Kennedy, Johnson, and Nixon years help to recapture their colorful language and reveal how the assumptions, styles, and emotions of these leaders influenced their decisionmaking.

In preparing this edition, we once again immersed ourselves in the memoirs, diaries, letters, speeches, recorded tapes, and oral histories of U.S. and international leaders. We often let them speak for themselves in the frankest terms, guarded and unguarded. We have sought to capture their anger and their humor, their cooperation and their competitiveness, their truths and their lies, their moments of doubt and times of confidence, their triumphs and setbacks. This brief edition, in short, strives to capture the erratic pulse of international relations through peoples' struggles to plan, decide, and administer. We study not only the leaders who made influential decisions, but also the world's peoples who welcomed, resisted, or endured the decisions that profoundly influenced their lives. In this regard, we have drawn on the growing scholarship that studies non-state actors, including peace groups, African Americans, and international bodies such as the World Health Organization.

Each chapter opens with a significant and dramatic event—a "Diplomatic Crossroad"—that helps illustrate the chief characteristics and issues of the era. The introductory and concluding sections of each chapter set the themes. Illustrations from collections around the world are closely tied to the narrative in image and caption description. The maps, graphs, and "Makers of American Foreign Relations" tables in each chapter provide essential information. The up-to-date chapter bibliographies guide further reading and serve as a starting point for term or research papers.

In the late 1970s, the People's Republic of China adopted a new system for rendering Chinese phonetic characters into the Roman alphabet. Called the Pinyin method, it replaced the Wade-Giles technique, which had long been used in English. Use of the Pinyin method is now common, and we use it in *American Foreign Relations.* Many changes are minor—Shantung has become Shandong and Mao Tsetung has become Mao Zedong, for example. But when we have a possibly confusing Pinyin spelling, we have placed the Wade-Giles spelling in parentheses—for example, Beijing (Peking) or Jiang Jieshi (Chiang Kai-shek).

Instructors and students interested in the study of foreign-relations history are invited to join the Society for Historians of American Foreign Relations (SHAFR). This organization publishes a superb journal, *Diplomatic History,* and a newsletter; offers book, article, and lecture prizes and dissertation research grants; and holds an annual conference where scholars present their views and research results. Dues are very reasonable. For information, contact the SHAFR Business Office, Department of History, Ohio State University, 106 Dulles Hall, 230 West 17th Avenue, Columbus, OH 43210, or visit their website, *http://www.shafr.org.*

Another informative website is H-Diplo: Diplomatic History, found at *http://www.h-net.org/~diplo/.* Besides presenting provocative on-line discussions on foreign-relations history, this site also provides research and bibliographic aids and an extensive list of links to other useful resources, including journals, newspapers, archives and presidential libraries, research organizations such as the National Security Archive, and government agencies such as the Central Intelligence Agency and Department of State.

Many colleagues, friends, students, and editors contributed to this brief edition and to earlier editions of *American Foreign Relations* by providing research leads, correction of errors, reviews of the text, library searches, documents and essays, and editorial assistance. At Houghton Mifflin we give our heartiest thanks to Jean L. Woy, senior consulting editor; Frances Gay, senior development editor; Jeff Greene, senior development editor; Kerry Doyle, project editor; and Nancy Benjamin at Books By Design.

We are also eager to thank the many people who helped us in the previous editions of the longer book: Philip J. Avillo, Jr., Richard Baker, Ann Balcolm, Michael A. Barnhart, Derick Becker, Robert Beisner, R. Christian Berg, Kenneth J. Blume, Mark Boyer, Richard Bradford, Kinley J. Brauer, John Burns, Richard Dean Burns, Michael Butler, Robert Buzzanco, Charles Conrad Campbell, Chen Jian, John Coogan, Alejandro Corbacho, Frank Costigliola, Carol Davidge, Mark Del Vecchio, Ralph Di Carpio, Justus Doenecke, Michael Donaghue, Regina Egan, Robert H. Ferrell, David S. Foglesgong, Xavier Franco, Irwin Gellman, Paul Goodwin, James Gormly, Eric Hafter, Peter Hahn, Robert E. Hannigan, Hope M. Harrison, Alan Henrikson, Gregg Herken, George Herring, Ted Hitchcock, Joan Hoff, Kristin Hoganson, Reginald Horsman, Michael Hunt, Edythe Izard, Holly Izard, Richard Izard, Leith Johnson, Burton Kaufman, Melville T. Kennedy, Jr., Thomas Lairson, Lester Langley, Thomas M. Leonard, Li Yan, Terrence J. Lindell, Florencia Luengo, Martha McCoy, David McFadden, Charles McGraw, Elizabeth McKillen, Matt McMahon, Robert McMahon, Elizabeth Mahan, Paul Manning, Herman Mast, Dennis Merrill, Jean-Donald Miller, William Mood, Jay Mullen, Carl Murdock, Brian Murphy, R. Kent Newmyer, Arnold Offner, John Offner, Marc O'Reilly, Chester Pach, Jerry Padula, Carol Petillo, David Pletcher, Salvadore Prisco, Stephen G. Rabe, Carol S. Repass, Wayne Repeta, Barney J. Rickman III, Michael Roskin, John Rourke, Nicholas Evan Sarantakes, Kenneth E. Shewmaker, Kent M. Schofield, David Sheinin, Anna Lou Smethurst, Elbert B. Smith, Kevin Smith, Thomas G. Smith, Larry Spongberg, Jennifer Sterling-Folker, Kenneth R. Stevens, Mark A. Stoler, Stephen M. Streeter, William W. Stueck, Jr., Duane Tananbaum, George Turner, Jonathan G. Utley, Thomas Walker, Wang Li, Kathryn Weathersby, Ralph E. Weber, Edmund S. Wehrle, Immanuel Wexler, Lawrence Wittner, Sol Woolman, Sherry Zane, and Thomas Zoumaras.

We welcome comments and suggestions from students and instructors.

T. G. P.
J. G. C.
S. J. M.
D. K.
K. J. H.

CHAPTER ✤ 1

Imperialist Leap,
1895–1900

✖ *The* Maine, *McKinley, and War, 1898*

THE SLEEK U.S. BATTLESHIP *Maine* steamed into Havana harbor on January 25, 1898. "A beautiful sight," reported the American consul-general Fitzhugh Lee, who had requested the visit ostensibly to protect Americans living in war-torn Cuba. Spain was then in its third year of attempting to suppress Cuban rebels fighting for national independence. The *Maine* was to stay three weeks and then depart for New Orleans in time for Mardi Gras. But at 9:40 P.M. on February 15, a "dull sullen" roar followed by massive explosions ripped through the 6,700-ton ship, killing 266 Americans. President William McKinley, who had been taking drugs to sleep, awoke an hour before dawn for a phone call from Secretary of the Navy John D. Long. "The *Maine* blown up! The *Maine* blown up!" the stunned president kept muttering. Even though "the country was not ready" for it, the war with Spain that McKinley was laboring so hard to avoid would occur within three months.

McKinley ordered an official investigation of the *Maine* disaster and tried to gain time. With no evidence but with considerable emotion, many Americans assumed that the *Maine* had been "sunk by an act of dirty treachery on the part of the Spaniards." In early March U.S. Minister Stewart L. Woodford protested strongly to the Spanish about the *Maine*. "End it at once—*end it at once—end it at once!*" he exhorted Madrid regarding the war in Cuba. On March 6 the president met with Joe Cannon, chair of the House Appropriations Committee, and asked for $50 million for war preparedness. Congress enthusiastically obliged three days later.

In mid-March Senator Redfield Proctor of Vermont, a friend of McKinley reportedly opposed to war, graphically told his colleagues about his recent visit to Cuba. He recounted ugly stories about the forced concentration of Cubans into fortified camps: "Torn from their homes, with foul earth, foul air, foul water, and foul food or none, what wonder that one-half died and one-quarter of the living are so diseased that they cannot be saved?" Shortly after this moving speech, which convinced many members of Congress and business leaders that Spain could not restore order to Cuba, the U.S. court of inquiry on the *Maine* concluded that an external

1

U.S.S. *Maine* Entering Havana Harbor. The gleaming white battleship, commanded by Captain Charles Sigsbee, arrived in Havana on January 25, 1898, ostensibly to protect American citizens caught up in the Cuban rebellion against Spanish rule. Because a few sailors had been swept overboard and drowned on earlier missions, the *Maine* had the reputation of being a "Jonah" or "Hoodoo" ship. (Courtesy National Archives—SC-94543)

mine of unknown origin had destroyed the vessel. A Spanish commission at about the same time attributed the disaster to an internal explosion. (More than a century later, after several more investigations, experts still disagree whether the *Maine* blew up because of "a coal bunker fire" or from an "undership mine.") In 1898 vocal Americans pinned "the crime" squarely on Spain. "Remember the *Maine,* to hell with Spain" became a popular slogan.

A decorated veteran of the Civil War, President McKinley once asserted: "I have been through one war; I have seen the dead piled up, and I do not want to see another." He quietly explored the possibility of purchasing Cuba for $300 million— or some other means "by which Spain can part with Cuba without loss of respect and with certainty of American control." But a jingo frenzy had seized Congress. Interventionist critics increasingly questioned the president's manhood, claiming, as did Assistant Secretary of the Navy Theodore Roosevelt, that he "had no more backbone than a chocolate eclair." One member of Congress called McKinley's policies on Cuba "lame, halting, and impotent," while another claimed: "He wobbles, he waits, he hesitates. He changes his mind." Following one stormy Senate session, Vice President Garrett Hobart warned: "They will act without you if you do not act at once." "Say no more," McKinley responded.

On March 27, the president cabled his demands to Madrid: an armistice, Cuban-Spanish negotiations to secure a peace, McKinley's arbitration of the conflict if there was no peace by October, termination of the forced concentration policy, and relief aid to the Cubans. Implicit was the demand that Spain grant Cuba its independence under U.S. supervision. As a last-ditch effort to avoid American military intervention, the scheme had little chance of success. The Cubans had already vowed to accept "nothing short of absolute independence." Hoping to elicit European backing, Madrid's answer held some promise: Spain had already ended concentration, would launch reforms, and would accept an armistice if the rebels did so first. Yet by refusing McKinley's mediation and Cuban independence, the Spanish reply fell short. McKinley began to compose a war message in early April. On April 9, Spain declared a unilateral suspension of hostilities "for such a length of time" as the Spanish commander "may think prudent." The declaration still sidestepped Cuban independence and U.S. mediation. Any chance of European support for Spain faded when the British told Washington that they would "be guided [on Cuban issues] by the wishes of the president." On April 11, McKinley asked Congress for authority to use armed force to end the Cuban war. Since neither Cubans nor Spaniards could stem the blood-letting, Americans would do so because of the "cause of humanity" and the "very serious injury to the commerce, trade, and business of our people, and the wanton destruction of property." Conspicuously, he made no mention of Cuban independence, defining the U.S. purpose as "forcible intervention . . . as a neutral to stop the war." At the very end of the message, McKinley asked Congress to give "your just and careful attention" to news of Spain's recently offered armistice.

As Congress debated, McKinley beat back a Senate attempt to recognize the rebels. He strongly believed that Cuba needed American tutelage to prepare for self-government. And he wanted a Cuba subservient to the United States. Congress did endorse the Teller Amendment, which disclaimed any U.S. intent to annex the island. Even Teddy Roosevelt supported the amendment lest "it seem that we are merely engaged in a land-grabbing war." On April 19 Congress proclaimed Cuba's independence (without recognizing the Cuban junta), demanded Spain's evacuation from the island, and directed the president to use force to secure these goals. Spain broke diplomatic relations on April 21. The next day U.S. warships began to blockade Cuba; Spain declared war on April 24. Congress issued its own declaration the next day.

Because of the Teller Amendment, the choice for war seemed selfless and humane, and for many Americans it undoubtedly was. But the decision had more complex motives. McKinley cited humanitarian concern, property, commerce, and the removal of a threat. Politics also mattered. Senator Henry Cabot Lodge told the White House that "if the war in Cuba drags on . . . we [Republicans] shall go down to the greatest defeat ever known." Important business leaders, initially hesitant, shifted in March and April to demand an end to Cuban disorder. Farmers and entrepreneurs ogling overseas markets thought a U.S. victory over Spain might open new trade doors by eliminating a colonial power. Republican senator George F. Hoar of Massachusetts, later an anti-imperialist, could not "look idly on while hundreds of thousands of innocent human beings . . . die of hunger close to our doors.

William McKinley (1843–1901). In one of his last speeches before his death in 1901, McKinley peered into the next century: "How near one to the other is every part of the world. Modern inventions have brought into close relations widely separated peoples . . . distances have been effaced. . . . The world's products are being exchanged as never before . . . isolation is no longer possible or desirable." (Library of Congress)

If there is ever to be a war it should be to prevent such things." Another senator claimed that "any sort of war is better than a rotting peace that eats out the core and heart of the manhood of this country." Christian missionaries dreamed of new opportunities to convert the "uncivilized." Imperialists hoped that war would add new territories to the United States and encourage the growth of a larger navy.

Emotional nationalism also made an impact. The *Maine* ignited what one educator called the "formidable inflammability of our multitudinous population." Imperialist senator Albert Beveridge waxed ebullient: "At last, God's hour has struck. The American people go forth in a warfare holier than liberty—holy as humanity." Excited statements by people such as Roosevelt, who regarded war as a sport, stirred martial fevers. War would repudiate those "old women of both sexes, shrieking cockatoos" who made virile men "wonder whether" they lived "in a free country or not." Newspapers of the "yellow press" variety, such as William Randolph Hearst's *New York Journal,* sensationalized stories of Spanish lust and atrocities. The American public, already steeped in a brash nationalism and prepared by earlier diplomatic triumphs, reacted favorably to the hyperbole.

Both Washington and Madrid had tried diplomacy without success. McKinley wanted "peace" and independence for Cuba under U.S. tutelage. The first Spain could not deliver because the Cuban rebels sensed victory and complete independence. The second Spain could not grant immediately because ultranationalists might overthrow the Bourbon constitutional monarchy. When Spain promised to fight the war more humanely and grant autonomy, McKinley and Congress wanted more, and they believed they had the right and duty to judge the affairs of Spain and Cuba.

Well-meaning or not, American meddling prevented Cubans and Spaniards from settling their own affairs. Dispatching the *Maine* and asking Congress for $50 million probably encouraged the Cuban rebels to resist any compromise. McKinley could have given Spain more breathing space. Spain, after all, did grant partial autonomy, which ultimately might have led to Cuban independence. Some critics said the president should have recognized the Cuban insurgents and covertly aided them. American materiél, not men, might have liberated Cuba from Spanish rule. By April 1898, one U.S. official concluded that Spain had become "absolutely hopeless, . . . exhausted financially and physically, while the Cubans are stronger." McKinley chose war reluctantly only after trying other options. That he adamantly refused to recognize the insurgency indicates also that he did not endorse outright Cuban independence. He probably had two goals in 1898: to remove Spain from Cuba and to control Cuba in some manner yet ill defined. When the Spanish balked at a sale and both belligerents rejected compromise, McKinley chose war—the only means to oust Spain *and* to control Cuba. A new and enlarged American empire was about to be created.

The Venezuela Crisis of 1895

Three years earlier, during the administration of an avowedly anti-imperialist president, a seemingly insignificant cartographic controversy in South America had served as a catalyst for empire. In July 1895, Secretary of State Richard Olney personally delivered a 12,000-word draft document to President Grover Cleveland on the Venezuelan boundary dispute. Deeming it "the best thing of its kind I ever read,"

"The Real British Lion." A popular American depiction of the British global presence during the crisis over Venezuela. A few years later, President Cleveland himself recalled British behavior as "mean and hoggish." (*New York Evening World*, 1895)

the president directed Olney to send the document to London, which he did on July 20.

What became known as Olney's "twenty-inch gun" was aimed at Great Britain, which had long haggled with Venezuela over its boundary with British Guiana. The British drew a line in the 1840s, but nobody liked it. In the 1880s, the discovery of gold in the region in question raised the stakes. Since the 1870s Venezuela had remonstrated against Britain's alleged violation of the Monroe Doctrine. Washington repeatedly asked the British to submit the issue to arbitration but met constant rebuff. London's latest refusal in December 1894 led to Olney's "twenty-inch gun" answer.

The Venezuelans had hired William L. Scruggs, a former U.S. minister to Caracas, to propagandize their case before the American public. His widely circulated pamphlet *British Aggression in Venezuela, or the Monroe Doctrine on Trial* (1895) stirred considerable sympathy for the South American nation. Stereotypes soon congealed: The land-grabbing British were robbing a poor hemispheric friend of the United States. A unanimous congressional resolution of February 1894, calling for arbitration, underscored growing U.S. concern. Cleveland's Democratic party had lost badly in the 1894 elections, and Republicans were attacking his administration as cowardly for not annexing Hawai'i. Bold action might recoup Democratic losses. As one Democrat advised Cleveland, "Turn this Venezuelan question up or down, North, South, East or West, and it is a 'winner.'"

The global imperial competition of the 1890s also pushed the president toward action. The British, already holding large stakes in Latin America, seemed intent on enlarging them. Like the French intervention in Mexico a generation earlier, London's claim against Venezuela became a symbol of European intrusion into the hemisphere. The economic depression of the 1890s also caused concern. Many Americans, including Cleveland, thought that overproduction had caused the slump and that expanding foreign trade could cure it. The National Association of Manufacturers, organized in 1895 to encourage exports, chose Caracas for its first overseas display of U.S. products. Might the British close this potential new market?

Cleveland also disliked bullies. He had already rejected Hawaiian annexation in part because he thought Americans had bullied the Hawaiians. Now the British were arrogantly slapping the Venezuelans. Defense of the Monroe Doctrine became his and Olney's maxim. In unvarnished language, the "twenty-inch gun" of July 20, 1895, warned that European partition of Africa should not repeat itself in Latin America. The "safety," "honor," and "welfare" of the United States were at stake, and the Monroe Doctrine stipulated that "any permanent political union between a European and an American state [was] unnatural and inexpedient." The Cleveland-Olney message stressed that Latin American countries "are friends and allies, commercially and politically, of the United States. To allow the subjugation of any one of them by a European power . . . signifies the loss of all the advantages incident to their natural relations with us." The forceful overriding theme of the note boldly addressed an international audience. "To-day the United States is practically sovereign on this continent, and its fiat is law upon the subjects to which it confines its interposition." And more: The United States's "infinite resources combined with its isolated position render it master of the situation and practically invulnerable as against any or all other powers." Finally, the message demanded arbitration and requested a British answer before Cleveland's annual message to Congress in December.

British prime minister Lord Salisbury received the missive with some surprise and sent it to the Foreign Office for study. Distracted by crises especially in Africa, Salisbury saw no urgency. In the late nineteenth century Anglophobic bombast was not unusual, especially before U.S. elections. Thus the British reply did not arrive until after Cleveland's annual message, which was actually quite tame on Venezuela. Salisbury's note, which smacked of the "peremptory schoolmaster trying—with faded patience—to correct the ignorance of dullards in Washington," denied the applicability of the Monroe Doctrine and dismissed any U.S. interest in the controversy.

On reading the note, Cleveland became "mad clean through." His special message to Congress on December 17 rang the alarm bell: England must arbitrate; the United States would create an investigating commission to set the true boundary line; then American action would follow. The message seemed an ultimatum, with the danger of war lurking throughout. Congress quickly voted funds for the commission. Republicans and Democrats rallied behind the president, and New York City police commissioner Theodore Roosevelt boomed: "Let the fight come if it must; . . . we would take Canada." With Irish-Americans volunteering to fight their ancient foe, the British ambassador reported: "Nothing is heard but the voice of the Jingo bellowing defiance to England."

War fevers cooled rapidly in early 1896. Many business leaders grew alarmed when the stock market plummeted, in part because British investors were pulling out. The *New York World* put out a special Christmas issue under the headline "PEACE AND GOOD WILL," suggesting the irrationality of war with Britain, a country so close in race, language, and culture. Even the U.S. ambassador in London feared the president had been "too *precipitate*" in joining "the camp of aggressiveness." But Cleveland never wanted war. He wanted peace on his terms.

What followed seemed anticlimactic. The British cabinet in early January 1896 decided to seek an "honourable settlement" with the United States. Facing a new dispute with Germany over South Africa, England needed friends, not enemies.

Formal talks continued until November 1896, when London and Washington agreed to set up a five-person arbitration board to define the boundary. Finally, in October 1899, that tribunal rejected the extreme claims of either party and generally followed the original line from the 1840s. The mouth of the Orinoco went to Venezuela, which came out of the dispute rather well, considering that neither the United States nor Britain cared much about Venezuela's national interest. In fact, both parties excluded Venezuela's duly accredited minister in Washington from the talks. Lobbyist William Scruggs complained that the United States sought to "*bulldoze* Venezuela." He had it right, but Washington's "sledgehammer subtlety" targeted others besides that South American nation. The overweening theme of the "twenty-inch gun" merits repeating: "To-day the United States is practically sovereign on this continent, and its fiat is law upon the subjects to which it confines its interposition."

Men of Empire

The Venezuelan crisis and the war with Spain punctuated an era of imperialist competition when, as one senator grandly put it: "The great nations are rapidly absorbing . . . all the waste areas of the earth . . . for civilization and the advancement of the race." Cleveland and McKinley helped move the United States toward world-power status. As examples of forceful, even aggressive, diplomacy, both events accelerated important trends. Besides ignoring the rights and sensibilities of small countries, both episodes revealed a United States more certain about the components of its "policy" and more willing to confront rivals. Both episodes stimulated what critics at the time called "jingoism." The Monroe Doctrine gained new status as a warning to European nations to curb their activities in the Western Hemisphere. Just as Cleveland went to the brink of war over Venezuela without consulting Congress, so McKinley, despite a jingo Congress and inflamed public opinion, reinforced presidential control over foreign policy.

In both crises Latin Americans learned again that the United States sought supremacy in the Western Hemisphere and would intervene when it saw fit. The Venezuela crisis and the outbreak of revolution in Cuba in 1895 intensified North American interest in the Caribbean, a significant dimension of which was economic. Coinciding with a severe economic depression at home, the potential loss

Makers of American Foreign Relations, 1895–1900

Presidents	Secretaries of State
Grover Cleveland, 1893–1897	Walter Q. Gresham, 1893–1895
	Richard Olney, 1895–1897
William McKinley, 1897–1901	John Sherman, 1897–1898
	William R. Day, 1898
	John Hay, 1898–1905

of markets in Venezuela and Cuba brought more attention to the theory of over-production as a cause of depression, which exports could allegedly cure. Commercial expansion received another boost.

The discord over Venezuela also helped foster Anglo-American rapprochement. Cooperation and mutual interest increasingly characterized relations thereafter between Washington and London. British diplomats cultivated U.S. friendship as a possible counterweight to growing German power, and Britain's support over Cuba and its subsequent deference regarding the Caribbean facilitated the emerging entente.

The chief way the United States could manage events in that area was through naval power. The Venezuelan crisis, joined by crises in Asia and the belief that naval construction would employ those idled by the depression, stimulated additional naval expansion. The Navy Act of 1896, for example, provided for three new battleships and ten new torpedo boats, several of which contributed to naval victories over Spain two years later.

By the end of the decade the United States had gained new U.S. colonies in the Pacific, Asia, and the Caribbean, a protectorate over Cuba, and Europe's recognition of U.S. hegemony in the Caribbean. By 1900, too, the United States had pledged to preserve the "Open Door" in China; its navy had just annihilated the Spanish fleet and ranked sixth in the world; and its export trade had grown to $1.5 billion. Steel and iron production almost equaled that of Britain and Germany combined. The postwar acquisition of new colonies suggests that *only then,* about 1898, did the United States become an imperialist world power. Having taken halting steps toward a larger empire before the depression of the 1890s, the United States then took the leap.

Theodore Roosevelt described the anti-imperialists in 1897 as "men of a bygone age" and "provincials." Indeed, anti-imperialism waned through the late nineteenth century. Increasing numbers of educated, economically comfortable Americans made the case for formal empire (colonies or protectorates) or informal empire (commercial domination). Naval officers, diplomats, politicians, farmers, skilled artisans, business leaders, and clergy made up what political scientists call the "foreign-policy public." Having access to lecterns to disperse their ideas, this "elite" helped move America to war and empire. Neither "public opinion" nor the jingoistic "yellow press" in the 1890s compelled the United States to war. Rather, two key elements stand out: a McKinley administration very much in charge of its diplomacy through skillful maneuvering, and a majoritarian view within the articulate "foreign-policy public" in favor of a vigorous outward thrust.

Analysis of the phrase "public opinion" helps explain the *hows* as distinct from the *whys* of decisionmaking. One often hears that "the man in the street" influenced a leader to follow a certain course of action. But "public opinion" did not comprise a unified, identifiable group speaking with one voice. Further, political leaders and other articulate, knowledgeable people often shaped the "public opinion" they wanted to hear by their very handling of events and their control over information—that is, leaders *led*. Social-science studies demonstrate that in the 1890s the people who counted, the people who expressed their opinion publicly in order to influence policy, numbered no more than 1.5 million to 3 million, or between 10 and 20 percent of the voting public. These upper- and middle-income groups, educated, active politically, constituted the "foreign-policy public." The "public opinion" the president heard in the 1890s did not come from the "people," but rather from a small, articulate segment alert to foreign-policy issues. Although this educated public counted anti-imperialists among them, the "foreign-policy public" leaned heavily toward the side of imperialism.

The president often dominates policymaking, even thwarting the advice of the "foreign-policy public" itself. President Cleveland, for example, successfully resisted pressure to annex Hawai'i and withdrew the treaty from the Senate, and he never let Congress or influential public opinion shape policy toward the Venezuelan crisis. Clamorous jingoes and a sensationalist press intruded in the 1890s, but the initiative in foreign affairs, unlike in the 1860s and 1870s, remained largely in executive hands, with Cleveland and McKinley "unabashed in their resistance" to "public opinion." In most historical periods, the public *reacts* to *immediate* events; the executive *acts* and *manages* with *long-term* policy considerations.

Cleveland and McKinley Confront *Cuba Libre,* 1895–1898

The year 1895 brought momentous events. The Venezuelan crisis, Japan's defeat of China in the Sino-Japanese War, and the outbreak of revolution in Cuba—all carried profound meaning for U.S. foreign relations. The sugar-rich island of Cuba, following its unsuccessful war for independence (1868–1878), suffered political repression and poverty. From 1880 to 1895, the Cuban national hero José Martí plotted from exile in the United States. In 1892 he organized the Cuban Revolutionary party, using U.S. territory to recruit men and money. Martí's opportunity came when Cuba's economy fell victim in 1894 to a new U.S. tariff, which raised duties on imported sugar and hence reduced Cuban sugar shipments to the United States. On February 24, 1895, with cries of *"Cuba Libre,"* the rebels opened their drive for independence.

Cuban revolutionaries kept a cautious eye on the United States, well known for its relentless interest in their nation's destiny. José Martí's fifteen-year stay in the United States had turned him into a critic of what he called "the monster,"—an "aggressive" and "avaricious" nation "full of hate" and "widespread spiritual coarseness." He asked rhetorically: "Once the United States is in Cuba, who will drive them out?" On May 19 Martí died in battle.

Cuban and Spanish military strategies produced destruction and death. Led by General Máximo Gómez, the *insurrectos* burned cane fields, blew up mills, and disrupted railroads, with the goal of rendering Cuba an economic liability to Spain. Spain, in turn, vowed to "use up the last peseta in her treasury and sacrifice the last of her sons" to retain Cuba. Although outnumbered (about 30,000 Cuban troops fought 200,000 Spanish) and lacking adequate supplies, the insurgents, with the sympathy of the populace, wore the Spanish down through guerrilla tactics. By late 1896 rebels controlled about two-thirds of the island, with the Spanish concentrated in coastal and urban enclaves. That year, to break the rebel stronghold in the rural areas, Governor General Valeriano y Nicolau Weyler instituted the brutal reconcentration program. He divided the island into districts and then herded one-half million Cubans into unsanitary fortified camps, where perhaps 200,000 people soon died. Weyler's soldiers regarded any Cubans outside the camps as rebels and hence targets for death; they also killed livestock, destroyed crops, and polluted water sources. This effort to starve the insurgents, combined with the rebels' destructive behavior, made a shambles of Cuba's society and economy.

The Cleveland administration could have recognized Cuban belligerency. But such an act, Olney noted, would relieve Spain of any responsibility for paying claims filed by Americans for properties destroyed in Cuba. Cleveland and Olney found recognition of Cuban independence even less appetizing, for they believed the Cubans ("the most inhumane and barbarous cutthroats in the world") incapable of self-government and feared anarchy and even racial war. Olney toyed with buying the island at one point. The Cleveland administration settled on hostility to the revolution and pressure on Spain to grant some autonomy. Lecturing to a foreign government seemed to work in the Venezuelan crisis; perhaps it would work with Cuba.

Prodded by a Republican Congress and by Spanish obstinacy in refusing reforms and adhering to force, Olney sent a note to Spain in April 1896. He urged a political solution that would leave "Spain her rights of sovereignty . . . yet secure to the [Cubans] all such rights and powers of local self-government as they [could] ask." Spain should initiate reforms short of independence. When Spain rejected Olney's advice, the Cleveland administration seemed stymied. It did not desire war, but it meant to protect U.S. interests. Congress kept asking for firm action. And in Havana, hotheaded Consul-General Fitzhugh Lee clamored for U.S. annexation. Cleveland did not feel he could fire Lee, nephew of General Robert E. Lee, because the incumbent president needed political friends at a time when Democrats were dumping him in favor of William Jennings Bryan. Consul-General Lee also warned that "there may be a revolution within a revolution," noting that Cuban insurgents vowed to redistribute property, which U.S. officials (and Creole elites) would not tolerate. It further nettled Cleveland and Olney that Spain had approached the courts of Europe for diplomatic support, with the argument that the Monroe Doctrine threatened all European powers.

British ambassador to Spain H. Drummond Wolff accurately claimed that for Cuba the United States wanted "peace with commerce." In December 1896, Cleveland reported that neither the Spanish nor the Cuban rebels had established their authority over the island. Americans felt a humanitarian concern, he said, and their trade and investments ("pecuniary interest") faced destruction. Further, the United States had to police the coastline to intercept unlawful expeditions. Spain must grant "home rule," but not independence, to "fertile and rich" Cuba to end the bloodshed and devastation. Otherwise, having thus far acted with "restraint," Washington might abandon its "expectant attitude." But Cleveland had more bark than bite. Through Olney he successfully buried a Senate resolution urging recognition of Cuban independence and acknowledged limited Spanish reforms of February 1897. Thereafter he bequeathed Cuba to the incoming McKinley administration.

President William McKinley had defeated William Jennings Bryan in the election of 1896. The teetotaling Ohioan seemed a stable, dignified figure in a time of crisis. He projected deep religious conviction, personal warmth, sincerity, party loy-

Uncle Sam—"All That You Need Is Backbone." This cartoon depicts a tall, erect Uncle Sam shoving a rifle down President McKinley's coat to provide him with a backbone. As the historian Kristin Hoganson points out in *Fighting for American Manhood* (1998), expansionist critics of McKinley often accused the president of being weak, flabby, and vacillating because he did not immediately leap into war with Spain. (*Chicago Chronicle,* in *Cartoons of the War of 1898 with Spain,* Chicago, 1898)

alty, and support for expansion abroad. Yet McKinley often gave the appearance of being a pliant follower, a mindless flunky of the political bosses. Cartoonists often depicted him in women's dress and called him a "goody-goody" man. Such an image was created in large part by bellicose imperialists who believed that McKinley was not moving fast enough. Certainly a party regular and friend of large corporations, the president was no lackey. A manager of diplomacy, who wanted a settlement of the Cuban question without U.S. military intervention, McKinley acted as his own man.

McKinley shared America's image of itself as an expanding, virile nation of superior institutions and as a major power in Latin America. He agreed that the United States must have a large navy, overseas commerce, and foreign bases. As a tariff specialist who wanted America to export its surplus, he favored high tariffs on manufactured goods, low tariffs on raw materials, and reciprocity agreements. The Republican party platform of 1896 overflowed with expansionist rhetoric. It urged American control of Hawai'i, a Nicaraguan canal run by the United States, an enlarged navy, purchase of the Virgin Islands, and Cuban independence. Before inauguration, however, McKinley quietly joined Cleveland in sidetracking a Senate resolution for recognition of Cuba. He wanted a free hand, and he did not believe that Cubans could govern themselves. His inaugural address vacuously urged peace, never mentioning the Cuban crisis.

Beginning in March 1897, resolutions on Cuba sprang up repeatedly, but McKinley managed to kill them. He did satisfy imperialists by sending a Hawaiian annexation treaty to the Senate. In June, Madrid received a nonpublic American rebuke for Weyler's uncivilized warfare and for his disruption of the Cuban economy. Spain, however, showed no signs of tempering its military response to the insurrection. U.S. citizens languished in Spanish jails; American property continued to be razed. In July, McKinley instructed Minister Woodford to demand that the Spanish stop the fighting. Increasingly convinced that the Cuban *insurrectos* would not compromise, the president implored Spain to grant autonomy. A new Spanish government soon moderated policy by offering Cuba a substantial degree of self-government. Even more, it removed the hated Weyler and promised to end reconcentration. Such reforms actually encouraged intransigence, as Cuban leaders saw them as "a sign of Spain's weakening power and an indication that the end is not far off."

McKinley's annual message to Congress in December discussed the Cuban insurrection at great length. Voicing the "gravest apprehension," McKinley rejected annexation as "criminal aggression." He opposed recognition of belligerency, because the rebels hardly constituted a government worthy of recognition. And he ruled out intervention as premature while Spain traveled the "honorable paths" of reform. Asking for patience, he promised to keep open all policy options, including intervention "with force."

By mid-January it became apparent that Spanish reforms had not moderated the crisis; in fact, insurgents, conservatives, and the Spanish army all denounced them. After antireform Spaniards rioted in Havana, McKinley sent the *Maine*. On February 9, the State Department received a copy of a private letter written in late 1897 by the Spanish minister to the United States Enrique Dupuy de Lôme. Intercepted by a rebel sympathizer who forwarded it to the Cuban junta in New York City, the letter was published that same day by William Randolph Hearst's flamboyant *New York Journal* under a banner headline: "Worst Insult to the United States in its History." De Lôme had labeled McKinley "weak," a "bidder for the admiration of the crowd," and a "would-be politician." McKinley particularly resented another statement—that Spain did not take its reform proposals seriously and would persist in fighting to defeat the rebels. Spain, it appeared, could not be trusted. De Lôme's hasty recall hardly salved the hurt. Less than a week later the *Maine* blew up, setting in motion events and decisions that led to war and overseas empire for the United States.

The Spanish-American-Cuban-Filipino War

Americans enlisted in what they trumpeted as a glorious expedition to demonstrate U.S. right and might. They were cocky. Theodore Roosevelt, who resigned as assistant secretary of the navy to lead the flashy but overrated Rough Riders, said that it was not much of a war but it was the best Americans had. It was a short war, ending August 12, but 5,462 Americans died in it—only 379 of them in combat. Most met death from malaria and yellow fever. Camera operators for Thomas Edison and Biograph shot "moving pictures" of the war, as crowds flocked to see flickering images of battleships at sea, the wreck of the *Maine,* and triumphant victory parades.

"Cuba Reconciling the North and South." Captain Fritz W. Guerin's 1898 photograph depicted nationalism in the Spanish-American-Cuban-Filipino War. Golden-haired Cuba, liberated from her chains by her North American heroes, oversees the reconciliation of the Union and Confederacy in a splashy display of patriotism. (Library of Congress)

Led by officers seasoned in the Civil War and in campaigns against Native Americans, the new imperial fighters embarked from Florida in mid-June. Seventeen thousand men, clutching their Krag-Jörgensen rifles, landed on Cuban soil unopposed because Cuban insurgents had driven Spanish troops into the cities. Cubans and Americans cooperated warily. Yet the big news had already arrived from the Philippine Islands, Spain's major colony in Asia. Only days after the U.S. declaration of war, Commodore George Dewey sailed his Asiatic Squadron from Hong Kong to Manila Bay, where he smashed the Spanish fleet with the loss of one sailor. Slipping by the Spanish guns at Corregidor, Dewey entered the bay at night. Early in the morning of May 1, with the laconic order, "You may fire when ready, Gridley," his flagship *Olympia* began to demolish the ten incompetently handled Spanish ships. Some people, ignorant of American interests in the Pacific, wondered how a war to liberate Cuba saw its first action in Asia. Naval officials had pinpointed the Philippines in contingency plans as early as 1896. Often credited alone with ordering Dewey on February 25, 1898, to attack Manila if war broke out, Assistant Secretary of the Navy Theodore Roosevelt actually set in motion preexisting war plans already known and approved by the president.

By late June, U.S. troops in Cuba had advanced toward Santiago. Joined by experienced Cuban rebels, the North Americans on July 1 battled for San Juan Hill. American forces, spearheaded by the Rough Riders and the black soldiers of the Ninth Cavalry, finally captured the strategic promontory overlooking Santiago after suffering heavy casualties. Two days later the Spanish fleet, penned in Santiago harbor for weeks by U.S. warships, made a desperate daylight break for open sea.

U.S. vessels hurried to sink the helpless Spanish craft, which went down with 323 dead. Its fleet destroyed, Spain surrendered—but only to the Americans. Cubans were forbidden from entering towns and cities to celebrate.

U.S. troops also invaded another Spanish colony, Puerto Rico, which expansionists such as Roosevelt coveted as a Caribbean base that might help protect a Central American canal. In nineteen days General Nelson A. Miles, losing only three soldiers, captured the sugar- and coffee-exporting island. At least at first, the Puerto Rican elite welcomed their new North American masters as an improvement over their Spanish rulers.

Manila capitulated in mid-August, after the Spanish put up token resistance in a deal with Dewey that kept Filipino nationalist Emilio Aguinaldo from the walled city. Washington soon ordered Aguinaldo and other Filipino rebels, who had fought against the Spanish for independence since 1896, to remain outside the capital and to recognize the authority of the United States.

In July, to ensure uninterrupted reinforcement of Dewey, the United States officially absorbed Hawai'i, where ships took on coal en route to Manila. From 1893 to 1897, when Cleveland refused annexation, politics in Hawai'i had changed little. The white revolutionaries clung to power. After negotiating a new treaty with the white-led Hawaiian government, McKinley adopted the ploy of asking for a joint resolution. On July 7, 1898, Congress passed the resolution for annexation by a majority vote, thereby formally attaching the strategically and commercially important islands to the United States. Annexation was "not a change" but "a consummation," said McKinley.

Peace and Empire: The Debate in the United States

Spain sued for peace, and on August 12 the belligerents proclaimed an armistice. To negotiate with the Spanish in Paris, McKinley appointed a "peace commission" loaded with imperialists and headed by Secretary of State William R. Day, friend and follower of the president's wishes. After McKinley tested public opinion by touring the Midwest, he demanded all of the Philippines, the island of Guam in the Marianas, and Puerto Rico, as well as independence for Cuba. Articulate Filipinos pleaded for their country's freedom but met a stern U.S. rebuff. Spanish diplomats accepted this American land grab and the U.S. offer of $20 million in compensation. In early December, U.S. delegates walked out of the elegant French conference room with the Philippines, Puerto Rico, and Guam.

Anti-imperialists howled in protest. They had organized the Anti-Imperialist League in Boston in November 1898 and counted among their number such unlikely bedfellows as the steel magnate Andrew Carnegie, the labor leader Samuel Gompers, the agrarian spokesman William Jennings Bryan, the Massachusetts senator George Hoar, Harvard president Charles W. Eliot, and the humorist Mark Twain—people who had often disagreed on domestic issues. Hoar, the most outspoken senator against the treaty, had voted for war and annexation of Hawai'i. An expansionist, Carnegie apparently would accept colonies if they could be taken without force. He even offered to write a personal check for $20 million to buy the independence of the Philippines. But the anti-imperialists could not overcome the *fait accompli*, possession and occupation of territory, handed them by McKinley. After all, argued the president, could America really let loose of this real estate so nobly taken in battle?

The anti-imperialists denounced the thesis that greatness lay in colonies. Some of them wanted trade too, but not at the cost of subjugating other peoples. Quoting the Declaration of Independence and Washington's Farewell Address, these critics recalled America's tradition of self-government and *continental* expansion. Some anti-imperialists insisted that serious domestic problems demanded attention. The racist South Carolina representative "Pitchfork" Ben Tillman opposed annexing ten million "barbarians of the lowest type." Mark Twain wrote a scathing parody of the "Battle Hymn of the Republic": "Mine eyes have seen the orgy of the launching of the Sword;/He is searching out the hoardings where the strangers' wealth is stored;/He has loosed his fateful lightning, and with woe and death has scored;/His lust is marching on."

Prominent women also joined the debate, hoping to build a distinct foreign-policy constituency out of existing networks of women's clubs and organizations. The New Hampshire pacifist Lucia True Ames Mead pronounced it immoral for "any nation . . . which buys or takes by conquest another people . . . without promise of granting them independence." The social reformer Jane Addams saw children playing war games in the streets of Chicago. The kids were *not freeing Cubans,* she protested, but rather *slaying Spaniards* in their not-so-innocent play. Although unsuccessful in the fight against empire, tens of thousands of women became activists over the next decade.

The imperialists, led by Roosevelt and McKinley, and backed strongly by business leaders, engaged their opponents in vigorous debate in early 1899. These empire builders stressed pragmatic considerations, although they communicated common ideas of racial superiority and national destiny. "We are a conquering race," boasted Senator Albert Beveridge, and "we must obey our blood and occupy new markets, and, if necessary, new lands." The Philippines provided stepping-stones to the rich China market and strategic ports for the expanding navy that protected American commerce. International competition also dictated that the United States keep the fruits of victory, argued the imperialists; otherwise, a menacing Germany or expansionist Japan might pick up what America discarded. Few believed that the United States should relinquish territory acquired through blood. To the charge that no one had asked the Filipinos if they desired annexation to the United States, Roosevelt delighted in telling Democratic anti-imperialists that Thomas Jefferson took Louisiana without a vote by its inhabitants. McKinley put it simply: "Duty determines destiny."

Pro-imperialist Senator Lodge described the treaty fight in the Senate as the "closest, most bitter, and most exciting struggle." Shortly before the vote, word reached Washington that Filipino insurrectionists and American soldiers had begun to fight. The news apparently stimulated support for the Treaty of Paris. Democrats tended to be anti-imperialists and Republicans imperialists, yet enough of the former endorsed the treaty on February 6, 1899, to pass it by a bare two-thirds vote,

Emilio Aguinaldo (1869–1964). Of mixed Chinese and Tagalog ancestry, this Filipino nationalist was exiled by the Spanish from his country in 1897. He returned with American forces and later clashed with them when he declared independence for the Philippines. Captured in 1901, he then declared allegiance to the United States. During World War II, however, he favored the Japanese, who occupied the islands, and American authorities briefly imprisoned him in 1945 when they reestablished U.S. power over Manila. (Library of Congress)

57 to 27. William Jennings Bryan, believing that rejection of the treaty would prolong the war and that the Philippines could be freed after terminating the hostilities with Spain, urged an aye vote on his anti-imperialist friends. The Republicans probably had enough votes in reserve to pass the treaty even if Bryan had opposed it.

Imperial Collisions in Asia: The Philippine Insurrection and the Open Door in China

Controlling, protecting, and expanding the enlarged U.S. empire became a major chore. The Filipinos proved the most obstructionist. By the end of the war, Aguinaldo and rebel forces controlled most of the islands, having routed the Spanish and driven them into Manila. Aguinaldo believed that American leaders, including Dewey, had promised his country independence if he joined U.S. forces in defeating the Spanish. Ordered out of Manila by U.S. authorities after the Spanish-American armistice, he and his cohorts had to endure racial insults, as American soldiers considered the Filipinos inferior, the equivalent of Indians and blacks at home. The Treaty of Paris angered the Filipinos, as did McKinley's decree asserting the supreme authority of the United States in the Philippines. In open defiance of Washington, Aguinaldo and other prominent Filipinos organized a government at Malolos, wrote a constitution, and proclaimed the Philippine Republic in late January 1899.

McKinley believed his new subjects to be ill-fitted for self-government. In February 1899 the Filipinos began fighting better-armed American troops. After bloody struggles, Aguinaldo was captured in March 1901. Before the insurrection collapsed in 1902, some 4,165 Americans and more than 200,000 Filipinos died. One hundred twenty-five thousand American troops quelled the insurrection, which cost the United States at least $160 million. In Batangas province south of Manila, General J. Franklin Bell drove insurrectionists into the hills and killed their livestock. Then malaria-transmitting mosquitoes infected people instead of cattle. The result: an epidemiological catastrophe wherein the Batangas population declined by 90,000 over a six-year period. The Harvard philosopher William James denounced Filipino pacification as "the big, hollow, resounding, corrupting, sophisticating, confusing torrent of brutal momentum and irrationality that brings forth fruits like this!"

This savage contest saw both sides commit atrocities. After Filipinos massacred an American regiment on Samar and stuffed molasses into disemboweled corpses to attract ants, General Jacob Smith told his officers: "I wish you to kill and burn, the more you kill and burn the better you will please me." U.S. soldiers burned *barrios* to the ground, placing villagers in reconcentration camps like those that had defaced Cuba. To get information, Americans administered the "water cure," forcing prisoners to swallow gallons of water and then punching the swollen stomach to empty it quickly. Racist notions of white superiority surfaced. "Civilize 'em with a Krag" went a popular army song, as one officer urged the same "remedial measures that proved successful with the Apaches." The civil governor of the Philippines from 1901 to 1904, William Howard Taft, put it less crudely when he described the American mission: to "teach those people individual liberty, which shall lift them up to a point of civilization . . . and which shall make them rise to call the name of the

William Howard Taft (1857–1930) and Animal. The first U.S. civil governor of the Philippines, Taft weighed more than 300 pounds. He once proudly reported to Washington that he had ridden twenty-five miles to a high mountain spot. Secretary of War Elihu Root replied: "HOW IS HORSE?" (U.S. Army Military History Institute)

United States blessed." In fact, Taft administered a sedition act that censored newspapers and jailed dissenters. For years, the Moros would not submit to American rule. One military expert predicted that "the Moro question will eventually be settled in the same manner as the Indian question, that is by gradual extermination." In a June 1913 battle on the island of Jolo, U.S. forces killed 500 Moros. The army's premier "guerrilla warrior," General John J. Pershing, called that bloody encounter "the fiercest [fighting] I have ever seen."

The carrot joined the stick to pacify the Philippines. Local self-government, social reforms, and American schools, which taught Filipinos of all social classes English and arithmetic, helped win over elites and key minorities. A general amnesty proclaimed by President Theodore Roosevelt on July 4, 1902, also encouraged accommodation. By restricting suffrage at the outset to Filipinos with wealth, education, and previous government service, U.S. administrators successfully wooed Filipino elites, including former revolutionaries. American roads, bridges, port improvements, and sanitation projects soon followed. At the St. Louis World's Fair in 1904, a thousand Filipinos were put on display as "living exhibits," and photographs and dioramas depicted their "rapid social, educational and sanitary development" under "the kindly tutelage of the United States." By 1911, Cebu City could boast telephone service, English-language newspapers, Fords and Buicks, movie houses, and a baseball park, but "the poor are still poor," as one Cebuano put it. The Jones Act of 1916 promised eventual Philippine independence. It did not occur until 1946.

The proximity of the Philippines to China whetted commercial appetites. In early 1898 business leaders organized the American Asiatic Association to stimulate, protect, and enlarge U.S. interests in China. Treasury official Frank Vanderlip typically lauded the Philippines as the "pickets of the Pacific, standing guard at the entrances to trade with the millions of China." Although China attracted only 2 percent of U.S. foreign commerce, American traders had long dreamed of an unbounded China market, and missionaries romanticized a Christian kingdom. These dreams spurred action, and during the 1890s the United States, despite limited power, sought to defend its Asian interests, real and imagined.

In that decade imperial powers and Japan were dividing China, rendered helpless in 1895 after the Sino-Japanese War, into exclusive spheres of influence. The McKinley administration in early 1898 watched anxiously as Germany grabbed Jiaozhou (Kiaochow) and Russia gained a lease at Port Arthur on the Liaodong Peninsula. France, already ensconced in Indochina, leased Guangzhou Bay in southern China in April. Japan already had footholds in Formosa and Korea. The British in March 1898 suggested a joint Anglo-American declaration on behalf of equal commercial opportunity in China. Distracted by the Cuban crisis, Washington gave little attention to the request. Britain, which already had Hong Kong, then forced China to give up part of the Shandong Peninsula.

American interests in China seemed threatened. The American Asiatic Association and missionary groups appealed to Washington for help. Drawing on recommendations from William W. Rockhill, adviser on Asian policy, who in turn consulted his British friend and officer of the Chinese customs service, Alfred Hippisley, Secretary of State John Hay tried words. Hay sent an "Open Door" note on September 6, 1899, to Japan, Germany, Russia, Britain, France, and Italy, asking them to respect equal trade opportunity for all nations in their spheres. It was, of course, a traditional American principle. Noncommittal replies trickled back, but Hay read into them what he wanted and proclaimed definitive acceptance of the Open Door proposal.

Although frail, the Open Door policy carried meaning. Despite less leverage than the other imperialists, Americans discerned a delicate balance of power in Asia that the United States could upset. Excluding American commerce altogether from China might cause Washington to tip that balance by joining one of the powers against the others. A world war might erupt from competition in Asia. Americans hoped the Open Door policy would serve their goals in an area where they had little military power. The United States wanted the commercial advantages without having to employ military force, as it did in Latin America. The policy did not always work, but it fixed itself in the American mind as a guiding principle for Chinese affairs.

The Open Door note notwithstanding, the Manchu dynasty (1644–1912) neared death, unable to cope with the foreign intruders. Resentful nationalistic Chinese, led by a secret society called *Yihequan* ("Boxers"), undertook in 1900 to throw out the imperialist aggressors. The Boxers murdered hundreds of Christian missionaries and their Chinese converts and laid siege to the foreign legations in Beijing (Peking). To head off a complete gouging of China by vengeful imperialists, McKinley sent 2,500 American troops to Beijing from the Philippines to join 15,500 soldiers from other nations to lift the siege. Hay then issued another Open Door note on July 3, 1900. He redefined U.S. policy as the protection of American life and property, maintenance of "equal and impartial trade," and preservation of China's "territorial and administrative entity." In short, keep the trade door open by keeping China intact.

Certainly these actions did not save China, which had to pay more than $300 million for the Boxers' damages. Thereafter Washington buttressed its support for the Open Door by increasing the Asiatic Squadron to forty-eight warships and ear-marking army forces in the Philippines for future emergency deployment in China. Even Buffalo Bill Cody extended America's frontier to China by reenacting the suppression of the Boxer Rebellion in his Wild West Show to depict the "triumph of Christian civilization over paganism."

The Elbows of a World Power, 1895–1900

Venezuela, Cuba, Hawai'i, the Philippines, Open Door notes—an unprecedented set of commitments brought new responsibilities for the United States. Symbolic of this thrust to world-power status was the ascendancy of the imperialists' imperialist, Theodore Roosevelt, to the presidency in 1901. TR warned Americans to avoid "slothful ease and ignoble peace." Never "shrink from the hard contests"; "let us therefore boldly face the life of strife." Indeed, many diplomats regarded the 1890s as a testing time when the United States met the international challenge and right-fully asserted its place as a major world power. Europeans watched anxiously. Some, especially Germans, spoke of the "American peril." The United States, European leaders pointed out, had become a factor in the "balance of power." With whom would the nation ally itself?

The odds seemed to favor Britain, although the Anglo-American courtship would be prolonged and marriage something for the future. Ever since the eye-opening Venezuelan crisis, the British had applauded Washington for "entering the lists and sharing the task which might have proved too heavy for us alone." Look-ing for support against an expansionist Germany, John Bull thought Uncle Sam a fit partner. During the Spanish-American-Cuban-Filipino War the British conspicu-ously tilted toward the American side and encouraged the subsequent absorption of Spanish colonies. U.S. leaders, in turn, compared the British suppression of the Boers in South Africa (1899–1902) with their own war against the Filipinos, saying that both peoples were equally "incapable of statehood." Articulate Americans wel-comed Britain's implicit acceptance of their imperialism. "Germany, and not Eng-land, is the power with whom we are apt to have trouble over the Monroe Doctrine," wrote Roosevelt in 1898.

Britain still ranked first in naval power, but the United States stood sixth by 1900. In 1898 alone, spurred by the war with Spain, the United States added 128 vessels to its navy, at a cost of $18 million. As one scholar put it: "Every nation el-bows other nations to-day." The steel magnate Andrew Carnegie boasted that "the old nations of the earth creep at a snail's pace," but the United States "thunders past with the rush of the express." Southern racists and northern imperialists now had something in common: the need to keep inferior peoples in their place. Befitting their new imperial status, U.S. leaders often used gendered and age-based language that presumed superiority over peoples deemed "emotional, irrational, irresponsible, unbusinesslike, unstable, childlike." If Americans played "the part of China, and [were] content to rot by inches in ignoble ease within our borders," warned Roosevelt, they will "go down before other nations which have not lost the manly and adventurous qualities." Imperial annexation, bragged Senator Beveridge in 1900, "means opportunity for all the glorious young manhood of the republic, the most virile, ambitious, impatient, militant manhood the world has ever seen."

The events of the 1895–1900 period further altered the process of decision-making. Both Cleveland and McKinley conducted their own foreign policies, often thwarting or manipulating Congress. Woodrow Wilson, then president of Princeton University, later noted that 1898 had "changed the balance of powers. Foreign questions became leading questions again. . . . Our President must always, henceforth, be one of the great powers of the world." From "a provincial huddle of petty sovereignties held together by a rope of sand," one editor exulted, "we rise to the dignity and prowess of an imperial republic incomparably greater than Rome."

Indeed, the allure of empire seemed to offer an exceptionalist mission for the "most merciful of the world's great race of administrators," that of "teaching the world how to govern dependent peoples through uplift, assimilation, and eventual self-government." Thus did the optimistic leaders of the "new world power" after 1900 see themselves as reforming an international system that seemed to be "working in their favor." After 1900 the task of managing the expansive empire and the global responsibilities that came with it preoccupied U.S. leaders.

FURTHER READING FOR THE PERIOD 1895–1900

For the 1890s push for empire and the coming and waging of the Spanish-American-Cuban-Filipino War, see Ada Ferrer, *Insurgent Cuba* (1999); Linda Guerra, *The Myth of José Martí* (2005); Robert E. Hannigan, *The New World Power* (2002); Kenneth E. Hendrickson, Jr., *The Spanish-American War* (2003); Sylvia Hilton and S. J. Ickringell, eds., *European Perceptions of the Spanish-American War* (1999); Kristin L. Hoganson, *Fighting for American Manhood* (1998); John L. Offner, *An Unwanted War* (1992); Louis A. Pérez Jr., *The War of 1898* (1998), *Cuba and the United States* (1997), and *Cuba Between Empires, 1878–1902* (1983); Peggy Samuels and Harold Samuels, *Remembering the* Maine (1995); Thomas Schoonover, *Uncle Sam's War and the Origins of Globalization* (2003); Angel Smith and Emma Davila-Cox, eds., *The Crisis of 1898* (1999); and Warren Zimmermann, *First Great Triumph* (2002).

For U.S. leaders, see H. W. Brands, *T.R.* (1997); Kathleen Dalton, *Theodore Roosevelt* (2002); and H. Wayne Morgan, *William McKinley and His America* (1963).

Anti-imperialism is treated in Robert L. Beisner, *Twelve Against Empire* (1968); Amy Kaplan, *The Anarchy of Empire in the Making of U.S. Culture* (2002); and Frank Ninkovich, *The United States and Imperialism* (2001).

The Open Door policy and Asia are discussed in Paul A. Cohen, *History in Three Keys* (1997) (Boxers); Michael Hunt, *Frontier Defense and the Open Door* (1973) and *The Making of a Special Relationship* (1983); Thomas McCormick, *China Market* (1967); and Marilyn Blatt Young, *The Rhetoric of Empire* (1968).

The Philippine rebellion and the American debate receive scrutiny in Vincent Cirillo, *Bullets and Bacilli* (2004); Michael Cullinane, *Illustrado Politics* (2005); Brian M. Linn, *The Philippine War* (2000); Glenn A. May, *Social Engineering in the Philippines* (1980); Stuart C. Miller, *"Benevolent Assimilation"* (1982); Resil B. Mojares, *The War Against the Americans* (1999); Daniel B. Schirmer, *Republic or Empire* (1972); Angel Velasco Shaw and Luis Francia, eds., *Vestiges of War* (1999); and Richard E. Welch, *Response to Imperialism* (1979).

For the Venezuelan crisis and Anglo-American relations, see Judith Ewell, *Venezuela and the United States* (1996); Richard B. Mulanax, *The Boer War in American Politics and Diplomacy* (1994); Thomas J. Noer, *Briton, Boer, and Yankee* (1978); Bradford Perkins, *The Great Rapprochement* (1968); and Joseph Smith, *Illusions of Conflict* (1979).

See also Robert L. Beisner, ed., *Guide to American Foreign Relations Since 1600* (2003).

For comprehensive coverage of foreign-relations topics, see the articles in the four-volume *Encyclopedia of U.S. Foreign Relations* (1997), edited by Bruce W. Jentleson and Thomas G. Paterson.

CHAPTER 2

Managing, Policing, and Extending the Empire, 1900–1914

DIPLOMATIC CROSSROAD

✳ *Severing Panama from Colombia for the Canal, 1903*

"REVOLUTION IMMINENT" WARNED the cable from Colón, a normally quiet Colombian seaport on the Atlantic side of Panama. Acting Secretary of State Francis B. Loomis quickly fired off an inquiry to the U.S. consul at Panama City, on the Pacific slope: "Uprising on Isthmus reported. Keep Department promptly and fully informed." The response came back in four hours: "No uprising yet. Reported will be in the night." Loomis's anxiety soon increased when he learned that troops of the Colombian government had landed in Colón.

In Washington, D.C., it was now 8:20 P.M., November 3, 1903. As far as Loomis knew, a revolution had not yet broken out on the isthmus. Nonetheless, he hurriedly drafted instructions for the consuls at Panama and Colón. "Act promptly" to convey to the commanding officer of the U.S.S. *Nashville* this order: "Make every effort to prevent [Colombian] Government troops at Colón from proceeding to Panama [City]." Loomis agonized for another hour. Finally, a new cable arrived: "Uprising occurred to-night . . . no bloodshed. . . . Government will be organized to-night." Loomis had done his part in the scheme to acquire a canal controlled by the United States.

November 3 was far more hectic for the conspirators in Panama. A tiny band of Panamanians and Americans living on the isthmus had actively plotted revolution since August, when the Colombian congress rejected the treaty that would have permitted the United States to construct an isthmian canal. By late October, they had become convinced that the North American colossus, frustrated in its overtures to Colombia, would lend them moral and physical support. Confident that U.S. naval vessels would be at hand, they selected November 4 for their coup d'état. To their dismay, however, the Colombian steamer *Cartagena* disembarked about 400 troops at Colón early on November 3. Because Washington's order to prevent the

"The Thirteenth Labor of Hercules." With this official poster by Perham Nahl, the Panama-Pacific Exposition in San Francisco in 1915 celebrated the opening of the Panama Canal. The artist commemorates the ten-year construction project using symbols that reflect the era's themes of empire-building and male hegemony: A powerful, muscular Hercules (the United States) forcibly parts the land (a yielding Panama) to make space for the canal. (Library of Congress)

"landing of any armed force . . . at Colón" had not reached him, Commander John Hubbard of the *Nashville* did not interfere.

Forced to improvise, the conspirators deviously separated the Colombian commanding general from his troops, lured him aboard a train, and sped him across the isthmus to Panama City, where they arrested their guest, formed a provisional government, and paraded before a cheering crowd at the Cathedral Plaza. Back in Colón, the insurgents gave the colonel in charge $8,000 in gold, whereupon he ordered his remaining troops aboard a departing steamer. The U.S. consul at Panama City cabled: "Quiet prevails." At noon the next day, Secretary of State John Hay officially recognized the sovereign Republic of Panama.

The new Panamanian government appointed as its minister plenipotentiary a Frenchman, Philippe Bunau-Varilla, an engineer of an earlier failed Panama canal project. With Gallic flourish, Bunau-Varilla congratulated Secretary Hay for rescuing Panama "from the barbarism of unnecessary and wasteful civil wars to consecrate it to the destiny assigned to it by Providence, the service of humanity, and the progress of civilization." On November 18, 1903, less than two weeks after U.S. recognition of Panama, Hay and Bunau-Varilla signed a new treaty by which the United States would build, fortify, and operate a canal linking the Atlantic and Pacific oceans. Washington also guaranteed the "independence of the Republic in Panama," thereby ensuring against any retaliation from Colombia.

Theodore Roosevelt the Pirate. The Colombian minister called the United States a "pirate." When Roosevelt asked about legal precedents for his Panama policy, Attorney General Philander C. Knox replied, "Oh, Mr. President, do not let so great an achievement suffer from any taint of legality." (Frank Nankivell, Swann Collection of Caricature and Cartoon)

Hay had at last achieved a goal set by his chief, President Theodore Roosevelt, several years earlier. If an unfortified, neutral canal had existed in Central America during the recent war with Spain, Roosevelt had argued, the United States would have spent the war in "wild panic," fearful that the Spanish fleet would slip through the waterway and rush to the Philippines to attack Commodore Dewey. "Better to have no canal at all, than not give us the power to control it in time of war," Roosevelt concluded.

The Clayton-Bulwer Treaty of 1850, stipulating joint Anglo-American control of any isthmian canal, seemed to block the way. In December 1898, flushed with victory over Spain, President William McKinley had directed Secretary Hay to modify that agreement. The ensuing Hay-Pauncefote Treaty of February 1900 permitted the United States to build a canal but forbade its fortification, much to the dismay of Roosevelt who spearheaded an attack that defeated the treaty in the Senate. On November 18, 1901, with Roosevelt now president, Hay and Pauncefote signed a satisfactory new pact.

Then began the complex process of determining the route. The decisive criterion—cost—seemed exorbitant for Panama because of the New Panama Canal Company, a French-chartered firm that held the Colombian concession for canal rights. The company estimated its assets at $109 million—machinery, property, and excavated soil left by the defunct de Lesseps organization in 1888. Purchase of the company's rights and holdings would make a Panama canal prohibitively expensive if technologically easier. For these reasons, plus travel accounts that depicted Panama as "a hideous dung heap of physical and moral degradation," the House passed the Hepburn Bill in January 1902 authorizing a canal through Nicaragua.

The New Panama Canal Company's American lawyer, William Nelson Cromwell, schemed to sell the assets of his French client for the highest possible price. Lobbying hard, Bunau-Varilla even exposed the unsuitability of Nicaraguan terrain by deluging Congress with Nicaraguan postage stamps that depicted a belching volcano. The company also lowered its price to $40 million. Guided by Roosevelt and Cromwell, Congress reversed itself and chose the Panama route. The State Department soon opened negotiations with Colombia. The annual rent became a stumbling block, which Hay removed only by delivering an ultimatum to the Colombian chargé d'affaires, Tomás Herrán, in January 1903. On January 22 he and Hay signed a treaty granting Colombia an initial payment of $10 million and $250,000 annually. The United States would control the six-mile-wide canal zone for one hundred years, renewable at the "sole and absolute option" of the North American republic.

The U.S. Senate approved the Hay-Herrán Treaty on March 17, 1903, but the Colombian government attempted to extract a $10 million payment from the New Panama Canal Company for selling its assets to the U.S. government. Cromwell promptly cried foul, whereupon Hay bluntly announced that any payment to Colombia was "not permissible." The Colombians next tried to raise the initial American cash payment from $10 million to $15 million. Roosevelt exploded against "those contemptible little creatures in Bogotá." TR's intransigence and Hay's extraordinary intercession on behalf of a privately owned foreign corporation so angered the Colombian congress that it unanimously defeated the treaty on August 12, 1903.

Panama Canal. The U.S.S. *Ohio* passes through the Culebra Cut (now called the Gaillard Cut) of the Panama Canal about a year after the canal opened to traffic—both warships and commercial vessels. (Library of Congress)

Roosevelt was already pondering undiplomatic alternatives. In June the ubiquitous Cromwell had met with Roosevelt and then planted a story in the *New York World* reporting that, if Colombia rejected the treaty, Panama would secede and grant "absolute sovereignty over the Canal Zone," and that "President Roosevelt is said to strongly favor this plan." By now the president was privately castigating Colombia for its "squalid savagery . . . dismal ignorance, cruelty, treachery, greed, and utter vanity."

Roosevelt now considered seizure of Panama by force or instant recognition and support for any revolutionary regime in Panama. The president inclined sharply toward the latter course after a meeting with Bunau-Varilla on October 10, during which the Frenchman predicted an uprising. When Bunau-Varilla asked what the United States would do, TR replied: "Colombia by her action has forfeited any claim upon the U.S." One week later, on October 16, Secretary Hay informed Bunau-Varilla that American naval vessels were heading toward the isthmus. Calculating the steaming time, Bunau-Varilla cabled his fellow plotters on the isthmus that warships would arrive by November 2. Early that evening the U.S.S. *Nashville* dropped anchor at Colón as predicted. As a Colombian diplomat rightfully complained, "The Americans are against us. What can we do against the American Navy?"

Roosevelt urged swift ratification of the Hay–Bunau-Varilla Treaty, claiming that Colombia had forced him "to take decisive steps to bring to an end a condition of affairs which had become intolerable." When critics complained about his "Bowery-boy" behavior toward Colombia, Roosevelt denounced the "small body of shrill eunuchs who consistently oppose" his "righteous" policies. On February 23, 1904, the Senate approved the treaty by a vote of 66 to 14. The treaty granted the United States "power and authority" within the zone "in perpetuity" as "if it were the sovereign of the territory." Later, in 1911, TR reportedly boasted that "I took the Canal Zone and let Congress debate; and while the debate goes on the Canal does also."

Construction began in mid-1904, and the fifty-mile-long canal opened on August 15, 1914. During the first year of operation alone, 1,058 merchant vessels slid through the locks, while the Atlantic and Pacific fleets of the U.S. Navy freely exchanged ships. In 1922 the United States paid "conscience money" or "canalimony" of $25 million to Colombia but did not formally apologize for having taken the canal zone. Despite critics, most Americans have applauded Roosevelt's bold venture against Colombia. The canal, Woodrow Wilson later asserted, shifted "the center of gravity of the world."

The Conservative Shapers of Empire

The taking of Panama symbolized the new activism characteristic of American foreign policy after 1898, and construction of the canal ensured virtual U.S. hegemony over Latin America. It also intensified Washington's participation in the global contest for empire among the great powers. "The United States will be attacked as soon as you are about to complete the canal," Germany's Kaiser Wilhelm II predicted in 1907, identifying Japan as the most likely culprit. Britain, which had the power to challenge U.S. preeminence in the hemisphere, chose to acquiesce in the face of a growing threat from Germany. In turn, the vigorous German Empire, having expanded its markets and investments in Central and South America to more than 2 billion marks by 1900, seemed "desirous of obtaining a foothold in the Western Hemisphere," noted the General Board of the U.S. Navy. Revolutionary upheavals in Russia, China, and Mexico produced further shifting in the international balance of power. As European alliances consolidated and lurched toward a world war, TR and his successors had to defend, develop, and enlarge the new U.S. empire in an era of tumultuous transformation.

Makers of American Foreign Relations, 1900–1914

Presidents	Secretaries of State
Theodore Roosevelt, 1901–1909	John Hay, 1898–1905
	Elihu Root, 1905–1909
	Robert Bacon, 1909
William Howard Taft, 1909–1913	Philander C. Knox, 1909–1913
Woodrow Wilson, 1913–1921	William Jennings Bryan, 1913–1915

In the late nineteenth century, Roosevelt corresponded regularly with Alfred Thayer Mahan, the navalist who tirelessly touted the strategic advantages of a canal. During the war of 1898, the warship *Oregon* dashed at full speed from San Francisco around South America to Cuba in time to help destroy the Spanish fleet off Santiago. The race of more than 14,000 miles fired American imaginations, but it also consumed sixty-eight days and underscored the need for an interoceanic canal across Central America.

Roosevelt's sense of isthmian strategic necessity reflected a broad worldview he shared with many "progressives" in the early twentieth century. A conservative patrician reformer, he "feared that unrest caused by social and economic inequities would impair the nation's strength and efficiency." With similar danger lurking in unrest abroad, he sought U.S. influence to create order on a global scale through "proper policing." Imbibing Darwinist doctrines of "natural selection," Roosevelt proclaimed "our duty toward the people living in barbarism to see that they are freed from their chains, and we can free them only by destroying barbarism itself." Anglo-Saxon superiority was best expressed in war, he said. Not all Progressive-era reformers joined TR in advocating a vigorous activism abroad. Wisconsin's Senator Robert M. La Follette, for example, opposed imperialism and contended that the same corporate monopolists they battled at home were dragging the United States into perpetual intervention overseas. Activists in women's organizations bemoaned the "present intoxication with the hashish of conquest" as they urged "women's values" on a male government so as to rein in the "champing steeds" of militarism and empire.

Roosevelt vigorously debated his critics. Exuberant and calculating, he centralized foreign-policy decisionmaking, frequently bypassed Congress, and believed "the people" too ignorant about foreign affairs to guide an informed president like himself. Nonetheless, he kept favorite journalists and other "intelligent observers sufficiently enlightened to prevent their going wrong." Seeking world stability, Roosevelt advocated "multiplying the methods and chances of honorably avoiding war in the event of controversy." TR disliked pomp and ceremony and once broke up a state luncheon by demonstrating jujitsu holds on the Swiss minister. "The biggest matters," this progenitor of the imperial presidency later wrote, "I managed without consultation with anyone."

Roosevelt and other shapers of American foreign policy before World War I were members of an American quasi-aristocracy who moved comfortably in the affluent, cosmopolitan society of the Atlantic seaboard. Roosevelt, a graduate of Harvard College and prolific author, had served as assistant secretary of the navy and governor of New York. His successor, Ohioan William Howard Taft, a graduate of Yale, had served as a federal circuit court judge, governor of the Philippines (1901–1904), and secretary of war (1904–1908). Woodrow Wilson earned a Ph.D. from Johns Hopkins, wrote books on government and history, presided over Princeton, and governed New Jersey before entering the White House. Each president believed that "we owe to our less fortunate [international] neighbors" the same "neighborly feeling and aid that a successful man in a community owes to his less fortunate fellow citizens."

Their secretaries of state, with one exception, belonged to the same elite. John Hay, secretary from 1898 to 1905, was educated at Brown University. A poet, novelist, biographer, and editor, the wealthy Hay had served as Lincoln's personal secretary during the Civil War and later as McKinley's ambassador to Great Britain. His successor, Elihu Root (1905–1909), graduated from Hamilton College, took a law degree at New York University, and became one of America's most successful corporation lawyers. As secretary of war from 1899 to 1904, he created mechanisms, such as the Platt Amendment for Cuba, for managing the American empire. Like TR, he believed that the "main object of diplomacy is to keep the country out of trouble." Philander C. Knox (1909–1913) followed Root. A corporation lawyer, Knox served as attorney general and U.S. senator before heading the State Department. He liked to play golf at Chevy Chase, spend summers with his trotters at his Valley Forge Farms estate, and delegate departmental work to subordinates. He advocated "dollar diplomacy" to stabilize revolution-prone areas—that is, using private financiers and business leaders to promote foreign policy, and using diplomacy to promote American commerce and investment abroad. As his *second* secretary of state President Wilson named New Yorker Robert Lansing (1915–1920), a graduate of Amherst College, son-in-law of a former secretary of state, and practitioner of international law. Reserved and conservative, Lansing also abhorred disorder in the U.S. sphere of Latin America.

William Jennings Bryan, Wilson's *first* appointment (1913–1915), lacked such conservative elite status. The "boy orator" of Nebraska could mesmerize crowds but could not win a presidential election in 1896, 1900, and 1908. The "Great Commoner" languished for years as the most prominent has-been of the Democratic party until Wilson named him secretary of state as a reward for support at the convention of 1912. The president let Bryan appoint "deserving Democrats" to diplomatic posts, but Wilson bypassed him in most important diplomatic decisions, even to the point of composing overseas cables on his own White House typewriter.

The conservative managers of American foreign policy believed that a major component of national power was a prosperous, expanding economy invigorated by a healthy foreign trade. The principle of the "Open Door"—to keep open trade and investment opportunities—became a governing tenet voiced globally, if often tarnished in application. In 1900 Americans exported goods valued at $1.5 billion. By 1914 that figure stood at $2.5 billion. Exports to Latin America increased markedly from $132 million at the turn of the century to $309 million in 1914. Investments there in sugar, transportation, and banking shot up. By 1913 the United Fruit Company, the banana empire, had some 130,000 acres in cultivation in Central America, a fleet of freighters, and political influence as well. By 1914 U.S. entrepreneurs dominated nickel mining in Canada and sugar production in Cuba, and total investments abroad equaled $3.5 billion.

But those statistics meant more than fat pocketbooks. Americans believed that economic expansion also carried abroad positive values of industriousness, honesty, morality, and private initiative. Thus Yale University-in-China and the Young Men's Christian Association (YMCA) joined Standard Oil Company and Singer Sewing in China as advance agents of civilization. And Taft said about the Chinese: "The more civilized they become the more active their industries, the wealthier they become, and the better market they will become for us." President Wilson, adding missionary paternalism to the quest for order, said simply that he would "teach the

South American Republics to elect good men." Not all Americans were seen as benevolent. One Venezuelan writer characterized "Yanquis" as "rough and obtuse Calibans, swollen by brutal appetites, the enemies of idealism, furiously enamored of the dollar," whiskey-soaked sots, "overwhelming, fierce, [and] clownish." Whatever their intentions, American efforts to shape the lives of other peoples while denying any desire to dominate brought mixed results.

Cuba Under the Platt Amendment

In December 1898, President McKinley promised "free and independent" status for Cuba once the U.S. occupation had established "complete tranquility" and a "stable government." To accelerate Cuban democracy and stability, he appointed General Leonard Wood the military governor of the island. A Harvard graduate with a degree in medicine, Wood favored outright annexation of Cuba, but he loyally carried out the administration's policy of patrician tutelage. During his tenure (1899–1902), he worked to eradicate yellow fever, Americanize education, construct highways, and formulate an electoral law. He even added "before" and "after" photos of public toilets in his reports. "When money can be borrowed at a reasonable rate of interest and when capital is willing to invest in the Island," the general predicted, "a condition of stability will have been reached." Only the North Americans had the resources to reconstruct war-ravaged Cuba. Those Cuban elites who spoke English and knew American ways could serve as local managers, traders, agents, and advisers. The occupation thus stressed English in public schools because "the Cuban people will never understand the people of the United States until they appreciate our institutions."

Secretary of War Elihu Root sought a Cuban-American political relationship that would weather the storms of independence. Working closely with Senator Orville Platt, Root fashioned the Platt Amendment to the Army Appropriation Bill of 1901. By the amendment's terms, Cuba could not make a treaty with any nation that might impair its independence. Should Cuban independence ever be threatened, or should Cuba fail to protect "life, property, and individual liberty," Washington had the right to intervene. For these purposes, Cuba would cede to the United States "lands necessary for coaling or naval stations."

Cubans protested. On Good Friday 1901, Havana's *La Discusión* carried a cartoon of "The Cuban Calvary" depicting the Cuban people as Christ and Senator Platt as a Roman soldier. Root piously denied any "intermeddling or interference with the affairs of a Cuban government," but Wood privately conceded that "little or no independence [was] left Cuba under the Platt Amendment." A reluctant Cuban convention adopted the measure as an amendment to the new constitution on June 12, 1901, and the two governments signed a treaty embodying the Platt Amendment on May 22, 1903. That same year the U.S. Navy constructed a naval base at Guantánamo Bay; "Gitmo," as the marines christened it, was leased to the United States in perpetuity for a small annual fee. With North American investments pouring into capital-starved Cuba, extending control over sugar, tobacco, mining, transportation, utilities, and cattle ranching, the Reciprocity Treaty of 1902 permitted Cuban products to enter the United States at specially reduced tariff rates, thereby further interlocking the two economies.

The first president of the Republic of Cuba, Tomás Estrada Palma, acted "more plattish than Platt himself" until discontented Cuban nationalists revolted. In September 1906, the U.S. consul general in Havana reported Estrada Palma's inability to "protect life and property." "I am so angry with that infernal little Cuban republic," exploded Roosevelt, "that I would like to wipe its people off the face of the earth." All he wanted was that the Cubans "should behave themselves." Into this turmoil stepped the portly secretary of war, William Howard Taft, sent by TR to mediate between the warring factions. Estrada Palma resigned, permitting Taft to establish a new government with himself as governor. He returned home in mid-October, leaving behind a government headed by an American civilian, administered by U.S. Army officers, and backed by 5,000 American soldiers. For twenty-eight months Governor Charles E. Magoon attempted to reinstate Leonard Wood's electoral and humanitarian reforms, while Roosevelt worried that "those ridiculous dagoes would flare up over some totally unexpected trouble and start to cutting one another's throats."

Under his successor Taft, and under Taft's successor Woodrow Wilson, U.S. policy toward Cuba reflexively supported existing governments, by force if necessary. No serious effort was made to reform Cuba in the North American image. Through "dollar diplomacy," Washington sought order in Cuban politics and security for investments and commerce, particularly in sugar. The $50 million invested by Americans in 1896 jumped to $220 million in 1913. By 1920 American-owned mills produced about half of Cuba's sugar. Exports to the United States in 1900 equaled $31 million, by 1914 $131 million, and by 1920 $722 million, thus confirming the Cuban patriot José Martí's dictum that "*el pueblo que compra, manda*" ("the country which buys, commands"). U.S. entrepreneurs helped establish missionary schools that, in effect, trained Cubans for employment in North American companies. When revolution threatened, as in May 1912 and February 1917, marines went ashore. After Havana followed Washington's lead and declared war against Germany in April 1917, some 2,500 American troops went to the island, ostensibly to protect the sugar plantations that helped feed the Allied armies.

The Constable of the Caribbean

In his first annual message, on December 3, 1901, President Roosevelt called the Monroe Doctrine "a guarantee of the commercial independence of the Americas." The United States, however, as protector of that independence, would "not guarantee any state against punishment if it misconducts itself, provided that punishment does not take the form of the acquisition of territory by any non-American power." If a Western Hemispheric country misbehaved toward a European nation, Roosevelt would "let the European country spank it."

The president was thinking principally of Germany and Venezuela. The flamboyant Venezuelan dictator Cipriano Castro had perpetually deferred payment on $12.5 million in bonds held by European investors. In December 1902, after clearing the way with Washington, Germany and Britain delivered an ultimatum demanding immediate settlement of their claims, seized several Venezuelan vessels, bombarded two forts, and blockaded all ports. To all of this Roosevelt initially acquiesced. In mid-January 1903, however, the German navy bombarded two more forts. This time the president delivered a quiet warning to desist. He also sent Admiral George Dewey on naval maneuvers in the Caribbean, which were intended as "an object lesson to the Kaiser." Impressed by the U.S. reaction, the kaiser replaced his ill-informed ambassador with Hermann Speck von Sternberg, an old friend of Roosevelt. The president urged on him a quick settlement. Thereupon, Britain and Germany in February lifted the blockade and submitted the dispute to the Permanent Court at The Hague. Speck von Sternberg averred that the kaiser "would no more think of violating that [Monroe] doctrine than he would of colonizing the moon." When the Hague arbiters found in favor of Germany and England in early 1904, a State Department official complained that this decision put "a premium on violence" and made likely similar European interventions in the future.

TR also fretted about the Dominican Republic, revolution-torn since 1899. "I have about the same desire to annex it," Roosevelt said privately, "as a gorged boa constrictor might have to swallow a porcupine wrong-end to." An American firm claimed damages of several million dollars, and European creditors demanded action by their governments. The president prayed that the Dominicans "would behave so that I would not have to act in any way." By spring 1904 he thought he might have to do "what a policeman has to do." On December 6, 1904, Roosevelt described to Congress his conception of the United States as hemispheric policeman. "Chronic wrongdoing, or an impotence which results in a general loosening of the ties of civilized society," he proclaimed, may "ultimately require intervention by some civilized nation, and in the Western Hemisphere the adherence of the United States to the Monroe Doctrine may force the United States, however reluctantly . . . to the exercise of an international police power." James Monroe "certainly would no longer recognize" his own doctrine because TR had transformed the ban on European meddling into a brash promise of U.S. hegemony over the Americas.

The Rough Rider soon donned his constable's badge. He assigned a U.S. collector of Dominican customs. "The Constitution," Roosevelt later explained, "did not explicitly give me the power to bring about the necessary agreement with Santo Domingo," but it did "not forbid me." Yet "policing" and "civilizing" the Dominican Republic by presidential order provoked nationalist resentment, as Dominicans soon quieted "their children with the threat 'There comes an American. Keep quiet or he will kill you.' " Taft's secretary of state, Philander C. Knox, applauded the customs receivership for curing "century-old evils" and halting corruption. The assassination of the Dominican president in November 1911 suggested that Knox spoke prematurely. And in 1912 revolutionaries operating from contiguous Haiti marauded throughout the Dominican Republic, forcing the closure of several customshouses. To restore order, Taft in September 1912 sent a commission backed by 750 marines. The commissioners redefined the Haitian-Dominican border, forced the corrupt Dominican president to resign, and avoided direct interference in a new election.

Despite his denunciation of "dollar diplomacy," President Wilson's search for stability in Latin America retraced familiar steps. When, in September 1913, revolution again threatened the Dominican government, Secretary Bryan promised "every legitimate means to assist in the restoration of order and the prevention of further insurrections." Ordering naval intervention after further Dominican disorders in May 1916, Wilson said: "If a man will not listen to you quietly in a seat, sit on his neck and make him listen." Marines brought a new treaty that gave the United States full control over Dominican finances. In November, as U.S. participation in the European war became increasingly probable, Wilson proclaimed the formal military occupation of the Dominican Republic, ostensibly to suppress revolutionaries suspected of a pro-German bias. The U.S. Navy formally governed the country until 1922. The main legacy of the occupation, in one historian's terse judgment, was "a strong anti-U.S. feeling" among the Dominican people.

The Quest for Order in Haiti and Nicaragua

The Dominican Republic shares the island of Hispaniola with Haiti, where revolution became an increasingly popular mode of changing governments. In contrast to large French and German assets, U.S. investments in Haiti were limited to ownership of a small railroad and a one-third share in the Haitian National Bank. After the outbreak of World War I, the Wilson administration worried about "the ever present danger of German control" of Haiti and its deepwater harbor of Môle Saint Nicolas. Given the precedent of the German cruiser *Panther* sinking of a Haitian gunboat in 1902, the State Department offered to buy the Môle "to take it out of the market." Wilson also pressed for an American customs receivership on the Dominican model.

The Haitians resisted successfully until July 1915, when the regime of Guillaume Sam fell in an orgy of grisly political murders. Wilson ordered the navy to "amicably take charge" of the "dusky little republic." As 2,000 troops imposed martial law, one marine recorded that "the opaque eyes in the black faces were . . . as indifferent as the lenses of cameras." Subsequent fighting between occupiers and native guerrillas killed more than 2,250 Haitians compared to 16 marine casualties. Until the marines finally departed in 1934, U.S. officials noted "the intense feeling . . . practically everywhere against the American occupation."

The United States also intervened, virtually at will, in Nicaragua. In 1907 Roosevelt proposed a peace conference to end the incessant warfare among Central American states. As Secretary Root explained, their conduct mattered because the Panama Canal put them "in the front yard of the United States." When President José Santos Zelaya solicited funds to build a second interoceanic canal, especially from Germany, Washington turned against a leader whom some Nicaraguans had compared to Roosevelt himself. For Zelaya's crime of seeking a "better economic position for Nicaragua outside the U.S. economic subsystem," the State Department labeled him "the most reprehensible ruler that ever oppressed an aspiring people."

After Zelaya "yanked Mr. Taft by the ear" by executing two Americans, Washington broke diplomatic relations in November 1909, sent a battleship for "moral effect," forced Zelaya into exile, and threatened to "knock heads together until they should maintain peace." Secretary Knox then negotiated a treaty with the victorious conservatives led by Adolfo Díaz, providing for U.S. customs control and an American loan. Instead of gratitude, "the natural sentiment of an overwhelming majority of Nicaraguans is antagonistic," the U.S. envoy reported. Rebuffed by the U.S.

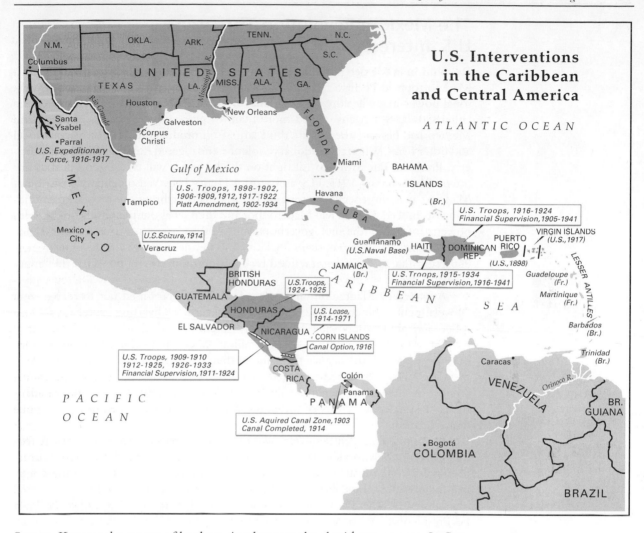

U.S. Interventions in the Caribbean and Central America

ATLANTIC OCEAN

N.M.

Columbus

OKLA. ARK.

TENN.

N.C.

S.C.

UNITED STATES

TEXAS

LA. MISS. ALA. GA.

Houston

FLORIDA

Santa
Ysabel

Galveston

New Orleans

Corpus
Christi

Parral

*U.S. Expeditionary
Force, 1916-1917*

Miami

Gulf of Mexico

BAHAMA

ISLANDS

(Br.)

M E X I C O

Tampico

U.S. Troops, 1898-1902,
1906-1909, 1912, 1917-1922
Platt Amendment, 1902-1934

Havana

CUBA

U.S. Troops, 1916-1924
Financial Supervision, 1905-1941

VIRGIN ISLANDS
(U.S., 1917)

Mexico
City

U.S. Seizure, 1914

Guantánamo
(U.S. Naval Base)

HAITI

PUERTO
RICO

Veracruz

DOMINICAN
REP.

(U.S., 1898)

JAMAICA
(Br.)

C A R I B B E A N

U.S. Troops, 1915-1934
Financial Supervision, 1916-1941

Guadeloupe
(Fr.)

L E S S E R   A N T I L L E S

BRITISH
HONDURAS

U.S. Troops,
1924-1925

Martinique
(Fr.)

GUATEMALA

S E A

HONDURAS

U.S. Lease,
1914-1971

Barbados
(Br.)

EL SALVADOR

NICARAGUA

CORN ISLANDS
Canal Option, 1916

Trinidad
(Br.)

U.S. Troops, 1909-1910
1912-1925, 1926-1933
Financial Supervision, 1911-1924

COSTA
RICA

Colón

Caracas

VENEZUELA

Orinoco R.

BR.
GUIANA

P A C I F I C

O C E A N

Panama

PANAMA

U.S. Aquired Canal Zone, 1903
Canal Completed, 1914

Bogotá

COLOMBIA

BRAZIL

Senate, Knox and a group of bankers simply went ahead without a treaty. In September 1912, 354 U.S. marines rushed into battle on behalf of the Díaz regime, which the State Department deemed representative of "the ablest people of the country." After routing the newest revolutionary army, the leathernecks returned home, leaving one hundred behind as a legation guard in Managua.

Bryan in spring 1913 dusted off a draft treaty granting the United States a canal option in Nicaragua in exchange for $3 million. The secretary also added a clause similar to the Platt Amendment before sending the Bryan-Chamorro Treaty to the Senate. When the upper house balked, Bryan deleted the U.S. right of intervention. Ratification in February 1916 did help Nicaragua's finances. The treaty also effectively excluded European powers from naval bases in the Gulf of Fonseca, and thus U.S. warships pointedly cruised offshore during the 1916 Nicaraguan presidential campaign. Although nominally independent, Nicaragua remained a U.S. protectorate until 1933.

The Mexican Revolution Threatens U.S. Interests

Revolution in Mexico posed major problems for Washington. In 1911 Francisco I. Madero toppled Porfirio Díaz, the aged dictator who had maintained order, personal power, and a healthy environment for North American investments since the late 1870s. U.S. citizens owned more than 40 percent of Mexico's property, and Mexico had become the world's third largest oil producer, thanks to Standard Oil and other firms. When revolutionary violence endangered American lives and property, President Taft vowed to "sit tight on the lid and it will take a good deal to pry me off." In February 1913, U.S. ambassador Henry Lane Wilson encouraged one of Madero's trusted generals, Victoriano Huerta, to overthrow the revolutionary nationalist. Indeed, Huerta had Madero shot and then set about to consolidate his own power. But one of the state governors, Venustiano Carranza, organized the "Constitutionalist" revolt on February 26. With U.S. residents caught in the crossfire, the departing Taft administration refused recognition until Huerta punished the "murderers of American citizens."

Appalled by Madero's murder, President Wilson promised not to recognize a "government of butchers." He denounced Huerta as a "diverting brute! . . . seldom sober and always impossible." Seemingly unconcerned about private American properties in Mexico worth some $1.5 billion, Wilson refused to act as "the servant of those who wish to enhance the value of their Mexican investments." When Ambassador Wilson continued to urge recognition of Huerta to protect those U.S. interests, the president peremptorily recalled him in July 1913. The president thereafter treated with Mexico through special emissaries, only one of whom spoke fluent Spanish.

In August one such representative, John Lind, arrived in Mexico City. A former governor of Minnesota without diplomatic experience, Lind delivered Wilson's proposal for an armistice, "an early and free election," and Huerta's promise not to run for president. In exchange, Wilson offered recognition and aid to any elected government. "Where in the hell does he get the right to say who shall or shall not be President of Mexico," wrote one Mexican after Wilson's "counsels" were rebuffed. After this snub, Wilson announced a restrained policy of "watchful waiting." Undeterred, Huerta in October held a special election, which returned an entirely submissive congress ready to extend his presidency indefinitely. Wilson then turned to Carranza in northern Mexico, but the latter contemptuously refused Wilsonian mediation and rejected any solution short of his own triumph. Wilson then announced in November a renewed policy "to isolate General Huerta entirely . . . and so to force him out."

Most European powers, especially Germany, had recognized Huerta in defiance of Wilson. The British, however, their navy relying on Mexican oil, did not want to antagonize Wilson, with tensions mounting in Europe. London therefore notified Huerta that it would not support him against the United States, and urged him to resign—all the while viewing Wilson's policies as "most impractical and unreasonable."

With British compliance assured, Wilson lifted the U.S. arms embargo in February 1914. As Carranza's resupplied forces pushed south, the president sent U.S.

naval vessels to the oil-producing town of Tampico on the Gulf of Mexico. On April 9, at Tampico, Huerta's troops arrested several U.S. sailors loading gasoline aboard a whaleboat docked provocatively near the Mexican outpost. The Mexican colonel in charge quickly freed the bluejackets and apologized orally. Hotheaded Admiral Henry T. Mayo nonetheless demanded a formal twenty-one-gun salute because Mexico had insulted the flag. When Huerta refused, the president on April 20 asked Congress to authorize force "to obtain . . . the fullest recognition of the rights and dignity of the United States." Wilson then ordered U.S. warships to the port of Veracruz to stop a German arms shipment intended for Huerta.

On April 21, 1914, 800 American sailors and marines landed. Huerta's troops withdrew but cadets from the naval academy put up a bloody resistance. Nineteen Americans and several hundred Mexicans died. Despite Wilson's intent to undermine Huerta, the capture of Veracruz temporarily united Mexicans behind the dictator. Rejecting advice from his military advisers, who wanted to march to Mexico City, Wilson accepted mediation when proposed by Argentina, Brazil, and Chile (the ABC powers) on April 25. These mediation talks, held on the Canadian side of Niagara Falls that summer, accomplished little, but in mid-July Huerta fled to Europe, and on August 20 a triumphant Carranza paraded before enthusiastic throngs in Mexico City.

The Constitutionalist triumph did not last. One of Carranza's northern generals, Francisco (Pancho) Villa, soon broke from the ranks, marched south, and in December occupied Mexico City. Wilson saw Villa as "the only instrument of civilization in Mexico" who could "educate the turbulent masses of peons so prone to pillage." The president thus eased arms exports to him and refused to recognize Carranza. To prevent a military clash with any Mexican faction, all American troops withdrew from Veracruz on November 23, 1914. Once again, Wilson watched and waited.

Relations remained tense during early 1915. Carranza's forces gradually drove Villa north, but in the process Mexico City became a no-man's-land, with bread riots and starvation threatening its inhabitants, including 2,500 Americans and 23,000 other foreign residents. Further complications arose along the Mexico-U.S. borderland, especially in southern Texas, where the massive influx of refugees and revolutionaries exacerbated local tensions between Anglos and *Tejanos*. The ensuing raids and counterraids turned south Texas into a war zone as vigilantes and Texas rangers killed at least 150 Mexicans. Preoccupied by the *Lusitania* crisis with Germany after May 1915, Wilson reluctantly concluded that "Carranza will somehow have to be digested." With U.S. oil fields under Carranza's protection, Wilson extended de facto recognition to the Constitutionalist regime in June 1915, permitted arms exports (while banning them to opponents), and beefed up the U.S. military presence along the border.

Egged on by German agents, Villa denounced *Carranzistas* as "vassals" of the United States. In the predawn hours of March 9, 1916, Villa led a band of *Villistas* across the border into Columbus, New Mexico, leaving seventeen Americans and more than a hundred Mexicans dead. Within hours, Wilson unleashed the Punitive Expedition of 7,000 soldiers, commanded by General John J. Pershing, which soon penetrated 350 miles into Mexico in a vain search for Villa. Nonetheless, a clash

Francisco (Pancho) Villa (1878–1923). The intelligent, dedicated revolutionary nationalist bedeviled both Mexico and the United States. His daring raid on an American town was calculated to outrage President Wilson, whom he mocked as "an evangelizing professor of philosophy who is destroying the independence of a friendly people." (El Paso Public Library, Southwest Collection)

with *Carranzista* troops occurred at Carrizal in June 1916. Wilson resisted demands to withdraw Pershing's troops until February 1917. Later that month, the secret Zimmermann telegram, proposing an anti-American alliance between Germany and Mexico, came into the hands of the State Department, courtesy of British intelligence. This German threat prompted the United States to extend de jure recognition of Carranza's government on August 31, 1917, in order to ensure Mexican neutrality during the fight against Germany. After four futile years, Wilson had finally given up trying to tutor the Mexicans.

Japan, China, and Dollar Diplomacy in Asia

Managing Asian affairs proved even more difficult. Secretary of State John Hay's Open Door notes did not prevent the further humiliation of China. During the Boxer Rebellion Russia stationed 175,000 troops in Manchuria and demanded exclusive rights from China, including a commercial monopoly. Roosevelt and Hay acquiesced because the Open Door had "always recognized the exceptional position of Russia" in Manchuria. Thinking it folly "to play the role of an Asian power without military power," Roosevelt retreated because the American people would not fight for nebulous principles of Chinese integrity in Manchuria.

Japan viewed the question quite differently. Russia blocked Japanese economic expansion into Manchuria, posed a potential naval menace, and endangered the Japanese position in Korea. Tokyo covered its flanks with an Anglo-Japanese Alliance in 1902 and prepared for war. On February 8, 1904, the Japanese navy destroyed Russia's Asian fleet in a surprise attack at Port Arthur. At first Roosevelt cheered privately, "for Japan is playing our game," but he worried about "the creation of either a yellow peril or a Slav peril." By spring 1905, Japanese soldiers had taken Mukden, where Russia lost 97,000 men. Revolutionary stirrings had hit St. Petersburg, and Admiral Heihachiro Togo had sunk the Russian Baltic fleet at Tsushima. On May 31, Japanese envoy Kogoro Takahira requested Roosevelt "to invite the two belligerents to come together" for direct peace negotiations.

Hoping to balance the belligerents and thus protect U.S. interests in the Pacific and Asia, Roosevelt invited Japanese and Russian diplomats to meet at Portsmouth, New Hampshire, in August 1905. Japan demanded Russia's leasehold on the Liaodong Peninsula and the railroad running from Harbin to Port Arthur, evacuation of Russian troops from Manchuria, and Japan's control of Korea. The Russians quickly conceded these points but rejected demands for an indemnity and cession of the island of Sakhalin. Roosevelt then proposed dividing Sakhalin and agreement "in principle" on an indemnity. Tsar Nicholas II agreed to partition but "not a kopeck of compensation." Japan yielded and in late August signed a peace treaty. Roosevelt had earned the Nobel Peace Prize.

The president's search for equipoise in East Asia did not end at Portsmouth. As early as March 1904, TR had conceded to Japan a relationship with Korea "just like we have with Cuba." Secretary of War Taft reaffirmed the concession with Prime Minister Taro Katsura on July 27, 1905, whereby Japan denied any designs on the Philippines, and Taft acknowledged Japanese control of Korea. A year later Tokyo

reopened southern Manchuria to foreign and American trade but discouraged foreign capital investments. Japan formally annexed Korea in 1910.

A domestic dispute in California soon soured Japanese-American cordiality. On October 11, 1906, the San Francisco School Board created a special "Oriental Public School" for all Japanese, Chinese, and Korean children. Japan immediately protested, and TR denounced the "infernal fools in California" whose educational exclusion of Japanese was "as foolish as if conceived by the mind of a Hottentot." Given existing federal-state jurisdictions, however, he could do little more than rail against the recalcitrant school board and apply political pressure to the California legislature to prevent statewide discriminatory measures. Defending segregation, the *San Francisco Examiner* editorialized:"Californians do not want their growing daughters to be intimate in daily school contact with Japanese young men. Is this remarkable?" Always the political realist, Roosevelt accepted what he personally disliked and in February 1907 reached a "Gentlemen's Agreement" with Tokyo, sharply restricting Japanese immigration on a voluntary basis.

Because "the Japanese jingoes are . . . about as bad as ours," the president shrewdly pressed for more battleships and fortification of Hawai'i and the vulnerable Philippines, now America's "heel of Achilles," so that the United States would "be ready for anything that comes." He also dramatized the importance of a strong navy to Congress and to Japan by ordering the battle fleet in 1907 to the Pacific and around the world. Just after the "Great White Fleet" visited Tokyo in October 1908, Ambassador Takahira received instructions to reach an agreement with the United States recognizing the Pacific Ocean as an open avenue of trade, pledging the integrity of Japanese and American insular possessions in the Pacific, and promising equal opportunity in China. The ensuing Root-Takahira declaration of November 30, 1908, seemed to restore Japanese-American harmony.

Conflicting Japanese-American goals toward China spoiled the new epoch. Despite the Open Door notes, American commerce with China stalled during the Roosevelt era, in part because of resurgent nationalism. When Congress barred Chinese immigration in 1904, the Chinese staged a short-lived boycott of American goods. Because Roosevelt viewed the Chinese as passive and effete, "sunk in Oriental stagnation and corruption," he placed strategic interests first and refused to antagonize Japan over China. TR's successor thought otherwise. Instead of a decrepit China in decay, Taft envisaged expanded trade with a "young China, rousing from a centuries-old slumber and rubbing the sand of its past from its eyes." During a 1905 trip to East Asia, Taft met the intensely anti-Japanese American consul general in Mukden, Willard Straight. Two years later Straight proposed the creation of a Manchurian bank, to be financed by the American railroad magnate E. H. Harriman. Under Taft, Straight and the State Department quickly inspired several New York banks to serve as the official agency of American railroad investment in China. As acting chief of the department's new Far Eastern Division, Straight demanded admission of the American bankers into a European banking consortium undertaking construction of the Huguang Railway linking Beijing and Guangzhou (Canton). Straight then resigned from the State Department to become the consortium's roving representative.

In November 1909, Washington had proposed to Britain the neutralization of Manchurian railroads through a large international loan to China for the purchase of the lines. Britain, however, joined both Japan and Russia to reject the proposal. Instead of an open door in Manchuria, Secretary of State Knox had "nailed that door closed with himself on the outside." In fall 1910, an agreement expanded the Huguang Railway consortium to include American bankers, but the Chinese Revolution broke out in May 1911 and delayed railroad construction until 1913. "Dollar diplomacy," Straight ruefully admitted, "made no friends" in the Huguang matter.

Hoping to reap tangible benefits by dissociating from the other powers, President Wilson repudiated American participation in the international consortium in March and then extended formal diplomatic recognition to the Chinese Republic in May. He had thereby renewed America's commitment to the political integrity of China, a goal pragmatically abandoned by Roosevelt, unsuccessfully resuscitated by Taft, and consistently opposed by Japan.

Events at home soon made Wilson's Asian policy resemble Taft's more than Roosevelt's. In April 1913, politicians placed before the California legislature a bill denying residents "ineligible to citizenship" the right to own land. The measure struck directly at the 50,000 Japanese living in California. Racist passions erupted, with one farmer recoiling from the prospect of racial intermarriage: "What is that baby? It isn't a Japanese. It isn't white." Basically sharing the Californians' anti-Japanese prejudices, and sensitive to states' rights, Wilson nonetheless sent Secretary Bryan to Sacramento to beg for a less harsh statute. But the California legislature passed the offensive bill on May 3, 1913. When Japan protested, Wilson and Bryan lamely argued that one state's legislation did not constitute a "national discriminatory policy."

Wilson's antipathy toward Japan reappeared in fall 1914 when Japan declared war on Germany, seized the German Pacific islands north of the equator, and swept across China's Shandong Peninsula to capture the German leasehold of Jiaozhou. "When there is a fire in a jeweller's shop," a Japanese diplomat theorized, "the neighbours cannot be expected to refrain from helping themselves." Tokyo immediately followed with the Twenty-One Demands of January 18, 1915, claiming extensive political and economic rights in Shandong, southern Manchuria, and Mongolia. Preoccupied with Mexico and the *Lusitania* crisis, the Wilson administration refused to recognize Japan's gains, which amounted to a repudiation of the Open Door policy.

Wilson's nonrecognition policy ran counter to secret treaties in which the European Allies promised to support Japan's conquests at the peace conference after World War I. Washington soon compromised. In an agreement with Viscount Kikujiro Ishii in November 1917, Secretary Lansing acknowledged that "territorial propinquity creates special relationships between countries, and consequently . . . Japan has special interests in China," while Ishii pledged his nation's dedication to the Open Door and integrity of China. The Wilson administration also revived the international banking consortium as the only way to check further unilateral Japanese economic penetration of China proper. The wheel had turned full circle for Wilson. Like Taft before him, Wilson failed to protect China's fragile sovereignty without conciliating or blocking Japan.

Anglo-American Rapprochement and Empire-Building

American policies toward Asia and Latin America often fell short of their proclaimed goals because of the pseudoscientific race thinking of the early twentieth century. Americans viewed Asians as "inscrutable and somnolent," depicted Latin Americans as black children or alluring maidens, imagined Africa as the "dark continent" of "savage beasts and beastly savages," and referred to Filipinos as "our little brown brothers," and these biased stereotypes inevitably aroused resentment from Bogotá to Beijing, from Managua to Manila. Yet such Darwinist racial attitudes also facilitated much closer relations between the United States and Great Britain. Because victory "in the international competition among the races" might go to the most populous and unscrupulous countries, England and the United States might then need "to cultivate a sense of solidarity and a capacity for cooperation." Theodore Roosevelt certainly thought so when he predicted that the "twentieth century" would "still be the century" of "men who speak English." So too did the British, as shown by their willingness to accept exclusive U.S. control of a canal in Panama. Also prompted by a search for allies against Germany, London's pursuit of "the most

John Bull in Need of Friends.
Battered by criticism over its war against the Boers in South Africa and challenged by a rising Germany, Great Britain found a new friend in the United States. (*Des Moines Leader* in *Literary Digest*, 1901)

cordial and constant cooperation" with the United States led to a celebrated "great rapprochement."

The new Anglo-American affinity, however, nearly dissolved in 1903 over the Alaska boundary controversy, which stemmed from Canadian claims to large areas of the Alaskan panhandle. As the power responsible for the Dominion's foreign relations, Britain found itself backing Ottawa's dubious contention that much of the panhandle's coastline actually belonged to Canada. Expostulating that Canada had less right "than the United States did to Cornwall or Kent," Roosevelt refused arbitration and sent 800 soldiers to Alaska to awe his opponents. London finally agreed in January 1903 to a mixed boundary commission composed of six jurists, three from each side. Taking no chances, Roosevelt appointed Senator Henry Cabot Lodge and Secretary Root, hardly disinterested judges, to the commission. He told London he would run the line himself if the commissioners failed to agree. One British commissioner sided with the Americans, and in October 1903, by a vote of 4 to 2, the commission officially decided for the United States. The British "made the inevitable choice to please a power ten times the size of Canada and with more than ten times the wealth."

Anglo-American entente also characterized the settlement of the North Atlantic fisheries dispute. Since 1782, American fishermen had insisted on retaining their pre-Revolutionary privileges off Canada's Newfoundland. Indeed, a gilded wooden cod still hung from the ceiling of the Massachusetts State House. The modus vivendi of 1888, under which they had fished for several years, collapsed in

1905 when Newfoundland placed restrictions on American fishing vessels. Senator Lodge cried for warships to protect his constituents' livelihood. Instead, Roosevelt proposed, and London accepted, arbitration at The Hague Tribunal. In 1910 the tribunal ruled that Britain could oversee fishing off Newfoundland under reasonable regulations, that a fisheries commission would hear cases, and that Americans could fish up to three miles from shore. This compromise defused the oldest dispute in American foreign relations and symbolized London's political withdrawal from the Western Hemisphere.

The naval retrenchment had occurred earlier, when the Admiralty abolished the North Atlantic station based at Jamaica. After 1902 the Royal Navy patrolled the Caribbean only with an annual visit by a token squadron of cruisers. Admiral Sir John Fisher wanted to concentrate his heavy ships in the North Sea as monitors of the growing German navy. He regarded the United States as "a kindred state with whom we shall never have a parricidal war."

Even the aggressive hemispheric diplomacy of Taft and Wilson did not undermine Anglo-American rapprochement. Foreign Secretary Sir Edward Grey tersely laid to rest all talk of a challenge: "His Majesty's Government cannot with any prospect of success embark upon an active counterpolicy to that of the United States, or constitute themselves the champions of Mexico or any of these republics against the United States." In reciprocation, Wilson protected British oil interests and made it a "point of honor" to eliminate the one potentially dangerous British grievance inherited from his predecessor. Because Taft's exemption of American intercoastal vessels from payment of Panama Canal tolls unfairly discriminated against foreign (and British) shipping, Wilson persuaded Congress to revoke the law in June 1914.

In the end, rapprochement meant mutual respect for each other's empires. Roosevelt, for example, encouraged London to frustrate native aspirations for independence in India, while the British accepted the American suppression of the Filipinos and U.S. hegemony in Latin America. U.S. leaders usually spoke favorably of independence for colonial peoples—but only after long-term tutelage to make them "civilized" enough to govern. In 1910 in Egypt, where Roosevelt applauded Britain's "great work for civilization," the ex-president even lectured Muslim nationalists about Christian respect for womanhood. In unstable Liberia, where the United States in 1912 instituted a financial receivership in the African nation like that in the Dominican Republic, the British encouraged Washington to use a strong hand in America's African "protectorate."

While building an empire, policymakers largely adhered to the tradition of aloofness from continental European affairs. Even Roosevelt overtly tampered only once with Europe's balance of power. In 1904 France acquiesced in British control of Egypt in exchange for primacy in Morocco. A year later, Germany tested the solidity of the new Anglo-French entente by challenging France's claims in Morocco. The kaiser belligerently demanded a German political role in Morocco, which France at once refused. After a brief European war scare, in which Britain stood by its ally, Germany asked Roosevelt to induce France and England to settle Morocco's future. Worried about Kaiser Wilhelm's "violent and often wholly irrational zigzags," Roosevelt accepted the personal invitation only after assuring Paris that his "sympathies . . . at bottom [were] with France." During the ensuing conference, held in early 1906 at Algeciras, Spain, Roosevelt devised a pro-French compromise and persuaded the kaiser to accept it. This political intervention isolated Germany and reinforced the Anglo-French entente, but it generated criticism at home. Roosevelt's successors made sure they did not violate the American policy of nonentanglement with Europe during the more ominous second Moroccan and Balkan crises preceding the First World War.

Nonentanglement also doomed the sweeping arbitration treaties that Secretary Hay negotiated with several world powers. When the Senate attached crippling amendments, Roosevelt withdrew the treaties because they did "not in the smallest degree facilitate settlements by arbitration." After 1905 Secretary Root persuaded Roosevelt to accept watered-down bilateral arbitration treaties, and Secretary Bryan later negotiated a series of "cooling-off" treaties that pledged nations to refrain from war during international investigations of serious disputes. None of these arrangements, however, effectively bound signatories, and like the Permanent Court of Arbitration at The Hague, they represented a backwater in international diplomacy. Ambassador Whitelaw Reid compared U.S. participation in the Hague Peace Conference of 1907 to a farmer taking his hog to market: "That hog didn't weigh as much as I expected he would, and I always knew he wouldn't."

The mainstream of American foreign policy between 1900 and 1914 flowed through the Panama Canal, a momentous political, military, and technological achievement. The United States became the unchallenged policeman of the Caribbean region, empowering Washington, in Taft's words, "to prevent revolutions" so that "we'll have no more." Despite a two-ocean navy, the United States still lacked the power to challenge Japan or Britain. As Roosevelt understood, the Open Door "completely disappears as soon as a powerful nation determines to disregard it." One military officer told Congress in 1910: "We have grown from a little frontier army to one spread all over the world—in America, Puerto Rico, Hawai'i, Alaska, the Philippines, and sometimes in Cuba—and we have not got the officers and men to do it."

American insensitivity to the nationalism of other peoples became another imperial legacy. Filipino resistance to American domination, Cuban anger against the Platt Amendment, Colombian outrage over Panama, and Mexican rejection of Wilsonian intervention bore witness to the depth of nationalistic sentiments. Like the European powers carving up Asia, Africa, and the Middle East, the United States was developing its empire and subjugating peoples and compromising their sovereignty in Latin America and the Pacific. As a Panamanian diplomat later explained, "When you hit a rock with an egg, the egg breaks. Or when you hit an egg with a rock, the egg breaks. The United States is the rock. Panama is the egg. In either case, the egg breaks." With the exception of the Virgin Islands, purchased from Denmark for $25 million in 1917 to forestall any wartime German seizure, the empire grew little from outright territorial gains. It was, instead, an informal empire administered by troops, financial advisers, and reformers who showed contempt for native peoples' culture, politics, and economies through a paternalistic discourse.

Puerto Rico thus seemed the "good" territorial possession, as political cartoons portrayed the populace as a "polite schoolchild, sometimes female, in contrast to ruffian boys" in Cuba and the Philippines. Under the Foraker Act (1900), Puerto

Rico and its naval base on Culebra became a "new constitutional animal"—an "unincorporated territory" subject to the will of the U.S. Congress and governed by the War Department (until 1934). In a series of decisions called the Insular Cases (1901–1904), the Supreme Court upheld the Foraker Act, providing Washington with a means to govern people it did not wish to organize as a state. In March 1917, Congress granted Puerto Ricans U.S. citizenship just in time for them to be drafted into the U.S. armed forces in the war against Germany. To this day, Puerto Rico remains a colony, or "commonwealth," and Puerto Ricans remain divided in their views about statehood, independence, and commonwealth status.

The adventures of American foreign relations under an imperial ideology and the male ethos in the years 1900–1914 attracted many capable, well-educated young men to diplomatic service. "It was TR's call to youth which lured me to Washington," the diplomat William Phillips recalled. Several of these young foreign-service professionals, virtually all graduates of Ivy League colleges, including Phillips, Joseph Grew, Willard Straight, former Rough Rider Henry P. Fletcher, and soldier-diplomat Frank R. McCoy, lived in an exclusive bachelors' townhouse at 1718 H Street during their Washington service. Dubbed "the Family," these youthful professionals blended camaraderie with careers and "became the elite or legendary 'inner circle' of the State Department" for the next forty years. The New York attorney Henry L. Stimson, a protégé of Elihu Root, served as secretary of war under Taft (1911–1913) and continued this tradition of recruiting some of the brightest public servants in a succession of high-level posts through the end of World War II.

Cultural foreign relations also flourished during these years. Just as Buffalo Bill Cody's Wild West Show had "hyped" American cultural myths abroad since the 1890s, Wilbur Wright's airplane tour of Europe in 1908 set records, thrilled crowds, and impressed military strategists. The cruise of the "Great White Fleet" provided as much pageantry as statecraft—"a feast, a frolic, or a fight," as one admiral put it. Colonial subjects became popular on college campuses, as anthropologists and ethnographers offered courses on "Savage Childhood" and "Peoples of the Philippines."

Hundreds of thousands of U.S. tourists ("the world's wanderers") traveled abroad clutching their Baedeker guidebooks, spending American dollars, and sometimes acquiring foreign titles through marriage, as in the case of Jennie Jerome and Lord Randolph Churchill, whose son Winston valued Anglo-American partnership. Civic leaders took pride in hosting the Olympic Games in St. Louis in 1904, hailed an American victory in the 1908 Round-the-World Automobile Race, and cheered the gold medals won by Native American Jim Thorpe at the Stockholm Olympics in 1912. Just as they seemed to take up the great game of empire from Great Britain, so too did Americans become proficient in that most diplomatic of athletic competitions, the royal and ancient Scottish sport of golf. For some Americans, true Anglo-American entente did not occur until young Francis Ouimet bested British champions Harry Vardon and Ted Ray in the U.S. Open at Brookline, Massachusetts, in 1913.

Yet beneath the glitter lurked danger. Winston Churchill later wrote of living in two different worlds: "the actual, visual world with its peaceful activities" and "a hypothetical world 'beneath the threshold'"—"a world at one moment utterly fantastic, at the next seeming to leap into reality—a world of monstrous shadows moving in convulsive combination through vistas of fathomless catastrophe." Once the world started spinning around Sarajevo, Bosnia, it became impossible for the growing American empire to escape the maelstrom of world war.

FURTHER READING FOR THE PERIOD 1900–1914

See studies listed in the last two chapters and Michael C. C. Adams, *The Great Adventure: Male Desire and the Coming of World War I* (1990); Gail Bederman, *Manliness & Civilization* (1995); Frances A. Boyle, *Foundations of World Order* (1999); Kurkpatrick Dorsey, *The Dawn of Conservation Diplomacy* (1999); Lloyd C. Gardner, *Safe for Democracy: The Anglo-American Response to Revolution, 1913–1923* (1984); Robert E. Hannigan, *The New World Empire* (2002); George R. Matthews, *America's First Olympics* (2005); Cyrus Veeser, *A World Safe for Capitalism* (2002); and Richard H. Werking, *The Master Architects* (1977) (foreign service).

Theodore Roosevelt is the subject of H. W. Brands, *T.R.* (1997); Richard H. Collin, *Theodore Roosevelt* (1985); Kathleen Dalton, *Theodore Roosevelt* (2002); Frederick W. Marks, *Velvet on Iron* (1979); Edmund Morris, *Theodore Rex* (2001); Natalie A. Naylor et al., eds., *Theodore Roosevelt* (1992); Patricia O'Toole, *When Trumpets Call* (2005); William N. Tilchin, *Theodore Roosevelt and the British Empire* (1997); and Sarah Watts, *Rough Rider in the White House* (2003).

For the Taft administration, see Paolo E. Coletta, *The Presidency of William Howard Taft* (1973); Ralph E. Minger, *William Howard Taft and American Foreign Policy* (1975); and Walter V. Scholes and Marie V. Scholes, *The Foreign Policies of the Taft Administration* (1970).

For Wilson policies, see the next chapter and Frederick S. Calhoun, *Power and Principle* (1986) and *Uses of Force and Wilsonian Foreign Policy* (1993); and Kendrick A. Clements, *The Presidency of Woodrow Wilson* (1990).

U.S. relations with Latin America are examined in Laura Briggs, *Reproducing Empire* (2002) (Puerto Rico); Bruce J. Calder, *The Impact of Intervention* (1984) (Dominican Republic); Raymond A. Carr, *Puerto Rico* (1984); Arturo M. Carrión, *Puerto Rico* (1983); Mark T. Gilderhus, *Pan American Visions* (1986) (Wilson); David Healy, *Drive to Hegemony* (1989) and *Gunboat Diplomacy in the Wilson Era* (1976) (Haiti); Lester D. Langley, *The Banana Wars* (2002); Lester D. Langley and Thomas Schoonover, *The Banana Men* (1995); Nancy Mitchell, *The Danger of Dreams* (1999); Thomas F. O'Brien, *The Revolutionary Mission* (1996); Brenda G. Plummer, *Haiti and the Great Powers, 1902–1915* (1988); Mary Renda, *Taking Haiti* (2001); Emily Rosenberg, *Financial Missionaries to the World* (1999) (dollar diplomacy); Thomas D. Schoonover, *The United States in Central America, 1860–1911* (1991); David Sheinin, *Searching for Authority* (1998) (Argentina) and *Beyond the Ideal* (2000) (Pan Americanism); and Richard P. Tucker, *Insatiable Appetite* (2000).

For the Panama Canal, see Richard H. Collin, *Theodore Roosevelt's Caribbean* (1990); Michael L. Conniff, *Panama and the United States* (2001); Richard L. Lael, *Arrogant Diplomacy* (1987); Walter LaFeber, *The Panama Canal* (1989); John Lindsay-Poland, *Emperors in the Jungle* (2003); John Major, *Prize Possession* (1993); David McCullough, *The Path Between the Seas* (1977); and Stephen J. Randall, *Colombia and the United States* (1992).

U.S. hegemony in Cuba is discussed in David Healy, *The United States in Cuba, 1898–1902* (1963); James H. Hitchman, *Leonard Wood and Cuban Independence, 1898–1902* (1971); Allan R. Millett, *The Politics of Intervention* (1968); and Louis A. Pérez, Jr., *Cuba and the United States* (2003) and *Cuba Under the Platt Amendment, 1902–1934* (1986).

Relations with Mexico are treated in Jonathan C. Brown, *Oil and Revolution in Mexico* (1993); Joseph M. Gilbert, *Revolution from Without* (1982); Mark T. Gilderhus, *Diplomacy and Revolution* (1977); John M. Hart, *Revolutionary Mexico* (1988) and *Empire and Revolution* (2002); Friedrich Katz *The Secret War in Mexico* (1981); Alan Knight, *U.S.–Mexican Relations, 1910–1940* (1987); Daniel Nugent, ed., *Rural Revolt in Mexico and U.S. Intervention* (1988); Robert L. Scheina, *Villa* (2004); and Joseph A. Stout, Jr., *Border Conflict* (1999).

For America's interactions with Asia and China, see Jongsuk Chay, *Diplomacy of Asymmetry* (1990) (Korea); Sharon Delmendo, *The Star Spangled Banner* (2004) (Philippines); Frank H. Golay, *Face of Empire* (2004) (Philippines); Jonathan Goldstein et al., eds., *America Views China* (1991); Michael H. Hunt, *The Making of a*

Special Relationship (1983); Eileen Scully, *Bargaining with the State from Afar* (2001) (Extraterritoriality); and Guanhua Wang, *In Search of Justice* (2002).

Japanese-American relations are studied in Raymond A. Esthus, *Double Eagle and Rising Sun* (1988) (Portsmouth) and *Theodore Roosevelt and Japan* (1966); Tsuyoshi Ishihara, *Mark Twain and Japan* (2005); Walter LaFeber, *The Clash* (1997); Charles E. Neu, *The Troubled Encounter* (1975); and E. P. Trani, *The Treaty of Portsmouth* (1969).

American missionaries, especially in Asia, are covered in Gael Graham, *Gender, Culture, and Christianity* (1995); Patricia R. Hill, *The World Their Household* (1985) (women); Jane Hunter, *The Gospel of Gentility* (1984) (women in China); and Xi Lian, *The Conversion of Missionaries* (1997).

U.S. relations with Europe and Great Britain, and rivalry with Germany, are discussed in Stuart Anderson, *Race and Rapprochement* (1981); Holger H. Herwig, *Politics of Frustration* (1976); Bradford Perkins, *The Great Rapprochement* (1968); Thomas and Kathleen Schaeper, *Rhodes Scholars, Oxford, and The Creation of an American Elite* (2004); and Hans-Jürgen Schröder, ed., *Confrontation and Cooperation* (1993) (Germany).

The peace movement and the role of The Hague are discussed in Calvin Davis, *The United States and the First Hague Conference* (1962) and *The United States and the Second Hague Peace Conference* (1975); Sondra R. Herman, *Eleven Against War* (1969); C. Roland Marchand, *The American Peace Movement and Social Reform, 1898–1918* (1973); and David S. Patterson, *Toward a Warless World* (1976).

See also Robert L. Beisner, ed., *Guide to American Foreign Relations Since 1600* (2003).

For comprehensive coverage of foreign-relations topics, see the articles in the four-volume *Encyclopedia of U.S. Foreign Relations* (1997), edited by Bruce W. Jentleson and Thomas G. Paterson.

CHAPTER ❋ 3

War, Peace, and Revolution in the Time of Wilson, 1914–1920

❋ *The Sinking of the* Lusitania, *1915*

"PERFECTLY SAFE; SAFER than the trolley cars in New York City," claimed a Cunard Line official the morning of May 1, 1915. More than twice as long as an American football field, the majestic *Lusitania,* with its watertight compartments and swiftness, seemed invulnerable. The British Admiralty had stipulated that the 30,396-ton vessel could be armed if necessary, but "Lucy's" priority was pleasure, not war. Resplendent with tapestries and carpets, the luxurious floating palace dazzled. One American found the ship "more beautiful than Solomon's Temple—and big enough to hold all his wives." A crew of 702 attended the 1,257 travelers who departed from New York's Pier 54 on May 1. Deep in the *Lusitania's* storage area rested a cargo of foodstuffs and contraband. The Cunarder thus carried, said a U.S. State Department official, both "babies and bullets."

In the morning newspapers of May 1 a rather unusual announcement, placed by the German Embassy, appeared beside the Cunard Line advertisement. The German "Notice" warned passengers that the waters around the British Isles constituted a war zone wherein British vessels were subject to destruction. The State Department did not intercede to warn the 197 American passengers away from the *Lusitania.* Most Americans accepted the Cunard Line statement: "She is too fast for any submarine. No German war vessel can get her or near her."

Captained by William T. Turner, the *Lusitania* steamed into the Atlantic at half past noon on May 1. Manned by an ill-trained crew (the best now on war duty), "Lucy" enjoyed a smooth crossing in calm water. Despite lifesaving drills, complacency about the submarine danger lulled captain, crew, and passengers alike. Passengers joked about torpedoes, played cards, consumed liquor, and listened to concerts on deck. On May 6, as the *Lusitania* neared Ireland, Turner received a warning from the Naval Centre at Queenstown: "Submarines active off south coast

46

Mass Grave of *Lusitania* Victims. In Queenstown, Ireland, a large burial ground holds more than a hundred victims of the *Lusitania* disaster of 1915, which rudely brought Word War I to American consciousness. (U.S. War Department, National Archives)

of Ireland." The captain posted lookouts but took no other precautions, despite follow-up warnings. He had standing orders from the Admiralty to take a zigzag path at full speed to make it difficult for lurking German submarines to zero in on their targets. But Turner steamed straight ahead.

Unusually good visibility, recorded Lieutenant Walter Schwieger in his log on May 7. The young commander was piloting his *U-20* submarine along the southern Irish coast. Schwieger surfaced at 1:45 P.M. and soon spotted a four-funneled ship in the distance. He quickly submerged and set a track toward the *Lusitania*. At 700 meters the *U-20* released a torpedo. The deadly missile dashed through the water tailed by bubbles. A watchman on the starboard bow of the *Lusitania* cried out. Captain Turner did not hear the megaphone one minute before the torpedo struck. Had he heard, the ship *might* have veered sharply and avoided danger. Turner felt the explosion as it ripped into the *Lusitania*. Panic swept the passengers as they stumbled about the listing decks. Steam whistled from punctured boilers. Less than half the lifeboats lowered; some capsized or embarked only partially loaded. Within eighteen minutes the "Queen of the Atlantic" sank, killing 1,198—128 of them Americans.

President Wilson had just ended a cabinet meeting when he learned of the disaster. His special assistant, Colonel Edward House, then in London, predicted: "We shall be at war with Germany within a month." Fearing war, Secretary Bryan told the president that "ships carrying contraband should be prohibited from carrying

The *Lusitania* and *U-20*.
The majestic passenger liner was sunk by German submarine *U-20* off the coast of Ireland on May 7, 1915. "Suppose they should sink the *Lusitania* with American passengers on board," King George V had mused to Colonel Edward M. House on that fateful morning. (Peabody Museum of Salem; Bundesarchiv)

passengers. . . . It would be like putting women and children in front of an army. " Ex-president Theodore Roosevelt soon bellowed that Germany had perpetrated "piracy on a vaster scale of murder than old-time pirates ever practiced." American after American voiced horror, but few wanted war. Wilson secluded himself to ponder a response. Just months before, he had promised to hold Berlin strictly accountable for the loss of any American ships or lives because of submarine warfare. Thereafter, Wilson found himself trying to fulfill America's "double wish"—"to maintain a firm front . . . [toward] Germany and yet do nothing that might by any possibility involve us in war."

Wilson spoke in Philadelphia on May 10. His words, much misunderstood, suggested he had no backbone: "There is such a thing as a man being too proud to fight. There is such a thing as a nation being so right that it does not need to convince others by force that it is right." The next morning he told the cabinet that he would send a note to Berlin insisting that Americans had a right to travel on the high seas and demanding a German disavowal of the inhumane acts of its submarine commanders. Secretary Bryan, long upset about an apparent double standard in protesting more against German than British violations of American neutral rights, pleaded with Wilson for a simultaneous protest to London. But only one note went out on May 13—to Berlin: "The Imperial Government will not expect the United States to omit any word or any act necessary to the performance of its sacred duty of maintaining the rights of the United States and its citizens and of safeguarding their free exercise and enjoyment." In short, end submarine warfare, or else.

The German government took little pleasure in the destruction of the *Lusitania*. Chancellor Theobald von Bethmann-Hollweg had more than once chastised the navy for inviting war with the United States through submarine attacks on neutral or Allied merchant vessels. On May 28 he sent an evasive reply to Wilson's note. Claiming that the ship was armed, carried munitions, and had orders to ram submarines, Germany asked Washington to investigate. That same day, in a secret meeting with German ambassador Johann von Bernstorff, Wilson proposed that if Germany would settle the *Lusitania* crisis favorably, he would press the British to suspend their blockade and then call a conference of neutrals to mediate an end to the war.

Wilson convened the cabinet on June 1. When one member recommended a strong note demanding observance of American rights, another suggested as well a note to England to protest British interference with American commerce. Debate became heated. A majority rejected simultaneous notes. When Germany did not immediately reply to his mediation proposal, Wilson sent a second "*Lusitania* note" that vigorously demanded an end to warfare by submarine. He rejected Bryan's plea for a warning to passengers and a protest note to England. The secretary of state then quietly resigned on June 8. Wilson himself went to the golf links to free himself from the blinding headaches of the past several days.

More correspondence on the *Lusitania* followed. Washington insisted that Germany admit it had committed an illegal act; but Germany, unwilling to abandon its one effective weapon against British mastery of the ocean, refused to admit wrongdoing and asked for arbitration. "Utterly impertinent," sniffed Kaiser Wilhelm II, who preferred victory to Wilson's mediation. Eventually Berlin sought compromise. In February 1916 it expressed regret over the American deaths and offered to pay an indemnity. Wilson accepted the German concession.

The horrible deaths from the *Lusitania* remained etched in American memories. The torpedoing of the magnificent Cunarder marked a "naval victory worse than a defeat," as Britons and Americans alike depicted the "Huns" as depraved. The sinking also hardened Wilson's opinion of Germany. His secret mediation offer spurned, Wilson no longer made diplomatic life easier for the Germans by simultaneously protesting British infractions. He also refused to warn Americans away from belligerent ships. In short, if a U-boat attacked a British ship with Americans aboard,

Germany would have to take the consequences. Wilson did not spell out those consequences, but the logical implication was war—just what Bryan feared. His successor, Robert Lansing, expected "that we would ultimately become an ally of Great Britain." The sinking of the *Lusitania* pointed up, for all to see, the complexities, contradictions, and uncertainties inherent in American neutrality during the European phase of the First World War, 1914–1917.

The Travails of Neutrality

Woodrow Wilson acted virtually as his own secretary of state during those troubled years. "Wilson makes confidant of no one. No one gets his whole mind," an aide wrote. The president defined the overall character of American foreign policy—what historians call "Wilsonianism." Above all else, Wilson stood for an *open* world unencumbered by imperialism, war, or revolution. Barriers to trade and democracy had to come down, and secret diplomacy had to give way to public negotiations. The right of self-determination would force the collapse of empires. Constitutional procedures would replace revolution. A free-market, humanized capitalism would ensure democracy. Disarmament programs would restrict weapons. The Open Door of equal trade and investment would harness the economic competition that led to war. Wilson, like so many Americans, saw the United States as exceptional—"a sort of pure air blowing in world politics, destroying illusions and cleaning places of morbid miasmic gasses." His "semi-divine power to select the right" blended with realism. The president calculated the nation's economic and strategic needs and devised a foreign policy to protect them. Yet many Americans feared that his world-reforming efforts might invite war, dissipate American resources, and undermine reform at home. Wilson led a divided nation.

Few Americans, Wilson included, desired war. Most watched in shock as the European nations savagely slashed at one another in 1914. The conviction that civilization had advanced too far for such bloodletting was ruthlessly challenged. Before 1914 the new machine guns, poison gas, submarines, and dreadnoughts seemed too awesome for leaders to launch them. The outbreak of World War I smashed illusions and tested innocence. Progressive-era Americans nonetheless exuded optimism, and the crusading Wilson sought to retrieve a happier past by assuming the role of civilized instructor: America would help Europe come to its senses by teaching it the rules of humane conduct. The war's carnage justified the mission. In 1915 alone France suffered 330,000 deaths, Germany 170,000, and Britain 73,000.

Makers of American Foreign Relations, 1914–1920

President	Secretaries of State
Woodrow Wilson, 1913–1921	William Jennings Bryan, 1913–1915
	Robert Lansing, 1915–1920
	Bainbridge Colby, 1920–1921

Americans had good reason, then, to believe that Europe needed help in cleaning its own house. The outbreak of the war seemed so senseless. By June 1914, the great powers had constructed two blocs, the Triple Alliance (Germany, Austria-Hungary, and Italy) and the Triple Entente (France, Russia, and Great Britain). Some called this division of Europe a balance of power, but an assassin's bullet unbalanced it. Between Austria and Serbia lay Bosnia, a tiny province in the Austro-Hungarian Empire. Slavic nationalists sought to build a greater Serbia by annexing Bosnia, which the Austro-Hungarian Empire had absorbed in 1909. A Slavic terrorist group, the Black Hand, decided to force the issue. On June 28 the heir to the Hapsburg Crown of Austria-Hungary, Archduke Franz Ferdinand, visited Sarajevo, the capital of Bosnia. As his car moved through the streets of the city, a Black Hand assassin gunned him down.

Austria-Hungary sent impossible demands to Serbia. The Serbs rejected them. Austria-Hungary had already received encouragement from Germany, and Serbia had a pledge of support from Russia, which in turn received backing from France. A chain reaction set in. On July 28 Austria-Hungary declared war on Serbia; on August 1 Germany declared "preventive" war on Russia and two days later on France; on August 4 Germany invaded Belgium, and Great Britain declared war on Germany. In a few weeks Japan joined the Allies (Triple Entente) and Turkey the Central Powers, and Italy entered on the Allied side the next year.

Wilson issued a Proclamation of Neutrality on August 4, followed days later by an appeal to Americans to be neutral in thought, speech, and action. Laced with patriotic utterances, the decree sought to cool the passions of immigrant groups who identified with the belligerents. America must demonstrate to a troubled world that it was "fit beyond others to exhibit the fine poise of undisturbed judgment, the dignity of self-control, the efficiency of dispassionate action." A lofty call for restraint, an expression of America as the beacon of common sense in a world gone mad, a plea for unity at home—but difficult to achieve.

Few Americans proved capable of neutral thoughts. Loyalties to fatherlands and motherlands did not abate. German Americans identified with the Central Powers. Many Irish Americans wished catastrophe on Britain. But Anglo-American traditions and cultural ties, as well as slogans such as "Remember Lafayette," pulled most Americans toward a pro-Allied position. Wilson himself harbored pro-British sentiment, telling the British ambassador that "everything I love is at stake" and that a German victory "will be fatal to our form of Government and American ideals." Wilson's advisers, House and Lansing, were ardently pro-British. Ambassador Page even wanted Americans "to hang our Irish agitators and shoot our hyphenates and bring up our children with reverence for English history."

German war actions, exaggerated by British propaganda, also undermined neutrality. To Americans, the Germans, led by arrogant Kaiser Wilhelm II, became symbols of the dreaded militarism of the Old World. Germany, too, seemed an upstart nation, a noisy intruder in the Caribbean where the British had already acknowledged U.S. hegemony. Eager to grasp world power and encouraging Austria-Hungary to war, Berlin certainly had little claim on virtue. On August 4, 1914, hoping to get at France, the Germans attacked Belgium and, angered that the Belgians resisted, ruthlessly proceeded to raze villages and unleashed firing squads against

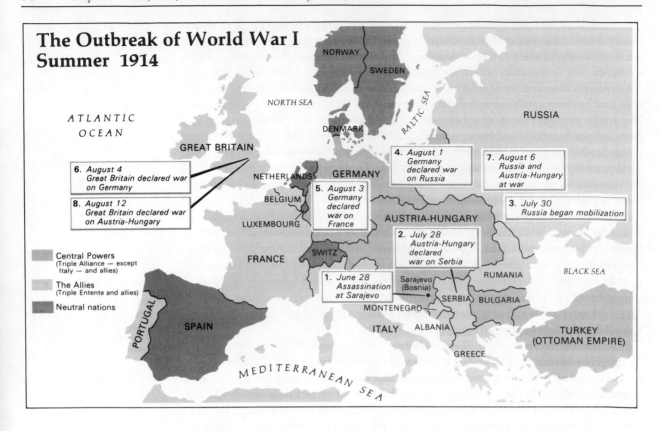

The Outbreak of World War I
Summer 1914

6. *August 4*
Great Britain declared war on Germany

8. *August 12*
Great Britain declared war on Austria-Hungary

5. *August 3*
Germany declared war on France

4. *August 1*
Germany declared war on Russia

7. *August 6*
Russia and Austria-Hungary at war

3. *July 30*
Russia began mobilization

2. *July 28*
Austria-Hungary declared war on Serbia

1. *June 28*
Assassination at Sarajevo

Central Powers
(Triple Alliance — except Italy — and allies)

The Allies
(Triple Entente and allies)

Neutral nations

townspeople. One magazine called Belgium "a martyr to civilization, sister to all who love liberty, or law; assailed, polluted, trampled in the mire, heel-marked in her breast, tattered, homeless." American hearts went out in the form of a major relief mission headed by a young, wealthy, and courageous mining engineer, Herbert Hoover.

U.S. economic links with the Allies also undercut neutrality. England had always been America's best customer, and wartime conditions simply intensified the relationship. The Allies needed both war matériel and consumer goods. Americans, inspired by huge profits and a chance to pull out of a recession, obliged. In 1914 U.S. exports to England and France equaled $754 million; in 1915 the figure shot up to $1.28 billion; and in 1916 the amount more than doubled to $2.75 billion. Comparable statistics for Germany reveal why Berlin believed the United States was taking sides. In 1914 exports to Germany totaled $345 million; in 1915 they plummeted to $29 million; and in 1916 they fell to $2 million. In 1914–1917 New York's banking house of J. P. Morgan Company served as an agent for England and France and arranged for the shipment of more than $3 billion worth of goods. By April 1917, British purchasing missions were spending $83 million a week for American copper, steel, wheat, oil, and munitions.

Britain and France sold many of their American securities to pay for these goods. This netted them several billion dollars. Next, in appeals to prominent American bankers and State Department officials, they also sought loans. In 1914 Bryan discouraged private American loans to the belligerents, because "money is the worst of all contrabands because it commands everything else." After Bryan's resignation, Robert Lansing argued that loans to the Allies would prevent "restriction of output, industrial depression, idle capital, idle labor, numerous failures, financial demoralization, and general unrest and suffering among the laboring classes." Because U.S. industries "will burst their jackets" without "free outlet to the markets of the world," Wilson thus approved $2.3 billion in loans to the Allies during 1914–1917—a sharp contrast to loans of only $27 million to Germany. Once it joined the war as a belligerent, the American economic powerhouse became even more the dispenser of munitions, food, and money to the Allies. Berlin, of course, protested such "unneutral" economic ties. Yet curbing trade with Britain, which ruled the seas, would have constituted unneutral behavior in favor of the Germans, for under international law a belligerent could buy, at its own risk, contraband and noncontraband goods from a neutral. Neutral or not, the United States had become the arsenal of the Allied war effort.

Submarines, Neutral Rights, and Mediation Efforts

To strangle Germany, the British invoked legal doctrines of retaliation and contraband without ever technically declaring a blockade. They mined the North Sea, expanded the contraband list to include foodstuffs and cotton, forced American ships into port for inspection, seized "contraband" from neutral vessels, halted American trade with Germany's neutral neighbors Denmark and Holland, armed British merchant ships, used decoy ships to lure U-boats into traps, flew neutral (often American) flags, and rammed whenever possible any U-boats that complied with international law by surfacing to warn of an imminent attack. The Wilson administration issued protests against these illegalities. The Foreign Office usually paid appropriate verbal deference to international law and went right on with its restrictive behavior. Britain sometimes compensated U.S. businesses for damages and purchased large quantities of goods at inflated prices. Americans thus came to tolerate the indignities of British economic warfare. Britain managed brilliantly to sever American economic lines to the Central Powers without rupturing Anglo-American relations.

Germans protested vehemently against American acquiescence in the British "hunger" blockade. To continue the war, Germany had to have imports and had to curb the flourishing Anglo-American trade that fueled the Allied war machine. The German surface fleet, bottled up in ports, seemed inadequate for the task, so German leaders hesitantly turned to a relatively new experimental weapon of limited maneuverability, the submarine. At the start they possessed just 21 U-boats, and only 127 at peak strength in October 1917. On February 4, 1915, Berlin retaliated by declaring a war zone around Britain. All *enemy* ships in the area would be destroyed. It warned neutral ships to *stay out* of the zone because of possible mistaken identity. Passengers from neutral countries were urged, moreover, to *stay off* enemy passenger vessels. Six days later Wilson held Germany to strict accountability for the loss of American life and property.

The British continued to arm their merchant vessels, which thereby became warships and theoretically ineligible to take on munitions in neutral ports. But Washington invoked a fine distinction between offensive and defensive armaments and permitted such "defensively" armed British craft to carry war supplies from U.S. ports. Crying foul, the Germans also argued that old international law, which Wilson invoked, did not fit the submarine. Rules adopted during the sailing-ship era held that an attacking cruiser about to sink or capture enemy merchant vessels had to give adequate warning so as to ensure the safety of passengers and crew. Yet if a submarine surfaced in its sluggish fashion, the merchant ship's crew might sink it with a deck gun. Imagine the problem for Schwieger of *U-20* when he spotted the *Lusitania*. Had he surfaced to warn the ship, the *Lusitania* probably would have attempted to ram *U-20* or send distress signals to British warships in the vicinity. Even if the *Lusitania* had stopped, it might have taken an hour for passengers to get into lifeboats before Schwieger could torpedo the Cunarder, by which time British warships might have closed in. In short, from the German point of view, to comply with an international law that failed to anticipate the submarine was not possible.

Secretary Bryan tried diplomacy in early 1915, asking Germany to give up use of unannounced submarine attacks in exchange for a British promise to disarm its merchant carriers and permit food to flow to Germany. The Germans seemed interested, but London refused. In March 1915, Wilson did send Colonel House to Europe to sound out possibilities for mediation, but to no avail. Wilson thus failed to adjust or shelve ancient international law, which had no provision for the submarine. He accepted British alterations but not German ones, for reasons of both morality and economics.

Between February and May 1915, marauding submarines sank ninety ships in the war zone. One American, on the British passenger ship *Falaba,* died in the sinking of that vessel on March 28. Then came the *Lusitania* in May. Through Wilson's many protest notes, a U.S. posture took shape: uneasy tolerance of British violations of property rights and rejection of German violations of human rights. Despite secret German orders to avoid a repetition of the *Lusitania* incident, on August 19 the *Arabic,* another British liner, was torpedoed with the loss of two American lives. A worried Ambassador Bernstorff publicly pledged that U-boats would now spare passenger ships.

In early 1916, calling the United States the "mediating nation of the world," Wilson tried to bring the warring parties to the conference table. Colonel House talked with British officials in London but left with no promises for peace. He journeyed next to Berlin, where German leaders gave no assurances. Both sides would fight on—"Hell will break loose in Europe this spring and summer as never before." House then traveled to Paris, where he rashly informed his skeptical French hosts: "If the Allies obtain a small success this spring or summer, the U.S. will intervene to promote a peaceful settlement, but if the Allies have a setback, the United States will intervene militarily and will take part in the war against Germany." House did not report his prediction to the president.

House returned to London to press Sir Edward Grey, British foreign secretary, for a peace conference. The presidential envoy recorded their apparent agreements in the House-Grey Memorandum of February 22, 1916, a document loaded with "ifs." The first paragraph read: "Colonel House told me that President Wilson was ready, on hearing from France and England that the moment was opportune, to propose that a Conference should be summoned to put an end to the war. Should the Allies accept the proposal, and should Germany refuse it, the United States would probably enter the war against Germany." House also said that the peace conference would secure terms "not unfavourable to the Allies" or else "the United States would leave the Conference as a belligerent on the side of the Allies, if Germany was unreasonable." Wilson pronounced the memorandum a diplomatic triumph, but he clouded its meaning all the more by inserting a "probably" before the word "leave" in the sentence quoted above. He took the document much more seriously than did the British or French, who shelved it, snubbed American mediation, and vowed victory over Germany.

As House moved among European capitals, Lansing offered a modus vivendi to defuse naval crises: The Allies would disarm merchant vessels, and the Germans would follow international law by warning enemy merchant ships. This suggestion revealed that Wilson understood the German argument that armed merchant vessels actually operated as offensive craft—that is, warships. The British and Colonel House protested when the Germans seemed to endorse the proposal by declaring on February 10 that submarines would henceforth attack only *armed* merchant ships without warning. Suddenly Wilson reversed policy. He abandoned the modus vivendi in order to restore his standing with the British and sustain House's mediation efforts in London.

Edward M. House (1858–1938). This Texas "colonel" served as Wilson's trusted emissary abroad. In the House-Grey Memorandum of 1916 he showed signs of the deviousness that led to his break with the president after the Versailles conference. An opponent called House "an intimate man . . . even when he was cutting your throat." (National Portrait Gallery, Smithsonian Institution/Art Resource, N.Y.)

Wilson Leads America into World War

Why let one American passenger and a trigger-happy U-boat captain start a war? Why not ban Americans from belligerent ships and require them instead to sail on American vessels? From August 1914 to mid-March 1917 only three Americans had lost their lives on an American ship torpedoed by a U-boat. In contrast, about 190 Americans, including the *Lusitania*'s 128, died on belligerent ships. After the *Falaba* was sunk, Bryan had acknowledged the right of neutrals to travel on belligerent vessels, but he wanted Wilson to forgo that right. Americans on belligerent ships seemed no different than "those who by remaining in a belligerent country assume risk of injury." Ambassador James W. Gerard in Berlin also wondered: "Why should we enter a great war because some American wants to cross on a ship where he can have a private bathroom?"

In January 1916, Representative Jeff McLemore of Texas, a Democrat, introduced a resolution to prohibit Americans from travelling on armed belligerent vessels. In February, Senator Thomas P. Gore of Oklahoma, another Democrat, submitted a similar resolution in his chamber. Wilson bristled at this challenge from Congress, flexing patronage muscle on timid legislators and insinuating that Gore-McLemore was a pro-German ploy. To forego American passage on belligerent ships, Wilson declared, would amount to national humiliation and destruction of the

Permeating Wilson's policies was the traditional American belief that its ideals served as a beacon for the world. "We created this Nation," the president once proclaimed, "not to serve ourselves, but to serve mankind." When the Germans defied America's ideals, destroyed its property, and threatened its security through a proposed alliance with Mexico, they had to be punished. Here was an opportunity to protect both humane principles and commercial interests. When Wilson spoke passionately of the right of a neutral to freedom of the seas, he demonstrated the interconnections among American moral, economic, and strategic interests. Wilson sought the role of peacemaker and promised to remake the world in the American image—world order in which barriers to political democracy and the Open Door came down, in which revolution and aggression no longer threatened. As the philosopher John Dewey put it, war came at a "plastic juncture" in history in which Americans could fight to reshape the world according to progressive principles.

The Debate Over Preparedness

Berlin's assumption that U.S. soldiers could not reach France fast enough to reverse an expected German victory proved a gross misjudgment. American military muscle and economic power, in fact, decisively tipped the balance against Germany. In early 1917, however, the German calculation did not seem so unrealistic. In April the United States had no capacity to send a major expedition to the western front. The Regular Army counted only 130,000 officers and men, backed by 180,000 national guardsmen. Despite earlier interventions in Cuba, the Philippines, and Mexico, many soldiers lacked adequate training. Arsenals had meager supplies of such modern weapons as the machine gun. The "Air Service," then part of the army, did not have a plane of modern design with a machine gun, and some warships had never fired a gun.

An American "preparedness movement" had been under way for months, encouraged by prominent Americans such as General Leonard Wood, who argued that America's military weakness invited attack. After 1914, Wood, Theodore Roosevelt, the National Security League, the Army League, and the Navy League lobbied for bigger military appropriations with the argument that "preparedness" offered insurance against war. When the pacifist song "I Didn't Raise My Boy to Be a Soldier" became a hit in 1915, preparedness proponents countered with "I Didn't Raise My Boy to Be a Coward." One propaganda film, *The Battle Cry of Peace* (1916), depicted spike-helmeted soldiers rampaging through New York City. That same year a U.S. admiral claimed that a single hostile dreadnought could "knock down all the buildings in New York . . . , smash all the cars, break down all the bridges, and sink all the shipping." Convinced that "a great standing army" was "antidemocratic," Wilson belatedly sought moderate preparedness. His request for a half-billion-dollar naval expansion program in late 1915, including ten battleships, promised a new force that would surpass Britain as "incomparably the greatest navy in the world." He also urged that land forces be enlarged and reorganized.

Senator La Follette, Representative Claude Kitchin, and prominent reformers such as William Jennings Bryan, Lillian Wald, and Oswald Garrison Villard spurred a movement against these measures. These peace advocates, especially the Women's Peace Party, argued that war would interrupt reform at home, benefit big business, and curtail civil liberties. The American Union Against Militarism agitated against preparedness with its papier-mâché dinosaur, "Jingo," whose collar read "ALL ARMOR PLATE—NO BRAINS." Because his support of mediation, disarmament, and a postwar association of nations appealed to antiwar liberals and socialists, Wilson hoped that moderate preparedness would not alienate them. Chicago's famed social reformer Jane Addams remembered "moments of uneasiness," but she and others endorsed Wilson in the 1916 presidential campaign, for it seemed "at last that peace was assured and the future safe in the hands of an executive who had received an unequivocal mandate from the people 'to keep us out of war.'"

In January 1916, Wilson set out on a two-month speaking tour, often criticizing members of his own party for their opposition to a military buildup. U-boat sinkings aided the president's message. In May 1916, Congress passed the National Defense Act, increasing the Regular Army to some 200,000 men and 11,000 officers, and the National Guard to 440,000 men and 17,000 officers. The act also authorized summer training camps, modeled after one held in Plattsburg, New York, in 1915 for the social and economic elite. The navy bill passed in August 1916. Theodore Roosevelt thought both measures inadequate, but the anarchist Emma Goldman saw no difference between Roosevelt, "the born bully who uses a club," and Wilson, "the history professor who uses the smooth polished mask."

Once in the war, after learning that the Allies "want and need . . . men, whether trained or not," Wilson relied on the Selective Service Act of May 1917. National military service, proponents believed, would not only prepare the nation for battle but also instill respect for order, democracy, and sacrifice. Under the selective service system, 24,340,000 men eventually registered for the draft. Some 3,764,000 men received draft notices, and 2,820,000 were inducted. Over all, 4,744,000 soldiers, sailors, and marines served. The typical serviceman was a white, single, poorly educated draftee between twenty-one and twenty-three years of age. Officer training camps turned out "ninety-day wonders," thousands of commissioned officers drawn largely from people of elite background. Although excluded from combat, women became navy clerks, telephone operators in the Army Signal Corps, and nurses and physical therapists to the wounded and battle-shock cases.

With the Allies begging for soldiers, General John J. "Black Jack" Pershing, now head of the American Expeditionary Force to Europe, soon sent a "show the flag" contingent to France to boost Allied morale. Neither Wilson nor Pershing, however, would accept the European recommendation that U.S. troops be inserted in Allied units. The U.S. Army would remain separate and independent. National pride dictated this decision, but so did the realization that Allied commanders had for years wasted the lives of hundreds of thousands in trench warfare. Soldiers jumped out to charge German lines, also a maze of trenches. Machine guns mowed them down; chlorine gas, first used by Germany in 1915, poisoned them. Nor did Wilson wish to endorse exploitative Allied war aims. Thus did the United States call itself an "associated" rather than an "allied" power in the war.

Red Cross Postcard. Women served in many roles in the war. They became workers in weapons factories. They sold Liberty Bonds and publicized government mobilization programs as members of the Women's Committee of the Council of National Defense. In France, women nurses and canteen workers became envoys of the U.S. home front, representing the mothers, wives, and sisters left behind. As the historian Susan Zeiger has written, the government's sponsorship of these wartime roles for women cleverly blunted the feminist-pacifist claim that women were "inherently more peaceful than men and would oppose war out of love for their children." (Library of Congress)

The Doughboys Make the Difference in Europe

On July 4, 1917, General Pershing reviewed the first battalion to arrive in France, as nearly a million Parisians tossed flowers, hugged the "doughboys," and cheered wildly. *"Lafayette, nous sommes ici!"* ("we are here") shouted Pershing's aide.

To the dismay of American leaders, taverns and brothels quickly surrounded military camps. "Fit to Fight" became the government's slogan, as it moved to close "red-light districts," designated "sin-free zones" around camps, and banned the sale of liquor to men in uniform. Government signs declared: "A German Bullet Is Cleaner Than A Whore." The YMCA and the Jewish Welfare Board sent song leaders to camps. Movies, athletic programs, and well-stocked stores sought to keep soldiers on the base by making them feel "at home."

Success against venereal disease contrasted with a major flu epidemic, which first struck camps in spring 1918. At Camp Sherman, Ohio, one of the bases hit hardest, 1,101 people died between September 27 and October 13. Whereas about 51,000 soldiers died in battle during the war, some 62,000 soldiers died from diseases. "Doughboys" infected with the virus carried the flu with them to the European war, where it ignored national boundaries and turned into a global pandemic that killed more than 21 million people by spring 1919.

Approximately 400,000 African-American troops suffered discrimination during this war "to make the world safe for democracy." Camps were segregated and "white only" signs posted. In 1917 in Houston, Texas, whites provoked blacks into a riot that left seventeen whites and two blacks dead. In the army, three out of every four black soldiers served in labor units, where they wielded a shovel, not a gun. African Americans endured second-class citizenship and the contradiction between America's wartime rhetoric and reality. A statistic revealed the problem: 382 black Americans were lynched in the period 1914–1920.

The first official American combat death in Europe came only ten days after Congress declared war—that of Edmund Charles Clinton Genet, the great-great-grandson of French Revolutionary diplomat Citizen Genet and member of the famed American volunteer air squadron, the Lafayette Escadrille. Despite Allied impatience, General Pershing hesitated to commit his green soldiers to full-scale battle. Great numbers of troops shipped over in British vessels and had to borrow French weapons. By early 1918 the Allies had become mired in a murderous strategy of throwing ground forces directly at enemy ground forces. German troops were mauling Italian forces, and the French army was still suffering from mutinies of the year before. In March, after Germany swallowed large chunks of European Russia through the Brest-Litovsk Treaty, Wilson warned of a German "empire of force" out to "dominate the world itself" and urged Americans to "contest the mastery of the world." In April he called for "Force, Force to the utmost, Force without stint or limit." Pershing's doughboys soon trooped into battle in greater numbers.

In March the German armies, swollen by forty divisions from the Russian front, launched a great offensive. Allied forces retreated, and by late May the kaiser's soldiers surged to less than fifty miles from Paris. Saint-Mihiel, Belleau Wood, Cantigny, Château-Thierry—French sites where U.S. soldiers shed their blood— soon became household words for Americans. In June at Château-Thierry the doughboys dramatically stopped a German advance. In mid-July the Allies launched a counteroffensive; nine American divisions fought fiercely, helping to lift the German threat from Paris. In the Meuse-Argonne offensive, begun in late September, more than 1 million American soldiers joined French and British units to penetrate the crumbling German lines. "The American infantry in the Argonne [Forest] won the war," German marshal Paul von Hindenburg later commented.

On October 4, the German chancellor asked Wilson for an armistice. German troops had mutinied; revolution and riots plagued German cities; Bulgaria had left the war in September. Then Turkey dropped out in late October, and Austria-Hungary surrendered on November 3. Germany had no choice but to seek terms. The kaiser fled to Holland. On November 11, in a railroad car in the Compiègne Forest, German representatives capitulated.

The Fourteen Points
and the Peace Conference

During the combat, President Wilson had begun to explain his plans for the peace. He trumpeted his vision most dramatically in his "Fourteen Points" speech before Congress on January 8, 1918. The first five points promised an "open" world after the war, a world distinguished by "open covenants, openly arrived at," freedom of navigation on the seas, equal trade opportunity and the removal of tariffs, reduction of armaments, and an end to colonialism. Points six through thirteen called for self-determination for national minorities in Europe. Point fourteen stood paramount: a "general association of nations" to ensure "political independence and territorial integrity to great and small states alike." His Fourteen Points signaled a generous, nonpunitive postwar settlement. They served too as effective American propaganda against revenge-fed Allied aims and Russian Bolshevik appeals for European revolution.

Despite secret treaties that promised German colonies and other territorial gains, Allied leaders feared that Wilson would deny them the spoils of war. In view of the comparative wartime losses, Europeans believed that Wilson "had bought his seat at the peace table at a discount." When, in September and October 1918, Wilson exchanged notes with Germany and Austria-Hungary about an armistice, the Allied powers expressed strong reservations about the Fourteen Points. Wilson hinted at a separate peace with the Central Powers and even threatened to publicize the exploitative Allied war aims. Also facing possible reduced U.S. shipments to Europe, London, Paris, and Rome reluctantly accepted, in the armistice of November, peace negotiations on the basis of the Fourteen Points.

Wilson relished his opportunity. The United States could now claim a dominant role in deciding future international relations. The pictures of dying men dangling from barbed-wire fences and the battle-shock victims who staggered home persuaded many Americans of the need to prevent another conflagration. Wilson's call for a just peace commanded the backing of countless foreigners as well. Italians hoisted banners reading *Dio di Pace* ("God of Peace") and *Redentore dell' Humanità* ("Redeemer of Humanity") to welcome Wilson to Europe.

Yet the president weakened his position even before the peace conference. Congressional leaders wanted him to stay home to handle domestic problems. Lansing feared that Wilson would have only one vote in the day-to-day conference bickering, whereas from Washington he could symbolically marshal the votes of humankind. Wilson retorted that "England and France have not the same views with regard to peace that we have," so he had to attend personally to defend the Fourteen Points.

Domestic politics soon set Wilson back. In October 1918, Wilson "hurled a brick into a beehive" by asking Americans to return a Democratic Congress loyal to him. Partisan Republicans proceeded to capture the November election and majorities in both houses of Congress; they would sit in ultimate judgment of Wilson's peacemaking. The president also made the political mistake of appointing neither an important Republican nor a senator to the American Peace Commission. Wilson, House, and Lansing sat on it; so did Henry White, a seasoned diplomat and nominal Republican. Some concessions to his political opposition, and to senatorial pre-rogatives in foreign affairs, might have smoothed the path later for his peace treaty.

On December 4, with great fanfare, Wilson departed from New York aboard the *George Washington*. He settled into a quiet voyage, surrounded by advisers and nearly 2,000 reports on issues likely to arise at the peace conference. Confident that "we can force" the Allies "to our way of thinking" because they will be "financially in our hands," the president had made few concrete plans. After reaching France on December 15, Wilson basked in the admiration of enthusiastic Parisian crowds, and later thousands in Italy and England cheered him with near religious fervor. Wilson assumed that this generous outpouring meant that *his* peace aims were universally popular and that Americans "would be the only disinterested people" at Versailles. Such "man-in-the-street" opinion, however, did not impress David Lloyd George, prime minister of Britain, French premier Georges Clemenceau, or Italian prime minister Vittorio Orlando, Wilson's antagonists at the peace conference.

David Lloyd George (1863–1945). "America," said the British prime minister referring to the League of Nations, "had been offered the leadership of the world, but the Senate had tossed the sceptre into the sea." (Getty Images)

Excluding Germany and Bolshevik Russia, thirty-two nations sent delegations, which essentially followed the lead of the "Big Four." Most sessions worked in secrecy, hardly befitting Wilson's first "point." Clemenceau resented Wilson's "sermonettes" and preferred the more compliant Colonel House. "The old tiger [Clemenceau] wants the grizzly bear [Wilson] back in the Rocky Mountains before he starts tearing up the German Hog," commented Lloyd George, who sought to build a strong France and to ensure German purchases of British exports. A fervent nationalist, Orlando concerned himself primarily with enlarging Italian territory. These leaders sought a vengeful peace. Lloyd George complained of a chameleon-like Wilson—"the noble visionary, the implacable and unscrupulous partisan, the exalted idealist and the man of rather petty personal rancour." Wilson, in turn, thought the Europeans "too weatherwise to see the weather."

Much wrangling occurred over the disposition of colonies and the creation of new countries. "Tell me what's right and I'll fight for it," said Wilson as he appealed for self-determination. After hard negotiating, the conferees allocated former German and Turkish colonies to the countries that had conquered them, to be loosely supervised under League of Nations auspices. Under the mandate system—a compromise between outright annexation and complete independence—France (with Syria and Lebanon) and Britain (with Iraq, Trans-Jordan, and Palestine) received parts of the Middle East. Japan acquired China's Shandong Province and some of Germany's Pacific islands. Regarding Shandong, the president deemed it "the best that could be accomplished out of a 'dirty past'" and planned to "let the League of Nations decide the matter later." Wilson also ignored a petition calling for self-determination in French Indochina and signed by, among others, Nguyen Ai Quoc—later famous under the name Ho Chi Minh. France gained the demilitarization of the German Rhineland and a stake in the coal-rich Saar Basin. Italy annexed South Tyrol and Trieste from the collapsed Austro-Hungarian Empire. Newly independent countries also emerged from the defunct Austro-Hungarian Empire: Austria, Czechoslovakia, Hungary, Romania, and Yugoslavia. The Allies further recognized a ring of hostile states already established around Bolshevik Russia: Finland, Poland, Estonia, Latvia, and Lithuania, all formerly part of the Russian empire. The mandate system smacked of imperialism, but the new states in Europe fulfilled

Wilson's self-determination pledge. To assuage fears of a revived Germany, Britain and the United States signed a security pact with France guaranteeing its border, but Wilson never submitted it for Senate approval.

Reparations proved a knotty issue. The United States wanted a limited indemnity for Germany to avoid a harsh peace that might arouse long-term German resentment or debilitate the German economy and politics. "Excessive demands," Wilson had predicted, "would most certainly sow the seeds of war." To cripple Germany, France pushed for a large bill of reparations. The conferees wrote a "war guilt clause," which held Germany responsible for all of the war's damages. Rationalizing that the League would ameliorate any excesses, Wilson gave in on both reparations and war guilt. The Reparations Commission in 1921 presented a hobbled Germany with a huge reparations bill of $33 billion, thereby helping to destabilize international economic relations for more than a decade.

The Allies played to Wilson's priorities: "Give him the League of Nations and he will give us all the rest." Drafted largely by Wilson, the League's covenant provided for an influential council of five big powers (permanent) and representatives from smaller nations (by election) and an assembly of all nations for discussion. Wilson saw the heart of the covenant as Article 10: "The Members of the League undertake to respect and preserve as against external aggression the territorial integrity and existing political independence of all Members of the League." In case of aggression or threat, "the Council shall advise upon the means by which this obligation shall be fulfilled." Wilson persuaded the conferees to merge League covenant and peace terms in a package, with the charter comprising the first 26 articles of a 440-article Treaty of Paris. Wilson deemed the League covenant the noblest part of all—"It is practical, and yet it is intended to purify, to rectify, to elevate."

The Germans signed sullenly on June 28 in the elegant Hall of Mirrors at Versailles. By stripping Germany of 13 percent of its territory, 10 percent of its population, and all of its colonies, and by demanding reparations, the treaty humiliated the Germans without crushing them. In one historian's words, the treaty contained "a witches' brew" with "too little Wilsonianism to appease, too little of Clemenceau to deter; enough of Wilson to provoke contempt, enough of Clemenceau to inspire hatred." When Wilson died on February 3, 1924, the German Embassy in Washington broke custom by not lowering its flag to half-mast.

Principle, Personality, Health, and Partisanship: The League Fight

Wilson spent almost six months in Europe. From February 24 to March 14, 1919, however, he returned to the United States for executive business. On arrival, he asserted that any U.S. failure to back the League "would break the heart of the world." In Washington, Republicans peppered Wilson with questions about the degree to which the covenant limited American sovereignty. In early March, Republican senator Henry Cabot Lodge of Massachusetts engineered a "Round Robin," a statement by thirty-nine senators (enough to deny the treaty a two-thirds vote) that questioned the League covenant and requested that the peace treaty and the covenant be acted on separately.

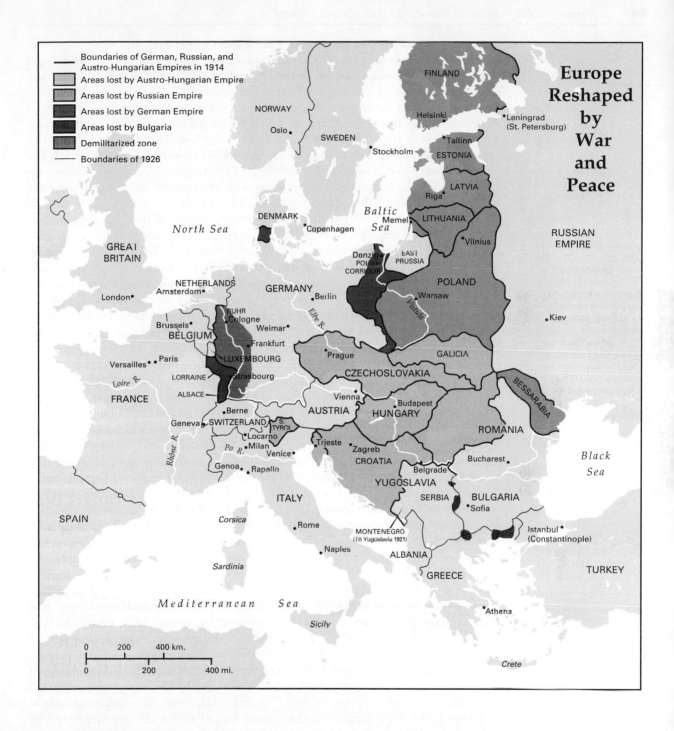

Europe
Reshaped
by
War
and
Peace

Boundaries of German, Russian, and
Austro-Hungarian Empires in 1914
Areas lost by Austro-Hungarian Empire
Areas lost by Russian Empire
Areas lost by German Empire
Areas lost by Bulgaria
Demilitarized zone
Boundaries of 1926

NORWAY
Oslo
SWEDEN
Stockholm
DENMARK
Copenhagen
FINLAND
Helsinki
Leningrad
(St. Petersburg)
Tallinn
ESTONIA
LATVIA
Riga
LITHUANIA
Memel
Vilnius
RUSSIAN
EMPIRE
Baltic
Sea
North Sea
GREAT
BRITAIN
NETHERLANDS
Amsterdam
London
Brussels
BELGIUM
GERMANY
Berlin
Danzig
POLISH
CORRIDOR
EAST
PRUSSIA
POLAND
Warsaw
Kiev
Elbe R.
Vistula
RUHR
Cologne
Weimar
Frankfurt
LUXEMBOURG
Versailles
Paris
LORRAINE
Strasbourg
ALSACE
Loire R.
FRANCE
Prague
CZECHOSLOVAKIA
GALICIA
BESSARABIA
Berne
Geneva
SWITZERLAND
S.
TYROL
Locarno
Milan
Po R.
Venice
Genoa
Rapallo
Rhône R.
Vienna
AUSTRIA
HUNGARY
Budapest
ROMANIA
Bucharest
Black
Sea
Trieste
Zagreb
CROATIA
YUGOSLAVIA
Belgrade
SERBIA
BULGARIA
Sofia
SPAIN
ITALY
Corsica
Rome
Naples
Sardinia
MONTENEGRO
(To Yugoslavia 1921)
ALBANIA
GREECE
Istanbul
(Constantinople)
TURKEY
Mediterranean Sea
Sicily
Athens
Crete

0   200   400 km.
0   200   400 mi.

A defiant Wilson sailed again for France, determined that "little Americans," full of "watchful jealousies [and] of rabid antagonisms," would not destroy his beloved League. Still, he was politician enough to seek changes in Paris. He amended the covenant so that League members could refuse mandates, League jurisdiction over purely domestic issues was precluded, and the Monroe Doctrine was safeguarded against League interference. But he would not alter Article 10. When he returned to the United States in July, Wilson submitted the long Treaty of Versailles to the Senate on July 10, with an address that resembled an evangelical sermon: "It has come about by no plan of our conceiving, but by the hand of God, who led us into this way." Asked if he would accept senatorial "reservations" to the treaty, Wilson snapped: "Anyone who opposes me in that, I'll crush."

Wilson, against strong odds, gained a good percentage of his goals as outlined in the Fourteen Points. Self-determination for nationalities advanced as never before in Europe, and the League ranked as a notable achievement. But Wilson did compromise, especially with Clemenceau. Both Italy and Japan also had threatened to walk out unless they realized some territorial goals. Still, Wilson had so built up a case for an unselfish peace that when hard bargaining and harsh terms dominated the conference, observers could only conclude that the president had betrayed his millennial rhetoric. Critics said that Wilson should have left Paris in protest, refusing to sign, or that he might have threatened the Allies with U.S. economic pressure. Believing desperately that the League, with Article 10, would rectify all, Wilson warned Congress that without it, "the United States and every other country will have to arm to the teeth."

He would not compromise at home, however. And he seldom provided systematic, technical analysis to treaty clauses. He simply expected the Senate dutifully to ratify his masterwork. Yet his earlier bypassing of that body and his own partisan speeches and self-righteousness ensured debate. Henry Cabot Lodge asked a key question: "Are you willing to put your soldiers and your sailors at the disposition of other nations?" Article 10 seemed to rattle everybody. The article did not require members to use force, but it implied they should. Senator William Borah complained that "I may be willing to help my neighbor," but he should not "decide for me when and how I shall act." Senator Hiram Johnson of California claimed that Article 10 would "freeze the world into immutability," keeping "subject peoples . . . subject until the crack of doom." The article seemed too open-ended to most opponents.

Republican Henry Cabot Lodge towered as Wilson's chief legislative obstacle. Chair of the Senate Foreign Relations Committee, nationalist-imperialist, author, like Wilson a scholar in politics, Lodge packed his committee with anti-League senators, dragged out hearings for weeks, and nurtured a personal animosity toward Wilson matched only by Wilson's detestation for Lodge. He attacked obliquely by offering "reservations" to the League covenant. They addressed the central question of American national interest—the degree to which the United States would limit its freedom of action by engaging in collective security. In fact, many of the fourteen reservations stated the obvious—that Congress would retain its constitutional role in foreign policy, for example. Another denied the League jurisdiction over American domestic legislation. The reservation on Article 10 disclaimed any obligation to preserve the territorial integrity or political independence of another country unless authorized by Congress. For Wilson this meant "nullification of the treaty."

The Senate divided into four groups. Wilson counted on about forty loyal Democrats called the Non-Reservationists. Another group, the Mild-Reservationists, led by Frank B. Kellogg, numbered about thirteen Republicans. The third faction, managed by Lodge, stood together as the Strong-Reservationists—some twenty Republicans and a few Democrats. The fourth group, consisting of sixteen Irreconcilables, ardently opposed the treaty with or without reservations. Most of them were Republicans, including La Follette, George Norris of Nebraska, and Hiram Johnson of California.

Wilson met individually with twenty-three senators over two weeks, but he suffered a minor stroke on July 19, 1919. He thereafter rigidly refused to accept any reservations. He argued that a treaty with reservations would have to be renegotiated and every nation would then rush in with its pet reservations—a hollow claim after the British announced that they would accept American reservations. In September 1919, Wilson set off on a 10,000-mile train trip across the United States. Growing more exhausted with each day, suffering severe headaches and nighttime coughing spells, Wilson pounded the podium in forty speeches. He blasted his traducers as "absolute, contemptible quitters." He confused his audiences when he stated that Article 10 meant that the United States had a moral but not legal obligation to use armed force. Failure to join the League, he prophesied in St. Louis, would result in a war "in which not a few hundred thousand fine young men from America will have to die, but as many millions as are necessary to accomplish the final freedom of the peoples of the world." On September 26, after an impassioned speech in Pueblo, Colorado, he awoke to nausea and uncontrollable facial twitching. When his doctor ordered him to cancel the rest of his trip, Wilson wept.

After Wilson returned to Washington, a massive stroke paralyzed his left side. He lay flat in bed for six weeks and saw virtually no one except his wife and Dr. Cary Grayson. For months Mrs. Wilson ran her husband's political affairs, screening messages and banishing House and Lansing, among others, from presidential favor. If the president had resigned, as Dr. Grayson advised him to do, the Senate and Vice President James Marshall almost certainly would have reached some compromise agreement on admission to the League with reservations. As it was, his concentration hampered and his stubbornness accentuated by the stroke, Wilson adamantly refused to change his all-or-nothing position.

In November 1919, the Senate balloted on the complete treaty *with* reservations and rejected it, 39 to 55 (Irreconcilables and Non-Reservationists in the negative). Then it voted on the treaty *without* reservations and also rejected it, 38 to 53 (Irreconcilables and Reservationists in the negative). The president had instructed loyal Democrats not to accept any "reserved" treaty. In March 1920, another tally saw some Democrats vote in favor of reservations. Not enough, the treaty failed, 49 to 35, short of the two-thirds majority required for approval. Still a fighter, the president claimed that the election of 1920 would be a "solemn referendum" on the treaty. Other questions actually blurred the League issue in that campaign, and Warren G. Harding, who as a senator had supported reservations, promptly condemned the League after his election as president. In July 1921, Congress officially terminated the war, and in August, by treaty with Germany, the United States claimed as valid for itself the terms of the Treaty of Versailles—exclusive of the League articles.

Woodrow Wilson After His Stroke. Recent scholarly assessments of medical evidence reveal that Wilson had a long history of cerebrovascular disease. Wilson remained in the White House after his massive stroke in October 1919, while his wife and doctor tried to keep secret the severity of his physical incapacity. (Library of Congress)

The memorable League fight had ended. The tragic denouement occurred because of political partisanship, personal animosities, senatorial resentments, the president's failing health, adherence to traditional unilateralism, and distraction and confusion in the public. Progressive internationalists, many of them harassed by wartime restrictions on civil liberties and disappointed by Wilson's compromises with the imperial powers, no longer backed a president they thought reactionary. Then, of course, there was Wilson himself—stubborn, pontificating, combative, and increasingly ill. He might have conceded that the peace had imperfections. He might have provided more careful analysis of a long, complicated document. Instead, he chose often shrill rhetoric and rigid self-righteousness. Most important, he saw the difference between himself and his critics as fundamental: whether it was in America's national interest to participate in collective security or seek safety unilaterally.

In fact, none of the great powers wished to bestow significant authority on the new League organization. Even if Washington had joined, it most likely would have acted outside the League's auspices, especially regarding its own empire in Latin America. No international association at that time could have outlawed war, dismantled empires, or scuttled navies. Wilson overshot reality in thinking that he could reform world politics through a new international body. Certainly the League represented a commendable restraint against war, but hardly a panacea for world peace.

Red Scare Abroad: Bolshevism and Intervention in Russia

"Paris cannot be understood without Moscow [Russia]," wrote Wilson's press secretary Ray Stannard Baker. Wilson himself depicted Bolshevism as "the poison of disorder, the poison of revolt, the poison of chaos." Revolutionary and anticapitalist, the Bolsheviks, or Communists, threw fright into the leaders of Europe and America. At home and abroad the peacemakers battled the radical left. In the United States the Wilson administration trampled on civil liberties during an exaggerated "Red Scare," which sent innocent people to jail or deported them. Wilson initially thought that "the only way to kill Bolshevism is . . . to open all the doors to commerce." Only belatedly, after authorizing secret aid and espionage against the "Reds," did the president openly "cast in his lot" with the other powers in a futile attempt to destroy the new revolutionary regime.

Most Americans applauded the Russian Revolution of March 1917, which toppled Tsar Nicholas II. But after the moderate Provisional government under Alexander Kerensky fell to the radical Bolsheviks in October, Americans were outraged when the new regime signed the Brest-Litovsk Treaty (March 1918) with Germany and ceded Ukraine and Finland, among other territories—one-third of Russia's best agricultural land. A necessary peace for a devastated Russia from the Bolshevik perspective, the treaty seemed a stab in the back for the Allies. Because German authorities had allowed Lenin to travel to Russia via Germany in 1917, some irate American officials even considered Bolsheviks pro-German. Others recoiled after Ambassador David Francis's testimony that Bolsheviks had "nationalized women."

Lenin actually treated the United States as a special, favored case, and he consistently sought accommodation with Washington. Soviet leaders held a series of cordial conversations from December 1917 to May 1918 with the Red Cross official Raymond Robins, a de facto U.S. representative, and reached agreements on food relief, purchase of strategic materials, and exemption of U.S. corporations from Bolshevik nationalization decrees. Prior to Brest-Litovsk, Robins urged prompt diplomatic recognition to keep Russia in the war, but President Wilson paid more heed to Francis's prediction that the Bolshevik regime would soon collapse.

Although U.S. officials in Russia engaged in espionage and cooperated with Allied and "White" agents in anti-Bolshevik activities after November 1917, Wilson knew only broad outlines of this "secret war" when he sent U.S. troops to Archangel in northern Russia in August 1918. Ordered to avoid military action in the Russian civil war, they inevitably cooperated with British and French forces in attempts to roll back Bolshevik influence. Wilson said publicly that he authorized the expedition only to prevent German seizure of military supplies, but he quickly approved $50 million in secret payments to White armies fighting the Bolsheviks. Wilson's motives were thus "simultaneously anti-German and anti-Bolshevik." Some 5,000 American troops suffered through a bitter winter of fifty-below-zero temperatures. Their morale sagged; mutiny threatened. U.S. soldiers did not leave Russia until June 1919; two hundred twenty-two of them died in what critics dubbed "Mr. Wilson's little war with Russia."

Wilson claimed to be "sweating blood over the question of what is right . . . in Russia." Pressure from the Allies and his own anti-Bolshevism inclined him to send another expedition, this time to Siberia. In July 1918 he approved the expedition, later officially explaining to the American people that he was sending 10,000 troops to rescue a group of 70,000 Czechs stranded in Russia. Organized earlier as part of the Tsarist Russian army to fight for a Czech homeland in Austria-Hungary, the Czech legion was battling Bolsheviks along the Trans-Siberian Railroad in an effort to reach Vladivostok and possible transportation to the western front. Wilson's avowed purpose of evacuating the Czech legion derived also from his "friendly feelings" for Professor Thomas Masaryk and Czechoslovakia's independence, which Wilson soon recognized in October.

Despite his disingenuous official explanation, Wilson believed that "a limited, indirect intervention to help the Russian people overcome domination by Bolsheviks and Germans would not contradict, but rather facilitate self-determination." Yet intervention in Siberia became openly anti-Bolshevik because the Czechs were fighting Lenin's forces. Once Wilson found it impossible to evacuate the Czechs in time to fight in Europe, he reluctantly bowed to Allied pressure and gave support to the anti-Bolshevik White Russian leader Admiral A. V. Kolchak in the hope that he could form a pro-Western constitutional government. Despite money and supplies from the Allies, Kolchak's armies were routed before they could reach Moscow in June 1919. U.S. troops finally withdrew from Siberia in 1920.

At the Paris peace conference, the victors tried to isolate what they considered revolutionary contagion. Accordingly, the conferees granted territory to Russia's neighbors (Poland, Romania, and Czechoslovakia) and recognized the nations of Finland, Estonia, Latvia, and Lithuania as a ring of unfriendly states around Russia.

A. Mitchell Palmer (1872–1936). When U.S. troops were intervening in Bolshevik Russia, Wilson's attorney general, A. Mitchell Palmer, was chasing suspected radicals at home. An architect of the "Red Scare," Palmer believed that the "blaze of revolution" was "eating its way into the homes of the American workmen, its sharp tongues of revolutionary heat . . . licking the altars of the churches, leaping into the belfry of the school bell, crawling into the sacred corners of American homes, burning up the foundations of society." In January 1920, the "Palmer Raids" put 4,000 people in jail. (Library of Congress)

During the conference, besides the military interventions, the Allies imposed a strict economic blockade on Russia, sent aid to the White forces, and extended relief assistance to Austria and Hungary to stem political unrest.

Even though Wilson found the anticlerical, anticapitalist Soviets distasteful, he never settled on a definitive, workable policy to co-opt or smash Bolshevism. Through "a reluctant, chaotic, and capricious process," the president allowed subordinates and circumstances to determine U.S. policy toward Russia. His growing estrangement at Versailles from Colonel House, a conduit for pro-Soviet liberals, meant that the interventionist Allies and the rabidly anti-Bolshevik Secretary Lansing exerted greater influence.

Wilson's one serious effort to end the civil war in Russia through diplomacy came in January 1919 when he invited the warring groups to meet on Prinkipo Island off the Turkish coast. The Bolsheviks cautiously accepted the invitation, but the anti-Bolsheviks refused. Next, in February, House helped arrange a trip by William C. Bullitt, a member of the U.S. delegation at Versailles, and Lincoln Steffens, the radical muckraking journalist, to Russia. Wilson envisioned only a fact-finding mission. The ambitious Bullitt nonetheless negotiated a proposal whereby the Allies would withdraw their troops, suspend military aid to White forces, and lift the economic blockade; in return the Soviets promised a cease-fire in which their opponents would hold the territories they occupied. Bullitt and Steffens returned to Paris convinced that their agreement would satisfy all parties. Lloyd George squelched it; Wilson ignored it. Bullitt resigned in protest.

The Allied counterrevolution proved costly. "It intensified the civil war and sent thousands of Russians to their deaths," the British official Bruce Lockhart later wrote. "Its direct effect was to provide the Bolsheviks with a cheap victory." Kremlin leaders also nurtured long memories. "Never have any of our soldiers been on American soil," Premier Nikita S. Khrushchev lectured Americans as late as 1959, "but your soldiers were on Russian soil." Participation by such young men as Allen and John Foster Dulles in Wilson's "secret war" against the Bolsheviks gave them expertise in "propaganda and covert action" when they later directed U.S. policies during the Cold War. Such tactics ultimately backfired, as Wilson recognized before his death. "Bolshevism is a mistake," Wilson said. "If left alone it will destroy itself. It cannot survive because it is wrong."

The Whispering Gallery of Global Disorder

More than 116,000 American soldiers died in World War I, which cost the U.S. government more than $30 billion. What President Dwight D. Eisenhower would later call the "military-industrial complex" had its origins in a high degree of government-business cooperation during the war; economic decisionmaking for the nation became centralized as never before; and the increased application of efficient methods in manufacturing contributed to U.S. economic power. The era of World War I witnessed other domestic events that impinged on foreign affairs: racial conflict, evidenced by twenty-five race riots in 1919; suppression of dissent under the Espionage and Sedition Acts; the stunting of radical commentary (Socialist leader Eugene Debs and the pacifist Alice Paul, among others, went to jail for opposing the war); and the withering of the reform impulse.

In foreign affairs, the White House assumed more authority in initiating policy and controlling execution. The State Department read diplomatic messages that Wilson had typed on his own machine. Wilson bypassed Congress on a number of occasions, failing to consult that body about the Fourteen Points, the goals at Versailles, and the intervention in Russia. The Senate finally rebelled by rejecting the League of Nations, but that negative decision did not reverse the trend of growing presidential power over foreign policy.

World War I took the lives of some 14,663,400 people—8 million soldiers and 6.6 million civilians. Russia led with 3.7 million dead; Germany followed with 2.6 million; then came France with 1.4 million, Austria-Hungary with 950,000, and Britain with 939,000. One out of every two French males between the ages of twenty and thirty-two (in 1914) died during the war. It had been a total war, involving whole societies, not merely their armies. Never before had a war left the belligerents so exhausted, so battered. New destructive weapons made their debut— "a preview of the Pandora's box of evils that the linkage of science with industry in the service of war was to mean." The war reinforced American desires to avoid foreign entanglement. Captain Harry S. Truman of Missouri claimed that most soldiers "don't give a whoop (to put it mildly) whether Russia has a Red Government or no government and if the King of the Lollipops wants to slaughter his subjects or his Prime Minister it's all the same to us." Disillusioned clergy regretted their participation in the "shrieking and hysterical patriotism." The war had ended "the artificial glow of past American idealism," wrote the novelist Ellen Glasgow.

World War I stacked the cards for an unstable future. Empires broke up—the Turkish, Austro-Hungarian, German, and Russian—creating new and weak nations, especially in central and eastern Europe. Nationalists in Asia, such as Mahatma Gandhi in British-dominated India, set goals of national liberation based in part on Wilson's ideal of self-determination. "Wilson's proposals, once set forth, could not be recalled," said Sun Zhongshan (Sun Yat-Sen) in 1924 as his China battled imperialist domination. In Latin America, prewar European economic ties withered, inviting the United States to expand its interests there, where nationalists resented the greater North American presence. The rise of Bolshevism in Russia and the hostility it aroused around the world made an already fluid international system even more so. Because of fear of a revived Germany, leaders tried to strip it of power, creating bitter resentments among the German people. Facing reconstruction problems at home, the victors tagged Germany with a huge reparations bill that would disorient the world economy. Nobody seemed happy with the postwar settlement; many would attempt to recapture lost opportunities or to redefine the terms.

World War I made the United States the world's leading economic power. As Wilson confidently put it, "The financial leadership will be ours. The industrial primacy will be ours. The commercial advantage will be ours." During the war years, to meet the need for raw materials, American companies expanded operations in developing nations. Goodyear went into the Dutch East Indies for rubber, Swift and Armour reached into South America, tin interests tapped Bolivia, copper companies mined in Chile, and oil firms sank new wells in Latin America and in the Middle East. Washington encouraged this economic expansion by building up the merchant marine, which by 1919 had grown 60 percent larger than its prewar size. By 1920, the United States produced about 40 percent of the world's coal and 50 percent of its pig iron.

Because the U.S. government and American citizens loaned heavily to the Allies during the war, the nation shifted from a debtor to a creditor, with Wall Street replacing London as the world's financial center. Whereas before the war Americans owed foreigners some $3 billion, after the conflict foreigners owed Americans and the U.S. government about $13 billion. Americans had devised plans to seize the apparent economic opportunities given them by the war—the Edge Act to permit foreign branch banks, and the Webb-Pomerene Act to allow trade associations to combine for export trading without fear of antitrust action, for example. How could Europeans pay back their debt to the United States? The answer lay somewhere in a complicated tangle of loans, reparations, tariffs, and world trade.

Economic disorder and political instability thus became the twin legacies of global war. "The world is all now one single whispering gallery," Wilson asserted in September 1919. "All the impulses . . . reach to the ends of the earth; . . . with the tongue of the wireless and the tongue of the telegraph, all the suggestions of disorder are spread." More than most Americans, Woodrow Wilson understood that global interdependence exposed America to "disorder and discontent and dissolution throughout the world." And "democracy has not yet made the world safe against irrational revolution," he admitted.

FURTHER READING FOR THE PERIOD 1914–1920

Many of the works listed in the last chapter also explore the themes, events, and personalities in the era of World War I. See also Anthony Boyle, *Foundations of World Order* (1999); Robert E. Hannigan, *The New World Power* (2002); Tony Smith, *America's Mission* (1994); David Stevenson, *The First World War and International Politics* (1988); Hew Strachan, *Over There* (2004); and Spencer C. Tucker, *The Great War* (1998).

For Woodrow Wilson and his foreign-policy views, consult Lloyd E. Ambrosius, *Wilsonianism* (2002); Louis Auchincloss, *Woodrow Wilson* (2000); H. W. Brands, *Woodrow Wilson* (2003); Thomas J. Knock, *To End All Wars* (1992); Arthur S. Link, *Woodrow Wilson* (1979); Jan Willem Schulte Nordholt, *Woodrow Wilson* (1991); and John A. Thompson, *Woodrow Wilson* (2001).

Wilson's health problems and their relationship to decisionmaking are examined in Robert H. Ferrell, *Ill-Advised* (1992), and Edwin A. Weinstein, *Woodrow Wilson* (1981). See also Bert E. Park, *Ailing, Aging, and Addicted* (1993) and *The Impact of Illness on World Leaders* (1986).

For European questions and the neutrality issue on the U.S. road to World War I, see John W. Coogan, *The End of Neutrality* (1981); Robert H. Ferrell, *Woodrow Wilson and World War I* (1985); Ross Gregory, *The Origins of American Intervention in the First World War* (1971); and Ernest R. May, *The World War and American Isolation, 1914–1917* (1959).

The German-American relationship is spotlighted in Reinhard R. Doerries, *Imperial Challenge* (1989); Manfred Jonas, *The United States and Germany* (1984); and Hans-Jürgen Schröder, ed., *Confrontation and Cooperation* (1993).

The Anglo-American relationship is featured in Kathleen Burk, *Britain, America, and the Sinews of War, 1914–1918* (1985); G. R. Conyne, *Woodrow Wilson: British Perspectives, 1912–21* (1992); and Joyce G. Williams, *Colonel House and Sir Edward Grey* (1984).

For the peace movement, see Frances H. Early, *A World Without War* (1997); Barbara S. Kraft, *The Peace Ship* (1978); Kathleen Kennedy, *Subversive Mothers and Scurrilous Citizens* (1999); Erika A. Kuhlman, *Petticoats and White Feathers* (1997); and Ernest A. McKay, *Against Wilson and War* (1996).

America's preparedness and warmaking experiences are discussed in Robert B. Bruce, *A Fraternity of Arms* (2003); Carol Byerly, *Fever of War* (2005) (influenza); John W. Chambers, *To Raise an Army* (1987); Byron Farrell, *Over There* (1999); Jennifer D. Keene, *The Doughboys, the Great War, and the Remaking of America* (2002); Thomas C. Leonard, *Above the Battle* (1978); Bullitt Lowry, *Armistice, 1918* (1997); David F. Trask, *The AEF and Coalition Warmaking* (1993) and *Captains & Cabinets* (1980); David R. Woodward, *Trial by Friendship* (1993); Susan Zeiger, *In Uncle Sam's Service* (1999) (women); and Robert H. Zieger, *America's Great War* (2001).

For the wartime home front, civil-liberties issues, and propaganda, see Allan M. Brandt, *No Magic Bullet* (1985) (venereal disease); Alfred W. Crosby, *America's Forgotten Pandemic* (1989); Leslie Midkiff DeBauche, *Reel Patriotism* (1997); Mark Ellis, *Race, War, and Surveillance* (2002); Joseph A. McCartin, *Labor's Great War* (1998); Elizabeth McKillen, *Chicago Labor and the Quest for a Democratic Diplomacy* (1995); John A. Thompson, *Reformers and War* (1986); and Stephen Vaughn, *Hold Fast the Inner Lines* (1980) (Committee on Public Information).

The Versailles peacemaking and League debate are discussed in Lloyd E. Ambrosius, *Wilsonian Statecraft* (1991) and *Woodrow Wilson and the American Diplomatic Tradition* (1987); Manfred F. Boeneke et al., eds., *The Treaty of Versailles* (1998); John M. Cooper Jr., *Breaking the Heart of the World* (2002); Inga Floto, *Colonel House in Paris* (1973); Warren F. Kuehl and Lynne K. Dunne, *Keeping the Covenant* (1997); Margaret MacMillan, *Paris 1919* (2002); Herbert F. Margulies, *The Mild Reservationists* (1989); Klaus Schwabe, *Woodrow Wilson, Revolutionary Germany, and Peacemaking* (1985); Alan Sharp, *The Versailles Settlement* (1991); Marc Trachenberg, *Reparations in World Politics* (1986); and Arthur Walworth, *America's Moment, 1918* (1977) and *Wilson and His Peacemakers* (1986).

The U.S. response to Bolshevism, intervention in Russia, and the Red Scare are investigated in Leo Bacino, *Reconstructing Russia* (1999); Donald E. Davis and Eugene P. Trani, *The First Cold War* (2000); Victor M. Fic, *The Collapse of American Policy in Russia and Siberia, 1918* (1995); David S. Foglesong, *America's Secret War Against Bolshevism* (1995); Lloyd Gardner, *Safe for Democracy* (1984); Linda Killen, *The Russian Bureau* (1983); Arno Mayer, *Politics and Diplomacy of Peacemaking* (1967); David W. McFadden, *Alternative Paths* (1993); Benjamin D. Rhodes, *The Anglo-American Winter War with Russia, 1918–1919* (1988); Neil V. Salzman, *Reform and Revolution* (1991) (Robins); Norman Saul, *War and Revolution* (2001); Ilya Somin, *Stillborn Crusade* (1996); John Thompson, *Russia, Bolshevism, and the Versailles Peace* (1966); and Betty Miller Unterberger, *America's Siberian Expedition* (1956) and *The United States, Revolutionary Russia, and the Rise of Czechoslovakia* (1989).

Also see Robert L. Beisner, ed., *Guide to American Foreign Relations Since 1600* (2003).

For comprehensive coverage of foreign-relations topics, see the articles in the four-volume *Encyclopedia of U.S. Foreign Relations* (1997), edited by Bruce W. Jentleson and Thomas G. Paterson.

CHAPTER 4

Descending into Europe's Maelstrom, 1920–1939

DIPLOMATIC CROSSROAD

✳ Roosevelt's Attempt to Extend America's Frontier to the Rhine, 1939

DAUBED WITH RED, white, and blue paint, the new A-20 ("Boston") twin-engine light bomber performed high-speed acrobatics over Los Angeles's municipal airport on January 23, 1939. The sleek craft climbed to 3,000 feet at more than 300 miles per hour. The test pilot then apparently cut one motor to attempt a climb on half power. Suddenly the plane went into a spin and hurtled toward the ground. The pilot bailed out at 400 feet but died on impact.

Onlookers extricated a civilian-clad survivor from the crashed bomber before it burst into flames. Reporters soon learned that the man with the broken leg belonged to a secret French purchasing mission sent to buy American-made warplanes for the French air force. The French were getting ready for World War II, which finally began in September.

Controversy soon engulfed Washington. General Henry "Hap" Arnold of the U.S. Army Air Corps was testifying before the Senate Military Affairs Committee. One senator asked how a French officer could be aboard the "secret" bomber that had just crashed. Arnold disingenuously replied that the Frenchman had gone "out there under the direction of the Treasury Department with a view of looking into possible purchase of airplanes by the French Mission." The War Department, he added, had removed all secret equipment from the plane before the French saw it.

Senator Gerald P. Nye of North Dakota then summoned Treasury Secretary Henry Morgenthau, Jr., and Secretary of War Harry Woodring for further grilling. Morgenthau acidly pointed out that the plane, which remained the sole property of the Douglas Company, could hardly be termed "secret" if flown from a municipal airport where anyone could see it. Woodring, however, admitted that the air corps had originally opposed the French mission but that "everyone [was] . . . in accord before the French went to the West Coast." President Franklin D. Roosevelt muddied matters further by denying to the press that "this Government [had] taken any

A-20 Boston Attack Bomber. Nearly fifty feet long, this mid-wing, twin-engine, medium bomber was the most-produced attack bomber built during World War II, with more than 7,000 constructed in the United States. President Franklin D. Roosevelt hoped to expedite rearmament in 1938 by secretly selling hundreds of these planes to the French. Some 162 of the aircraft on route to France in 1940 were diverted to the British Royal Air Force. More than half of the Boston bombers went into the service of other countries, especially the Soviet Union. The plane earned a reputation for returning its crews home safely. The bomber pictured here was being serviced at Langley Field, Virginia, in 1942. (Library of Congress)

steps to assist or facilitate France in buying planes in this country." But French plane purchases "would be an excellent idea" for "building up" U.S. foreign trade, he noted blandly.

A devotee of poker, the president "wasn't ready publicly to show his hand." In seeking to deter war through nonmilitary methods, he had talked publicly in recent years about quarantines against aggression, held secret naval talks with the British, and toyed with calling a conference in Washington of major world leaders. His invitation to the king and queen of England to visit America in June 1939 seemed a clever way of "dramatizing Anglo-American solidarity for the benefit of the dictators and the American public." Roosevelt had mentioned "methods short of war" to Congress in early January but gave no details of what would amount to a shift in foreign policy in the months prior to World War II.

Ever since the disastrous Munich Conference of September 1938, when England and France had agreed to German territorial demands against Czechoslovakia, FDR had seized on air power as a possible deterrent against another European war. "Had we . . . 5,000 planes and the immediate capacity to produce 10,000 per year," he had mused, "[Adolf] Hitler would not have dared to take the stand he did." When the French financier-diplomat Jean Monnet visited in October 1938, the president confided that France and England needed to acquire "20–30,000" more planes per year "to achieve decisive superiority over Germany and Italy; and they'll have to be found here, in the United States." He urged England and France to place orders, thereby stimulating the lagging U.S. aviation industry and jump-starting military rearmament. When War Department officials balked at showing top-secret prototypes to foreign buyers, Roosevelt argued that "the only check to a world war, which would be understood by Germany, would be the creation of a great [French] air force and a powerful force in this country." Only after a direct presidential order did General Arnold permit the French to inspect the Douglas bomber.

Franklin D. Roosevelt (1882–1945).   Although stricken by polio in the 1920s, Roosevelt remained energetic and optimistic. A talented politician who won four presidential elections, he moved haltingly to shore up Britain and France as they faced an aggressive Germany. Here FDR relaxes with stamp collecting, his favorite hobby. During World War II the president once showed British prime minister Winston Churchill a favorite stamp "from one of your colonies." Churchill asked: "Which one?" Roosevelt replied: "One of your last. . . . You won't have them much longer, you know." (Franklin D. Roosevelt Library)

FDR also wanted to revise America's neutrality laws to permit the sale of arms and munitions to belligerents on a cash-and-carry basis. France and Britain could buy weapons legally in peacetime, but the current law forbade such sales in wartime. The president had secretly promised British prime minister Neville Chamberlain "the industrial resources of the American nation . . . in the event of war with the dictatorships." The crash of the plane with the French officer aboard put Roosevelt's plans in jeopardy. The choice of his close friend Morgenthau to oversee all foreign purchases had aroused criticism. The bespectacled Treasury secretary served as an "intellectual rough-neck" who "bulled things through" with little regard for red tape. In this instance, the chief obstruction proved to be Secretary of War Woodring, a "fourth-rate" former governor of Kansas, "who not only couldn't see that our frontier was the Rhine, but couldn't see across the Hudson River."

Roosevelt invited the Senate Military Affairs Committee to the White House on January 31, 1939. FDR asked for confidentiality so as not "to frighten the American people." During the meeting, he asserted that the growing menace from Germany, Italy, and Japan necessitated fundamental changes in U.S. policies. "We can [not] draw a line of defense around this country and live completely and solely to ourselves," he said. Americans might hope that "somebody would assassinate Hitler or that Germany will blow up from within." Or they could "try to prevent the domination of the world—prevent it by peaceful means."

Strengthening America's "first line of defense" offered the best approach. In the Pacific, that defense consisted of "a series of islands, with a hope that through the Army and Navy and the airplanes we can keep the Japanese" from dominating the Pacific. In the Atlantic, the line of defense rested on "the continued independence" of countries from Finland to Turkey. If England and France fell, however, the others would "drop into the [German] basket." Colonial Africa would "automatically" capitulate. The president claimed that the Germans could grab South and

Central America through subversion and economic penetration. He warned: "The Germans have 1,500 bombing planes that can go from Germany to Colombia inside of forty-eight hours. We have, I think, about eighty that can go down there."

Roosevelt emphatically defended the sale of aircraft, saying that "it is to our interest . . . to help the British and French maintain their independence." The American aviation industry also needed foreign orders to expedite mass production and "turn out nine or ten thousand planes per year" without at the same time delaying the buildup of U.S. air forces. He vowed to send them "all they can pay for on the barrelhead. . . . Now, that is the foreign policy of the United States."

A bravura performance, to be sure. Yet when asked if he meant that the United States had the "duty" to "maintain the independence of these nations," Roosevelt shot back: "No. No! Listen: I probably saw more of the war [World War I] in Europe than any other living person." Describing his three month tour of the battle zones as assistant secretary of the navy in 1918, "I spent days on the Belgian front, on the British front, on the French front, and on the American front." Thus "the last thing this country should do is ever to send an army to Europe again." Senator Nye, listening intently, went back to his office and recorded his thoughts. "Get the uniforms ready for the boys," he noted. "I saw troops moving even though the Pres[ident] had declared he had no intent to go to war."

The next day word leaked to the press that FDR had proclaimed that "the frontiers of the United States are on the Rhine." The president angrily called the leak "a deliberate lie" that "some boob got off." Accusing isolationists of making "political capital" out of words he never spoke, he specifically singled out Senator Nye as "an unscrupulous person."

Did FDR lie? According to a stenographic transcript of his meeting with the senators, he never said exactly that America's frontier extended to the Rhine, but his argument that the nation's first line of defense depended on the independence of England and France carried the same meaning. Several times, Morgenthau later recalled, the president did say privately: "Our frontier is on the Rhine." Yet in all likelihood Roosevelt believed he spoke the truth. A deft "juggler" who always kept options open, the smiling squire of Hyde Park wanted above all else to deter a European war while at the same time to prepare for possible U.S. participation. He sought "methods short of war" because "sending a large army abroad was . . . politically out of the question." Roosevelt persisted in selling aircraft to the French and British, even threatening to exile General Arnold to Guam if he did not "play ball." Although the 555 combat planes eventually delivered to France did not deter war, the French orders quadrupled airplane production and laid the foundation "for the gigantic later expansion of the U.S. aircraft industry."

The bomber affair also caused FDR to abandon any sustained personal effort to educate Congress and public opinion about revising American neutrality laws before the outbreak of war in Europe. Only after the German invasion of Poland in September 1939 did Congress repeal the arms embargo, and even then the president remained conspicuously in the background. The French airplane fiasco reinforced his timidity. "Recall the colorful and untrue reports of over a year ago about our frontier being on the Rhine; . . . about the death of a French officer caused by the crash of an airplane in California," he told a prominent publisher in June 1940.

"The government . . . cannot change its 'editorial' policy overnight. . . . Governments, such as ours, cannot swing so far or so quickly." Of course, the Frenchman had not died, but Roosevelt sometimes exaggerated for effect.

Six years and two months after FDR's alleged remarks about an American frontier on the Rhine, U.S. soldiers seized the bridge at Remagen and crossed the Rhine into Germany. Another European war, which American diplomacy had failed to prevent, then definitively extended the frontiers of the United States.

The Independent Internationalists

The French airplane incident of 1939 illustrates salient themes of interwar foreign relations. It demonstrates that even on the eve of World War II in Europe, the United States still sought methods short of war to deter potential aggressors in areas vital to the national interest. Because foreign airplane orders also meant "prosperity in this country and we can't elect a Democratic Party unless we get prosperity," as Roosevelt put it, the episode reveals the impact of the Great Depression on foreign trade, domestic politics, and international security. Even in failure, it shows how an activist president can use subterfuge and surrogates to circumvent bureaucratic rivalries and congressional opposition. The episode underlines the lessons learned from World War I and the determination to avoid the mistakes attributed to Woodrow Wilson. FDR's claim that America's national security had become tied to the independence of France and England suggested that important U.S. leaders recognized global interdependence and rejected an ostrichlike course during the interwar years.

The United States had emerged from World War I a recognized world power. Postwar diplomats, closer to a global perspective than ever before, knew that even if they wanted to, Americans could not be bystanders in world affairs. True, between World Wars I and II Americans hoped to avoid foreign entanglements and concentrate on domestic matters. But, within the limits of U.S. power, U.S. leaders pursued an active foreign policy befitting their nation's high international status. They worked to create a community of peaceful nations characterized by legal and orderly processes, the Open Door, and economic and political stability. Washington emphasized nonmilitary means—treaties, conferences, disarmament, economic and financial agreements, banking reform—in its pursuit of world order. America between the wars wanted to isolate itself from war, to scale down foreign military interventions, and to preserve the freedom to make independent decisions in international affairs. "Independent internationalism," rather than "isolationism," best characterizes American practice—active on an international scale, but independent in action.

Where the United States lacked viable power, such as in Asia, it moved haltingly. Where it possessed power, as in Latin America, it moved vigorously. As for Europe, until 1933 the Republican administrations seriously worked to contain but rehabilitate Germany, relieve French strategic anxieties, tame Soviet radicalism while seeking to integrate Russia into the community of nations, advance disarmament, resolve controversies over war debts and reparations, stabilize European currencies, foster U.S. exports, and systematize the flow of private American capital abroad. In seeking peace and prosperity, the U.S. government encouraged private experts in business, finance, labor, and agriculture to cooperate with public officials in a system of "corporatism." By the mid-1930s, with international stability shattered by the Great Depression, Americans tried to protect themselves from war through neutrality laws. Not until 1939 did policymakers again risk war to achieve world order.

In the 1920s especially, weak presidential leadership, congressional-executive competition, and increased professionalism in the Foreign Service characterized U.S. policymaking. Presidents Warren G. Harding and Calvin Coolidge gave minimal attention to foreign affairs. Harding's world was his hometown of Marion, Ohio. Wilson's League of Nations fiasco persuaded Harding to eschew a conspicuous role in foreign policy. "I don't know anything about this European stuff," he once said.

Calvin Coolidge managed in his autobiography to avoid mentioning foreign policy. The taciturn president once shocked the British ambassador by saying he would "never visit Europe because he could learn everything he needed to know by remaining in America." Coolidge's relaxed style, exemplified by long afternoon naps in the White House and by his fawning worship of American business, created a deceptively passive image. The simple man from Vermont, preaching self-reliance, complained that Europeans always looked to the United States to bail them out. "We couldn't help people very much until they showed a disposition to help themselves," he noted in 1926.

Herbert Hoover adopted a more active presidential role. His distinguished career included experience in international business (mining), food relief (Belgium and Russia), and diplomacy (reparations adviser at Versailles). As secretary of commerce under Harding and Coolidge, he energetically expanded American economic interests abroad. Hoover had a telephone installed at his elbow in the White House, further enhancing his reputation for administrative efficiency. A plodding speaker with a shy personality, Hoover entered the presidency as the Great Depression struck, wrecking his political career. True to his Quaker background, he sought nonmilitary, noncoercive solutions to international crises and emphasized cooperative economic relations.

The secretaries of state in the 1920s often compensated for presidential shortcomings. Magisterial Charles Evans Hughes was a distinguished jurist (Supreme Court), an experienced politician (Republican candidate for president in 1916), and

Makers of American Foreign Relations, 1920–1939

Presidents	Secretaries of State
Woodrow Wilson, 1913–1921	Bainbridge Colby, 1920–1921
Warren G. Harding 1921–1923	Charles E. Hughes, 1921–1925
Calvin Coolidge 1923–1929	Frank B. Kellogg, 1925–1929
Herbert C. Hoover 1929–1933	Henry L. Stimsom, 1929–1933
Franklin D. Roosevelt 1933–1945	Cordell Hull, 1933–1944

**Herbert Hoover
(1874–1964).** The thirty-first
president graduated from Stanford
University. Cautious and stubborn,
Hoover advocated healthy trade
relations, military retrenchment,
and foreign loans for "reproductive
purposes" as routes to peace.
(Library of Congress)

a confirmed nationalist and expansionist. Under Harding and Coolidge the patient,
pragmatic Hughes enjoyed considerable freedom in diplomacy, receiving little presidential instruction. International law and the sanctity of treaties served as his primary guides to world order. Frank B. Kellogg succeeded Hughes. Ingloriously
called "Nervous Nellie" because of a trembling hand, the former senator and ambassador to Britain moved cautiously, often consulting a major critic of interventionism, William Borah, chair of the Senate Foreign Relations Committee. Because
of jurisdictional disputes with the Commerce Department, one of Kellogg's subordinates commented: "diplomatic functions today are mainly economic; this places
the Department of Commerce in control of the substance of diplomacy, and leaves
the State Department with social relationships."

President Hoover named as secretary of state mustachioed Henry L. Stimson,
one of America's most distinguished public servants. The strong-willed, confident,
reserved, punctual, sexist, mannered, wealthy Stimson lived on his Long Island estate like an English squire. His resumé included Phillips Andover Academy, Yale
University, and Harvard Law School. Formerly secretary of war under Taft, Stimson in 1927 went as a diplomatic troubleshooter to Nicaragua and later served as
governor-general of the Philippines. He had been Colonel Stimson in World
War I—and let few forget it.

Franklin D. Roosevelt came to office with some foreign-affairs experience,
having served in the Navy Department under Woodrow Wilson. He admired both
the big-sticking of his cousin Theodore and the liberal internationalism of Wilson.
As a vice-presidential candidate in 1920, Roosevelt had defended the League of Nations, but in the 1932 campaign he repudiated the League to garner the endorsement of the influential newspaper magnate William Randolph Hearst. "I am not a
Wilsonian idealist, I have problems to solve," he once said. Fully conscious of the
war clouds billowing in Europe and Asia, FDR nonetheless gave priority to his
domestic New Deal recovery program. With his "happy-go-lucky, snap-of-the-
moment style," FDR relished personal diplomacy, often taking command of negotiations and neglecting to tell the Department of State what he was doing. He centralized decisionmaking in the White House; but too often he possessed only a
superficial understanding of other national cultures and histories. Sometimes he
misled diplomats with his easy smile; sometimes his agreements lacked precision, de-
pending for their authority on the honor of gentlemen's words; sometimes U.S.
diplomacy moved forward with the dizziness of a confused bureaucracy. A consum-
mate politician, Roosevelt compromised frequently and resorted to deception if it
served his goals.

Roosevelt chose Tennessean Cordell Hull as his secretary of state. A respected
senator devoted to free trade, the chronically ill sexagenarian reluctantly accepted.
FDR picked Hull because the appointment would please old Democratic party
members, southern conservatives, and unreconstructed Wilsonians. Roosevelt often
undercut him, although Hull and the State Department remained dominant in for-
mulating Asian and Latin American policy. The president sent Hull to the World
Economic Conference in London in June 1933 without consulting him on the
makeup of the delegation, and then embarrassed him by rejecting a currency stabilization plan and effectively ending the conference. Once dubbed "Miss Cordelia

Dull" for his "congenital procrastination," Hull's deliberate methods wearied the president, who preferred quickness and repartee. The secretary resented the president's practice of dispatching personal envoys overseas, and his reliance on friends such as Henry Morgenthau instead of Hull himself. But he stayed on until 1944, the longest tenure of any secretary of state, always charming listeners with his hill-country drawl, and impressing all with his deep commitment to the premise that wars grew out of international economic competition.

The Foreign Service over which Hull presided improved during the interwar period. It certainly needed reform. Frequenting the ornate State, War, and Navy Building on Pennsylvania Avenue were U.S. diplomats noted for their elite backgrounds (urban, wealthy, eastern, and Ivy League–educated). Some derided them as "cookie pushers" and purveyors of "pink peppermint and protocol." Foreign Service Officers nonetheless believed that "they belonged to a pretty good club" with "a healthy *esprit de corps.*" Under the spoils system, faithful politicians still received top diplomatic posts and seldom spoke the language of their assigned countries.

The heavy work load imposed on Foreign Service personnel during World War I had exposed the shortcomings. The immigration laws of 1921 and 1924, establishing quotas, demanded a more efficient consular staff; revolutions in Russia and China required observers who could intelligently interpret those convulsions; and economic expansion depended on sound reporting about overseas markets. The Rogers Act of 1924 merged the previously unequal consular and diplomatic corps into the Foreign Service and provided for examinations, increased salaries, promotion by merit, and overseas living allowances. Fledgling diplomats began training as specialists in Soviet affairs, with George F. Kennan and Charles E. Bohlen (both later ambassadors to the Soviet Union) among the initiates who mastered the language and culture of Russia. Despite persistent cliques, political favoritism, snobbery, sexism, anti-Semitism, and lower salaries and staff cutbacks during the depression, the Foreign Service slowly became more efficient and professional.

Economic and Cultural Expansion in a Rickety World

The Foreign Service helped facilitate conspicuous American economic expansion abroad after World War I. Measured by statistics, the United States had become the most powerful nation in the world, accounting for 70 percent of the world's petroleum and 40 percent of its coal production. Most impressive, the United States produced 46 percent of total world industrial goods (1925–1929 figures). It also ranked first as an exporter, shipping more than 15 percent of total world exports in 1929, and it replaced Britain as the largest foreign investor and financier of world trade. Throughout the decade the United States enjoyed a favorable balance of trade, exporting more than it imported. In the period 1914–1929, the value of exports more than doubled, to $5.4 billion, and U.S. private investments abroad grew from $3.5 billion in 1914 to $17.2 billion by 1930.

As the historian Mira Wilkins has noted, U.S. companies in the 1920s "were (1) going to *more countries,* (2) building *more plants* in a particular foreign country,

(3) manufacturing or mining *more end products* in a particular foreign land, (4) investing in a single alien nation in a *greater degree* of integration, and (5) diversifying on a *worldwide* basis." U.S. Rubber bought its first Malayan plantation; Anaconda moved into Chilean copper mining; General Electric invested heavily in Germany; oil companies began to drill in the Middle East; Americans controlled 83 percent of the automobile industry in Canada; General Motors purchased Opel, by 1929 the best-selling automobile in Germany; and Henry Ford helped build an automobile plant in Soviet Russia.

American culture—including household appliances, foods, language, music, film, and appreciation for machines—also spread worldwide. "Today we go to America as the Japanese once came to Germany," an industrialist from Weimar Germany wrote after visiting Detroit to observe American mass-production techniques. U.S. government support for the growing communications industry helped International Telephone and Telegraph (ITT), Radio Corporation of America (RCA), Associated Press (AP), and United Press (UP) become international giants by 1930. American movies so dominated the global market that the "sun . . . never sets on the British Empire and the American motion picture." Indeed, as "the most pervasive and persuasive of American contributions to European culture," Hollywood movies "epitomized American culture in its mass orientation, tempo, monumentalism, sensationalism and profit urge." Thus did street urchins in London adopt American slang: "O.K., kid" and "What are you doing tonight, babe?" In 1929 alone, some 251,000 American tourists visited Europe, where they spent $323 million. For German women "Americanization" produced, among other things, an advertisement from Siemens describing "How the Buschmüllers Got a Vacuum." Despite elitist fears of being "swamped" by a vulgar *Unkultur,* American products from jazz to gym shoes claimed an eager international clientele.

Through philanthropic programs in preventive medicine and public health in Eastern and Central Europe in the 1920s, the Rockefeller Foundation also introduced America to foreigners. Under Rockefeller auspices, for example, "Kentucky closets" (outdoor toilets) became ubiquitous in Croatian villages. The foundation also battled yellow fever in Latin America and supported colleges to train doctors in Lebanon and China—all under the philosophy that culture adoption, economic expansion, and political stability went hand in hand.

This expansion did encounter obstacles. Mexican nationalism, confiscation of property in Soviet Russia, European resentments, a wrecked German economy, wartime destruction in Europe, growing tariff walls, and the dislocation of international finance caused by war debts and reparations—all hindered enterprising Americans. U.S. government decisions offered welcome but limited help. The Webb-Pomerene Act (1918) permitted American companies to combine for purposes of foreign trade without prosecution under the antitrust laws; the Edge Act of 1919 legalized branch banks abroad; and the Merchant Marine Act of 1920 authorized the federal government to sell vessels to private companies and to make construction loans for new ships. New tax laws also permitted foreign tax credits for American investors abroad. The Department of Commerce provided businesses with research data and advice. To help financiers avoid unproductive foreign lending, official Washington tried to oversee loans and bond sales but did so unevenly.

The Weight of the United States in the World Economy

Relative Value of Industrial Production, 1925–1929

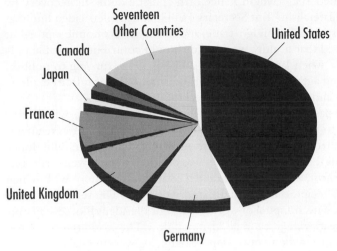

Source: U.S. Department of Commerce, *The United States in the World Economy* (Washington, D.C.: Government Printing Office, 1943), p. 28.

For example, the government discouraged investment in a Czech brewery because it violated the "spirit" of prohibition laws but tolerated an unproductive loan for a sports palace in Germany.

Believing trade essential to domestic prosperity, the United States continued to proclaim the Open Door policy but applied it selectively. U.S. officials usually invoked the policy where the United States faced vigorous competition, as in Asia and the Middle East. In Latin America and the Philippines, however, where American capital and trade dominated, something approximating a "closed door" developed. Europeans also resented American tariff policy, which made it difficult to sell to the United States—as they had to do in order to obtain the dollars necessary to buy American goods. The tariff acts of 1922 (Fordney-McCumber) and 1930 (Hawley-Smoot) raised duties to protect domestic producers and invited retaliation against American products. Economists anticipated "a tariff war" that would disturb world peace. Some twenty-five nations by 1932 had retaliated against American imports. Hoover insisted that high tariffs and overseas economic expansion could proceed hand in hand, and until the Great Depression struck in 1929 the seeming contradiction appeared to work.

The depression raised havoc with the international economy. Economic nationalism guided most countries as they tried to protect themselves from the cataclysm with higher tariffs and import quotas. World trade declined 40 percent in value and 25 percent in volume from 1929 to mid-1933. In 1933 the United States exported goods worth $2.1 billion, down from the 1929 figure of $5.4 billion. American capital stayed at home, and foreign holders of American loans defaulted. American private investments abroad slumped to $13.5 billion, down from the

$17.2 billion figure of 1930. President Hoover flatly—and wrongly—called it a "patently European crisis." Even FDR, confronting 13 million unemployed Americans in 1933, succumbed to economic nationalism as he created his New Deal recovery program. He abruptly sabotaged the London Economic Conference, indicating that the United States would henceforth "pursue domestic recovery by means of a policy of unilateralism." But Secretary Hull gradually persuaded him that lowered tariffs would spur U.S. foreign trade and spark an economic upturn at home. Hull also preached that healthy world trade would contribute to stable politics and peace at a time when Japan, Germany, and Italy were turning to political extremes and threatening aggression. It would also deter Bolshevism from exploiting Europe's economic and social turmoil. Or so Hull hoped.

In 1934 Congress passed the Reciprocal Trade Agreements Act, which empowered the president to reduce tariffs by as much as 50 percent after agreements with other nations under the doctrine of the most-favored nation. This long-standing principle meant that the United States was entitled to the lowest tariffs imposed by a country (in short, the best favor granted to any other nation) with which the United States had a reciprocal agreement, and vice versa. The reciprocal trade program did slow the downward spiral of world trade, but President Roosevelt complained: "Those trade treaties are just too goddamned slow. The world is moving too fast." Hull also created in 1934 the Export-Import Bank, a governmental agency designed to provide loans to expand foreign trade. By 1937, however, FDR concluded that "an economic approach to peace is a weak reed."

The reciprocal trade program and the bank came too late to help solve the interwar debts-reparations tangle. Whereas before the war U.S. citizens owed some $3 billion to Europeans, after the war European citizens owed private Americans $3 billion and their governments owed another $10 billion, largely because of wartime loans. But how would Europeans earn dollars to pay such a huge sum? American investments, sale of goods to the United States, U.S. tourist spending, and income from German reparations payments ranked as the most promising sources. But the Germans refused to meet the indemnity of $33 billion, so in the early 1920s the British began quoting Scripture: "Forgive us our debts," arguing that Americans should write them off as a contribution to the Allied victory. Europeans pointed out that they had suffered huge losses of lives and property, while Americans, neutral until 1917, had enjoyed prosperity and profits from sales to the Allies financed by loans. Washington indignantly rejected this argument, prompting one British leader to note that "even in its gifts and its goodness" the United States "has an attitude and a spirit that makes one's soul shrink up and shrivel." Congress created the War Debt Commission in 1922 to negotiate full payment. The commission ultimately forgave or canceled about half of the Allied debts. From 1918 to 1931 the United States actually received only $2.6 billion in Allied debts payments.

By stabilizing European finances, restoring trade, and encouraging the flow of private capital to Germany, U.S. diplomats sought to "harness Germany's resources to the cause of European recovery" without "reinvigorating the economic nationalism and autarky" that could lead to war. The debts-reparations imbroglio eventually undercut this strategy. Wild inflation, a crippled economy, inadequate exports, and anti-Versailles hostility prompted the Germans to default on reparations payments in 1922–1923. France and Belgium thereupon aggravated Germany's plight by seizing the rich Ruhr Valley. In 1924 the State Department encouraged the businessman Charles G. Dawes to negotiate the Dawes Plan, whereby American investors loaned millions to Germany, and Berlin accepted a revised reparations payment schedule. But the European economy simply could not bear the heavy debts and reparations. Nor could American capital keep Europe afloat. Under the Young Plan of 1929, another salvaging effort reduced German reparations to $9 billion. That year, too, Hoover informed the British that he would cancel their debt if they transferred Bermuda, British Honduras (Belize), and Trinidad to the United States. London refused. In 1931 he declared a one-year moratorium on debts payments. Thereafter only Finland met its debt obligations, forever winning a place in American hearts. Debtors defaulted, Germany stopped paying reparations, and the world settled into the devastating depression of the 1930s. The threat of war increased.

Peace Seekers for a World Without War

Despite the international economic turmoil, peace sentiment ran high in the United States between the wars. In 1923, when the publisher Edward Bok sponsored a contest for the best peace plan, he received more than 22,000 entries. Some peace advocates, such as the Carnegie Endowment for International Peace, placed their hopes in such global institutions as the World Court and League of Nations. Pacifists in the Fellowship of Reconciliation, the War Resisters League, and the Women's Peace Union, in contrast, renounced individual participation in war. Religious groups pointed to the un-Christian character of war. Salmon Levinson, a Chicago lawyer who organized the American Committee for the Outlawry of War, argued that war "will never cease to be an institution until it becomes illegal." Women gravitated to their own organizations, such as the Committee on the Cause and Cure of War and the Women's International League for Peace and Freedom (WILPF), because they lacked influence in male-dominated groups and because of their belief that women—as life givers and nurturing mothers—had a unique aversion to violence and war. Radical pacifists and antiwar advocates agitated for fundamental social and economic change in order to remove social injustice, which they saw as the capitalist wellsprings of imperialism and war. The National Council for the Prevention of War, founded in 1921, served as an organizational umbrella for the divergent peace groups.

Most peace activists hoped that the United States could regenerate habitually war-prone Europe. In the 1920s, such reformist ideas did not seem farfetched: technology had not yet produced global bombers or atomic weapons; domestic economies still did not rely heavily for their prosperity on defense production; the revulsion against World War I remained intense; and few warmongers had yet seized governments. Yet when Dorothy Detzer of WILPF threatened the loss of a million female votes if President Hoover did not name Mt. Holyoke College president Mary Wooley as a delegate to the Geneva Disarmament Conference, Secretary Stimson grumbled that Wooley "knows nothing about the subject. I presume, however, that she can read." Notwithstanding Wooley's active participation, and a WILPF-sponsored Transcontinental Peace Caravan that forwarded several hundred thousand

"Come on In. I'll treat you right. I used to know your daddy." C. D. Batchelor's cartoon won a Pulitzer Prize in 1937. As the historian Michael Sherry has noted, the depiction of war as "a diseased whore luring men to their death" revealed the "strikingly—sometimes maliciously—gendered ways in which war was often portrayed in modern American culture." (Library of Congress)

signatures to Geneva, the disarmament talks ran afoul of the Manchurian crisis (see Chapter 5) and accomplished little.

One of the peace movement's few achievements was the Kellogg-Briand Pact of 1928. France, prodded by James T. Shotwell, a trustee of the Carnegie Endowment for International Peace, asked the United States to sign a bilateral treaty renouncing war between the two nations. The security-conscious French, ever worried about a revived Germany, seemed to want an "American Locarno," in which Washington would support the European guarantee of France's eastern boundary as stipulated in the Locarno Treaty of 1925. Washington coolly received the request. But a publicity campaign for a multilateral treaty launched by Shotwell, Salmon Levinson, and Senator William Borah, as well as pressure from women's delegations prodded Secretary Kellogg into action. In February 1928 he sent a draft treaty to France and other powers. Foreign Minister Aristide Briand fumed; Kellogg and the peace advocates had transformed his Franco-American security treaty into a universal declaration against war. That August in Paris, sixty-two signatories agreed to renounce war as an "instrument of national policy."

The Kellogg-Briand Pact required no real sacrifices and established no precise responsibilities. On January 15, 1929, the Senate approved it 85 to 1. With one supporter dismissing the treaty as "the last stage of nervous and degenerate effeminacy," the Senate that same day approved funds for fifteen new cruisers. Peace advocates did not naively believe that Kellogg-Briand guaranteed a peaceful world. Dorothy Detzer, for one, regarded it as a first step in a long process and championed the pact as a way of alerting the American people to think once again of the costs of war. Thus it held educational value. And the pact gave the Allies the legal grounds after World War II to punish Axis leaders for plotting aggressive war.

The League of Nations, itself designed to check wars, opened in Geneva without the United States. By 1930, however, unofficial American "observers" had attended more than forty League conferences on such questions as health, prostitution, obscene materials, codification of international law, and opium. In October 1931, U.S. envoy Prentiss B. Gilbert formally participated in League Council meetings on the Manchurian crisis, urging the League to cite the Kellogg-Briand Pact and condemn Japan for aggression (see Chapter 5). The United States almost joined the League-sponsored World Court, which sought to arbitrate international disputes when requested to do so. In 1935 a treaty of membership nearly gained the two-thirds vote, aided by FDR's claim that "the sovereignty of the United States [would] in no way be diminished or jeopardized." That eminent jurists such as Charles Evans Hughes did sit as judges in the World Court offered internationalists some solace.

Participation in disarmament conferences in 1922 (Washington), 1927 (Geneva), 1930 (London), 1932–1933 (Geneva), and 1935–1936 (London) also demonstrated America's international but independent diplomatic course. At those conferences, the United States sought arms limitations, especially on navies, in part because it hoped to shackle others at a time when a parsimonious Congress restrained U.S. military growth. Except for some naval restrictions negotiated at the Washington and London conferences, little was accomplished. Without building to treaty limits, the United States sought to curb other navies; France would not endorse disarmament until it received security guarantees; the British had a huge empire to protect and police by sea; Italy and Germany plotted military buildups; Japan eyed naval expansion in the Pacific. German rearmament under Adolf Hitler after 1933 and Japanese renunciation of Washington treaty provisions in 1934 signaled the failure of the peace seekers as the world lurched toward global war.

Cold as Steel: Soviet-American Encounters

Soviet Russia signed the Kellogg-Briand Pact and joined the League of Nations in 1934. Yet most nations, including the United States, treated Bolshevik Russia as a revolutionary disease to be isolated. It was like "having a wicked and disgraceful neighbor," Hoover wrote. "We did not attack him, but we did not give him a certificate of character by inviting him into our homes." Only when Europe tottered on the brink of war in 1939 did Germany on the one hand and France and Britain on the other seriously woo Soviet Russia. Only grudgingly did the United States establish contacts with the Soviets during the interwar years.

Washington in the 1920s adhered to the nonrecognition policy set by Woodrow Wilson. The Bolsheviks had confiscated American-owned property valued at $336 million, and Russia owed another $299 million in Tsarist and Provisional government debts. Until Moscow paid, recognition would be denied. Many Americans, moreover, saw the Bolsheviks as godless, uncivilized, anticapitalist, violent revolutionaries who chained their workers like slaves to an authoritarian system. Secretary Stimson, wary of the American Communist party, promised in 1930 to deny recognition until Russia "ceased to agitate for the overthrow of American institutions by revolution." Some Americans, such as Senator Borah and the International Ladies Garment Workers Union, urged tolerance and recognition while they criticized the Soviet system.

Contacts occurred nevertheless. In 1921 Russia suffered a devastating famine, and Secretary of Commerce Hoover organized shipments of food and medicine to needy areas. Moved by humanitarianism, Hoover also believed that this aid would help implant American influence in Russia and serve as a counterrevolutionary force. From 1921 to 1924 the American Relief Administration collected $50 million from the federal government and private citizens for assistance to 10 million Russians.

American businesses also seemed willing to "sell the misguided fanatics all they are willing to pay for." International Harvester, General Electric, and Du Pont signed trade and technical assistance contracts with the Soviet government, often through its purchasing agency in New York, the Amtorg Trading Corporation. By 1924 Soviet purchases of U.S. products had jumped seven times over the 1923 figure. The entrepreneur W. Averell Harriman obtained monopolistic rights to rich manganese deposits in Soviet Georgia valued at $1 billion, from which Harriman eventually earned a "reasonable profit." In 1928, Americans accounted for 24 percent of all foreign investment in Soviet Russia. Communist plans for industrialization and collectivization could not have advanced without American machinery, technology, and engineers (1,000 by 1931). Moscow's contract in 1929 with the fiercely anticommunist Henry Ford seemed remarkable. Yet the auto magnate agreed to supply technical information needed for the large Nizhny-Novgorod automobile factory, which would buy Ford parts and produce a car like the Model A and a truck like the Model AA. Although Ford eventually lost $578,000 on this multimillion-dollar venture, he did sell the Soviets on mass-production techniques (*Fordizatsia*). By 1927, 85 percent of the Soviets' tractors were "Fordsons." Once Moscow acquired Western skills and technology, the Soviet leader Leon Trotsky predicted, "Americanized Bolshevism will defeat and crush imperialist Americanism."

American-Russian economic ties began to fray in the early 1930s. With the Great Depression causing widespread unemployment, U.S. officials resented Soviet announcements that jobs were available in Russia. Russia also "dumped" goods on the world market well below American prices. Washington banned imports of Soviet paper pulp, claiming that convict labor produced it. The Soviets retaliated by drastically cutting their purchase of American products. By 1932 U.S. exports to Russia had declined 90 percent from the 1931 trade. Business executives eager for markets began to argue that official diplomatic recognition might restart stalled commercial relations. The Reconstruction Finance Corporation, a U.S. government agency, helped by extending Russia a $4 million credit for the purchase of American cotton.

The Roosevelt administration, because it wanted to improve trade and deter further Japanese encroachment on China, formally recognized the Soviet Union in November 1933. Roosevelt himself conducted the negotiations. But the exchange of embassies did not smooth relations or halt Japan. American trade with Russia improved little, despite a trade treaty in 1935 and the establishment of the Export-Import Bank. Disagreement over compensation for Russian debts prevented any loans or credits to the Soviets. When American communists spoke critically of the United States at Moscow's Seventh International Communist (Comintern) Congress in 1935, Secretary Hull charged a violation of Russia's no-propaganda pledge.

Named the first ambassador to Moscow, William Bullitt left America in 1933 as a friend of Russia. Two years later he resigned, convinced that the Soviet government "is a conspiracy to commit murder and nothing else." He had changed his mind because of difficult living conditions in Moscow, spies among his servants, indignities inflicted by rude Soviet bureaucrats, his own volatile prejudices, and the ubiquitous Soviet tyranny. Bullitt soon "deviled the Russians. I did all I could to make things unpleasant." The ghastly purges that began in 1935 also moved Bullitt and others to a hard line. "The last mass trials were a great success. There are going to be fewer but better Russians," quipped an unsmiling Greta Garbo in the movie *Ninotchka* (1939). Bullitt's successor as ambassador, the wealthy Joseph E. Davies, thought Soviet Premier Joseph Stalin "cold as steel" and the trials "a nightmare." George F. Kennan, a member of the embassy staff, attended the purge trials and witnessed the "horrors of Stalinism" in person. So appalled were Kennan, Bullitt, and others at official Soviet cruelties that they resembled spurned suitors thwarted in their wooing of the Russian people.

The Nazi-Soviet Pact of August 1939 also caused outrage. Stalin believed that the Western European powers and the United States had let Hitler expand uninhibited to encourage the German's design to conquer Russia. And Stalin had so depleted the officer ranks of his army through the purges that he was in no position to stave off an expected German attack. In the United States, the nonaggression pact, which secretly divided Poland, reinforced charges that Stalin had become Hitler's friend. When World War II erupted in September 1939, many Americans blamed the Soviet Union.

Hitler's Germany, Appeasement, and the Outbreak of War

By exploiting the depression-afflicted economy and resentment against the Versailles treaty in Germany, the Nazi leader Adolf Hitler came to power in January 1933. Racist toward Jews and emphatically anti-Bolshevik, Hitler quickly alarmed diplomats with his fanatic chauvinism. In October 1933, Hitler withdrew Germany from the faltering League of Nations, telling an associate that the European powers would "never act! They'll just protest. And they will always be too late." Indeed, France and Britain settled on a timid policy of "appeasement," hoping to satisfy what they thought were Hitler's limited goals and avert another European war. By 1935 Britain, France, Italy, and the League of Nations had censured Germany for building a huge army and air force. Yet at the same time, Britain agreed that Germany could rebuild its navy to 35 percent of the size of the British navy, another costly concession to German militarism.

Adolf Hitler (1889–1945). When Hitler took power in 1933, some Americans likened his mustachioed face to that of the actor Charlie Chaplin. In this propagandistic German painting, the anticommunist, anti-Semitic Nazi leader is surrounded by swastikas and saluting followers. (U.S. Army)

Hardly adjusted to the rise of Nazi Germany, the world watched as Italy invaded the African state of Ethiopia in October 1935. The fascist Benito Mussolini had governed Italy since 1922, long nurturing dreams of an Italian empire. Already holding Somaliland and Eritrea as African colonies, Mussolini harassed Ethiopian leader Haile Selassie until military skirmishes broke out. Then Mussolini invaded and annexed Ethiopia. The League imposed an embargo on the shipment of war-related goods (except oil) to Italy. But the French and the British, fearing for their own African colonies, seemed willing to sacrifice Ethiopia, a mere "corridor for camels." They also worried that further hostilities would "play into Germany's hands" and "might mean a general war in Europe."

Apparently encouraged by Anglo-French docility over Ethiopia, Hitler in March 1936 ordered his goose-stepping troops into the Rhineland, the area bordering Belgium and France that the Versailles treaty had declared permanently demilitarized. By seizing the Rhineland, Germany could outflank the Maginot Line, a series of fortified bunkers along the German-French border. The French, fearful of igniting another war, did not resist the German advance. That same fall, after Hitler signed the Rome-Berlin Axis agreement with Italy and the Anti-Comintern Pact with Japan, U.S. military attachés sent ominous reports on German military maneuvers, including *Panzer* brigades, warning of "a revolution in military methods."

Spain became contested ground, too. "Nationalist" soldiers under General Francisco Franco started the Spanish civil war in July 1936 by attacking the "Loyalist" Republican government. Hitler and Mussolini poured military equipment and troops in support of Franco. The tepid Anglo-French response produced an International Non-Intervention Committee of twenty-seven nations, remarkably including Germany and Italy. Hitler and Mussolini continued covert aid, and France and Britain lived with the fiction that they had isolated the Spanish civil war. The Soviet Union and Mexico sent help to the Republicans, and some 3,000 Americans fought alongside them in the Abraham Lincoln Brigade. Franco and his brand of fascism nonetheless prevailed in early 1939.

When Neville Chamberlain became British prime minister in 1937, he enshrined the appeasement policy. He believed that Germany had good reason to want to reject the humiliating Versailles treaty and to claim status as a major power. Tolerant of Hitler's demand for mastery over people of German descent living in Austria, Czechoslovakia, and Poland, Chamberlain also judged that Germany could be "weaned from aggression by his blend of conciliation and firmness, carrot and stick." An appeased Germany could also serve as a useful restraint on Soviet Russia.

In March 1938, German troops crossed into Austria and annexed it to the German Reich. Hitler next demanded the Sudeten region of Czechoslovakia, where 3 million ethnic Germans lived. Hitler assured Chamberlain that this marked his last territorial demand. At the Munich Conference of September 29–30, 1938, Italy, Germany, France, and Britain agreed never to make war against one another and to sever the Sudetenland from Czechoslovakia. The Czechs were not consulted. Unwilling to wage "a war today in order to prevent a war hereafter," Chamberlain proclaimed "peace for our time." Hitler soon accelerated his persecution of German Jews and in March 1939 swallowed the rest of Czechoslovakia. The following month Italy absorbed Albania.

Poland came next. Refusing Hitler's demands for the city of Danzig, the Poles soon faced German pressure. But London and Paris announced in March 1939 that they would stand behind an independent Poland. The Soviet Union then emerged as a central actor in the European tumult. Germany, Britain, and France opened negotiations with Moscow in attempts to gain Soviet allegiance. Stalin chose Germany. "Britain and France wanted us to be their hired hand . . . and without pay," he remarked. On August 23, Nazi Germany and Soviet Russia signed the nonaggression pact. On September 1, German soldiers invaded Poland. Two days later Britain and France declared war against Germany. On September 17, Soviet troops struck Poland, taking half the nation.

Throughout these years of descent into World War II, Hitler both admired and underrated the United States. Impressed by anti-Semite Henry Ford and his production techniques, he sent German car designers to Detroit before launching the *Volkswagen*. Nonetheless, he scorned U.S. influence in world affairs. Although his advisers warned that American isolationism might not last, he deemed the United States "incapable of conducting war"—a "Jewish rubbish heap," incapacitated by economic and racial crises, crime, and inept political leadership. Hitler's Nazis also viewed emancipated American women as "egoistic, manipulative, overly sexual, and unerotic," in stark contrast to "the Nazi ideal of a devoted Gretchen bearing future soldiers for the Third Reich's wars of conquest." Despite the popularity of "swing" music and American films, the Nazis outlawed "Nigger-Jew jazz" and soon banned Hollywood imports. Although the *Fuehrer's* long-range goals probably included aggressive war against the United States, his initial perceptions of America as a "half-Judaized, half negrified" country with a large navy and minuscule army caused him to discount growing U.S. support for England and France.

American Isolationism and the Neutrality Acts

"This nation will remain a neutral nation," President Roosevelt announced on September 3, 1939, "but I cannot ask that every American remain neutral in thought as well." Second thoughts about neutrality came only late in the decade. During the early 1930s the United States attempted to remain rigidly neutral. Although most Americans strongly disapproved of Hitler and his "brutal, beer swilling people," they tried to isolate themselves from a continent they thought prone to self-destruction. If Britain and France could not handle German aggression in their own backyards, America could not do the job for them.

Americans also drew lessons from World War I. Disillusioned writers and "revisionist" historians argued that Germany had not solely precipitated war in 1914, that business leaders and propagandists had influenced a pro-British Wilson, and that the costs and results of war did not justify U.S. participation. In 1934 the best-selling book *Merchants of Death* argued that profiteering arms manufacturers had exploited the American economic and political system to compromise U.S. neutrality. Encouraged by President Roosevelt, Senator Gerald P. Nye headed a special committee that held hearings during 1934–1936 to determine if munitions makers and bankers had lobbied Wilson into war. The committee never proved the allegation but did uncover substantial evidence that these entrepreneurs had exerted influence on behalf of the Allies. Popular sentiment held that World War I had been a tragic blunder and that Americans "must think of the next war as they would of suicide."

A diverse coalition of isolationists and peace advocates shared the traditional belief in political and military nonentanglement—"a north star, constant and steady, which will hold us true to our course." Antiwar sentiment grew strong on college campuses and among women. Princeton University students organized the Veterans of Future Wars in 1936 and demanded $1,000 each as a bonus *before* going into battle, because few would live through the next war. The journalist William Allen White predicted that "the next war will see . . . the same bowwow of the big dogs to get the little dogs to go out and follow the blood scent and get their entrails tangled in the barbed wire." In 1938, Representative Louis Ludlow of Indiana introduced a constitutional amendment calling for a national referendum on decisions for war. Roosevelt claimed that the amendment "would cripple any President in his conduct of our foreign relations." A motion to discharge Ludlow's resolution from the Rules Committee failed by only 209 to 188.

Many progressive isolationists believed that American entry into a European war would undercut the New Deal's attempts to recover from the depression. They also remembered how the Wilson administration had savaged critics in World War I. Convinced that business expansionists helped create the conditions that spawned war, progressive isolationists sought to curb business adventures abroad that entangled the United States. By 1937, in fact, twenty of the top one hundred American corporations had negotiated important agreements with Nazi Germany, some with the core of the German military machine, the I. G. Farben Company. Du Pont, Union Carbide, and Standard Oil signed contracts, with Standard Oil helping Germany develop synthetic rubber and aviation fuel. Peace progressives worked also behind the scenes on behalf of the Nye Committee and neutrality legislation.

Roosevelt wanted a neutrality law that would permit him to ban sales of arms to aggressors. Congress instead passed the Neutrality Act of 1935, requiring an arms embargo against all belligerents after the president had officially proclaimed the existence of war. "Leave as little to the discretion of the President as possible," urged Dorothy Detzer of the WILPF. Subsequent legislation banned loans to belligerents (Act of 1936) and required that belligerents wishing to trade with the United States must carry away U.S. goods in their own ships ("cash and carry"), after payment on delivery (Act of 1937). The latter also forbade U.S. citizens to travel on belligerent vessels. An amendment of 1937 made the United States neutral in the Spanish civil war.

The Neutrality Acts erred in providing for no discrimination among the belligerents, no punishment of the aggressor. They denied the United States any leverage over the cascading events in Europe. They amounted to an abdication of power. Yet much of what the isolationists said about the fruits of war rang true. Their criticisms of imperialism and business expansion were honest and telling. They scorned the British Empire and U.S. intervention in Latin America. They compared Italy's subjugation of Ethiopia to Britain's supremacy in India. Many of them warned about increasing the power of the president in foreign affairs beyond congressional reach. Denounced by Neville Chamberlain as "those pig-headed and self-righteous nobodies," isolationists nonetheless comprised "a large, responsible, and respectable segment of the American people." In condemning all imperialism—American, British, or German—the isolationists often refused to make the choice of the lesser of two or three evils. However praiseworthy their aims, their formulas for the 1930s proved as misguided as Britain's appeasement policy.

Roosevelt Shifts and Congress Balks on the Eve of War

President Roosevelt, sensitive to American sentiment against U.S. entanglement in Europe, responded haltingly to the events of the 1930s. His foreign policy fed appeasement. When Italy attacked Ethiopia, Roosevelt stated that the United States sought above all to avoid war. America would set a peaceful example for other nations to follow. He and Hull invoked the Neutrality Act, warned Americans not to travel on belligerent ships, and suggested a moral embargo against trade with the warring parties. Actually, American businesses ignored the moral embargo and increased commerce with Italy, especially in oil. In August 1936, the president gave a stirring speech at Chautauqua, New York, recalling World War I: "I have seen war. . . . I have seen men coughing out their gassed lungs. . . . I hate war."

In January 1937, Roosevelt asked Congress for an arms embargo against Spain. Congress obliged by enacting a "malevolent neutrality" that worked against the "Loyalist" Republican government and in favor of Franco. In this case, many isolationists protested the sacrifice of Spanish democracy. Roosevelt and Hull chose strict neutrality, in essence backing feeble British-French efforts to contain the civil war and aligning themselves with the pro-Franco views of the Catholic hierarchy at home. Yet Roosevelt privately pondered ways to curb the aggressors.

In July, when Japan plunged into undeclared war against China, Roosevelt favored China by not invoking the Neutrality Act, thereby permitting the Chinese government to buy and import American war goods (see Chapter 5). Then in October he delivered his famous "quarantine" speech, calling for the isolation of international lawbreakers. FDR also approached the British ambassador about a joint cruiser blockade against Japan and sent a naval officer to London for secret staff talks. Under Secretary of State Sumner Welles then proposed a world conference on disarmament and international law in Washington, at which Roosevelt might quietly stiffen British diplomacy. Chamberlain, however, convinced that he could "count on nothing from the Americans but words," rejected such a meeting in early 1938 because it interfered with his efforts to appease the aggressors.

During the Czech crisis of 1938 the United States kept at a safe distance. The president appealed for negotiations to head off war, while telling Hitler that the United States "will assume no obligations in the conduct of the present negotiations." "Good man," Roosevelt cabled Chamberlain when he heard that the prime minister would go to Munich. Yet the dismemberment of Czechoslovakia soon prompted FDR to confess privately that Munich had failed and that Hitler was "a pure unadulterated devil" who must be stopped.

In October 1938, Roosevelt asked Congress for $300 million for national defense. He quietly asked for repeal of the arms embargo law. In November, in protest against Hitler's vicious persecution of the Jews, he recalled Ambassador Hugh Wilson from Berlin and never let him return. That same month, FDR requested more than 10,000 warplanes per year, in order "to have something to back up my words." He also secretly arranged for the French government to place orders for planes.

In January 1939, Roosevelt again urged revision of the Neutrality Act so that it would not "actually give aid to an aggressor and deny it to the victim." The crash of the A-20 bomber in Los Angeles stalled this initiative. The president thus delayed until March the introduction of a bill specifically repealing the arms embargo, and throughout the spring he allowed others to direct legislative strategy. Reluctant to risk battle against sizable political odds, FDR failed to lead at a critical time. In April he asked Hitler and Mussolini to refrain from attacking countries named on a list, but his request met open derision. The Senate Foreign Relations Committee, by a 12 to 11 vote, refused in July to report out a bill repealing the arms embargo. "I've fired my last shot," the president groaned. Not until November 1939—after Germany's conquest of Poland—did Congress finally revise the Neutrality Act so that England and France, as belligerents, could purchase American arms on a cash-and-carry basis.

Even in fall 1939, however, most Americans joined their president in wanting to avoid participation in World War II. "We cannot expect . . . the United States to evolve quicker than we did," the British ambassador reported. By sending Sumner Welles to Berlin, London, Paris, and Rome in the winter of 1940, FDR evidently thought he might "intervene as a kind of umpire." Hitler's *blitzkrieg* in the west that spring killed any such possibility. The Democratic party platform of 1940, on which Roosevelt ran for a third term, reflected the American desire to avoid war but also to prepare for it: "We will not participate in foreign wars, and we will not send our army, naval or air forces to fight in foreign lands outside of the Americas except in case of attack." As in World War I, because of their international interests, because U.S. power became intertwined in the war, and because they gradually abandoned neutrality to aid the Allies, Americans once again found themselves risking major war. The interwar quest for world order and peace had failed; the several Neutrality Acts had failed; independent internationalism had failed.

FURTHER READING FOR THE PERIOD 1920–1939

Overviews include Warren I. Cohen, *Empire Without Tears* (1987); Justus D. Doenecke and John E. Wilz, *From Isolation to War* (2003); Margaret Louria, *Triumph and Downfall* (2001); Brenda Gayle Plummer, *Rising Wind* (1996) (African Americans); Benjamin D. Rhodes, *United States Foreign Policy in the Interwar Period, 1918–1941* (2001); and Geoffrey S. Smith, *To Save a Nation* (1992).

The presidents and their presidencies are treated in Martin Fausold, *The Presidency of Herbert C. Hoover* (1985); Robert H. Ferrell, *The Presidency of Calvin Coolidge* (1998); Ellis W. Hawley, ed., *Herbert Hoover: Secretary of Commerce* (1981); and Robert K. Murray, *The Harding Era* (1969).

For Franklin D. Roosevelt, see Wayne S. Cole, *Roosevelt and the Isolationists* (1983); Robert Dallek, *Franklin D. Roosevelt and American Foreign Policy, 1933–1945* (1979); Kenneth R. Davis, *FDR* (1972–1993); Frank Freidel, *Franklin D. Roosevelt* (1990); Alonzo L. Hamby, *For the Survival of Democracy* (2004); Frederick W. Marks III, *Wind over Sand* (1988); George McJimsey, *The Presidency of Franklin Delano Roosevelt* (2000); and David F. Schmitz, *Franklin D. Roosevelt and the International Crisis of the 1930s* (2006).

For the secretaries of state, see Michael Butler, *Cautious Visionary* (1998) (Hull); L. Ethan Ellis, *Frank B. Kellogg and American and Foreign Relations* (1961); and David F. Schmitz, *Henry L. Stimson* (2001).

Other diplomats and politicians are studied in Fred A. Bailey, *William Edward Dodd* (1997); Will Brownell and Richard N. Billings, *So Close to Greatness* (1988) (Bullitt); Ralph de Bedts, *Ambassador Joseph Kennedy* (1985); Wayne S. Cole, *Senator Gerald P. Nye and American Foreign Relations* (1962); Irwin Gellman, *Secret Affairs* (1995) (Hull and Welles); Betty Glad, *Key Pittman* (1986); Kenneth P. Jones, *Diplomats in Europe, 1919–1941* (1981); Richard C. Lower, *A Bloc of One* (1993) (Hiram Johnson); Elizabeth K. MacLean, *Joseph E. Davies* (1992); Peter Schlinger and Holman Hamilton, *Spokesman for Democracy: Claude G. Bowers* (2000); Jesse H. Stiller, *George S. Messersmith* (1987); and Benjamin Welles, *Sumner Welles* (1997).

Economic foreign relations receive attention in Frederick Adams, *Economic Diplomacy* (1976); Joseph Brandes, *Herbert Hoover and Economic Diplomacy* (1962); Patricia Clavin, *The Failure of Economic Diplomacy* (1996); Michael J. Hogan, *Informal Entente* (1977); Charles P. Kindleberger, *The World in Depression, 1929–1939* (1986); Stephen J. Randall, *United States Foreign Oil Policy, 1919–1948* (1986); William Stivers, *Supremacy and Oil* (1982); Mira Wilkins, *The Maturing of Multinational Enterprise* (1974) and *The History of Foreign Investment in the United States, 1914-1945* (2004); and Gilbert Ziebura, *World Economy and World Politics, 1924–1931* (1990).

The German reparations issue is explored in Bruce Kent, *The Spoils of War* (1989); Stephen Schuker, *American "Reparations" to Germany* (1988); and Marc Trachtenberg, *Reparation in World Politics* (1980).

Cultural issues and industries are highlighted in Frank Costigliola, *Awkward Dominion* (1984) (Europe); Harvey Levinstein, *We'll Always Have Paris* (2005); Emily S. Rosenberg, *Spreading the American Dream* (1982); Thomas J. Saunders, *Hollywood in Berlin* (1994); Lawrence Spinelli, *Dry Diplomacy* (1989) (Prohibition); and Richard W. Steele, *Propaganda in an Open Society* (1985).

Defense preparedness and arms–control questions are discussed in Thomas Buckley, *The United States and the Washington Conference* (1970); Roger Dingman, *Power in the Pacific* (1976); Richard W. Fanning, *Peace and Disarmament* (1995); Emily O. Goldman, *Sunken Treaties* (1994) (naval arms control); Robert Kaufman, *Arms Control During the Pre-Nuclear Age* (1990); Paul A. C. Koistinen, *Planning War, Pursuing Peace* (1998); Ernest R. May, *Knowing One's Enemy* (1984) (intelligence assessment); Stephen Pelz, *Race to Pearl Harbor* (1974) (Second London Naval Conference); and Michael S. Sherry, *The Rise of American Air Power* (1987).

For peace advocates and the League of Nations, see Harriet H. Alonso, *The Women's Peace Union and the Outlawry of War* (1989); Blanche Wiesen Cook, *Eleanor Roosevelt* (1992, 1999); Charles DeBenedetti, *Origins of the Modern American Peace Movement, 1915–1929* (1978); Michael Dunne, *The United States and the World Court* (1988); Carrie Foster, *The Women and the Warriors* (1995); Catherine Foster, *Women for All Seasons* (1989); Robert D. Johnson, *The Peace Progressives and American Foreign Relations* (1995); Harold Josephson, *James T. Shotwell and the Rise of Internationalism in America* (1976); Warren F. Kuehl and Lynne K. Dunn, *Keeping the Covenant* (1997) (League); Cecilia Lynch, *Beyond Appeasement* (1999); Gary B. Ostrower, *Collective Insecurity* (1979) (League); Linda K. Schott, *Reconstructing Women's Thoughts* (1997) (WILPF); and Lawrence S. Wittner, *Rebels Against War* (1984).

For American isolationism, see Thomas Guinsburg, *The Pursuit of Isolationism* (1981); Manfred Jones, *Isolationism in America* (1981); and John Wiltz, *In Search of Peace* (1963) (Nye Committee).

Relations with Europe and Germany and the coming of World War II are studied in many of the works cited above and in Alfred M. Beck, *Hitler's Ambivalent Attaché* (2005); Bernard Burke, *Ambassador Frederick Sackett and the Collapse of the Weimar Republic* (1995); Barbara R. Farnham, *Roosevelt and the Munich Crisis* (1997); John Haight Jr., *American Aid to France, 1938–1940* (1970); Linda Killen, *Testing the Peripheries* (1994) (Yugoslavia); Melvyn Leffler, *The Elusive Quest* (1979) (France); Brian McKercher, ed., *Anglo-American Relations in the 1920s* (1991) and *Transition of Power* (1999); John E. Moser, *Twisting the Lion's Tail: American Anglophobia between the World Wars* (1999); Mary Nolan, *Visions of Modernity* (1994) (American business in Germany); Arnold Offner, *American Appeasement* (1969); R. A. C. Parker, *Chamberlain and Appeasement* (1993); Stanley G. Payne, *The Spanish Civil War, the Soviet Union, and Communism* (2004); Neal Pease, *Poland, the United States, and the Stabilization of Europe, 1919–1933* (1986); David Reynolds, *The Creation of the Anglo-American Alliance, 1937–41* (1982); William R. Rock, *Chamberlain and Roosevelt* (1988); David F. Schmitz, *The United States and Fascist Italy* (1988); David F. Schmitz and Richard D. Challener, eds., *Appeasement in Europe* (1990); Dan P. Silverman, *Reconstructing Europe After the Great War* (1982); Henry Ashby Turner, *General Motors and the Nazis* (2005); D. C. Watt, *How War Came* (1989); Gerhard Weinberg, *The Foreign Policy of Hitler's Germany* (1970, 1980); and Marvin Zahniser, *Then Came Disaster: France and the United States, 1918–1940* (2002).

Soviet-American relations and recognition are discussed in Edward Bennett, *Recognition of Russia* (1970) and *Franklin D. Roosevelt and the Search for Security* (1985); Peter G. Boyle, *American-Soviet Relations* (1995); Dennis Dunn, *Caught Between Roosevelt and Stalin* (1998); Keith D. Eagles, *Ambassador Joseph E. Davies and American-Soviet Relations, 1937–1941* (1985); Jonathan Haslam, *The Soviet Union and the Struggle for Collective Security in Europe* (1984); Melvyn Leffler, *The Specter* (1994); David Mayers, *The Ambassadors and America's Soviet Policy* (1995); Bertrand Patenaude, *The Big Show in Bololand* (2002) (Relief for Russia); Katherine Siegel, *Loans and Legitimacy* (1996), and Christine A. White, *British and American Commercial Relations with Soviet Russia* (1993).

For the Spanish civil war, see Michael Alpert, *A New International History of the Spanish Civil War* (1998); Peter N. Carroll, *The Odyssey of the Abraham Lincoln Brigade* (1994); and Douglas Little, *Malevolent Neutrality* (1985).

See also "Further Reading" in Chapters 5 and 6, and Robert L. Beisner, ed., *Guide to American Foreign Relations Since 1600* (2003).

For comprehensive coverage of foreign-relations topics, see the articles in the four-volume *Encyclopedia of U.S. Foreign Relations* (1997), edited by Bruce W. Jentleson and Thomas G. Paterson.

best-selling *The Good Earth* (1931), made into a powerful movie six years later, captured for Americans the romance of hard-working, persevering Chinese peasants. This "righteous infatuation" with China, stemming from years of religious missionary activity and a self-congratulatory belief that the United States had become China's special friend by virtue of the Open Door, meant that in Asia, "Washington preached to everyone, including the Chinese," recalled one diplomat.

Washington sermonized most fervently to the Japanese, Soviets, and Chinese Nationalists, all of whom strove to check Western imperialists in Asia. For the United States, peaceful change, the Open Door, protection of American property and citizens, and the treaty rights of trade and judicial extraterritoriality seemed threatened. Sun Zhongshan, leader of the Chinese Revolution until his death in 1925, bristled when U.S. gunboats visited Guangzhou in 1923 to halt a potential Chinese takeover of foreign-dominated customshouses. Instead of "an American Lafayette" who would "fight on our side in this good cause," the Christian, English-speaking Sun lamented, "there comes not a Lafayette but an American Admiral with more ships of war than any other nation in our waters."

Washington did little to assist Chinese Nationalists and insisted on U.S. treaty privileges. The Chinese turned instead to another possible means of support, the Soviet Union. Seeking to restrain Japan, spank imperialist capitalists, and implant communism, Moscow sent Michael Borodin to help the Nationalists centralize the structure of the Guomindang party. Americans understood neither the depth of Chinese nationalism nor Sun's use of Soviet agents for Chinese purposes; some U.S. officials attributed China's intense antiforeign sentiment to Bolshevik agitation.

In 1925, Sun died and the Nationalist outpouring in the May 30th Movement of that year led to attacks on foreign nationals and missionaries. Lieutenant Colonel George C. Marshall summed up his experience in China over the next two years: "We are either just out of near trouble with the Chinese or trouble is just hovering near us." The outbreak of civil war within the Nationalist ranks prompted Washington to reconsider treaty privileges. The ambitious Guomindang leader Jiang Jieshi turned fiercely on his communist allies in 1926–1927, booting Borodin back to Moscow and killing Chinese communists by the thousands. The communist leader Mao Zedong fled south to Kiangsi Province, where he set up a rebel government. Jiang told U.S. officials that only American assistance could buttress China in "holding off" Japan and Soviet Russia and averting "a great war in the Pacific." Washington signed a trade treaty in 1928 that restored tariff autonomy to China and granted most-favored-nation treatment. By 1930 more than 500 American companies were operating in China, with investments amounting to $155 million, still only 1 percent of total American foreign investments. From 1923 to 1931 the United States sent only 3 percent of its exports to China. American trade with Japan totaled twice as much.

Washington nonetheless waxed hopeful because American-trained Chinese "cosmopolitans" such as H. H. Kung, Hu Shi, and T. V. Soong were gaining influence in the Guomindang. Jiang had joined the crusade against communism. In 1930, furthermore, he converted to Christianity and married Meiling Soong, daughter of the U.S.-educated, prominent Chinese businessman Charles Soong. The Wellesley College honors graduate spoke impeccable English and soon established ties with prominent Americans, later called the China Lobby. The beautiful, intelligent, and "Westernized" Madame Jiang became the perfect "damsel in distress" as she—and the new God-fearing China—appealed to American notions of "mission, chivalry, and machismo."

Japan's Footsteps Toward a New Pacific Order

Zealous expansionists, the Japanese feared the future. With 65 million people living in an area smaller than Texas in 1931, they had become dependent on outside sources for vital raw materials. Japan sought self-sufficiency because "a tree must have its roots," citing U.S. "roots" in Latin America as an example. Japan was only doing what the Western powers had done, Tokyo explained. The imperialists had taught Japan the game of poker but then, after winning most of the chips, pronounced the game immoral and took up contract bridge. In August 1936 Tokyo secretly adopted the "Fundamental Principles of National Strategy," which called for both southern expansion by peaceful "footsteps" toward the British, Dutch, and French empires of Southeast Asia (favored by the navy) and a northern advance into China and Mongolia (favored by the army). Three years later Japan announced its imperial ambitions by defining the "Greater East Asia Co-Prosperity Sphere."

Japan ranked the United States first on its list of potential enemies. A Japanese navy study of 1936 stated that "in case the enemy's [America's] main fleet is berthed at Pearl Harbor the idea should be to open hostilities by surprise attacks from the air." U.S. naval leaders likewise used Japan as the enemy on the war-game board at the Naval War College. Naval competition intensified in 1935–1936 when the London conference aborted and Japan announced its withdrawal from earlier treaties. The Immigration Act of 1924, blatantly discriminatory in excluding Japanese citizens from entering the United States, rankled Tokyo "right down to the bone." Trade disputes also intensified. Inexpensive Japanese goods, especially textiles, entered the American market, undercutting some domestic producers. "Buy America" campaigns and public boycotts of Japanese goods followed. Japan began to close the trade and investment door in China.

President Franklin D. Roosevelt continued Stimson's nonrecognition policy. This policy reflected American weakness in Asia. But at least until 1937, the long lull in fighting between China and Japan did not seem to require U.S. action. Roosevelt did move to bring the navy up to treaty strength. Under New Deal programs in 1933, the president allocated funds for thirty-two new vessels, including two aircraft carriers, and by 1937 naval appropriations had doubled. The United States also staged large-scale naval maneuvers near Midway Island in the Pacific to impress the Japanese. Instead, these naval activities reinforced Japan's secret decision in May 1937 to outbuild the Americans and construct warships well beyond treaty limits—including the huge 64,000-ton battleships *Yamato* and *Musashi*. FDR's diplomatic recognition of the Soviet Union in 1933 aimed in part to cow Japan with the suspicion that Moscow and Washington had linked arms in Asia. Four years later, Captain Claire Chennault, retired from the U.S. Army Air Corps, joined the Chinese air force as chief adviser. By 1940 U.S. volunteer pilots manned his "Flying Tigers" unit.

Shanghai, China, 1937. This photograph of a baby amid the ruins of North Station after Japanese bombing galvanized American opinion. Senator George Norris, who gradually abandoned his isolationism because of scenes like this, denounced the Japanese as "disgraceful, ignoble, barbarous, and cruel, even beyond the power of language to describe." (© Copyright United Press International. All rights reserved. Distributed by Valeo IP.)

On July 7, 1937, Japanese and Chinese troops clashed at the Marco Polo Bridge near Beijing. This skirmish grew quickly into the "China Incident" (not a "war" because the Kellogg-Briand Pact outlawed wars). Fighting spread throughout China. Shanghai fell to Japan in November after the cruel bombing of civilians. The "rape" of Nanjing followed in December, as Japanese soldiers raped 80,000 women and massacred some 300,000 residents of China's then capital city.

The civil war between Jiang's Guomindang forces and Mao Zedong's communists further sapped China. The communists had declared war on Japan in 1932, charging Jiang with appeasing Tokyo. Until 1937 Jiang fought the communists more than he fought the Japanese. From 1935 to 1937, the communists took the dramatic "Long March" of 6,000 miles to Yan'an (Yenan) in the north. In late 1936 dissident Chinese army forces in Manchuria kidnapped Jiang, hoping to end the civil war by creating a coalition government. Joseph Stalin and the Chinese communists soon secured his release and persuaded him to institute a tenuous united front against Japan in early 1937. Thereafter Moscow increased arms sales and technical assistance to Jiang and Soviet troops delivered a "firm rebuff" to the Japanese in border clashes along the Manchurian and Mongolian frontiers in 1938 and 1939.

Having refused to invoke American neutrality after the Marco Polo Bridge incident, thereby permitting valuable trade to continue with China, Roosevelt addressed a Chicago audience on October 5, 1937. He called vaguely for a "quarantine" on aggressors to check the "epidemic of world lawlessness." After the speech, FDR privately toyed with economic warfare—a naval blockade or embargo—but drew back following isolationist protests. In November Roosevelt sent representatives to a conference in Brussels, but it disbanded without action— only the Soviet Union pushed for reprisals against Japan. In December the American

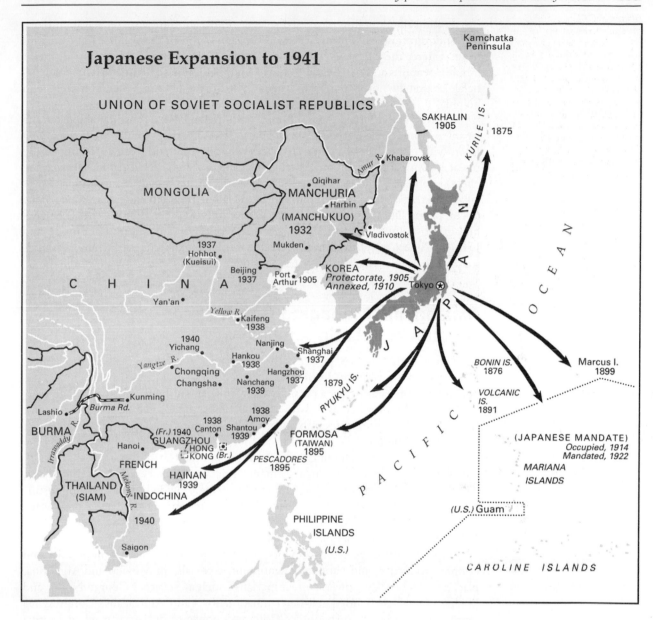

Japanese Expansion to 1941

gunboat *Panay,* escorting on the Yangtze River three Standard Oil Company tankers flying American flags, took destructive fire from Japanese pilots. Two U.S. sailors died. With Secretary Hull blasting the perpetrators as "wild, runaway, half-insane men," Tokyo quickly apologized and paid an indemnity.

As Japan plunged deeper into China in 1938, Washington cautiously initiated new measures. By purchasing Chinese silver, the United States gave China dollars with which to buy American military equipment. Secretary Hull imposed a "moral embargo" on the sale of aircraft to Japan, while a naval bill authorized two new carriers and the doubling of naval airplanes. FDR also sent a secret naval emissary to London to discuss contingency plans in case of war in the Pacific. These actions did not deter the Japanese, who by the end of 1938 controlled virtually all major Chinese seaports and had begun to install a puppet Chinese regime. A U.S. trade official accurately noted that the "Open Door" was being "banged, barred, and bolted."

With war clouds billowing in Europe in summer 1939, Roosevelt abrogated the Japanese-American commercial treaty of 1911. With the United States supplying Japan with nearly half of its imports, especially oil, iron, and steel, FDR hoped the threat of economic pressure might temper Japan's onslaught in China. The abrogation, effective January 1940, did not immediately limit bilateral trade. Ambassador Grew's talks with the Japanese foreign minister in the fall of 1939 did elicit a Japanese pledge to curtail brutalities against foreigners in China. In November 1939 another U.S. naval bill authorized two more battleships. By then World War II had begun in Europe, and Japanese-American relations had stalemated. Unwilling to fight over China, Washington had to decide what to do if Japan expanded beyond China.

Making and Managing Good Neighbors in Latin America

In contrast with Asia, U.S. power in the Western Hemisphere remained unmatched. Indeed, shortly after World War I, U.S. armed forces used the Caribbean for maneuvers—as preparation for a possible war with Japan in the Pacific. And when Germany and Japan marched aggressively in the 1930s, the United States brought most of the Latin American states into a virtual alliance to resist foreign intrusions in the hemisphere. The imperial net in Latin America had been stitched before and during World War I, especially in Central America and the Caribbean, through military occupations, Panama Canal, management of national finances, and economic ties. The Roosevelt Corollary to the Monroe Doctrine provided the overriding justification for U.S. hegemony. Swaggering American marines in the streets of Havana, Managua, or Port-au-Prince represented only the most conspicuous evidence of North American imperial management.

The use of troops as instruments of policy, however, became unpopular and counterproductive, and nationalist sentiment, especially in Mexico and Argentina, placed limits on U.S. power. Anti-imperialists such as Senators George Norris and William Borah demanded self-determination for Latin Americans. Congress resented the president's usurpation of Congress's power to declare war when he unilaterally dispatched troops to the Caribbean. Business leaders came to believe that military expeditions, because they aroused anti-U.S. violence, endangered rather than protected their properties. Referring to Japan's seizure of Manchuria, and alert to a double standard, Secretary Stimson commented in 1932: "If we landed a single soldier among those South Americans now . . . it would put me absolutely in the wrong in China, where Japan has done all this monstrous work under the guise of protecting her nationals."

Between the world wars, therefore, the United States increasingly used nonmilitary methods to maintain its hegemony in Latin America. Washington forswore armed interference and employed economic penetration, political subversion, non-recognition, support for dictators who kept order, arbitration treaties, PanAmericanism, financial supervision, Export-Import Bank loans, and the training of national guards. At times U.S. officials pressed for negotiated settlements, as when, in 1929, Secretary Kellogg helped settle the Tacna-Arica dispute between Chile and Peru. These tactics translated into a catchy phrase popularized by Franklin D. Roosevelt— the Good Neighbor policy. FDR hailed in early 1933 "the policy of the good neighbor . . . who respects his obligations and respects the sanctity of his agreements in and with a world of neighbors." Although Latin Americans welcomed the new spirit, the goal of U.S. hegemony in the hemisphere had not changed, only the means for maintaining it. As the Axis specter loomed larger in the late 1930s, the Good Neighbor policy came to mean cooperation against the aggressors.

Economic decisions by U.S. leaders, private and governmental, held immense importance for Latin American nations. In the Dominican Republic and Haiti, for example, officials had to obtain U.S. consent before borrowing foreign capital. In Cuba, where North American interests accounted for about two-thirds of sugar production, U.S. investments helped lock the country into a risky one-crop economy subject to fluctuating world sugar prices. In Honduras, U.S. companies provided cannon and machine guns to one political group that conducted a successful coup in 1924. In 1929 U.S. firms produced more than half of Venezuela's oil. Their bribery of Venezuelan government officials, including the president, was not uncommon.

In a process sometimes called "colonialism by contract," professional economists such as Edward Kemmerer of Princeton University served as financial advisers to Colombia, Chile, Ecuador, and Peru during the 1920s, usually recommending gold-exchange currency reforms managed by a central bank, new taxes, revised tariffs, and private American loans for public-works projects tied to U.S. firms. Popular at first, such programs aroused nationalist backlashes in the 1930s when declining exports, excessive indebtedness, and contracting capital markets caused massive defaults throughout Latin America, where "money doctors" were once again seen as Wall Street, Yankee imperialists.

The Argentine writer Manuel Ugarte bluntly identified a "new Rome" in the mid-1920s. The United States, he explained, annexed wealth rather than territory, thus enjoying the "essentials of domination" without the "dead-weight of areas to administrate and multitudes to govern." U.S. economic penetration always "invoked peace, progress, civilization and culture; but its motives, procedure, and results have frequently been a complete negation of these premises." Nonetheless, President Roosevelt's smiling personification of the Good Neighbor seemed to make the Yankee presence more palatable—"a gringo in the Latin mold, a man they could understand and empathize with as a projection of their own political style," according to one historian.

Still, too many North Americans resembled the boorish member of Congress who insulted a Latin American diplomat's wife: "Señora, I regret that I know only two words of your beautiful language: mañana, which means tomorrow, and pyjama,

Nelson A. Rockefeller (1908–1979) and Anastasio Somoza García (1896–1956). The grandson of Standard Oil millionaire John D. Rockefeller, Sr., Nelson (second from right) served as director of the family oil business in Venezuela during the 1930s. An advocate of improved U.S. cultural, scientific, and educational relations within the hemisphere, Rockefeller served as coordinator of the Office of Inter-American Affairs for the State Department during World War II and later became vice president in 1974 under President Gerald Ford. Rockefeller is dining here with Nicaraguan strongman Somoza, who ruled from 1937 to 1956, aligned himself with the United States, and created a corrupt family dynasty in his country. (National Archives)

which means tonight." When a young Nelson Rockefeller visited Venezuela in the early 1930s to look after his oil investments, he noticed that U.S. citizens there seldom learned Spanish. Rockefeller thereupon hired twelve Berlitz instructors to begin Spanish classes for company employees. A decade earlier the Rockefeller Foundation had begun to spend millions to destroy the mosquito in Latin America to combat yellow fever and succeeded in "unhooking the hookworm" in Colombia.

U.S. investments in and trade with Latin America reached a "boom" stage after World War I. The direct investments of U.S. citizens jumped from $1.26 billion in 1914 to $3.52 billion in 1929, mostly in electric power, railroads, bananas, sugar, oil, and minerals. By 1936, because of the devastating impact of the global depression, the amount dropped to $2.77 billion. These figures represented about one-third of total U.S. investments abroad. One of the nation's largest corporations, Standard Oil of New Jersey, operated in eight countries, and United Fruit Company held a large stake in the "banana republics" of Central America. International Telephone and Telegraph controlled communications in Cuba, where, between 1919 and 1933, overall U.S. investments increased 536 percent. Worried about diminishing domestic oil reserves after World War I, Washington urged U.S. firms to preempt foreign competitors in South America. "A conference of the leading oil producers was called," recorded Commerce Secretary Hoover, and "most of the available oil lands in South America were acquired by Americans." In the late 1920s, the average annual income outflow from U.S. investments in Latin America totaled $100 million more than the U.S. capital inflow.

With trade following investments, U.S. exports to Latin America tripled in value from 1914 to 1929, reaching the billion-dollar figure, approximately 20 percent of total U.S. exports. Although this impressive trade slumped during the Great Depression, for many Latin American countries commercial relationships with the United States remained critical. Nicaragua, for example, shipped 96 percent of its exports to the United States by 1941. In 1920 the United States supplied Cuba with 73 percent of its imports; that trade shrank to 59 percent in 1929 because of the depressed Cuban sugar economy. Cuba's exports to the United States also dropped off, although they still comprised 68 percent of all the island's exports. American investments in and trade with Venezuela helped that country to become the world's leading oil exporter. Trade with Chile in nitrates and copper jumped after U.S. investments there grew to $400 million in 1928. To stem declining world trade during the 1930s, Secretary Hull sought wider markets in Latin America when he launched the Export-Import Bank (directing loans to inter-American commerce) and the Reciprocal Trade Agreements Program. His efforts helped increase exports to Latin America from $244 million in 1933 to $642 million in 1938.

Creating Dictators in the Dominican Republic, Nicaragua, and Haiti

Until World War I corrupt politics in the Dominican Republic and mismanagement of national revenues produced economic stagnation, political factionalism, foreign indebtedness, and U.S. intervention (see Chapter 2). In May 1916, to quell local disorder, American marines went ashore. Although U.S. forces occupied the major cities and established martial law, the peasants and caudillos in the mountainous east waged bloody guerrilla war from 1917 to 1922. The marines retaliated in kind against insurgents who "are almost all touched with the tarbrush," as Military Governor Harry Knapp crudely put it. Marine atrocities against Dominican people of color usually went unpunished. Sumner Welles, the American commissioner to the Dominican Republic (1922–1924), later criticized the U.S. officers who ran the occupation— "the great majority of whom could not even speak the language of the country."

The military intervention in the Dominican Republic became a hot political issue at home and abroad. Warren G. Harding accused Wilson of the "rape of Haiti" in the 1920 campaign but continued the Dominican and Haitian occupations as president. When Washington ended the occupation in 1924, after forcing on the Dominican government a stabilization loan to liquidate past debt, and when the new national guard consumed a quarter of the Dominican budget, Secretary Hughes disingenuously claimed that the departure proved that the United States was "anti-imperialistic." Franklin D. Roosevelt agreed in a 1928 article in *Foreign Affairs:* "We accomplished an excellent piece of constructive work, and the world ought to thank us." With Americans running the country's fiscal affairs until 1941, FDR ignored "the lasting hostility towards the American people which the occupation created in the hearts of . . . the Dominican people."

The U.S. occupation also begot Rafael Leonidas Trujillo. In early 1919 he received a commission as a second lieutenant in the U.S.-created National Guard. The one-time pimp earned high marks from U.S. military officers and became chief of staff of the army in 1928. Through the rigged election of 1930, Trujillo won the presidency. The State Department initially looked on Trujillo as "a kind of Frankenstein, brought to life by the marines" but gradually warmed to him when his strong-arm tactics created internal order and precluded U.S. military intervention. Thanks to beneficent U.S. control of the customs, Trujillo could divert funds to his army for the suppression of internal dissent. Political corruption, military muscle, torture, murder, nepotism, commercial monopolies, and raids on the national treasury enabled Trujillo to quiet opponents and amass a fortune of $800 million.

Until his assassination in 1961, sometimes as president, sometimes through puppets, Trujillo became "the dictatingest dictator who ever dictated," as *Time* called him. U.S. military arms filled Dominican arsenals. U.S. business leaders, who dominated sugar production, endorsed him. The National City Bank became the official depository for Dominican revenues. By World War II the Dominican Republic stood as a success story for the new Good Neighbor policy. But good neighbors with whom? Roosevelt reportedly gave an answer in reference to Trujillo: "He may be an S.O.B., but he is our S.O.B."

Nicaragua, like the Dominican Republic, developed under the weight of U.S. military occupation and the Good Neighbor policy. From 1912 to 1925 the United States ruled Nicaragua and kept in power the pliant Conservative party. With the country apparently solvent, secure, and stable by 1925, the marines departed, but in late 1926 they returned because, in President Coolidge's words, Nicaragua "went to hell in a hack." In an overstated report titled "Bolshevik Aims and Policies in Mexico and Latin America" Secretary Kellogg alleged that communists were fomenting trouble in Nicaragua. The U.S. embassy in Mexico had greatly exaggerated the activities of American leftists in Mexico, and Washington found the anti-Bolshevik rationale irresistible. In fact, Nicaraguan Liberals had used Mexico as a sanctuary to challenge the Conservatives. "We are not making war on Nicaragua," Coolidge opined, "any more than a policeman on the street is making war on passersby." Nicaraguans in the Coco River basin saw it differently: "The Machos are coming," they said of the marines. "They will burn our houses."

The Nicaraguan intervention generated rancorous debate in the United States. The assertion of a communist plot persuaded few. Senator Burton K. Wheeler suggested that if U.S. soldiers intended to "stamp out banditry, let's send them to Chicago to stamp it out there." Bloodshed and destruction in Nicaragua raised further outcries after Secretary of the Navy Curtis D. Wilbur matter-of-factly reported in 1928: "Several houses were destroyed . . . to prepare a landing field for airplanes so that 19 wounded Marines could be evacuated to a hospital." From 1927 to 1933 the Liberal insurgent César Augusto Sandino, who railed against the "dastardly invaders," earned an international reputation as he waged guerrilla war against U.S. troops, which numbered 50,000 in early 1929.

With critics urging Washington to trade the "big bully" for the "big brother" in Nicaragua, special emissary Henry L. Stimson brought Liberals and Conservatives together in the "Peace of Tipitapa" (1927) and provided for U.S. supervision of elections in 1928. Most important, he and General Frank R. McCoy created an American-trained national guard to perpetuate the domestic order that the marines had imposed. Shortly after U.S. troops withdrew in 1933 General Anastasio Somoza, who had studied at a business school in Philadelphia, gained command of the U.S.-trained Guardia Nacional. Somoza then captured and executed Sandino, notwithstanding his "word of honor" that no harm would come to the insurgent leader. Somoza seized power in 1936 and established a self-enriching family dictatorship that lasted until 1979. A U.S. collector-general remained to handle customs collections until 1944. The Roosevelt administration in 1939 constructed an interoceanic highway (the Rama Road) to spur economic development.

Few benefits accrued to Washington from its years of interference in Nicaragua. Trade never reached important levels, and from 1914 to 1930 U.S. investments grew from $4.5 million to a meager $13 million. As for the vaunted Good Neighbor policy, that policy for Nicaraguans meant continued foreign financial management and replacement of the U.S. Marine Corps by a home-grown dictator who was insistently "*Americanista*" in following Uncle Sam.

Haiti, too, drew Washington's hegemonic attention. A marine officer depicted the Haitians as "real nigger and no mistake." When U.S. soldiers went abroad, of course, they carried American prejudices as well as canteens. For nineteen years, from 1915 to 1934, marines governed the tiny black French-speaking nation of Haiti in the Caribbean. The venture only deepened Haiti's distress. The Wilson administration ordered U.S. marines into Haiti on July 28, 1915, because it feared German intrigue during World War I, sought to protect American financial interests, and insisted on order in the Caribbean.

The occupation built highways, technical schools, lighthouses, hospitals, and railroads. Americans improved public health and sanitation, but never eradicated Haiti's profound human squalor. By the mid-1960s Haiti had the lowest life expectancy (thirty-five years) and the lowest literacy rate (10 percent) in Latin America. Many roads had been built in 1916–1918 through the *corvée* system, which forced workers into labor gangs. The NAACP official James Weldon Johnson, who toured Haiti, compared the "maltreated, beaten and terrorized" workers to "convicts in the Negro chain gangs that are used to build roads in many of our southern states." Haitians rebelled against the *corvée;* in 1919 alone the marines killed 2,000 to crush the insurrection.

American racism reached into Haiti, as U.S. personnel introduced words like "nigger" and "coon" and enforced segregation between blacks and whites. When an aide objected to inviting Haitian diplomats to tea, Secretary Hull responded in both race and class terms: "When they [blacks] speak French, that's different." Americans bestowed higher status on the mulattoes (the "elites") than on the *authentiques* (blacks) but neither wooed nor fraternized with the Haitian bourgeoisie. Anthropological research in the 1930s showed complex linkages among African, European, and indigenous cultures but could not displace the prevailing Hollywood film stereotype of Haiti as "America's Africa"—the land of voodoo and zombies.

Transportation improvements expanded commercial contacts between cities and rural farmers. Pan American Airways began flights between Miami and Port-au-Prince. Sugar and cotton exports increased, although the heavy dependence on one crop, coffee, left Haiti susceptible to fluctuations in world prices. With the Banque Nacional owned by the National City Bank of New York, American capital investments grew from $11.5 million in 1914 to $28.5 million in 1930. Under U.S. financial supervision, Haiti actually paid its foreign debts ahead of schedule.

U.S. military authorities trained a national guard, the Garde d'Haiti. The first commandant, Major Smedley D. Butler of the marines worked "hard with my little black Army" which did well "as long as white men lead them." The *gendarmerie*

César Augusto Sandino (1895–1934). President Hoover called him a "cold-blooded bandit," but Nicaraguans have hailed Sandino as a hero. Determined that Nicaragua control its natural resources and help the poor, Sandino blasted the Monroe Doctrine as meaning "America for the Yankees." The revolutionaries who overthrew the Somoza dictatorship in 1979 called themselves "Sandinistas." (Library of Congress)

served as judges and tax collectors, enforced martial law, and wielded deciding political force.

The United States failed to establish respect for honest government. Washington officials drafted the 1918 constitution, forced it on Haitians, and then suspended the legislature for thirteen years. When President Philippe Sudre Dartiguenave's term ended in 1922, Americans jilted him in favor of Louis Borno, an acquiescent lawyer who collaborated with the American high commissioner, General John H. Russell of Georgia, to rule Haiti from 1922 to 1930. Borno "has never taken a step without first consulting me," Russell boasted. The marines had made Haiti "safe for almost everybody but the Haitians," gibed *The Nation* in 1926.

Haitians resented their colonial status. A slump in coffee exports and exposure of Borno's political machinations ignited widespread protests and strikes in 1929. President Hoover appointed an investigating commission chaired by W. Cameron Forbes, former governor-general of the Philippines. His report of 1930 noted "the failure of the Occupation to understand the social problems of Haiti" and promoted "Haitianization" to ease Haitians into positions of responsibility. Hoover started the withdrawal; Roosevelt completed it in 1934.

Thereafter strong-arm presidents ruled with the help of Export-Import Bank loans and ties with Washington. During World War II the United States used Haitian bases and supervised Haitian national finances. A revolution in 1956–1957 produced the callous dictatorship of Dr. François ("Papa Doc") Duvalier, who ruled with the ruthless help of his secret police force, the Touton Macoutes, until his death in 1971, when his son "Baby Doc" assumed power. Driven out in 1986, he left behind abject poverty and rampant civil strife. In both 1994 and 2004 U.S. armed forces again invaded Haiti to stabilize politics (see Chapter 12).

Subverting Nationalism in Cuba and Puerto Rico

Cubans bristled under the Platt Amendment. Through the 1920s and into the 1930s the United States helped conduct elections, enlarged the national army, managed the national budget, and maintained economic control over the island. North American investment, particularly in sugar, soared to $1.5 billion in 1929. Approximately half a million fun-seeking Americans a year visited the capital city of Havana, where, as Irving Berlin's lyrics suggested, "dark-eyed Stellas/Light their fellers' panatelas."

Gerardo Machado ruled from 1924 to 1933; he suppressed free speech, jailed or murdered opponents, and used the army as a political weapon. Obtaining loans from U.S. bankers, he prohibited strikes and looked after North American business interests "as if they were my own." After sugar prices slumped in the late 1920s, Cuba sank further into economic crisis when Washington instituted the restrictive Smoot-Hawley Tariff of 1931. Unemployment rates shot up. Machado's army beat back protesters. Because armed intervention would violate the newly stated Good Neighbor policy, Roosevelt and his advisers chose to ease out the unpopular Machado.

Suave Sumner Welles, a Groton School friend of Roosevelt, went as ambassador to Havana in 1933. While U.S. warships patrolled Cuban waters and a general strike rocked the country, Welles persuaded Machado to flee. But Welles's hand-picked government lasted less than a month. Military dissidents, commanded by Sergeant Fulgencio Batista, staged the "Sergeants' Revolution" of September 1933 and installed Professor Ramón Grau San Martín as president.

An exile under Machado and critic of the Platt Amendment, Grau stood as "the hope and the symbol of the forces of nationalism, patriotism, and reform." Yet Welles refused recognition because "we owe it to the Cuban people not to assist in saddling upon them . . . a government which every responsible element in the country violently opposed." When Grau suspended payment on Chase National Bank loans and seized some North American–owned sugar mills, Welles decried the "confiscatory" decrees of this "social revolution" and conspired with Batista who toppled Grau in January 1934. A Batista-backed president took over, and the United States quickly granted recognition.

Batista ruled Cuba, sometimes as president, sometimes from the shadows, from 1934 to 1959. At the start of the Batista era, the United States abrogated the unpopular Platt Amendment (1934), lowered the sugar tariff, granted a favorable quota to Cuban sugar imports (1934), and issued Export-Import Bank loans. In 1940, Cuba granted U.S. armed forces the use of ports and airfields (besides Guantánamo) in exchange for military aid. Even popular Hollywood movies influenced Cuban politics, as *gangsterismo* passed into the vernacular to describe political violence in the Batista era.

Elsewhere in the Caribbean, Puerto Rico stagnated under American paternalism. Throughout the interwar years, mediocre U.S. governors castigated Puerto Ricans as "unsteady, unprincipled children" unable to govern themselves. Washington stiff-armed requests for independence or statehood, and Puerto Ricans did not gain the right to elect their own governor until 1947. Absentee American landowners and sugar barons ran the island's economy. Despite improved roads and new schools, Governor Theodore Roosevelt, Jr. (1929–1932) observed "lean underfed women and sickly men" with "little food and no opportunity to get more." Eighty percent of peasants remained landless and many crowded into urban slums.

During the 1930s the Harvard-educated lawyer Pedro Albizu Campos headed the Nationalist party, which advocated the violent overthrow of U.S. rule. On Palm Sunday, 1937, police fired on unarmed Nationalist marchers, killing nineteen in the "Ponce Massacre." Albizu went to federal prison until 1947. Other Puerto Ricans rallied behind the socialist Luis Muñoz Marín, whose Popular Democratic party ultimately advocated "commonwealth" status (attained in 1952). New Deal projects brought in $1 million a month, along with funds to attract mainland tourists to Puerto Rico—to don a "coat of tan" and to mingle with "beautiful señoritas" on San Juan's beaches. Yet in 1941 Governor Rexford Tugwell found the island "still sunk in hopeless poverty."

Fulgencio Batista (1901–1973). Born of farm folk in the United Fruit Company town of Banes, Batista joined the Cuban army at age twenty. A smiling, ruthless dictator, he became a staunch U.S. ally, bought real estate in Daytona Beach, Florida, and turned Havana into a playground of casinos and brothels for American tourists. Fidel Castro's 26th of July Movement overthrew the corrupt regime in 1959. Batista died in exile in Portugal. (National Archives)

Compromising with Mexico: Oil and Nationalism

The ongoing Mexican Revolution, which began in 1910, challenged the United States. Before the 1920s it had appeared that Mexico would share the fate of other

U.S. neighbors—invaded, occupied, and owned by Americans, who by 1910 controlled 43 percent of Mexican property and produced more than half of Mexico's oil. Hollywood films perpetuated stereotypes by portraying the Mexican as a bandit or villainous "greaser." To counter such negative images, Professor Herbert E. Bolton of the University of California, Berkeley, emphasized a shared borderlands history in his popular course on "Greater America." In the 1930s at U.S. universities, the Mexican artist José Clemente Orozco painted colorful murals of revolutionary struggle. Such contacts encouraged an environment of tolerance and understanding based on mutual experience that undercut war hawks bent on military confrontation.

The Mexican Constitution of 1917 alarmed capitalist Americans, because its Article 27 held that all subsoil raw materials belonged to the Mexican nation, thereby jeopardizing American investments in oil and mines. Mexico also began to tax American oil producers heavily. Washington continued to claim economic rights for its nationals in Mexico and refused to recognize the government of Alváro Obregón. In 1923, however, the two countries signed the Bucareli Agreements. In exchange for U.S. recognition, Mexico agreed that Americans who held subsoil rights before 1917 could continue those concessions and owners of expropriated agricultural lands would receive Mexican bonds in compensation. But a new Mexican law passed in 1925 stated that oil lands secured before 1917 could be held for a maximum of only fifty years. With U.S. oil companies shifting to the oil fields of Venezuela, Washington rejected intervention and resorted to diplomacy instead.

In early 1927, President Coolidge selected Dwight W. Morrow, an old college chum and Wall Street banker, as the new ambassador to Mexico City. Learning a little Spanish, having "Lone Eagle" Charles Lindbergh fly nonstop from Washington, D.C., and even bringing the humorist Will Rogers to the Mexican capital, Morrow ingratiated himself. Morrow then negotiated a compromise that confirmed *pre-1917* ownership of petroleum lands and tacitly conceded that Mexico legally controlled its own raw materials. This arrangement lasted until 1938, when President Lázaro Cárdenas defiantly expropriated the property of all foreign oil companies. "No more humble pie, no more kowtowing to arrogant foreign officials," crowed one Mexican journalist.

Ambassador Josephus Daniels did his best to effuse the crisis. He balked at Hull's "get tough" policies, softening an intemperate State Department blast when he delivered it to the Mexican foreign minister and opposing any reduction of U.S. purchases of Mexican silver. For their part American oil companies refused to sell petroleum equipment to Mexico and persuaded shipping firms not to transport Mexican oil. Standard Oil of New Jersey financed false propaganda in the United States with the message that Cárdenas plotted to turn Mexico communist. In 1938 Daniels cabled Hull that "some of the oil men are predicting revolution" so that they can "return to conditions here as existed under Díaz or Huerta."

Viewing Cárdenas as "actually preaching and trying to practice democracy," FDR ruled out intervention and sought compensation. Increased purchases of Mexican oil by Germany, Italy, and Japan underscored the urgent need for a diplomatic settlement. Indeed, once war broke out in Europe in September 1939, FBI director J. Edgar Hoover reported false rumors about 250 Nazi pilots in Mexico and

With President Cardenas, of Mexico.

Lázaro Cárdenas (1895–1970) and Josephus Daniels (1862–1948). A former newspaper publisher and secretary of the navy during the Wilson administration, Daniels (second from left) donned Mexican national costumes, adopted a warm, folksy style, and became a popular ambassador to Mexico (1933–1941) under his friend President Franklin D. Roosevelt. As president of Mexico (1934–1940), Cárdenas (center with mustache) attempted to regain control of his nation's oil resources from multinational corporations. Daniels assured FDR that Cárdenas was simply another "New Dealer" trying to improve his country's living conditions. (Library of Congress)

Hitler's promise of British Honduras if Mexico agreed to supply Germany with petroleum. Protracted negotiations produced an agreement in 1941 that recognized Mexico's ownership of its own raw materials, plus Mexico's promise to pay for expropriated properties. The Export-Import Bank then extended a $30 million loan. Compromise with Mexican nationalism became a strategic necessity as the United States readied itself for World War II.

Pan Americanism and the Approach of the Second World War

Notwithstanding occasional conferences, elegant architecture, and high hopes for improved trade and hemispheric solidarity, the Pan American movement had accomplished little, as indicated by the declarations of neutrality by seven Latin American governments during World War I. At the Fifth International Conference of American States in Santiago, Chile (1923), the United States controlled the agenda, and the delegates endorsed the Gondra Treaty to Avoid or Prevent Conflicts Between the American States. The Havana conference of 1928 proved quite different, because it convened shortly after U.S. troops had landed in Nicaragua. Anticipating trouble, the popular former secretary of state Hughes headed the U.S. delegation, and even President Coolidge traveled to Cuba to address the conference with soothing banalities. At the conference, the delegate from El Salvador boldly moved that "no state has the right to intervene in the internal affairs of another." Mexico and Argentina backed this challenge to Washington. Hughes valiantly defended the right of "interposition of a temporary character," and he manipulated the conference to table the resolution.

The seventh Pan American conference, in Montevideo, Uruguay (1933), met under the aura of the Good Neighbor policy. The nonintervention resolution was once again introduced. Secretary Hull cast an affirmative vote but retained a U.S.

right to intervene "by the law of nations as generally recognized and accepted." The U.S. definition, however, intended to outlaw *military* intervention, whereas many Latin American countries wanted to proscribe economic or political pressure when countries nationalized American-owned property.

Pan Americanism took a decided turn toward hemispheric security in the late 1930s, as Germany, Italy, and Japan attempted to improve their standing in Latin America. As Germany's trade with Latin America climbed, Hull saw the most "acute" threat "in its indirect form of propaganda, penetration, organizing political parties, buying some adherents, and blackmailing others." With Adolf Hitler dreaming of "a new Germany" in Brazil and instigating subversive activities there and in Uruguay, Argentina, and Mexico, Washington tried to form "a north-south axis" at the Lima Pan American conference of 1938, despite opposition from Argentina, Uruguay, and Chile. The anti-German sentiment of most delegates, aroused by the recent Munich crisis, helped Hull to fashion the Declaration of Lima, a pledge to resist foreign intervention in the Americas. In autumn 1939 the Declaration of Panama established a security belt around the Western Hemisphere to rebuff possible Axis intrusions. At the same time, Latin American nations agreed to reduce or cease trade with the Axis powers and to ship strategic materials to the United States.

The post–World War I search for international order had broken down by 1939. In both Asia and Latin America, fervent nationalists challenged the United States. In both areas the viability of American diplomacy derived from the power Americans possessed and exercised. In Asia, after the Manchurian crisis of 1931–1932, the United States sought, without success, to build a counterforce to Japan. Even the Philippines became a virtual hostage that the U.S. military said it could not defend. By spring 1939 the possibility of a two-ocean war prompted the U.S. Joint Army-Navy Board to modify war plan ORANGE (which emphasized a naval offensive in the Pacific) in favor of RAINBOW plans for hemispheric defense based on the primacy of the Atlantic and Caribbean approaches.

The Great Depression prostrated international relations. World trade and investment collapsed; tariffs went up. The trade-conscious Japanese accelerated efforts to build a "co-prosperity" sphere in Asia. In Latin America, where many countries depended on the exportation of one commodity, revolutions and coups erupted, feeding on incipient nationalism. Social unrest and political instability rocked the area from which U.S. marines were withdrawing. Political upheavals in the Dominican Republic, Argentina, Brazil, and Chile in 1930, Peru in 1931, Cuba in 1933—all threatened U.S. hegemony. Devastated by the depression, Latin Americans gained a new awareness of the extent to which foreigners made their national choices and drained profits from them. By World War II, Latin Americans held a more favorable image of the Good Neighbor policy, which seemed to have eschewed military intervention. Would invigorated inter-American economic relations continue U.S. hegemony? Yankeephobia simmered even as Latin Americans joined the United States in the fight against the Axis.

FURTHER READING FOR THE PERIOD 1920–1939

For general studies and biographies for this period, see works cited in Chapter 4.

For Asia, see Tokomo Akami, *Internationalizing the Pacific* (2000); Akira Iriye, *The Origins of the Second World War in Asia and the Pacific* (1987); Greg Kennedy, *Anglo-American Strategic Relations and the Far East, 1933–1939* (2002); Brian M. Linn, *Guardians of Empire* (1997); John Mecham, *The Dominion and the Rising Sun* (2004); William R. Nestor, *Power Across the Pacific* (1996); and Haruo Tohmatsu and H. P. Willmott, *A Gathering Darkness: The Coming of War to the Far East and the Pacific, 1921–1942* (2004).

For relations with Japan, consult Michael Barnhart, *Japan Prepares for Total War* (1987); Justus D. Doenecke, *When the Wicked Rise* (1984) (Manchurian crisis); Peter Duus et al., eds., *The Japanese Wartime Empire, 1931–1945* (1996); Carol Gluck and Stephen Graubard, eds., *Showa: The Japan of Hirohito* (1992); Izumi Hirobe, *Japanese Pride, American Prejudice* (2001) (Exclusion Clause); Walter LaFeber, *The Clash* (1997); James W. Morley, ed., *Deterrent Diplomacy: Japan, Germany and the U.S.S.R., 1934–1940* (1977); Ian Nish, *Japanese Foreign Policy in the Interwar Period* (2002); Nicholas Tarling, *A Sudden Rampage* (2001); Jonathan G. Utley, *Going to War with Japan, 1937–1941* (2005); and Dandra Wilson, *The Manchurian Crisis and Japanese Society, 1931–1933* (2002).

China and the United States are explored in Mary B. Bullock, *An American Transplant* (1980) (Rockefeller Foundation); Warren I. Cohen, *The Chinese Connection* (1978); Bernard Cole, *Gunboats and Marines* (1983); John W. Garver, *Chinese-Soviet Relations, 1937–1945* (1988); David H. Grover, *American Merchant Ships on the Yangtze* (1992); Robert E. Herzstein, *Henry Luce, Time, and the American Crusade in Asia* (2005); Shizhang Hu, *Stanley K. Hornbeck and the Open Door Policy* (1995); T. Christopher Jespersen, *American Images of China* (1996); Karen Leong, *The Chinese Mystique* (2005); Fei Fei Li et al., *Nanking 1937* (2002); Youli Sun, *China and the Origins of the Pacific War* (1993); and Stephen J. Valone, *A Policy Calculated to Benefit China* (1991).

Inter-American relations and the Good Neighbor policy are treated in Marcos Cueto, ed., *Missionaries of Science* (1994) (Rockefeller Foundation); Max Paul Friedman, *Nazis and Good Neighbors* (2003); Irwin F. Gellman, *Good Neighbor Diplomacy* (1979); Mark T. Gilderhus, *The Second Century* (2000); Kenneth J. Grieb, *The Latin American Policy of Warren G. Harding* (1976); David G. Haglund, *Latin America and the Transformation of U.S. Strategic Thought, 1936–1940* (1984); Gilbert M. Joseph et al., *Close Encounters of Empire* (1998); Thomas L. Karnes, *Tropical Enterprise: The Standard Fruit and Steamship Company in Latin America* (1978); Michael L. Krenn, *U.S. Policy Toward Economic Nationalism in Latin America* (1990); Lester D. Langley, *America and the Americas* (1989); John Major, *Prize Possession* (1993) (Panama Canal); Thomas O'Brien, *The Revolutionary Mission* (1996); Fredrick B. Pike, *FDR's Good Neighbor Policy* (1995); Emily S. Rosenberg, *Financial Missionaries to the World* (1999); David F. Schmitz, *Thank God They're on Our Side* (1999) (dictatorships); Lars Schoultz, *Beneath the United States* (1998); James Schwoch, *The American Radio Industry and Its Latin American Activities* (1990); Sarah E. Sharbach, *Stereotypes of Latin America* (1993); Peter H. Smith, *Talons of the Eagle* (1996); and Joseph Tulchin, *The Aftermath of War: World War I and U.S. Policy Toward Latin America* (1971).

For the Caribbean and Central America, see G. Pope Atkins and Larman C. Wilson, *The Dominican Republic and the United States* (1998); Bruce Calder, *The Impact of Intervention* (1984) (Dominican Republic); Raymond Carr, *Puerto Rico* (1984); Arturo Morales Carrión, *Puerto Rico* (1983); Paul J. Dosal, *Doing Business with the Dictators* (1993) (United Fruit, Guatemala); Ronald Fernandez, *The Disenchanted Island* (1992) (Puerto Rico); Walter LaFeber, *Inevitable Revolutions* (1993); Brenda G. Plummer, *Haiti and the United States* (1992); Mary Renda, *Taking Haiti* (2001); Eric Paul Roorda, *The Dictator Next Door* (1998) (Trujillo); and Hans Schmidt, *Maverick Marine* (1987) (Butler).

For Nicaragua and the U.S. intervention, see Paul C. Clark Jr., *The United States and Somoza* (1992); Thomas J. Dodd, *Managing Democracy in Central America* (1992); Marco Aurelia Narro-Genie, *Augusto "Cesar" Sandino* (2002); and Knut Walter, *The Regime of Anastasio Somoza* (1993).

For South America, see Elizabeth A. Cobbs, *The Rich Neighbor Policy* (1992); Paul W. Drake, *The Money Doctor in the Andes* (1988); Michael Grow, *The Good Neighbor Policy and Authoritarianism in Paraguay* (1981); Michael Montéon, *Chile in the Nitrate Era* (1982); and Stephen G. Rabe, *The Road to OPEC* (1982) (Venezuela).

Studies of U.S.-Mexican relations include John A. Britton, *Revolution and Ideology* (1995); Helen Delpar, *The Enormous Vogue of Things Mexican* (1992) (culture); Linda B. Hall, *Oil, Banks, and Politics* (1995); Catherine E. Jayne, *Oil, War, and Anglo-American Relations* (2001); Dan LaBotz, *Edward L. Doheny* (1991) (oil); Stephen R. Niblo, *War, Diplomacy, and Development* (1995); W. Dirk Raat, *Mexico and the United States* (1996); Friedrich E. Schuler, *Mexico Between Hitler and Roosevelt* (1998); and Daniela Spencer, *The Impossible Triangle* (1999).

For Cuba, see Jules R. Benjamin, *The United States and Cuba* (1978); Irwin F. Gellman, *Roosevelt and Batista* (1973); and Louis A. Pérez Jr., *Becoming Cuban* (1999).

See also Robert L. Beisner, ed., *Guide to American Foreign Relations Since 1600* (2003).

For comprehensive coverage of foreign-relations topics, see the articles in the four-volume *Encyclopedia of U.S. Foreign Relations* (1997), edited by Bruce W. Jentleson and Thomas G. Paterson.

CHAPTER ✳ **6**

Survival and Spheres: The Allies and the Second World War, 1939–1945

DIPLOMATIC CROSSROAD

✳ *The Atlantic Charter Conference, 1941*

PRESIDENT FRANKLIN D. ROOSEVELT slowly limped the entire length of the battleship H.M.S. *Prince of Wales.* More than 1,500 men, including British prime minister Winston S. Churchill, stood at rigid attention as the president took his tortured steps. Roosevelt finally reached his seat near the bow, next to Churchill. British and American chiefs of staff stood behind them. Roosevelt and Churchill were attending church services in Placentia Bay near the harbor of Argentia, Newfoundland, on August 10, 1941.

The Sunday services aboard the *Prince of Wales* marked the "keynote" of the four-day summit meeting between the two leaders (August 9–13, 1941), four months before Pearl Harbor catapulted the United States into World War II as a formal belligerent. The sermon, from Joshua 1:1–9, seemed directed at the president: "As I was with Moses, so I will be with thee: I will not fail thee, nor forsake thee." Suggesting the need for U.S. aid in the war against Hitler was the hortatory hymn, "Onward Christian Soldiers," with its call for "marching as to war." Roosevelt, who had already supplied destroyers, Lend-Lease, and other aid short of war, later told his son, "That . . . cemented us. 'Onward Christian Soldiers.' We *are,* and we *will,* go on, with God's help." Churchill found symbolic unity that morning—"the Union Jack and the Stars and Stripes draped side by side. . . . British and American sailors . . . joining fervently in the prayers and hymns familiar to both." Nobody aboard the *Prince of Wales* could know that Japanese bombs would destroy the majestic battleship off the coast of Malaya on December 10, 1941.

The four-day meeting in Placentia Bay was the first of many between Roosevelt and Churchill during World War II. Notwithstanding fears about a clash of "prima donnas," the personalities blended nicely. Churchill's willingness to defer to a man he regarded "almost with religious awe" and his own pride in being half-American (his mother) made him an ardent advocate of Anglo-American solidarity.

Church Service on the Prince of Wales.   On August 10, 1941, President Franklin D. Roosevelt and Prime Minister Winston S. Churchill, with their staffs, attended a stirring service aboard the British warship during the Atlantic Charter Conference. (Franklin D. Roosevelt Library)

Roosevelt reciprocated Churchill's friendship. Under their leadership the two countries became "mixed up together . . . for mutual and general advantage" to a degree unmatched in modern times. "No lover ever studied the whims of his mistress as I did those of President Roosevelt," Churchill later boasted.

Aside from the personal equation, Argentia produced few decisive results. The British asked for men, ships, planes, and tanks. Churchill urged that the U.S. navy extend its convoying of British vessels farther into the German submarine-infested North Atlantic. The British military chiefs, citing the frightful casualties of World War I, argued that bombing, blockades, and propaganda might so weaken the Germans that they would surrender without a full-scale invasion. Insisting on large ground armies, Army chief of staff General George C. Marshall declared that a U.S. military buildup had to take priority over British requests for weapons and equipment; otherwise "we might have lost everything we owned, including our pants." FDR did promise to convoy British merchant ships as far as Iceland, but he delayed any public declaration until September, when a German submarine fired torpedoes at the U.S. destroyer *Greer* near Iceland. Neglecting to mention that the *Greer* had shadowed the U-boat for three hours prior to the attack, Roosevelt announced on September 11 that henceforth American naval vessels would shoot at German submarines. Undeclared naval action was as far as Roosevelt would go in the months before Pearl Harbor.

At Argentia, discussions about Japan exposed British and American differences. Foreign Office diplomats argued that Japan, which had recently occupied the southern half of French Indochina, should receive an explicit U.S. warning against further encroachments, and that the United States should commit to war if the Japanese attacked British or Dutch territory in Southeast Asia. Roosevelt did promise a "mighty swat" at Japan, but instead of announcing that continued Japanese aggression would cause the United States to take measures that "might result in war," the watered-down statement merely read that Washington would take steps necessary "toward insuring the safety and security of the United States." Roosevelt preferred to delay a confrontation in the Pacific until he strengthened his army and navy and cultivated a more favorable public opinion. He also intended to beat Hitler first.

The most famous result of the summit came in the eight-point statement of war aims—the Atlantic Charter. Reminiscent of Woodrow Wilson's Fourteen Points, the charter reaffirmed the principles of collective security, national self-determination, freedom of the seas, and liberal trading practices. The signatories also disclaimed any territorial aggrandizement. Behind the shared vision of a postwar world, however, lay key differences. The Americans pressed for a statement explicitly endorsing freer trade. The British wanted to protect their discriminatory system of imperial preferences. The compromise called for "access, on equal terms, to the trade and to the raw materials of the world," leaving the British an escape clause that promised "due respect for their existing obligations." Churchill failed to gain Roosevelt's backing for a new League, as FDR endorsed only "the establishment of a wider and permanent system of general security." As "both realist and idealist, both fixer and preacher, both a prince and a soldier," the president was as cautious as he was eloquent about postwar goals.

The Atlantic Charter became a propaganda tool against the Axis. Soon Voice of America radio broadcasts hailed the charter's call to "fight on all the world's battlefields for these essential liberties: liberty of expression, of religion, and the right to live protected from need and from fear." In September 1941, representatives of the nations battling Hitler formally adhered to the "common principles" set forth in the Atlantic Charter. Twenty-six nations, on January 1, 1942, signed the Declaration of the United Nations, which pledged cooperation in achieving the aims of the Atlantic Charter. Churchill and Roosevelt, however, provided no procedures for enforcement or implementation. Indeed, the prime minister insisted that the charter applied only to nations "now under the Nazi yoke," not to "peoples [who] owe allegiance to the British Crown." Roosevelt came to view the principles as a "beautiful idea" rather than as set rules, and he seemed willing to postpone their application to accommodate pressing military and diplomatic priorities. "I dream dreams but am, at the same time, an intensely practical person," he once said.

By meeting secretly with Churchill on a British battleship, Roosevelt demonstrated America's commitment to the defense of Britain by all means short of war. Whatever his hopes that the theatrics of Argentia would galvanize American opinion for a firmer stance, Roosevelt maintained a "policy of influence without belligerence." Yet the Atlantic Charter, the Churchill-Roosevelt friendship, the

Anglo–American strategic conversations, even the divergent views on international organization and postwar economic policy—all struck chords that would echo through the next four years of war. That the Soviet Union, invaded by Germany six weeks earlier, sent no representatives to Argentia did not inhibit discussion of Soviet cooperation against the Axis. Presidential aide Harry Hopkins had visited Moscow two weeks before the Argentia conference, and his assurances that the USSR would withstand the Nazi onslaught buoyed the two leaders. In a joint communication to Joseph Stalin from Argentia, Churchill and Roosevelt hailed "the splendid defense that you are making against the Nazi attack" and promised the "very maximum" of supplies. This commitment to the Soviet Union also carried large implications for the future.

Juggling Between War and Peace, 1939–1941

The conversations at Placentia Bay exemplified Roosevelt's distinctly personal approach to diplomacy during World War II. FDR delighted in face-to-face confrontations, always confident in his ability to charm even those who accused him of "messianic" delusions. It mattered little that Secretary Hull learned of the conference when he read about it in the newspapers. With selfless subordinates such as Sumner Welles and Harry Hopkins to do his bidding, Roosevelt relished the spotlight on himself. British foreign secretary Anthony Eden once compared FDR to "a conjurer, skillfully juggling with balls of dynamite, whose nature he failed to understand."

The juggling act had begun two years earlier, when Germany started World War II by attacking Poland. FDR had avowed that "this nation will remain a neutral nation." Still, "I cannot ask that every American remain neutral in thought as well." Thus, in words pointedly different from Wilson's in 1914, did Roosevelt project the next twenty-six months of U.S. policy toward the war in Europe. Roosevelt proceeded from neutrality to nonbelligerency to undeclared war in the Atlantic and finally, after Pearl Harbor, to full-scale war against the Axis. Hoping to avoid war while giving as much aid as possible to Hitler's opponents, FDR did not always speak candidly about the ultimate contradiction between these two goals.

On September 21, 1939, Roosevelt asked Congress to repeal the arms embargo in the Neutrality Act as the best way to stay out of the war. He stressed this deceptive argument, knowing that his real purpose was to permit England and France, with their superior sea power, to purchase arms and munitions on a cash-and-carry basis. Although isolationists opposed "our changing the rules after the war has broken out," FDR's tactics worked. By a vote of 63 to 30 in the Senate and 243 to 181 in the House, the revised Neutrality Act became law on November 4, thus permitting Britain and France to buy arms.

The Pan American Conference at Panama City (September 23–October 3, 1939) also signaled the pro-Allied emphasis of U.S. policy. The conferees proclaimed neutrality and created a neutral zone 300 miles wide along the entire coast of the Western Hemisphere (except Canada), in which belligerent naval operations were prohibited. Roosevelt had told his cabinet in April 1939 that the Atlantic fleet would patrol such areas and "if we fire and sink an Italian or German [submarine] . . . we will say it the way the Japs do, 'so sorry.' 'Never happen again.' Tomorrow we sink

Makers of American Foreign Relations, 1939–1945

Presidents	Secretaries of State
Franklin D. Roosevelt, 1933–1945	Cordell Hull, 1933–1944
	Edward R. Stettinius, Jr., 1944–1945
Harry S. Truman, 1945–1953	James F. Byrnes, 1945–1947

two." These "neutrality patrols" actually became the first step toward Anglo-American naval cooperation. By late summer 1940, conversations between staff officers began in London, soon followed by exchanges of cryptographic intelligence, actual coordination against German naval operations, and, in autumn 1941, convoying merchant ships across the Atlantic. Such naval measures led the chief of naval operations, Admiral Harold R. Stark, to conclude in early 1941: "We cannot avoid having it [war] thrust upon us or our deliberately going in."

Germany's *blitzkrieg* humbled Poland in two weeks, and then from November 1939 to March 1940 the Soviet Union defeated Finland in the "Winter war." Roosevelt sent his sympathies but little else to Finland. The fall of France in June 1940 stung FDR into bolder measures. In a speech on June 10, Roosevelt condemned Italy for holding the dagger that "struck . . . the back of its neighbor," and he pledged to England "the material resources of this nation." A week later he named the prominent Republicans Henry L. Stimson and Frank Knox, both vocal advocates of aid to Britain, as secretary of war and secretary of the navy, respectively. Then, after intricate negotiations, the president announced on September 3, 1940, that he was transferring to England fifty old destroyers in exchange for leases to eight British bases stretching from Newfoundland to British Guiana. Two weeks later, he signed into law the Selective Service Act of 1940, the first peacetime military draft in American history.

That Roosevelt could accomplish so much during his campaign for a controversial third presidential term testifies to his political astuteness. Not only did FDR ascertain that his Republican presidential rival, Wendell L. Willkie, would not make either the draft or the destroyers campaign issues, but in both cases he also encouraged influential citizens groups to lobby for his objectives. The Committee to Defend America by Aiding the Allies soon rallied behind the president to counter the isolationist America First Committee set up in September 1940. FDR bypassed Congress in the destroyers deal by presenting it as an executive agreement, and he deflected political opposition to conscription by having Secretary Stimson and General Marshall attest to the military's need for a draft. Further, Roosevelt continued to promise that he would keep America out of war. Although Germany could regard the destroyers deal as an act of war, FDR called it instead "the most important action in the reinforcement of our national defense . . . since the Louisiana Purchase." At the end of the fall campaign Roosevelt promised American mothers: "Your boys are not going to be sent into any foreign wars." Willkie exploded: "That hypocritical son of a bitch! This is going to beat me!" It did.

After the election Churchill cabled: "The moment approaches when we shall no longer be able to pay cash for shipping and other supplies." Roosevelt soon held one of his breezy, jaunty press conferences, saying that he favored lending or leasing supplies to Britain. He likened it to lending a garden hose to a neighbor whose house was burning. Once the fire is out, "he gives it back to me and thanks me very much." In a fireside chat on December 29, FDR claimed that the "sole purpose" of sending arms to Britain was "to keep war away from our country and our people." Then, in a ringing phrase, Roosevelt called on the United States to "become the great arsenal of democracy."

Over the next two months, Americans debated the Lend-Lease bill "in every newspaper, on every wave length—over every cracker barrel in all the land." Despite a favorable vote of 60 to 31 in the Senate and 317 to 71 in the House, the White House did not win easily. Senator Burton K. Wheeler, an isolationist Democrat from Montana, warned: "You can't put your shirt tail into a clothes wringer and pull it out suddenly when the wringer keeps turning." Right-wing women's groups accused interventionists of "'bundling,' 'balling,' and curtseying for Britain." The Lend-Lease Act nonetheless became law on March 11, 1941. Under its terms the president could "sell, transfer title to, exchange, lease, lend, or otherwise dispose of" defense articles to "any country whose defense the President deems vital to the defense of the United States." Although the initial appropriation totaled $7 billion, by war's end the United States had expended more than $50 billion on Lend-Lease. England eventually received $31.6 billion of that amount.

With German U-boats sinking 500,000 tons of shipping a month, it seemed logical that the United States would use its navy to ensure that Lend-Lease supplies reached England safely. Instead, FDR extended naval "patrols" halfway across the Atlantic, announcing in April that U.S. vessels would monitor German warships. "We have got a tadpole that someday may be a frog," noted Secretary Hull. U.S. troops also occupied Greenland the same month. The president declared a national emergency in late May but took no new action. He told the cabinet that "he expected a clash sooner or later but said the Germans would have to fire the first shots."

When Hitler invaded the Soviet Union in June 1941, the president announced that 4,000 American marines would occupy Iceland for hemispheric defense. Roosevelt also began military Lend-Lease aid to the USSR in November, notwithstanding opinions from State Department and military advisers that the Soviet Union would quickly fall. "Now comes this Russian diversion," FDR wrote four days after the German assault. "If it is more than just that it will mean the liberation of Europe from Nazi domination." He insisted that supplies be sent to the USSR "even if the Army and Navy authorities in America did not like it." Then came FDR's dramatic meeting with Churchill at Placentia Bay, and in early September, he publicly ordered naval convoys as far as Iceland and issued a "shoot-on-sight" command to the navy.

By autumn 1941, Roosevelt probably anticipated an "incident" to induce U.S. entry into the war against Hitler. At Argentia the president told Churchill that "he would wage war, but not declare it, and that he would become more and more provocative. If the Germans did not like it, they could attack American forces." When a U-boat torpedoed the destroyer *Kearny* off Iceland on October 17, Roo-

The German Onslaught
1939–1942

sevelt seized the moment: "The shooting has started. And history has recorded who fired the first shot." The president hoped to persuade Congress to repeal the sections of the 1939 Neutrality Act that prohibited the arming of merchant ships and banned such vessels from war zones. After a U-boat sank the destroyer *Reuben James* on October 31, killing more than one hundred men, the isolationist America First Committee charged the White House with issuing "an engraved drowning license to American seamen." Following bitter debate, repeal passed in November by narrow margins, 50 to 37 in the Senate and 212 to 194 in the House. U.S. merchant vessels could now legally carry munitions to England.

Roosevelt charted an oblique course toward war because he believed he had no other choice. "Haranguing the country doesn't help," he said. "It will take a 'shock' like 1932" to change isolationist attitudes. If he asked for "a declaration of war," he said "he wouldn't get it, and opinion would swing against him." FDR thus chose indirection over candor and relied on events and his own manipulative ability to inch ahead. By autumn 1941, 80 percent of the American people still opposed entering the war, while a higher percentage wanted an Axis defeat. So long as the president touted aid to the Allies as the best way to avoid war, Americans could apparently fulfill both goals. The narrow vote over repeal of the Neutrality Act in November reinforced his reluctance to ask for outright intervention. "The day of the white rabbits has passed," one senator wrote, "and the great magician who could pull them out of any silk hat . . . cannot find the rabbit."

Asian Collision Course: Japanese-American Relations, 1939–1941

Events in Asia, not Europe, plunged the United States into World War II. Ambassador Joseph C. Grew expressed surprise at increased anti-Japanese sentiment during a trip home in the summer of 1939, when President Roosevelt talked truculently of intercepting the Japanese fleet if it moved against the Dutch East Indies. With the announcement in July that the 1911 commercial treaty with Japan would terminate in six months, Grew feared that economic sanctions and war might follow. "Sparks will fly before long," he predicted.

Grew misjudged the Europe-first emphasis of Roosevelt's foreign policy. After 1937, when Japan marched deeper into China, Washington angrily protested but lacked the power to challenge Japanese predominance in East Asia. Even Roosevelt's much-heralded refusal to apply the Neutrality Act to the "incident" in China, thus making it legal to sell arms to Jiang Jieshi's government, could not obscure the fact that U.S. trade with Japan was nearly three times greater than with China until 1940. Ending the 1911 commercial treaty permitted economic sanctions against Japan, but oil, the most vital ingredient in Japan's war machine, flowed until July 1941. Reflecting Roosevelt's policy of aid to England short of war, the navy revised its strategic thinking in November 1940. "Plan Dog" called for a defensive posture in the Pacific, depicted Germany as America's primary enemy, and made preservation of England its principal goal. Roosevelt still hoped to avoid a confrontation, because "I simply have not got enough Navy to go around."

Japanese movement into Southeast Asia placed Washington and Tokyo on a collision course. With the Asian colonies of France and the Netherlands lying unprotected, Japanese expansionists demanded a thrust southward, thus strangling China and transforming the whole region into the Greater East Asia Co-Prosperity Sphere. Japan pressed England and France to close down supply routes through Burma and Indochina and demanded economic concessions from the petroleum-rich Dutch East Indies. Then, only four days after occupying northern Indochina, Japan signed the Tripartite Pact with Germany and Italy on September 27. With the signatories pledged to aid one another if attacked by a nation not currently involved in the war, Washington had no doubt about being its target. A new, more militant Japanese government, with Prince Fumimaro Konoe as prime minister and General Hideki Tojo as war minister, took the fateful steps. Foreign Minister Yosuke Matsuoka intended the Tripartite Pact to deter the United States from intervening in the Atlantic or the Pacific, and to facilitate a rapprochement between Japan and the Soviet Union, which remained aligned with Germany in the Nazi-Soviet Pact.

Washington flashed warnings. In July 1940, Roosevelt withheld aviation fuel and top-grade scrap iron from Japan. In September, after the Tripartite Pact, he extended the embargo to all scrap metals. Even Grew urged firmness, labeling Japan "one of the predatory powers," lacking "all moral and ethical sense." Administration "hawks" pressed the president to end oil exports as well. Backed by Hull and the Joint Chiefs, however, Roosevelt kept the oil flowing to Japan and expedited aid to China to keep Japan's army "busy and more or less tied up" so it could not "move southward in full force." The president hoped to aid England while avoiding a showdown in the Pacific, which an oil embargo would likely precipitate.

In February 1941, Admiral Kichisaburo Nomura became ambassador to Washington. A personal friend of President Roosevelt, Nomura accepted the appointment only when assured by Konoe and Matsuoka that peace with the United States took precedence over Japan's commitment to the Axis. Notwithstanding protracted negotiations between Hull and Nomura that spring and summer, Japan's determination to hold China and to expand farther doomed any diplomatic solutions. In early July 1941, Roosevelt thought the Japanese were about to decide "which way they are going to jump—attack Russia, attack the South Seas . . . or whether they will sit on the fence and be more friendly with us." When Japanese troops occupied the rest of Indochina in late July, FDR signed an order freezing all Japanese funds. Hard-line bureaucrats interpreted the order to mean stopping all trade with Japan—including oil.

Unless the sale of American oil resumed, Japan determined to seize Dutch and British petroleum fields. "If we are going to fight," the navy chief of staff told Emperor Hirohito, "then the sooner . . . the better because our supplies are dwindling anyway." But the United States would not turn on the oil spigot until Tokyo agreed to respect China's sovereignty and territorial integrity. Key American officials also knew from cracking the Japanese diplomatic code (Operation MAGIC) that Japan's forces were massing to strike southward after mid-November, although most officials did not think Japan would attack the United States. As late as November 27, when MAGIC intercepts revealed the imminence of a Japanese strike somewhere, Asian expert Stanley K. Hornbeck challenged his colleagues: "Tell me of one case in history when a nation went to war out of desperation." Amid this atmosphere, the urging of army and navy leaders to string out negotiations until the Philippines could be reinforced went unheeded. An eleventh-hour U.S. modus vivendi envisioned a trickle of oil to Japan and negotiations between Chongqing and Tokyo, while maintaining American aid to China; Japan would have to abrogate the Tripartite Pact and accept basic principles of international conduct. Exhausted from months of negotiations, Hull shelved the proposal. "It is now in the hands of . . . the Army and Navy," he said.

Pearl Harbor. A Japanese pilot's perspective on Ford Island, Pearl Harbor, Hawai'i. The three Pacific U.S. aircraft carriers were not in port and escaped the attack. Of the eight battleships hit at Pearl Harbor, six were repaired and eventually participated in the war. (Navy Department National Archives)

After months of discussion, the Japanese Imperial Conference of September decided to fight if Washington did not lift its embargo by October 15—a date later extended to November 29. Tokyo's final decision to attack the United States did not stem from irrationality or suicidal tendencies. Japan required 12,000 tons of oil each day, and desperate moderates and militants alike read U.S. pressure as provocative and life-strangling. In a choice between fighting the United States or pulling out of China, no Japanese leader recommended the latter. They knew America's power and industrial potential well enough, but as Tojo (who replaced Konoe as prime minister) put it: "You have to plunge into war if there is some chance, however slight, of winning victory." The Japanese hoped that a stalemated war of endurance might persuade tired Americans to negotiate a compromise peace. "We would become a third-class nation . . . if we just sat tight," asserted Tojo.

On November 25, 1941, a huge task force that included six carriers bearing some 350 airplanes headed across 3,000 miles of the Pacific Ocean. The target: Pearl Harbor, Hawai'i. Every ship maintained radio silence to avoid detection and ensure complete surprise. In the early morning of Sunday, December 7, the carriers launched their planes. After a flight of 220 miles, the aircraft swept down on the unsuspecting American naval base. Within a few hours eight U.S. battleships had been sunk or damaged and 2,403 Americans had died. The stunning news shot around the world. In London, Churchill thought: "So we had won after all!" In Chongqing, Jiang Jieshi "played the Ave Maria all that day," also rejoicing in his new ally.

Critics have charged that Roosevelt and his top advisers deliberately sacrificed the Pacific fleet to get into the war with Hitler via the "back door." Most scholars reject the conspiracy theory and explain Pearl Harbor as the consequence of missed clues, overconfidence, and plain bad luck. Better intelligence from Washington might have alerted Hawai'i, but American errors weighed less than the enormous care with which the Japanese planned the attack. MAGIC intercepts on November 30, for example, read that "war may suddenly break out between the Anglo-Saxon nations and Japan . . . ; this war may come quicker than anyone dreams." Yet the intercepts never revealed military plans, and Washington thought Japan would strike Southeast Asia, where troop ships were spotted heading for Malaya. As to hints of major Japanese interest in Pearl Harbor, including Grew's warning in February 1941 of a possible sudden attack, one scholar has written: "After the event a signal is always crystal clear. . . . But before the event it is obscure and pregnant with conflicting meanings. . . . In short, we failed to anticipate Pearl Harbor not for want of the relevant materials, but because of a plethora of irrelevant ones." Many "ifs" cloud the question. If the radar operator had been able to convince his superiors on Oahu that the blips really were planes, if General Marshall had sent his last-minute warning by navy cable instead of Western Union telegraph, if MAGIC could have read Japan's naval communications as well as its diplomatic cables, if . . .

For Japan, Pearl Harbor proved a tactical victory but a strategic disaster. When President Roosevelt, referring to the "date which will live in infamy," asked for a declaration of war, Congress responded on December 8 with a unanimous vote in the Senate and only one dissent in the House. For Senator Arthur H. Vandenberg, the Japanese attack on Hawai'i "ended isolationism for any realist." In the mistaken belief that Japan "would keep the bulk of American power tied up" indefinitely, Hitler declared war on the United States on December 11. Congress's immediate declaration of war on Germany confronted Americans with a daunting two-theater conflict.

The Big Three: Strategies and Fissures, 1941–1943

The Atlantic Charter Conference and the events of 1939–1941 foreshadowed the themes of wartime diplomacy. Giving material aid to Hitler's opponents became the main U.S. contribution to victory in Europe. Washington's "Europe First" strategy derived from Anglo-American staff discussions prior to Pearl Harbor, as did the different American and British conceptions of that strategy. Americans favored a "massive thrust at the enemy's heart," and the British preferred "successive stabs around the periphery . . . like jackals worrying a lion before springing at his throat." During the war Americans also revived Wilsonianism but with a pragmatic determination to avoid Wilson's mistakes. This time the United States would join an international organization, even if it meant adding blatant balance-of-power features, through Roosevelt's "Four Policemen" (United States, USSR, Britain, and China), each of which would maintain peace in a sphere of influence. This time there would be no debts-reparations tangle because Lend-Lease would eliminate the dollar sign. This time the enemy must surrender unconditionally. This time tariff walls must fall and trade doors must open. This time there would be postwar cooperation with the Soviets.

Global war brought new power and confidence to U.S. diplomacy. The Atlantic Charter reflected a commitment to shaping the postwar world in an American image. As Henry Luce's best-selling *American Century* phrased it in 1941, the United States must "exert upon the world the full impact of our influence, for such purposes as we see fit and by such means as we see fit." By rearming, acquiring new bases, raising an army of more than 2 million, welding hemispheric unity, and revving up its industries, the United States built the sinews of global power even before Pearl Harbor. Churchill told Roosevelt in 1944: "You have the greatest navy in the world . . . the greatest air force . . . the greatest trade. You have all the gold." But Churchill hoped that "justice and fair-play will be the lights that guide" Americans. FDR often irritated his European allies by his anticolonial pronouncements, claiming, for example, that "after 100 years of French rule in Indochina, the inhabitants were worse off than they were before." Churchill retorted: "I have not become the King's First Minister in order to preside over the liquidation of the British Empire."

American-British-Soviet diplomacy in the "Grand Alliance" centered on boundaries in Eastern Europe and the timing of an Anglo-American "second front" in Western Europe. Shortly after Pearl Harbor, Stalin said he had no objections to the Atlantic Charter, but he preferred an agreement guaranteeing Soviet boundaries with Eastern Europe as they stood prior to Hitler's attack in 1941. The British seemed agreeable, but Roosevelt vetoed any secret or public treaty on boundaries "until the war had been won." Content with "a free hand," Stalin noted that "our frontiers" would be "decided by force."

FDR viewed the second front with great urgency. The Soviets, fighting some 200 German divisions, pleaded for a cross-channel attack as quickly as possible. When V. M. Molotov visited Washington in May 1942, Harry Hopkins urged the Soviet diplomat to paint a deliberately "gloomy picture of the Soviet position to make the American generals understand the gravity of the situation." Roosevelt promised Molotov a second front that year, but the Anglo-American invasion of France did not take place until June 6, 1944. In the interim, as the president acknowledged, "the Russian armies are killing more Axis personnel and destroying more Axis material than all other twenty-five United Nations put together." The delay produced serious fissures in the Grand Alliance.

American military leaders urged a cross-channel attack by spring 1943 at the latest, but the British decided otherwise. A new plan, Operation TORCH, called for the invasion of French North Africa in November 1942, a decision that led logically to operations against Sicily and Italy in summer 1943 and effectively postponed a cross-channel attack until 1944. At numerous military conferences in 1942–1943, the Americans always suspected that British fixation on the Mediterranean demonstrated a desire to shore up imperial lifelines and not, as the British claimed, a coherent strategy to bloody Germany on the periphery before launching a full-scale invasion of France. British strategy predominated in the two years after Pearl Harbor because England had fully mobilized, whereas America had not, and any combined operation had to depend largely on British troops, shipping, and casualties. U.S. matériel and forces, moreover, were being diverted to the Pacific theater at the insistence of General Douglas MacArthur and Admiral Ernest King. Once American production and manpower surged by 1943, combined strategy gradually shifted toward a cross-channel invasion.

Roosevelt and Churchill knew how intensely Stalin wanted a second front in France, not in North Africa or Italy. The Red Army had stopped the Germans short of Moscow in 1941, but in summer 1942 German *panzers* drove into the Caucasus oil fields and laid siege to Stalingrad. Churchill told Stalin in August 1942 that a cross-channel attack was planned for spring 1943. Not until June 1943 did the Soviets learn officially that a cross-channel assault would not happen at all that year. Kremlin officials suspected that their capitalist allies were "striving for the maximum exhaustion and wearing down" of the USSR "in order to diminish its role in deciding postwar problems."

Tensions increased that summer, when the Soviet Union broke off diplomatic relations with the Polish exile government in London after the Poles asked the International Red Cross to investigate charges that the Russians had murdered more than 10,000 Polish prisoners in the Katyn Forest in 1941. Stalin claimed the victims had escaped "to Manchuria," but Russian archives later revealed that he had ordered the murders. The Soviets also protested when the Allies suspended convoys carrying vital Lend-Lease supplies to Murmansk because of shipping needs in the Mediterranean and Pacific. In August 1943, Stalin complained to Roosevelt that he was only "informed" about separate peace talks with Italy. The Italians formally surrendered in early September, then declared war against Germany, only to have German forces occupy most of the peninsula before Anglo-American troops could land in force.

Stalin had to be "courted, wooed, constantly chatted up," so Churchill urged the Poles not to protest because "nothing you can do will bring them [the dead POWs] back." FDR expedited Lend-Lease supplies to Russia without the usual quid pro quo arrangements. At the Casablanca Conference in January 1943, he announced the goal of "unconditional surrender by Germany, Italy, and Japan." Coming shortly after an agreement with the Vichy French collaborator Admiral Jean-François Darlan to gain French cooperation in North Africa, Roosevelt's "unconditional surrender" announcement signaled to a suspicious Stalin that Britain and the United States would not make a separate German peace with one of Hitler's subordinates. The doctrine brought a modicum of Allied unity by concentrating on a total military victory over Hitler, deferring troublesome peace terms until afterward.

The foreign ministers' meeting in Moscow (October 19–30) established an Advisory Council for Italy to coordinate Allied policy and a European Advisory Commission to make recommendations for a final peace settlement. The Soviets told Hull that the 200,000 American battle casualties did not amount to much—"we lose that many each day before lunch." Hull replied: "I knew a bully in Tennessee. He used to get a few things his way by being a bully and bluffing other fellows. But he ended up by not having a friend in the world." Suffering from tuberculosis, the seventy-two-year-old Hull got what he wanted: a Declaration of Four Nations on General Security (China included), the first definite commitment to a postwar replacement for the defunct League of Nations.

The Moscow Conference seemed a mere appetizer for "the turning point" at Teheran, Iran, November 28–December 1, 1943. Meeting the Soviet leader for the first time, FDR thought Stalin "very confident, very sure of himself." Stalin emphatically told Churchill and Roosevelt that he favored a firm commitment to OVERLORD (the cross-channel attack) as opposed to any Anglo-American operations in the Balkans. The Soviet leader asked: "Do the British really believe in OVERLORD or are they only saying so to reassure the Russians?" Churchill lamely promised to "hurl every scrap of strength across the channel." Later Stalin playfully advocated the summary execution of 50,000 German officers, whereupon the prime minister protested that the British would "never tolerate mass execution." When Roosevelt joked that only 49,500 should be shot, Churchill walked out in a huff.

At Teheran, FDR called for a new international organization dominated by the "Four Policemen," who would deal immediately with threats to peace. The president anticipated sending only air and naval support in the event of a crisis in postwar Europe; troops would have to come from Britain and the USSR. The conferees also discussed the postwar status of Eastern Europe and Germany. Churchill had proposed moving Poland's boundaries a considerable distance to the west, incorporating German lands. Polish territory in the east would pass to the Soviets to secure their western frontier. Roosevelt acquiesced in these plans for Poland but could not say so publicly "at the present time." The election of 1944 loomed, and "as a practical man," he would not risk the votes of millions of Polish-Americans. When he mentioned self-determination for the Baltic states, Stalin insisted that they belonged to the Soviet Union. To Roosevelt's remark that the American people "neither knew nor understood," Stalin shot back that "some propaganda work should be done." But FDR never did explain publicly the differences between the Atlantic Charter and Soviet demands for security in Eastern Europe. On Germany, the conferees debated ways to divide the nation, but they left specific plans for "retribution" to the future.

Although inconclusive on many points, the Teheran discussions pleased the Americans, especially because Stalin had confirmed that, once Hitler was defeated, the USSR would fight against Japan. Stalin's preference for OVERLORD instead of a Balkans operation also resolved the Anglo-American debate over strategy. A peace dictated by the big powers, an international organization, and a weakened postwar Germany signified important Allied cohesion. Stalin also paid tribute to Lend-Lease: "Without these planes from America the war would have been lost." After Teheran the president remarked: "We are going to get along very well with him [Stalin] and the Russian people—very well indeed." The Grand Alliance had temporarily closed some fissures.

In Search of a China Policy

Visiting Washington in December 1941, Winston Churchill was astonished that his hosts "rated the Chinese armies as a factor to be mentioned in the same breath as the armies of Russia." America's infatuation with China, the legacy of the Open Door, the false image of China as "one of the great democracies of the world"—all reinforced the view that China should be a high wartime priority. Some Americans, President Roosevelt included, even envisioned a strong, united China as a postwar client of the United States and a bridge to Asian peoples freeing themselves from colonialism. China's military importance soon diminished, however, as Japanese victories in early 1942 sent the British and Americans reeling. The fall of Burma in May closed the last remaining land route to Chongqing. The Americans wanted to

Major Wartime Conferences, 1941–1945

Conference	Date	Participants	Results
Argentia, Newfoundland	August 9–12, 1941	Roosevelt, Churchill	Atlantic Charter
Washington, D.C.	December 22, 1941– January 14, 1942	Roosevelt, Churchill	Combined Chiefs of Staff; priority in war effort against Germany; United Nations Declaration
Washington, D.C.	June 19–25, 1942	Roosevelt, Churchill	North African campaign strategy
Moscow, USSR	August 12–15, 1942	Churchill, Stalin, Harriman	Postponement of second front
Casablanca, Morocco	January 14–24, 1943	Roosevelt, Churchill	Unconditional surrender announcement; campaign against Sicily and Italy
Washington, D.C.	May 12–25, 1943	Roosevelt, Churchill	Scheduling of cross-channel landing for May 1, 1944
Quebec, Canada	August 14–24, 1943	Roosevelt, Churchill	Confirmation of cross-channel landing (OVERLORD)
Moscow, USSR	October 19–30, 1943	Hull, Eden, Molotov	Postwar international organization to be formed; Soviet promise to enter the war against Japan after Germany's defeat; establishment of European Advisory Commission
UNRRA, Washington, D.C.	November 9, 1943	44 nations	Creation of UNRRA
Cairo, Egypt	November 22–26, 1943	Roosevelt, Churchill, Jiang	Postwar Asia: China to recover lost lands; Korea to be independent; Japan to be stripped of Pacific islands
Teheran, Iran	November 27– December 1, 1943	Roosevelt, Churchill, Stalin	Agreement on cross-channel landing and international organization; Soviet reaffirmation of intent to enter the war against Japan
Bretton Woods, New Hampshire	July 1–22, 1944	44 nations	Creation of World Bank and International Monetary Fund
Dumbarton Oaks, Washington, D.C.	August 21– October 7, 1944	U.S., Britain, USSR, China	United Nations Organization
Quebec, Canada	September 11–16, 1944	Roosevelt, Churchill	"Morgenthau Plan" for Germany
Moscow, USSR	October 9–18, 1944	Churchill, Stalin	Spheres of influence in Balkans (percentage scheme)
Yalta, USSR	February 4–11, 1945	Roosevelt, Churchill, Stalin	Polish governmental structure, elections, and boundaries; United Nations; German reparations; USSR pledge to declare war against Japan and to recognize Jiang's government; some Japanese territories to USSR
San Francisco, California	April 25–June 26, 1945	50 nations	United Nations Organization Charter
Potsdam (Berlin), Germany	July 17– August 2, 1945	Truman, Churchill/Attlee, Stalin	German reconstruction and reparations; Potsdam Declaration to Japan; Council of Foreign Ministers established

keep China in the war, yet Roosevelt could not send troops needed elsewhere. He sent General Stilwell instead.

Joseph W. Stilwell arrived in Chongqing with the impressive title of Commanding General of the United States Forces in India, Burma, and China. As a junior officer he had served two tours of duty in China, had become fluent in Chinese, and had developed great admiration for the Chinese people. But he thought Jiang an untrustworthy scoundrel. In Chongqing "Vinegar Joe" sought to train and equip Chinese divisions. With these modernized forces, plus British help from India, Stilwell planned to reopen Burma, increase supplies to China, and thus make the mainland the staging point for the final invasion of Japan.

Stilwell's plans for military reform cut at the heart of the Guomindang system. The general sputtered in his diary: "Why doesn't the little dummy [Jiang] realize that his only hope is the 30-division plan, and the creation of a separate, efficient, well-equipped, and well-trained force?" Most of Jiang's armies were actually controlled by twelve commanders, several of them virtually autonomous warlords. Before making a decision, the generalissimo always had to ask: "What orders will my generals accept from me?" Some 500,000 of Jiang's best troops were blockading the communists in Yan'an as he waited out the war and mustered his strength for a final showdown with Mao Zedong. Jiang refused to fight in Burma without more Allied support, and the British balked at a Burma campaign. Shortly after the landings in North Africa, Stilwell described his strategic dilemma: "Peanut [Jiang] and I are on a raft, with one sandwich between us, and the rescue ship is heading away from the scene."

President Roosevelt sought conciliation. To Chongqing he sent personal emissaries to buoy Chinese morale. Jiang received a half-billion dollar loan in 1942, and a 1943 treaty abolished the U.S. right of extraterritoriality in China. Next Roosevelt hosted Madame Jiang at the White House. The Wellesley College alumna addressed Congress and garnered applause for speaking "not only the language of your hearts, but also your tongue." At the Cairo Conference in November 1943, Churchill and Roosevelt met with Jiang and formally pledged the return, after the war, of Taiwan, Manchuria, and other areas "stolen by Japan." In December Congress repealed the exclusion laws, which had prohibited Chinese immigration. FDR talked confidently of postwar China as one of his "Four Policemen" that would keep the peace.

FDR also endorsed a plan of General Claire Lee Chennault. The famed "Flying Tiger" claimed that with "a very modest American air force equipped with modern airplanes" he could destroy Japanese air power in "six months." When Chennault's bombers began to draw blood in spring 1944, Japanese armies launched a massive counterattack and nearly overran all U.S. air bases. Jiang then refused to fight. This time Roosevelt made the extraordinary proposal that Jiang give Stilwell unrestricted command of all forces, Chinese and foreign, in China. Stilwell delivered the ultimatum himself. "I handed this bundle of paprika to the Peanut and then sank back with a sigh. The harpoon hit the little bugger right in the solar plexus, and went right through him," he wrote in September. Rather than antagonize Jiang further after such humiliation, FDR soon replaced Stilwell.

In November, General Patrick J. Hurley became ambassador to China and concentrated on forming a coalition between Jiang's nationalists and the communists. Even though the Soviets, like the Americans, sent military supplies to Jiang's forces and not to Mao Zedong's communists, the communist-led troops had waged successful guerrilla war against the Japanese. The Yan'an communists had an effective intelligence network that extended behind Japanese lines. Members of the U.S. "Observer Mission" to Yan'an found it easier to talk with Mao and Zhou Enlai "than with the Nationalists. You knew the Nationalists were lying most of the time." The

Mao Zedong (1893–1976) and Patrick J. Hurley (1883–1963). The Chinese communist leader (second from left) seems less than moved by Ambassador Hurley's dramatic gesture of welcome at Chongqing in 1945. Mao thought Hurley a "clown" who favored Jiang. Hurley once bellowed that Mao was a "motherfucker." In November 1945, Hurley suddenly resigned and flung wild charges at Foreign Service Officers who had disagreed with him. (National Archives)

communists, according to Foreign Service Officer John S. Service, "are certain to play a large, if not dominant, part in China's future." Because most Americans in China thought the communists might defeat Jiang in a postwar struggle for power, Hurley's initial efforts at coalition received unified support.

On Hurley's first visit to communist Yan'an, in November 1944, the "genbassador" alighted from his plane "with enough ribbons on his chest to represent every war . . . in which the United States had ever engaged except possibly Shays's Rebellion." Then he completely discombobulated Zhou Enlai by letting out Choctaw war whoops. Later, after the communists rejected Jiang's offer of a virtually worthless seat on the National Military Council in return for merging the Yan'an army under Nationalist control, Hurley first accepted and then rejected Mao's counterproposal for full coalition and communist sharing in Lend-Lease supplies.

At this point Hurley began to diverge markedly from the Foreign Service Officers. The ambassador decided on his own that his objective was not to mediate but rather to "sustain" Jiang Jieshi and "to prevent the collapse of the Nationalist government." During an earlier visit to Moscow in August 1944, Molotov had told Hurley that the Chinese communists "had no relation whatever to Communism" and the Soviets would support Jiang Jieshi. Other U.S. officials in China feared that if denied aid, Mao would obtain assistance from Moscow and thus create a postwar squabble with the USSR over China. Contrary to Hurley, these "China hands" believed that the rift between the communists and Guomindang ran deep, and that they could obtain Chinese unity only by dealing with Yan'an separately as a way of pressing Jiang. In January 1945, the head of the American Military Observers Mission cabled that "Mao and Zhou will be immediately available . . . should President Roosevelt express desire to receive them at White House as leaders of a primary Chinese party." "Clearly offering himself," Mao hoped that if American forces landed in China Roosevelt would abandon the "militarily impotent Nationalists" and choose "military cooperation" with the communists.

The predictable explosion occurred when Hurley returned to Washington in February 1945 after the Yalta Conference. In Hurley's absence, the embassy officers at Chongqing cabled the president to inform Jiang "in definite terms that we are required by military necessity to cooperate with and supply the communists against Japan." These young "China hands" did not know that Stalin had reaffirmed future Soviet entry into the Japanese war at Yalta and, accordingly, that the military rationale for a Guomindang-communist coalition now became less urgent. When Hurley read the telegram, he charged that his subordinates had betrayed him. The dying president gave Hurley what he wanted—unqualified backing for Jiang's regime. The embassy diplomats soon found themselves transferred out of China as a timid State Department bowed to the demands of the rambunctious ambassador. Mao's communists grew more suspicious.

Roosevelt's wartime policy toward China exposed the disparity between his military strategy and postwar political goals. When it became obvious in 1944 that China would not play a major role in the Japanese war, Roosevelt faced a choice. He could accelerate American military activities in China and press Jiang to undertake the reforms necessary to maintain him in power. Or he could scale down his political expectations for China and limit military operations there. In fact, Roosevelt "tried to do both and ran the risk of succeeding in neither." He kept hyping China as a great power while giving higher and higher military priorities to other theaters. When the feud between Hurley and the "China hands" ignited, moreover, Roosevelt drifted with existing policy rather than take a hard look at Chinese politics.

Bystanders to the Holocaust

Another problem finessed for the future was that of hundreds of thousands of Jewish refugees from Nazi-occupied territories. Many sought asylum in the United States. Although most Americans denounced Hitler's crusade to preserve the purity of the "Aryan race" through the persecution and extermination of European Jews, translating moral revulsion into effective policy proved difficult. U.S. immigration laws, traditional anti-Semitism, the depression, bureaucratic procedures, wartime fear of spies, and domestic politics shaped the timid American response.

The dark story began in 1933 when Hitler initiated his attacks on "non-Aryans." Throughout the 1930s, the Nazis systematically eliminated Jews from the professions and denied them ownership of businesses. In 1935 the Nuremberg Laws stripped Jews of their civil and political rights. Hatemongers plastered signs on buildings: "Whoever buys from a Jew is a traitor." In November 1938 a distraught Jewish youth living in Paris killed a German official. Nazi thugs beat up Jews on the streets, sacked and burned synagogues, and destroyed Jewish shops. After this *Kristallnacht* the German government fined its Jewish subjects $400 million and sent 50,000 Jews to concentration camps at Dachau and Buchenwald, detention centers where tortures and executions became common. Roosevelt called the U.S. ambassador home in protest, saying that he "could scarcely believe that such things could occur in a twentieth century civilization."

Such brutal events occurred again in Austria, Czechoslovakia, Poland, Hungary, and elsewhere as the Third Reich overran Europe. Urgent requests for visas flooded U.S. embassies and consulates. American immigration law, however, prescribed a quota for each country. The National Origins Act of 1924 openly discriminated against immigrants from eastern and southern Europe. The annual quota for Great Britain and Ireland was 83,575, for Germany and Austria 27,370, for Poland 6,000, for Italy 5,500, and for Romania 300. Potential immigrants had to present documents attesting to their birth, health, financial status, and crime-free background. Many of these papers had to be obtained from uncooperative Nazi officials. Americans also rigidly denied entry to people "likely to become a public charge," which meant admitting only those who proved that they could support themselves once in the United States. Yet under Nazi law Jews could not take their property or savings from Germany. These restrictions, plus the loss of American jobs during the depression, meant that, for the period 1933–1938, 174,067 people entered the United States and 221,239 departed, or a net *loss* of 47,172. To have opened America's doors to refugees, in short, would not have inundated a nation of 130 million.

The American Federation of Labor lobbied against any quota changes, claiming that foreigners should not compete with U.S. citizens for scarce jobs—a telling argument during the depression. Longstanding anti-Semitism fed such nativist thought. Father Charles E. Coughlin, a fiery Catholic priest from Michigan, equated Judaism and communism in his radio broadcasts, which reached 3.5 million listeners a week. Opinion polls revealed that more than 80 percent of Americans opposed revision of the quotas to admit European refugees. Congress stood firmly behind the quota system. Already blistered by charges that his domestic reform program was a "Jew Deal," a label attached because he appointed Jews to prominent positions, the president played it safe.

Roosevelt mostly left the refugee problem to a timid Department of State. Despite his own wife's Jewish heritage, Secretary Hull opposed boycotts organized by American Jews against German products because such behavior interrupted normal trade. FDR quietly manipulated at the margins with executive orders that combined German and Austrian quotas in 1938–1939 and temporarily relaxed enforcement of the "likely to become a public charge" clause, but many Jews still could not obtain documents. The result: the German-Austrian quota went unfilled in 1933–1938 and 1940–1945.

In 1938 Roosevelt did call for an international conference on refugees, which met in Evian, France, to establish an Intergovernmental Committee on Refugees (IGC). Plans for refugee havens in Latin America and central Africa faltered. Hitler sneered that "the entire democratic world dissolves in tears of pity, but then . . . closes its heart to the poor, tortured people." In early 1939 a proposed bill would have allowed 20,000 German refugee children to enter above the quota. With revision of the Neutrality Act then pending, the president scratched "File No action FDR," and the bill died in committee.

The plight of Jewish refugees deepened after the outbreak of war. State Department visa regulations actually tightened. Refugee questions came under the jurisdiction of Breckinridge Long, who feared a potential fifth column of refugees in the United States. He and other officials blocked private efforts to save them and

Buchenwald Concentration Camp, Germany. This large Nazi concentration camp held Jews and others who served as slave labor for local factories during World War II. Although Buchenwald did not have death-dealing gas chambers, many prisoners died there from disease, malnutrition, beatings, medical experiments, and executions. Representative Henry M. Jackson (Democrat of Washington), visiting Buchenwald after its liberation, reported: "The atrocities are the most sordid I have ever imagined." Thereafter Jackson became a staunch supporter of Israel. (Library of Congress)

later erected a "wall of silence" about Hitler's genocidal policies. U.S. consuls increasingly rejected visa applications, and ships returned to America half empty. Of Latin American countries, only the Dominican Republic gave asylum to 235 Jewish refugees. Resettlement proposals for Portuguese Angola, British Guiana, French Madagascar, and the Philippines also fell through; Britain restricted the movement of Jews to Palestine.

Reliable reports reached Washington in August 1942 that Germany had begun to exterminate the entire Jewish population in Europe. When Jan Karski, a Pole who had witnessed mass executions at Belzec and Treblinka, briefed FDR and Hull, they could not grasp the enormity of the Holocaust. Even Justice Felix Frankfurter, a Zionist, confessed that "he didn't believe what he was being told." Yet the evidence mounted. The Jewish ghetto in Warsaw, with only 70,000 of its 380,000 residents still alive, desperately rebelled in the spring of 1943. Using Zyklon B gas and large crematoria, Nazi officials murdered a million victims in the most notorious extermination camp at Auschwitz, Poland. Scholars have debated the feasibility of bombing Auschwitz and surrounding rail lines. The U.S. Air Force probably could have destroyed these installations by August 1944, but the War Department rejected any "diversions" that would delay victory, seen as the best hope for the Jews. Perhaps only the assassination of Hitler in 1943 or 1944 could have saved hundreds of thousands of Jews, if not more, but the Allies never tried, and attempts by German dissidents failed. By war's end at least 5.5 million Jews in Nazi-occupied Europe had been murdered.

Secretary of the Treasury Henry Morgenthau Jr. did what he could. At his request, Treasury general counsel Randolph Paul submitted the *Report to the Secretary on the Acquiescence of This Government in the Murder of the Jews,* a blistering critique of the State Department. "It takes months and months to grant the visa and then it usually applies to a corpse," Paul wrote. The rescue of Jews should not "remain in the hands of men indifferent, callous and perhaps hostile," warned Morgenthau, who persuaded FDR to create the War Refugee Board, outside the auspices of the State Department. Using private and public funds, board operatives established refugee camps in Italy, Morocco, Hungary, Sweden, Palestine, and Switzerland. The board thus saved some 200,000 Jews and 20,000 non-Jews by war's end. "What we did was little enough. . . . Late and little," its director concluded. Jewish refugees themselves took command of their survival after the war by leading the "exodus" to Palestine and creating the new nation of Israel in 1948. Nearly a half century later the film director Steven Spielberg in *Schindler's List* (1993) underscored what a few heroic individuals might have done to save thousands more.

Planning the Postwar Peace, 1943–1945

The great European military battles of 1944, wherein the D-Day invasion of France in June coincided with a massive Soviet offensive into Poland by August, gave postwar planning higher priority. Taking advantage of a "second chance" to overcome isolationism, economic depression, and war, U.S. officials helped launch several international organizations to secure peace and prosperity. Indeed, when FDR saw the Hollywood film *Wilson* (1944), with vivid scenes of his predecessor losing his health and the League, he exclaimed, "By God, that's not going to happen to me." During 1943–1945 the United Nations Relief and Rehabilitation Administration (UNRRA), World Bank, International Monetary Fund, and United Nations Organization took form. Unlike World War I, this time postwar planning would not await the grand deliberations of one conference.

On November 9, 1943, at the White House, forty-four nations signed the UNRRA agreement for the "relief of victims of war . . . through the provision of food, fuel, clothing, shelter and other basic necessities." Some leaders feared that hungry, displaced people might, in desperation, turn to political extremes like communism; food and medicine would help stem postwar political chaos. Operating until mid-1947, UNRRA dispensed 9 million tons of food; built hundreds of hospitals; prevented epidemics of diphtheria, typhoid, cholera, and venereal disease; revived transportation systems; and cared for at least a million displaced persons. China, Italy, Greece, and Austria absorbed about half of UNRRA's assistance. The other half went to Poland, other Eastern European nations, and the Soviet Union. American critics protested that an international organization was spending taxpayers' dollars to shore up communist governments. In fact, UNRRA refused to apply political tests to the needy. But Americans expected food aid to bring political returns. When it did not, Washington killed UNRRA in 1947 by cutting off funds.

United Nations Symbol.
A sign of peace for the new
international organization.
(United Nations)

Two other organizations proved more permanent. In July 1944, the delegates of forty-four nations met at Bretton Woods in New Hampshire and created the International Bank for Reconstruction and Development (World Bank) and the International Monetary Fund (IMF). The World Bank could extend loans to "assist in the reconstruction and development" of members, to "promote private investment," and to "promote the long-range balanced growth of international trade." The IMF was intended to facilitate world trade by stabilizing the international system of payments through currency loans. After much debate Congress passed the Bretton Woods Agreement Act by margins of 345 to 18 and 61 to 16 in July 1945.

From the start, U.S. economic power dominated both organizations. Located in Washington, D.C., the World Bank has always had an American as president. The United States also possessed one-third of the votes in the bank by committing $3.175 billion of the total of $9.100 billion initial subscriptions. With one-third of the votes in the fund as well, the United States would pay the "piper" and "call the tune." The USSR did not join the bank or fund because the Soviets practiced state-controlled trade and finance, feared having to divulge economic data, and rejected the emphasis on "private" enterprise. Moscow's absence augured poorly for postwar Allied cooperation.

From August to October 1944, representatives of the United States, Britain, the Soviet Union, and China met in the Dumbarton Oaks mansion in Washington, D.C., to shape the United Nations Organization (UN). Public opinion polls strongly endorsed a new collective-security organization, and Congress had passed favorable resolutions. The conferees hammered out the UN's charter, providing for a powerful Security Council dominated by the great powers and a weak General Assembly. The Security Council, empowered to use force to settle crises, had five permanent members. When the United States pushed China as a permanent member, Churchill proposed France, calling China a "faggot vote on the side of the United States."

Two other issues also proved contentious: voting procedures in the Security Council and membership in the Assembly. The Soviet Union advocated an absolute veto for permanent members, whereas the United States argued that parties to a conflict should not veto discussion or action. Not until the Yalta Conference in early 1945 did the Allies agree that the veto would apply only to substantive but not to procedural questions. As for Assembly membership, Moscow brazenly requested seats for all sixteen Soviet republics, claiming to be badly outnumbered in the Assembly by the British Commonwealth "bloc" and the U.S.–Latin America "bloc." At Yalta the Soviets accepted a compromise of three votes in the Assembly.

Seeking bipartisan support, Secretary Hull successfully appealed to GOP presidential candidate Thomas E. Dewey to keep international organization out of the 1944 political campaign. The resulting nonpartisanship and the inclusion of senators in the Dumbarton Oaks delegation helped the Roosevelt administration build its case for the UN. On January 10, 1945, the influential Senator Arthur H. Vandenberg of Michigan, an arch prewar isolationist, delivered a stunning speech urging U.S. participation in collective security as a curb on aggression. Vandenberg could accept membership in the United Nations because "this is anything but a wild-eyed internationalist dream of a world State."

Vandenberg served as a delegate to the San Francisco Conference of April–June 1945, convened to launch the United Nations. The new secretary of state, Edward

R. Stettinius, Jr., managed the conference. The 282 delegates did not make decisions without prior approval of the representatives of the big powers, who met each evening in Stettinius's penthouse at the Fairmont Hotel. The United States refused to admit Poland, because its government had not reorganized as required by Yalta. But then Stettinius shocked all by requesting participation for Argentina, which had only declared war against Germany in March. The United States, believing that the Latin American republics would not vote for three Soviet seats in the Assembly unless Argentina was included, would not relent. By the lopsided vote of 32 to 4, with 10 abstentions, Argentina won its seat.

Journalists detected an American "steamroller" at San Francisco. So did the Soviet Union, which objected in blunt language. And so did smaller states, which protested their impotence in the new United Nations Organization. Fifteen nations abstained in the vote on the veto formula. The UN Charter, as finally adopted, created the Economic and Social Council and the Trusteeship Council. The latter looked to the eventual independence of colonial areas but left the British and French empires intact and permitted the United States to absorb former Japanese-dominated islands in the Pacific (Marianas, Carolines, and Marshalls). The Charter also included Article 51, which permitted regional alliances such as that the United States and Latin America outlined in the Act of Chapultepec in March. The United States would "have our cake and eat it too"—freedom of action in the Western Hemisphere and an international organization to curb aggression in Europe. Amid memories of 1919, the Senate approved the UN Charter on July 28, 1945, by a vote of 89 to 2.

While these plans for the victors unfolded, the debate over the fate of a defeated Germany centered on a "constructive" policy (rehabilitation, economic unity, and integration into the European economy) or a "corrective" policy (strict reduction of industry, large reparations, and a decentralized economy). At the center of the controversy stood Treasury Secretary Morgenthau. In early September 1944 he had advised Roosevelt that the coal- and iron-rich Ruhr area should be stripped of industry. At the Quebec Conference in September 1944, the president gained Churchill's reluctant signature to a memorandum "eliminating the war-making industries in the Ruhr and in the Saar" and "converting Germany into a country primarily agricultural and pastoral in its character." Churchill apparently had approved the Morgenthau scheme in exchange for the promise of a postwar American loan.

Leaked to the press, the Morgenthau Plan caused "a hell of a hubbub" because Secretaries Hull and Stimson both opposed a harsh economic peace. Because "poverty in one part of the world induces poverty in other parts," Hull and Stimson believed that Germany had to revive to spur postwar prosperity in Western Europe. Morgenthau nonetheless persuaded Roosevelt to approve an interim Joint Chiefs of Staff directive (JSC/1067), which ordered denazification and demilitarization, the dismantling of iron, steel, and chemical industries, a controlled economy, and limited rehabilitation. The new president, Harry S. Truman, however, thought "Morgenthau didn't know sh—from apple butter" and began a gradual retreat from the Morgenthau Plan and JCS/1067, especially after he eased Morgenthau out of office in July 1945. By the end of the war, then, U.S. plans for postwar Germany remained unsettled.

"The Two Thousand Yard Stare." Combat artist Tom Lea captures the zombie-like demeanor of a young marine who has endured too much. Lea painted this portrait during the battle for Peleliu in the Palau Islands (September–November 1944), in which 2,000 Americans were killed and more than 8,500 were wounded. Some 11,000 Japanese also died. (U.S. Army, Center of Military History)

Compromises at Yalta

Near the end of the European war Churchill, Roosevelt, and Stalin met once again, at the Livadia Palace near Yalta in the Crimea. Meeting from February 4 to 11, 1945, the Big Three, after considerable compromise, made important decisions for the war against the Axis and for the postwar configuration of international affairs. Yalta subsequently sparked heated controversy akin to the Munich Conference. To some critics, Yalta symbolized a "sell-out" to the Soviets. Worn low by the illness that would take his life two months later, critics have claimed, Roosevelt gave in to a guileful Stalin and failed to use superior U.S. economic power to force concessions. The president's detractors also pointed an accusing finger at Alger Hiss, a U.S. official at Yalta who later went to jail on a perjury charge for testifying that he had not served Moscow as a spy.

The Big Three approached the conference with different goals. Britain sought a zone in Germany for France, a curb on Soviet expansion into Poland, and protection of the British Empire. The Soviet Union wanted reparations to rebuild its devastated economy, possessions in Asia, influence over Poland, and a Germany too weak ever again to march eastward. Washington wanted a U.S.-managed United Nations, a Soviet declaration of war against Japan, a reduction of communist political power in Poland, and elevation of China to big-power status. Despite mutual suspicions, Yalta did reach agreements.

The "consensus" at Yalta reflected the military and diplomatic realities of the moment. Just prior to Yalta, Anglo-American troops had bogged down in the Bat-

The Yalta Conference. In this meeting with Churchill, a haggard Roosevelt betrayed symptoms of the cardiovascular disease that would kill him in April 1945. Robert H. Ferrell's *The Dying President* (1998), utilizing the records and diaries of FDR's heart doctor, concludes that the president was "arguably as incapacitated as President Wilson had been, a shell of his former self, unable to keep abreast of the great decisions he had left to the end of the war, too ill or too arrogant to inform his successor about them." (Franklin D. Roosevelt Library)

tle of the Bulge in Belgium. Asked to take pressure off the western front by stepping up the Soviet winter offensive in the east, Stalin obliged on January 12. "I am most grateful to you for your thrilling message," a relieved Churchill replied. Indeed, Russian soldiers were sweeping westward along a wide front through Poland, Czechoslovakia, and Hungary, with Romania already freed from German clutches. The Red Army, not Roosevelt, gave the Soviet Union dominance in Eastern Europe.

Asian military realities also shaped diplomatic decisions. Japan was fiercely battling American forces in Luzon and the Marianas, and still had 1 million soldiers in China, 2 million in the home islands, and another 1 million in Manchuria and Korea. With some 54 percent of American battle deaths in the Pacific occurring in the last year of the war, both sides fought with increasing savagery. "We shot prisoners in cold blood, wiped out hospitals, strafed lifeboats," one U.S. war correspondent admitted, and "boiled the flesh off enemy skulls to make table ornaments for sweethearts, or carved their bones into letter openers." Japan's suicidal *Kamikaze* resistance on Okinawa still lay in the future. In short, Roosevelt and Churchill still needed Soviet help to defeat Japan.

The Yalta meetings proceeded amicably, although Stalin once became ruffled when he took Roosevelt's name for him—"Uncle Joe"—as ridicule rather than as a term of endearment. At the final dinner, Churchill informed Stalin that with general elections scheduled soon "I shall have to speak very harshly about the Communists. . . . You know we have two parties in England." "One party is much better," Stalin deadpanned.

For Churchill, Poland counted as "the most urgent" issue. The British and Americans recognized the conservative exiled government in London, led by Stanislaw Mikolajczyk. Moscow recognized the communist-led provisional government in Lublin. Repeatedly reminding everyone that Germany had attacked the Soviet Union through the Polish corridor twice in the century, Stalin insisted not only on Allied recognition of the Lublin government but also "a mighty, free and independent Poland" that included part of Germany but gave Russia Polish territory in the east (the Curzon line). Churchill and Roosevelt had little bargaining power because Soviet troops occupied much of the country. Roosevelt invoked several million Polish voters back home who demanded a more representative Polish government. Stalin remained adamant.

Compromises emerged. The Curzon line was temporarily set as the eastern boundary. The Yalta agreement stipulated also that the provisional government should be "reorganized on a broader democratic basis with the inclusion of democratic leaders from Poland itself and from Poles abroad," with "free and unfettered elections" held as soon as possible. Until such an election the communist Lublin group would comprise the nucleus of the Polish government. When later asked about the Polish agreement, FDR said it was "the best I could do." Churchill swallowed the bitter pill, in part because Stalin assured him that the Soviet Union would not intrude in British-dominated Greece, then rocked by civil war. Compromises on other issues also made the Polish settlement tolerable.

Britain reluctantly accepted Germany's dismemberment so long as France received a zone of occupation. Noting that Roosevelt had said that American troops would not long remain in Europe, Churchill cited France as a bulwark against Germany. Stalin grudgingly accepted a French zone. Britain and America agreed to Soviet demands for German reparations "in kind," but they refused to set a figure until they determined Germany's ability to pay.

The conferees reached compromises on Asia and the Pacific. By February 1945, the Japanese home islands were under sustained attack by U.S. heavy bombers, but the Americans still feared very high casualties in the planned invasion of Japan. Soviet intervention across Manchuria would draw off defenders and materially reduce U.S. casualties during the landings in Kyushu and Honshu. A grateful FDR won Stalin's pledge to declare war against Japan three months after Hitler's defeat, enough time to transfer his troops to Asia. Stalin also agreed to sign a pact of friendship with Jiang Jieshi's regime, not with Mao Zedong's rival communists. In return, the Soviet Union was promised the southern part of Sakhalin, Dairen (Dalian) as a free port, Port Arthur as a naval base, joint operation of Manchurian railroads, and the Kurile Islands. On these issues the Big Three never consulted China, a clear loser at Yalta.

Yalta marked the "dawn of the new day," said Harry Hopkins. "We were absolutely certain that we had won the first great victory of the peace." "Poor Neville Chamberlain believed he could trust Hitler," Churchill commented after Yalta. "He was wrong. But I don't think I'm wrong about Stalin." Roosevelt, Churchill, and Stalin had deftly played the great-power game of building spheres of influence. Each went home with some major objectives satisfied. Although they had postponed some tough questions and written some vague language, they had faced military and political realities.

Later, when the Yalta agreements collapsed, critics ignored U.S. gains from the conference—broadening of the Polish government, a UN voting formula, the significant Soviet pledge to enter the Pacific war—and charged that FDR had conceded too much in "saying 'nice kitty' to Stalin." The United States might have used reconstruction aid as a diplomatic weapon, but such tactics would have spoiled the spirit of compromise at Yalta, which served American interests. Churchill recognized the necessity of conciliation: "What would have happened if we had quarreled with Russia while the Germans still had three or four hundred divisions on the fighting front?" The spheres-of-influence agreement, the Yalta signators believed, would serve as a transition to peace.

To Each Its Own: Allied Divergence and Spheres of Influence

Throughout World War II, the Allies attempted to protect and, if possible, extend their spheres of influence. Churchill's defense of the British Empire, from Argentia through Yalta, reflected this characteristic of wartime diplomacy. "If the Americans want to take Japanese islands," he remarked, "let them do so with our blessing. . . . But 'Hands Off the British Empire' is our maxim." Some Americans suspected that Churchill's constant postponement of the second front and his strategies for North Africa and Italy aimed at preserving British interests. His advice to U.S. military leaders, near war's end, that they drive quickly to Berlin to beat the Soviets there also aroused suspicion.

The Churchill-Stalin percentage agreement of October 1944 was emblematic. In early 1944 Churchill concluded that "we are approaching a showdown with the Russians" in the Balkans. Instability plagued Romania, where Soviet troops dominated; Yugoslavia, where independent communist Josip Tito and his Partisans were emerging; Bulgaria, where an indigenous communist movement grew with Soviet influence; and Greece, a British-dominated area plagued by civil war. At an October conference with Stalin in Moscow, Churchill scribbled some percentages on a piece of paper. In Romania, Russia would get 90 percent of the power and Britain 10 percent; in Greece, Britain would enjoy 90 percent and Russia 10 percent; in Yugoslavia and Hungary, a 50–50 split; and in Bulgaria, 75 percent would go to Russia and 25 percent to "others." Churchill "pushed this across to Stalin," who "took his blue pencil and made a large tick upon it." Stalin liked this arrangement that granted the Soviets predominant influence in Eastern Europe. Roosevelt did not protest.

Soviet support for the Lublin government, demands for Polish and Romanian territory, and efforts to exclude the United States and Britain from the joint control commissions in Eastern Europe underscored the growing power of the Soviet Union over its neighbors. Soviet handling of the Warsaw uprising of July 1944 alarmed Western observers. With Soviet armies some twelve miles from Warsaw, the Polish underground gambled and attacked German forces, hoping that Soviet troops would dash to their aid. But the Red Army stopped. Over the next two months the Germans leveled half the city and killed 166,000 Poles, most of whom owed allegiance to the exiled government in London. Stalin dropped supplies to the besieged city in September but refused at first to let Allied planes land at Soviet airfields after carrying supplies to Warsaw. He called the uprising a "reckless and fearful gamble" by "power-seeking criminals." Stalin's callous contempt for the Warsaw Poles

The Allies Push Japan Back, 1942–1945

Japanese-held areas

Limit of Japanese conquest

Norman Adams

prompted Ambassador W. Averell Harriman to view the Soviets as a "world bully" who "misinterpreted our generous attitude toward them." The liberation of Poland by Soviet forces in 1944 ultimately fixed a communist regime in Warsaw—one that Roosevelt's compromises at Yalta essentially recognized.

The United States itself was expanding and building spheres of influence during the war. Having drawn most of the Latin American states into a defense community at the Lima Conference (1938) and in the Declaration of Panama (1939), Washington moved to drive German investments and influence from the Western Hemisphere. The Export-Import Bank loaned $130 million to twelve Latin American nations in 1939–1941 to help them oust German businesses, cut trade with the Axis, stabilize their economies, and bring them into alignment with U.S. foreign policy. During the war, the United States increased its stake in Bolivian tin, helped build Brazilian warships, expanded holdings in Venezuelan oil, acquired bases in Panama and Guatemala, and dispensed arms and training to Latin American forces. During the war Latin America shipped 50 percent of its exports, largely much needed raw materials, to the United States. At the Rio de Janeiro Conference (January 15–28, 1942), all but Chile and Argentina voted to break diplomatic relations with the Axis nations. In March 1945, in the Act of Chapultepec, the United States and Latin America took another step toward a regional defense alliance.

U.S. leaders also sought to direct events in postwar Italy and Asia. They essentially excluded the Soviets from the Italian surrender agreement in 1943 and denied them a role in the control commission, thereby setting a precedent for later Soviet predominance in Romania and Hungary. U.S. officials also insisted on unilaterally governing postwar Japan. With American forces spearheading the counteroffensive in the southwest Pacific, Australian prime minister John Curtin acknowledged allegiance "to America, free of any pangs to our traditional links with the United Kingdom." Thus did Washington envisage closer postwar ties with India, Australia, New Zealand, and Jiang's China.

In the Middle East the United States also expanded. In 1939 the Arabian-American Oil Company (Aramco) began to tap its 440,000-square-mile concession in Saudi Arabia's rich oil fields. By 1944 U.S. corporations controlled 42 percent of the proved oil reserves of the Middle East, a nineteen fold increase since 1936. In 1944, American companies, with Washington's encouragement, applied for an oil concession in Iran, then occupied by British and Soviet troops and used as a corridor for Lend-Lease shipments to the Soviet Union. This request touched off a three-cornered competition for influence in the heretofore British-dominated country. Churchill sarcastically thanked FDR "for your assurances about no sheeps' eyes at our oil fields in Iran and Iraq. Let me reciprocate by giving you fullest assurance that we have no thought of trying to horn in upon your interests or property in Saudi Arabia."

With Germany's surrender on May 8, 1945, the Third Reich collapsed in the rubble of bombed-out Berlin. President Harry S. Truman quickly ended Lend-Lease aid to the Soviet Union, thereby stirring up a hornet's nest in Moscow. With this issue and the Polish question troubling Soviet-American relations, the president sent Harry Hopkins to see Stalin in May, to "use diplomatic language or a baseball bat." An irate Stalin warned the Americans had made "a fundamental mistake" in halting Lend-Lease "as pressure on the Russians in order to soften them up." Hopkins expressed growing U.S. dismay about Stalin's obstruction of the Yalta agreement on elections in Poland—a symbol of Soviet-American trust. Stalin would not permit the anti-Soviet London Poles (the most likely winners of an election) to govern postwar Poland, because Poland had twice "served as a corridor for German

Harry Hopkins (1890–1946).
A progressive reformer, the Iowa-born Hopkins became one of Franklin D. Roosevelt's most trusted New Deal administrators and advisers. During World War II, Roosevelt sent Hopkins on special missions and utilized his counsel at international conferences, including Yalta. When he traveled to Moscow for Truman in May 1945, Hopkins was suffering from the cancer that would cause his death within months. (Courtesy of FDR Library)

attacks. . . . It is therefore in Russia's vital interest that Poland should be both strong and friendly." Stalin did agree that a few ministries should go to non-Lublin Poles. He also reiterated his Yalta promises that he would enter the war against Japan and respect Jiang's government. Truman then noted in his diary: "I'm not afraid of Russia. . . . They've always been our friends and I can't see any reason why they shouldn't always be."

The Potsdam Conference and the Legacy of the Second World War

The Big Three next gathered near Berlin for the Potsdam Conference (July 16–August 2, 1945). Truman's first impression of his Soviet counterpart was favorable: "I can deal with Stalin. He is honest—but smart as hell." That impression soon changed, as Truman wrote that "you never saw such pigheaded people as are the Russians." Churchill took a liking to the new president, whom he described as a "man of exceptional character and ability . . . and a great deal of self-confidence." Reports of the successful explosion of an atomic device in New Mexico had "tremendously pepped up" the president, Churchill noticed

By Potsdam, American intentions toward postwar Germany had moved a good distance from the Morgenthau Plan and JCS/1067. Reconstruction now became the watchword. U.S. officials saw Germany as a vital link in the economic recovery of Western Europe. When Germany came up for discussion, Truman thus resisted dismemberment and large reparations. The final Potsdam accord stated that Germany would be managed by military governors in four zones, treated as "a single economic unit," and permitted a standard of living higher than its low level of 1945. Transportation, coal, agriculture, housing, and utilities industries were to be restored. As for reparations, desired by the Soviet Union for both revenge and the recovery of its hobbled economy, Stalin had to settle for an agreement that each occupying power would take reparations from its own zone and that the USSR would get some industrial equipment from the Western zones. In return, the Soviet Union would send food to the other three zones.

When Churchill complained about no elections in Poland, Stalin mentioned the British domination of Greece. They did agree, however, to set the Oder-Neisse line as Poland's temporary western boundary, thereby granting Poland large chunks of German territory. The big powers also established the Council of Foreign Ministers to continue discussion on issues not resolved at Potsdam: peace treaties for the former German satellites; withdrawal of allied troops from Iran; postwar control of the Dardanelles; internationalization of inland waterways; and disposition of Italian colonies. After learning that they had successfully tested a new atomic weapon, Britain and the United States issued the "Potsdam Declaration," demanding Japan's unconditional surrender and threatening it with destruction.

The seemingly minor issue of waterways became for Truman a test of Soviet intentions. At Potsdam he pushed for an international authority to govern the 800-mile-long Danube River, which wound its way through several countries, including the Soviet Union, to the Black Sea. Essentially combining two traditional American principles—free navigation and the Open Door—the proposal antagonized Moscow, which countered with a commission limited to those states through which the river flowed. The president simplistically concluded that Stalin's attitude on waterways showed "what he was after. . . . The Russians were planning world conquest." For his part, Stalin thought London and Washington wanted to "force us" to accept "their plans on questions affecting Europe and the world. Well, that's not going to happen."

Potsdam left the world much as it had found it—divided and devastated. World War II ended on August 14, 1945, with Japan's surrender after Soviet intervention and two atomic bombs decimated Hiroshima and Nagasaki. But peace remained elusive because of the war's vast social, economic, and political dislocations in Europe and Asia. World War II claimed the lives of at least 55 million people—27 million in the USSR. Poland and Germany lost 6 million each; Yugoslavia suffered at least 1.6 million dead; Britain lost 400,000. The toll mounted in Asia, too: 15 million Chinese, 4 million Indonesians, 3 million Japanese, 1 million Vietnamese, 120,000 Filipinos, and more. A total of 405,395 Americans died fighting in the war—approximately one American death for every fifteen Germans and fifty-three Russians. Millions of displaced persons became separated from their homelands. Transportation systems, communications networks, and factories shut down. Cities entered the postwar era as rubble heaps. The incendiary "area raid" on Tokyo in March killed at least 83,793 civilians and left more than 1 million homeless. An unprecedented reconstruction task lay ahead.

With the imperial powers in disarray, their Asian colonies soon grew rebellious. Without the necessary resources and manpower to curb the nationalist revolutions, the European empires began to crumble. The Dutch battled their Indonesian subjects; France fought the Vietnamese in Indochina; Britain reluctantly began its exit from Burma, India, and Ceylon (Sri Lanka).

The rise of the Soviet Union counts as another legacy of World War II. Thanks to Hitler, said Truman at Potsdam, "we shall have a Slav Europe for a long time to come." Reeling from heavy wartime losses, the Soviets asked for much—"like a greedy kid, never satisfied," noted one U.S. official. "Whoever occupies a territory imposes on it his own social system," said Stalin. "It cannot be otherwise."

The USSR rose, Britain declined, China floundered, and the United States galloped. "Unbombed, unoccupied, and relatively unbloodied," America had its economy moving in high gear at war's end. The U.S. gross national product jumped from $90.5 billion in 1939 to $211.9 billion in 1945. Observers spoke of an American production miracle. By the end of the war the United States had become "the global workshop and banker, umpire and policeman, preacher and teacher."

Alone in a position to provide the capital and goods for recovery abroad, Washington felt flushed with power. Americans looked forward to creating the stable world order that had eluded them between the two world wars. State Department official Dean Acheson observed that "peace is possible only if countries work together and prosper together. That is why the economic aspects are no less important than the political aspects of the peace." Through the war years the United States had constructed institutions—UNRRA, World Bank, International Monetary Fund, United Nations—to ensure that peace.

The war also wrought changes in the decisionmaking process in the United States. Government agencies handling national security matters ballooned in size. The defense establishment became more active in making diplomatic choices. "Obstruction, understaffing, and rival ambitions" distracted a State Department too often bypassed by FDR. The war spawned a large espionage establishment, beginning with the Office of Strategic Services (OSS) in 1942 and culminating in the Central Intelligence Agency (CIA) five years later. The president centralized decisionmaking in the White House, while Congress neglected its foreign-affairs prerogatives in the constitutional system and applauded bipartisanship. Another consequence of the war was an enlarged "military-industrial complex," a partnership between business executives eager for lucrative defense contracts and military brass eager for increased budgets. The recruitment of universities bequeathed a long-term legacy. Science professors had developed the atomic bomb at the Universities of Chicago and California, Berkeley. Princeton received grants for ballistics research. Postwar federal subsidies flowed to colleges for arms development, research on Soviet studies, and intelligence gathering.

"The world was fluid and about to be remade" in 1945, the journalist Theodore White remembered. After the setbacks of depression and war, the historian Allan Nevins wrote, "the old self-confident America is coming into its stride again." But it did so now as the world's strongest power.

FURTHER READING FOR THE PERIOD 1939–1945

Biographical studies include Rudy Abrahamson, *Spanning the Century* (1992) (Harriman); Conrad Black, *Franklin Delano Roosevelt* (2003); Dik Alan Daso, *Hap Arnold and the Evolution of American Air Power* (2000); Kenneth R. Davis, *FDR* (1972–1993); Justus D. Doenecke and Mark A. Stoler, *Debating Franklin D. Roosevelt's Foreign Policies, 1933–1945* (2005); Martin Gilbert, *Winston S. Churchill* (1983); Warren F. Kimball, *The Juggler* (1991) (FDR); John Lukacs, *Churchill* (2002); George McJimsey, *Harry Hopkins* (1987); Forrest C. Pogue, *George C. Marshall* (1963–1987); Robert Service, *Stalin* (2005); Mark A. Stoler, *George Marshall* (1989); and works cited in Chapters 4 and 5.

FDR's health is the subject of Robert H. Ferrell, *The Dying President* (1998) and *Ill-Advised* (1992); and Bert E. Park, *The Impact of Illness on World Leaders* (1986).

For the United States and Europe, 1939–1941, and debates at home, see J. Garry Clifford and Samuel R. Spencer Jr., *The First Peacetime Draft* (1986); Wayne S. Cole, *Roosevelt and the Isolationists* (1983); Justus Doenecke, *The Battle Against Intervention* (1997) and *Storm on the Horizon* (2001); Richard F. Hill, *Hitler Attacks Pearl Harbor* (2002); Thomas Mahl, *Desperate Deception* (1998); Thomas Mahnken, *Uncovering Ways of War* (2002); Norman Moss, *Nineteen Weeks* (2003); Anthony Read and David Fisher, *The Deadly Embrace* (1989) (Nazi-Soviet Pact); David Reynolds, *The Creation of the Anglo-American Alliance, 1937–1941* (1982) and *From Munich to Pearl Harbor* (2001); James C. Schneider, *Should America Go to War?* (1989); Ivo Tasovac, *American Policy and Yugoslavia, 1939–1941* (1999); D. C. Watt, *How War Came* (1989); and Theodore A. Wilson, *The First Summit* (1991).

For the advent of war with Japan, see Michael A. Barnhart, *Japan Prepares for Total War* (1987); Hilary Conroy and Harry Wray, eds., *Pearl Harbor Reexamined* (1990); Henry G. Gole, *The Road to Rainbow* (2003); Akira Iriye, *The Origins of the Second World War in Asia and the Pacific* (1987); Walter LaFeber, *The Clash* (1997); James Morley, ed., *The Fateful Choice* (1980), ed., *The Final Confrontation* (1994), and, ed., *Japan's Road to the Pacific War: Japan's Negotiations with the United States, 1941* (1994); Gordon W. Prange, *At Dawn We Slept* (1981) and *Pearl Harbor* (1986); Emily Rosenberg, *A Date Which Will Live* (2003); Youli Sun, *China and the Origins of the Pacific War* (1993); Nicholas Tarling, *A Sudden Rampage* (2001); and Jonathan Utley, *Going to War with Japan* (2005).

Allied relations and postwar planning are explored in David Alvarez, *Secret Messages* (2000) (codebreaking); Alan H. Bath, *Tracking the Axis Enemy* (1998); Edward M. Bennett, *Franklin D. Roosevelt and the Search for Victory* (1990); David Bercuson and Holger Herwig, *A Christmas in Washington* (2005); Michael Beschloss, *The Conquerors* (2002); Richard Breitman et al., *American Intelligence and the Nazis* (2005); Susan A. Brewer, *To Win the Peace* (1997); Douglas Brinkley and David Facey-Crowther, eds., *The Atlantic Charter* (1994); Marius Broekmeyer, *Stalin, the Russians, and their War, 1941–1945* (2004); Mark J. Conversino, *Fighting with the Soviets* (1997); Alan P. Dobson, *U.S. Wartime Aid to Britain* (1986); Robin Edmonds, *The Big Three* (1991); Lloyd C. Gardner, *Spheres of Influence* (1993); David Glantz, *Colossus Reborn* (2005) (Red Army); Mary E. Glantz, *FDR and the Soviet Union* (2005); Patrick Hearden, *Architects of Globalism* (2002); George C. Herring Jr., *Aid to Russia, 1941–1946* (1973); Gary R. Hess, *The United States at War, 1941–1945* (1986); Gregory Hooks, *Forging the Military-Industrial Complex* (1990); Barry M. Katz, *Foreign Intelligence* (1989); Warren F. Kimball, ed., *America Unbound* (1992); Paul A. C. Koistinen, *Arsenal of World War II* (2004); Eric Larrabee, *Commander in Chief* (1987); Christopher Mauch, *The Shadow War Against Hitler* (2003); Steven M. Miner, *Between Churchill and Stalin* (1988) and *Stalin's Holy War* (2003); David Murphy, *What Stalin Knew* (2005); Williamson Murray and Allen Millett, *A War to Be Won* (2000); Arnold A. Offner and Theodore A. Wilson, eds., *Victory in Europe 1945* (2000); William O'Neill, *A Democracy at War* (1993); Septimus Paul, *Nuclear Rivals* (2002); Robert Persico, *Roosevelt's Secret War* (2001); R. C. Raack, *Stalin's Drive to the West, 1938–1945* (1995); David Reynolds et al., eds., *Allies at War* (1994) and *Rich Relations: The American Occupation of Britain* (1995); Ronald Schaffer, *Wings of Judgment* (1985) (U.S. bombing); Stephen C. Schlesinger, *Act of Creation* (2003) (UN); Michael S. Sherry, *Preparing for the Next War* (1977); Bradley F. Smith, *Sharing Secrets with Stalin* (1996); Gaddis Smith, *American Diplomacy During the Second World War* (1985); Mark A. Stoler, *Allies and Adversaries* (2000); Dwight W. Tuttle, *Harry L. Hopkins and Anglo-American-Soviet Relations, 1941–1945* (1983); Gerhard L. Weinberg, *A World at Arms* (2004); Steve Weiss, *Allies in Conflict* (1996); and Randall B. Woods, *A Changing of the Guard* (1990) (U.S.-Britain).

For the Churchill–Roosevelt relationship, see Paul Addison, *Churchill* (2005); Warren F. Kimball, *Forged in War* (1997); Keith Sainsbury, *Churchill and Roosevelt at War* (1994); and David Stone, *War Summits* (2005).

Big Three summit meetings are treated in Russell O. Buhite, *Decisions at Yalta* (1986); Keith Eubank, *Summit at Teheran* (1985); and Keith Sainsbury, *The Turning Point* (1985) (Cairo and Teheran).

For the creation of new international organizations, see Robert C. Hilderbrand, *Dumbarton Oaks* (1990); Townsend Hoopes and Douglas Brinkley, *FDR and the Creation of the U.N.* (1997); and Greg Schild, *Bretton Woods and Dumbarton Oaks* (1995).

Propaganda and the mobilizing of public opinion in the era of World War II are studied in Steven Casey, *Cautious Crusade* (2001); Nicholas Cull, *Selling War* (1995) (British propaganda in the United States); Thomas Doherty, *Projections of War* (1999); Clayton Koppes and Gregory Black, *Hollywood Goes to War* (1987); Clayton Laurie, *The Propaganda Warriors* (1996); George H. Roeder Jr., *The Censored War* (1993); Holly C. Shulman, *The Voice of America* (1991); Bruce Smith, *The War Comes to Plum Street* (2005); Richard Steele, *Propaganda in an Open Society* (1985); and Michael S. Sweeney, *Secrets of Victory* (2000).

For the Pacific theater, China, and decolonization, see Wesley M. Bagby, *The Eagle-Dragon Alliance* (1992); Günter Bischof and Robert Dupont, eds., *The Pacific War Revisited* (1997); Herbert P. Bix, *Emperor Hirohito and the Making of Modern Japan* (2001); John W. Dower, *War Without Mercy* (1986); T. Fujitani et al., *Perilous Memories: The Asia-Pacific War(s)* (2001); Tsuyoshi Hasegawa, *Racing the Enemy* (2005); Akira Iriye, *Power and Culture* (1981); Xiaoyuan Liu, *A Partnership for Disorder* (1996) (China); Mark Roehrs and William Renzl, *World War II in the Pacific* (2003); Peter Schrijvers, *The GI War Against Japan* (2002); Michael M. Sheng, *Battling Western Imperialism* (1997); Leon V. Sigal, *Fighting to the Finish* (1988); Ronald H. Spector, *Eagle Against the Sun* (1984); Christopher Thorne, *Allies of a Kind* (1977) and *The Issue of War* (1985); Odd Arne Westad, *Cold War and Revolution* (1993) (China); H. P. Wilmott, *The Battle of Leyte Gulf* (2005); and Thomas Zeiler, *Unconditional Defeat* (2003).

For wartime relations with Latin America, see Max Paul Friedman, *Nazis and Good Neighbors* (2003); Michael Grow, *The Good Neighbor Policy and Authoritarianism in Paraguay* (1981); Stephen R. Niblo, *War, Diplomacy, and Development* (1995) (Mexico); María Emilia Paz, *Strategy, Security, and Spies* (1997) (Mexico); and Randall B. Woods, *The Roosevelt Foreign Policy Establishment and the "Good Neighbor"* (1980) (Argentina).

For U.S. interest in the Middle East and oil, consult Irvine H. Anderson, *Aramco, the United States, and Saudi Arabia* (1981); Philip J. Baram, *The Department of State in the Middle East, 1919–1945* (1978); Aaron D. Miller, *Search for Security* (1980) (Saudi Arabia); and Michael B. Stoff, *Oil, War, and American Security* (1980).

The Holocaust and refugee problem are recounted in Robert H. Abzug, *Inside the Vicious Heart* (1985); Yehuda Bauer, *Jews for Sale?* (1994) and *Rethinking the Holocaust* (2001); Richard Breitman, *Official Secrets* (1998); Richard Breitman and Alan M. Kraut, *American Refugee Policy and European Jewry* (1987); Christopher Browning, *The Path to Genocide* (1992); Leonard Dinnerstein, *America and the Survivors of the Holocaust* (1982); Henry L. Feingold, *Bearing Witness* (1995); Carole Fink, *Defending the Rights of Others* (2005); Deborah E. Lipstadt, *Beyond Belief* (1993); Louise London, *Whitehall and the Jews, 1933–1948* (2002); William E. Nawyn, *American Protestantism's Response to Germany's Jews and Refugees* (1982); Verne Newton, ed., *FDR and the Holocaust* (1995); Monty N. Penkower, *The Jews Were Expendable* (1983); David Wyman, *The Abandonment of the Jews* (1984), and ed., *The World Reacts to the Holocaust* (1996); and David S. Wyman and Rafael Medoff, *A Race Against Death* (2002).

See also Robert L. Beisner, ed., *Guide to American Foreign Relations Since 1600* (2003).

For comprehensive coverage of foreign-relations topics, see the articles in the four-volume *Encyclopedia of U.S. Foreign Relations* (1997), edited by Bruce W. Jentleson and Thomas G. Paterson.

CHAPTER 7

All-Embracing Struggle: The Cold War Begins, 1945–1950

DIPLOMATIC CROSSROAD

The Atomic Bomb at Hiroshima, 1945

THE CREW OF the B-29 group on Tinian scrawled graffiti on the "Little Boy." A major, thinking about his son and a quick end to the war, scratched "No white cross for Stevie" on the 10,000-pound orange and black bomb. At last, the United States's secret atomic development program (Manhattan Project) neared fruition. In the evening of August 5, 1945, Colonel Paul Tibbets informed his crew that their rare cargo was "atomic." He did not explain the scientific process in which two pieces of uranium (U-235), placed at opposite ends of a cylinder, smashed into one another to create tremendous energy. Yet they knew what the equivalent of 20,000 tons of TNT meant.

At 2:45 A.M. on August 6, Tibbets's heavily laden B-29, the *Enola Gay,* named after his mother, lifted ponderously off the Mariana island runway. The six-hour flight was uneventful except for the nerve-wracking final assembly of the bomb's inner components. The *Enola Gay* spotted the Japanese coast at 7:30 A.M. A weather plane assigned to Hiroshima, the primary target, reported that "everything was peachy keen." Tibbets headed for that city.

"This is history," he intoned over the intercom, "so watch your language." At 31,600 feet and 328 miles per hour the *Enola Gay* began its run on Hiroshima. Bombardier Thomas Ferebee prepared to cross the hairs in his bombsight. At 8:15 A.M. he shouted "bombs away." "Little Boy" fell for fifty seconds and then exploded about 2,000 feet above ground, a near perfect hit at hypocenter. A brilliant flash temporarily blinded the fliers. The aircraft trembled. "It looked like a pot of black, boiling tar," thought navigator Theodore Van Kirk, as he watched the huge cloud of smoke, dust, and debris rise 40,000 feet.

Hiroshima ranked as Japan's eighth largest city, with 250,000 people. Manhattan Project director Lieutenant General Leslie Groves had put it first on the target

Atomic Blast. The second atomic bomb fell on Nagasaki August 9, 1945, killing at least 60,000. When the renowned scientist Albert Einstein heard that Japan had been blasted with an atomic bomb, he said: "Ach! The world is not ready for it." (U.S. Air Force)

list because it housed regional military headquarters, even though it was largely a residential and commercial city. On the cloudless, warm morning of August 6, 1945, few of Hiroshima's inhabitants heard the *Enola Gay* overhead. Suddenly a streak of light raced through the sky. A blast of lacerating heat traveling near the speed of light rocked the city. The temperature soared to suffocating levels. Trees were stripped of their leaves. Buildings blew apart like firecrackers. Debris shot through the air like bullets. Permanent shadows etched themselves into concrete. The sky grew dark, lighted only by the choking fires that erupted everywhere. In an example of "psychic numbing," one survivor recalled that the agony around him "no longer moved me" because people "on the point of death were no longer human: they became mere substance."

As the giant mushroom cloud churned above, a Japanese child "clearly saw the demonic faces of our enemies, Roosevelt and Churchill, looking down on me." Other victims remembered skin peeling off like ribbons, gaping wounds, vomiting

Office of War Information Bombing Leaflet. This photo of five airborne B-29 bombers appeared on approximately 1 million leaflets prepared by the Office of War Information (OWI) and dropped on Hiroshima, Nagasaki, and thirty-three other Japanese cities on August 1, 1945. The reverse side of the leaflet printed the following Japanese text: "Read this carefully as it may save your life. . . . In the next few days some or all of the cities named on the reverse side will be destroyed by American bombs. . . . Heed this warning and evacuate these cities immediately." (Official Report to U.S. Information Service)

and diarrhea, intense thirst. The nightmare registered in statistics: about 130,000 dead, as many wounded, and 81 percent of the city's buildings destroyed. Some twenty-three U.S. prisoners of war also perished there. Nine days later in Fukuoka, Japan, seventeen captured American airmen were beheaded by Japanese soldiers, allegedly in retaliation for the "indiscriminate bombing" of civilians.

On August 9, a second atomic bomb smashed Nagasaki, killing at least 60,000. The next day, shaken after "killing all those kids," President Harry S. Truman decided not to unleash a third atomic bomb. The Japanese surrendered four days later. "We cried with relief and joy," a young American lieutenant recalled. "We were going to grow up to adulthood after all." Presidential aide Admiral William D. Leahy later regretted that "in being the first to use it, we had adopted the ethical standard common to the barbarians of the Dark Ages." No military or naval adviser, however, told Truman before Hiroshima that "the use of the A-bomb was unnecessary, or that the weapon should not be used, or both."

Although Truman later defended his atomic bomb decision as necessary to end the war and thus save American lives, some advisers and scientists disagreed. They suggested viable alternatives to dropping the bomb on a civilian population: (1) follow up Japanese peace feelers; (2) blockade and bomb Japan conventionally; (3) have the USSR declare war on Japan; (4) warn Tokyo about the bomb and threaten its use; (5) demonstrate the bomb on an unpopulated island or area with international observers, including Japanese; (6) conduct a military landing on the outlying Japanese island of Kyushu. Many scientists believed that use of the bomb would constitute a moral blot on the American record, that it would jeopardize chances of postwar international control of the awesome weapon, and that it was unnecessary because Japan tottered on the verge of surrender.

Those who approved the use of the bomb stressed the need to save U.S. lives, "to prevent an Okinawa from one end of Japan to the other," in Truman's words. Told that an invasion might cost "500,000 to 1,000,000 American lives," the president thought first "of the kids who won't be killed." That simple reason helps to explain the decision, but decisions seldom derive from single factors and this one is no exception. Three primary and intertwined motives induced policymakers to inflict atomic horror on the citizens of Japan. Together, the three suggest that Truman found no compelling reasons against dropping atom bombs on Hiroshima and Nagasaki and important advantages in doing so.

The first motive—emotion—dated from December 7, 1941, when the Japanese bombed Pearl Harbor without warning. Vengeful Americans never forgot or forgave that disaster. Nor did they forget Japanese atrocities. Racialized American images of the Japanese as treacherous agents of a "Yellow Peril" strengthened this popular wartime attitude. *Kamikaze* air attacks in 1945 persuaded many that the Japanese, suicidal and bloodthirsty, deserved the worst of punishments. Americans hated the Japanese more than they hated the Germans, and 13 percent in a Gallup Poll of December 1944 recommended the extermination of all Japanese. This angry emotion carried influence. Truman himself said on August 11, 1945: "When you have to deal with a beast you have to treat him as a beast."

The second motive—military momentum—merged with the first and derived from the Manhattan Project. This program began after European scientists, through a letter from Albert Einstein to President Roosevelt, warned that Germany might develop a nuclear device for military purposes. Officials in charge of the $2 billion project always assumed that once they developed a bomb they would use it to end the war. Truman inherited this assumption from the Roosevelt administration. Put another way, Truman really did not *decide* to drop the bomb. Rather, the president practiced "noninterference—basically a decision not to upset the existing plans." By August 1945, however, compelling momentum had taken on an irrational quality, for the Germans had surrendered and Japan faced certain defeat.

The third factor that helped unleash the atomic bomb was the diplomatic "bonus" that might accrue to the United States. This opportunity beckoned after the successful test explosion at Alamogordo, New Mexico, on July 16, 1945. "Japs will fold up before Russia comes in," Truman wrote on learning the details. "I am sure they will when Manhattan appears over their homeland." Throughout the war, Churchill and Roosevelt tried to keep the bomb a secret from the Soviet Union, in part to use it for diplomatic leverage in the postwar period. At Potsdam, Truman did cryptically inform Stalin that the United States had "a new weapon of unusual destructive force." In fact, despite Soviet penetration of the Manhattan Project through espionage, Stalin did not grasp the importance of atomic weapons until Hiroshima and Nagasaki had "shaken the whole world." He quickly authorized an accelerated program to catch up. Churchill noted at Potsdam that when Truman heard the news from Alamagordo, "he was a changed man" who "told the Russians just where they got on and off." Two diplomatic advantages suggested themselves. First, the bomb might strengthen Washington's negotiating position vis-à-vis the Soviets. An intimidated USSR might offer concessions on Eastern Europe if the bomb revealed its destructive power on a Japanese city. Second, the bomb might end the war in the Pacific before the Soviets could intervene. Even though Americans had sought Soviet participation prior to Alamogordo, quick use of the bomb might deny the USSR any part of the postwar control of Japan. In fact, Moscow's declaration of war on August 8 caused greater alarm in Tokyo than did news of Hiroshima, as Emperor Hirohito soon maneuvered the deadlocked Supreme War Council into accepting surrender.

James F. Byrnes (1879–1972) and Harry S. Truman (1884–1972). Both the secretary of state and the president, here on their way back from the Potsdam Conference, welcomed the atomic bomb as a diplomatic bargaining weapon in the postwar period. (U.S. Navy, courtesy of the Harry S. Truman Library)

All three factors—emotion, military momentum, and diplomatic advantage—explain the tragedies at Hiroshima and Nagasaki. To have decided against dropping the atomic bomb, Truman would have had to deny the growing passion and momentum of mid-summer 1945. He could avenge Pearl Harbor, end the war quickly, save American lives, and shore up the U.S. diplomatic position—the advantages far outweighed the disadvantages in his mind. Still, the costs were not inconsequential. Some of the alternatives might have terminated the war without the heavy death toll and the grotesque suffering of the survivors. The failure to discuss atomic issues with the Soviets during the war bequeathed to the postwar generation both division and fear.

The Big Two and the International System

Because World War II left the international system in disarray, the transition to peace proved rough and contentious. Broken societies and economies needed repair, and competing models for a new future produced wrenching political turmoil. Some 35 million people died in Europe during the war, and homeless survivors struggled to live in the rubble. The contrast with prosperous America, untouched by enemy bombers or soldiers, became stark. The war so weakened the French, British, and Dutch, moreover, that they began to retreat from empire. Britain granted independence to India in 1947 and Burma in 1948, and the Dutch left Indonesia a year later. The French clung precariously to Indochina in the face of nationalist rebellion.

Joseph Stalin (1879–1953)
General secretary of the Soviet Communist party since 1922, he ran an authoritarian state and conducted a foreign policy of suspiciousness. Because Stalin often played "good cop" to Molotov's "bad cop," President Truman once called the Soviet dictator a "prisoner of the Politburo," and Ambassador W. Averell Harriman wrote that if "it were possible to see [Stalin] more frequently . . . many of our difficulties would be overcome." (*The Reporter*, 1952. Copyright 1952 by Fortnightly Publishing Co., Inc.)

As Washington moved to fill the power vacuums left by the defeated Axis and retreating colonial powers, it encountered an obstreperous competitor in Joseph Stalin's Soviet Union. Soon a bipolar international structure emerged from the Soviet-American rivalry—the Cold War. The Soviets' pushy behavior, suspiciousness, and blunt language rankled Americans. At the end of the war, the Soviet Union had troops in several Eastern European countries and part of Germany. It lacked an effective navy or air force and had no atomic bomb, but it possessed strong regional power by virtue of its military exploits. Motivated by traditional Russian nationalism and communist ideology, craving security against a revived Germany and facing a major task of reconstruction, the Kremlin determined to make the most of its limited power. Still, compared with the United States, as the diplomat George F. Kennan reported from Moscow, the Soviet Union stood as the "weaker force."

In fact, an asymmetry—not a balance—of power existed. Washington flexed its multidimensional muscle to build even more power. Because of domestic public pressure, Washington may have demobilized its troops faster than Truman wished, but the Soviet Union also demobilized millions of soldiers. With troops in Asia and Europe, the world's largest navy and air force, a monopoly of the atomic bomb, and a high-gear economy, the United States claimed first rank in world affairs. In contrast, a Moscow study estimated that total Soviet war damages surpassed "the national wealth of England or Germany" and constituted "one-third of the overall national wealth of the United States." So devastated, "Russia couldn't turn a wheel in the next ten years without our aid," bragged Truman.

American ideology held that world peace and order depended on the existence of prosperity and political democracy. Poverty and economic depression bred totalitarianism, revolution, communism, the disruption of world trade, and war. Prosperity became the handmaiden of stability, political freedom, unrestricted trade, and peaceful international relations. Americans had long believed that they were prosperous because they were democratic and democratic because they were prosperous.

American leaders determined that *this time,* unlike after World War I, the United States would seize the opportunity to fulfill its ideological premises. As the diplomat Dean Acheson saw it, "only the United States had the power to grab hold of history and make it conform." The lessons of the 1920s and 1930s taught the leaders of the 1940s to make the most of a "second chance" and to install America's concept of "peace and prosperity" as the world's way.

Makers of American Foreign Relations, 1945–1950

President	Secretaries of State
Harry S. Truman, 1945–1953	Edward R. Stettinius, Jr., 1944–1945
	James F. Byrnes, 1945–1947
	George C. Marshall, 1947–1949
	Dean G. Acheson, 1949–1953

Economic needs also influenced postwar expansionism. Truman frankly stated that the United States *had* to export American goods and *had* to import strategic raw materials. By 1947 U.S. exports accounted for one-third of total world exports at $14 billion a year. Pivotal industries, such as automobiles, steel, and farm machinery, relied heavily on foreign trade for their well-being. Farmers exported about half of their wheat. Many Americans, remembering the Great Depression, predicted economic catastrophe unless foreign trade continued and expanded. Further, imports of manganese, tungsten, and chromite had become essential to America's industrial system. Foreign trade, however, was threatened by the sickness of America's best customer, Europe, which lacked the resources to purchase American products, and also by nationalists in former colonial areas, who controlled raw materials sources for both Europe and America.

President Truman felt the flush of American power, shared the ideology, and knew well the economic needs of the country. A Democratic party regular from the Pendergast machine in Kansas City, Missouri, Truman had long experienced rough-and-tumble politics. "The buck stops here" read a sign on his desk. He prided himself on blunt language and quick decisions. With intense eyes peering through thick lenses, Truman relished the verbal brawl. His peppery style spawned jokes that often fit the truth. Somebody rewrote a proverb: "To err is Truman." Although intelligent and energetic, Truman was a provincial nationalist of narrow vision who believed he could win the Cold War through the projection of U.S. power, and he expected the world to go America's way. When it did not, he sometimes lost his temper.

In April 1945, Soviet foreign minister V. M. Molotov visited the White House. President Truman gave him a vigorous tongue-lashing, charging that Moscow had not honored the Yalta accords. After the encounter, the first meeting between the new president and a high-ranking Soviet official, Truman gloated to a friend: "I gave it to him straight 'one-two to the jaw.' I let him have it straight." Truman told Ambassador W. Averell Harriman that he did not fear the Soviets, because they "needed us more than we needed them." He did not expect to win 100 percent of the American case, but "we should be able to get 85 percent."

The confrontation between the United States and the Soviet Union derived from the different postwar needs, ideology, style, and power of the two rivals. Each saw the other, in mirror image, as the world's bully. Each charged the other with assuming Hitler's aggressive mantle. Americans compared Nazism and communism, Hitler and Stalin, and coined the phrase "Red Fascism." Moscow and Washington became trapped in a "security dilemma": Every step taken by one side to ensure its security appeared to the other to be provocative.

The advent of the air and nuclear ages made all nations vulnerable to surprise attack. "We are for all time de-isolated," wrote one observer. And the Soviet and American quests for spheres of influence kindled a global contest for advantage— an "all embracing struggle" with an expensive arms race, military alliances, trade restrictions, and repeated interventions and proxy wars. The Cold War era lasted more than forty years, claimed the lives of millions of victims, and nearly bankrupted the main protagonists.

"Red Fascism."   This popular notion among Americans suggested that German Nazism and Soviet communism were really one and the same and that the 1940s would suffer totalitarian aggression like that of the 1930s. Such thinking aroused fears of another "Munich" or "appeasement" and thereby hindered negotiations. (*The Reporter*, 1950. Copyright 1950 by Fortnightly Publishing Co., Inc.)

Challenging the Soviet Sphere in Eastern Europe

The Soviet presence in Eastern Europe before 1947–1948 was neither uniform nor consistent. Soviet documents from 1945–1946 suggest that Stalin acted as a "ruthless opportunist rather than a revolutionary ideologue." A "freely elected government in any of these countries would be anti-Soviet," he stated bluntly, "and that we cannot allow." Yet he also urged local communists not to "precipitate conflict, alienate the Americans, or challenge the British" so long as "time was on his side." Poland, with the Lublin communists in control, fell firmly within the Soviet grasp, as did Romania, where the Red Army imposed communist rule. In Bulgaria, indigenous communists easily won elections.

Hungary and other nations developed differently. The conservative Hungarian Smallholders' party of Ferenc Nagy won national elections in November 1945 by routing the communists, who gained only 17 percent of the vote. Toward Finland, Stalin practiced "generosity by calculation," telling Finnish leaders "when we treat our neighboring countries well, they respond in kind." So long as Helsinki remained neutral vis-à-vis the Soviet-American confrontation, the Finns retained their independence and in 1948 even ousted the lone communist from their cabinet. In Czechoslovakia, democratic socialist officials sought to steer a middle course in the developing Cold War. A coalition government under noncommunist president Eduard Benes and Foreign Minister Jan Masaryk assumed office after free elections in May 1946. With Czech communists holding a minority position in the Prague government, the Soviet Union refrained from meddling directly in Czech affairs until a communist coup in February 1948 sharply intensified the Cold War. Yugoslavia, although a communist state, established its independence from Moscow under the leadership of Josip Broz Tito. When Belgrade and Moscow bitterly split in 1948, U.S. officials noted that the "germ of Titoism is growing" and planned "the judicious use of covert operations applied at the appropriate time" to roll back Soviet influence in the region.

The Soviet presence in Eastern Europe before 1948, then, became conspicuous and often repressive, but not absolute. Staggering from the loss of 27 million dead during the recent war, Soviet leaders above all else demanded security. "Give them twelve to fifteen years and they'll be on their feet again," Stalin said of the Germans. He said repeatedly that Poland had been a corridor for attack and that a secure Poland meant life or death for the Soviets. Moscow also believed that the Yalta accords acknowledged its primary position in Eastern Europe.

Washington sought "free elections" and the "Open Door" for trade. The Soviets signed bilateral trade treaties with many Eastern European states, which established favors anathema to America's multilateral approach to trade. Despite minimal commercial ties with Eastern Europe, U.S. diplomats preached the Open Door as a way of driving a wedge into the area. "Free elections" proved difficult because open elections in most of Eastern Europe would have produced strongly anti-Soviet governments threatening Soviet security. In Hungary, for example, it was the *noncommunist* Nagy who delayed elections in 1946 because he knew that the communists would lose badly, alarming Moscow and perhaps triggering Soviet intervention.

Truman grew impatient. In early 1946 he instructed Byrnes to "stiffen up," to make no compromises with the Soviets. News of a Canadian spy ring that had sent atomic secrets to Moscow broke in February, about the time that Stalin gave a speech that persuaded some Americans that the Soviets had become intractable. From Moscow, on February 22, chargé d'affaires George F. Kennan wrote an alarmist cable that described an adversary "committed fanatically to the belief that with [the] US there can be no permanent modus vivendi." Widely read in Washington, this "long telegram" depicted, in gendered terms, a rapacious, aggressive, hypermasculine Soviet Union, guided by an implacable communist ideology and a "neurotic view of world affairs." To reassure the "tired and frightened" Europeans, Kennan urged the United States to "tighten" up, assert greater "cohesion, firmness and vigor," and rely on the manly virtues of "courage, detachment, [and] objectivity" in dealing with Moscow.

On March 5, Winston Churchill, no longer prime minister, spoke in Fulton, Missouri. President Truman heard the eloquent orator lash out at the Soviets: "From Stettin in the Baltic to Trieste in the Adriatic, an iron curtain has descended across the Continent." Most Americans liked his stern anti-Soviet tone, but they warmed much less to his call for an Anglo-American alliance outside the fledgling United Nations Organization. The British ambassador called the Fulton speech the "sharpest jolt to American thinking of any utterance since the end of the war."

The Iranian crisis disturbed Soviet-American relations at the same time. The crisis began quietly in 1944 when British and American oil companies applied for Iranian concessions. In a classic example of competition for spheres of influence, the Soviet Union soon applied as well. By 1944 U.S. corporations controlled 42 percent of the "proved" oil reserves of the Middle East, a nineteenfold increase since 1936. A 1942 treaty with Iran allowed the British and Soviets to occupy the country and required them to leave six months after the end of the war. U.S. personnel also went to Iran, primarily to facilitate Lend-Lease shipments to the Soviet Union. After the Soviets backed an indigenous rebellion in northern Iran (Azerbaijan) against the central government, Iran took the question to the new United Nations Organization in January 1946. Teheran and Moscow could not reach an accord by March 2, when all foreign troops, by treaty, had to depart. With U.S. and British troops already gone, the remaining Soviet forces, in Truman's exaggerated view, threatened a "giant pincers movement" toward the Mediterranean and the Near East. In April, however, Soviet forces agreed to withdraw; in exchange, Iran offered to establish a joint Iranian-Soviet oil company, subject to approval by its parliament. Stalin abandoned his Azerbaijani clients. In late 1946, Iranian troops, advised by U.S. Army officers, crushed the insurrection in northern Iran. Not until October 1947 did Iran's legislature consider the joint oil company, rejecting it by a vote of 102 to 2.

The Soviets exploded in anger. They had departed Iran while Britain and the United States had driven in stakes. Moscow wanted what the British and Americans already had—oil and influence—and feared the foreign penetration of a neighboring state. Years later, Truman embellished the Iranian story by claiming that he had sent the Soviets an ultimatum to get out of Iran or face U.S. troops; no record of such a message exists. Yet this myth suggests the simple lesson Americans drew: "Get tough" and the Soviets will give way. Secretary Wallace, however, told a Madison

**W. Averell Harriman
(1891–1986).**   Graduate of
Yale, heir to the Harriman railroad
empire, investment banker of
Brown Brothers, and diplomat,
Harriman was one of America's
great public servants in the
twentieth century. He served as
ambassador to Russia
(1943–1946), ambassador to
Great Britain (1946), secretary of
commerce (1946–1948), and U.S.
representative in Europe for the
Marshall Plan. Later he advised
Presidents John F. Kennedy and
Lyndon B. Johnson. (*The
Reporter,* 1950. Copyright 1950
by Fortnightly Publishing Co., Inc.)

Square Garden audience in September 1946: 'Getting tough' never brought anything real and lasting. . . . The tougher we get, the tougher the Russians will get." Truman fired Wallace, lumping the "cat bastard" with "parlor pinks and soprano-voiced men" as a "national danger" and "a sabotage front for Uncle Joe Stalin."

Other fractious issues in 1946 illustrated Truman's "get tough" policy. During the war, Moscow asked Washington for a major postwar reconstruction loan. Seeing U.S. aid as one of America's cards in the Cold War game, Truman decided to treat assistance for the USSR's massive reconstruction task as a weapon rather than as a tool. But as Ambassador Harriman admitted, U.S. rejection of the Soviet loan request in early 1946 actually "may have contributed to their avaricious policies" in Eastern Europe. In contrast, Washington granted Britain a $3.75 billion loan in mid-1946 in return for British promises to open trade in their Sterling Bloc.

The Baruch Plan of July 1946 also divided Washington and Moscow. The plan emerged from months of intra-administration talks, but its final touches belonged to Bernard Baruch, the uncompromising American negotiator. He outlined the proposal for control of atomic weapons: (1) creation of an international authority; (2) international control of fissionable raw materials by this authority; (3) inspections to prevent violations; (4) no Security Council vetoes of control or inspections; (5) global distribution of atomic plants for peaceful purposes; (6) cessation of the manufacture of atomic bombs; (7) destruction of existing bombs; (8) these procedures to occur in stages, with abandonment of the U.S. atomic bomb monopoly coming last.

Not until after the Soviets had given up all fissionable materials and submitted to inspections would the United States relinquish its "winning weapon." "We are telling the Russians that if they are 'good boys' we may eventually turn over our knowledge of atomic energy to them," Wallace wrote to the president. About the same time, the Soviet ambassador in Washington, Nikolai Novikov, warned his superiors that the United States was "striving for world supremacy." Moscow rejected the Baruch Plan, and the stalemate persisted until 1949, when the Soviets successfully exploded their first atomic device.

The issue of Germany—zones, reparations, central administration, demilitarization, and the dismantling of war-oriented factories—deepened the schism. The Allied occupation consisted of British, French, American, and Soviet zones, wherein each occupying power did what it liked. The vengeful French proved the most obstructionist, refusing to permit any centralized German agencies and pushing for permanent dismemberment. The Soviets tried with mixed success to grab reparations, thereby weakening the entire German economy. The British generally wanted a strong Germany. The United States sought to treat Germany as one economic unit to speed reconstruction. With the Morgenthau Plan shelved, new plans evolved to reconstruct steel- and coal-rich Germany as the vital center of a revived European economy. Thousands of GIs, meanwhile, "fraternized" or "went frattin" with German *frauleins* in the U.S. zone, while Project Paperclip recruited ex-Nazi scientists to assist in the "development of new types of weapons."

The dismantling of industrial plants slowed, and in May 1946 U.S. military governor Lucius Clay halted all reparations shipments from the American zone until the Soviets contributed to German economic unity. In December 1946, the British and

Americans combined their zones into "Bizonia." "We really do not intend to accept German unification in any terms that the Russians might agree to," one U.S. diplomat wrote privately. The Federal Republic of Germany (West Germany), a consolidation of "Bizonia" and the French zone, was formed in May 1949. The Soviets, after looting their zone, created their own client, the German Democratic Republic (East Germany), in October 1949.

Perhaps we can kick them out, Stalin told a German communist as he initiated the Berlin blockade (June 1948–May 1949) to impede unification of the western zones. Fearful of a Germany linked to the West, the Soviets sealed off land, rail, and water access to Berlin (inside the Soviet zone). Truman answered with an airlift. U.S. planes soon swept into the western part of the city with food, fuel, and other supplies. He also ordered B-29 bombers to England, concealing the fact that they went without any of the fifty atomic bombs then in the U.S. arsenal. The Soviet ambassador reported a "war psychosis" rampant in Washington. Yet Stalin never interfered with the airlift and even permitted a half-million tons of supplies to reach Berlin from the Soviet zone. Moscow eventually lifted the blockade, but only after suffering worldwide reproach and the creation of the West Germany it had so wanted to prevent. Americans drew another Cold War lesson: To win, never flinch in the face of communist aggression.

The Truman Doctrine, Israel, and Containment

On March 12, 1947, President Harry S. Truman spoke dramatically to a joint session of Congress. Unless the United States offered help to Greece and Turkey, "we may endanger the peace of the world—and we shall surely endanger the welfare of this Nation." His most famous words became known as the Truman Doctrine: "It must be the policy of the United States to support free peoples who are resisting attempted subjugation by armed minorities or by outside pressures." Truman asked for $400 million to ensure this policy's success. The president's address was short on analysis of alleged threats to Greece and Turkey, but long on clichés and alarmist language. He played on the words *free* and *democratic,* implying that they fit the Greek and Turkish governments. Presidential aide Clark Clifford called it "the opening gun in a campaign to bring the people up to [the] realization that the war isn't over by any means."

A British request for help in Greece and a lingering squabble over the Dardanelles served as immediate catalysts for the Truman Doctrine. When the Germans withdrew from Greece in 1944, much of the countryside had come under the control of communist and other leftist Greek nationalist resistance fighters. Intent on preserving their influence in the eastern Mediterranean, the British soon reinstated the Greek government-in-exile. Violence erupted in December 1944. British troops, transported to Greece on U.S. ships, engaged the leftists in vicious warfare. The rebels, hoping to gain political power through elections, signed a peace treaty in February 1945.

From then until March 1946, when civil war flared again, the British-sponsored Athens regime persecuted its political foes. The United States sent warships to Greek ports and aid through the Export-Import Bank. In September, Navy Secretary

Forrestal announced a permanent U.S. fleet in the Mediterranean. Despite a Greek government that was reportedly "weak, stupid, and venal," Washington still preferred a friendly regime to a leftist or communist one. Greece limped along, staggered by war-wrought devastation and civil turmoil. On February 21, 1947, the economically hobbled British informed Washington that they were pulling out. Truman's special message to Congress answered London's appeal with uncommon alacrity.

Critics charged that Truman backed a ruthless Greek regime. Others urged economic over military aid, recommended UN action, and feared that the Soviets would interpret the Truman Doctrine as threatening a world crusade. Critics also doubted that Soviet aggression threatened Greece and Turkey. Greek leftists, though communist-led, had minimal ties with the Soviet Union. Churchill always credited Stalin for keeping the bargain he made at their 1944 Moscow conference to stay out of the Greek imbroglio. In fact, Stalin disliked the nationalist Greek communists because the independent-minded Yugoslav leader Tito gave them aid. Yet Truman claimed that all communists took their orders from Moscow.

The Dardanelles question also had more complexity than Truman acknowledged. The Soviets complained that the Turks had permitted German warships to pass through the straits into the Black Sea during World War II. As Stalin insisted at Yalta, he could not "accept a situation in which Turkey had a hand on Russia's throat." When Turkey refused joint control with the Soviets, Moscow threatened to take action. The presence of Soviet troops near the Turkish border in August 1946 prompted the State-War-Navy Coordinating Committee to assert that "the only thing which will deter the Russians will be the conviction that the United States is prepared . . . to meet aggression with the force of arms." The ostentatious dispatch of a U.S. carrier task force to Istanbul may have caused the Soviets to moderate their demands. Ignoring legitimate Soviet concerns about the Dardanelles, Truman drew the simplistic conclusion that Stalin sought to subjugate Turkey. Aid to Turkey under the Truman Doctrine soon pulled that Soviet neighbor into the U.S. orbit.

American aid and advisers flowed to Greece after 1947, with U.S. officials taking charge of the Greek government. More than 350 American officers accompanied the Greek army in its counter-insurgency campaign. Truman claimed another Cold War victory, but the Greek rebels lost in October 1949 not only because of U.S. intervention but because the Soviet Union refused to help them and Tito sealed off the Yugoslav border to deny them a sanctuary.

U.S. interest in the Mediterranean region also entangled Washington in the Palestine question. Zionists had long sought a Jewish homeland, and at the end of World War II they pressed London and Washington to open British-mandated Palestine to Holocaust survivors. When the British blocked immigration and turned back ships such as the *Exodus* loaded with Jewish refugees, extremist Zionists resorted to arms. At first, U.S. Mideast policy sought to satisfy the Arabs, who opposed increased Jewish immigration and a new Jewish state, because Washington valued Mideast oil and Arab anticommunism. Yet many Americans, including President Truman, welcomed the humanitarian opportunity to assist displaced persons once terrorized by Nazism. The astute politician in Truman also spoke: "I do not have hundreds of thousands of Arabs among my constituents." The beleaguered British referred the Palestine question to the United Nations, whose special commission recommended partition into Jewish and Arab states, with 56 percent of the mandate area assigned to the Zionists. Truman groped for a policy while he exploded against Zionists who castigated him for not backing an independent Jewish nation: "Neither Hitler nor Stalin has anything on them for cruelty or maltreatment of the underdog." The president still hoped to win the large Jewish vote in the forthcoming presidential election, and he resented State Department predictions that partition would alienate Arabs. In fall 1947 Truman chose partition. Fighting between Arabs and Jews escalated, and millions of private dollars from Jewish Americans flowed to co-religionists in Palestine to buy weapons.

Truman tilted further toward the Zionists after a visit from Chaim Weizmann in March 1948. This Zionist leader (soon to be the first president of Israel) had once thought Truman "will never jeopardize his oil concessions for the sake of the Jews, although he may need them when the time of election arrives." For reasons of politics and Cold War strategy, Truman formally extended diplomatic recognition to the new Jewish state on May 14, 1948. Zionist sympathizers had persuaded Truman that Israel would "line up on the side of the United States a far abler force" than the Arabs, thereby bolstering the American position vis-à-vis the Soviet Union in the Middle East. Despite Secretary of State George Marshall's blunt warning that he "would vote against you" in the election if Truman recognized Israel, subsequent Israeli military victories over the armies of five Arab states prompted even the State Department to reassess Israel's importance as a potential ally in the containment of the Soviet Union. By war's end in early 1949, some 780,000 of 1,300,000 Arab residents had become refugees in Lebanon and Jordan, whereas Israel came to occupy 77 percent of Palestine.

Containment became the byword of the time, and George F. Kennan, director of the State Department's Policy Planning Staff, wrote the definitive statement. The July 1947 issue of the prestigious journal *Foreign Affairs* carried "The Sources of Soviet Conduct," written by a mysterious Mr. "X," soon revealed as Kennan. The United States must adopt a "policy of firm containment," he wrote, "designed to confront the Russians with unalterable counterforce, at every point where they show signs of encroaching upon the interests of a peaceful and stable world." Such pressure might force the "mellowing" of Soviet policy. Kennan sketched a picture of an aggressive, uncompromising Soviet Union driven by ideology, moving "inexorably along a prescribed path, like a persistent toy automobile wound up and headed in a given direction, stopping only when it meets some unanswerable force." Even though Kennan actually opposed military means to implement containment, his muscular language suggested otherwise.

One of Kennan's most vocal critics, the journalist Walter Lippmann called containment a "strategic monstrosity" because it did not distinguish vital from peripheral areas. Lippmann prophetically observed that the "policy can be implemented only by recruiting, subsidizing and supporting a heterogeneous array of satellites, clients, dependents and puppets." Instead, he proposed the removal of all foreign troops from Europe to ease tension. Denying that Soviet forces stood poised to attack Western Europe, Lippmann sadly concluded that Truman and Mr. "X" had abandoned their essential responsibility—diplomacy. "For a diplomat to think that rival and unfriendly powers cannot be brought to a settlement is to forget what diplomacy is about."

George F. Kennan (1904–2005). Graduate of Princeton, Pulitzer Prize–winning historian, career diplomat, and recognized expert on Soviet affairs, Kennan was Mr. "X" in 1947 when he articulated the containment doctrine. This brilliant man served Ambassador Harriman in Moscow and then headed the State Department's Policy Planning Staff (1947–1949). Later he became ambassador to Russia (1952) and Yugoslavia (1961–1963). In the 1970s and 1980s he emerged as a leading critic of the nuclear arms race. (Getty Images)

On Its Feet and Off Our Backs: The Marshall Plan, NATO, and the Division of Europe

V. M. Molotov (1890–1986). Popularly known as "stone ass," the Soviet foreign minister (1939–1949; 1952–1956), a tough-minded negotiator, cleared most decisions with Stalin. When he became angry, a bump appeared on his forehead, alerting adversaries of trouble. In his memoirs Molotov stressed *realpolitik:* "What we did . . . we did superbly, we strengthened the Soviet state. That was my chief task. My task as minister of foreign affairs was to see to it that we weren't cheated." (*The Reporter,* 1956. Copyright 1956 by The Reporter Magazine Co.)

In 1947–1948, under the banner of containment, U.S. goals for Western Europe crystallized: economic reconstruction and hunger relief, linkage of Germany's western zones with a Western European economic system, reinvigorated trade with the United States, prevention of leftist political gains, ouster of communists in Italy and France, settlement of colonial disputes, blockage of neutralist tendencies, and building military allies. By 1947 the United States had already spent $9 billion in the region. Despite assistance through the United Nations Relief and Rehabilitation Administration (UNRRA), the World Bank, and the International Monetary Fund, plus the loan to Britain and expenditures for the military occupation of Germany, Europe's continued economic prostration left it vulnerable to communist exploitation. A multibillion-dollar deficit also meant that Europeans could not buy American products unless they received dollars from the United States.

On June 5, 1947, at Harvard University, Secretary of State George C. Marshall called for a comprehensive, coordinated program to put Europe back on its feet. A halting orator, Marshall delivered his monumental message in only 1,500 words. Europe needed help to overcome "economic, social and political deterioration of a very grave character." He urged the European nations to initiate a collective plan. British foreign secretary Ernest Bevin and French foreign minister Georges Bidault conferred and soon accepted Marshall's proposal, ultimately shaping it according to American specifications. They reluctantly invited Soviet foreign minister V. M. Molotov to join them for a meeting in Paris in June.

Smelling a capitalist trap, Molotov suggested loosely structured arrangements designed to protect national sovereignties. Bevin and Bidault, knowing that Washington insisted on an integrated effort, rejected national shopping lists. Molotov then abruptly left Paris. Believing that aid would "raise the Iron Curtain," Truman had never wanted Soviet participation in the European Recovery Program (ERP), as the Marshall Plan became known. Moscow rejected the Marshall Plan because Eastern Europe was expected to ship raw materials to industrial Western Europe, thereby becoming "a tool against the USSR," because a large influx of dollars into the Soviet sphere of influence would directly challenge Soviet interests, and because the plan sought to revive West Germany. In any case, Congress would probably have voted against a recovery program that included the Soviet Union and its neighbors. In response, Stalin demanded "total conformity" from his allies, divided the world into "two camps," and instituted a feeble Molotov Plan for Eastern Europe.

Congress in March 1948 passed the Economic Cooperation Act. The coup in Czechoslovakia, elections in Italy, and the growing crisis over Germany, together with a bellicose Truman speech to a joint session of Congress, garnered the Marshall Plan a vote of 69 to 17 in the Senate and 329 to 74 in the House. Congress approved $4 billion for the program's first year. Before ending in December 1951, the Economic Cooperation Administration had sent $12.4 billion into the needy European economy.

The Marshall Plan sparked impressive Western European industrial production and investment and started the region toward self-sustaining economic growth. The ERP, noted the administrator Paul Hoffman, "got Europe on its feet and off our backs." It stimulated the U.S. economy by requiring recipients to spend some aid in the United States on American goods; in this way, the profitable flow of American exports to traditional European markets continued. The program accelerated the anti-Communist shift of the European trade union movement, and it won votes for political parties that backed the generous U.S. project.

The Marshall Plan had shortcomings, too. Europe became dependent on American aid, less able to make its own choices. The French complained about "Coca-colonization." Some American money funded European resistance to colonial wars. The program bypassed the United Nations and the Economic Commission for Europe, where it might have operated with less divisiveness. The ERP encouraged restrictions on East–West trade and helped revive West Germany, thereby arousing Moscow's fears of its nemesis. In 1951 the Economic Cooperation Administration merged into the Mutual Security Administration, with 80 percent of American aid to Western Europe becoming military in nature.

Believing the Soviets capable of overrunning Western Europe in six months, the Pentagon sought greater rearmament without knowing that "the Soviet army in Germany was configured for defensive operations." In July 1947, Congress passed the National Security Act, which streamlined the military establishment. The act created the Department of Defense, the National Security Council (NSC) to advise the president, and the Central Intelligence Agency (CIA) to gather and collate information. The CIA's Office of Policy Coordination soon recruited ex-Nazis and other agents for subversive activities in Eastern Europe. In Europe in March 1948, Britain, France, and the three Benelux nations, with U.S. encouragement, signed the Brussels Treaty for collective defense. In June the Senate passed (64 to 4) Vandenberg's resolution applauding that effort and suggesting American participation.

The United States also implemented the Fulbright Program in 1948. The brainchild two years earlier of Senator J. William Fulbright, Democrat of Arkansas and a former Rhodes scholar, this example of "public diplomacy" sought to breach cultural barriers and inculcate a favorable image of the United States among foreign peoples. The Fulbright Program sponsored educational exchanges; faculty and students went abroad to teach and study, and their counterparts from other countries came to the United States. By 1953 elites in twenty-eight nations participated in the program in Europe, Asia, and the Middle East. In some countries, former Fulbrighters achieved political prominence and helped keep their governments friendly to Washington. To combat anti-American propaganda in what President Truman described as a "great campaign of truth," some American and European intellectuals organized the Congress of Cultural Freedom in 1950; the CIA secretly subsidized this effort to promote America in Europe.

The United States also endorsed in 1948 the World Health Organization (WHO), a specialized United Nations agency that fulfilled a "two-pronged strategy of education and disease-fighting." Targeting borderless epidemic diseases such as malaria, tuberculosis, and syphilis, with a "sense of international fellowship," WHO physicians blanketed the earth to promote prevention and administer vaccines. Washington has traditionally supplied the largest share of WHO's budget.

Truman summarized American foreign policy in his inaugural address of January 20, 1949, by listing four central points. First, he endorsed the United Nations. Second, he applauded the European Recovery Program. Third, he announced that the United States was planning a North Atlantic defense pact. And fourth, "we must embark on a bold new program" of technical assistance for "underdeveloped areas," a reference to the Point Four Program, launched in 1950. Under Point Four, countries such as Afghanistan received millions in Export-Import Bank loans for hydroelectric dams and other modernization projects to create "an environment in which societies which directly or indirectly menace ours will not evolve."

On April 4, 1949, the United States, Canada, and ten European countries signed the North Atlantic Treaty in Washington. Article 5 provided "that an armed attack against one or more . . . shall be considered an attack against them all." Senator Robert Taft of Ohio saw NATO as a threat to the Soviet Union that would eventually force the United States to send military aid to Europe and spur an arms race; the president could commit American troops almost at will without constitutional restraint. Some dissenters questioned the precise nature of the Soviet threat: Was it military, political, or ideological? After all, no Soviet military attack seemed imminent. Others thought that the United States was overextending itself. The Truman administration welcomed NATO as much for political as for military purposes. A popular saying explained that NATO kept the Soviets out, the Americans in, and the Germans down. In other words, the alliance permitted the United States to rearm West Germany while reassuring Europeans that Germany would be controlled by a multinational organization. U.S. officials also believed that Western Europe needed a "general stiffening of morale" through the creation of NATO, not only to deter the Soviets, but also to stimulate capital investment and encourage an energetic reconstruction effort. Depicting new allies as insecure members of the same family, Kennan recommended that "we must exhibit more confidence in them than we may actually feel—string them along a little."

On July 21, 1949, the Senate approved the NATO Treaty by an 82 to 13 margin. Two days later, Truman also sent the Mutual Defense Assistance Bill to Congress requesting more than a billion dollars for European military aid. Containment had taken a distinct turn to military means, and the stakes became bigger. After the Soviets exploded an atomic device in August 1949, Truman ordered development of a thermonuclear or hydrogen "superbomb." By mid-1950 the U.S. arsenal already included some 300 atomic bombs and more than 260 aircraft that could drop them on Soviet targets. The Soviets responded to NATO with the Warsaw Pact in 1955, the same year that they detonated their first hydrogen bomb, three years after the U.S. H-bomb.

In January 1950, Truman ordered a comprehensive review of U.S. military and foreign policy. Eventually tagged National Security Council Paper Number 68 (NSC-68), the April report predicted prolonged global tension, Soviet military expansion, and relentless communist aggression. Washington had to persuade the public to support larger defense budgets and higher taxes. Paul Nitze, who replaced

Kennan as head of the Policy Planning Staff, wrote most of NSC-68, and he glossed over complexities. The document treated communism as a monolith. It spoke of the "free world," overlooking the many undemocratic nations allied with the United States. It postulated that communism orchestrated the world's troubles, ignoring the indigenous origins of anticolonial rebellions. It made sweeping assumptions about Soviet motives and capabilities without evidence. The report, in short, exaggerated the "threat," as Washington prepared to become the world's policeman. But how to convince Americans to support the report's prescriptions? "We were sweating over it, and then—with regard to NSC-68—thank God Korea came along," recalled an aide to Secretary of State Dean Acheson. Shortly thereafter Truman ordered NSC-68's implementation.

Stalin initially responded to NATO with disdain. "America, though it screams war, is actually afraid of war," he told Mao Zedong in December 1949. Yet, as the two sides consolidated their respective spheres, Moscow appealed in spring 1950 for a dialogue to reduce tensions. Secretary Dean Acheson ridiculed the Soviet "Trojan dove," vowing to contest the Soviets by building U.S. "situations of strength" throughout the world. As Lippmann had predicted, diplomacy became a victim of the Cold War.

Asian Allies: Restoring Japan and Backing Jiang in China

Asia experienced a major reconfiguration after World War II. In Indochina, Burma, and Indonesia the old imperial system crumbled. The colonial powers looked to the United States to help them salvage what they could. Japan suffered defeat and occupation. Korea, formerly dominated by Japan, was divided along the thirty-eighth parallel by the Soviet Union and the United States. Civil war loomed in China.

The Pacific Ocean was becoming an "Anglo-Saxon lake." If the Soviets ran some of the Eastern European countries, the Supreme Commander for the Allied Powers, General Douglas MacArthur, ran Japan. Unlike Germany, Japan had no zones. Despite a Far Eastern Advisory Commission with Soviet membership, MacArthur treated Stalin's representative like "a mere piece of furniture." The United States also assumed control over Micronesia (the Marianas, Marshalls, and Carolines), Okinawa, Iwo Jima, and more than a hundred other Pacific outposts. As if to demonstrate the point, on July 7, 1946, the United States tested an atomic bomb on the Marshall Island of Bikini.

The first two years of occupation brought *demokurashii* to Japan: a new constitution, war crimes trials, women's rights, dismantling of feudal landownership, even American censorship of Japanese films so as to depict Emperor Hirohito not as a god but as a constitutional monarch. Millions learned conversational English from the radio program "Come, Come English," and "Tokyo Boogie-Woogie" became the hit song of 1948. Japan seemed to bury its militarism as a more pacifist culture emerged. Then U.S. officials reversed course as the Cold War escalated. Americans now needed a "stable Japan, integrated into the Pacific, friendly to the U.S." During 1947–1950, labor unions were restricted, production controls in war-related

General Douglas MacArthur (1880–1964) and Emperor Hirohito (1901–1989). This famous photograph of the first meeting of the Japanese emperor and the American supreme commander on September 27, 1945, has been called the "wedding photo" because, as Yoshikuni Igarashi points out in *Bodies of Memory* (2000), it suggests the "sexualized power relations" between a conquering United States and a submissive Japan. The meeting provided "the necessary ingredients for a melodrama—humiliation and the heroic acceptance of humiliation" by Hirohito. (Courtesy of the General Douglas MacArthur Foundation)

industries relaxed, the antitrust program suspended, communists barred from government and university positions, and former Japanese leaders reinstated. In the end, as the historian John W. Dower has noted, "the ideals of peace and democracy took root in Japan—not as a borrowed ideology or imposed vision, but as a lived experience and a seized opportunity."

The restoration of Japan brought international ramifications. The Chinese communists feared a devilish scheme to rebuild Japan for aggression against China. Japanese recovery, U.S. officials argued in early 1950, also required the development of Asian markets for Japanese products and thus the application of the containment doctrine to undercut communists. Moscow suspiciously eyed U.S. expansion in Asia and protested separate peace negotiations with Japan. In September 1951, the United States and fifty other nations signed a peace treaty that restored Japanese sovereignty, gave the United States a base on Okinawa, and permitted the retention of foreign troops in Japan. Stalin refused to sign. A bilateral security pact also permitted U.S. troops and planes on Japanese soil. From Pearl Harbor, a merciless war, and the atomic blasts to a peaceful occupation and Japanese-American cooperation— how to explain the dramatic shift? Continued demonic images and punishment no longer served the interests of either party. Americans sought a Cold War ally, and the Japanese sought a helping hand. The same stereotypes that spawned racial hatred could facilitate cooperation. For example, Americans considered the Japanese, in MacArthur's words, "like a boy of twelve" and able to become "good pupils" under U.S. tutelage. And the Japanese philosophy of "proper place" meant that the Japanese could become "good losers" who win by diplomacy after "losing in war."

Americans wanted a peaceful China within their sphere of influence too. For decades they had preached the Open Door, dreamed of vast Chinese markets and Christian converts, and considered China a special friend. A recovering Japan also needed Asian markets. The Chinese communists had other ideas, challenging the American-backed regime of Jiang Jieshi. During 1945–1949, the United States became a counterrevolutionary force in a revolutionary country.

American postwar goals sought a united noncommunist country under Jiang as a U.S. ally. At the end of the war, American forces transported Jiang's soldiers to Manchuria in a race to beat Mao Zedong's communists there. As he promised at Yalta, Stalin signed a treaty of friendship with Jiang's regime in August 1945 to deter a Japan expected to "restore her might in 20, 30 years." He pressed Mao to cooperate with Jiang. Thinking Mao too "Titoist," Stalin preferred a cooperative China that would pose no threat along the 4,150 miles of the Sino-Soviet border. U.S. Foreign Service officers reported from China that relations between Moscow and Mao remained fractious and that the communists would probably defeat Jiang without much help from Soviet troops in Manchuria.

Swashbuckling Ambassador Patrick J. Hurley managed to bring Mao and Jiang together for talks in fall 1945, but Jiang refused to make concessions, confident of American backing. The talks failed. In November, Hurley, with his typical blast-furnace approach, resigned and charged that pro-communist diplomats were plotting in favor of "Mouse Dung" and "Joe N. Lie" (as he called Mao and Zhou Enlai). Hurley's attack on the professional diplomats provided scapegoats for the American frustration over China. The "China experts" had not preferred Mao; they had simply reported that Jiang was corrupt, reactionary, and unlikely to gain the allegiance of the Chinese people, and that the communists would thus triumph. Paying for their accuracy, the China hands eventually were forced from the State Department under pressure from red-baiting Senator Joseph McCarthy.

After the Hurley debacle, in December 1945, Truman sent the "Marshall Mission" to China. Headed by the highly respected General George C. Marshall, it sought to unite the factions under a noncommunist government. The communists, seeing coalition government as a nonviolent route to power, accepted Marshall's cease-fire in January 1946. By May 1946, after Soviet forces had pulled out, 90 percent of Manchuria rested in communist hands. Jiang's decision to storm into Manchuria to challenge Mao doomed the cease-fire. Marshall and the 1,000 U.S. military and naval personnel could not restrain the overconfident generalissimo. "We were taken in," said Mao of U.S. mediation efforts; "We won't be cheated again." A chagrined Marshall returned to Washington in January 1947 to become secretary of state.

Still hopeful of preventing a communist victory, Truman dispatched the "Wedemeyer Mission" to China in July 1947. General Albert C. Wedemeyer criticized the disarray of the Nationalists but concluded that China, like Greece, needed an aid program to curb the communist menace. Secretary Marshall did release undelivered Lend-Lease goods to Jiang, and sent more arms, advisers, and ammunition that autumn. In part to answer critics who wondered why Greece but not China should be saved from communism, the White House asked Congress in early 1948 for $570 million in China aid. China obtained $400 million in April.

Despite $3 billion in aid to Jiang since V-J Day, Washington failed to stop Mao's ascent. Jiang let inflation run rampant, neglected tax and land reforms, launched risky military expeditions, tolerated corruption, and rejected negotiations. Dispirited soldiers defected, as U.S. military equipment fell into communist hands; ironically, in this roundabout way, Mao's troops got more aid from America than from the Soviet Union. "We picked a bad horse," the president lamented.

The People's Republic of China and U.S. Nonrecognition

In June 1949, Mao Zedong stated that he was leaning to the side of socialism (the Soviet Union) against that "one great imperialist power" (the United States). For many Americans, Mao's strident address simply confirmed Moscow's creation of another puppet state. Despite "limited" Soviet military aid ("not even a fart," Mao complained), Americans preferred Acheson's words, in the *China White Paper* of August 1949, that "the Communist regime serves not [Chinese] interests but those of Soviet Russia." The *White Paper* documents showed little the United States could have done because Jiang himself would do so little. In January 1949 he sent China's gold supplies to the island of Formosa (Taiwan); in December, his Nationalist government followed. Mao's People's Republic formally assumed power in October.

Critics charged that "China had been sold down the Yangtze" by the Democrats. Senator Styles Bridges and Representative Walter Judd headed an informal and influential "China Lobby," which for years had advocated a major U.S. intervention in the Chinese civil war. They asked: If Truman sought to contain communism without geographical limit, as stated in the Truman Doctrine, why no intervention in China? Truman officials answered that China was too large, a land war in Asia unthinkable, Jiang unmanageable, and the monetary costs prohibitive. Jiang's mishandling of U.S. funds confirmed Truman's private view of the Guomindang as "grafters and crooks."

After Mao's victory, Washington refused to recognize the People's Republic of China. Behind the nonrecognition policy lay mounting Sino-American animosities. In June 1949 when communist leaders asked to meet American ambassador J. Leighton Stuart, Truman vetoed contact. He resented bombastic communist speeches that reminded Americans of their imperialist past, including military participation in the Boxer Rebellion and naval gunboat patrols on Chinese rivers in the 1920s and 1930s. Confiscating American property, the Chinese communists kept the U.S. consul general at Mukden under house arrest for two years before expelling him as a spy in October 1949.

From December 1949 through February 1950, in Moscow, Mao negotiated a treaty of friendship and alliance. Fearful of a revived Japan and of the expanded U.S. presence in Asia, Mao needed an ally. In spite of frosty personal relations with Stalin, Mao eventually obtained an alliance obligating both parties to come to each other's assistance if attacked by a third party. U.S. observers played down both the meager foreign aid that Moscow promised and Sino-Soviet differences over Mongolia and Manchuria. Truman publicly stressed Sino-Soviet ideological affinity and denounced the treaty as the Soviet conquest of China. The "Chi Commies" did not merit U.S. diplomatic recognition. As Assistant Secretary of State Dean Rusk bluntly put it in early 1951: "The Peiping regime may be a colonial Russian government— a Slavic Manchukuo on a larger scale. It is not the Government of China. It does not pass the first test. It is not Chinese."

A Cold War Culture Emerges

"We were heirs to a smiling and victorious confidence," noted a U.S. writer who recalled the end of World War II. Liberated countries usually welcomed the American presence. In addition to soldiers and dollars, Washington exported jazz and baseball, "blue jeans and T-shirts, Coca-Cola and chewing gum, U.S. comics and movie stars." "The American occupation [in Austria] cannot be complete without Mickey Mouse and Donald Duck," an official cabled Washington in 1945. Japanese radio called a child fathered in 1946 by a U.S. serviceman a "rainbow across the Pacific," the first of some 200,000 Japanese-American children born during the occupation, with many destined to endure racial discrimination from both cultures. The roughly 94,000 offspring of GIs in Germany by 1949 prompted a German joke that in the event of another war, Americans would not need to "send any troops—just the uniforms." Because Western Europeans had "invited" the United States to create an empire and include them within it, some scholars have argued, Washington pursued its economic, ideological, and strategic goals all the more zealously.

The Soviet threat seemed to justify Washington's expansive behavior. Americans came to believe that the Soviet Union had launched a crusade to communize the world. Appearances fed such a notion. Austere, intransigent, and ruthless, Stalin became in American eyes an obstructionist. Soviet diplomatic machinations and strong-arm rule in Eastern Europe alarmed Washington, and simple-minded communist propaganda offended. With threats more common than compromises, the rude Soviet diplomatic style caused Western diplomats to respond in the same "crabbed and rancorous" manner. In the turmoil of the immediate postwar years, Americans exaggerated the Soviet/communist threat, imagining an omnipresent force. Americans made the communist adversary into something it was not, claiming for it a strength it did not possess, blaming it for trouble it did not start, and identifying a monolith that did not exist. True, the tough-talking Soviets eventually turned Eastern Europe into client states and probed in Berlin, but right after World War II the Soviets acted cautiously because they lacked a long-range air force, air defenses, the atomic bomb, and a surface fleet. Moscow actually snubbed independent communists such as Tito and Mao and could not control communists in Western Europe.

Americans nonetheless came to believe that Moscow ignited, fueled, and exploited unrest around the world, including revolutions. Most upheaval actually sprang from indigenous sources—colonial, tribal, ethnic, religious, cultural, economic. Erecting a global wall against communism, the United States supported imperialist allies such as France, which attempted to restore its colonial power in Vietnam against a popular nationalist movement. Believing that the Soviet Union masterminded revolutions, Washington sniffed international conspiracy and refused to recognize the People's Republic of China, hardly a Soviet puppet. Dependent on imports of uranium from South Africa to sustain a Cold War nuclear strategy and economy, the Truman administration backed white, anticommunist regimes that suppressed black nationalism, acting "as a reluctant uncle—or godparent—at the baptism of apartheid."

Even in Latin America, indirect U.S. intervention to oust communists from the Costa Rican government in 1948 "mirrored the hardening" of Washington's Cold War policies elsewhere. In 1945–1946 Washington had given tacit support for democratic interventions by exile groups against Caribbean dictatorships, but by the end of the decade it "placed a premium on stability out of concern that Communists might exploit situations of unrest." Thus did Panama receive Point Four assistance in 1950 to combat "Communist-influenced subversive elements," and military aid flowed to the Perón regime in Argentina after 1947 because of Cold War fears.

The Cold War mentality framed discourse in a "system of symbolic representation that defined America's national identity by reference to the un-American 'other,' usually the Soviet Union." Federally funded behavioral scientists used statistical models that always posited the Soviets as a "predatory expansionist power" and the United States always as a "defensive status quo power." The expansive term "national security" took on an almost sacred aura, justifying huge military budgets that starved the infrastructure, the suspension of diplomacy in favor of confrontation, interventions far distant from the United States, a secrecy that undermined constitutional procedures, and actions Americans condemned others for—manipulating foreign governments, assassinating political foes abroad, and disseminating false information ("disinformation"). Because the Soviets acted similarly, they share responsibility for the extremes of the long Cold War.

"Uncle Sam's World Wide Umbrella." The United States undertook new global responsibilities after World War II. The depiction of smaller countries as children and Uncle Sam as the adult protector suggests a favorite American image/metaphor of family in which difficult allies were seen as naive children in need of tutelage and nurturing from the altruistic United States. (*The Reporter,* 1950. Copyright 1950 by Fortnightly Publishing Co., Inc.)

American diplomats in the early Cold War pursued a self-conscious, expansionist, often unilateral foreign policy. In a world ravaged by war, business and government officials cooperated to expand U.S. foreign trade. By 1947 the United States accounted for one-third of the world's exports. Americans exploited Middle Eastern oil and tapped the raw materials of the Third World, importing manganese ore from Brazil and India, for example. Open Door pronouncements helped spur this trade and facilitate the investment of $12 billion abroad by 1950. Stalin thought the "Open Door policy as dangerous to a nation as foreign military invasion."

The containment doctrine became commanding dogma. "Like medieval theologians," Senator Fulbright noted, "we had a philosophy that explained everything to us in advance, and everything that did not fit could be readily identified as a fraud or a lie or an illusion." Americans henceforth applied the historical lessons of the 1940s, failing to define precisely the "threat." Whereas Washington explained its mission as containment, Moscow charged "strangulation."

Cold War competition also reshaped political priorities at home. The rhetoric of defending freedom abroad exposed America's "Achilles heel" of institutionalized racism. With the United Nations calling racial discrimination a "burning question" of "immense importance," the President's Committee on Civil Rights warned that "the treatment which our Negroes receive" plays "into the hands of the Communist propagandists." In a brilliant stroke, he appointed Eleanor Roosevelt to the United Nations, where she exhibited "the will, the clout, and the skill" to push through the UN Declaration on Human Rights, adopted in 1948. Yet too often Truman's administration used scare tactics ("clearer than truth," as Acheson put it) to get its way. Most foreign policy debates centered on how much to spend, not whether to spend. Presidential authority expanded accordingly. Bipartisanship also allowed Truman to depict any critic as "a son-of-a-bitch and not a true patriot." If people "will swallow that," Acheson observed, "then you're off to the races."

People swallowed it. Debate became shallow. Tolerance of dissenting views and the fearless inquiry so essential to democracy deteriorated during the early Cold War. Unprincipled demagogues exploited public anxiety about national security, charging that communist conspiracies wormed through official Washington. During the 1948 campaign, the president himself practiced the "red-baiting" so common to Cold War politics when he deliberately linked Progressive party candidate Henry A. Wallace, a dissenter from the "get-tough" policy, to the communists. Three years before demagogic Senator Joseph McCarthy charged government officials with treason, the Truman administration itself instituted a federal employee loyalty program to identify and ferret out suspected subversives. By not clearly distinguishing dissent from subversion, Truman opened the door for McCarthyism.

As the Cold War grew more perilous, so too did the ominous presence of the atomic bomb. Military estimates projected that growing Soviet stockpiles of "10, 50, 100" atomic bombs could devastate American cities and kill tens of millions by 1953. Government officials, magazine editors, strategic analysts, scientists, and fiction writers alike, again and again, issued doomsday forecasts, sketching pictures of a radioactive global wasteland if nuclear weapons were not controlled. "The best way to be alive when an atomic bomb goes off in your neighborhood is not to be there," a civil defense official disingenuously suggested. In late 1949, after the Soviet atomic success, the *Bulletin of the Atomic Scientists* moved the hands of its "doomsday clock" to three minutes before midnight. A few months after the United States exploded the first hydrogen bomb in 1953, the hands moved to two minutes before midnight.

FURTHER READING FOR THE PERIOD 1945–1950

Some works cited in Chapter 6 cover particular leaders and the transition from war to peace.

For general studies of the Cold War era relevant to this chapter and others that follow, see S. J. Ball, *The Cold War* (1998); H. W. Brands, *The Devil We Knew* (1993); Robert W. Cherny et al., *American Labor and the Cold War* (2004); John Lewis Gaddis, *We Now Know* (1997); Allen Hunter, ed., *Rethinking the Cold War* (1998); Robert David Johnson, *Congress and the Cold War* (2006); Robert H. Johnson, *Improbable Dangers* (1994); Walter LaFeber, *America, Russia, and the Cold War* (2001); Klaus Larres and Ann Lane, eds., *The Cold War* (2001); Deborah W. Larson, *Anatomy of Mistrust* (1997); David Leebaert, *The Fifty-Year Wound* (2002); Stuart W. Leslie, *The Cold War and American Science* (1994); Ralph Levering, *The Cold War* (1994); Thomas J. McCormick, *America's Half Century* (1994); Robert J. McMahon, *The Cold War* (2003); Martin Medhurst and H. W. Brands, eds., *Critical Reflections on the Cold War* (2001); David S. Painter, *The Cold War* (1999); Thomas G. Paterson, *Meeting the Communist Threat* (1988) and *On Every Front* (1992); James T. Patterson, *Grand Expectations* (1996); David Reynolds, *One World Divisible* (2000); Michael S. Sherry, *In the Shadow of War* (1995); and Marc Trachtenberg, ed., *Between Empire and Alliance* (2003).

U.S. leaders in the early Cold War period are studied in Rudy Abrahamson, *Spanning the Century* (1992) (Harriman); Kai Bird and Martin Sherwin, *American Prometheus* (2005) (J. Robert Oppenheimer); Allida Black, *Casting Her Own Shadow* (1995) (Eleanor Roosevelt); Douglas Brinkley, ed., *Dean Acheson and the Making of U.S. Foreign Policy* (1993); David Callahan, *Dangerous Capabilities* (1990) (Nitze); James Chace, *Acheson* (1998); John C. Culver and John Hyde, *American Dreamer* (2000) (Henry Wallace); Irwin F. Gellman, *The Contender* (1999) (Nixon); Mary Ann Glendon, *A World Made New* (2001) (Eleanor Roosevelt); James G. Hershberg, *James B. Conant and the Birth of the Nuclear Age* (1993); Townsend Hoopes and Douglas Brinkley, *Driven Patriot* (1992) (Forrestal); Walter Isaacson and Evan Thomas, *The Wise Men* (1986); Peter C. Kent, *The Lonely Cold War of Pope Pius XII* (2002); Nelson D. Lenkford, *The Last American Aristocrat* (1996) (David Bruce); David McCullough, *Truman* (1992); John T. McNary, *Acheson and Empire* (2001); Arnold Offner, *Another Such Victory* (2002) (Truman); William E. Pemberton, *Harry S. Truman* (1989); Forrest C. Pogue, *George C. Marshall* (1963–1987); Darlene Rivas, *Missionary Capitalist* (2002) (Nelson Rockefeller); David Robertson, *Sly and Able* (1994) (Byrnes); T. Michael Ruddy, *The Cautious Diplomat* (1986) (Charles Bohlen); Ronald Steel, *Walter Lippmann and the American Century* (1980); Mark A. Stoler, *George C. Marshall* (1989); and J. Samuel Walker, *Henry A. Wallace and American Foreign Policy* (1976).

Many books, all with the main title *Stalin,* include and critique the Soviet leader's foreign policy: Robert Conquest (1991); Isaac Deutscher (1967); Walter Laqueur (1990); Robert H. McNeal (1988); Edward Radzinsky (1996); Robert Service (2005); and Dmitri Volkogonov (1991).

The ideas and career of George F. Kennan are explored in Walter Hixson, *George F. Kennan* (1990); David Mayers, *George Kennan and the Dilemmas of U.S. Foreign Policy* (1988); Wilson D. Miscamble, *George F. Kennan and the Making of American Foreign Policy* (1992); and Anders Stephanson, *George Kennan and the Art of Foreign Policy* (1989).

For the origins of the Cold War, see Kendrick A. Clements, ed., *James F. Byrnes and the Origins of the Cold War* (1982); John Lewis Gaddis, *The United States and the Origins of the Cold War* (1972); Francesca Gori and Silvio Pons, *The Soviet Union and Europe in the Cold War* (1996); James L. Gormly, *The Collapse of the Grand Alliance* (1987); Michael J. Hogan, *A Cross of Iron* (1998); John Ikenberry, *After Victory* (2001); Deborah W. Larson, *Origins of Containment* (1985); Melvyn P. Leffler, *A Preponderance of Power* (1992) and *The Specter of Communism* (1994); Ralph B. Levering et al., *Debating the Origins of the Cold War* (2002); Vojtech Mastny, *The Cold War and Soviet Insecurity* (1996); Robert Messer, *The End of an Alliance* (1982); Chester J. Pach, *Arming the Free World* (1991); David S. Painter and Melvyn P. Leffler, *Origins of the Cold War* (2005); Thomas G. Paterson, ed., *Cold War Critics* (1971); David Reynolds, ed., *The Origins of the Cold War in Europe* (1994); and Vladislav Zubok and Constantine Pleshakov, *Inside the Kremlin's Cold War* (1996).

For the early years of the United Nations Organization, see Robert C. Hilderbrand, *Dumbarton Oaks* (1990); Townsend Hoopes and Douglas Brinkley, *FDR and the Creation of the U.N.* (1997); and George Mazuzan, *Warren R. Austin at the U.N., 1946–1953* (1977).

The atomic bomb, nuclear questions, and their cultural impact are discussed in Gar Alperovitz, *The Decision to Use the Atomic Bomb* (1995); Kai Bird and Lawrence Lifschultz, eds., *Hiroshima Shadows* (1998); Paul Boyer, *By the Bomb's Early Light* (1986) and *Fallout* (1998); McGeorge Bundy, *Danger and Survival* (1990); Hugh Gusterson, *People of the Bomb* (2000); Tsuyoshi Hasegawa, *Racing the Enemy* (2005); Jonathan E. Helmreich, *Gathering Rare Ores* (1986); Margot A. Henriksen, *Dr. Strangelove's America* (1997); Gregg Herken, *The Winning Weapon* (1981); Michael J. Hogan, ed., *Hiroshima in History and Memory* (1996); David Holloway, *Stalin and the Bomb* (1994); Robert Jay Lifton and Greg Mitchell, *Hiroshima in America* (1995); M. Susan Lindee, *Suffering Made Real: American Science and the Survivors at Hiroshima* (1994); Robert J. Maddox, *Weapons for Victory* (2004); Robert P. Neuman, *Truman and the Hiroshima Cult* (1995); Robert S. Norris, *Racing for the Bomb* (2002) (Leslie Groves); Joe O'Donnell, *Japan 1945* (2005); Martin Sherwin, *A World Destroyed* (2003); Ronald Takaki, *Hiroshima* (1995); J. Samuel Walker, *Prompt and Utter Destruction* (2005); Samuel R. Williamson and Steven L. Rearden, *The Origins of U.S. Nuclear Strategy* (1993); Allan M. Winkler, *Life Under a Cloud* (1993); and Lawrence S. Wittner, *The Struggle Against the Bomb* (1993) (disarmament movement). The H-bomb is treated in Richard Rhodes, *Dark Sun* (1987), and Herbert F. York, *The Advisors* (1975).

Studies that focus on Eastern Europe and Finland include Debra J. Allen, *The Oder-Neisse Line* (2003); Michael M. Boll, *Cold War in the Balkans* (1984); James Jay Carafano, *Waltzing into the Cold War* (2002) (Austria); Jussi M. Hanhimäki, *Containing Coexistence* (1997) (Finland); Lorraine M. Lees, *Keeping Tito Afloat* (1997); Richard Lukacs, *Bitter Legacy* (1982) (Poland); Eric Roman, *Hungary and the Victor Powers* (1996); and Patricia Ward, *The Threat of Peace* (1979).

Anglo-American relations are discussed in Terry H. Anderson, *The United States, Great Britain, and the Cold War* (1981); Richard A. Best, Jr., *"Co-operation with Like-Minded Peoples"* (1986); Robin Edmonds, *Setting the Mould* (1987); Fraser J. Harbutt, *The Iron Curtain* (1986); Robert M. Hathaway, *Ambiguous Partnership* (1981); Michael H. Hopkins, *Oliver Franks and the Truman Administration* (2003), and *Cold War Britain, 1946–1961* (2003); John Kent, *British Imperial Strategy and the Origins of the Cold War* (1993); Arieh Kochavi, *Post-Holocaust Politics* (2002) (Britain and U.S.); Klaus Larres, *Churchill's Cold War* (2002); W. Roger Louis and Hedley Bull, eds., *The Special Relationship* (1986); Ritchie Overdale, *The English Speaking Alliance* (1985); Kenneth W. Thompson, *Winston Churchill's World View* (1983); and Randall B. Woods, *A Changing of the Guard* (1990).

The United States in the world economy and economic expansion are treated in Irvine H. Anderson, *Aramco, the United States, and Saudi Arabia* (1981); Alfred E. Eckes Jr., *A Search for Solvency* (1975) (Bretton Woods) and *The United States and the Global Struggle for Minerals* (1979); Diane Kunz, *Butter and Guns* (1997); Aaron D. Miller, *Search for Security* (1980) (Saudi Arabia's oil); David S. Painter, *Oil and the American Century* (1986); Stephen J. Randall, *United States Foreign Oil Policy, 1919–1984* (1985); and Thomas Zeiler, *Free Trade, Free World* (1999).

Cultural relations are specifically explored in Christian G. Appy, *Cold War Constructions* (2000); David Caute, *The Dancer Defects* (2005); Stanley Corkin, *Cowboys as Cold Warriors* (2004); Kyle Cuordileone, *Manhood and American Political Culture in the Cold War* (2005); Victor DeGrazia, *Irresistible Empire* (2005); Thomas Doherty, *Cold War Cool Medium* (2005) (television); Chistopher Endy, *Cold War Holidays* (2004); Benjamin O. Fordham, *Building the Cold War Consensus* (1998); John Fousek, *To Lead the Free World* (2000); Jessica C. E. Gienow-Hecht, *Transmission Impossible* (1999); Kyoko Hirano, *Mr. Smith Goes to Tokyo* (1992) (cinema in Japan); Christina Klein, *Cold War Orientalism* (2003); Michael Krenn, *Fall Out Shelters for the Human Spirit* (2005) (art); Peter J. Kuznick and James Gilbert, eds., *Rethinking Cold War Culture* (2001); Raina Mitter and Patrick Major, eds., *Across the Blocs* (2004); Richard Pells, *Not like Us* (1997); Uta G. Poiger, *Jazz, Rock, and Rebels* (2000); Frances Stoner Saunders, *The Cultural Cold War* (1999); William W. Savage, Jr., *Commies, Cowboys, and Jungle Queens* (1998); and Reinhold Wagnleitner, *Coca-Colonization and the Cold War* (1994) (Austria).

For Western European issues, including economic reconstruction, Austria, and the Marshall Plan, see John Bledsoe Bonds, *Bipartisan Strategy* (2002); Anthony Carew, *Labour Under the Marshall Plan* (1987); Jill

Edwards, *Anglo-American Relations and the Franco Question, 1945–1955* (1999); David W. Ellwood, *Rebuilding Europe* (1992); Chiarello Esposito, *America's Feeble Weapon* (1994) (Marshall Plan); Haim Genizi, *America's Fair Share* (1993) (displaced persons); John L. Harper, *America and the Reconstruction of Italy* (1986) and *American Visions of Europe* (1994); William I. Hitchcock, *France Restored* (2001); Michael J. Hogan, *The Marshall Plan* (1987); John Killick, *The United States and European Integration, 1945–1960* (1998); Deborah Kisatsky, *The United States and the European Right, 1945–1955* (2005); James E. Miller, *The United States and Italy* (1986); Alan S. Milward, *The Reconstruction of Western Europe, 1945–51* (1984); Thomas G. Paterson, *Soviet-American Confrontation* (1973); Sallie Pisani, *The CIA and the Marshall Plan* (1991); Robert A. Pollard, *Economic Security and the Origins of the Cold War* (1985); Mark Trachtenberg, *A Constructed Peace* (1999); Irwin M. Wall, *The United States and the Making of Postwar France* (1991); and Imanuel Wexler, *The Marshall Plan Revisited* (1983).

For Germany, see Tom Bower, *The Paperclip Conspiracy* (1988); Jeffrey M. Diefendorf et al., eds., *American Policy and the Reconstruction of West Germany* (1993); Carolyn Eisenberg, *Drawing the Line* (1996); Petra Goedda, *GIs and Germans* (2003); Maria Hohn, *GIs and Frauleins* (2002); Bruce Kuklick, *American Policy and the Division of Germany* (1972); James McAllister, *No Exit: America and the German Problem, 1943–1954* (2002); David Monod, *Settling Scores* (2005); Norman Naimark, *The Russians in Germany* (1995); Thomas Parrish, *Berlin in the Balance, 1945–1949* (1998); Thomas A. Schwartz, *America's Germany* (1991); Avi Shlaim, *The United States and the Berlin Blockade, 1948–1949* (1983); Christopher Simpson, *Blowback* (1988) (recruitment of Nazis); and John Willoughby, *Remaking the Conquering Heroes* (2001).

For the Truman Doctrine and containment, consult G. M. Alexander, *The Prelude to the Truman Doctrine* (1984); John Lewis Gaddis, *Strategies of Containment* (1981); John O. Iatrides, ed., *Greece at the Crossroads* (1995); Judith S. Jeffery, *Ambiguous Commitments and Uncertain Policies* (1999); Howard Jones, *"A New Kind of War"* (1989); Jon V. Kofas, *Intervention and Underdevelopment* (1989) (Greece); Bruce R. Kuniholm, *The Origins of the Cold War in the Near East* (1980); and Lawrence S. Wittner, *American Intervention in Greece, 1943–1949* (1982).

NATO and military questions are studied in Timothy P. Ireland, *Creating the Entangling Alliance* (1981); Lawrence S. Kaplan, *The United States and NATO* (1984), *NATO and the United States* (1988), and *The Long Entanglement: NATO's First Fifty Years* (1999); S. V. Papacosma et al., *NATO After Fifty Years* (2001); Steven L. Rearden, *History of the Office of the Secretary of Defense* (1984); Gustav Schmidt, *A History of NATO* (2001); Edward J. Sheehy, *The U.S. Navy, the Mediterranean, and the Cold War* (1992); E. Timothy Smith, *The United States, Italy, and NATO* (1991); and Joseph Smith, ed., *The Origins of NATO* (1990).

U.S. relations with Asia, including decolonization, are discussed in Kenton J. Clymer, *Quest for Freedom* (1995) (India); Nick Cullather, *Illusions of Influence* (1994) (Philippines); Hal M. Friedman, *Creating an American Lake* (2000); Marc S. Gallicchio, *The Cold War Begins in Asia* (1988); Gary Hess, *The United States' Emergence as a Southeast Asian Power, 1940–1950* (1987); Akira Iriye and Warren Cohen, eds., *American, Chinese, and Japanese Perspectives on Wartime Asia, 1931–1949* (1990); Robert J. McMahon, *Colonialism and Cold War* (1981) (Indonesia), *The Cold War on the Periphery* (1994) (India and Pakistan), and *The Limits of Empire* (1999) (Southeast Asia); Allan R. Millett, *Their War for Korea* (2005); Andrew Roadnight, *United States Policy Toward Indonesia in the Truman and Eisenhower Years* (2002); Andrew J. Rotter, *Comrades at Odds* (2000) (India); Anita I. Singh, *The Limits of British Influence* (1994) (South Asia); William Stueck, *The Road to Confrontation* (1981); John Swenson-Wright, *Unequal Allies?* (2005); and Nicholas Tarling, *Britain, Southeast Asia and the Onset of the Cold War, 1945–1950* (1998). For works on Vietnam and Indochina, see Chapter 9.

For Japan and the American occupation, see Ian Buruma, *Inventing Japan* (2003); William S. Borden, *The Pacific Alliance* (1984); Roger Buckley, *Occupation Diplomacy* (1982); John W. Dower, *Embracing Defeat* (1999); Robert D. Eldridge, *The Origins of the Bilateral Okinawa Problem* (2001); Richard B. Finn, *Winners in Peace* (1992); D. Clayton James, *The Years of MacArthur* (1985); Yukiko Koshiro, *Trans-Pacific Racisms and the U.S. Occupation of Japan* (1999); Walter LaFeber, *The Clash* (1997); Tim Maga, *Judgment at Tokyo* (1999); Michael S. Molasky, *The American Occupation of Japan and Okinawa* (1999); Nicholas E. Sarantakes, *Keystone* (2000) (Okinawa); and Michael Schaller, *The American Occupation of Japan* (1985).

For China and the recognition question, see Dorothy Borg and Waldo Heinrichs, eds., *Uncertain Years* (1980); Carolle J. Carter, *Mission to Yenan* (1997); Gordon Chang, *Friends and Enemies* (1990); Thomas J. Christensen, *Useful Adversaries* (1996); Sergei Goncharov, John Lewis, and Xue Litai, *Uncertain Partners* (1993); Harry Harding and Yuan Ming, eds., *Sino-American Relations, 1945–55* (1989); Michael H. Hunt, *The Genesis of*

Chinese Communist Foreign Policy (1996); T. Christoper Jesperson, *American Images of China* (1996); Chen Jian, *Mao's China and the Cold War* (2001); Ronald C. Keith, *The Diplomacy of Zhou Enlai* (1989); Paul G. Lauren, ed., *The China Hands' Legacy* (1987); Robert P. Newman, *Owen Lattimore and the "Loss" of China* (1992); Michael M. Sheng, *Battling Western Imperialism* (1998); William Stueck, *The Wedemeyer Mission* (1984); Nancy B. Tucker, *Patterns in the Dust* (1983) and *Taiwan, Hong Kong, and the United States* (1994); Odd Arne Westad, *Cold War and Revolution* (1993) and *Decisive Encounters: The Chinese Civil War* (2003); and Shu Guang Zhang, *Deterrence and Strategic Culture* (1992).

For the Middle East, Iran, and the new state of Israel, see books on oil cited above and Michael J. Cohen, *Palestine and the Great Powers* (1983) and *Truman and Israel* (1990); Leonard Dinnerstein, *America and the Survivors of the Holocaust* (1982); Bruce J. Evensen, *Truman, Palestine, and the Press* (1992); Louise L. Fawcett, *Iran and the Cold War* (1992) (1946 crisis); James F. Goode, *The United States and Iran, 1946–51* (1989); Peter L. Hahn, *The United States, Great Britain, and Egypt* (1991), *Caught in the Middle East* (2004), and *Crisis and Crossfire* (2005); Burton I. Kaufman, *The Arab Middle East and the United States* (1996); George Lenczowski, *American Presidents and the Middle East* (1989); Douglas Little, *American Orientalism* (2002); William Roger Louis, *The British Empire in the Middle East, 1945–1951* (1984); William Roger Louis and Robert W. Stookey, eds., *The End of the Palestine Mandate* (1986); Mark H. Lytle, *The Origins of Iranian-American Alliance, 1941–1953* (1987); John Quigley, *Palestine and Israel* (1990); and David Schoenbaum, *The United States and the State of Israel* (1993).

Relations with other Third World nations, including Latin America, are explored in Charles D. Ameringer, *The Caribbean Legion* (1996); Scott L. Bills, *Empire and Cold War* (1990) and *The Libyan Arena* (1995); Thomas Borstelmann, *Apartheid's Reluctant Uncle* (1993) (South Africa); Mary Ann Heiss and Peter L. Hahn, eds., *Empire and Revolution* (2001); Zachary Karabell, *Architects of Intervention* (1999); Michael L. Krenn, *The Chains of Interdependence* (1996) (Central America); Thomas M. Leonard, *The United States and Central America, 1944–1949* (1984); Kyle Longley, *The Sparrow and the Hawk* (1997) (Costa Rica); Stephen Schwartzberg, *Democracy and U.S. Policy Toward Latin America in the Truman Years* (2003); and Gaddis Smith, *The Last Years of the Monroe Doctrine* (1994).

For Canada-U.S. relations, see Greg Donaghy, ed., *Canada and the Early Cold War, 1943–1957* (1998); Joseph Jockel, *No Boundaries Upstairs* (1989); Denis Smith, *Diplomacy of Fear* (1988); and John H. Thompson and Stephen J. Randall, *Canada and the United States* (1998).

For espionage and the origins of the Central Intelligence Agency, see Richard Aldrich, *The Hidden Hand* (2001); Arthur B. Darling, *The Central Intelligence Agency* (1990); Peter Grose, *Operation Rollback* (2000); John Earl Haynes and Harvey Klehr, *Venona* (1999); Gregory Mitrovich, *Undermining the Kremlin* (2000); Katherine S. Olmsted, *Red Spy Queen* (2002) (Elizabeth Bentley); David F. Rudgers, *Creating the Secret State* (2000); Athan Theoharis, *Chasing Spies* (2002); Evan Thomas, *The Very Best Men* (1995); Thomas F. Troy, *Wild Bill and Intrepid* (1996); and Hugh Wilford, *The CIA, the British Left, and the Cold War* (2003).

For domestic politics, anticommunism, interest groups, and public opinion in the early Cold War period, see Carol Anderson, *Eyes Off the Prize* (2003); Bruce E. Field, *Harvest of Dissent: The National Farmers Union and the Early Cold War* (1998); Richard M. Fried, *Nightmare in Red* (1990) and *The Russians Are Coming! The Russians Are Coming!* (1998); Aaron L. Friedberg, *In the Shadow of the Garrison State* (2003); Robert Griffith and Athan Theoharis, eds., *The Specter* (1974); John E. Haynes, *Red Scare or Red Menace?* (1996); William Keller, *The Liberals and J. Edgar Hoover* (1989); Harvey Klehr and Ronald Radosh, *The Amerasia Spy Case* (1996); David F. Krugler, *The Voice of America and the Domestic Propaganda Battles, 1945–1953* (2000); Azza Salama Layton, *International Politics and Civil Rights in the United States, 1941–1960* (1999); Scott Lucas, *Freedom's War* (1999); William L. O'Neill, *A Better World: Stalinism and the American Intellectuals* (1983); Brenda G. Plummer, *Rising Wind* (1996) (African Americans) and *Window on Freedom* (2003); Ron Robin, *The Making of a Cold War Enemy* (2001); Jonathan Rosenberg, *How Far the Promised Land?* (2005) (civil rights); Katherine A. S. Sibley, *Red Spies in America* (2004); Timothy E. Smith, *Opposition Beyond the Water's Edge* (1999); and Penny von Eschen, *Race Against Empire* (1997) (African Americans).

See also Robert L. Beisner, ed., *Guide to American Foreign Relations Since 1600* (2003).

For comprehensive coverage of foreign-relations topics, see the articles in the four-volume *Encyclopedia of U.S. Foreign Relations* (1997), edited by Bruce W. Jentleson and Thomas G. Paterson.

CHAPTER 8

Global Watch: The Korean War and Eisenhower Foreign Relations, 1950–1961

✳ *The Decision to Intervene in the Korean War, 1950*

AT 4:00 A.M. that rainy Sunday morning of June 25, 1950, some 75,000 troops of the Democratic People's Republic of Korea (North Korea) bolted across the thirty-eighth parallel into South Korea. North Korean units "struck like a cobra" with armor and heavy artillery along a 150-mile front. As Soviet-made tanks rumbled forward, South Korean forces collapsed in a rout.

Around 10:00 p.m. the bad news reached Secretary of State Dean Acheson, resting at his Maryland farm. Acheson quickly convened an emergency session of the United Nations Security Council. The United States dominated that body, and the principle of collective security in the face of aggression seemed at issue. At 11:20 P.M. Acheson rang up President Harry S. Truman, at home in Independence, Missouri, and advised him to come to Washington the next day. State Department personnel worked through the night drafting a Security Council resolution that charged North Korea with a "breach of the peace." The Pentagon and State Department debated courses of action. Orders went out to evacuate Americans from Seoul. World War III, thought some officials, had started.

President Truman possessed "an appetite, too much of one, really, for unhesitating decision." He stood low in opinion polls at the time, in part because Senator Joseph McCarthy of Wisconsin charged Truman with "softness toward communism." Former State Department official Alger Hiss, to right-wing critics the ultimate "sell-out" spy, had been convicted of perjury in January, and China had "fallen" a few months before. Bold action now would disarm the president's critics. Truman pondered history and drew facile lessons from the past. "Communism was acting in Korea just as Hitler, Mussolini, and the Japanese had acted ten, fifteen, and twenty years earlier." No appeasement this time! Meanwhile, the Security Council passed the U.S. resolution condemning North Korea. Except for Yugoslavia's abstention, all

United Nations Leaflet in Korean War.   This leaflet, dropped by UN forces over North Korea, aimed to incite hostility in the Korean War among Chinese "volunteer" forces against their nation's leaders. The flyer shows a "Soviet advisor" manipulating the "Chinese Puppet" marionettes Liu Shaoqi, Mao Zedong, and Zhou Enlai. Such "psychological warfare," according to the scholar Ron Robin, was a "futuristic strategy for defeating the enemy by words" and images "rather than bullets." This propaganda piece reflected the widespread U.S. assumption that Joseph Stalin and his cohorts pulled the strings in China, North Korea, and other communist regimes. During the first eighteen months of the Korean War, U.S. aircraft dropped a billion leaflets on North Korean and Chinese forces. (Courtesy General Douglas MacArthur Foundation)

members present voted "yes." The Soviet delegation, which could have vetoed the measure, remained surprisingly absent, boycotting the U.N. over its refusal to seat China's new communist government.

A stern, short-tempered Truman deplaned in Washington and headed for a meeting with top officials. Nobody present doubted that the Soviet Union had engineered the attack, using its North Korean allies to probe for a soft spot in the American containment shield. The relationship between the Soviet Union and North Korea, one official remarked, was like "Walt Disney and Donald Duck." "If we let Korea down," Truman predicted, "the Soviet [*sic*] will keep right on going and swallow up one piece of Asia after another. . . . [Then] the Near East would collapse and no telling what would happen in Europe." Truman ordered General Douglas MacArthur in Japan to send military equipment to the South Koreans and to use U.S. war planes to attack the North Korean spearhead. He sent the Seventh Fleet into the waters between the Chinese mainland and Formosa to forestall conflict between the two Chinas.

Despite strong bipartisan support for Truman's decisions, some conservative Republicans indulged in McCarthyite recriminations. "The Korean debacle," Senator William E. Jenner of Indiana blustered, "reminds us that the same sell-out-to-

Stalin statesmen . . . are still in the saddle, riding herd on the American people." By Monday evening, North Korean forces neared Seoul. Truman learned about a downed North Korean plane, which he hoped "was not the last." Diplomats and military leaders believed that the United States' reputation stood at risk. To falter would forfeit world leadership, Truman officials claimed.

Truman ordered U.S. aircraft and warships into full-scale action below the thirty-eighth parallel; he declared Formosa (Taiwan) off limits to the mainland Chinese; and he dispatched military aid to Indochina and the Philippines. The president informed key legislators about his decision, but he did not request a congressional declaration of war. Senator Tom Connally of Texas, chair of the Foreign Relations Committee, reasoned: "If a burglar breaks into your house, you can shoot him without going down to the police station and getting permission." While Senator Robert A. Taft complained that the president had done "the right thing the wrong way," most Americans applauded Truman's response. The United Nations passed another U.S.-sponsored resolution urging members to aid South Korea, in essence endorsing actions the United States had already taken. Seoul nonetheless fell.

The continued North Korean push into the South sparked talk on June 28 and 29 of sending U.S. troops. Presidential supporters cited historical precedent: Jefferson had ordered action against the Barbary pirates and McKinley had sent troops into China during the Boxer Rebellion without prior congressional sanction. On the twenty-ninth, Truman ordered U.S. pilots to attack above the thirty-eighth parallel. On Friday, June 30, after visiting the war front, MacArthur asked Truman to send U.S. soldiers to Korea. The president gave the order amid reports of a North Korean surge southward into the Pusan perimeter. "We will hurl back the North Koreans, and if the Russkies intervene we will hurl them back, too!" declared one general. The nation mobilized for an undeclared but initially popular war against communism. Truman tagged it a "police action."

Dean Acheson (1893–1971). He, like the president, assumed that Moscow had initiated the Korean War and urged resolute American reaction. The new crisis, coming after Acheson's National Press Club speech of January 12, 1950 and other foreign-policy woes such as the communist victory in China, emboldened some critics to ask once again for his resignation. (*The Reporter,* 1952. Copyright 1952 by Fortnightly Publishing Co., Inc.)

Korea, the Cold War, and the "Trojan Horse" of National Security

At first the war went badly for the United States, South Korea, and the small number of allied troops, all nominally under U.N. auspices. America's combat units took heavy losses, buying time to equip and transport a substantial offensive force. Discussions began on whether U.S. troops should cross the thirty-eighth parallel and attempt to liberate the North from communism. In August the president approved this drastic change in U.S. war aims.

Meanwhile, MacArthur persuaded the reluctant Joint Chiefs of Staff to approve a difficult amphibious assault at Inchon, hundreds of miles behind North Korean lines. On September 15, U.S. marines landed at Inchon, pushed the North Koreans back, and quickly cut to Seoul. North Korean troops retreated north. "We want you to feel unhampered tactically and strategically to proceed north of the 38th Parallel," Secretary of Defense George C. Marshall cabled MacArthur.

The Chinese warily watched events. When Truman sent the Seventh Fleet to neutralize Formosa on June 27, Beijing railed that U.S. "armed aggression" had exposed the United States' "true imperialist face." Shortly after the Inchon landing,

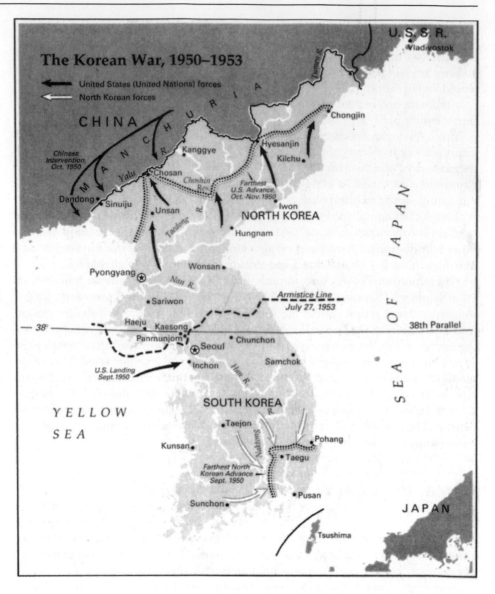

The Korean War, 1950–1953

← United States (United Nations) forces
← North Korean forces

Mao Zedong, vowing not to wait "year after year unsure of when the enemy will attack us," prepared to send "volunteers" into Korea. Mao and Zhou Enlai also told the United States to keep away from the Yalu River boundary. MacArthur dismissed Chinese warnings as bluffs. Stalin cabled Mao on October 1, urging the Chinese to "move at least five or six divisions toward the 38th parallel at once." Mao cabled back the next day, ruling out an intervention that would provoke "open conflict" with the United States. "The wounds inflicted on the people by the [Chinese Civil] war have not healed, we need peace." Stalin then promised Soviet air support: "If war is inevitable, then let it be waged now, and not in a few years, when Japanese militarism will be restored as an ally of the USA." After intense debate in Beijing, Mao reversed course because the "Americans would run more rampant" unless stopped.

On October 8, United Nations forces under U.S. command trooped across the thirty-eighth parallel and marched deep into North Korea. Some 250,000 Chinese troops quietly crossed the Yalu on October 19, even after Stalin reneged on his promise of air support. On October 26, Chinese forces attacked. After fierce fighting, they retreated—"purposely showing ourselves to be weak," as their commander put it, "increasing the arrogance of the enemy, letting him run amuck, and luring them deep into our area." U.S. officials abandoned caution. On November 8, for the first time, B-29 bombers struck bridges across the Yalu—bridges that linked North Korea and China. Then, on November 24, MacArthur launched a major offensive that would "have the boys home by Christmas." Two days later, what one U.S. general called "a glut of Chinamen" swept down on MacArthur's unsuspecting armies. Within weeks Chinese engulfed the North, propelling UN forces southward. "We are not retreating," one harried commander told a reporter. "We are merely attacking in another direction." MacArthur unsuccessfully requested Washington's approval of air strikes against China, now branded an "aggressor" by the United Nations. Truman hinted publicly that nuclear retaliation was under "active consideration." "You can use the atomic bomb," Mao reportedly boasted. "I will respond with my hand grenade. I will catch the weak point on your part and defeat you." British prime minister Clement Attlee urged negotiations, not a dangerously expanded war. To Truman's assertion that the Chinese communists were "complete satellites" of Moscow, the British ambassador argued that war with China would tighten a Sino-Soviet alliance based "on a coincidence of Chinese and Russian views, not Chinese subservience to Russian views." In fact, Truman and his advisers rejected a wider war because they deemed the nuclear arsenal too small and feared Soviet retaliation in Europe.

**Douglas MacArthur
(1880–1964).** The West Point graduate commanded U.S. troops in Asia during World War II, directed the postwar occupation of Japan, and headed forces in Korea until relieved of duty by the president in April 1951. MacArthur later said he could have ended the Korean War in ten days: "I would have dropped between 30 and 50 atomic bombs" on China. (Library of Congress)

By March 1951, MacArthur had shoved communist forces back across the thirty-eighth parallel. With fighting stabilized at roughly the prewar boundary, Truman contemplated negotiations, but the "obstreperous," "vain," and, "egotistical" general was hell-bent on reversing earlier defeats and slashing China on behalf of the crusade against international communism. MacArthur began publicly suggesting that his commander in chief preferred appeasement. To Representative Joseph Martin, he wrote, in a letter made public in April: "There is no substitute for victory." On April 11 Truman, backed strongly by the Joint Chiefs, fired the seventy-one-year-old MacArthur for insubordination.

The general, who had so badly miscalculated Chinese reactions, returned home to ticker-tape parades. In a televised address he told Congress on April 19 that the war must be expanded. He closed famously: "Old soldiers never die; they just fade away." Congressional hearings soon revealed that many Americans shared MacArthur's frustrations over Truman's "limited war" in Korea. Debate focused on different strategies for rolling back communism. "There was MacArthur's, which resembled a locomotive with no brakes. And there was Acheson's, a controlled rollback limited to Korea."

Truman and Acheson pointed to the risk of world war. The Joint Chiefs of Staff Chairman, General Omar Bradley, warned that escalation might bring the Soviets in and cost the United States allies. A showdown with Soviet communism in Korea, he said, would be "the wrong war, at the wrong place, at the wrong time, and with the wrong enemy." As one scholar observes, Bradley implied that the *right war* should be against the Soviet Union, "the *right place* to fight it was not at the periphery, but at the heart of Soviet power," and the *right time* was only after a U.S. military buildup.

Peace talks began at Panmunjom in July 1951 but made little headway. Republican presidential candidate Dwight D. Eisenhower pledged in 1952, if elected, to go to Korea and seek an end to the conflict. Ike won, in part due to American frustration with limited war. He went to Korea, but found no easy solution. The most serious obstacle centered on prisoners of war (POWs). Thousands of Chinese and North Korean soldiers, encouraged by a "re-education" program in the South, refused repatriation. A few hundred captives in the North, having undergone communist "brainwashing," elected to remain above the thirty-eighth parallel. Despite the usual diplomatic practice of returning all prisoners, "the allure of many Chinese voting with their feet for Chiang [Jiang] rather than Mao apparently validated" Washington's pro-Nationalist policy.

By 1953 the military buildup under NSC-68 had erased doubts about U.S. capabilities that had earlier precluded escalation. Announcing that the United States considered "the atomic bomb as simply another weapon in our arsenal," Eisenhower tried to intimidate the Chinese. Jiang Jieshi's forces attacked the mainland, with Washington's approval. The death of Stalin in March probably helped bring the peace talks to a conclusion. A more flexible Moscow urged Beijing to settle the prisoner question. When South Korean president Syngman Rhee tried to sabotage the talks by releasing thousands of North Korean POWs, the Chinese launched a final offensive against South Korean positions.

On July 27, 1953, the adversaries signed an armistice. They agreed to turn over the POW issue to a committee of neutral nations (ultimately the POWs stayed where they chose—including twenty-one Americans in North Korea). The conferees drew a new boundary line close to the thirty-eighth parallel, which gained South Korea 1,500 square miles of territory. The agreement also provided for a demilitarized zone between the two Koreas.

The Korean War ranks as one of the costliest in twentieth-century history. More than 4 million died: 2 million North Korean civilians and 500,000 North Korean soldiers; 1 million South Korean civilians and some 47,000 South Korean soldiers; and official Chinese statistics list 148,000 dead. The United States, with 54,246 dead and 105,000 wounded, spent some $20 billion. The United States supplied 80 percent of the naval power and 90 percent of the air support, as well as 90 percent of foreign combat troops, in this "United Nations" effort.

The Korean War has left many questions, some of which the partial opening of Chinese and Russian archives are helping to answer. Did Moscow start the Korean War? Truman officials claimed that the Soviet Union induced its North Korean client to attack. Perhaps Moscow sensed an opportunity because Acheson had, in a speech of January 12, 1950, implied that South Korea lay outside the American defense perimeter. Acheson's remarks could have "produced a certain influence" on the North Korean leader Kim Il Sung, who visited Moscow in April and promised a surprise attack that would win the war in three days. A cautious Stalin told Kim to check with Mao, who anticipated American intervention but endorsed Kim's plans. Stalin then backed Kim's scheme, probably gambling that North Korea could score a quick victory.

The "gamble thesis" raises difficult questions. Moscow did provide secret air cover, supplies, and training to North Korean and Chinese forces, but only after China's intervention on October 19. If Stalin engineered the initial attack, why did the Soviets not veto the Security Council's June condemnation of North Korea, which paved the way for a UN-sponsored intervention? Why did Stalin delay aiding communist forces, and why was all such assistance kept covert? Why would Moscow launch a European movement for peaceful coexistence and then torpedo that effort by provoking war in Asia? "We are thus left to reconcile the ubiquitous American assumption that Stalin started the war," one scholar notes, "with the unambiguous evidence that he distanced Soviet interests, prestige, and armed might from the conflict, allowing the United States ultimately to pulverize North Korea."

Soviet relations with China influenced Stalin's decisions on Korea. If he refused to support Korean unification, Stalin invited charges that he hindered revolution in Asia and boosted Mao's China as a Soviet rival. Stalin may further have calculated that, even if the United States did not defend South Korea, Washington would never permit the additional loss of Taiwan. American efforts to protect Jiang Jieshi's government on Formosa would prevent rapprochement between Washington and Beijing and ensure China's continued reliance on Soviet economic and military aid. Whatever Stalin's motives, he knew that war in Korea risked Soviet economic and strategic interests in northeast Asia. As for Mao, who expected imminent U.S. aggression against China, he leaned toward intervention *after* Truman sent the Seventh Fleet into the Taiwan Strait and "exposed its [America's] imperialist face." The initiative, and probably the timing, for the war came from Pyongyang, not from Moscow or Beijing.

This interpretation seems plausible because since 1945 a two-part civil war had wracked Korea: the conflict in the South and the conflict between South and North. In the South, "people's committees" resisted the rightist state backed by the United States. Peasant uprisings, leftist-initiated labor strife, and guerrilla warfare claimed tens of thousands of lives. The North encouraged the rebellions in the South, and skirmishes between northern and southern soldiers intensified in 1949 along the dividing parallel. Both Kim's North Korean communist government and Rhee's Republic of Korea in the South craved national unification. Both tapped foreign sources for material aid. Rhee, who had lived in the United States for almost four decades, used his American political connections well. In February 1950, Congress authorized $60 million in economic aid for South Korea; in March it voted almost $11 million in military assistance; and on June 5 it added another $100 million in military aid. Although U.S. occupation troops had departed in mid-1949, a U.S. Military Advisory Group remained to train Rhee's forces. In May elections, Rhee lost control of the South Korean National Assembly. All the while, Rhee "seemed like a tethered hound, constantly pulling at the [U.S.] leash."

With a 150,000-soldier army well supplied with Soviet arms, including 150 T-34 tanks, Kim's authoritarian regime probably decided to strike before Rhee could utilize

U.S. aid and stabilize his precarious political position. In any case, scholars interpret the major war that exploded in June 1950 as an extension of the ongoing civil war waged by North and South Korea, not simply as a conflagration ignited by the two Cold War superpowers.

Despite uncertainty over the war's origins, we *can* measure its consequences. "Like the Trojan horse sent into Troy," writes one historian, "President Harry S. Truman's June 1950 decision to intervene" in Korea "laid the nation bare to a bombardment of economic, political, military, and social changes." The war "put an end to Truman's 'Fair Deal' [domestic reform program] and to a Democrat[ic] political hegemony that extended back two decades." Public exasperation with the Korean stalemate led to the repudiation of the Democrats and the election of the Republican Eisenhower in 1952. The war wounded bipartisanship and fueled McCarthyism. It helped set off a "great debate" in the early 1950s over whether Europe or Asia ranked higher in the campaign against communism and whether the United States had overcommitted itself globally. Truman's handling of the Korean War also confirmed presidential supremacy in foreign policy; he neither consulted Congress nor asked for a declaration of war. Acheson did not wish to answer "ponderous questions" in drawn-out hearings that might have "muddled up" Truman's policy.

The Korean War poisoned Sino-American relations and strengthened Japanese-American ties. The Taiwan question became "locked in place" as the United States continuously intervened in China's civil war by aiding Jiang and adamantly refusing to recognize Mao's government, which now had shed American blood. The war enabled the Chinese communists to consolidate their revolution at home and gain international prestige by battling the "American imperialists" to a draw. The conflict also bolstered Japan and its alliance with the United States. Some $3 billion in U.S. procurement orders during the war revived Japanese industry. The "seedbed" for the Japanese economic "miracle" of the 1960s and 1970s was "planted."

The Korean War further divided the world into two competing camps and drew Third World nations into the Cold War's destructive wake. "We are fighting in Korea," Truman proclaimed, "so we won't have to fight in Wichita, or in Chicago, or in New Orleans, or on San Francisco Bay." South Korea became a key ally, receiving, in 1953–1972, $5.5 billion in foreign aid. Viewing nationalist movements as potential Soviet allies, and determined to back allies in the enlarged Cold War, Washington increased aid to the French in their battle against Vietnamese nationalists (see Chapter 9).

The Korean War also "gave teeth to the mobilization planning process" already begun during Truman's presidency. The Defense Department budget for fiscal year 1953 reached $52.6 billion, up from $17.7 billion in 1950. U.S. military expansion included a much enlarged army; development of tactical nuclear weapons; four more army divisions for Europe, making a total of six there; the 1952 maiden flight of a new jet bomber, the B-52; the explosion of a thermonuclear device in November 1952; and expansion of the Strategic Air Command (SAC) to 1,600 aircraft (nearly all atomic capable). The United States also acquired bases in Saudi Arabia and Morocco, began successful talks with fascist Spain for an air base, and initiated plans for the rearmament of West Germany. In 1951 the United States, Australia, and New Zealand formed the ANZUS Pact. The United States created a military alliance with

Makers of American Foreign Relations, 1950–1961

Presidents	Secretaries of State
Harry S. Truman, 1945–1953	Dean G. Acheson, 1949–1953
Dwight D. Eisenhower, 1953–1961	John Foster Dulles, 1953–1959
	Christian A. Herter, 1959–1961

Pakistan in 1954. Strategies for psychological warfare and propaganda culminated in the creation of the United States Information Agency (USIA) in 1953. The Korean War's most lasting legacy was the quickened militarization of the Cold War.

Ambivalent Cold Warrior: Dwight D. Eisenhower

The stalemated Korean War and the "loss" of China fueled the 1952 Republican presidential race. Eisenhower conducted a smiling, moderate campaign, but his party's right wing vehemently attacked the Truman administration as "soft" on Communism. John Foster Dulles, who authored the Republican party platform condemning Truman's leadership, proposed the "liberation" of "captive peoples" in Eastern Europe as an alternative to "futile and immoral" containment. He never explained precisely how liberation would be achieved, but Eisenhower's promise to go to Korea helped the Republican candidate win 55 percent of the popular vote, and the rhyme "I like Ike" probably decided the election. The journalist David Brinkley recalled that Eisenhower frequently mangled syntax and grammar when he spoke, so that his "ad-libbed sentences bounced around like dodgem cars at a carnival." But Eisenhower appeared modest and sincere, with his homespun rhetoric and wholesome Midwestern image. Because the Cold War seemed more than ever a military matter, this professional soldier and war hero outshone the comparatively bland Democratic candidate Adlai Stevenson, who later wondered, "Who did I think I was, running against George Washington?"

The first Republican president since Hoover proved a skillful politician, whose "hidden-hand" leadership dominated the policy process. Raised in Abilene, Kansas, Eisenhower graduated from West Point and led an obscure military life until appointed the supreme allied commander in Europe during World War II. After the war he served as army chief of staff, president of Columbia University, and NATO commander. Eisenhower admired business leaders and appointed many to high policy offices. Believing in a "mutually cooperative, voluntarist society," Eisenhower and his advisers held that only through "free enterprise" could "democracy be preserved" and communism deterred. The president extended the reciprocal trade agreements program, expanded the lending authority of the Export-Import Bank, and relaxed controls on trade with Eastern European nations. Total American exports expanded from $15 billion in 1952 to $30 billion in 1960. During the 1950s,

Richard M. Nixon (1913–1994).
Before being elected vice president in 1952, Nixon graduated from Whittier College, earned a law degree from Duke University, and represented California in the U.S. House of Representatives (1947–1950) and Senate (1950–1953). An anticommunist alarmist who often used excessive language to score debating points, Nixon was, said Adlai Stevenson, "the kind of politician who would cut down a redwood tree, and then mount the stump and make a speech for conservation." (*The Reporter,* 1960. Copyright 1960 by The Reporter Magazine Co.)

the United States spent more than $3 billion a year in foreign military assistance under the Mutual Security program. The "Food for Peace" program, inaugurated in 1954, accounted for $12.2 billion in farm exports over ten years. Beginning in 1959 the Inter-American Development Bank spurred hemispheric economic projects.

Eisenhower waged "psychological warfare" against the Soviets and their allies through Voice of America, Radio Free Europe, Radio Liberty, and the United States Information Agency, which disseminated American "life and culture" in order to "facilitate understanding" of U.S. foreign policy overseas. His administration also elevated the CIA as a major instrument of foreign policy. Under its director Allen W. Dulles, brother of the secretary of state, the CIA gathered data on foreign countries and prepared "estimates" about their policies, motives, and capabilities. The agency also provided the president with the "quiet option" of "termination with extreme prejudice" or "health alteration"—that is, assassination. Among those included on the CIA's assassination hit list were the Congo's Patrice Lumumba and Cuba's Fidel Castro. The agency hired mercenaries, conducted sabotage, co-opted labor unions, planted news stories, and covertly bribed foreign leaders such as King Hussein of Jordan. The CIA also successfully staged coups in Iran (1953) and Guatemala (1954) but failed to overthrow Indonesia's government in 1958 or to counter a growing "Filipino First" movement.

At home, the CIA put American journalists and professors on its payroll, published books, recruited business executives as "fronts," financed the National Student Association, funded research projects at universities, and used philanthropic foundations to pass money to organizations for anticommunist activities. Under a program called MKULTRA, researchers subjected unwitting Americans to the mind-altering drug LSD. Other projects secretly exposed unsuspecting soldiers, prisoners, children, and sick people to radiation. While sometimes portrayed as a "rogue elephant" acting on its own, the CIA's "mahout, the driver who sits on top and steers," as two scholars put it, "is always the president."

Unlike Truman and Acheson, Eisenhower at least seemed willing to negotiate with the Soviets. Stalin's death in March 1953 removed one of the original Cold War instigators, and in April the president's earnest "Chances for Peace" speech revealed Ike's discomfort with militarism. "Every gun that is made, every warship launched, every rocket fired signifies, in the final sense, a theft from those who hunger and are not fed." But Soviet analysts deemed Eisenhower's remarks "irritating and provocative," unworthy of serious attention, while Secretary Dulles's tougher speech two days later confirmed Moscow's suspicion that the administration contained "resolute enemies" of peace. Fearing that "there aren't enough bulldozers to scrape the bodies off the street" following a nuclear war, especially once the Soviets exploded a thermonuclear device in August 1953, Eisenhower often recommended arms control measures. The president's "Atoms for Peace" speech in December 1953 led to America's signing agreements with thirty-nine nations to develop nuclear energy for peaceful purposes. In 1954 the president rejected advice to use nuclear weapons or send troops to Indochina to forestall a Vietnamese victory over France, and in 1958 he unilaterally halted atomic tests. In his "Farewell Address" of early 1961, Eisenhower warned against a "military-industrial complex" and a government-university scientific complex that threatened the "democratic process" and "possible domination of the nation's scholars by federal employment, project allocations, and the power of money."

But Ike's peace initiatives fizzled, and his antimilitarist sentiments seldom translated into effective policies. America's stockpile of nuclear weapons during his presidency rose from 1,200 to 22,229, and by 1959 a million Americans served overseas in forty-two countries. By 1960 the Defense Department controlled 35 million acres of land at home and abroad. Defense budgets averaged more than $40 billion a year, although Eisenhower, fearful of "busting ourselves" by overspending, angered generals who disputed his cuts in army personnel.

Dulles, McCarthyism, and the New Look

Although Secretary of State John Foster Dulles (1953–1959) seemed a less flexible and more articulate Cold Warrior than Eisenhower, the two "held strikingly parallel views," and "the documents confirm that it was the president who made the decisions." Forceful, ambitious, sharp, and self-righteous, Dulles blended moral "idealism" with hard-nosed political "pragmatism." Tutelage from his Presbyterian minister father, education at Princeton and George Washington Law School, service as a negotiator on reparations at the Paris Peace Conference at Versailles, membership in the prestigious Wall Street firm of Sullivan and Cromwell, and worldwide activity on behalf of the Federal Council of Churches gave Dulles varied international pre–World War II experience. After the war he promoted bipartisanship but in 1952 assailed the very policies of the Truman administration that he had helped to shape. He later admitted that his desire to elect Eisenhower had prompted this political gambit.

Prompted by Stalin's death and by growing Soviet nuclear capabilities that one early reassessment of defense strategy, code-named Solarium, predicted could cause as many as 12 million U.S. casualties if Moscow launched a surprise attack by 1955, Dulles helped Eisenhower craft a revised military strategy. The "New Look" coupled conventional military forces "adequate to deter" or to "counter aggression" with cost-saving "massive atomic capability" that permitted the United States to "respond vigorously" to threats "at places and with means of its own choosing." What Dulles called "massive retaliation," the president tersely described as "blow hell out of them in a hurry if they start anything." Ike's secretary of state also urged "brinkmanship." With its huge nuclear arsenal and strong armed forces, the United States could stand down opponents in a crisis, even if it meant going to the brink of war. "Victory goes to him who can keep his nerve to the last fifteen minutes," wrote Dulles. "Three brinks and he's brunk," jibed critics.

As for the Third World, Eisenhower in 1954 commented: "You have a row of dominoes set up, you knock over the first one, and . . . the last one . . . will go over very quickly." The 1957 "Eisenhower Doctrine" stipulated that the United States would intervene in the Middle East if any government threatened by a communist takeover requested aid. Sold as dynamic departures from Truman policies, such slogans offered only tactical changes in a continuing containment strategy.

Eisenhower once said that "sometimes Foster is just too worried about being accused of sounding like Truman and Acheson." Dulles had witnessed the harassment

John Foster Dulles (1888–1959). Watching Dulles "grapple with a problem," an aide recalled, "was like watching a bird dog sniffing for its prey. He got a little excited as he worked over a solution, breathed a little faster, and obviously enjoyed the thinking process." (*The Reporter*, 1956. Copyright 1956 by The Reporter Magazine Co.)

**Joseph McCarthy
(1909–1957).** Graduate of
Marquette University, judge, and
marine, the Republican senator
from Wisconsin was once known
as the "Pepsi-Cola Kid" for
protecting the interests of that
company. The scholar Ellen
Schrecker, noting that
anticommunist excesses were
widespread, argues that the
demagogic McCarthy was the
"creature" not the "creator" of the
1950s Red Scare. But as the
journalist Cabell Phillips wrote,
McCarthy used "lies, slander, and
innuendo to smash his opponents
and to build his own image of
invincibility." The Senate formally
condemned McCarthy in
December 1954. (*The Reporter,*
1951. Copyright 1951 by Fortnightly Publishing Co., Inc.)

of Acheson by Senator Joseph McCarthy and his backers. To avoid a similar fate, Dulles appointed an ex-FBI man and henchman of McCarthy, Scott McLeod, as the State Department's chief security officer. After seven months of tapping phones, McLeod's investigators fired 193 "security risks," only one of them a suspected subversive. A prominent and tragic case centered on Foreign Service Officer John Carter Vincent, an independent-minded "China hand" who during World War II reported that Jiang Jieshi would probably lose. McCarthyites took this professional analysis to mean that Vincent plotted to defeat Jiang. A State Department Loyalty Board cleared Vincent, but the Civil Service Loyalty Review Board, by a vote of 3 to 2, doubted his loyalty to the United States. Dulles forced Vincent out. Another China specialist, John Paton Davies, also lost his job even though nine security reviews had cleared him. McCarthyism left deep wounds. "The wrong done," the journalist Theodore H. White has written, "was to poke out the eyes and ears of the State Department on Asian affairs, to blind American foreign policy."

The Glacier Grinds On: Khrushchev, Eisenhower, and the Cold War

Like a huge glacier, the Cold War ground across the international landscape. After Stalin's death, early signs for improved Soviet-American relations seemed auspicious. Although the Soviets crushed an East Berlin riot in June 1953, Moscow helped end the deadlock over Korea, opened diplomatic relations with Yugoslavia and Greece, abandoned territorial claims against Turkey, toned down its anti-American rhetoric, launched a "peace offensive," and freed victims from forced labor camps. Soviet leaders scrambled for position in the post-Stalin succession crisis. Nikita S. Khrushchev, for years the Communist party boss of the Ukraine, climbed to the top of the Kremlin hierarchy. By September 1953, Khrushchev had become first secretary of the Central Committee of the party; five years later he became premier. Portly and amiable, Khrushchev impressed Americans as impulsive, competitive, and coarse. Eisenhower found him "tough, and coldly deliberate even when he was pretending to be consumed by anger."

Eisenhower and Khrushchev continued their nations' military buildups. While Soviet ground forces outnumbered the Americans' by a 2 to 1 margin, the United States possessed many more strategic bombers and nuclear weapons. In an attempt to bolster Western defenses through greater integration, Dulles promoted a European Defense Community (EDC) that included West German units. He warned that French resistance would prompt an "agonizing reappraisal" of U.S. security commitments. Paris called his bluff and rejected EDC, but in May 1955 the secretary gained West German membership in NATO. That same year the Southeast Asia Treaty Organization (SEATO) went into effect, the American defense treaty with nationalist China commenced, and the Baghdad Pact was created. The Soviets formed their own military organization, the Warsaw Pact of Eastern European states.

One "test case for détente" resulted in a rare display of Cold War cooperation. The two powers agreed in May 1955 to end their ten-year occupation of Austria and create an independent, neutral state. Both the Soviets and the Americans found elements of "victory": Each side effectively denied Austria to the other's sphere; Moscow demonstrated a commitment to peaceful coexistence; and Washington welcomed a possible model for Eastern European nations eager to roll back Soviet power.

Also in May 1955, the Soviet Union and the United States seemed close to a treaty to prohibit the use and manufacture of nuclear weapons, reduce conventional forces, and create an inspection system to monitor compliance—all terms that the United States had insisted on for years. Within months, however, Washington backed away from the disarmament proposal, convinced that the Soviets would cheat. Dulles and Eisenhower sought a "cold war victory," not merely a "thaw."

Throughout 1954–1955 came calls for a summit meeting of the great powers. Winston Churchill made an eloquent plea, and Democrats in Congress urged negotiations. Dulles countered: A summit conference would empower the Soviets and encourage neutralism, for other countries would fear less and align less. Soviet totalitarianism required an outside enemy, he said. But while Eisenhower agreed that Moscow should not be permitted to "hit the free world in the face," he thought the "present" a "propitious time" to negotiate.

The Soviet Union, the United States, Britain, and France met in Geneva, Switzerland, July 18–23, 1955. In the end, a participant recalled, "not much was achieved at the meeting except that it had occurred." Everybody tried to score points for prestige. East and West wanted Germany united, but each on its own terms. Both sides favored arms control but parted over methods. Eisenhower's dramatic "Open Skies" proposal called for the Soviet Union and the United States to exchange maps and submit their military installations to aerial inspection. Eisenhower later remarked: "We knew the Soviets wouldn't accept," but still "thought it was a good move." "A bald espionage plot," sniffed Khrushchev. The Soviets kept Americans guessing on whether Moscow had caught up in airborne striking power. That secrecy ended in 1956 when the United States began covert surveillance flights by high-altitude U-2 planes over the Soviet Union.

Eisenhower nonetheless applauded a "new spirit of conciliation and cooperation" and assured Americans that he had not penned any secret agreements. Soviets and Americans at Geneva drank "coexistence cocktails"—vodka and Coke. After the largely ceremonial conference, Moscow recognized West Germany and Khrushchev endorsed "détente." Yet, he added, "if anybody thinks" that now "we shall forget about Marx, Engels, and Lenin, he is mistaken. This will happen when shrimps learn to whistle."

The Geneva summit did initiate cultural exchanges, most notably Vice President Nixon's 1959 trip to the Soviet Union where, at a display of U.S. products in a Moscow exhibition, he engaged Khrushchev in the "kitchen debate" on capitalism, communism, and the "commodity gap." Even more impressive in spreading the U.S. message were goodwill jazz tours by American "jambassadors" such as Dizzy Gillespie, and Voice of America's "Music USA" program, which attracted far more listeners than did its political broadcasts. The Soviets responded with the Moscow Youth Festival of 1957, where some 30,000 young people danced to U.S. musicians, picking up slang ("see ya later, alligator"), and calling themselves *bitniki* (beatniks). Washington's containment strategists never imagined "rollback as rock 'n' roll back."

Nikita S. Khrushchev (1894–1971). "I made speeches to bolster the morale of my people," Premier Khrushchev recalled. "I wanted to give our enemy pause. . . . I exaggerated a little. I said that we had the capability of shooting a fly out of space with our missiles." He fell from power in 1964 and until his death aired his views through his memoirs. (*The Reporter,* 1956. Copyright 1956 by The Reporter Magazine Co.)

Preparation for the "Kitchen Debate." Khrushchev and Vice President Richard M. Nixon share a light moment at the American National Exhibition in Moscow in July 1959, just before their "kitchen debate" in which the Soviet leader admitted American superiority in consumer goods but boasted "when we catch you up, in passing you by, we will wave to you." (Getty Images)

Soviet-American relations over Europe nonetheless remained tense. In February 1956, Khrushchev, once the loyal supporter of Stalin's bloody purges of the 1930s, delivered a secret speech to the Twentieth Party Congress. He denounced Stalin as "monstrous" for his "grave abuse of power," initiated "de-Stalinization," embraced peaceful coexistence, and seemed to endorse different brands of communism. The abolition of the Cominform in April seemed to demonstrate Moscow's new tolerance for diversity. The CIA published Khrushchev's speech, thereby emboldening nationalists and victims of Stalinism to challenge autocratic leaders in Eastern Europe. In Poland, a labor dispute in mid-1956 evolved into national resistance to Soviet tutelage. After using force to put down riots, Moscow compromised with Polish nationalism by reluctantly accepting Wladyslaw Gomulka as the Polish Communist party chairman, heretofore denied influence because Stalin thought him too "Titoist." The United States, which had been giving aid to Tito himself for years, soon offered Poland economic assistance.

Revolt erupted next in Hungary. A new government, backed by Budapest street demonstrators and countrywide local revolutionary councils, dramatically announced Hungary's pullout from the Warsaw Pact and neutrality in the Cold War. Fearful that Soviet apparatchiks "would not understand a failure to respond with force in Hungary" and that a successful revolt would "give a great boost to Americans, English, and French," an initially reluctant Khrushchev endorsed intervention. The Anglo-French-Israeli invasion of Egypt on October 31 offered the Red Army a "favorable moment" to act. Some 20,000 under-armed Hungarian students and workers and 3,000 Soviet troops died in hand-to-tank combat in the streets of Budapest in early November.

The Polish and Hungarian rebellions seemed to satisfy Dulles's dream of "liberation." In 1953, Congress had passed the first annual Captive Peoples' Resolution to spur self-determination in Eastern Europe. The Eisenhower administration had been encouraging discontent in Eastern Europe through Voice of America and CIA-financed Radio Free Europe. And the covert CIA program RED SOX/RED CAP trained East European émigrés for paramilitary action. Hungary nonetheless exposed "liberation" as a sham slogan "fashioned to appeal to domestic ethnic audiences." To counter criticism, the administration permitted more than 20,000 Hungarian refugees to enter the United States and introduced a UN resolution condemning Soviet force. Still, condemnations "rained down upon the administration for publicly advocating" but not supporting liberation in Eastern Europe.

Missile Race, Berlin, and the U-2 Mess

In 1956–1957, the United States seemed on the defensive and the Soviets on the offensive. Washington hastened to patch up its crumbling European alliance, rocked by U.S. disapproval of British-French military actions in the Middle East. Washington reinvigorated NATO and deployed intermediate-range ballistic missiles in Britain and tactical nuclear weapons in Western Europe. The French foundered amidst a colonial war in Algeria and shifted key French NATO contingents to Africa. Many Western Europeans distrusted the U.S. push for German rearmament, worried about resurgent McCarthyism, and resented U.S. strictures on trade with communist countries. An American economic recession in 1957 further sapped Western vitality. John Foster Dulles's cancer surgery in November 1956 meant that President Eisenhower had to steer the United States through Eastern European and Mideast crises without his trusted adviser, who died in May 1959.

On October 4, 1957, the Soviets launched the world's first artificial space satellite, *Sputnik*. Two months earlier the Soviets had launched the first intercontinental ballistic missile (ICBM). Critics lambasted Eisenhower for allowing American power to slip. Even though the USSR had test-fired only six ICBMs, Khrushchev bragged about turning out rockets "like sausages." In fact, Khrushchev bluffed; he actually deployed only four unwieldy ICBMs by 1960. Eisenhower knew that *Sputnik* had not endangered U.S. security because high-flying U-2 spy planes had been photographing Soviet military capabilities since 1956. A presidential commission study, the Gaither Report of November 1957, nonetheless urged an expensive military buildup to improve U.S. "deterrent power." Eisenhower responded by building more missiles, dispersing Strategic Air Command bombers, improving radar technology, beefing up antimissile defense, and reorganizing the Defense Department. In January 1958, rocket scientists successfully launched an American satellite named Explorer I. In July, Congress created the National Aeronautics and Space Administration (NASA), which soon became, alongside the Pentagon, the chief federal funding source for high-tech government-sponsored research in universities such as Stanford and Massachusetts Institute of Technology. So that "Johnny" could keep up with "Ivan," the National Defense Education Act (NDEA), enacted in

September 1958, financed new educational programs in the sciences, mathematics, and foreign languages.

The continued militarization of the Cold War alarmed George F. Kennan, an earlier architect of containment. In 1957 Kennan, building on a proposal of Polish Foreign Minister Adam Rapacki earlier that year, delivered the "Reith Lectures" in London, calling for the "disengagement" of all foreign troops from Eastern Europe and Germany, restrictions on nuclear weapons in that area, and a unified, non-aligned Germany. Although Dulles and Eisenhower had already rejected Rapacki's plan for a "denuclearized zone" in Central and Eastern Europe as "highly danger-ous," Kennan urged the administration to "put our military fixations aside," to exer-cise diplomacy rather than to strengthen NATO.

Kennan's suggestions sparked furious debate. Should Kennan's plan become re-ality, former Secretary of State Dean Acheson scolded, the Soviet Union might rein-troduce troops into Eastern Europe, threaten Western Europe, and sign an anti-American military pact with the new united Germany. A rearmed West Ger-many must remain in the U.S. camp. The United States, Kennan answered, would never know Moscow's intentions unless it negotiated. The journalist Walter Lipp-mann, who had criticized Kennan's containment in 1947, stood with him in 1957. Lippmann compared Acheson and other hard-liners to "old soldiers trying to relive the battles in which they won their fame and glory. . . . Their preoccupation with their own past history is preventing them from dealing with the new phase of the Cold War."

A new crisis over Berlin demonstrated the importance of Kennan's call for de-fusing European issues. West Berlin, 110 miles inside communist East Germany, had become a "malignant tumor," in Khrushchev's words. Some 3 million East German defectors, many of them skilled workers, had used West Berlin as an escape route since 1949. For Americans and their allies, the city operated as an espionage and propaganda center. West Berlin's prosperity, induced by billions of dollars in U.S. aid, glittered next to drab East Berlin. Washington piqued Soviet tempers by crowing about West Berlin's economic success and applauding the East German exodus. The continued rearmament of West Germany, including U.S. planes capable of dropping nuclear bombs, further alarmed Moscow, which had endorsed the Rapacki Plan. The United States also insisted that the two Germanies unite under free elections and refused to recognize the East German government. In November 1958 the So-viet Union boldly issued an ultimatum. Within six months, warned Khrushchev, unless East-West talks on Germany had begun, Moscow would sign a peace treaty with East Germany, end occupation agreements still in effect from World War II, and turn East Berlin over to the East German regime. He recommended that Berlin be-come a "free city" without foreign troops. Washington knew that to deal with East Germany would confirm the Soviet claim of two Germanies and throw into ques-tion U.S. occupation rights in West Berlin and West Germany. Eisenhower feared that "if we let the [West] Germans down they might shift their own position and even go neutralistic." Urged to test Soviet intentions by sending U.S. military units through the corridors to West Berlin, the president stalled, fearful of war. Khrushchev wanted to talk, not fight. "Do not hurry. . . . The conditions are not ripe as yet for a new scheme of things," he told militant East German leaders. He agreed to a foreign ministers conference for May 1959, which proved inconclusive, a trip in September 1959 to the United States to speak directly with Eisenhower, and ultimately a Paris summit meeting in May 1960.

Warmly welcomed by Eisenhower, Khrushchev began his U.S. visit of September 1959 with a dramatic speech at the United Nations, where he proposed "general and complete disarmament in three years." Eisenhower, more in the forefront of diplomacy following Dulles's death in May, hoped that firsthand exposure to America's vastness and variety would make a "favorable chip in the granite." The portly premier inspected an IBM plant, marveled at the fecundity of Midwest grain fields, and visited a Hollywood movie set where he took offense at the bare legs exposed in a cancan dance—a sign to him of the decadence of Western capitalism. Khrushchev plugged "peaceful coexistence" and said that no one should take his "we will bury capitalism" statement in a literal or military sense: "You may live under capitalism and we will live under socialism and build communism. The one whose system proves better will win." After ten days on the road, the Soviet premier went to Camp David, a quiet, secluded presidential retreat near the Catoctin Mountains in Maryland. For two days the two leaders traded war stories and discussed Berlin. Eisenhower would not agree to a new summit meeting until Khrushchev abandoned his Berlin ultimatum. The premier agreed to do so, evoking the "Spirit of Camp David"—a willingness on both sides to talk their way to détente. Eisenhower "sincerely wanted to liquidate the 'cold war' and improve relations," Khrushchev later told the Politburo, adding that the moderates who advised Eisenhower had gained the upper hand over the "madmen."

In 1959–1960 Eisenhower himself took goodwill foreign trips in a deliberate effort to ease tensions. Just before Khrushchev's visit to the United States, the president flew to London, Paris, and Bonn for talks with European leaders. In December he traveled 22,000 miles to eleven nations in Europe, Asia, and North Africa. In February 1960, he toured Latin America for two weeks and encountered a mixed reception. And then he departed for the Paris summit meeting in May.

Two weeks before that summit meeting, on May 1, 1960, an American airplane carrying high-powered cameras and other reconnaissance instruments was shot down over Sverdlovsk in the Ural Mountains of northern Russia, 1,200 miles inside the Soviet Union. On a CIA mission, the U-2 intelligence plane flew from a base in Pakistan to one in Norway. Although such flights had gone on for four years and the Soviets knew about them, this was the first time that Soviet firepower had reached the high-altitude craft. Pilot Francis Gary Powers's U-2 evidently had engine trouble and dropped several thousand feet before being shot down. He parachuted and was captured immediately, unable or unwilling to kill himself by taking his CIA-issued poison. When Khrushchev declared that the downed U.S. plane had violated Soviet air space, the State Department fabricated a claim that a civilian weather plane had simply flown off course. On May 6, Khrushchev displayed photographs of the uninjured pilot, his spy equipment, and the crashed U-2. The president then defended the flights as necessary to prevent "another Pearl Harbor"—a "surprise attack" on "the United States and the Free World." But for many the affair "reinforced the prevailing view that Eisenhower was not minding the store."

Berlin and nuclear-weapons testing controls stood high on the Paris summit meeting's agenda. Apparently preferring to wait until a new president took office, perhaps seizing an opportunity to show domestic hard-liners and Chinese critics of peaceful coexistence that he could be tough, and certainly angry about U.S. violations of Soviet air space, Khrushchev denounced American aggression, demanded an apology for the U-2 flights, and stalked out. Thinking that a real opportunity to wind down the Cold War had been lost, Eisenhower bemoaned "the stupid U-2 mess" and looked forward to retirement on his Gettysburg farm.

To the Brink with China; To the Market with Japan

The Chinese communists did not mourn this deterioration in Soviet-American relations. From the mid-1950s onward, Beijing criticized Khrushchev for "yielding to evil" in dealing with the United States. John Foster Dulles seized opportunities to exploit the growing Sino-Soviet rift, which widened for many reasons, including Moscow's refusal to help China develop nuclear capability. The Eisenhower-Dulles "wedge" strategy instead strained Sino-American relations, further stalling progress toward détente.

In early 1953, to press the People's Republic of China to accept an armistice in the Korean War, President Eisenhower announced that the Seventh Fleet would no longer block Jiang Jieshi's attempts to attack the mainland. The decision alarmed Beijing, especially after Nationalist bombing raids began to hit the coast. Throughout the 1950s, Jiang pledged a return to China and received more than $250 million annually in U.S. economic and military aid. The Seventh Fleet remained in the Taiwan Strait to protect Formosa as a valued Asian military partner. In December 1954, Taiwan and the United States signed a mutual defense treaty. The following month, Congress, by a vote of 83 to 3 in the Senate and 410 to 3 in the House, authorized the president in the Formosa Resolution to "stand up to Communist aggression" by employing American troops as needed to defend Taiwan and the adjoining islands.

In 1954 the United States created the Southeast Asia Treaty Organization (SEATO), which formally allied France, Britain, Australia, New Zealand, Thailand, Pakistan, and the Philippines against "Red China" and its support of revolution in Indochina. Washington also forbade American journalists to accept Beijing's 1956 invitation to visit the mainland and prohibited the shipment of a panda to the United States from China. At the 1954 Geneva Conference on Indochina (see next chapter), Foreign Minister Zhou Enlai approached Secretary Dulles intending to shake hands, but Dulles turned away, lest photographers record this contaminating gesture. Washington further imposed a total trade embargo in order to increase China's "ostracism" from the world.

China and the United States lurched toward the brink in 1954–1955. Jinmen (Quemoy) and Mazu (Matsu) lay just a few miles off southeastern China in the Taiwan Strait, two of some thirty small offshore islands that the Nationalists had managed to hold when they fled to Taiwan in 1949. Jiang had fortified the two islands with thousands of troops and used the outposts to raid the mainland. As the United

States negotiated the defense treaty with Jiang in summer 1954, Beijing unfurled a "Liberate Taiwan" global propaganda campaign and prepared to invade another off-shore island group called the Dachens. Chinese shore batteries began to bombard Jinmen early in September. Although the Chinese did not intend to invade Jinmen, they did not anticipate the U.S. response.

Deeming the offshore islands militarily valuable to Taiwan (some 100 miles away), Washington cautioned Jiang against escalating coastal warfare. "Quemoy is not our ship," Eisenhower said at first. People would ask: "What do we care what happens to those yellow people out there?" But Senator William F. Knowland of California insisted: "The defense . . . cannot wait until the team with the ball crosses the line of scrimmage before resisting." Despite British warnings that Jiang might ignite war "through impulsiveness," the United States signed the defense treaty with Taiwan, and Congress gave the president a blank check in the Formosa Resolution. Mao also practiced brinkmanship. Claiming that "the U.S. cannot annihilate the Chinese nation with a small stack of atom bombs," Mao in mid-January 1955 sent his army to overrun the Dachens. Heeding U.S. advice, Jiang pulled his troops out; then Washington took up Mao's challenge. Eisenhower brandished nuclear weapons, stating publicly that he would use them "just exactly as you would use a bullet or anything else." The Joint Chiefs of Staff readied plans to drop several Hiroshima-size bombs on coastal cities with expected casualties in the millions.

Lacking guaranteed support from the Soviet Union and reacting to alarms voiced by Asian nations attending the Bandung Conference, China offered in April to discuss tensions with the United States. The crisis quickly quieted. At Geneva, and after 1958 in Warsaw, Chinese and American officials talked at the ambassadorial level about Taiwan, trade, and other topics. But relations soon ruptured once again.

After the deployment of U.S. tactical nuclear weapons on Taiwan, and after Jiang had augmented his forces to more than 100,000 on the offshore islands, Mao answered in August 1958 by shelling Jinmen and Mazu anew. Khrushchev leveled a "barrage of criticism" against Beijing, whose actions jeopardized Moscow's "peace offensive" with the West, while Soviet Foreign Minister Andrei Gromyko urged Mao to seek a peaceful settlement. Eisenhower nonetheless perceived a "long-range plan, 'with Soviet backing,' to retake Taiwan." Possibly heeding European allies' urging of caution, the president resisted military advice to strike China with "low yield" nuclear weapons. Eisenhower instead ordered airlifts and Seventh Fleet escorts for Nationalist supply ships while Beijing vowed "resolute blows" against Jiang's "clique." Mao told Gromyko that "it's getting so hot, and we want Eisenhower to take a shower." "Those damned little offshore islands," the president griped. "I wish they'd sink."

Eisenhower stepped back from the brink, as did Mao. After Dulles and Jiang agreed in October that Jiang would not use force against the mainland, the Nationalist leader withdrew some troops from Jinmen and Mazu, and Eisenhower suspended escorts of Nationalist vessels. Beijing relaxed bombardment of the islands. But the People's Republic accelerated efforts to acquire nuclear weapons "even if the Chinese people have to pawn their trousers for this purpose."

As it went to the brink with Beijing, the United States worked to "keep the Japanese on our side," all the while frightening China, the Soviet Union, the Koreas, and other past victims of Japan's aggression. Two September 8, 1951, agreements

Mao Zedong (1893–1976). Chief of the Communist party in "Red China," father of the successful Communist Revolution, and radical philosopher-poet, Mao said of the Taiwan Strait crisis: "I did not expect that the whole world would be so deeply shocked." (National Archives)

guided Japanese-American relations for the decade. The first, a peace treaty signed by the United States and forty-seven other nations, provided for the ending of American occupation on April 28, 1952. The second, the Mutual Security Treaty signed by Washington and Tokyo, provided for U.S. defense of Japan and the stationing of American arms and forces on Japanese soil. Japan agreed to create a 110,000-strong military (Self-Defense Forces), which could not be used outside the nation. Many Japanese resented the U.S. bases and the U.S. pressure to rearm, and throughout the 1950s, with popular opinion favoring "rice before guns," mass street demonstrations strained relations. Meanwhile, American leaders who insisted that Japan pay for more of its own defense sharply criticized the Tokyo government for obstructing rearmament.

The plight of the *Fukuryu Maru (Lucky Dragon),* a Japanese fishing boat, heightened debate. On March 1, 1954, the United States tested its new hydrogen bomb in the Bikini Atoll (Marshall Islands), near where the boat fished for tuna. A huge fireball sprinkled radioactive fallout on the crew, causing severe nausea, fever, and blisters, and eventually killing one crew member. Disparaging Japan's "fancied martyrdom," Washington waited months to compensate the victims. Widespread Japanese protests ensued. Two years later, the movie *Godzilla* eerily recalled the *Lucky Dragon* affair as a prehistoric monster, revived by atomic tests, rampaged through Tokyo.

After negotiators signed a renewed Japanese-American defense pact in January 1960, hundreds of thousands marched and rioted against the retention of U.S. bases. The Japanese government pushed the new treaty through the Diet (parliament), but the prime minister was forced to resign, and President Eisenhower cancelled his goodwill trip to Japan.

Even though huge U.S. military purchases in Japan during the Korean War—for Toyota trucks, for example—spurred economic recovery, Secretary Dulles complained in 1954 that Japan expected "merely to be taken care of by [the] U.S." Eager to lower the costs of subsidizing Japanese reconstruction and to blunt possible communist exploitation of economic instability, American officials encouraged Japan to develop a prosperous export-oriented economy. By the mid-1950s, Japan experienced double-digit economic growth by using substantial U.S. aid to buy and adapt American technology (Motorola helped start the electronics industry), improving labor-management coordination to enhance efficiency and quality, and investing in research and development rather than in weapons. With Japan's populace striving for the "three sacred treasures" (television, washing machine, and refrigerator), and with 2,500 Japanese intellectuals visiting the United States through academic exchange programs in the 1950s, Japan became not only America's military ally but also eventually its economic competitor.

The Third World Rises: Revolutionary Nationalism and Nonalignment

Between 1946 and 1960, thirty-seven new nations emerged from colonial status in Asia, Africa, and the Middle East. Eighteen countries gained independence in 1960 alone. In 1958, twenty-eight prolonged guerrilla insurgencies raged. Revolutions and the collapse of empires claimed a central place in global affairs. These great changes occurred in the "Third World"—a term for nations that belonged neither to the capitalist "West" nor to the communist "East." At first called "backward" and then "developing" countries, Third World nations generally consisted of nonwhite, agricultural peoples in the southern hemisphere. Such countries provided industrial nations with bountiful raw materials, military bases, intelligence facilities, and markets for manufactured goods. In 1959 more than one-third of American direct private investments abroad were in the Third World.

Volatile nationalist movements flourished in these "emerging" nations, often led by anticolonial revolutionaries who sought economic improvement without foreign ownership. Eisenhower wrote Churchill that "should we try to dam [nationalism] up completely it would, like a mighty river, burst through the barriers and could create havoc." Yet many U.S. leaders doubted darker-skinned peoples' capacity for self-government. Nixon in 1960 remarked that "some African peoples had only been out of the trees for fifty years." Anticolonial revolutions often produced undemocratic regimes that declared themselves "nonaligned" or "neutral" in the Cold War, a stance Washington condemned as helpful to communism. Convinced that "premature independence" would facilitate "Soviet colonialism," the administration endorsed a "middle path" of accepting continued colonial rule by anticommunist allies while verbally backing eventual self-determination in Africa and elsewhere. To blame communists for nationalist explosions, one scholar has written, "is like blaming the inherent danger in a huge mass of exposed combustible materials on the possible presence of arsonists."

Americans found that foreigners both envied and resented America's unmatched abundance. The image of the "Ugly American" exacerbated foreign resentment. In 1958 William J. Lederer and Eugene Burdick wrote a novel with that title to satirize "fat," "ostentatious," "loud," and "stupid" American tourists and U.S. diplomats. The authors appealed for Foreign Service Officers who spoke the language of the host country and moved more among "the people," or else Washington might lose the popular struggle against communism.

American racism, symbolized by Jim Crow practices, hovered like "the sword of Damocles . . . over American pretensions to world leadership after 1945." In December 1952, the attorney general asked the Supreme Court to strike down segregation in public schools, noting that "it is in the context of the present world struggle between freedom and tyranny that the problem of racial discrimination must be viewed." In 1955 the dark-skinned Indian ambassador G. L. Mehta was "racially abused" at an airport restaurant in Texas, and in 1957 a Howard Johnson's in Dover, Delaware, denied food to Ghana's finance minister, K. A. Gbedemah. That same year, the president sent federal troops to escort black children to school in Little Rock, Arkansas, amidst ugly white protests. Foreign observers concluded that "the United States has no moral claim to be leader of Western democracies," for "one can't be world champion of the colonial peoples while championing inequality in one's backyard." At the Brussels World's Fair of 1958, the State Department, itself largely "lily white," extolled "positive progress" on race with a controversial life-size photo of multiracial children playing ring-around-the-rosy. Despite favorable European reaction, Eisenhower withdrew the display when segregationists in

**Eisenhower and Prime Minister
Jawaharlal Nehru (1889–1964).**
The Indian prime minister and the American
president are shown during Nehru's U.S. visit
in 1956. As the historian Andrew Rotter has
observed, Nehru's wearing of the traditional
kurta, his preference for fruit juice instead of
alcohol, and above all his refusal to ally with
the West in the Cold War all invoked
subliminal stereotypes of Indians as lacking
decisiveness and male "potency." (Dwight D.
Eisenhower Library, White House Album)

Congress protested the "unimaginable stupidity" of America's government "[apologizing] for racial segregation in the United States."

Gender stereotypes joined racism and other cultural biases in shaping U.S. policies toward the Third World. In South Asia, for example, American officials thought that the "vigorous" and "virile" Pakistan, which had joined the Baghdad Pact and SEATO, showed "more masculinity" than the "mystics, dreamers, [and] hypocrites" of nonaligned India, which displayed an "almost feminine hypersensitiveness" regarding national prestige. Israel, having shed the stereotype of passive victim of the Holocaust for that of the "tough Jew" surrounded by "hostile enemies," likewise assumed the role of America's "democratic bulwark" in the Middle East. Arab states, despite their valuable oil, were portrayed as cowardly "marauders," "devious" and undisciplined soldiers, or "problem [children]" in need of "an intelligent parent."

When early-twentieth-century upheavals, as in Mexico, China, and Russia, rocked international equilibrium, the United States increasingly found itself a target rather than a model of revolution. Hence, in late 1960, when forty-three Afro-Asian states, led by India, sponsored a United Nations resolution championing decolonization, the United States abstained from voting, lest it offend such Cold War colonial allies as Portugal.

The Soviets paid attention to the Third World, too. Both Marxism and the USSR's professed anticolonialism enjoyed wide appeal. In the mid-1950s Khrushchev toured India, Burma, and Afghanistan. Moscow granted some quarter billion dollars to Indonesia between 1954 and 1959 and funded an Indian steel plant and the Aswan Dam in Egypt. The Soviets also praised the Bandung Conference of

April 1955, which convened twenty-nine "nonaligned" states (about one-quarter of the world's population) at the "first international conference of colored peoples in the history of mankind." Yet the Soviet Union also bumped up against Third World nationalism. When, during his 1955 trip to India, Khrushchev vehemently denounced the West, the neutralist Indians resented this blatant effort to bring the Cold War into their country. Arab nationalism, rather than Soviet communism, dominated the Middle East. And in Latin America, between 1945 and 1955, sixteen nations outlawed the Communist party. The Soviets, like the Americans, could not countenance independent nationalism or explain away the contradiction between their own "promise" of self-determination and their hypocritical suppression of independence, as in Eastern Europe. American officials remained fearful, however, that communists would exploit nationalism and poverty in the Third World. Foreign aid became a primary U.S. tool. Whereas during the 1949–1952 period some three-quarters of total U.S. economic assistance went to Europe, in the years 1953–1957 three-quarters flowed to developing countries. By 1961 more than 90 percent of U.S. aid targeted the Third World. Yet many recipients refused to choose sides in the Cold War. To Dulles, neutralism seemed but an "immoral and shortsighted" stage on the road to communism.

Stormy Weather: Nationalism in the Middle East and Latin America

Crises in the Middle East and Latin America strained U.S.–Third World relations and elevated covert action and propaganda as major instruments of foreign policy. In 1952, Colonel Nasser led young Egyptian army officers against King Farouk, who fled to Europe with his harem and his wealth. Nasser initiated land reform and pledged to end British control of the Suez Canal. London reluctantly agreed in 1954 to a phased withdrawal. To prevent a defense "vacuum" in the Middle East, Washington in 1955 promoted the Baghdad Pact, a military alliance of Britain, Turkey, Iran, Iraq, and Pakistan. An expansive "public diplomacy" campaign simultaneously used pamphlets, posters, media outlets, books, music, film, educational exchanges, and religion in order to guide "revolutionary and nationalistic pressures throughout the area into orderly channels not antagonistic to the West." Iran was won over in 1953 when the CIA, jointly with British intelligence, overthrew the nationalist regime of Mohammed Mossedegh, who had pushed to nationalize foreign oil interests. U.S. companies produced about 50 percent of the Middle East's petroleum. Eighty-nine percent of Europe's crude oil imports came from that region.

Israel drew closer to the United States through foreign aid totaling $374 million from 1952 to 1961. Yet bitter Arab-Israeli conflict thwarted U.S. hopes for order in the Middle East. After the Israelis raided the Gaza Strip in 1955 and exposed Egypt's military weakness, Cairo signed an arms agreement with Czechoslovakia, ending the Western arms sales monopoly in the Middle East. Meanwhile, Palestinian refugees languished in squalid camps, growing more militant each year. The State Department's Henry Byroade lectured Israelis to "drop the attitude of conqueror" toward their neighbors. But he also implored Arabs to accept the "accomplished fact" of Israel's existence.

Gamal Abdul Nasser (1918–1970). The bold Egyptian leader once told John Foster Dulles that the Russians "have never occupied our territory . . . but the British have been here for seventy years." Nasser went on: "How can I go to my people and tell them I am disregarding a killer with a pistol sixty miles from me at the Suez Canal to worry about somebody who is holding a knife a thousand miles away?" (*The Reporter,* 1956. Copyright 1956 by The Reporter Magazine Co.)

Despite his dislike for Nasser's Pan Arabism and neutralism, Dulles tried to entice him toward the West with foreign aid. In December 1955 the secretary offered to fund Nasser's dream of the Aswan Dam as a potential source of electricity and irrigation on the Nile. The next year the World Bank crafted a $1.3 billion project utilizing British, American, and World Bank monies. Egypt concurrently joined an anti-Israeli military alliance with Saudi Arabia, Syria, and Yemen. Jewish Americans protested in Washington, while southern members of Congress balked at a project that permitted Egypt to produce competitive cotton. Eisenhower and Dulles worried that a Czech-Egyptian arms deal signified alignment with the Soviets. Nasser countered that nationalism offered the best defense against communism and that Zionism and Western imperialism, not communism, ranked as Egypt's greatest enemies. But on July 19, 1956, a distrustful Dulles told the Egyptian ambassador that the United States had changed its mind about funding the Aswan Dam. The State Department publicly insulted the Egyptians by declaring their credit no good—despite the World Bank's decision that the dam represented a sound investment. "May you choke to death on your fury," Nasser fumed. He quickly seized the Suez Canal, intent on using its $25 million annual profit to help build the dam. Washington's hard-knuckled economic diplomacy had failed.

Without consulting Washington, the British and French huddled with Israel to plan a military operation. In late October and early November 1956, British, French, and Israeli forces invaded Egypt and nearly captured the canal. "Nothing justifies double-crossing us," Eisenhower raged. With Dulles in the hospital for cancer treatment, Eisenhower publicly upbraided the British and French for military action that invited Soviet interference in the Middle East and diverted attention from the simultaneous Soviet invasion of Hungary. Moscow, preoccupied with Eastern Europe, actually did little during the Suez crisis except rail against the invaders.

Suez accelerated Britain's postwar decline. U.S. officials introduced a UN resolution demanding withdrawal and refused Britain oil shipments to compensate for the closing of the Suez Canal and the destruction of oil pipelines. Washington also refused to aid Britain when its currency (the pound) faltered and Bank of England reserves dwindled because of a dollar drain. Bowing to U.S. pressure, French and British troops pulled out by late December. Only after Washington threatened sanctions (economic aid had already been suspended) did Israel disengage from the Sinai in March 1957. A UN peacekeeping force then took positions and returned the canal, now clogged with sunken ships, to Egypt.

Although retaining its oil interests, Washington after Suez failed to dissuade many Arabs from seeing Uncle Sam as anything more than another Western usurper. After all, the United States still stood at odds with the region's most popular figure, Nasser. After withdrawing the High Dam offer and letting Moscow build the imposing structure, Eisenhower urged a U.S. role as Middle East policeman—because "the Bear is still the central enemy." Anti-imperialist and anti-Israeli Arabs bristled at the U.S. presumption that they needed a protective sheriff. But Eisenhower coveted Israel as an anticommunist ally, and in August 1958 Washington made its first arms sale to the Jewish state.

Claiming that "it is 'curtains' for Israel" if the United States did not thwart Soviet-backed Arab radicals, the president and a recuperating Dulles revitalized containment in the Eisenhower Doctrine. On January 30, 1957, both houses approved Eisenhower's request (72 to 19 in the Senate and 350 to 60 in the House) militarily and economically to help Middle East nations resist "overt armed aggression from any nation controlled by International Communism." Although Iran and Lebanon endorsed the doctrine, Syria, Egypt, and Jordan soundly rejected it, while Iraq and Saudi Arabia seemed lukewarm. British Prime Minister Harold Macmillan called the policy a "gallant effort to shut the stable door after the horse had bolted."

Tests soon arose. In April 1957, when pro-Nasser Jordanians threatened to overthrow King Hussein, Eisenhower ordered the Sixth Fleet to patrol off the coast of Lebanon and suggested that he would send U.S. marines, too. Although the king had appealed for implementation of the Eisenhower Doctrine, this first application actually targeted Nasserite Arabs, not communists. In any case, the revolt failed. The second test came in Syria, where pro-Nasser radical military officers gained power and negotiated aid from the Soviet Union. Syrian officials exposed a CIA plot to oust them, and Dulles declared Syria a virtual Soviet satellite. In fact, the anticommunist Syrians looked mostly to Cairo, not Moscow. In February 1958, Syria and Egypt merged as the United Arab Republic; Nasser quickly banished the Communist party from Syria.

Iraq and Lebanon claimed attention next. In July 1958, Washington swallowed "a bitter pill" when Nasserites overthrew Iraq's government. Fearing that Arab radicalism could spread, the United States acted to save the Christian-led, pro-American government in multireligious Lebanon, where a civil war pitted Christians against pro-Nasser Muslims. On July 15, 14,000 U.S. marines waded ashore, "confronting ice-cream vendors, gawkers, and bikini-clad sunbathers, not hostile gunmen." Lebanese politicians soon resolved the dispute, and U.S. forces departed in fall 1958. This first instance of the Eisenhower Doctrine at work offered "little more than ideological window dressing for American action" on behalf of status quo forces, because, as Dulles privately acknowledged, the country was never "under the control of international communism." The incident thus set "dangerous precedents" by "misrepresenting the Third World nationalism as Soviet inspired, and by waging what amounted to a limited but undeclared presidential war."

Nationalism also challenged in Latin America. Through the Rio Pact (a defensive military alliance formed in 1947), the Organization of American States (launched in 1948 but formally established in 1951 to help settle inter-American disputes), investments of $8.2 billion by 1959, economic assistance totaling $835 million for the period 1952–1961, and support for military dictators such as Fulgencio Batista in Cuba, the United States perpetuated hegemony over its neighbors. But Latin American poverty remained stark; illiteracy rates stood high; health care proved inadequate; a population explosion threatened scarce resources; productivity showed minuscule growth; profits from raw materials such as sugar and oil flowed through American companies to the United States. To reverse the resulting "drift in the area toward radical and nationalistic regimes," Dulles said, the United States would intervene, the Good Neighbor policy notwithstanding.

Guatemala became a litmus test for combating Communism in Latin America. Jacobo Arbenz Guzmán won election as president by a wide margin, and after his inauguration in spring 1951, he set land reform as his central goal. Only 2 percent of the population owned 70 percent of the land. Under the agrarian reform law of mid-1952, Arbenz expropriated about one-quarter of the nation's arable land and distributed it to some 500,000 peasants. Food production increased. But Arbenz soon clashed with the United Fruit Company (UFCO), the U.S.-owned banana exporter and Guatemala's largest landholder. UFCO had to give up more than 400,000 acres of uncultivated land. When Arbenz offered compensation in government bonds, using the value of the land the company itself, for tax purposes, set at $1.2 million, UFCO claimed the expropriated properties represented $19 million. The State Department backed UFCO, and company propagandists spread the false word: Communism had secured a beachhead in Central America.

The Soviet Union actually showed little interest in Latin America in the 1950s. Still, Arbenz welcomed indigenous communists' help against entrenched interests, and he appointed some of them to administer land reform projects. Given their Cold War mentality, U.S. diplomats thought the worst. As Ambassador John Peurifoy remarked, Arbenz "talked like a Communist, he thought like a Communist, he acted like a Communist, and if he is not one . . . , he will do until one comes along."

Fearful that Arbenz's program of aid to workers and peasants could spread and threaten U.S. hegemony throughout the region, Eisenhower approved the CIA plan PBSUCCESS to overthrow the Guatemalan leader. CIA-recruited Guatemalan exiles trained in Nicaragua and Honduras for an invasion. Colonel Carlos Castillo Armas, a graduate of the army staff school at Fort Leavenworth, Kansas, won favor as the president-to-be. In early 1954 Washington prodded the Organization of American States to declare, by a 17 to 1 vote, that the domination of any American state by the international communist movement would constitute a threat to the hemisphere. When Washington also cut off technical assistance to Guatemala, Arbenz accepted a large arms shipment from Czechoslovakia. "If Paul Revere were living today," a member of Congress declared, "he would view the landing of Red arms in Guatemala as a signal to ride."

On June 18, after the CIA bribed Guatemalans, planted fictitious news stories about Arbenz's submission to the Soviets, and dropped supplies at United Fruit facilities, Castillo Armas's small force attacked from Honduras. U.S.-supplied rebel planes bombed Guatemala City. Abandoned by his military and fearful that Washington would order U.S. marines to Guatemala if Castillo Armas's invasion failed, an anguished Arbenz fled to Mexico, where he died in 1971. Castillo Armas soon returned UFCO lands, jailed his detractors, and set Guatemala on a course of government-sponsored terror that by 1990 had left 100,000 Guatemalans dead. In 1957 he fell to assassination, but the new regime remained a staunch U.S. ally.

Vice President Richard Nixon felt Latin American resentment firsthand in April–May 1958 when he traveled south on a goodwill tour. In Montevideo, Uruguay, anti-Yankee pickets mingled with the cheering crowds when Nixon motored through the city. In Venezuela all hell broke loose. Earlier in 1958 a military junta had overthrown the dictatorship of U.S. ally Marcos Pérez Jiménez ("P.J."), to whom the Eisenhower administration then gave asylum. Into a volatile environment of Venezualen bitterness stepped Nixon, emboldened by earlier tangles with protesting students at Uruguay's San Marcos University. "Communists, hoodlums, and thrill seekers" blocked Nixon's motorcade en route to a wreath-laying ceremony at Simón Bolívar's tomb. Demonstrators spit, threw stones, shattered windows, smashed fenders, rocked the automobile, and threatened the vice president's life. Nixon's car somehow sped away. But USIA Director George Allen worried that "we continue to act like adolescents. We boast about our richness, our bignesss, and our strength. . . . Nations, like people, who boast can expect others to cheer when they fail."

After Nixon's trip, Washington began to send more economic and military aid to the hemisphere while remaining mostly inflexible toward grassroots nationalism. In 1959 the United States subscribed $500 million to the new Inter-American Development Bank. U.S. infantry and Panamanian Zone police in 1959 beat back efforts by students and other nationalists to gain control of the Canal Zone. Eisenhower eventually permitted the Panamanian flag to fly over the zone for the first time since the early twentieth century. In Cuba, however, the United States prepared to resist Fidel Castro, who overthrew Batista and launched a revolution to expel U.S. economic and military interests from the island. "Batten down the hatches," Assistant Secretary Thomas Mann told Latin American specialists in the State Department. "There's going to be some real stormy weather."

Cultural Expansion and the Globalized Cold War

By decade's end, one of the most conspicuous signs of U.S. influence abroad came in the proliferation of American mass culture and the foreign adoption of American ways. As economies recovered in Western Europe and Japan, people spent proportionally more of their incomes on luxuries such as electrical appliances, hi-fi phonographs, televisions, leisurewear, even glossy, befinned American cars. Although some foreign elites sneered at "fast-food emporiums" and "sugar-saturated soft drinks," youth culture made clear choices—"worn-out jeans vs. neat trousers, 'Elvis-quiff' and ponytail vs. orderly . . . hairstyles, uninhibited rock'n'roll vs. civilized ballroom dancing, comic strips vs. Goethe." At trade fairs, the USIA touted "People's Capitalism," or middle-class consumerism. At the Moscow exhibition of 1959, site of the Nixon-Khrushchev debate, the Miracle Kitchen of Today served up "17,500 dishes ranging from ready-to-bake biscuits and oven-ready vegetable pies to instant coffee and Jello." The continued appeal of American films demonstrated what one Austrian scholar has called the "Marilyn Monroe Doctrine." "Is the World 'Going American'?" *U.S. News & World Report* asked, as it described Hula-Hoops in France, canned beer in British pubs, traffic jams in Rome, Bonn, and Sydney. Americanization became a component of national security policy, equating consumerism with freedom. Yet cultural expansion generated both adoption *and* rejection, setting off cultural wars, as demonstrated by the "Ugly American" complaints of Europeans who detested the "intellectual fodder offered to the American masses, from scandal magazines to digests of books."

The Eisenhower administration promoted the expansion of American culture and Americanization abroad as one of several means to contest and undermine the appeal of Arab nationalism, Latin American revolution, Third World neutralism, communism, the Soviet Union, and China. Despite the catchy phrases of the Eisenhower-Dulles years, however, no dramatic new departures occurred in foreign policy. "Liberation" and "rollback" had always been the ultimate goal of "containment." The "Eisenhower Doctrine" extended the "Truman Doctrine." Dulles's strictures against neutralism sounded very much like Truman's declaration that all nations must choose between two ways of life. The "domino theory" in Asia differed little from Truman's alarmist predictions that if Greece fell, the Middle East would fall and Europe would collapse. Eisenhower and Dulles reinforced the Truman-Acheson hostility to "Red China." Both administrations intervened, with different methods, in the Middle East. Both bolstered the nation's nuclear arsenal. Both nourished overseas economic interests as essential to U.S. and world stability. Both sought to draw West Germany into Western Europe. America's Cold War institutions, its high defense budgets, its large foreign-affairs bureaucracy, its assumptions from the past, its export of culture—all ground on.

But the world had changed. In 1945 the United States sat atop the international system. Few restraints obstructed its power. As the Soviet Union and the United States built their economies and military forces toward a stalemate, particularly in Europe, the bonds of stability loosened elsewhere. Throughout the 1950s new nations claimed independence, threw off colonialism, and charted an independent course in the Cold War. Troubles for the two major powers also erupted in their own spheres of influence, as client states and allies challenged great-power hegemony in Latin America, and political turmoil and anti-Yankeeism grew apace. The 1959 victory of nationalists in the Cuban Revolution symbolized the new challenge (see next chapter). Japanese rioters forced Eisenhower to cancel his trip to Japan, and Europeans such as Charles de Gaulle of France resisted U.S. influence. The Soviets faced growing discontent in Eastern Europe and the Sino-Soviet split. In short, Dulles and Eisenhower "overestimated the reach of communism" and "underestimated the power of nationalism." Nuclear proliferation scared both sides. "Soon even little countries will have a stockpile of these bombs," Eisenhower worried in 1954, "and then we *will* be in a mess." Britain (1952), France (1960), and China (1964) independently developed atomic bombs.

The world was becoming multipolar. Neither the Soviet Union nor the United States, tied to rigid policies and military programs, adjusted well to the more fluid international system. Although each professed sympathy with Third World needs and aspirations, both sought to curb national self-determination in decolonizing areas. U.S. antipathy toward revolutionary nationalism, socialism, and neutralism created an anti-American backlash among non-Western peoples. So did CIA activities in Iran and Guatemala, the training of counterrevolutionaries in South Vietnam (see next chapter), the sending of troops into Lebanon, and alliances such as SEATO and the Baghdad Pact. Both the United States and the Soviet Union, in their drive to win friends through foreign aid and subversion, saw Third World nations manipulate Cold-War rivalries to gain economic assistance and military hardware from both sides.

Unimaginative in dealing with the Third World, the Eisenhower administration also lacked innovation in its relations with the Soviet Union and China. The arms race evolved into a space race and missile race. Washington seemed only minimally interested in reducing tension in Central Europe and Germany, quickly rejecting the Rapacki Plan and "disengagement" proposals. The Soviet Union seemed serious about cooling the arms race, but Moscow, too, so distrusted the other side that negotiations produced little. Nonrecognition of China simply isolated the United States from one of the world's important nations. Standing firmly with Jiang on Formosa revealed obstinacy, not wisdom, when many other Western nations recognized Beijing and traded with the People's Republic.

McCarthyism inhibited movement toward détente, but it had waned by 1954. The president also deflected another challenge, a proposed amendment to the Constitution. The Bricker Amendment, first offered in 1951 by Republican senator John Bricker of Ohio, sought primarily to limit the effects in the United States of UN-sponsored agreements on human rights. But it also included restrictions on executive agreements to ensure that presidents did not skirt the treaty-making power of the Senate. Hoping to force the president to consult more with Congress on foreign-policy issues and to forestall another Yalta, the amendment's backers insisted that executive agreements be voted on like treaties. Vowing to "fight up and down the country" against this "stupid, blind violation of [the] Constitution by stupid, blind isolationists," Eisenhower, with help from liberal Democrats and moderate Republicans, beat back the amendment in a close Senate vote in February 1954. Eisenhower thereafter consulted regularly with legislators on major foreign policies, with the conspicuous exception of covert operations. Congress usually granted his requests. The Cold War consensus shaped in the 1940s continued strong. The Eisenhower administration failed to devise new policies for new realities, then, not because of Joe McCarthy and the China Lobby but because of its own uncompromising assumptions.

In the election of 1960, the Democrats claimed that the Cold War could be won. They differed from Eisenhower over methods to continue the old fight and to reverse the declining position of the United States in the Third World. The Democratic party and its presidential candidate, Senator John F. Kennedy, embraced the anticommunist absolutes of the era as heartily as John Foster Dulles ever had. Eisenhower's political critics charged that he and his secretary of state had caused the United States to fall behind in the missile race and that they had squandered American power.

Historical assessments of the Eisenhower administration used to stress its rigid conservatism, passive style, limited achievements, and hesitancy to adjust to new circumstances. More recently, scholars have emphasized Eisenhower's "prudence and sober judgment"—his moderate approach to most problems, his command of policymaking, his political savvy, and his commitment to arms control. Yet Eisenhower's loyalty program damaged the Foreign Service. His expansion of the CIA and covert operations proved dangerous and short-sighted. Whatever his doubts about the insanity of the nuclear arms race, he accelerated it and left a legacy of nuclear fear. Eisenhower distrusted Jiang's Nationalists and preferred a "two Chinas" policy, but a hard-line posture toward the People's Republic of China risked nuclear war more than once. Eisenhower revisionism has stimulated healthy reconsideration of the period. But while Ike did not stumble over the brink, he remained a zealous anticommunist of little flexibility and little innovation whose diplomatic record is at best mixed.

FURTHER READING FOR THE PERIOD 1950–1961

Some works cited in Chapter 7 also cover this period.

The Korean War is explored in Bruce Cumings, *The Origins of the Korean War* (1981 and 1990; rev. ed. 2004), *Korea's Place in the Sun* (1997), and ed., *Child of Conflict* (1983); Rosemary Foot, *The Wrong War* (1985) and *A Substitute for Victory* (1990); Sergei N. Goncharov, John W. Lewis, and Xue Litai, *Uncertain Partners* (1994); John Halliday and Bruce Cumings, *Korea* (1988); Jian Chen, *China's Road to the Korean War* (1994); Peter Lowe, *The Origins of the Korean War* (1997); Callum A. MacDonald, *Korea* (1987); John Merrill, *Korea* (1989); Allan R. Millett, *Their War for Korea* (2004); Bonnie B. C. Oh, ed., *Korea Under the American Military Government* (2002); Gordon L. Rottman, *The Korean War Order of Battle* (2002); Michael Schaller, *Douglas MacArthur* (1989); William Stueck, *Rethinking the Korean War* (2002) and *The Korean War in World History* (2004); Richard C. Thornton, *Odd Man Out* (2000); John Toland, *In Mortal Combat* (1991); Richard Whelan, *Drawing the Line* (1990); and Shu Guang Zhang, *Mao's Military Romanticism* (1996).

For the 1950s and President Dwight D. Eisenhower, see Craig Allen, *Eisenhower and the Mass Media* (1993); Stephen E. Ambrose, *Eisenhower* (1983–1984) and *Nixon* (1987); Michael R. Beschloss, *MAYDAY* (1986) (U-2); Günter Bischof and Stephen E. Ambrose, eds., *Eisenhower* (1995); Meena Bose, *Shaping and Signaling Presidential Policy* (1998) (Eisenhower and Kennedy); H. W. Brands, Jr., *Cold Warriors* (1988); Jeff Broadwater, *Eisenhower and the Anti-Communist Crusade* (1992); Ira Chernus, *General Eisenhower: Ideology and Discourse* (2002); Blanche W. Cook, *The Declassified Eisenhower* (1981); Mary L. Dudziak, *Cold War Civil Rights* (2002); Fred I. Greenstein, *The Hidden-Hand Presidency* (1982); Robert H. Johnson, *Improbable Dangers* (1994); Burton I. Kaufman, *Trade and Aid* (1982); Michael T. Klare, *American Arms Supermarket* (1985); Michael L. Krenn, *Black Diplomacy* (1998); Elaine Tyler May, *Homeward Bound* (1988); Chester J. Pach Jr., and Elmo Richardson, *The Presidency of Dwight D. Eisenhower* (1991); James T. Patterson, *Grand Expectations* (1996); William B. Pickett, *Dwight David Eisenhower and American Power* (1995); Brenda G. Plummer, *Rising Wind* (1996) (African Americans); Caroline Pruden, *Conditional Partners* (1998) (United Nations); Duane Tananbaum, *The Bricker Amendment Controversy* (1988); and Tom Wicker, *Dwight D. Eisenhower* (2002).

John Foster Dulles is studied in Richard H. Immerman, ed., *John Foster Dulles and the Diplomacy of the Cold War* (1990) and *John Foster Dulles* (1999); Frederick W. Marks, *Power and Peace* (1993); and Ronald W. Pruessen, *John Foster Dulles* (1982).

Other biographical studies include Jeff Broadwater, *Adlai Stevenson* (1994); Lee Feigon, *Mao* (2002); James T. Patterson, *Mr. Republican* (1972) (Senator Robert Taft); and William Taubman, *Khrushchev* (2003).

For the Soviet Union and Europe, consult Volker R. Berghahn, *America and the Intellectual Cold Wars in Europe* (2001); Günter Bischof and Saki Dockrill, eds., *Cold War Respite* (1999); Frank Costigliola, *France and the United States* (1992); Audrey K. Cronin, *Great Power Politics and the Struggle over Austria* (1986); Ennio Di Nolfo, ed., *Power in Europe? II* (1992); Alexander L. George et al., eds., *U.S.-Soviet Security Cooperation* (1988); Jeffrey Glen Giauque, *Grand Designs and Visions of Unity* (2002) (European Union); Robert P. Grathwol and Donita M. Moorhus, *Berlin and the American Military* (1998); William Glenn Gray, *Germany's Cold War* (2003); Wolfram F. Hanrieder, *Germany, America, Europe* (1989); Hope M. Harrison, *Driving the Soviets up the Wall* (2003) (East Germany); Ted Hopf, *Social Constructions of International Politics* (2002) (Soviet Union); Klaus Larres, *Churchill's Cold War* (2002); William Roger Louis and Hedley Bull, eds., *The Special Relationship* (1986) (Britain); Thomas Risse-Kappan, *Cooperation Among Democracies* (1995); and Irwin M. Wall, *France, the United States, and the Algerian War* (2001).

The nuclear arms race, missile development, and antinuclear views are treated in Timothy Botti, *Ace in the Hole* (1996) (why nuclear weapons were not used); Ian Clark, *Nuclear Diplomacy and the Special Relationship* (1994) (U.S.-Britain); Campbell Craig, *Destroying the Village* (1998); Robert A. Divine, *Blowing on the Wind* (1978) and *The Sputnik Challenge* (1993); Stephen Endicott and Edward Hagerman, *The United States and Biological Warfare* (1999); Sharon Ghemar-Tabrizi, *The Worlds of Herman Kahn* (2005); Peter Goodchild, *Edward Teller* (2005); Gregg F. Herken, *Counsels of War* (1985); Richard G. Hewlett and Jack M. Holl, *Atoms for Peace* (1989); Fred Kaplan, *The Wizards of Armageddon* (1983); Milton S. Katz, *Ban the Bomb* (1986); Dean W. Kohlhoff, *Amchitka and the Bomb* (2002); Walter A. McDougall, *The Heavens and the Earth* (1985); Peter Roman, *Eisenhower and the Missile Gap* (1995); David K. Stumpf and Jay W. Kelley, *Titan II* (2000); Marc Trachtenberg, *History and Strategy* (1991); Andreas Wenger, *Eisenhower, Kennedy, and Nuclear Weapons* (1997); and Lawrence S. Wittner, *The Struggle Against the Bomb* (1998).

For culture and cultural expansion, see works cited in Chapter 7 and Manuela Aguilar, *Cultural Diplomacy and Foreign Policy* (1996) (U.S.-Germany); Thomas Doherty, *Cold War Cool Medium* (2005) (television); Paul R. Edwards, *The Closed World* (1996) (computers); Robert H. Haddow, *Pavilions of Plenty* (1997); Margot A. Henriksen, *Dr. Strangelove's America* (1997); Walter L. Hixson, *Parting the Curtain* (1997); Michael Krenn, *Fall-Out Shelters for the Human Spirit* (2005); Rob Kroes, *If You've Seen One, You've Seen the Mall* (1996); Laura McEnany, *Civil Defense Begins at Home* (2000); Yale Richmond, *Cultural Exchange and the Cold War* (2003); Ron Robin, *The Making of the Cold War Enemy* (2001) (military-industrial complex); Kenneth D. Rose, *One Nation Underground* (2001) (fallout shelters); Victor Rosenberg, *Soviet-American Relations, 1953–1960: Diplomacy and Cultural Exchange During the Eisenhower Presidency* (2005); and Penny Von Eschen, *Satchmo Blows Up the World* (2004).

Asian questions, including China, the offshore islands crises, and Japan, are studied in Robert Accinelli, *Crisis and Commitment* (1996) (Taiwan); S. Mahmud Ali, *Cold War in the High Himalayas* (1999), Stanley D. Bachrack, *The Committee of One Million* (1976) (China Lobby); Roger Buckley, *U.S.-Japan Alliance Diplomacy, 1945–1990* (1992); Gordon H. Chang, *Friends and Enemies* (1990); Thomas J. Christensen, *Useful Adversaries* (1996); Warren I. Cohen, *America's Response to China* (1990); Nick Cullather, *Illusions of Influence* (1994) (Philippines); Harry Harding and Yuan Ming, eds., *Sino-American Relations, 1945–1955* (1989); Audrey R. Kahin and George McT. Kahin, *Subversion as Foreign Policy* (1995) (Indonesia); Mercy A. Kuo, *Contending with Contradictions* (2001); Peter Lowe, *Containing the Cold War in East Asia* (1997); David A. Mayers, *Cracking the Monolith* (1986); Nancy B. Tucker, *Taiwan, Hong Kong, and the United States* (1994); Odd Arne Wested, ed., *Brothers in Arms* (1999); Qiang Zhai, *The Dragon, the Lion, & the Eagle* (1994); and Shu Guang Zhang, *Deterrence and Strategic Culture* (1992) (China). Studies of Indochina/Vietnam appear in Chapter 9.

For the Third World, H. W. Brands, *The Specter of Neutralism* (1989); Gabriel Kolko, *Confronting the Third World* (1988); Robert J. McMahon, *The Cold War on the Periphery* (1994) (India and Pakistan); Thomas J. Noer, *Cold War and Black Liberation* (1985) (Africa); Andrew J. Rotter, *Comrades at Odds* (2000) (India); Peter J. Schraeder, *United States Foreign Policy Toward Africa* (1994); and Stanley Wolpert, *Nehru* (1997). See also works cited in Chapters 7, 9–12.

For U.S. relations with the Middle East, especially with Egypt and Israel, see Isaac Alteras, *Eisenhower and Israel* (1993); Nigel J. Ashton, *Eisenhower, Macmillan, and the Problem of Nasser* (1996); George W. Ball and Douglas B. Ball, *The Passionate Attachment* (1992) (Israel); Abraham Ben-Zvi, *Decade of Transition* (1998) (Israel); William J. Burns, *Economic Aid and American Policy Toward Egypt* (1985); Zvi Ganin, *An Uneasy Relationship* (2004) (Israel); Mark Gasiorowski, ed., *Mohammed Mossadeq and the 1953 Coup in Iran* (2004); Irene Gendzier, *Notes from the Minefield* (1997) (Lebanon); Peter L. Hahn, *Caught in the Middle* (2004); Parker T. Hart, *Saudi Arabia and the United States* (1999); Zach Levey, *Israel and the Western Power, 1952–1960* (1997); Douglas Little, *American Orientalism* (2002); Melani McAlister, *Epic Encounters* (2005); Michael Oren, *The Origins of the Second Arab-Israeli War* (1993); William R. Polk, *The Arab World Today* (1991); Cheryl Rubenberg, *Israel and the American National Interest* (1986); Bonnie Saunders, *The United States and Arab Nationalism* (1996) (Syria); David Schoenbaum, *The United States and the State of Israel* (1993); and Steven L. Spiegel, *The Other Arab-Israeli Conflict* (1985).

The Suez crisis is included in many of the works above, but especially see Steven Freiberger, *Dawn Over Suez* (1992); Diane B. Kunz, *The Economic Diplomacy of the Suez Crisis* (1991); William Roger Louis and Roger Owen, eds., *Suez 1956* (1989); and Selwyn Troen, ed., *The Sinai-Suez Crisis, 1956* (1990).

Latin American–U.S. relations and the intervention in Guatemala are treated in Elizabeth A. Cobbs, *The Rich Neighbor Policy* (1992); Nick Cullather, *Secret History* (1999) (CIA in Guatemala); Michael D. Gambone, *Eisenhower, Somoza, and the Cold War in Nicaragua* (1997); Piero Gleijeses, *Shattered Hope* (1991) (Guatemala); Michael R. Hall, *Sugar and Power in the Dominican Republic* (2000); Richard Immerman, *The CIA in Guatemala* (1982); Stephen Kinzer and Stephen Schlesinger, *Bitter Fruit* (1982) (Guatemala); John V. Kofas, *The Sword of Damocles* (2002) (Colombia, Chile); Walter LaFeber, *The Panama Canal* (1989) and *Inevitable Revolutions* (1993)

(Central America); Abraham F. Lowenthal, ed., *Exporting Democracy* (1991); A. W. Maldonado, *Teodoro Moscoso and Puerto Rico's Operation Bootstrap* (1997); Nicola Miller, *Soviet Relations with Latin America, 1959–1987* (1989); Thomas G. Paterson, *Contesting Castro* (1994); Stephen G. Rabe, *Eisenhower and Latin America* (1988); Darlene Rivas, *Missionary Capitalist* (2002) (Venezuela); David F. Schmitz, *Thank God They're on Our Side* (1999) (right-wing dictatorships); Lars Schoultz, *Beneath the United States* (1998); Gaddis Smith, *The Last Years of the Monroe Doctrine* (1994); and Peter H. Smith, *Talons of the Eagle* (1996).

For the Central Intelligence Agency and its covert activities, see Stephen E. Ambrose, *Ike's Spies* (1981); Sigmund Diamond, *Compromised Campus* (1992); Peter Grose, *Gentleman Spy* (1994) (Allen Dulles); Loch K. Johnson, *America's Secret Power* (1989); Ludwell L. Montagne, *General Walter Bedell Smith as Director of Central Intelligence* (1992); John Ranelagh, *The Agency* (1986); Frances Stoner Saunders, *The Cultural Cold War* (2000); Evan Thomas, *The Very Best Men* (1995); and Robin W. Winks, *Cloak & Gown* (1987).

For the impact of McCarthyism, consult works cited in Chapter 7 and Robert Griffith, *The Politics of Fear* (1987); M. J. Heale, *McCarthy's Americans* (1998); David K. Johnson, *The Lavender Scare* (2003); William W. Keller, *The Liberals and J. Edgar Hoover* (1989); Stanley I. Kutler, *The American Inquisition* (1982); Mary S. McAuliffe, *Crisis on the Left* (1978); Thomas C. Reeves, *The Life and Times of Joe McCarthy* (1982); Ellen W. Schrecker, *No Ivory Tower* (1986) and *Many Are the Crimes* (1998); Athan Theoharis and John S. Cox, *The Boss* (1988) (J. Edgar Hoover); Stephen Vaughn, *Ronald Reagan in Hollywood* (1994); and Stephen J. Whitfield, *The Culture of the Cold War* (1991).

See also Robert L. Beisner, ed., *Guide to American Foreign Relations Since 1600* (2003).

For comprehensive coverage of foreign-related topics, see the articles in the four-volume *Encyclopedia of U.S. Foreign Relations* (1997), edited by Bruce W. Jentleson and Thomas G. Paterson.

CHAPTER ✳ 9

Passing the Torch: The Vietnam Years, 1961–1969

✳ *The Tet Offensive in Vietnam, 1968*

"THEY'RE COMING IN! VC in the compound," the young MP shouted into his radio. Seconds later Vietcong (VC) commandos killed him. Moments before, about 3:00 A.M. that January 30, 1968, the U.S. Embassy in Saigon, South Vietnam, was quiet, the only noise coming from the air conditioners and the fireworks exploding in celebration of Tet, the Lunar New Year. Completed in 1967 at a cost of $2.6 million, the embassy building was protected by shatterproof windows, a concrete sun shield covering the entire structure, and a thick, eight-foot-high outer wall. The fortified building had become "the symbol of America's power" in Vietnam.

At 2:45 A.M., a taxi cab and truck exited a repair shop near the embassy. About fifteen Vietcong leaped out after a huge explosion blew a three-foot hole in the wall. The VC scrambled through, firing automatic rifles at two embassy MPs (military police), who radioed for help before they died. The invaders then unleashed their antitank guns and rockets, transported into Saigon weeks before under shipments of tomatoes and firewood. The thick embassy doors took a direct hit, sending the U.S. seal crashing to the ground. Inside, a crew of Central Intelligence Agency and Foreign Service officials felt as if they were "in a telephone booth in the *Titanic.*" A few blocks away, aides whisked Ambassador Ellsworth Bunker away to a secret hiding place.

The news of the attack quickly reached the United States. Few U.S. leaders could believe that the enemy had breached "Bunker's bunker." On January 17, in his State of the Union message, President Lyndon B. Johnson himself had called most of South Vietnam secure, and the embassy seemed the most secure of all.

In Saigon's dim morning light, American soldiers counterattacked. By 9:15 A.M., with the compound secure, General William C. Westmoreland counted nineteen dead Vietnamese, five dead Americans, and two Vietcong prisoners. He then declared an American victory. One reporter described the compound as a "butcher shop in Eden."

"Wise Men." From 1965 to 1968, President Lyndon Johnson periodically received advice on Vietnam from experienced members of the foreign policy establishment (most were Truman-era diplomats and generals)—a group christened the "Wise Men." Dean Acheson (with mustache) and Secretary of State Dean Rusk (on the far right) are pictured here in a meeting with Johnson and aides. This group's consistent support for escalation led Assistant Secretary of Defense John McNaughton to remark that "a feeling is widely and strongly held" around the country that "the Establishment is out of its mind." After the Tet Offensive, when the Wise Men reversed course and urged LBJ to withdraw, the president grudgingly accepted their advice. (Lyndon Baines Johnson Library)

The bold sally against the embassy comprised but one part of the massive, well-coordinated Tet offensive. The forays struck thirty-six of the forty-four provincial capitals, some one hundred other villages, the gigantic Tan Son Nhut air base, and numerous sites in Saigon (see map, page 241). The communist forces attacked after half of the South Vietnamese Army (ARVN) had gone on leave for the Tet holiday. The VC, or National Liberation Front (NLF), and North Vietnamese hoped to seize the cities, foment a general sympathetic uprising, force ARVN and U.S. troops to move to the cities—leaving a vacuum in the countryside—and disrupt the governmental bureaucracy. In the end, Washington would presumably negotiate American withdrawal.

Yet the ARVN and U.S. armies struck back: "Forced to fight in the cities, they bombed, shelled, and strafed the most populous districts as if they saw no distinction between them and the jungle." Americans at home recoiled from the carnage. To fight enemy troops in Hue, South Vietnam's old imperial capital, U.S. and ARVN forces used everything from nausea gas to rockets. After three weeks of vicious warfare, the communists fled, 100,000 people had become refugees, thousands lay dead, and American bombings had reduced a once-beautiful city to rubble. The NLF executed hundreds, perhaps thousands, of civilians, most of them connected with the South Vietnamese government or Americans. The NLF commander at Hue later wrote: "There is never an easy 'political' victory . . . without first having to shed blood and scatter bones on the battlefield."

"What the Hell's Ho Chi Minh Doing Answering Our Saigon Embassy Phone . . . ?"   Paul Conrad's cartoon of President Lyndon B. Johnson expressed well the startled American response to the attack on the U.S. Embassy in South Vietnam in January 1968. Johnson had earlier reported that most of South Vietnam had been secured against the Vietcong and North Vietnamese. But General Earl Wheeler explained that "in a city like Saigon people can infiltrate easily. . . . This is about as tough to stop as it is to protect against individual muggings in Washington, D.C." (© 1968, *Los Angeles Times.* Reprinted with permission Los Angeles Times Syndicate)

In the northwest corner of South Vietnam, U.S. soldiers bravely resisted a siege of their base at Khe Sanh, which, according to Westmoreland, "served to lure North Vietnamese to their deaths." Hundreds of Americans died during the first months of 1968, as enemy rockets zeroed in on the strategic but vulnerable position. American B-52s countered by dropping tons of bombs on the surrounding area. By April, remembered a colonel, "the jungle had become literally a desert . . . a landscape of splinters and bomb craters." Khe Sanh held, just barely.

The provincial capital of Ben Tre symbolized the costs of the Tet offensive. To ferret out the NLF, American and ARVN forces leveled Ben Tre, killing a thousand civilians. In unforgettable words, a U.S. officer declared that "it became necessary to destroy the town to save it." That statement joined a visual image to sear American memory. The NBC news program of February 2 showed a film clip of the national police chief of South Vietnam pointing a pistol at the head of a suspected VC. General Nguyen Ngoc pulled the trigger and blasted the young man. The fifty-two seconds of footage, said an NBC producer, broadcast the "rawest, roughest film anyone had ever seen."

The Johnson administration, having claimed before Tet that South Vietnam had gained the upper hand in the war, suffered an ever-growing "credibility gap." January proved a bad month for Lyndon B. Johnson. On the twenty-third the North Koreans captured the American spy ship *Pueblo* and its entire crew off the Korean coast. The international balance of payments for the United States, Johnson learned, was running at an annual deficit of $7 billion. And Senator Eugene McCarthy, a "dove" on Vietnam, challenged Johnson's renomination to the presidency.

Critics probed the administration's assertion that Tet counted as a triumph. Senator Robert F. Kennedy, soon to become a candidate for the Democratic presidential nomination, said: "It is as if James Madison [had claimed] victory in 1812 because the British only burned Washington instead of annexing it to the British Empire." After Secretary Robert S. McNamara recited enemy casualties, a reporter queried: "Isn't there something Orwellian about it, that the more we kill, the stronger they get?" When the popular television newscaster Walter Cronkite of CBS judged the war a stalemate, LBJ moaned: "If I've lost Cronkite, I've lost middle America."

Some 45,000 NLF, 2,000 ARVN, and 1,000 American soldiers died. More than 14,000 Vietnamese civilians died and 24,000 were wounded. One-eighth of the South Vietnamese people became homeless refugees in their own land. North Vietnamese General Vo Nguyen Giap "was callous," Westmoreland later charged. "Had any American general taken such losses he wouldn't have lasted three weeks." Giap had actually opposed an ambitious offensive when NLF military leaders first proposed it in April 1967. Ho Chi Minh, the most eminent figure in the North Vietnamese government, sympathized with the Southern cadres' impatience with protracted war and overruled his chief general. But seeing the NLF devastated as a fighting force in the wake of Tet staggered Ho, who "silently regretted not having listened to Giap." Ho's health declined and "[u]nable even to sleep, he died the next year."

Despite a brave front, the U.S. president also reeled from the impact of Tet. Johnson authorized 10,500 more troops for Vietnam, gave hawkish speeches against quitting under fire, and flamboyantly toured U.S. military bases. "Give me the lesser of evils," said LBJ as he asked the new secretary of defense, Clark Clifford, to undertake a major review of Vietnam policy. In late February General Westmoreland had recommended that an additional 206,000 American troops join the more than 500,000 already there. The generals planned a major new ARVN-U.S. offensive. Within the Pentagon, formerly timid dissenters pleaded for deescalation. "Let's go in and win or else get out," a group of U.S. governors recommended. In early March, too, Secretary of State Dean Rusk suggested curtailing the bombing of North Vietnam to induce peace talks. In the New Hampshire Democratic primary on March 12, McCarthy made a strong showing by polling 42 percent of the vote to Johnson's 49 percent. Speaking for the Wise Men, former secretary of state Dean Acheson put it bluntly: "We can no longer do the job we ought to do in the time we have left and we must begin to take steps to disengage."

Clifford came to the same conclusion. "Nothing had prepared me for the weakness of the military's case," he recalled. His Ad Hoc Task Force on Vietnam recommended in early March sending 20,000 additional American troops. But Clifford's group found "no reason to believe" that 206,000 more troops—"or double or triple that quantity"—could achieve victory. The strategy of attrition had created "a sinkhole," said the report. Johnson's advisers also expressed alarm that the Vietnam War had initiated a gold and dollar crisis that threatened the economic well-being of the United States. Nervous foreigners rushed to exchange their dollars for gold. On March 14 alone, international investors redeemed $372 million for gold. A post-Tet

Lyndon Baines Johnson (1908–1973). A tired president confers with Generals Creighton Abrams and Earl Wheeler at the National Security Council Meeting of March 27, 1968. A few days later Johnson removed himself as a candidate in the presidential race. Johnson once told his vice president, Hubert Humphrey, "I'm not temperamentally equipped to be Commander in Chief. . . . I'm too sentimental to give the orders." (Courtesy of the Lyndon Baines Johnson Library)

military buildup would cost billions more, further bloat the deficit-burdened budget, and panic foreign owners of dollars even more. Clifford's friends in the business community found America "in a hopeless bog." The "sheer accumulation" of negative views turned Johnson toward deescalation. In a dream he saw himself as Woodrow Wilson paralyzed from the neck down.

On March 31 LBJ spoke on television. "We are prepared to move immediately toward peace through negotiations," he announced. Although another 13,500 soldiers would go to South Vietnam, U.S. airplanes would halt their bombing of a major portion of North Vietnam. "Even this limited bombing of the North could come to an early end—if our restraint is matched in Hanoi [the North Vietnamese capital]." To the amazement of viewers, Johnson also declared that he would not seek reelection. On April 3 the North Vietnamese agreed to go to the conference table. Discussions began on May 14. The fighting and talking—and dying—would go on for several years more. Many GIs no longer thought the war worth fighting, as they said in their familiar slogan: "It don't mean nothin'."

Vietnamese Wars Before 1961

Why Vietnam? Why did this Southeast Asian land of peasant farmers become the site of America's longest war? The origins are found in the centuries-long story of Vietnamese resistance to foreigners—Chinese, French, Japanese, and American. In 1867 France colonized Vietnam and soon began to exploit the country's raw materials, as well as those of Laos and Cambodia, which became part of French Indochina in the 1890s. Rice, rubber, tin, and tungsten from the area flowed to

Ho Chi Minh (1890–1969). His name meant "enlightened one" and was merely the most famous of more than fifty shifting aliases he used throughout his life. Described by the journalist David Halberstam as "part Gandhi, part Lenin, all Vietnamese," Ho often used the United States as an example of a successful anticolonial revolution. His chief biographer, William Duiker, however, argues that Ho might not have been completely sincere in his overtures to Washington after World War II, contending that he "was quite willing to make tactical alliances with potential adversaries in the full understanding that such arrangements might only be temporary in character." After 1955, Ho delegated more and more authority to younger party members and took an increasingly ceremonial role in the affairs of North Vietnam. (© Picture Research Consultants)

European markets. France constructed a repressive imperial government and monopolized land holdings, while some 80 percent of the Vietnamese people subsisted as poor, rural peasants. From 1867 onward the embittered Vietnamese battled their French overlords.

Vietnam's most famous nationalist leader was Ho Chi Minh, born in 1890 to a low-level government employee. Described by a U.S. intelligence officer as a "wisp of a man . . . intelligent, well-versed in the problems of his country, rational, and dedicated," Ho traveled to Europe and at the time of World War I lobbied futilely for independence. Because the Communist party seemed the only political force vigorously denouncing colonialism, Ho and other nationalists joined it. Throughout the twenties and thirties he lived and agitated in China and Russia. In 1930–1931 the French brutally suppressed a Vietnamese peasant rebellion.

During 1940–1941 the Japanese took over Vietnam but left collaborating French officials in charge. Vietnamese nationalists, including Ho's communists, went underground, used China as a base, and in 1941 organized the Vietminh, a coalition of nationalist groups. In the final days of World War II, Vietminh guerrillas tangled with Japanese troops, liberated some northern provinces, and cooperated with the U.S. Office of Strategic Services (OSS). Agency officials judged Ho "a convinced

Democrat." Ho sent formal messages to Washington, asked for recognition, and often spoke in understandable English about America—its history and its support for "free, popular governments all over the world." In late August 1945, Ho's Vietminh organized the Democratic Republic of Vietnam (DRV) in Hanoi. On September 2, he proclaimed Vietnam's independence, borrowing phrases from America's document of July 4, 1776. Still, Ho remained privately suspicious of Americans as "only interested in replacing the French. . . . They are capitalists to the core."

During World War II, President Franklin D. Roosevelt often remarked that France should relinquish Indochina. He toyed with the idea of a trusteeship. The Department of State valued the Southeast Asian countries as "potentially important markets for American exports." Some American officials also worried that denying France its empire would alienate a potential European ally. Prime Minister Winston Churchill, moreover, informed Roosevelt in no uncertain terms that Britain opposed the breakup of empires. Just before he died, Roosevelt retreated. He "did not want to get mixed up in any Indochina decision" with an agitated Churchill at Yalta, he said.

The French, with British military help and American acquiescence, returned to Vietnam. Ignored by the United States, receiving no support from Moscow, and now facing French forces, the Vietminh accepted a compromise with France in March 1946: DRV status as a "free state" in the French Union and French military occupation of northern Vietnam. Vietminh and French soldiers clashed in December. One French bombardment of Haiphong killed several thousand civilians. The Vietminh responded with guerrilla terror. For the next eight years Vietnam endured bloody combat, with the French holding the cities and the Vietminh the countryside. One French military commander compared fighting the Vietminh "to ridding a dog of its fleas. We can pick them, drown them, and poison them, but they will be back in a few days."

To win Paris's favor for its postwar policies in Europe, Washington tolerated the return of French colonialism to Vietnam. As the Cold War intensified in 1946–1947, Ho's Moscow "training" became a topic of American discussion. The Department of State designated him an agent of international communism, although some diplomats pointed out that Vietnamese leaders were nationalists and that Ho stood as an Asian Tito. In 1948 the French installed Emperor Bao Dai, who had served the Japanese in World War II, as their Vietnamese leader. Paris actively lobbied for U.S. support of this puppet government, hoping that U.S. recognition would make the Vietnamese "more disposed to reach an agreement with France [and abandon the Vietminh]." In February 1950, in a move inspired by fear of Communist Chinese expansion, Washington recognized the Bao Dai government. In May, moreover, the Truman administration extended aid to the French for their war in Vietnam.

The Korean War accentuated Washington's interest in the Vietnamese rebellion. In 1950 Truman sent $150 million and military advisers to Vietnam. For 1945–1954 the United States gave $2 billion of the $5 billion that Paris spent to battle Ho's forces. In 1954 U.S. aid covered 78 percent of the cost of the war, and some 300 Americans went to Vietnam as part of the Military Assistance Advisory Group—all to no avail.

In spring 1954, at Dienbienphu, a fortress where the besieged French had chosen to stand or fall, Vietminh forces moved toward a major, symbolic victory. To save the fortress, the French sought U.S. intervention. President Eisenhower received conflicting advice. The chair of the Joint Chiefs of Staff, Admiral Arthur Radford, urged massive night attacks on Vietminh positions by 300 U.S. carrier aircraft, possibly including tactical nuclear weapons. Army chief of staff Matthew Ridgeway, however, judged intervention a "hare-brained tactical scheme." A Defense Department analyst agreed that "one cannot go over Niagara Falls in a barrel only slightly." Eisenhower cited the "falling domino" analogy to explain U.S. interests in Southeast Asia and then sounded out Congress, France, and Britain about internationalizing the war through "United Action." Members of Congress warned against an air strike that might lead next to ground troops and another Korea. London also balked. Without U.S. intervention, French forces at Dienbienphu surrendered on May 7.

A few days earlier, on April 26, 1954, representatives from France, the Soviet Union, Britain, China, the United States, Bao Dai's Vietnam, the DRV, Laos, and Cambodia met in Geneva. The Eisenhower administration, fearing a French retreat, reluctantly agreed to discuss Vietnam at the conference. In fact, a new French government came to power on June 12 and pledged to end the war. President Eisenhower expected to "gag" on any Geneva agreement but vowed to "salvage something." China's Zhou Enlai pressed Ho's Vietminh (now controlling two-thirds of Vietnam) to make peace so as to "consolidate and develop our forces in order to make further progress later on."

On July 20 the DRV and France signed the Geneva agreements. The terms: temporary partition of Vietnam at the seventeenth parallel; French withdrawal to below that latitude; neither North nor South Vietnam to sign military alliances or permit foreign bases on Vietnamese soil; national elections to be held in 1956; unification of the country after elections; and elections also in neighboring strife-torn Laos and Cambodia, the other territories in French Indochina. Refusing to endorse the accords, the United States did state that it would "refrain from the threat or the use of force." The National Security Council found the Geneva settlement a "disaster" that represented a "major forward stride of Communism which may lead to the loss of Southeast Asia."

To stop "losing areas of the free world forever," Eisenhower established the Southeast Asia Treaty Organization in September 1954 to protect Cambodia, Laos, and South Vietnam from communist subversion and aggression. SEATO violated the spirit of the Geneva Accords by specifying the defense of the southern half of Vietnam—now treated as a separate state. Although Great Britain, France, Pakistan, the Philippines, Thailand, Australia, and New Zealand joined the United States in the pact, only the last three later sent troops to fight in Vietnam. (SEATO disbanded in 1977.)

In the South, the United States backed the new government of Prime Minister Ngo Dinh Diem, a Vietnamese nationalist and Catholic who impressed U.S. diplomats as "a Messiah without a message." A four-year residence in the United States gained him prominent friends such as Cardinal Francis Spellman, Supreme Court Justice William O. Douglas, and Senators Mike Mansfield and John F. Kennedy. An enlarged contingent of American advisers, in violation of Geneva, began to train a South Vietnamese army, and millions of dollars in U.S. military and economic aid flowed to Diem. He and U.S. officials cooperated to displace Bao Dai

Eisenhower, Ngo Dinh Diem (1901–1963), and Dulles. The South Vietnamese nationalist Diem, from a mandarin and Catholic family, spent time in exile in the United States before returning to his country as premier (1954–1963). Dulles urged U.S. support of Diem when most people in the U.S. and West European foreign policy establishments dismissed him as "not overly intelligent" and "a fanatic." One American diplomat complained that Diem's "only present emotion, other than a lively appreciation of himself, is a blind hatred of the French." Although Diem claimed that many of the people imprisoned by his regime were communists, a large number had actually supported the French prior to 1954. (Dwight D. Eisenhower Library)

and the remnants of French influence. In mid-1955 the North proposed preliminary talks toward the national election scheduled by Geneva for 1956. Diem refused, and the Eisenhower administration, certain that Ho would win an election, endorsed cancellation of the electoral provisions of the Geneva Accords. In October 1955, Diem used blatant fraud to garner 98.2 percent of the vote in a referendum in the South.

The two Vietnams went their separate ways, with Ho's North receiving aid from both the Soviet Union and China, cautiously avoiding dependence on either. Ho launched land reform, ending a landlord system that had largely excluded peasants. Diem's Republic of Vietnam received U.S. aid of about $300 million a year (80 percent of it for the military). Working under CIA contract, Michigan State University police experts trained a "Civil Guard" to capture suspected Vietminh. Air Force colonel Edward Lansdale, on loan to the CIA, inaugurated a propaganda campaign. Slogans such as "Christ has gone to the South" along with disinformation about impending communist bloodbaths served to scare Catholics in the North into moving to the South. Some 900,000 people, most of them Catholics, made the trek. Lansdale directed sabotage operations in the North and helped Diem defeat local rivals through bribes and threats. In 1956 Diem jailed 20,000 to 30,000 suspected communists in "reeducation" camps. Torture became routine. In 1957 and 1958 southern rebels retaliated by killing village teachers, police, and government officials.

Capitalizing on general anti-Diem dissent, the Vietminh organized the National Liberation Front (NLF) in December 1960. Hanoi encouraged this communist-dominated group. In the rural areas, NLF cadres won favor from peasants

John F. Kennedy (1917–1963). Before becoming president, JFK represented Massachusetts in the House (1947–1953) and the Senate (1953–1961). His ghostwritten book *Profiles in Courage* (1957) won a Pulitzer Prize. One of the president's underpublicized achievements was the Trade Expansion Act of 1962 and the subsequent "Kennedy Round" of trade negotiations, which reduced tariffs. (*The Reporter,* 1962. Copyright 1962 by The Reporter Magazine Co.)

by distributing land and reducing rents. In contrast, Diem resisted land reform and placed family members in profitable positions. Ambassador Elbridge Durbrow criticized Diem and his brother Nhu for establishing a political party, the Can Lao, which "has created an authoritarian organization largely modeled on Communist lines" and served as a means to line the Ngo Dinh family's pockets. But U.S. military advisers continued to defend Diem.

U.S. officials charged that North Vietnamese aggression initiated this new war in the South, but most scholars conclude that the NLF sprang from the peculiar, repressive environment of Diem's regime. Vietnam's history had thus evolved from a colonial rebellion to expel the French into several interacting wars and revolutions: post-Geneva social revolution in the North; civil war within Diem's South; civil war between North and South; and, finally, an anti-imperialist war to force the Americans out. Imbued with the Cold War mentality that shoehorned events into an East-West frame, however, Americans failed to understand the singularly *Vietnamese* character of these conflicts. Senator John F. Kennedy in 1956 called Diem's Vietnam the "cornerstone of the free world in Southeast Asia, the keystone of the arch, the finger in the dike." In 1961, Kennedy became president.

John F. Kennedy and His "Action Intellectuals"

Vietnam figured little in the 1960 presidential contest between Richard M. Nixon and John F. Kennedy, who differed more in style than on policy. Kennedy, who won by a narrow margin, aroused support through the slogan "I think it's time America started moving again." Both Nixon and Kennedy belonged to the "containment generation" that imbibed the popular lessons of World War II and the Cold War. Both had won seats in Congress in 1946 and endorsed the Truman Doctrine. In 1960, Kennedy charged that the Eisenhower-Nixon administration had neglected the Third World, losing it to communism. With the U-2 affair, an adverse balance of payments, and crises in Cuba, the Congo, and Indochina as the immediate backdrop, Kennedy claimed that the United States was losing the Cold War. Warning that the country had "gone soft—physically, mentally, spiritually soft," he ridiculed Nixon for saying in the "kitchen" debate with Khrushchev that, although behind in space, "we were ahead in color television." Asserted Kennedy: "I would rather take my television black and white and have the largest rockets in the world."

Kennedy did not mind being called Truman with a Harvard accent. Born in 1917 to wealthy, Catholic, politically active parents, John Fitzgerald Kennedy graduated from Harvard College and served with honor in World War II. While his father served as ambassador to Great Britain, his senior thesis appeared as a book titled *Why England Slept* (1940), with the theme that England should have resisted Nazi aggression with force. For Kennedy's generation, "The 1930s taught us a clear lesson: aggressive conduct, if allowed to go unchecked and unchallenged, ultimately leads to war."

The new president exuded charisma. "All at once you had something exciting," recalled a student campaigner for Kennedy. Call it psychology, charm, image, or mystique, Kennedy had it. Photogenic and quick-witted, he became a television star. Handsome, articulate, dynamic, competitive, athletic, cultured, bright, self-

Kennedy and Kwame Nkrumah (1909–1972). Shown here greeting the president of Ghana in 1961, Kennedy won praise from African leaders because of his previous support of Algerian independence and for speeches advocating "a world safe for diversity." A student in the United States (1935–1945) before becoming his country's first president in 1957, Nkrumah welcomed American Peace Corps volunteers to train Ghana's educators and U.S. aid to build hydroelectric dams. While calling Kennedy "a real friend," Nkrumah also condemned Western imperialism and invited young Soviet "volunteers" to compete with the Peace Corps. On a visit to China in 1966 as a self-appointed mediator of the Vietnam War, Nkrumah was deposed by his own army. (John F. Kennedy Library)

confident, analytical, zealous—these were the traits universally ascribed to the president. People often listened not to what he said but to how he said it, and he usually said it with verve. Dean Rusk remembered him as an "incandescent man. He was on fire, and he set people around him on fire." For the historian and presidential assistant Arthur M. Schlesinger, Jr., JFK had "enormous confidence in his own luck," and "everyone around him thought he had the Midas touch and could not lose." Style and personality influence diplomacy. Many of his friends have commented that a desire for power drove John F. Kennedy, because power ensured victory. His father, Joseph P. Kennedy, "pressed his children hard to compete, never to be satisfied with anything but first place." Although Kennedy secretly suffered from near-fatal Addison's disease and received regular injections of potent drugs, JFK nonetheless projected the image of a healthy, vigorous man. His appearances with Hollywood actresses such as Marilyn Monroe and his frequent extramarital liaisons reflected his macho self-image. Kennedy also saw foreign affairs as an arena for proving his toughness. "Who gives a shit about the minimum wage?" he once asked. Kennedy soon gave Americans box scores on the missile race, the arms race, and the space race. He introduced new slogans: "The Grand Design" for Europe; the "New Africa" policy; "Flexible Response" for the military; and the "Alliance for Progress" for Latin America. Kennedy and his advisers were, as one official complained, "sort of looking for a chance to prove their muscle." Kennedy's alarmist inaugural address pledged that "the torch has been passed to a new generation" that had been "tempered by war" and "disciplined by a hard and bitter peace." Then came those moving, but in hindsight dangerously expansive, words: "We shall pay any price, bear any burden, meet any hardship, support any friend, oppose any foe to assure the survival and the success of liberty."

Makers of American Foreign Relations, 1961–1969

Presidents	Secretary of State
John F. Kennedy, 1961–1963	Dean Rusk, 1961–1969
Lyndon B. Johnson, 1963–1969	

The Kennedy people considered themselves "can-do" types who could manage crises and revive an ailing nation and world. Theodore H. White tagged them "the Action Intellectuals." They had an inordinate faith in data. When a White House assistant attempted to persuade Secretary of Defense Robert McNamara, the "whiz kid" from Ford Motor Company, that the Vietnam venture would fail, McNamara shot back: "Where is your data? Give me something I can put in the computer. Don't give me your poetry." Danger lurked in a heavy reliance on quantified information. "Ah, *les statistiques,*" said a Vietnamese general. "If you want them to go up, they will go up. If you want them to go down, they will go down." Despite McNamara's high standing with both JFK and LBJ, some experienced Washington hands were unimpressed. J. William Fulbright, chair of the Senate Foreign Relations Committee, recalled that McNamara "didn't know a thing" about international relations. "[H]e'd had a great success making cars" and then suddenly "he's running the whole military."

Kennedy's secretary of state, Dean Rusk, worked uncomfortably with the crusading "action intellectuals" but remained a loyal member of the team. Rusk had served as a military intelligence officer in Asia during World War II, as an assistant secretary of state under Truman, and as president of the Rockefeller Foundation in the 1950s. A native of Georgia and son of a Presbyterian minister, Rusk agonized over Vietnam, opposing Americanization of the war but refusing to advise withdrawal until a noncommunist government stood secure. So he ended up backing military escalation. Lyndon Johnson appreciated his loyalty: "He has the compassion of a preacher and the courage of a Georgia cracker."

Next to Attorney General Robert F. Kennedy, the president's brother, who served as troubleshooter and confidant, McGeorge Bundy became Kennedy's chief foreign-relations counselor. The brilliant forty-one-year-old former Harvard dean centralized decisionmaking in the White House. Colleagues stood in awe of Bundy's "mathematical mind . . . very clipped. Almost surgical," while others thought him "cold as ice and snippy about everything." A self-professed member of the well-born elite, Bundy arrogantly asserted that "the United States is the engine of mankind, and the rest of the world is the caboose."

Arms Buildup, Berlin, and Nation Building

The Kennedy administration emphasized military expansion. Kennedy had lambasted Eisenhower for tolerating a "missile gap" favorable to the Soviets. Eisenhower knew the politically motivated charge was nonsense. U-2 intelligence flights revealed a modest Soviet missile program. The United States had immense superiority. Kennedy and McNamara learned this, too, but, worried by Soviet boasting and Third World insurgencies, they began a mighty expansion of the military arsenal.

The administration called its defense strategy "flexible response," with a method for every kind of war. The Special Forces, or Green Berets, would conduct counterinsurgency against wars of national liberation; conventional forces would handle limited wars; more and better missiles would deter war or serve as primary weapons in nuclear war; at home, fallout shelters would protect Americans under a civil defense plan. In 1961 Kennedy increased the defense budget by 15 percent. By 1963 the United States had 275 major bases in 31 nations, 65 countries hosted U.S. forces, and the U.S. military trained soldiers in 72 countries. Also, one and a quarter million military-related American personnel were stationed overseas. In 1961 the United States had 63 ICBMs; by 1963, 424. During 1961–1963, NATO's nuclear firing power increased 60 percent. Kennedy also created the U.S. Arms Control and Disarmament Agency, but his military buildup took priority.

The more missiles Americans acquired, the more vulnerable Americans seemed to become, because the Soviets tried to catch up by also building more. With Khrushchev about to test a fifty-megaton bomb, Kennedy sought to reassure Americans about nuclear supremacy as well as to warn Moscow not to miscalculate. On October 21, 1961, Secretary McNamara's deputy, Roswell Gilpatric, announced that the United States had such a powerful nuclear retaliatory force that it could withstand a Soviet nuclear strike and still have enough missiles remaining to annihilate the Soviet Union. Moscow reacted by speeding up its ICBM program.

Kennedy met with Khrushchev at Vienna in June 1961 to discuss a test ban treaty, Berlin, and Laos. Aides warned that Khrushchev's moods ranged from "cherubic to choleric." Kennedy wanted to show the Soviets that they "must not crowd him too much." With 30,000 refugees each month escaping from East Germany to West Berlin, Khrushchev speculated that "soon there will be nobody left in the GDR [East Germany] except for [Communist boss Walter] Ulbricht and his mistress." Khrushchev told Kennedy that Berlin must become a "free city," thereby ending Western occupation. If the United States did not negotiate, Moscow would sign a separate treaty with East Germany, thus terminating the Soviet commitment to postwar occupation rights in Berlin. "Berlin is the testicles of the West," Khrushchev privately quipped. "Every time I want to make the West scream, I squeeze." Although the Kremlin leader may have left Vienna thinking that he had outdueled the young president, records of their meetings reveal that a tenacious Kennedy gave as good as he got. Still, because news accounts depicted Kennedy as "shaken and angry," the public perception developed that Khrushchev had pushed Kennedy around.

After Vienna the administration decided to force the Berlin question. On July 25, calling Berlin "the great testing place of Western courage and will," the president asked Congress for a $3.2 billion addition to the regular defense budget and authority to call up military reservists. He also requested $207 million to begin a civil defense, fallout shelter program. In a meeting with East German comrades, Khrushchev snorted that if Kennedy "starts a war then he would probably become the last president of the United States of America."

On August 13 the East Germans, backed by Moscow, suddenly put up a temporary barbed wire barricade, and later an ugly concrete barrier, between the two Berlins. Worried that his East German ally Walter Ulbricht might try to capture West Berlin, Khrushchev welcomed the wall as a solution to the crisis. The wall did shut off the exodus of refugees. Kennedy remarked that "it seems particularly stupid to risk killing millions of Americans . . . because Germans want Germany to be reunified." So he begrudgingly accepted the Wall. Unbeknownst to the president, his special representative in Berlin, General Lucius Clay, had armed U.S. tanks with bulldozer attachments to knock down the wall. Soviet intelligence learned of these preparations. Ten American M-48 tanks suddenly found themselves facing ten Russian tanks on opposite sides of Checkpoint Charlie on October 27, nearly precipitating "a nuclear-age equivalent of the Wild West Showdown at the OK Corral." With the NSC staff simulating war games in which European fatalities reached tens of millions, Kennedy used a secret channel to negotiate with Khrushchev. After sixteen tense hours, both Soviet and U.S. tanks withdrew and the crisis passed. Khrushchev later told a U.S. official that "it's been a long time since you could spank us like a little boy. Now we can swat your ass." Kennedy visited West Berlin in 1963 to assuage bruised West German feelings.

Kennedy also attended to the Third World, the region he thought most vulnerable to revolution and communism and at the same time most susceptible to U.S. influence. "Nation building" became his watchword. Recognizing the force of nationalism in the Third World, the "action intellectuals" sought to use or channel it. They hoped that through modernization, or what the Kennedy team called middle-class revolution, Third World nations would grow from economic infancy to maturity, and that evolutionary economic development would ensure noncommunist political stability. Kennedy targeted populous India because it followed a noncommunist model of economic development, bordered the People's Republic of China, and led the nonaligned movement. Although dollar assistance to India angered Pakistan, a U.S. ally, Washington nonetheless tilted toward New Delhi, especially during the Sino-Indian border war of fall 1962. In the early 1960s, India became the world's largest recipient of U.S. economic aid, for, if "we lose" the neutrals, "the balance of power could swing against us."

Khrushchev's pledge of January 1961 to support wars of national liberation seemed to raise the stakes in the Third World. To meet this test, U.S. counterinsurgency took several forms: the training of native police forces and bureaucrats, flood control, transportation and communications improvements, and community action projects. U.S. Special Forces units—Green Berets—received special attention. Kennedy personally elevated their status in the military and supervised their choice of equipment. Washington assumed it could apply America's finest technology in Vietnam to succeed where the French had failed.

Kennedy also created the Peace Corps. Established by executive order in 1961, this volunteer group of mostly young Americans numbered 6,646 by mid-1963 and 15,000 by mid-1966. Seeking "to live out the ideals of their culture," as one volunteer put it, they went into developing nations as teachers, agricultural advisers, and technicians. Peace Corps officials won plaudits for their efforts to improve Third World living conditions. Peace Corps monuments—irrigation systems, water

The New Frontier in the Third World. Tom Qualia, a Peace Corps volunteer in Bolivia, illustrates the belief, which the historian Fritz Fischer details in *Making Them Like Us* (1998), that the United States was "sending American youth into the new frontier of the third world." Not just a rhetorical device, "the volunteers were trained to expect conditions . . . similar to those of the mythic American West." The Peace Corps proved to be one of Kennedy's most popular programs and came to exemplify his reputed idealism. But he had little affection for the program, especially after the first director, his brother-in-law Sargent Shriver, persuaded Congress to make it independent of the State Department. After JFK lost that bureaucratic battle, Shriver complained that the president refused to give him any help, not even so much as a "light for a cigarette." (Courtesy of National Archives)

pumps, larger crops—arose throughout Latin America and Africa, but the corps's humanitarian efforts fell far short of eradicating the Third World's profound squalor.

The Kennedy administration also implemented the Alliance for Progress in Latin America to head off Cuban-style revolution and communist subversion. Launched in August 1961, the alliance envisioned spending $20 billion in funds from the United States and international organizations. In return, Latin Americans promised land and tax reform, housing, and health improvements. Initiated with great fanfare, the alliance soon sputtered. American businesses did not invest as expected; the State Department dragged its feet; Latin American nationalists disliked U.S. control; elites resisted reforms and pocketed U.S. dollars; middle-class Latin Americans, whom Washington counted on, proved selfish. In the end, adult literacy and infant mortality rates improved, but Latin American economies registered unimpressive growth rates, class divisions widened, unemployment climbed, and agricultural production per person declined. A U.S. embargo shut off the flow of Cuban sugar to the United States (see page 229) and made increased imports from other countries a political priority to prevent the "damaging prospect of skyrocketing prices for the key commodity."

The difficulties of nation building appeared dramatically in the Congo, which obtained hurried independence from Belgium in mid-1960. Civil war quickly erupted. Backed by U.S. and European mining interests, Moise Tshombe tried to detach Katanga Province from the new central government headed by Patrice Lumumba. The United States, fearing Soviet influence in "another Cuba," helped a UN mission quell the Katanga insurrection. Although Lumumba was killed in 1961, by early 1963 the central Congolese government had defeated Tshombe. About a year later, however, a major leftist revolt supported by the Soviet Union, China, and Ghana broke out. With UN forces gone, the CIA soon bolstered former enemy Tshombe as the new leader of the central government, and with direct U.S. aid, including military advisers, he recruited white mercenaries. The rebels responded by terrorizing white foreigners. In November 1964 a small force of Belgian paratroopers dropped from U.S. aircraft into the Congo to rescue Belgian and U.S. citizens. The historian Thomas Borstelmann has noted that "Africans, African Americans, and antiracists around the world condemned Tshombe as a stooge of Belgian mining interests and were outraged by Lumumba's assassination, which they likened to an international lynching." Nation building thus met resistance on both nationalist and racial grounds.

The Most Dangerous Area in the World: The Cuban Revolution and Latin America

In Latin America, the Cuban Revolution claimed center stage. Because Cuba might export revolution to its neighbors, Kennedy considered Latin America "the most dangerous area in the world." On July 26, 1953, a young Cuban nationalist, Fidel Castro, attempted to overthrow the American-backed regime of Fulgencio Batista. Imprisoned and later released, Castro fled to Mexico. In late 1956, he returned to Cuba. Almost captured, he escaped into the mountains, where for two years he augmented his guerrilla forces, gained popular support, and fought Batista's U.S.-supplied army. In January 1959, despite CIA plots to deny him power, the bearded rebel marched into Havana and initiated social and economic programs designed to reduce extensive U.S. interests that had developed since 1898 and had come to dominate Cuba's sugar, mining, and utilities industries. Determined to dilute the North American cultural influence that they believed had undermined Cuba's national identity, the Castroites crippled the gangster-run gambling casinos and ousted from government the *batistianos* who had profited from close contact with U.S. investors. Castro avowed that "we no longer live in times when one had to worry when the American Ambassador visited the [Cuban] Prime Minister." Indeed, "what happened in Guatemala will not happen here."

Fearing that a successful Cuban revolution would cause the United States to "get kicked around in the hemisphere," but finding no evidence that Castro was a communist, Washington soon applied a series of tests: Cuba must respect North American–owned property, continue alignment with the United States on international questions, and adhere to a democratic politics that permitted pro-U.S. "moderates" to sustain ties with Washington. Cuba failed the tests. Land reform struck at U.S. interests, the execution of Batista supporters reduced U.S. influence, and the moderates faltered in their competition with Castroite radicals. Castro postponed elections and evicted the U.S. military missions that had supported Batista. In vehement anti-Yankee orations, Castro also called for revolutions throughout Latin America. In late 1959 the CIA began to work with Castro's rivals to "replace" the revolutionary regime. In January 1960, a furious Eisenhower labeled Castro a "mad man . . . who is going wild and harming the whole American structure."

In March 1960, Ike ordered the CIA to train Cuban exiles for an invasion of their homeland—this shortly after Cuba signed a trade treaty with the Soviet Union. In mid-1960, as the revolutionary government nationalized foreign properties, Washington suspended imports of Cuban sugar and then forbade U.S. exports to the island. These measures pushed Cuba toward a new economic lifeline—the Soviet Union. As Khrushchev later told Kennedy, Castro was no communist but "you are well on your way to making him a good one." In the belief that Castro had moved from neutralism to communism, Washington broke diplomatic relations with Cuba in January 1961.

"The Castro regime is a thorn in the flesh," Senator J. William Fulbright argued, but "not a dagger in the heart." Still, President Kennedy defined Cuba as a test of will and gave the green light for a "covert" assault, dubbed "Operation Castration" by White House aide Arthur Schlesinger. The CIA assured him that it could deliver another Guatemala, as in 1954. The agency predicted that the Cuban people would rise up against Castro and a CIA-hired assassin's bullet would kill him. The CIA pinpointed Bahía de Cochinos (Bay of Pigs) as the invasion site and organized a Cuban Revolutionary Council to take office. Kennedy, without consulting Congress, approved the invasion plan. He also prohibited U.S. military participation. The CIA did not protest this prohibition because "we felt that when the chips were down . . . any action required for success would have been authorized [by the president] rather than permit the enterprise to fail." Kennedy also worried that the trained exiles would embarrass him politically if he scotched the expedition.

In mid-April 1961, 1,453 CIA-trained commandos departed from Nicaragua for Cuba. They met early resistance from Castro's militia, no sympathetic insurrection occurred, and within two days the invasion had become a fiasco. One hundred fourteen commandos died, and more than 1,100 were captured. Some 150 Cuban defenders were killed. Four American pilots also died in the operation. Kennedy fumed: "[E]very son of a bitch I checked with" said that "the plan would succeed." The adviser Walt Rostow reassured him that "we would have ample opportunity to prove we were not paper tigers in Berlin, Southeast Asia, and elsewhere." After the disaster, President Kennedy, who had vetoed a desperate CIA request for U.S. air attacks during the last hours of the failing invasion, blamed the CIA and Joint Chiefs of Staff for faulty intelligence and sloppy execution. Cuban exiles cried betrayal, saying it was "like John Wayne backing down from a gunfight with an evil dwarf." But even if the president had ordered more air strikes, then what? The brigade's meager forces would have had to face Castro's army of 25,000 and the nation's 200,000-strong militia.

Little sobered by the Bay of Pigs setback, the president issued secret orders making Cuba the "top priority . . . no time, money, effort, or manpower is to be spared." Under Operations Mongoose and Northwoods, the Pentagon and CIA planned anti-Castro assassination plots and invasions while cooperating with anti-Castro exiles to stage hit-and-run sabotage raids. Washington also tightened the economic embargo. This multitrack campaign did not knock Castro from his perch. What next? "If I had been in Moscow or Havana at that time," Secretary of Defense McNamara later remarked, "I would have believed the Americans were preparing for an invasion." And rightly so, given that the Joint Chiefs of Staff in the spring of 1962 vigorously advocated "early military intervention in Cuba" even if the United States had to foment an incident to justify war.

Spinning Out of Control: The Cuban Missile Crisis

Critical to understanding the missile crisis of fall 1962 is the relationship and timing between U.S. activities and Soviet/Cuban decisions to place on the island nuclear weapons that could strike heavily populated areas of the United States. In May 1962, Soviets and Cubans first discussed the idea of such weapons; in July, during a trip by Raúl Castro to Moscow, representatives initialed a draft agreement; in late August/early September, during a trip by the Cuban leader Che Guevara to Moscow, an accord became final. These steps were taken while Washington was pressing Cuba on all fronts.

Not only did Castro learn about the assassination plots and witness the sabotage attacks, but his spies reported possible U.S. military action against Cuba. The director of Operation Mongoose planned to ignite a revolt against Castro in October 1962 and recommended the use of U.S. forces to ensure success. American military maneuvers heightened Cuban fears. One well-publicized U.S. exercise, staged during April, included 40,000 troops and an amphibious landing on a small island near Puerto Rico. "Were we right or wrong to fear direct invasion?" Castro later asked. After the Bay of Pigs invasion, Moscow had begun military shipments that included small arms, howitzers, armored personnel carriers, patrol boats, MiG jet fighters, and tanks. Under the Moscow-Havana agreement, the Soviets intended to send surface-to-air missiles (SAMs), 48 medium-range (SS-4) missiles, 32 intermediate-range (SS-5) missiles, 48 light IL-28 bombers, tactical nuclear weapons, and nuclear warheads. By mid-October only the intermediate-range missiles had not reached Cuba.

Had there been no Bay of Pigs invasion, no destructive covert activities, no assassination plots, no military maneuvers and plans, and no economic and diplomatic steps to harass, isolate, and destroy the Castro government, there might have been

Soviet Missile Site at San Cristóbal, Cuba. This revealing U-2 photograph was taken in October 1962, when Soviet technicians were busily trying to assemble the various components of medium-range missiles. (U.S. Air Force)

no Cuban missile crisis. The origins of the October 1962 crisis derived largely from the concerted U.S. campaign to quash the Cuban Revolution and from the Soviet-Cuban effort to deter the United States through missile deployment. Scholars have attributed other motives to the Soviets, such as forcing negotiations on Berlin, compelling a trade for U.S. missiles stationed in Turkey, or undermining Chinese criticism that Moscow had become too tolerant of the West. Moscow also may have hoped to catch up in the nuclear arms race. But to stress only the global, Cold War dimension misses the central point: Khrushchev would never have had the opportunity to install dangerous nuclear weapons in the Caribbean if the United States had not been attempting to overthrow the Cuban government. The United States helped precipitate what Dean Rusk called "an utterly crashing crisis."

On October 14, a U-2 reconnaissance plane photographed medium-range (1,100-mile) missile sites under construction in Cuba. After gathering more data, American officials informed the president on October 16 that the Soviet Union had indeed placed missiles in Cuba. Kennedy created an Executive Committee of the National Security Council (Ex Comm), consisting of his "action intellectuals" and experienced diplomats from the Truman years. Joining McNamara, brother Robert, and McGeorge Bundy were Dean Acheson, Paul Nitze, and Robert Lovett, among others.

Kennedy's immediate preference became clear: "We're certainly going . . . to take out these . . . missiles." Ex Comm considered four options: "talk them out," "squeeze them out," "shoot them out," and "buy them out." Ex Comm advisers initially concentrated on military action. Acheson, among others, favored an air strike. Under Secretary of State George Ball countered that even a successful air strike would mean "carrying the mark of Cain on your brow for the rest of your life." Air force officials reported that some missiles might remain in place for firing against the United States. The Joint Chiefs recommended a full-scale military invasion. Although alluring, such a scheme could mean a prolonged war with Cuba, heavy U.S. casualties, and a Soviet retaliatory attack on Berlin. Ex Comm ruled out a private overture to Castro. Ambassador to the United Nations Adlai Stevenson's proposal that the United States publicly trade U.S. missiles in Turkey for those in Cuba met open derision. Ex Comm members, tired and irritable, finally settled on a naval blockade or quarantine of future arms shipments to Cuba. The quarantine left open options for further escalation.

Kennedy went on national television on October 22, announcing a blockade and insisting that Khrushchev "halt and eliminate this clandestine, reckless and provocative threat to world peace." More than 180 warships patrolled the Caribbean, and marines reinforced the U.S. naval base at Guantánamo, Cuba. A B-52 bomber force loaded with nuclear bombs took to the skies. On October 24, Soviet vessels approached the blockade, but the ships stopped. Assembly of the missiles already in Cuba continued. Secretary General of the United Nations U Thant urged talks; Khrushchev called for a summit meeting. Kennedy demanded removal of the missiles first. On October 26, in a confusing episode, ABC News correspondent John Scali heard a Soviet agent suggest one possible solution whereby Moscow would disengage its missiles if Washington publicly pledged not to invade Cuba. Scali reported the conversation to U.S. officials as a genuine Soviet proposal from "very high sources," but the KGB agent had not been authorized to make the offer. Yet a long letter from Khrushchev soon arrived proposing much the same settlement.

The next day, October 27, a Soviet surface-to-air missile shot down a U-2 plane over Cuba. The Americans prepared to retaliate, not knowing that Soviet commanders had tactical nuclear weapons ready to use against an invasion. More ominous, the commander of a Soviet submarine harassed by American warships prepared his nuclear torpedo, telling his crew "we will die but we will sink them all." Another officer fortunately persuaded the commander to await further instructions from Moscow. By this time U.S. officials were analyzing another Khrushchev letter. The premier raised the stakes: He would withdraw the missiles from Cuba if the United States removed its missiles from Turkey. Sidestepping this proposal, the president endorsed Khrushchev's first proposal: removal of the missiles in Cuba in exchange for a public U.S. pledge not to invade Cuba. Robert Kennedy assured the Soviets in private that the Jupiter missiles would be withdrawn from Turkey, but he warned that if Moscow divulged this secret deal, Washington would disavow it. A "very upset" Bobby said that "many unreasonable heads" are "itching for a fight," that "a chain reaction will start that will be very hard to stop," and "millions of Americans and Russians will die." If Khrushchev had balked, Rusk had secretly arranged for the United Nations to propose removing missiles from both Turkey and Cuba; "Kennedy would not let the Jupiters in Turkey become an obstacle," Rusk had insisted. When Khrushchev agreed to withdraw the missiles because Soviet forces could not prevent an invasion, a livid Castro led crowds in chanting "*Nikita, mariquita, lo que se da no se quita!*" ("Nikita, you little homosexual, what is given should not be taken back!"), while the Chinese charged the Soviets with both "adventurism" and "capitulationism." Having secured Cuba from invasion, Khrushchev said he was no "czarist officer who has to kill himself if I fart at a masked ball. It is better to back down than go to war."

"We were in luck," John Kenneth Galbraith later commented, "but success in a lottery is no argument for lotteries." As McGeorge Bundy remembered, the crisis came "so near to spinning out of control." Declassified recordings of the Ex Comm meetings confirm that Washington never had a firm handle on the crisis. As the scholar James Nathan noted: "The voices are halting. The sentences are incomplete. Thoughts ramble. Memories slip and options ooze into the ether." NATO allies, moreover, pointedly complained that they "can live with Soviet MRBMS, why can't [Americans]?" Why not reduce tensions by publicly trading missiles in Turkey that U.S. officials privately considered "worse than useless"? Even the aftermath proved messy. Washington demanded that the IL-28 bombers that the Soviets had given to Cuba must be removed along with the missiles. Not until November 13 did Khrushchev agree to pull the IL-28s out. The three protagonists, moreover, never signed a formal agreement, leaving enough ambiguity to cause later crises in Cuban-Soviet-American relations.

The missile crisis both slowed and accelerated the Cold War. Having found communication difficult during the event, the antagonists installed a "hot line" or Teletype link between the White House and Kremlin. Both sides seemed frightened enough by nuclear danger to move toward a more accommodating relationship, producing the Limited Test Ban Treaty of July 1963, which prohibited atmospheric and underwater nuclear testing. In a speech at American University in June ("the best . . . by any president since Roosevelt," according to Khrushchev) Kennedy revealed uneasiness with large weapons spending, appealed for arms control, and asked Americans to reexamine Cold War attitudes. Later Kennedy speeches, however, sounded hawkish once again.

The missile crisis carried long-term detrimental effects. The Soviet Union, revealed as a nuclear inferior, pledged to catch up in the arms race. That part of the Cold War contest was ratcheted up with new and more dangerous weapons systems. As for Cuba, despite a Castro initiative for rapprochement, U.S. officials vowed to intensify "our present nasty course." The CIA quickly launched new dirty tricks and revitalized its assassination option by making contact with a cooperative Cuban official, Rolando Cubela Secades. On the very day that President Kennedy fell to assassination, Secades rendezvoused with CIA agents in Paris, where he received a ballpoint pen rigged with a poisonous hypodermic needle. Like all other assassination plots against Castro, this one failed. The new Johnson administration put exploratory Cuban-American contacts at the United Nations on ice. Thereafter U.S.-Cuba relations remained frozen.

In the afterglow of the missile crisis, Kennedy's civilian advisers ignored the close calls of October and rationalized their improvisations as "crisis management." Proud of keeping their generals "on a short leash," they could confidently avoid nuclear holocaust, confine actual combat to Third World insurgencies, and win the Cold War through a calculated "display of superior American nerve and resolve." Or so they thought, until Vietnam challenged their hubris.

Laos, Vietnam, and the Kennedy Legacy

As continued unrest destabilized Laos and Vietnam, they climbed higher on President Kennedy's agenda. Rostow saw an opportunity to use "our unexploited counterguerrilla assets"—helicopters and Special Forces units. "We are not saving them for the Junior Prom," he told Kennedy. Laos, wracked by civil war, became a testing ground. Granted independence at Geneva in 1954, Laos chose nonalignment in the Cold War when the nationalist leader Souvanna Phouma organized a coalition government of neutralists and the procommunist Pathet Lao in 1957. The Eisenhower administration opposed the government and built up the right-wing Laotian army. In 1958, CIA-backed rightists ousted Souvanna Phouma and the Pathet Lao and installed a pro-U.S. government. Washington dispatched military advisers to the new regime. Souvanna Phouma did return to power after a coup in 1960, but the United States again undermined him by equipping rightist forces. Souvanna soon took assistance from Moscow and North Vietnam. But in December he fled his country. For Eisenhower, Laos constituted the "cork in the bottle."

The incoming Kennedy administration shared this perception of the Laotian problem. As conspicuous Soviet aid flowed to the Pathet Lao, Kennedy ordered the Seventh Fleet into the South China Sea and moved marines with helicopters into Thailand. Then the Bay of Pigs disaster struck. With one arm tied down in Cuba, Kennedy swung the other in Laos. The president instructed the several hundred U.S. military advisers in Laos, heretofore restricted to covert operations, to discard their civilian clothes and dress in more ostentatious military uniforms as a symbol of U.S. resolve. The Soviets wanted no fight in Laos. In April 1961 they endorsed Kennedy's appeal for a cease-fire. But the Pathet Lao battled on alone. The Joint Chiefs of Staff told Kennedy that they could win in Laos so long as they sent "120,000 to 140,000 men, with authority to use nuclear weapons if necessary." Kennedy, however, listened to those who considered it "a mistake to fight in Laos" because the Chinese threat would be too great.

After more than a year of hard bargaining in Geneva, W. Averell Harriman helped produce "a good, bad deal" among the major powers. Laos, under a government led by Souvanna Phouma, would become neutral. Still, peace did not last. Both the United States and North Vietnam quickly violated the accords. Hanoi continued to supply the Pathet Lao and failed to remove all its troops from Laos. Washington secretly shipped arms to Souvanna's government, and the CIA also armed and trained Hmong mountain clans. Without informing the American people, the United States began secret bombing raids against Pathet Lao forces in 1964. By then the problem of Laos derived from the country's proximity to Vietnam.

After the Bay of Pigs, the Berlin Wall, and the neutralization of Laos, Vietnam seemed to assume greater urgency. Kennedy advisers considered the corrupt Ngo Dinh Diem a liability, but as Vice President Lyndon B. Johnson put it, "Sh—, man, he's the only boy we got out there." Kennedy said he did not want a white man's war in Asia; Asians had to fight their own battles. But because he accepted the domino theory, thought that China fomented Vietnamese turmoil, and believed that nation building promised success, he expanded the U.S. presence. In January 1961, Kennedy authorized $28.4 million to enlarge the South Vietnamese army and

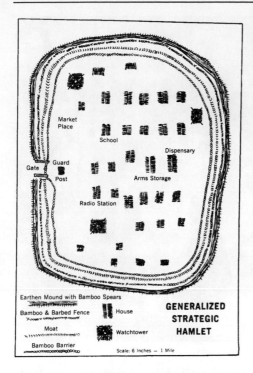

Strategic Hamlet, South Vietnam.
Introduced by the Diem regime in 1962 and funded by the United States, the strategic hamlet program sought to separate the NLF from its supporters among the people. The 6,000 hamlets, according to the historian David Trask, "isolated some Vietnamese from outside influences in ways reminiscent of reservations. . . . There was an effort to 'kill the Vietnamese' culturally that recalled earlier attitudes toward Native Americans." A Native American veteran agreed: "We were involved in the same kind of colonization process that was carried out by whites in this country." Many of the hamlets were poorly managed and defended, alienating the very people the Saigon government tried to win over. (Courtesy of M. W. Dow, from M. W. Dow, *Nation Building in Southeast Asia.* Boulder, Colo.: Pruett Press, 1966; rev. ed.)

another $12.7 million to improve the civil guard. In May he ordered 400 Special Forces soldiers and another 100 military "advisers" to South Vietnam. Meanwhile, the NLF captured more territory and accelerated the violence through assassinations of village chiefs. In October a U.S. intelligence study indicated that 80 to 90 percent of the 17,000 NLF in South Vietnam came from the South, not from North Vietnam, and that most of their supplies originated in the South.

The president in October dispatched two hawks, General Maxwell Taylor and Walt Rostow, to South Vietnam to study the war firsthand. Diem asked for more American military aid. The duo recommended sending 8,000 U.S. combat troops to avoid the "sickly pallor" of appeasement. Rusk questioned such a "major additional commitment of American prestige to a losing horse." Conscious that his decision violated the Geneva Accords but unwilling to say so publicly, Kennedy in November authorized an increase in U.S. forces or "advisers" in South Vietnam. During 1962 the numbers jumped to 9,000, and at the time of Kennedy's death in November 1963 these forces had reached 16,700. American troops, helicopter units, minesweepers, and air reconnaissance aircraft went into action. In 1962, 109 Americans died and in 1963, 489. The strategic hamlet program fortified villages but proved disruptive and unpopular with villagers and permitted the NLF to appear as Robin Hoods. In February 1963, Rusk nonetheless announced that the "momentum of the Communist drive has been stopped."

In May 1963 South Vietnamese troops opened fire on protesting and unarmed Buddhists in the city of Hue, massacring nine. The incident erupted after a Catholic provincial chief had enforced an old decree prohibiting the flying of Buddhist flags.

A Suicide in Protest, Saigon. Quang Duc, a Buddhist monk aged seventy-three, set his gasoline-drenched yellow robes afire in June 1963 to protest Diem's restrictions on Buddhists. (AP/Wide World Photos)

A Catholic oligarchy governed the predominantly Buddhist population. The Buddhist demonstrations also expressed longstanding nationalist sentiment, an appeal for peace talks with the NLF, and resentment against U.S. interference in Vietnamese politics. In early June a Buddhist monk sat in a Saigon street, poured fuel over his body, and immolated himself. Appalled, Kennedy reportedly told a confidant that the Vietnamese "hate us. . . . they'll kick our asses out of there." During summer and fall the protest spread; so did Diem's suppression. Kennedy publicly chastised Diem and reduced aid. Senior South Vietnamese generals, now aware that Diem no longer had American favor, asked U.S. officials how they would respond to a coup d'état. The new ambassador, Henry Cabot Lodge, wanted to dump Diem, but officials in Washington hesitated.

Washington continued cool relations with Diem, who proved increasingly resistant to U.S. advice. In early October 1963, as rumors swirled "about secret contacts between Diem-Nhu and Ho Chi Minh," the Vietnamese generals prepared a coup. Judging Diem's removal imperative to bring "this medieval country into the twentieth century," Lodge did not discourage them. On November 1, the generals easily took Diem prisoner and murdered him. A few weeks later, on November 22, Kennedy himself was assassinated in Dallas. The day before his trip to Texas, Kennedy had told an aide that "we have got to review this whole thing [Vietnam] from the bottom to the top." Scholars and former advisers have pointed to this and similar remarks to suggest that Kennedy would have withdrawn from Vietnam in 1965. Dean Rusk vigorously dissented, arguing that any president who left U.S. soldiers in danger merely to win reelection could not have lived "with himself or look[ed] his senior colleagues in the eye." Other scholars similarly point to

Kennedy's pledge as late as September 1963 that he was not in Vietnam "to see a war lost." They argue that given Kennedy's Cold War mentality, his personal aversion to defeat, and his fear of right-wing charges that he was soft on communism, he would have pushed on in Vietnam, much as did his successor, Lyndon B. Johnson.

Nose to Nose: Lyndon B. Johnson and the World

Johnson kept on many of Kennedy's advisers. McNamara stayed until early 1968; Rusk until the end; replacing Bundy in 1966 was the zealous Walt Rostow. Bundy called LBJ "a very majority leader president" who dealt with foreign leaders much as he had managed Senate committee chairmen from 1955 to 1961. Alliance partners immediately sensed the change in presidential style. A British diplomat commented: "President Johnson is not at home in international affairs." Less generous, French President Charles de Gaulle dismissed Johnson as "a cowboy radical" who "doesn't even take the trouble to pretend he's thinking."

An experienced political operator, Johnson came from the poor hill territory of Texas between Fort Worth and San Antonio. LBJ would thrust "his face close to the face of the person he was talking to, practically touching the other's nose," the Soviet ambassador wrote, "often pulling him closer by the lapel . . . in a heroic effort at persuasion." Dean Acheson once called Johnson "a real centaur—part man, part horse's ass." A "credibility gap" dogged the administration, not so much because Johnson told barefaced lies, but because he consciously downplayed his commitment to "that bitch of a war" lest it divert attention from the "woman I really loved—the Great Society" domestic reform program.

Johnson left relations with the Soviet Union and China much as he had found them—calmer after the Cuban missile crisis but still strained and based on intense military competition. In 1967, LBJ attempted to slow the arms race when he met with Soviet premier Aleksei Kosygin in Glassboro, New Jersey. But the movement toward negotiations stalled in June 1968 when the Soviets invaded Czechoslovakia the day before a Johnson-Kosygin summit was to be announced. The coincidence of these events, said Rusk, "was like throwing a dead fish" in the president's face. The United States, the Soviet Union, and more than fifty other nations signed a nuclear nonproliferation treaty in 1968 (ratified in 1969), a pledge not to spread nuclear weapons to other nations. But France and China, both members of the nuclear club, refused to sign.

In Latin America, smoldering nationalism, frequent military coups, and Castro's defiant survival defined Johnson's policies. Johnson put Assistant Secretary of State Thomas C. Mann in charge of the Alliance for Progress, and it soon withered away from neglect. Mann's declaration that the United States would support anticommunist military regimes received its first test in 1964, when the United States embraced a military coup in Brazil. That same year, Panamanians rioted against U.S. control of the Canal Zone. A macho LBJ claimed that "I know these Latin Americans. . . . They'll come right into your yard and take it over if you let them. . . . But if you say to 'em right at the start 'hold on, just a minute,' they'll know they're dealing with

Abe Fortas Gets the Johnson Treatment.
President Johnson used his formidable presence to cajole and persuade. Hubert Humphrey joked that LBJ at his most effective was like a "cowboy making love." Here the recipient of the famed treatment is Abe Fortas (1910–1982), Washington, D.C. lawyer, Supreme Court justice (1965–1969), and occasional presidential adviser on Vietnam. (Lyndon Baines Johnson Library)

somebody who'll stand up." Johnson had another opportunity to act on this self-proclaimed expertise when rebels launched a civil war in the Dominican Republic in 1965. Bragging that "Democratic presidents can deal with Communists as strongly as any Republican," he sent 24,000 soldiers to the Caribbean island. He wanted to prevent the return of Juan Bosch as president. Bosch had initially won an election in 1962, but a coup ousted him in 1963. LBJ believed that a small number of communists controlled the rebels ("Our choice is . . . Castro or intervention") even though McNamara scoffed, "I don't believe fifty-eight people" can control a rebellion. In the end, a military regime quashed the democratic rebellion with U.S. support. Proud of his actions, Johnson announced that the United States would henceforth prevent any communist government from taking office in the hemisphere. This frank statement of hegemony attempted to maintain the U.S. sphere in Latin America. (In 1968, the Soviets issued a similar statement after their invasion of Czechoslovakia, justifying their dominance of Warsaw Pact countries.)

"The Biggest Damned Mess": Johnson's Vietnam War

During Johnson's five years in office, Vietnam consumed his energies, his ambitions, and his reputation. After Diem's death, "the NLF was ready and eager" to form a neutralist coalition government, according to a former North Vietnamese diplomat. He chided Americans: "There was an opportunity and you missed it." Despite support for such a solution among American allies, the United Nations, and some U.S. officials, Johnson would have none of it. In December 1963, he insisted on "victory" to prevent "a communist takeover." For Johnson and his advisers, Vietnam occupied only one front in the Cold War; to falter in Southeast Asia, they believed, would send a false signal that the United States would retreat elsewhere, too.

   By early 1964, however, the war was going badly. "We ought [not] to take this government seriously," said Ambassador Lodge. "We have to do what we think we ought to do regardless of what the Saigon government does." The Army of the Republic of Vietnam (ARVN) proved ineffective in the field, and desertions ran high. The strategic hamlet program collapsed. A coup by General Nguyen Khanh brought little progress, as Secretary McNamara reported that the NLF controlled 40 percent of the South Vietnamese countryside by March 1964. "We're getting into another Korea," LBJ grumbled in May. "I don't think we can get out. It's just the biggest damned mess." The president worried a great deal about a resurgent right wing, arguing that the loss of China and the stalemate in Korea may have sparked McCarthyism, but they "were chicken shit compared to what might happen if we lost Vietnam." Deterioration in Vietnam gave Johnson's political foes an issue in the 1964 presidential campaign. Conservative Republican candidate Barry Goldwater urged military action against Ho Chi Minh's North. The president publicly branded Goldwater as a dangerous warmonger. But in private his administration was already developing new contingencies to increase the U.S. presence in South Vietnam and U.S. pressure against North Vietnam. In early 1964, Washington dispatched more military advisers (reaching 23,000 by the end of the year). Air strikes hit Laos, through which supplies flowed south. In February a covert operation began to air-drop commandos into the North to conduct sabotage. To stiffen the Khanh government, aides urged the president in June to ask Congress for a resolution "conveying our firmness of purpose in Southeast Asia."

On August 2, 1964, North Vietnamese torpedo patrol boats opened fire on the American destroyer *Maddox* some ten miles offshore. American aircraft from the U.S.S. *Ticonderoga* entered the fray. U.S. forces drove off the attackers, sinking one boat and damaging others, with no American casualties. The *Maddox* was on an espionage mission, called a "DeSoto patrol," collecting intelligence on radar and coastal defenses. As the president admitted privately, "we were playing around up there" in support of an operation against two islands, "and they came out, gave us a warning, and we knocked hell out of 'em." After the incident, almost as if to bait North Vietnam, the *Maddox* and *C. Turner Joy* steered to within four miles of the islands.

After dark on August 4, the captain of the *Maddox* interpreted his sonar data to mean that North Vietnamese gunboats had attacked the two ships. The *Maddox* and *C. Turner Joy* fired away wildly and American warplanes flew in to help. No evidence has ever confirmed a North Vietnamese attack. James B. Stockdale, who flew a Crusader jet from the *Ticonderoga* that night, saw "no boats, no wakes, no ricochets off boats, no boat impacts, no torpedo wakes—nothing but black sea and American firepower." Chinese intelligence correctly informed Hanoi that the second incident was "not an intentional act by the Americans" but caused by "mistaken judgment, based on wrong information."

Despite the CIA's report that the North Vietnamese were purely defensive, Johnson exploited the moment to punish North Vietnam and to seek passage of a congressional resolution. On August 4, the president announced air strikes against the North. Saying nothing about destroyer operations against the North, he charged the enemy with deliberate aggression in international waters. Johnson consciously misled the American people and the Congress. The "Tonkin Gulf Resolution" passed on August 7 by huge margins, 416 to 0 in the House and 88 to 2 in the Senate. The resolution authorized the president to "take all necessary measures to repel armed attack against the forces of the United States and to prevent further aggression." The resolution, said Johnson, was "like grandma's nightshirt—it covered everything." In 1970, regretting this open-ended concession to the president, the Senate repealed it.

After LBJ safely won reelection in November 1964, the Pentagon expected him to escalate quickly in Vietnam. But the president hesitated, seeming a "querulous wallflower, disappointingly reluctant to join the war dance in Southeast Asia." On February 7, 1965, the NLF attacked an American airfield at Pleiku and killed eight Americans. By March, the United States had initiated a sustained bombing program—Operation Rolling Thunder—against the North. When the Joint Chiefs of Staff in April urged calling up the reserves to "show the American people we were serious," the president said: "You leave the American people to me. I know more about . . . [them] than anybody in this room." With 80,000 U.S. troops in the South by July, the military asked for 100,000 more. On July 21 the president convened his high-level advisers. Only Under Secretary of State George W. Ball argued that the United States could not win a protracted war in an Asian jungle. Sending more troops

Caught in Battle. A Vietnamese peasant mother and her children emerge after battle between ARVN forces and Vietcong guerrillas near the village of Phung Hiep on July 23, 1965. Such a photograph is an exception to the caricatured images of the Vietnamese at war—"the shadowy foe darting through the underbrush or lying crumpled on the ground, the prostitute or crowd of children outside an American base camp, the venal official hobbling the Saigon government's war effort, the child in frightful flight from napalm," as the historian Michael H. Hunt has observed. (National Archives)

would be "like giving cobalt treatment to a terminal cancer case," he warned. Johnson jumped in: "But, George, wouldn't all these countries say that Uncle Sam was a paper tiger," with America losing its credibility? Ball answered, "The worse blow would be that the mightiest power on earth is unable to defeat a handful of guerrillas."

Friction between Johnson and his military advisers accompanied the decision to escalate. "Bomb, bomb, bomb. That's all you know," LBJ bellowed at one point. Unwilling to let "some military idiots talk him into World War III," the president once told the Joint Chiefs to "get the hell out of my office." Cowed by such tirades, the military professionals ("five silent men") never confronted Johnson with "the total forces they believed would ultimately be required in Vietnam." The result was a McNamara-dominated strategy of graduated pressure, in which ground forces went to Vietnam in increments. The defense secretary contended: "It won't be that the South Vietnamese can win. But it will be clear to Hanoi that Hanoi can't win." Incremental escalation also aimed at minimizing the chance of Chinese intervention. LBJ knew that all Pentagon war plans called for the use of nuclear weapons in such a contingency.

By the end of the year nearly 200,000 American troops were fighting in Vietnam; a year later the number reached 385,000. Not wanting to jeopardize Great Society reforms, Johnson built up forces without mobilizing the reserves or raising taxes. As Rusk later said: "In a nuclear world it is just too dangerous for an entire people to get too angry and we deliberately tried to do in cold blood what perhaps can only be done in hot blood."

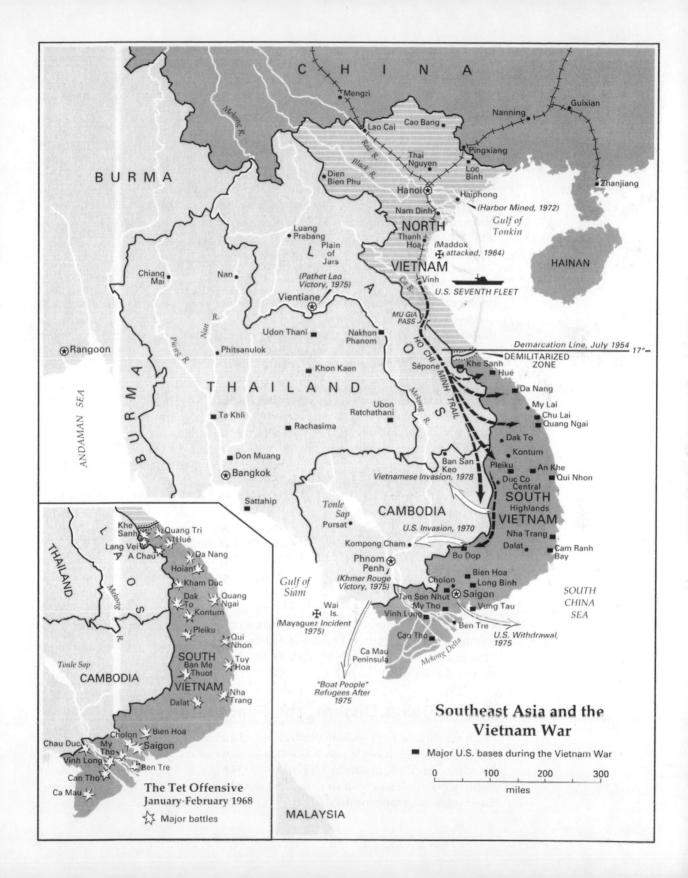

CHINA

Mengzi

Nanning · Guixian

Lao Cai · Cao Bang · Pingxiang

Thai Nguyen · Loc Binh

Dien Bien Phu

BURMA

Hanoi ⊛ · Haiphong · Zhanjiang

Nam Dinh

(Harbor Mined, 1972)

NORTH

Thanh Hoa ✝ *(Maddox attacked, 1964)* · Gulf of Tonkin · HAINAN

VIETNAM

Luang Prabang · Plain of Jars · L

Vinh

Ca R. · U.S. SEVENTH FLEET

Chiang Mai · Nan

(Pathet Lao Victory, 1975) · A

Vientiane ·

Nan R.

MU GIA PASS

HO CHI

Phitsanulok

Udon Thani · Nakhon Phanom

Demarcation Line, July 1954 — 17°—

MINH

Sépone · Khe Sanh · DEMILITARIZED ZONE

Ping R.

THAILAND

Hué

TRAIL · Da Nang

ANDAMAN SEA

Rangoon ⊛

Khon Kaen · S · My Lai · Chu Lai · Quang Ngai

Ta Khli

Ubon Ratchathani · Mekong R.

Dak To · Kontum

Rachasima

Ban San Keo · Pleiku · An Khe · Qui Nhon

Don Muang

Vietnamese Invasion, 1978 · Duc Co · Central Highlands

Bangkok ⊛

SOUTH

Sattahip · Tonle Sap · CAMBODIA · VIETNAM

Pursat · *U.S. Invasion, 1970* · Nha Trang · Cam Ranh Bay

Phnom Penh ⊛ · Bu Dop · Dalat

Gulf of Siam · *(Khmer Rouge Victory, 1975)* · Kompong Cham

Bien Hoa · Long Binh

Cholon · SOUTH CHINA SEA

Wai Is. · Tan Son Nhut · Saigon ⊛

(Mayaguez Incident 1975) · My Tho · Vung Tau

Vinh Long · Ben Tre

U.S. Withdrawal, 1975

Can Tho

Ca Mau Peninsula · Mekong Delta

"Boat People" Refugees After 1975

Southeast Asia and the Vietnam War

■ Major U.S. bases during the Vietnam War

0   100   200   300

miles

Khe Sanh · Quang Tri · Hué

Lang Vei · A Chau

THAILAND · Da Nang

L · Hoian

O · Kham Duc

Mekong · Dak To · Quang Ngai

S · Kontum

Pleiku

Qui Nhon

SOUTH

Tonle Sap · Ban Me Thuot · Tuy Hoa

CAMBODIA · VIETNAM · Nha Trang

Dalat

Cholon · Bien Hoa

Chau Duc · My Tho · Saigon

Vinh Long · Ben Tre

Can Tho

Ca Mau

The Tet Offensive
January–February 1968

☆ Major battles

MALAYSIA

In 1966 American bombers hit oil depots in the North, and by midyear 70 percent of the North's storage capacity had been destroyed. With North Vietnamese and NLF forces increasing from 116,000 to 282,000 during the 1965–1967 period, the heavy bombing apparently had little impact on the enemy's ability to resist. During 1965–1968 the United States tried, in Air Force General Curtis Lemay's infamous phrase, "to bomb them back into the stone age" by dropping 400 tons of ordnance per day. But the United States lost 918 aircraft valued at $6 billion. By war's end more than 7 million tons of U.S. bombs had battered Vietnam, the equivalent of 400 Hiroshima atomic blasts. General William Westmoreland kept asking for more troops, even though Secretary McNamara reported in October 1966 that "pacification has, if anything, gone backward." The president nonetheless kept sending troops—peaking at 543,400 in early 1969.

In this period of escalation, 1965–1968, the bloodshed and dislocation staggered the Vietnamese people. Under General Westmoreland's ("Waste-more-men") questionable strategy of "attrition," U.S. and South Vietnamese forces bombed and destroyed villages that harbored suspected Vietcong, the "Charlie." Hundreds of thousands of civilians died, many from fiery napalm attacks in areas called "free fire zones." "After . . . a while you forget that there are people down there," an American pilot explained. Counting enemy bodies became "a macabre statistical competition" for Captain Colin Powell. To deny the enemy food and to expose hideouts, American defoliation teams sprayed chemicals such as Agent Orange on crops and forests, denuding the landscape and inadvertently exposing GIs to the dioxin-tainted herbicide. Beginning in 1967 the CIA supervised the Phoenix program, in which South Vietnamese operatives infiltrated rural areas and "neutralized" thousands of suspected Vietcong. "Infiltration of a couple of guys into our ranks created tremendous difficulties," a NLF leader later admitted.

To many Americans, the My Lai massacre of March 16, 1968, where a U.S. Army platoon commanded by Lieutenant William Calley shot to death scores of helpless women and children represented a depravity unbecoming a civilized nation. Because of official cover-ups, the My Lai story did not become public until twenty months later. Despite documented incidents of the deliberate shooting, raping, and torturing of civilians and prisoners, however, most U.S. soldiers were not committing atrocities. They were trying instead to save their young lives—the average age of the Vietnam GI was only nineteen—from snipers, booby traps, ambushes, mortar attacks, and firefights. Etched in their memories, too, was the inhospitable environment, "as if the sun and land were in league with the Vietcong," recalled the marine officer Philip Caputo in *A Rumor of War* (1977), "wearing us down, driving us mad, killing us."

As the Doves Dissent, the Peace Efforts Fail

"Can the tortoise of progress in Vietnam stay ahead of the hare of dissent at home?" one official asked. It could not. Students and faculties at universities began to hold "teach-ins" in 1965, first at the University of Michigan in March. Hundreds refused military draft calls and went to jail or fled to Canada. Others obtained deferments. Sit-ins greeted representatives of major corporations such as Dow Chemical, a maker of napalm, when they attempted to recruit on campus. In early 1967, 300,000 demonstrators marched in New York City; in November, 100,000 surrounded the Pentagon. Fed misleading information from the FBI and CIA, LBJ told sympathetic senators that communists "were going into colleges" to stir up these protests.

Prominent intellectuals, such as the linguist Noam Chomsky, the political scientist Hans Morgenthau Jr., and the disaffected Arthur M. Schlesinger Jr., called for withdrawal from Vietnam. Business executives, lawyers, and members of the clergy, too, joined antiwar groups. The pediatrician Benjamin Spock and Dr. Martin Luther King Jr., the civil rights crusader, added their voices to the protest, as did the singers Pete Seeger and Joan Baez. Radical pacifists, liberal reformers, conservative constitutionalists, strategic realists, religious moralists, hippies, trade unionists, and many others melded into a national, largely unstructured antiwar movement. Often stereotyped as the haven for long-haired, bearded college-age youth, the movement actually encompassed a wide spectrum of people. The strongest opposition to the war came from four groups: older, black, female, and lower-class Americans. Younger, white, male, and middle-class citizens tended to support escalation of the war and follow the president's lead—at least until 1968. In February of that year, after Tet, a majority of polled Americans for the first time said that the United States had made a "mistake" in sending troops to Vietnam.

The critics offered multifaceted arguments: the war cost too much and weakened needed reform at home; America's youth was dying—30,000 by 1968; inflation and a worsening balance of payments undermined the economy; the ghastly bloodshed and U.S. conduct of the war were immoral; the war damaged relations with allies and foes alike; Washington and Saigon could not win the war; the president was undermining the constitutional system of checks and balances; U.S. behavior in Vietnam debased the American principles of fair play and right to self-determination; and dissension was ripping domestic America apart. Above all else, the United States had succumbed to a debilitating globalism of anticommunism, overcommitment, and overextension. In short, some critics complained about how the war was being conducted, whereas others criticized globalism and the containment doctrine itself.

The growing public disaffection encouraged dissent in Congress. Lingering doubts about the Tonkin Gulf Resolution prompted Senator Fulbright to hold publicly televised hearings before his committee. LBJ ridiculed him as Senator "Half Bright." The president also used threats to quash questions from Congress, shouting at Senator Robert Kennedy, "I'll destroy you and every one of your dove friends." But dissenting senators kept asking the administration to explain exactly what in Vietnam the United States was trying to contain. The Soviet Union? China? North Vietnam? The Vietcong? Rusk settled on China as the main culprit, especially after the Chinese leader Lin Biao declared in 1965 that China would encourage wars of national liberation in the Third World. China did urge a protracted struggle in Vietnam. But Hanoi and Beijing proved to be "both comrades and adversaries" in a contentious relationship. Through 1966, China sent supplies along with 320,000 noncombat troops. Mao also assured Hanoi that more would be forthcoming if the U.S. forces crossed into North Vietnam. Hanoi's distrust of Beijing's intentions surfaced

"Black Power" and the War. At the March on the Pentagon in 1967, a protester carries a sign symbolizing the coincidence of the civil rights and antiwar movements. Beginning in 1965, the slogan Black Power marked a more radical turn in the fight to end racial discrimination. New groups such as the Black Panther Party protested racism and the war, stating that "we will not fight and kill other people of color in the world, who like black people, are being victimized by the white racist government in America." (Frank Wolfe, LBJ Library Collection)

immediately, with a Chinese official sarcastically querying Hanoi, "Are you suspicious of us because we have so much enthusiasm? Do the Chinese want to take control over Vietnam?" By 1966, North Vietnam tilted toward Moscow in the Sino–Soviet split and dubbed China "La Grand Impuissance" (Great Non–Power). Moscow, Beijing, and Washington attempted to manipulate events in Vietnam to serve their national interests, but Hanoi acted as no one's puppet.

The administration's warning about Beijing carried little weight with Congress, especially after George F. Kennan testified that containment would not work in Asia and recommended gradual withdrawal. By early 1968, Senators Eugene McCarthy and Robert F. Kennedy mounted antiwar candidacies to displace LBJ as the Democratic nominee. Despite Johnson's insistent claims of victory over this "raggedy-ass little fourth-rate country," doubters grew more numerous within administration ranks. McNamara's increasing disenchantment and 1967 resignation angered the president, who blamed the defense secretary's departure on Robert Kennedy's telling McNamara he was "a murderer." Yet Johnson resisted anything that would appear to be defeat in Vietnam.

Throughout the 1965–1968 escalation period, international groups suggested avenues for peace. "Everybody thinks Hanoi is ready; the Pope, the Poles, the Russians, but when you really get down to it," Johnson lamented, Hanoi would not "budge." Moscow pushed negotiations to eliminate the war as an obstacle to warmer ties with Washington and out of fear that China would not "show restraint if the war continued to escalate." Although the United States and North Vietnam continued to make gestures toward negotiations, mistrust and fears about the consequences of compromise hindered success. Johnson believed that "we know, from Munich on, that when you give, the dictators feed on raw meat." The NLF leadership felt similarly "haunted" by the Geneva Conference, where they believed Ho Chi Minh had treated the South "as a sacrificial animal," and the North Vietnamese leadership feared that talks with the United States could prompt NLF "accusations of 'selling' their interests in return for ending the bombing in the North." Despite internal divisions among the Vietnamese, Washington appears to bear the greatest responsibility for squandering opportunities to end the war in 1966 and 1967. Two promising initiatives, MARIGOLD and SUNFLOWER, collapsed because Washington insisted on "capitulation by a Communist force that is far from beaten." The bombing of the North and Hanoi's aid to the NLF proved to be key sticking points. MARIGOLD died when LBJ failed to call off a previously scheduled round of bombings, and SUN-FLOWER withered when the United States insisted that Hanoi would have to prove it had stopped sending personnel and supplies down the jungle paths known as the Ho Chi Minh Trail (see map, page 241) before Washington ceased its aerial bombardment.

And then the Tet offensive wrought its havoc; military escalation and Johnson's political career derailed; the bombing scaled down; and the peace talks finally began in Paris. In November, Richard M. Nixon defeated Vice President Hubert Humphrey for the presidency. In 1961 John F. Kennedy had asked Americans to "pay any price" and "bear any burden." By 1969, many refused. The new Nixon administration faced the task of maintaining U.S. interests abroad while at the same time mollifying public discontent with globalism and the Vietnam War.

FURTHER READING FOR THE PERIOD 1961–1969

Several works cited in Chapters 7 and 8 on the Cold War and the Third World also survey this period, and not all are repeated here.

For John F. Kennedy and his foreign relations, see Nigel J. Ashton, *Kennedy, Macmillan, and the Cold War* (2002); Michael Beschloss, *The Crisis Years* (1991); Douglas Brinkley and Richard T. Griffiths, eds., *John F. Kennedy and Europe* (1999); Robert Dallek, *An Unfinished Life* (2003); Lawrence E. Freedman, *Kennedy's Wars* (2000); James N. Giglio and Stephen G. Rabe, *Debating the Kennedy Presidency* (2003); Seymour Hersh, *The Other Side of Camelot* (1997); Noam Kochavi, *A Conflict Perpetuated: China Policy During the Kennedy Years* (2002); Timothy P. Maga, *John F. Kennedy and New Frontier Diplomacy* (1994); Thomas G. Paterson, ed., *Kennedy's Quest for Victory* (1989); Richard Reeves, *President Kennedy* (1993); Thomas C. Reeves, *A Question of Character* (1991); W. J. Rorabaugh, *Kennedy and the Promise of the Sixties* (2002); and Mark J. White, *Kennedy* (1998). For Kennedy and specific countries and crises, see below.

For Lyndon B. Johnson and his administration (see Vietnam below), see Irving Bernstein, *Guns or Butter* (1996); H. W. Brands, *The Wages of Globalism* (1995) and ed., *The Foreign Policies of Lyndon Johnson* (1999); Warren I. Cohen and Nancy B. Tucker, eds., *Lyndon Johnson Confronts the World* (1995); Robert Dallek, *Flawed Giant* (1998); Robert A. Divine, ed., *The Johnson Years* (1987–1994); John Dumbrell, *President Lyndon Johnson and Soviet Communism* (2005); Diane Kunz, ed., *The Diplomacy of the Crucial Decade* (1994); and Mitchell Lerner, ed., *Looking Back at LBJ* (2005).

For other prominent Americans, see Leroy Ashby and Rod Gramer, *Fighting the Odds* (1994) (Frank Church); James A. Bill, *George Ball* (1997); Kai Bird, *The Color of Truth* (1998) (Bundy); Douglas Brinkley, *Dean Acheson* (1992); Jeff Broadwater, *Adlai Stevenson* (1994); David L. DiLeo, *George Ball, Vietnam, and the Rethinking of Containment* (1991); Gilbert C. Fite, *Richard B. Russell, Jr.* (1991); Robert A. Goldberg, *Barry Goldwater* (1995); Walter Isaacson and Evan Thomas, *The Wise Men* (1986); Robert David Johnson, *Ernest Gruening and the American Dissenting Tradition* (1998); John B. Martin, *Adlai Stevenson and the World* (1977); Jonathan Nashel, *Edwin Lansdale's Cold War* (2005); Richard Parker, *John Kenneth Galbraith* (2005); John Prados, *Lost Crusader* (2003) (William Colby); Howard B. Schaffer, *Ellsworth Bunker* (2004); Deborah Shapley, *Promise and Power* (1993) (McNamara); Ronald Steel, *Walter Lippmann and the American Century* (1980); Scott Stossel, *Sarge* (2004) (Shriver); Evan Thomas, *Robert Kennedy* (2000); Randall B. Woods, *Fulbright* (1995); and Thomas W. Zeiler, *Dean Rusk* (1999).

Economic issues and trade policy are scrutinized in David P. Calleo, *The Imperious Economy* (1982); Frances J. Gavin, *Gold, Dollars, and Power* (2003); and Thomas Zeiler, *American Trade and Power in the 1960s* (1992).

Europe, the Berlin crisis, and the nuclear arms race are the subjects of McGeorge Bundy, *Danger and Survival* (1988), Frank A. Mayer, *Adenauer and Kennedy* (1996); Kendrick Oliver, *Kennedy, Macmillan, and the Nuclear Test Ban Treaty* (1998); Christopher A. Preble, *John F. Kennedy and the Missile Gap* (2005); Thomas Risse-Kappen, *Cooperation Among Democracies* (1995); Thomas A. Schwartz, *Lyndon Johnson and Europe* (2003); Glenn T. Seaborg and Benjamin S. Loeb, *Stemming the Tide* (1987) (arms control); Jeremi Suri, *Power and Protest* (2003); Andreas Wenger, *Living with Peril* (1997); and Peter Wyden, *The Wall* (1989).

Aspects of relations with the Third World in the 1960s include Warren Bass, *Support Any Friend* (2003) (Israel); Evelyn Goh, *Constructing the U.S. Rapprochement with China, 1961–1974* (2004); Gabriel Kolko, *Confronting the Third World* (1988); Michael F. Latham, *Modernization as Ideology* (2000); Mitchell Lerner, *The Pueblo Incident* (2003); Timothy P. Maga, *John F. Kennedy and the New Pacific Community* (1990); Robert J. McMahon, *Cold War on the Periphery* (1994) (India and Pakistan) and *The Limits of Empire* (1999); Michael B. Oren, *Six Days of War* (2002) (Middle East); David L. Schalk, *War and the Ivory Tower* (1991) (Algeria); and Penny M. von Eschen, *Race Against Empire: Black Americans and Anticolonialism* (1998).

For the Cuban Revolution, Fidel Castro, Bay of Pigs, and missile crisis, see Jules Benjamin, *The United States and the Origins of the Cuban Revolution* (1990); James G. Blight, *The Shattered Crystal Ball* (1990); Don Bohning, *The Castro Obsession* (2005); James G. Blight and Philip Brenner, *Sad and Luminous Days* (2002); James G. Blight and Peter Kornbluh, eds., *Politics of Illusion* (1998) (Bay of Pigs); James G. Blight and David A.

Welch, *On the Brink* (1989); James G. Blight et al., *Cuba on the Brink* (1993); Don Bohning, *The Castro Obsession* (2005); Jorge Domínguez, *To Make a World Safe for Revolution* (1989); Alexander Fursenko and Timothy Naftali, *"One Hell of a Gamble"* (1997); Raymond L. Garthoff, *Reflections on the Cuban Missile Crisis* (1989); Alice L. George, *Awaiting Armageddon* (2003); Trumbull Higgins, *The Perfect Failure* (1987) (Bay of Pigs); Donna R. Kaplowitz, *Anatomy of a Failed Embargo* (1998); Richard Lebow and Janice G. Stein, *We All Lost the Cold War* (1994); Ernest R. May and Philip D. Zelikow, eds., *The Kennedy Tapes* (1997); Philip Nash, *The Other Missiles of October* (1997) (Jupiters); James A. Nathan, *Anatomy of the Cuban Missile Crisis* (2001); Scott D. Sagan, *The Limits of Safety* (1993); Sheldon M. Stern, *Averting "The Final Failure"* (2003) and *The Week the World Stood Still* (2005); Tad Szulc, *Fidel* (1986); Victor A. Triay, *Fleeing Castro* (1998); Lucien S. Vandenbroucke, *Perilous Options* (1993) (Bay of Pigs); Robert Weisbrot, *Maximum Danger* (2002); and Mark J. White, *The Cuban Missile Crisis* (1996) and *Missiles in Cuba* (1997).

U.S.–Latin America relations, including the Alliance for Progress, are explored in Eric Thomas Chester, *Rag-Tags, Scum, Riff-Raff, and Commies* (2001) (Dominican Republic); Piero Gleijeses, *The Dominican Crisis* (1978); Walter LaFeber, *Inevitable Revolutions* (1993); Ruth Leacock, *Requiem for Revolution* (1990) (Brazil); Stephen G. Rabe, *The Most Dangerous Area in the World* (1999) (JFK); L. Ronald Scheman, ed., *The Alliance for Progress* (1988); and W. Michael Weis, *Cold Warriors & Coups D'État* (1993) (Brazil).

Studies of U.S. relations with Africa include David N. Gibbs, *The Political Economy of Third World Intervention* (1991) (Congo); Richard D. Mahoney, *JFK* (1983); Thomas J. Noer, *Cold War and Black Liberation* (1985); and Joseph E. Thompson, *American Policy and African Famine* (1990) (Nigeria).

For the Peace Corps, see Julius A. Amin, *The Peace Corps in Cameroon* (1992); Fritz Fischer, *Making Them Like Us* (1998); Elizabeth Cobbs Hoffman, *All You Need Is Love* (1998); and Gerald T. Rice, *The Bold Experiment* (1985).

For Vietnam, especially the experience of the 1960s, see David L. Anderson, ed., *Shadow on the White House* (1993); Loren Baritz, *Backfire* (1985); David M. Barrett, *Uncertain Warriors* (1993); Larry Berman, *Planning a Tragedy* (1982) and *Lyndon Johnson's War* (1989); Anne Blair, *Lodge in Vietnam* (1995); Robert K. Brigham, *Guerrilla Diplomacy* (1999); Robert Buzzanco, *Vietnam and the Transformation of American Life* (1999); Robert Buzzanco and Marilyn Young, eds., *Companion to the Vietnam War* (2002); Larry Cable, *Unholy Grail* (1991); Philip E. Catton, *Diem's Final Failure* (2002); Andreas Daum et al., *America, the Vietnam War, and the World* (2003); Gerard DeGroot, *A Noble Cause?* (2000); William J. Duiker, *U.S. Containment Policy and the Conflict in Indochina* (1994); John Ernst, *Forging a Fateful Alliance* (1998) (Michigan State University contracts and Vietnam); Ilya V. Gaiduk, *The Soviet Union and the Vietnam War* (1996) and *Confronting Vietnam* (2003); Lloyd C. Gardner, *Pay Any Price* (1995); Lloyd C. Gardner and Ted Gittinger, eds., *The Search for Peace in Vietnam, 1964–1968* (2005); William C. Gibbons, *The U.S. Government and the Vietnam War* (1986–1994); Patrick L. Hatcher, *The Suicide of an Elite: American Internationalists and Vietnam* (1990); George C. Herring, *LBJ and Vietnam* (1994) and *America's Longest War* (1996); Paul Hendrickson, *The Living and the Dead* (1996); Gary R. Hess, *Vietnam and the United States* (1998); Michael H. Hunt, *Lyndon Johnson's War* (1996); Seth Jacobs, *America's Miracle Man in Vietnam* (2005) (Diem); Susan Jeffords, *The Remasculinization of America* (1989); Howard Jones, *Death of a Generation* (2003); George McT. Kahin, *Intervention* (1986); David Kaiser, *American Tragedy* (2000); Stanley Karnow, *Vietnam* (1991); Yuen Foong Khong, *Analogies of War* (1992); Gabriel Kolko, *Anatomy of a War* (1985); A. J. Langguth, *Our Vietnam* (2000); Mark A. Lawrence, *Assuming the Burden* (2005); David W. Levy, *The Debate over Vietnam* (1991); Fredrik Logevall, *Choosing War* (1999); Robert Mann, *A Grand Delusion* (2001); H. R. McMaster, *Dereliction of Duty* (1997); Robert S. McNamara et al., *Argument Without End* (1999); Edwin F. Moïse, *Tonkin Gulf and the Escalation of the Vietnam War* (1996); Joseph G. Morgan, *The Vietnam Lobby* (1997); Charles Neu, *America's Lost War* (2005); John M. Newman, *JFK and Vietnam* (1992); Caroline Page, *U.S. Official Propaganda During the Vietnam War* (1996); Douglas Pike, *Vietnam and the Soviet Union* (1987); Gareth Porter, *Perils of Dominance* (2005); William J. Rust, *Kennedy in Vietnam* (1985); Robert D. Schulzinger, *A Time for War* (1997); Orrin Schwab, *Defending the Free World* (1998); Neil Sheehan, *A Bright Shining Lie* (1988); Melvin Small, *At the Water's Edge: American Politics and the Vietnam War* (2005); Ronald H. Spector, *After Tet* (1993); Sandra Taylor, *Vietnamese Women at War* (1999); William S. Turley, *The Second Indochina War* (1986); Brian VanDeMark, *Into the Quagmire* (1991) (Johnson); Frank E. Vandiver, *Shadows of Vietnam* (1997); Jayne S. Werner and

Luu Doan Huynh, eds., *The Vietnam War* (1992); James J. Wirtz, *The Tet Offensive* (1992); Randall B. Woods, ed., *Vietnam and the American Political Tradition* (2003); Marilyn Young, *The Vietnam Wars* (1991); and Qiang Zhai, *China and the Vietnam Wars* (2000).

Laos and Cambodia are discussed in many of the studies above and in Timothy N. Castle, *At War in the Shadow of Vietnam* (1993) (Laos); David P. Chandler, *The Tragedy of Cambodian History* (1991); Michael Haas, *Cambodia, Pol Pot, and the United States* (1991); Jane Hamilton-Merritt, *Tragic Mountain* (1993) (Laos); Marie A. Martin, *Cambodia* (1994); and William Shawcross, *Sideshow* (1979) (Cambodia).

The colonial history of Vietnam, its wars against foreigners, and the development of its politics are examined in Mark Bradley, *Imagining Vietnam and America* (2000); Arthur J. Dommen, *The Indochinese Experience of the French and the Americans* (2001); William J. Duiker, *The Communist Road to Power in Vietnam* (1981) and *Ho Chi Minh* (2000); Bernard Fall, *The Two Viet-Nams* (1967); David Marr, *Vietnamese Anti-Colonialism, 1885–1925* (1971) and *Vietnamese Tradition on Trial, 1920–1945* (1981); and Douglas Pike, *History of Vietnamese Communism* (1978) and *Viet Cong* (1972).

Specific studies of the Truman and Eisenhower administrations and Vietnam are David L. Anderson, *Trapped by Success* (1991) (Eisenhower); Melanie Billings-Yun, *Decision Against War* (1988) (Dienbienphu); Lloyd C. Gardner, *Approaching Vietnam* (1988); Lloyd C. Gardner and Ted Gittinger, eds., *Vietnam: The Early Decisions* (1998); Lawrence S. Kaplan et al., eds., *Dien Bien Phu and the Crisis of Franco-American Relations* (1990); David G. Marr, *Vietnam 1945* (1995); Andrew J. Rotter, *The Path to Vietnam* (1987); Martin Shipway, *The Road to War* (1996) (French policy); and Stein Tönnesson, *The Vietnamese Revolution of 1945* (1991).

For the My Lai massacre, see David L. Anderson, *Facing My Lai* (1998); Seymour M. Hersh, *Cover-Up* (1972); James S. Olson and Randy Roberts, *My Lai* (1998); and Kevin Sim and Michael Bilton, *Four Hours in My Lai* (1992).

For province- and village-level studies that probe American interactions with a peasant society, see William Andrews, *The Village War* (1973); Eric M. Bergerud, *The Dynamics of Defeat* (1991); Jeffrey Race, *War Comes to Long An* (1972); and James W. Trullinger Jr., *Village at War* (1980).

Military decisions and operations and the soldier's experience in Vietnam are studied in Christian G. Appy, *Working Class War* (1993) and *Patriots* (2003); Robert Buzzanco, *Masters of War* (1996); Jeffrey J. Clarke, *United States Army in Vietnam* (1988); Mark Clodfelter, *The Limits of Power* (1989) (bombing); Eric Dean, *Shook Over Hell* (1997) (post-traumatic stress disorder); Douglas Kinnard, *The Certain Trumpet* (1991) (Taylor); Andrew F. Krepinevich, Jr., *The Army and Vietnam* (1986); Otto J. Lehrack, *No Shining Armor* (1992) (marines); Donald J. Mrozek, *Air Power & the Ground War in Vietnam* (1989); Douglas Pike, *PAVN: People's Army of Vietnam* (1986); John Prados and Ray Stubbe, *Valley of Decision* (1991) (Khe Sanh); Jeffrey Record, *The Wrong War* (1998); Ronald H. Spector, *United States in Vietnam* (1983); Shelby Stanton, *The Rise and Fall of an American Army* (1985); and Harry G. Summers, *On Strategy* (1981).

American public opinion, media, and the antiwar movement are discussed in many of the works above and specifically in Milton J. Bates, *The Wars We Took to Vietnam* (1996); Charles DeBenedetti and Charles Chatfield, *An American Ordeal* (1990) (antiwar movement); Terry Dietz, *Republicans and Vietnam* (1986); Kenneth J. Heineman, *Campus Wars* (1993); Rhodri Jeffreys-Jones, *Peace Now!* (1999); Katherine Kinney, *Friendly Fire* (2000); William Prochnau, *Once Upon a Distant War* (1995) (journalists); Melvin Small, *Johnson, Nixon, and the Doves* (1988) and *Antiwarriors* (2002); Melvin Small and William D. Hoover, eds., *Give Peace a Chance* (1992); Amy Swerdlow, *Women Strike for Peace* (1993); Robert R. Tomes, *Apocalypse Then: American Intellectuals and the Vietnam War, 1954–1975* (1998); Kathleen J. Turner, *Lyndon Johnson's Dual War* (1985); Jeremy Varon, *Bringing the War Home* (2004); Tom Wells, *The War Within* (1994); Philip West et al., *America's Wars in Asia* (1998); Clarence R. Wyatt, *Paper Soldiers* (1993); and Nancy Zaroulis and Gerald Sullivan, *Who Spoke Up?* (1984).

See also Robert L. Beisner, ed., *Guide to American Foreign Relations Since 1600* (2003).

For comprehensive coverage of foreign-related topics, see the articles in the four-volume *Encyclopedia of U.S. Foreign Relations* (1997), edited by Bruce W. Jentleson and Thomas G. Paterson.

CHAPTER 10

Détente and Disequilibrium, 1969–1977

Diplomatic Crossroad

Richard M. Nixon's Trip to China, 1972

"THERE IS NO crowd," the advance man radioed from the Beijing airport. "Did you say, 'No crowd'?" the presidential plane replied. Indeed, when President Richard M. Nixon's jet, the *Spirit of '76,* touched down that wintry morning of February 21, 1972, the reception was decidedly restrained. Apparently the Chinese wanted to show that Nixon desired this dramatic meeting more eagerly than did the People's Republic of China (PRC). Instead of cheering schoolchildren, only "a vast silence" welcomed Nixon. Greeting Nixon was trim seventy-three-year-old Premier Zhou Enlai, who had served Chairman Mao Zedong as key administrator since the success of the Chinese Revolution in 1949. Nixon and Zhou formally shook hands—the very gesture that Secretary John Foster Dulles had spurned at Geneva in 1954. The television cameras whirred, sending back home, via satellite, picture postcards of the historic encounter. Portraits of Mao and political signs hung everywhere. The Chinese had painted over one poster that read: "We Must Defeat the U.S. Aggressors and All Their Running Dogs."

Nixon's "journey for peace" contrasted sharply with the previous quarter-century of no formal diplomatic relations between the two countries. They had harangued each other as warmongers and had fought one another in Korea. Washington maintained close ties with the PRC's archenemy Jiang Jieshi in Taiwan, while China aided America's foe in Vietnam. Despite this history of hostility, Nixon and Zhou now recognized that cooperation best served their countries' interests.

In 1969, newly inaugurated President Nixon had asked his assistant for national security affairs, Henry A. Kissinger, to review relations with China. When border fighting between the Soviet Union and China broke out that year, Nixon told his cabinet: "The worst thing . . . would be for the Soviet Union to gobble up Red China." He soon sent signals to Beijing by scaling back U.S. Seventh Fleet operations in the Taiwan Strait and relaxing trade restrictions with China. Early in 1970 PRC diplomats once again began meeting with U.S. officials in Warsaw—talks that China had suspended two years earlier as a protest against American warfare in

Richard M. Nixon (1913–1994) and Zhou Enlai (1898–1976), 1972. During his historic trip to China in February 1972, President Nixon met with the Chinese premier. Zhou asked at one point: "Can [the] U.S. control the 'wild horse' of Japan?" Nixon replied: "The United States can get out of Japanese waters, but others will still fish there"— a veiled reference to the Soviet Union. (Nixon Presidential Materials Project/ National Archives)

Vietnam. In December, Mao told the visiting American journalist Edgar Snow that he would welcome Nixon to China, "either as a tourist or as President." In April 1971 a U.S. table tennis team competing in Japan accepted an invitation to visit China. Quips about "Ping-Pong diplomacy" did not detract from the symbolic significance of the team's trip. Kissinger made plans to go to China himself. In Islamabad, Pakistan, in early July, he secretly boarded a plane for Beijing. Kissinger soon reported that "the process we have now started will send enormous shock waves around the world." On July 15, President Nixon made the startling announcement that he would go to China to "seek the normalization of relations."

Renewed relations seemed to promise advantages. Because the Soviets had become China's "most dangerous and most important enemy," U.S. ties with Beijing might keep Moscow off balance. "We're using the Chinese thaw to get the Russians shook," Nixon told an aide. With the U.S. economy sagging, moreover, the legendary China market once again loomed large in American imaginations. Because China, a member of the nuclear club since 1964, had rejected the 1968 Treaty on the Nonproliferation of Nuclear Weapons, Washington sought Beijing's adherence. U.S. recognition of China might also influence Beijing to press North Vietnam to accept a political settlement of the Vietnam War.

The China trip also promised Nixon political profits at home. With antiwar Democrats campaigning against Nixon's continued intervention in Vietnam, New Hampshire would hold the first presidential primary of 1972 in March. Even though "the libs [liberals] will try to piss on it as an election year gimmick," Kissinger frankly remarked that Nixon's "political ass was on the line." Having urged relations with China for years, liberal-left Americans soon applauded the China trip. At the same time, the right wing of the Republican party could hardly charge that Nixon, a proven anticommunist, had turned soft on communism. Finally, the China journey was central to the general Nixon-Kissinger policy of "détente"—the relaxation of international tensions with communist nations to protect U.S. interests.

The Chinese, still reeling from their destructive internal Cultural Revolution, now perceived the Americans as changing from a "monkey" to a "human being." Sino-Soviet skirmishes in 1969 on the shared 4,150-mile border alarmed many Chinese, who recalled the Soviet invasion of Czechoslovakia in 1968. As the Soviets constructed an air base in Mongolia, the Chinese dug bomb shelters and tunnel networks. Renewed ties, then, might deter the "polar bear" to the north. "We can work together to commonly deal with a bastard," Mao told Kissinger. A Sino-American rapprochement might also keep a revived Japan off guard and cautious. Or it might, as actually happened, lead to the opening of Sino-Japanese relations, thereby strengthening China against Moscow. Finally, China wanted trade and a reduced U.S. commitment to Taiwan.

On the flight to China, Nixon studied notebooks about Chinese politics, culture, and diplomacy. Included were CIA analyses of Mao and Zhou and "talking points" that Nixon committed to memory. Joining the presidential party was a press corps of eighty-seven, heavy with television news personalities. Telling CBS reporter Dan Rather that there would be "tough, hard bargaining between people who have very great differences," the president carefully staged his pageant for prime-time screens back home.

Nixon soon met Chairman Mao. Seated in overstuffed chairs, Nixon, Kissinger, Mao, and Zhou talked warmly for about an hour. Seventy-eight-year-old Mao, although suffering from congestive heart disease, remained an imposing figure, esteemed by the Chinese as the father of the People's Republic. "Your book, *Six Crises,* is not a bad book," Mao bantered. Responding to that lukewarm review of his prepresidential memoirs, Nixon looked at Zhou and joked: "He reads too much." Born into a well-to-do mandarin family, Zhou spoke English, Russian, French, and Japanese as well as his native Chinese. U.S. diplomats contrasted Zhou's quiet, patient style with the blunt, haggling manner of Soviet officials.

That evening, in the Great Hall of the People, Zhou hosted a banquet for 800 guests. Sipping glasses of *mao tai,* a 150-proof rice liquor, Americans and their hosts toasted each other in the traditional "*gan bei*" ("dry glass") fashion. The Chinese military band played "America the Beautiful"—as "a toast to your next Inaugural," Zhou whispered to Nixon. The president called for a "long march together," even quoting Mao himself: "Seize the day, seize the hour. This is the hour."

While Nixon privately assured Zhou on February 22 that "I am removing this irritant [Vietnam] as fast as anyone in my position could," journalists filed reports on the Chinese lifestyle—clean streets, gauze masks to prevent infectious diseases, acupuncture techniques, anti-imperialist banners, expertise in table tennis, regimented schools, puritanical social habits, bicycles, the monotony of blue dress. After years of thinking the Chinese a bestial enemy, Americans now found them living and suffering like the rest of humanity. Whereas in the 1960s Americans used words such as "ignorant, warlike, treacherous, and sly" to describe the "Red Chinese," after the 1972 trip they described them as "hard-working, intelligent, progressive, artistic, and practical."

After late-night social events, an exhausted Kissinger helped fashion language for a joint communiqué that followed Zhou's formula of "seeking common ground while reserving differences." Affirming existing ties with South Korea and Japan, Nixon assured his hosts that a continued U.S. military presence in Asia was "China's [best] hope for Jap restraint." The Americans then stated their opposition to "outside pressure or intervention" in Asia—meaning Vietnam. The Chinese declared that they would continue to support "the struggles of all oppressed people" against large nations that attempt to "bully" the small. All foreign troops should withdraw from Asia, especially Vietnam. As for Taiwan, which the United States still recognized as the official government of China, the Chinese part of the communiqué urged the withdrawal of all U.S. military forces from the island. There was only one China. The Americans advocated a "peaceful settlement of the Taiwan question by the Chinese themselves." Both parties agreed, however, that "neither should seek hegemony in the Asia-Pacific region" and both opposed "efforts by any other country" to establish "such hegemony"—a slap at the Soviet Union. Finally, both sides appealed for increased cultural and commercial contacts.

Diplomacy done, on the seventh day of his trip, February 28, the president proclaimed that "this was the week that changed the world." Kissinger privately boasted that Washington and China had become "in plain words . . . tacit allies." One negative headline proclaimed: "They Got Taiwan, We Got Eggroll."

Nixon, Kissinger, and Their Critics

Nixon and Kissinger orchestrated this surprising turnabout in Sino-American relations. Richard Milhous Nixon, the grocer's son from Whittier, California, relished the big play in politics. Nixon also wanted the Soviets and North Vietnamese to think him irrational and unpredictable. This self-professed "madman theory" would supposedly deter adversaries or cause them to settle on American terms. A secretive, suspicious man, Nixon raged at his many domestic "enemies." "One day we will get them," he told an aide, "get them on the floor and step on them, crush them, show no mercy . . . stick our heels in . . . and twist."

His administration guarded itself against its critics through secrecy and executive crimes and corrupt political practices later known collectively as Watergate. Because he wanted documentation for his memoirs, Nixon secretly recorded conversations in the White House. When made public by court order, the tapes inspired an impeachment process that Nixon himself, caught in lies, terminated by resigning from the presidency on August 8, 1974, thereby elevating Vice President Gerald Ford to the White House. Exposure of criminality weakened the executive branch in its ongoing struggle with Congress over foreign policy. Watergate also caused bewilderment abroad, as Soviet leaders could not comprehend how the president could be forced to resign over what they viewed as a "small matter."

Pinocchio and Jiminy Cricket. "A two-fisted, bare-faced liar"—so Republican Senator Barry Goldwater described Nixon before the Watergate crisis forced him from office. Using characters from the popular story of Pinocchio, the cartoonist Robert Grossman depicts Nixon as the untruthful youngster and Henry A. Kissinger as his faithful adviser. (© Robert Grossman)

After Nixon's ignoble departure, Henry A. Kissinger stayed on. Presidential assistant for national security affairs (1969–1976) and secretary of state (1973–1977), Kissinger thought Nixon an "egomaniac" who did not get "adequate credit" for foreign-policy triumphs such as the change in China policy. Having escaped from Nazism in 1938, this ambitious, witty, energetic, persistent, and vain political scientist became one of the most traveled diplomats in history. He reveled in personal diplomacy, in the give-and-take, the manipulation of power and people. His "devilish nimbleness" and evident rapport with people of different cultures brought him negotiating successes. Kissinger managed an impressive number of roles: theorist, policymaker, negotiator, presidential adviser, bureaucratic infighter, and public spokesperson. He and Nixon agreed early that they would make policy in the White House, often sidestepping the foreign-affairs bureaucracy. William P. Rogers served as a loyal secretary of state until 1973, but Nixon granted him little authority. Resenting its exclusion from policymaking, Congress reasserted its prerogatives by passing the War Powers Resolution (1973): The president could commit U.S. troops abroad for no more than sixty days, after which he had to obtain congressional approval. Congress also vexed Kissinger by cutting foreign aid to Turkey, Cambodia, South Vietnam, and Angola. Without Watergate and without congressional meddling, Kissinger lamented, he could have accomplished so much more. Nonetheless, he and North Vietnamese negotiator Le Duc Tho shared the Nobel Peace Prize in 1973.

Kissinger still remained a popular figure. He charmed journalists and leaked secret information to generate favorable newspaper stories. A self-proclaimed "swinger" prior to his 1974 marriage, Kissinger once accused Anne Armstrong, the first U.S. woman ambassador to Britain, of crying when he excluded her from negotiations. "I might have bitten him," recalled Armstrong, "but I wasn't going to cry." Critics argued that Kissinger followed the ruthless maxim that the ends justify the means: He wiretapped aides and journalists; he defended the president in the lowest days of Watergate; he relied recklessly on huge arms sales; he sponsored CIA plots abroad that held America up to ridicule for advocating democracy but under-

Makers of American Foreign Relations, 1969–1977

Presidents	Secretaries of State
Richard M. Nixon, 1969–1974	William P. Rogers, 1969–1973
Gerald Ford, 1974–1977	Henry A. Kissinger, 1973–1977

mining it; and he approved the deadly bombing of the peoples of Southeast Asia. "One must not confuse the intelligence business with missionary work," Kissinger explained. He similarly urged the military leaders of Argentina to get the "terrorist problem under control as quickly as possible"; his main concern was not human rights but that they "get it over quickly."

Kissinger and Nixon considered themselves pragmatists, not ideologues. The term that most generally described the thrust of their diplomacy was "détente": limited cooperation with the Soviet Union and the People's Republic of China within a general environment of rivalry. Détente became a means, a process, a climate in which to reduce international tensions and sustain U.S. leadership in world politics. Détente was supposed to produce a geopolitical "equilibrium" by containing the Soviet Union and China and curbing radical revolution. To Nixon, the world divided into roughly five power centers (including Japan and Western Europe) with each keeping order among smaller states and clients in its region and each respecting one another's sphere. Nixon and Kissinger saw Soviet-American competition as the primary element in world affairs. They understood that by 1970 the Soviet Union had achieved nuclear parity or equality with the United States, that the Soviets suffered severe internal economic problems and needed outside help, that the Sino-Soviet split had widened, and that world power (capital and weaponry) had become diffused as nations had recovered from World War II and colonies had broken away from empires. Because Washington could not "conceive *all* the plans, design *all* the programs, execute *all* the decisions," the duo sought to change containment through confrontation to containment through negotiation.

Détente, SALT, and the Nuclear Arms Race

The Nixon administration emphasized the triangular relationship formed by the Soviet Union, China, and the United States and attempted to play the two communist states against one another, to keep one worrying about what the United States was doing with the other. For the Soviets there would be both incentives (capital and trade) to encourage restraint and penalties (large arms sales to Soviet adversaries and closer ties to China) to punish unacceptable behavior. Détente made sense to European allies who abhorred the U.S. "obsession with Southeast Asia." Moscow and Beijing might help the United States extricate itself from war in Vietnam. Détente supposedly offered a cheaper way of pursuing containment by reducing the necessity for interventions, spiraling military expenditures, and new nuclear weapons systems. The Nixon administration cut the armed forces from 3.5 million in 1968 to 2.3 million in 1973, ended the draft, and in 1972 negotiated a strategic arms limitation treaty. To reduce a billion-dollar deficit in the balance of payments, détente conjured up images of expanded markets. Massive grain shipments flowed to the Soviet Union, and corporations such as Pepsi-Cola and Chase Manhattan Bank started operations in the USSR. Exports to the Soviet Union reached $2.3 billion in 1976. "They want credits, they want trade, and we'll give it all to 'em," said Nixon. "But for a price. We don't give it away cheap."

The Nixon-Kissinger grand strategy rested on some questionable assumptions. It overestimated the usefulness of China as a check on Moscow. It assumed wrongly that the Soviets could manage their "friends" in North Vietnam or the Middle East and that great-power cooperation could calm Third World problems. Still viewing small states as proxies of the great powers, Nixon paid too little attention to the local sources of disputes. Kissinger spent much of his time trying to keep détente glued together in the face of conflicts in Asia, Africa, and the Middle East, and economic challenges from the Organization of Petroleum Exporting Countries (OPEC). Even America's friends caused difficulty: Iran insisted on huge arms shipments but raised oil prices, threatening the U.S. economy; Saudi Arabia demanded sophisticated weaponry but refused to help resolve the Arab-Israeli conflict.

Détente also ran afoul of domestic dissenters. In 1974 conservatives and liberals in Congress cooperated to deny most-favored-nation trade status to the Soviet Union until it permitted Jewish emigration. Americans of Eastern European descent berated détente as an abandonment of their homelands to Soviet domination. Liberals criticized Kissinger's tolerance of authoritarian regimes that trampled on human rights. The Nixon and Ford administrations contradicted themselves by appealing for arms control while they broke records for arms sales abroad ($10 billion in 1976 alone). Hard-line anticommunists labeled Kissinger an appeaser who squandered U.S. supremacy in the international system.

The Nixon administration nonetheless claimed diplomatic triumphs. The opening to China ranked highest. The turnaround helped thwart reconciliation between the two communist giants. Moscow deployed more divisions in Asia—away from NATO. China received top-grade intelligence on the Soviets. New ties between China and Japan contributed to Asian stability. Sino-American trade flourished, reaching $700 million in 1973. Also, cultural exchanges and travel between the once-distant nations reduced mutual ignorance. In 1973 Washington and Beijing exchanged "Liaison Offices" or mini-embassies. Formal diplomatic relations had to wait until 1979, after Watergate, Nixon's resignation, the 1976 presidential election, the deaths of Mao and Zhou, and new political alignments within China.

The Sino-American rapprochement did have some tragic side effects. In 1971 the Bengalis of East Pakistan rebelled against the military dictatorship of (West) Pakistan and declared the independent nation of Bangladesh. The Pakistani government attempted to crush the revolution through what U.S. officials at the scene called "selective genocide." India, which had just signed a treaty of friendship with the Soviet Union, intervened on behalf of the rebels. The White House thereupon ordered a "tilt" in favor of Pakistan. As an ally, Pakistan had granted bases for U-2 flights over the Soviet Union and intelligence-gathering posts to monitor Soviet nuclear testing. American weapons soon flowed to Pakistan, foreign aid to India stopped, and

The Nuclear Arms Race: A Glossary

Anti-ballistic missile (ABM): A defensive missile designed to destroy an incoming enemy ballistic missile before its warhead reaches its target.

Ballistic missile: A rocket-propelled missile that leaves the atmosphere and returns to earth in a free fall.

Cruise missile: A guided missile that flies to its target within the earth's atmosphere, close to the surface. The cruise missile can carry a nuclear warhead and can be launched from the air, land, or sea.

Delivery vehicle: A missile or strategic bomber that delivers a warhead to its target.

Deployment: Installing weapons, making them ready for action.

First strike: An initial nuclear attack by one country intended to destroy an adversary's strategic nuclear forces.

Intercontinental ballistic missile (ICBM): A land-based missile capable of traveling more than 3,000 nautical miles to deliver one or more warheads.

Intermediate-range nuclear forces (INF): Sometimes called theater nuclear forces, these weapons have a range of about 3,000 miles.

Missile experimental (MX): An American ICBM capable of carrying as many as ten MIRVs.

Multiple independently targetable reentry vehicle (MIRV): A vehicle loaded with a warhead and mounted, along with similar vehicles, on one ballistic missile. Once separated from the missile, each MIRV can be directed against a different target.

Mutual assured destruction (MAD): The ability of both the United States and the Soviet Union to inflict damage so severe that neither is willing to initiate a nuclear attack.

Neutron bomb: An "enhanced radiation weapon," this nuclear bomb is designed primarily to kill people and to inflict less damage on buildings than other bombs.

Nuclear freeze: The immediate halt to the development, production, transfer, and deployment of nuclear weapons.

Second strike: A retaliatory nuclear attack launched after being hit by an opponent's first strike.

Strategic Defense Initiative (SDI): Popularly known as "Star Wars," SDI was President Ronald Reagan's 1983 proposal to build a space-based, defensive system that could establish a protective shield over the United States and its allies with the capability to shoot down incoming ballistic missiles.

Strategic weapons or arms: Long-range weapons capable of hitting an adversary's territory. ICBMs, SLBMs, and strategic bombers are so classified.

Submarine-launched ballistic missile (SLBM): A ballistic missile carried in and launched from a submarine.

Surface-to-air missile (SAM): A missile launched from the earth's surface for the purpose of knocking down an adversary's airplanes.

Tactical nuclear weapons: Low-yield nuclear weapons for battlefield use.

Triad: The three-part structure of American strategic forces (ICBMs, SLBMs, and strategic bombers).

Warhead: The part of a missile that contains the nuclear explosive intended to inflict damage.

a naval task force steamed into the Bay of Bengal. The White House took a global rather than regional view of the crisis and saw India acting as Moscow's pawn trying to "goat" Pakistan into full-scale war. But India never attacked West Pakistan, and the Soviet Union never encouraged it to attack. Pakistan, India, China, and the Soviet Union all had indicated support for an agreement that matched the outcome: an end to hostilities and independence for Bangladesh.

Despite blunt exchanges over the hot line during the Indo-Pakistani conflict, détente remained U.S. policy. At a summit meeting in Moscow in May 1972, Nixon told USSR president Leonid Brezhnev that capitalism and communism could "live together and work together." They struck agreements on cooperation in space exploration (culminating in a joint space venture in 1975) and trade (large grain sales soon followed). On Vietnam, they concluded that small nations should not disrupt détente. Only a few weeks earlier, when Nixon had escalated the bombing of North

Vietnam, he feared that an angry Moscow might cancel the summit. The Soviets did not; détente came first.

The Strategic Arms Limitation Talks (SALT) agreements dominated the summit. When the Nixon administration entered office, it inherited a legacy of doctrines and missiles that defined U.S. nuclear strategy. In the 1960s, the doctrine of "massive retaliation" evolved into the concept of "mutual assured destruction," or MAD. MAD's viability depended on each side's "second-strike capability": the capacity to absorb a first strike and still destroy the attacker with a retaliatory or second strike. By 1969 American strategists sought superiority through the triad: land-based intercontinental ballistic missiles (ICBMs), long-range B-52 bombers, and submarine-launched ballistic missiles (SLBMs), all armed with nuclear weapons. To help guarantee superiority, the United States had also begun to flight-test the "multiple independently targetable reentry vehicle" (MIRV). Finally, Nixon inherited plans for an "anti-ballistic missile" (ABM) system to defend cities and ICBMs vulnerable to Soviet attack. Because ABMs theoretically protected offensive weapons from attack, critics feared that they would stimulate the Soviets to build more missiles to overwhelm the ABM protection, thus further accelerating the nuclear arms race.

By 1968 Washington had deployed 1,054 ICBMs to the Soviets' 858; the United States also led in SLBMs 656 to 121, and in long-range bombers 545 to 155. The United States ranked first in total nuclear warheads, about 4,200 to 1,100, and in the accuracy of its weapons systems. Yet U.S. officials knew that the Soviets were constructing new missiles, submarines, and bombers at a pace that would soon give the Soviets nuclear parity with the United States. President Nixon soon abandoned the untenable doctrine of superiority and accepted parity of forces with the Soviet Union. Still, he decided to phase in the ABM system and ordered the installation of MIRVs. Thus the United States could enter the SALT talks, he said, from a position of strength.

The SALT-I talks began in Helsinki in November 1969 and culminated at the Moscow summit in May 1972 with two agreements. The first, a treaty, limited the deployment of ABMs for each nation to two sites. In essence the accord sustained the MAD doctrine by leaving urban centers in both countries vulnerable. The other accord, an interim agreement, froze the existing number of ICBMs already deployed or in construction. At the time, the Soviet Union led 1,607 to 1,054. The interim agreements also froze SLBMs at 740 for the USSR and 656 for the United States. SALT-I did not limit the hydra-headed MIRVs, thus leaving the United States superior in deliverable warheads, 5,700 to 2,500. Nixon and Kissinger underestimated the speed with which the Soviets would deploy their own MIRVs on heavier missiles, and by not seeking a ban on MIRVs, they soon rendered American ICBMs theoretically vulnerable to a first strike. Kissinger later regretted that he had not "thought through the implications of a MIRVed world more thoughtfully." Nor did the agreement restrict long-range bombers, in which the United States held a 450 to 200 advantage. Finally, SALT-I did not prohibit the development of new weapons. The United States, for example, moved ahead on the Trident submarine (to replace the Polaris-Poseidon fleet), the B-1 bomber (to replace the B-52), and the cruise missile.

Still, SALT-I did begin frank talks to place limits on nuclear weapons. In August 1972, the Senate passed the ABM treaty by an 88 to 2 vote; a joint congressional resolution later endorsed the interim agreement. Détente's reputation soared. Conservative critics charged, however, that the United States still lagged behind the Soviet Union in delivery vehicles (ICBMs, SLBMs, and strategic bombers). "What in the name of God is strategic superiority?" Kissinger challenged his detractors. "What do you do with it?"

Subsequent negotiations on SALT-II moved slowly. At Vladivostok, in November 1974, Presidents Ford and Brezhnev agreed on two principles to guide the talks—a ceiling of 2,400 on the total number of delivery vehicles permitted each side and no more than 1,320 missiles equipped with MIRVs. Thereafter the SALT-II talks bogged down over which types of weapons should count in the 2,400 ceiling, with Washington insisting that the new Soviet Backfire bomber be included and the Soviets demanding inclusion of the U.S. cruise missile. By 1977 the United States wielded 8,500 warheads, compared with 5,700 in 1972; comparable Soviet figures equaled 4,000 and 2,500. Total strategic delivery vehicles by 1978 numbered 2,059 for the United States and 2,440 for the Soviet Union. Détente had not stopped the nuclear arms race.

In Europe, however, détente worked to ease tensions. Willy Brandt, the West German chancellor, pursued a policy of *Ostpolitik* to remove the two Germanies from great-power competition. A West German–Soviet treaty of August 1970 identified détente as the goal of both countries and recognized the existence of two Germanies. A few months later Brandt signed an agreement with Poland that confirmed the latter's postwar absorption of German territory to the Oder-Neisse line. Then, in June 1972, the four powers occupying Berlin signed an agreement wherein the Soviet Union guaranteed Western access to the city. Finally, in December 1972, the two Germanies themselves initialed a treaty that provided for the exchange of diplomatic representatives and membership in the United Nations for both (effected in 1973). European East-West trade boomed, with the West German economy the chief beneficiary.

At the Conference on Security and Cooperation in Helsinki, Finland, in summer 1975, delegates from thirty-five nations accepted the permanence of existing European boundaries, including adjustments made in Germany and Eastern Europe three decades earlier. The conferees pledged themselves to détente and endorsed human rights for all Europeans. While right-wing critics complained of another Yalta sell-out, so-called Helsinki groups pressed communist governments to honor their pledge about human rights. Such groups included Charter 77, headed by Václav Havel in Czechoslovakia, and Solidarity, led by Lech Walesa in Poland. Instead of the "consolidation of the postwar order that Moscow had so long desired," a Kissinger aide later noted, "the political status quo in Eastern Europe began to unravel."

Regional Tails Wagging the Superpower Dogs: The Middle East

The Nixon Doctrine, announced in July 1969, declared that henceforth the United States would supply military and economic assistance but not soldiers to help nations defend themselves. To prevent new Vietnams, Washington sought to build up regional surrogate powers, such as Iran and Israel, thus apparently retiring its badge

Golda Meir (1898–1978), Nixon, and Kissinger. In early 1973, the prime minister of Israel met with the president, who promised more U.S. airplanes. On the Nixon-Meir relationship, White House counsel Leonard Garment later wrote: "How could Nixon resist this mother of all mothers, Hannah Nixon squared—smart, spiky, and resolute in her simple schoolteacher frock?" (Department of State *Newsletter*)

as the world's policeman. Third World countries still mattered because of their vulnerability to destabilizing radicalism and hence to pernicious Soviet influence. Moscow's endorsement of national liberation movements, according to Kissinger, connected the internal politics of developing nations with the "international struggle." When troubles arose in the Third World, Nixon, Ford, and Kissinger reflexively interpreted them as moves in the game of great-power politics.

Problems in the Middle East sorely tested détente. Basic U.S. goals since World War II had been consistent for the region: ensure oil supplies; contain the Soviet Union; protect Israel; challenge neutralism; and blunt the appeal of Arab nationalism. After the 1956 Suez crisis, the Soviet Union and the United States armed Egypt and Israel respectively. In June 1967, after years of threats and counterthreats, Israel attacked Egypt and Syria. In the Six-Day War, the Israelis, using American-supplied weapons, captured the West Bank (including Jerusalem) from Jordan, the Golan Heights from Syria, and the entire Sinai Peninsula, including the eastern bank of the Suez Canal, from Egypt. Half of the Arab states broke diplomatic relations with Washington. Soviet vessels obtained access to Arab ports. Washington, in turn, sold fifty F-4 Phantom jets to Israel in December 1968 and winked at Israel's development of nuclear weapons.

Nixon's administration worried that the persistent Arab-Israeli "powder keg" would open a Soviet avenue into the Middle East. As the Israelis deployed U.S. Phantom jets on bombing raids deep into Egypt in January 1970, the Soviets shipped surface-to-air missiles (SAMs) to Egypt to defend against the Phantoms. Thousands of Soviet troops, advisers, and pilots answered Egypt's call for assistance. Washington gave Israel more planes and more arms with military credits amounting to $1.2 billion from 1971 to 1973.

Meanwhile, Palestinian Arabs, many of them refugees ousted from their homes in 1948 when Israel won nationhood, grew more frustrated. The Palestine Liberation Organization (PLO), formed in 1964, came under the aggressive leadership of

Yasir Arafat. Many Arab leaders backed the organization's demands for destruction of the Jewish state and for creation of a Palestinian homeland. In 1970 a radical wing of the PLO hijacked airliners and seized hostages. Palestinian terrorists murdered Israeli athletes at the 1972 Olympic Games in Munich. The Israelis retaliated, targeting PLO figures abroad.

From 1970 to 1973, the Nixon administration's "standstill diplomacy" seemed to work. Israel possessed military superiority, Moscow displayed restraint, and a new, seemingly more moderate Egyptian government under the leadership of Anwar el-Sadat came to power after Nasser's death in September 1970. Fearful that détente would condemn Egypt to a "no war, no peace" paralysis, Sadat plotted a new strike against Israel. After thwarting a Soviet-supported coup, he abruptly expelled several thousand Soviet technicians and military advisers in summer 1972. Then on October 6, 1973 (Yom Kippur), Egyptian forces struck across the canal into Sinai while Syrian troops attacked Israel's northern border. Taken by surprise, the Israelis suffered heavy losses, and the Arabs regained land lost in 1967. Nixon promised Tel Aviv more Phantoms. Moscow rushed arms to Syria.

In a massive airlift of supplies, President Nixon ordered "everything that will fly" to Israel on October 14. Soviet premier Aleksei Kosygin flew to Cairo to persuade Sadat to accept a cease-fire. Kissinger flew to Moscow on October 20, learning en route that the Saudis had embargoed oil to the United States. Other Arab states soon joined the embargo. With Nixon increasingly distracted by the Watergate crisis, Kissinger and the Soviets finally arranged a cease-fire on October 22. But the Israelis ignored the truce and surrounded the Egyptian Third Army. When Moscow pressed for Soviet and U.S. troops to enforce the truce jointly, Washington overreacted. An inebriated Nixon blurted: "Words won't do the job. We've got to act." Kissinger thereupon ordered all U.S. forces on nuclear alert, a calculated ploy to shock Soviet decisionmakers. Angry Kremlin leaders chose not to intervene unilaterally. Kissinger pressed the Israelis to honor the truce. A new cease-fire held.

The Arab-Israeli contest had far-reaching economic repercussions. Arab states such as Saudi Arabia, which for years had supplied Western nations with inexpensive petroleum, now used their black riches as a weapon: They embargoed petroleum shipments to the United States and quadrupled the price of crude oil for Western Europe and Japan. The United States, importing between 10 and 15 percent of its oil from the Middle East, suffered an energy crisis. Gasoline prices spun upward, as anxious drivers lined up for hours to fuel their automobiles. The embargo ended in March 1974, but prices remained high and U.S. vulnerability had been exposed.

Kissinger launched "shuttle diplomacy" to prevent another Mideast blowup. With impressive stamina, he bargained in Cairo and Tel Aviv and other capitals intermittently for two years. Finally, on September 1, 1975, Egypt and Israel initialed a historic agreement that provided for an eventual Israeli pullback from part of the Sinai, created a United Nations–patrolled buffer zone, and placed U.S. technicians in "early warning" stations to detect military activities. Washington also promised substantial aid to both Egypt and Israel.

Thorny problems remained. The Palestinian Arabs still demanded a homeland, while Israelis entrenched themselves in occupied territories, building farms and houses. Jordan still demanded return of the West Bank, and Syrian hostility persisted with the Golan Heights in Israel's hands. A bloody civil war broke out in Lebanon, which prompted Syria to send in troops in 1976. In 1976, Sadat, who wanted U.S. technology and mediation, denounced Moscow, saying that "99 percent of the cards in the game are in America's hands whether the Soviet Union likes it or not." Once Cairo turned emphatically toward Washington, U.S. Mideast policy looked more like old-fashioned containment than détente. Excluding the Soviets and Palestinians in Mideast diplomacy prevented a full Arab-Israeli settlement. The spectacular rescue by Israeli commandos of 259 hostages held captive by Palestinian terrorists in Entebbe, Uganda, on July 4, 1976, also galvanized U.S. public support for Israel. After Entebbe, it became axiomatic that "the United States should not only act *with* Israel on foreign policy but *like* Israel in matters of unconventional warfare." Moscow, in turn, gave more support to Libya's president Moammar Gadhafi, a radical Pan Arabist who came to power in 1969 and denounced all Mideast peace efforts.

As a counterweight to the Soviets and radical Arabs, Washington fashioned a closer alliance with the Shah of Iran. After 1972 the Shah's military gorged itself on modern American arms, paid for by galloping oil revenues ("petro-dollars"). American corporate executives rushed to Iran to display their submarines, fighter aircraft, assault helicopters, and missiles. In 1977 his nation ranked as the largest foreign buyer of American-made arms, spending $5.7 billion that year alone. But doubters thought such excessive military spending foolhardy when the Iranian per capita income stood at only $350. Ruthlessly suppressing all dissent, the Shah hired a New York advertising agency to enhance his image as America's "unconditional ally" in the turbulent Middle East. Washington did not see that "Iran was the regional tail wagging the superpower dog."

Covert Action and Economic Relations in Latin America and Africa

Latin America remained an area of intense interest to the United States. Latin American military officers still trained at the Inter-American Defense College in Washington, D.C., where they learned urban counterinsurgency and jungle warfare techniques. In the early 1970s one-third of Latin American exports went to the United States and two-fifths of the region's imports came from the United States. In 1976, Latin American countries supplied 34 percent of U.S. petroleum imports, 68 percent of its coffee, 57 percent of its sugar, 47 percent of its copper, and 98 percent of its bauxite. In that year U.S. direct investments in its southern neighbors totaled $17 billion. Latin American governments nonetheless increasingly challenged Washington. Soon after taking office, Nixon sent New York governor Nelson Rockefeller on a fact-finding mission to Latin America that sparked protests. The governor reported in August 1969 that Latin Americans resented Washington's "paternalistic" efforts to "direct the internal affairs of other nations to an unseemly degree."

Mexico refused to honor the economic blockade of Cuba, boldly proclaimed the economic independence of small states and their right to expropriate foreign enterprises, and urged that developed nations share their wealth with poorer countries. In 1974 the United Nations approved these views by a 120 to 6 vote, with Washington voting no. The United States also engaged Peru and Ecuador in a "tuna war," after those nations declared a 200-mile territorial limit and began seizing American fishing vessels in coastal waters. After 1968, a new, radical (noncommunist) military government in Peru nationalized an Exxon oil subsidiary and defiantly purchased Soviet MiGs. Venezuela, a founding member of the Organization of Petroleum Exporting Countries (OPEC) in 1960, joined the Arabs in drastically raising petroleum prices in the 1970s. In 1976 Caracas too nationalized American-owned oil companies.

Chile attracted Washington's rapt attention in September 1970. That month Chileans elected as their president Salvador Allende, a physician by profession and a founder of Chile's Socialist party. The CIA had sent hundreds of thousands of dollars in bribe and propaganda money to Chile to back a right-wing candidate. Fearing a "democratically elected version of Fidel Castro," Nixon personally gave CIA official Richard Helms full authority to undermine the Allende government. Following presidential instructions to "make the economy scream" in Chile in order to block the nationalization of American-owned copper corporations (Kennecott and Anaconda), the CIA worked with U.S. companies to stop the shipment of spare parts. Washington also cut off economic aid and denied Export-Import Bank loans to Chile. Military assistance continued as the CIA conspired with Chilean army officers and spent $6 million to subsidize newspapers and political parties opposed to Allende.

In 1973 a military junta overthrew Allende. In the chaos, military officers murdered him. Declassified documents indicate that "sectors of the U.S. government" were directly involved in operations designed to create a "coup climate" in which the overthrow of Chilean democracy "would and could take place." Vivid images of Allende's ouster recurred in the 1982 film *Missing,* a taut thriller in which Chilean authorities kill an American journalist fingered by the U.S. Embassy because he detected U.S. machinations. The new junta returned companies to private hands, suspended freedom of speech and press, and tortured and killed political opponents. When Congress threatened to cut off arms sales in 1976, Kissinger assured Chilean dictator Augusto Pinochet that "your greatest sin was to overthrow a government that was going Communist."

The Nixon and Ford administrations also sought to keep Cuba isolated. Still seeing Castro as a Soviet puppet, Nixon concluded in 1970 from sketchy U-2 evidence that the Soviets were building a nuclear submarine base at Cienfuegos, Cuba, in violation of their understanding after the 1962 missile crisis to refrain from placing offensive weapons on the island. When Moscow denied building a submarine facility, Nixon claimed a victory that "reaffirmed," "clarified," and "amplified" the 1962 understanding by prohibiting Soviet nuclear submarine facilities in Cuba. Still seeking some accommodation with North America in the early 1970s, Castro deemphasized the export of revolution and aid to insurgencies, and in 1973 he signed an antihijacking treaty with Washington to discourage terrorism in the airways. Two years later the Organization of American States lifted its economic blockade of Cuba. Following secret talks to explore possibilities for détente, Kissinger rejected baseball commissioner Bowie Kuhn's efforts in 1975 to arrange games between the United States and Cuba. When Cuban troops in Africa helped Angolan radicals come to power, hopes for a Cuban-American normalization faded.

Frank Church (1924–1984). Democratic senator from Idaho (1957–1981), Church became a major figure on the Foreign Relations Committee, serving as its chair (1979–1981). A critic of the Vietnam War and a great orator, Church chaired Senate investigations that revealed U.S. complicity in the overthrow of Chile's Salvador Allende and exposed CIA abuses such as assassination attempts on foreign leaders. (Frank Church Collection, Boise State University Library)

Until the mid-1970s, Africa stood low on the Nixon-Ford-Kissinger list of diplomatic priorities. Initially Nixon pursued a "Southern Africa" strategy by cozying up to white minority regimes in Portuguese Angola, Rhodesia, and South Africa. The National Security Council explained in a memorandum (NSSM 39) that the entrenched whites would approve only moderate change, and that the black majorities, fearing white military superiority, would refrain from major violent confrontation. Washington thus relaxed the arms embargo to white South Africa; Congress in 1971 passed the Byrd Amendment permitting the United States to buy chromium from Rhodesia despite UN sanctions against Ian Smith's white minority government. The Black Congressional Caucus blasted the "stifling hypocrisy" of Nixon's policies toward Africa, while dollar-conscious observers cited the more than $2 billion invested in black Africa and U.S. purchases of cobalt, oil, manganese, and platinum.

Events in Angola eventually shattered American complacency. Since the early 1960s, black rebel groups had battled the Portuguese in Angola. Playing a double game, the CIA channeled funds to a faction of independence fighters while Washington officially backed Portugal and sold it military equipment to quell the nationalist rebellion. The Soviets began to support another guerrilla group, the Popular Movement for the Liberation of Angola (MPLA). When the CIA spent $32 million in 1975 on covert operations to defeat the MPLA, the State Department official in charge of African affairs, Nathaniel Davis, argued that such actions could not control the revolution or local events in Africa, but would stimulate increased Soviet activity. Davis urged a diplomatic solution. For "a test of strength with the Soviets," he advised Kissinger, "we should find a more advantageous place." "You may be right in African terms, but I'm thinking globally," Kissinger retorted. Davis soon resigned.

In November 1975, Portugal granted independence to Angola. The insurgent factions then fought one another in a civil war, with the U.S. clients doing poorly. South Africa and Zaire also dispatched troops, as did Cuba. Moscow hesitated (lest it scuttle détente) but also sent arms and advisers when South African forces intervened. Davis's resignation and leaks about the secret intervention stirred Congress. Another Vietnam? President Ford asked for $25 million for arms, but Congress "pulled the plug" by voting to stop military expenditures for Angola in January 1976.

Kissinger raged at "the probable loss to communism of a key developing country at a time of great uncertainty over our will and determination." Yet critics thought it misleading to view an African civil war through a Cold War prism. The MPLA, after all, did not molest American oil companies and never became a Soviet puppet. Washington hurt itself by choosing the losing side. Discussions with the MPLA—preventive diplomacy—might have reduced the violence. Cuba's conspicuous intervention actually goaded Moscow, heretofore very cautious about backing revolutionary movements "outside its neighboring countries," to defend "global anti-imperialism" in far-off Angola. This success fueled further "limited interventions" in Africa and Asia, ultimately leading to the Soviet disaster in Afghanistan in the 1980s (see Chapter 11).

Ford's ban on using the word *détente* after Angola pointedly exposed the differing Soviet and American interpretations of that concept. What Nixon-Kissinger-Ford had intended as codes of conduct that would restrain Soviet expansion, Moscow saw as "the natural result of the correlation of forces in the world arena," nothing that would "change the laws of the class struggle." Thus, as Washington sustained its regional clients in the Mideast peace process, for example, the Brezhnev regime sought "to perform our international duty" by assisting national liberation movements.

In addition to Angola, the outbreak of racial violence in South Africa prompted a reappraisal of U.S. policy toward Africa. The United States, reasoned Kissinger, "must grab the initiative" or "we will be faced with the Soviets, and Cuban troops," even race wars. Arms shipments went to Kenya and Zaire. Economic ties were strengthened through investments by companies such as Bethlehem Steel and Kaiser Aluminum, in pursuit of titanium and bauxite, respectively. Kissinger began to disengage from white minority regimes in Rhodesia and South Africa, urging the latter to abandon its segregationist policy of apartheid. Such changes underscored the fact that Africa had become a Cold War arena.

Economic Competition, Environmental Distress, and the North-South Debate

"It's terribly important we be number one economically," said Nixon, "because otherwise we can't be number one diplomatically or militarily." In the 1970s the international economic order created after World War II foundered. The Bretton Woods monetary arrangements for currency stability faltered; the dollar skidded; famines starved millions; dwindling natural resources spawned political tensions; and the former colonies of the Third World challenged the industrial nations to share power. The global recession of the early 1970s became the worst since the 1930s. Inflation raised the cost of industrial goods for developing countries. Protectionist barriers rose. Dramatically climbing oil prices hit poor and rich nations alike, while the price of other commodities, such as copper, slumped, causing economic downturns in nations dependent on the export of one product. Economists coined the term "Fourth World"—poor, less developed countries (LDCs) that lacked profitmaking raw materials and built up large foreign debts. The Soviet Union and the People's Republic of China engaged in world trade as never before, in quest of agricultural products and high technology, and enlarged East-West trade became a headline issue.

In this chaotic economy, the United States produced about one-third of all the world's goods and services and remained the world's largest trading nation. In 1970 U.S. exports stood at $27.5 billion; by 1977 they had climbed to $121.2 billion. Coca-Cola, Gillette, and IBM earned more than half of their profits abroad. Many American jobs depended on healthy foreign trade. In 1976, for example, one out of every nine manufacturing workers produced goods for export. Exports accounted for one out of every four dollars of agricultural sales in 1977.

American industry also relied on imports of raw materials. 75 percent of the tin, 91 percent of the chrome, 99 percent of the manganese, and 64 percent of the zinc consumed by Americans in 1975 came from foreign sources. In 1977 the nation imported more than 40 percent of its petroleum. These import needs had become conspicuous in 1971 when, for the first time since the 1930s, the United States suffered a trade deficit, importing more than it exported. Six years later, the trade imbalance reached $26.5 billion, due mainly to oil imports. U.S. direct investments abroad—about half of the world's total of foreign direct investments—equaled $75.5 billion in 1970 and $149.8 billion in 1977. The greatest part of these investments remained in developed countries (73 percent in 1975). Some investments faced political unrest, terrorist acts, and nationalization.

Despite its commanding status, the United States seemed to be losing its competitive edge. In the 1970s, ninety-eight nations had higher rates of economic growth. Japan and West Germany, strategic allies but commercial rivals, challenged America in the international marketplace. In fact, Japanese automobiles, televisions, and electronic equipment seized a large share of the U.S. market. Once dominant, American producers of computers, high technology, and aerospace machinery now struggled to retain high rank. Would wealthy Arabs buy up American banks, companies, and real estate?

The descent of the once mighty dollar further suggested decline. A "dollar glut" developed abroad, induced by U.S. foreign-aid programs, military expenditures ($90 billion in 1970 alone), private investments, inflation, and purchases of higher-priced oil. Foreigners held $78 billion in 1969; by 1977 the figure had jumped to $373 billion. Foreign holders of dollars exchanged them for gold, thus putting pressure on America's diminishing gold stock. The dollar declined in value against currencies such as the German mark and Swiss franc. Washington faced a serious balance-of-payments crisis.

The Nixon administration responded with unilateral economic measures. In August 1971, after the dollar had fallen to its lowest point since World War II, Nixon devalued the dollar (by increasing the dollar price of an ounce of gold) and suspended its convertibility into gold. He also cut foreign aid by 10 percent and imposed a 10 percent surtax on all imports, seeking thereby to reduce the influx of Japanese and European goods and to put diplomatic pressure on other nations to revalue their currencies to make them less competitive with the dollar. "We'll fix those bastards," vowed Nixon.

In December, representatives of ten leading trading nations gathered in Washington to try to stabilize the international monetary system. After stormy sessions, America's economic competitors agreed to revalue their currencies to bring them more into line with the dollar. The United States then lifted its import surcharge and once more made the dollar exchangeable for gold. But this agreement did not work for long; in early 1973 the United States again devalued the dollar, this time letting it "float," its value determined by supply and demand in the monetary marketplace. Efforts by the International Monetary Fund to restore an orderly system fell short.

International money problems intersected with foreign trade problems. Higher priced American goods could not easily compete with Japanese or European products, and the European Common Market engaged in preferential trade arrangements and export subsidies that hurt U.S. sales abroad. Japan too was highly protectionist at home yet was aggressively penetrating global markets. When Nixon in 1971 threatened to "stick it to Japan" with quotas, Tokyo averted a trade war by voluntarily limiting textile exports to America. Multilateral trade negotiations, un-

Famine In Chad, Africa. Drought-stricken Chad was only one of many poor nations that suffered in the world hunger crisis of the 1970s. Millions died. (Photo courtesy of CARE, New York)

der the auspices of the long-working General Agreement on Tariffs and Trade (1947), began in Tokyo in 1974. Five years later the "Tokyo Round" of negotiations finally produced accords that shrank tariffs about 30 percent. The signatories, including the United States, also wrote codes to regulate subsidies and dumping, but without liberalizing trade in agriculture.

In 1972, the developing world had 74 percent of the world's population but accounted for only 17 percent of the world's combined gross national product (GNP). From the perspective of the developing nations (the "South"), it seemed imperative that wealthier industrial nations (the "North") charge less for manufactured goods and technology, offer foreign assistance and loans at low rates, reduce tariffs, pay more for raw materials through commodity price agreements, and allow Third World nations to restrict foreign-owned corporations. Developing countries also insisted on a greater voice in international institutions such as the World Bank. "The object is to complete the liberation of the Third World countries from external domination" by changing the "structure of power," explained Tanzania's Julius K. Nyerere.

The Group of 77, a coalition of developing nations organized in 1964, articulated these economic demands. More than one hundred countries by the 1970s, this consortium dominated the UN General Assembly, and in 1974 that body endorsed a New International Economic Order. The United States, Japan, and Western European nations agreed to talk and struck some compromises. Charges of American greed rang hollow when many Third World leaders indulged in financial corruption and wasted resources on weaponry. India, for example, allotted billions to produce a nuclear bomb in 1974 instead of devoting those funds to alleviate severe food shortages.

Famine intensified. Insufficient fertilizer, inadequate farm acreage, pollution, droughts, and shrinking fish supplies condemned one-quarter of humankind to hunger. The drought that swept Africa in the early 1970s caused at least 10,000 deaths a day. A high birth rate and falling death rate put severe pressure on available food supplies. In 1975 the world's population passed 4 billion. Nutritionists estimated that nearly a quarter of the world's people ate less than the calories required to sustain ordinary physical activity.

At the 1974 World Food Conference in Rome, the United States voted to help finance an International Fund for Agricultural Development to expand food production in developing countries. But Americans continued to market surplus food for profit, most notably in large grain sales to the dollar-paying Soviet Union. And food aid, always political, became more so; in 1973–1974 most U.S. food assistance went to clients South Vietnam, Cambodia, and South Korea. At the same time, because of rising oil costs, the United States reduced its exports of petroleum-derived fertilizers, thus contributing to a worldwide decline in grain production in 1974.

U.S. foreign-aid strategy in the early 1970s aimed to assist especially the most impoverished people through projects to improve nutrition, family planning, health, education, and food production. Although total foreign aid (economic and military) had increased from $6.6 billion in 1970 to $7.8 billion in 1977, the proportion of GNP devoted to development assistance actually decreased. In 1977 Americans spent about four times as much on tobacco products as their government expended on development aid. Kissinger attempted to meet some of the developing nations' demands; he nonetheless voiced a growing American impatience with their "confrontational" manner.

North-South relations also became contentious over environmental issues. In the United States, books such as Rachel Carson's *Silent Spring* (1962), Paul Ehrlich's *The Population Bomb* (1968), and Barry Commoner's *The Closing Circle* (1971) raised public consciousness about environmental degradation and the growing imbalance between food supplies and burgeoning populations. In 1969 Greenpeace organized to protest nuclear-weapons tests, and the following year Americans celebrated the first Earth Day. Nixon bowed to congressional pressure to create the Environmental Protection Agency (EPA). Oil spills from oceangoing tankers, unsafe disposal of hazardous wastes, and the contamination of water sources underscored these borderless, transnational issues requiring international attention. Environmental groups around the world pressed for action.

The United Nations sponsored the Conference on the Human Environment in Stockholm in 1972. More than one hundred nations, 19 intergovernmental organizations (IGOs), and 400 nongovernmental organizations (NGOs) attended. Third World nations feared that measures to protect the environment would slow their economic development. The South demanded compensation for stricter environmental controls as well as more Northern aid earmarked for environmental projects. Developed nations in turn worried that Third World industrialization would overwhelm the biosphere. "People don't give a shit about the environment," said Nixon privately as he pledged U.S. monies to the new environmental fund and backed a moratorium on commercial whaling. But he balked at more financial assistance to Third World countries and bristled at complaints that Washington had degraded the natural environment in Indochina. Still, the global conference spurred national environmental reforms, set up Earthwatch to monitor environmental conditions, and spotlighted transboundary pollution.

In the 1960s a new question became urgent: Who owned the rights to the gas, petroleum, and minerals such as manganese and nickel that rested in the deep seabed? Offshore oil drilling was well advanced, but the exploitation of the ocean's mineral riches was just beginning. American companies invested large sums in new technology for the ocean floor. Washington endorsed the principle that seabed resources were "a common heritage of mankind" in 1970, but at the UN-sponsored Law of the Sea Conference, which opened in 1973, U.S. officials rejected the South's call for a powerful international seabed agency with exclusive rights over the mining of ocean resources. Because the new authority would operate on a one-nation, one-vote basis, industrial nations would lose their competitive advantage. In 1976–1977 Washington proposed a dual system: private development and an international authority, the latter to be assigned exclusive exploitation of certain mining sites. Until such an agreement, Kissinger insisted, the United States would explore and mine on its own.

The South and North also debated multinational corporations, the South seeking tighter controls and a larger proportion of profits earned from operations in developing nations. Ten of the top twelve multinationals in the mid-1970s were U.S.-based, including General Motors, Exxon, and Ford Motor. Lockheed Aircraft and Exxon, among others, spent millions to bribe overseas politicians—a practice Congress tried to halt through the 1977 Foreign Corrupt Practices Act. The multinationals' economic decisions—where to locate a plant, for example—held real importance for developing nations that welcomed multinational investments but resented outside control. The South also protested that the multinationals employed too few "locals" in high positions and exploited natural resources without adequate compensation. Defenders replied that multinational enterprises brought benefits to developing nations in higher wages, tax revenues, and technology transfers. Beneficient or not, multinational corporations by the early 1970s had become major actors in the international system.

Vietnamization, Cambodia, and a Wider War

"What we are doing now with China is so great, so historic, the word 'Vietnam' will be only a footnote when it is written in history," Kissinger boasted in 1971. Yet America's longest war continued to claim rapt attention until 1975. Nixon constantly worried that the persistent war could undermine support at home and spoil détente. "I'm not going to end up like LBJ," he assured his advisers. "I'm going to stop that war. Fast." But under what terms would the United States withdraw?

At the outset, Nixon weighed his options. He could simply pull out of the war, "lock, stock and barrel." But Nixon would not sacrifice an ally. He vowed to end the war not so much to defeat North Vietnam but "to avoid [the] defeat of America." He hoped to capitalize on détente by persuading China and the Soviet Union to force Hanoi to compromise. Through military escalation, he signaled Ho Chi Minh that he intended to punish the enemy harshly where Johnson had not.

Nixon's "madman" strategy sought concessions from Hanoi through hints of atomic blackmail. The president would strengthen South Vietnam through huge infusions of foreign aid and the training of a larger South Vietnamese army (ARVN). He gradually withdrew U.S. troops from Vietnam and gave flag-waving speeches to counteract growing public disapproval of the war. In the cynical belief that most antiwar protesters simply feared "getting their asses shot off," he cut back draft calls, announced a draft lottery in May 1969, and promised to end the draft.

The multifaceted scheme did not work. Hanoi's leaders did not bow to foreign wishes, whether from Washington, Moscow, or Beijing. Having outlasted the French, Ho's legions had no intention of surrendering to the Americans. As for dissent at home, every new escalation swelled the ranks of the critics and finally prompted Congress to limit the president's ability to enlarge the war. Although U.S. ships, planes, helicopters, rifles, and millions of dollars poured in, South Vietnam became dependent on U.S. aid to keep its army in the field, thus undermining the ultimate objective of standing on its own feet. Aid sustained the corrupt regime of General Nguyen Van Thieu, a government of self-serving officials, unpopular and ultimately incapable of conducting a winning effort. Finally, Vietnamization diminished *American* military effectiveness. "Why get killed now?" a U.S. marine recalled. "You didn't have that 'let's go out and find them' attitude anymore."

In early 1969 the Paris peace negotiations stalled over Nixon's demand for North Vietnam to pull its forces out of the South and for the survival of the Thieu government. With infiltration continuing, Nixon decided to bomb communist sanctuaries in Cambodia—but secretly, so that neither Congress nor the American people knew about it. The bombing of Cambodia began in March 1969 with punishing B–52 sorties. But leaks soon brought the story out. Nixon ordered the FBI to wiretap several journalists and government officials in a futile attempt to catch the leakers.

Kissinger, in August 1969, began a series of secret meetings with North Vietnamese representatives that lasted into 1973. Both sides repeatedly accused the other of negotiating in bad faith. Meanwhile, U.S. soldiers were coming home, so that by the end of 1971 the troop level had dropped to 139,000. Protest against the war continued nonetheless. On October 15, 1969, a quarter-million people peacefully marched in Washington, calling for a moratorium on the war. The president asked the "great silent majority of my fellow Americans" to back him, and he urged Vice President Spiro Agnew to attack the news media.

Events in Cambodia actually prompted Nixon to expand the war. In March 1970, a pro-American general, Lon Nol, overthrew the neutralist government. Nixon saw new opportunities: Aid Lon Nol against the Khmer Rouge (Cambodian communists) and the North Vietnamese, who used Cambodian territory as a staging area to attack South Vietnam; step up the attack on the North Vietnamese in Cambodia, already targets of American bombing raids; send unmistakable signals to Hanoi that it had better relent; and show his critics "who's tough." He ordered U.S. troops to invade Cambodia in late April.

A cascade of protest rolled across America. Antiwar demonstrations rocked college campuses, as inexperienced National Guard troops killed four students at Kent State University in Ohio. Two students at all-black Jackson State College in Mississippi died when state police fired on a women's dormitory. Within the administration, three Kissinger aides resigned in protest against Cambodia. After the Senate terminated the Tonkin Gulf Resolution of 1964 and Congress nearly cut off funds for military operations in Cambodia, a "siege mentality" gripped the White House.

Nixon declared the Cambodian operation a success in terms of arms captured and enemy troops killed. Although the invasion probably bought time for Vietnamization, the venture also widened the war, caused the sanctuaries to spread out, and further ravaged Cambodia. Hanoi substantially increased its aid to the Khmer Rouge insurgents, who gained new recruits radicalized by the U.S. invasion. Lon Nol became another besieged Asian leader dependent on U.S. assistance. Both negotiations and the war dragged on. Nixon ordered "protective reaction strikes" against North Vietnam after U.S. reconnaissance planes were shot down. In early 1971, he approved a South Vietnamese invasion of Laos, where in six weeks of heavy fighting ARVN forces "got their tail beat off," thus turning Vietnamization's "first test" into its "biggest failure."

At home the wider war wrought more turmoil. After a court-martial in March 1971 found First Lieutenant William Calley guilty of murdering unresisting children, women, and old men at My Lai in 1968, Nixon ordered him released from jail (Calley won parole in November 1974). Army officials dismissed murder and cover-up charges against all other personnel connected with the massacre. In June 1971, the *New York Times* printed the *Pentagon Papers,* a long, secret Defense Department history of U.S. intervention in Vietnam. Leaked by a former Pentagon official, Daniel Ellsberg, the papers fortified critics in their argument that U.S. presidents consistently had tried to win a military victory and frequently had withheld facts from the American public. After the Supreme Court refused to halt publication of the *Pentagon Papers,* Nixon set up a "plumbers" group to stop leaks and to find ways to discredit Ellsberg. Watergate soon followed.

The year 1972 saw the presidential trip to China and SALT-I—and even greater escalation in Vietnam. In Paris, Kissinger continued to meet with North Vietnamese representatives, always rejecting the communist demand that the United States abandon Thieu. Hanoi launched a full-scale offensive in March that threw the Saigon government into disarray. Nixon ordered American B-52 bombers to pummel fuel depots around Hanoi and Haiphong, where four Soviet merchant ships were sunk. In May the president announced the mining of Haiphong harbor and more massive bombing raids code-named LINEBACKER-I. "We've got to use the maximum power of this country against a shit-asshole country [North Vietnam] to win the war," he growled. Supplies to the South slowed but did not stop.

The Jabberwocky Peace Agreement, Withdrawal, and Defeat

In early October 1972, Kissinger and the North Vietnamese negotiator Le Duc Tho finally reached an agreement that provided for U.S. withdrawal sixty days after a cease-fire, the return of U.S. prisoners of war, and a political arrangement in the South that ultimately included elections. In short, North Vietnam gave up its demand that Thieu resign, and Washington dropped its insistence that North Vietnamese

"Une Grande, une Immense Majorité Silencieuse."
President Nixon claimed support for his policies from the majority of Americans who remained silent during the vocal protests of the 1960s and 1970s. In this harsh sketch, Vazquez de Sola portrays Nixon's "silent majority" as war dead who cannot protest. (Swann Collection of Caricature and Cartoon)

troops pull out of the South. When Kissinger traveled to Saigon, however, Thieu balked. Resentful at not having been consulted, the South Vietnamese president said "we have been sold out by the U.S." and "if we accept the document as it stands, we will be committing suicide." The communists, suspecting trickery, published the agreement that they had crafted with Kissinger. Still, on October 31, Kissinger told the press "peace is at hand." Not quite.

Back in Paris, on November 20, Kissinger and Le Duc Tho resumed their meetings. In early December they reached terms very much like those Thieu and Nixon had torpedoed in October. But a final agreement faltered over the status of the Demilitarized Zone (DMZ). The carrot for Saigon (more arms), the stick for Hanoi. From December 18 to 28, LINEBACKER-II planes pounded North Vietnam hour upon hour in what Nixon told the Joint Chiefs was "your last chance to use military power to win this war." Everything from factories to water supplies took hits in the "Christmas bombing." Fifty-foot bomb craters gaped in Hanoi and Haiphong. At least 2,000 civilians perished.

On December 22, Washington offered to stop the bombing if Hanoi agreed to reopen negotiations. Prodded by Zhou Enlai to "let the Americans leave," Le Duc Tho resumed talks with Kissinger, and on January 27, 1973, the two men signed what has been termed a "Jabberwocky" peace accord. The United States promised to withdraw its remaining troops within sixty days; both sides would exchange prisoners; an international commission would oversee the cease-fire; and a coalition would conduct elections in the South. New language settled the DMZ issue. When Thieu again demurred, Nixon gave his secret promise that "we will respond with full force" if Hanoi violated the agreement. "Ah, these great powers who divide the world among themselves!" Thieu remarked. In the four years of the Nixon-Kissinger war, 20,553 Americans and half a million Vietnamese had died when "we could have gotten essentially the same deal anytime after the 1968 bombing halt," as one diplomat judged. Indeed, a Kissinger aide concluded: "We bombed the North Vietnamese into accepting our concessions."

The cease-fire broke down quickly as each side moved to strengthen itself militarily. The United States maintained military and CIA "advisers" in Vietnam and transferred equipment and bases to the Saigon regime. One peace provision called for U.S. reconstruction funds for Hanoi, but that promise died when the cease-fire collapsed. U.S. warships still cruised off the coast, and the bombing of Cambodia continued. Congress acted again, this time against a president weakened by Watergate, voting in June 1973 to require the president to cease military actions in all parts of Indochina. Nixon vetoed the measure but accepted a compromise deadline of August 15. In November came the War Powers Resolution. In 1974 Congress rejected Kissinger's appeal for $1.5 billion in military aid for Thieu's collapsing government, voting $700 million instead.

Pressed by North Vietnamese advances, Thieu and his coterie seemed paralyzed by early 1975. Then the communists launched an offensive whose swift success surprised even themselves. Many ARVN troops deserted, were captured, or were killed. Refugees clogged highways; the turmoil in the countryside and cities left some civilians near starvation.

On April 30, 1975, the victorious Vietcong and North Vietnamese streamed into Saigon. For days, frantic Vietnamese had surged toward the Tan Son Nhut air base near Saigon, where U.S. planes loaded evacuees. Thousands of scrambling, crying Vietnamese engulfed the U.S. Embassy, whose roof served as a landing pad for helicopters from offshore ships. Thieu, the generals, and other high-ranking officials had managed to escape earlier, but many Vietnamese compromised by their years of cooperation with the United States were later sent to communist "reeducation camps." Approximately 1 million Vietnamese escaped as "boat people" and sailed away in unseaworthy craft with inadequate water and food. Human tragedy also struck Cambodia and Laos, where, in 1975, the communist insurgents also triumphed. In Cambodia the Khmer Rouge imposed a genocidal regime that killed millions.

The Americans exited from their longest war without victory. Some 58,219 Americans died in battle. At least 3 million Vietnamese died. Hundreds of thousands of people were maimed, and millions became refugees. Civilian deaths in Cambodia and Laos also numbered in the millions. The United States spent at least $170 billion in Southeast Asia. The prolonged Vietnam War alienated U.S. allies, undercut détente, and spoiled relations with the Third World. At home the war fueled inflation and political instability. Nixon's Watergate abuses stemmed in large part from the strains the war placed on the White House and from frustrations over leaks. Believing that their highest officials had too often lied, Americans' trust in their government plummeted. Blaming others rather than his own flawed policies for failure in Vietnam, Nixon added to the bitterness and confusion that fueled debates over American foreign policy in the years ahead.

The Many Lessons and Questions of Vietnam

Americans only reluctantly searched for lessons after the Vietnam debacle, apparently more relieved that the war had ended than inquisitive about consequences. The 1976 presidential campaign passed with barely a word uttered about Vietnam.

Hawkish leaders feared that defeat had weakened U.S. credibility, lamenting a "Vietnam syndrome" that allegedly prevented America from sustaining its role as world leader. "Sir, do we get to win this time?" asked the fictional John Rambo as he returned to Vietnam in the popular film *Rambo II* (1985). Hawks claimed that they could have gained victory if only the American people had not suffered a failure of will during the Tet offensive: Just let the military do its job next time, unencumbered by fickle public opinion, inquisitive journalists, and congressional watchdogs. "We didn't know our ally [South Vietnam]," General Maxwell Taylor later admitted, but "we knew even less about the enemy. And, the last, most inexcusable of our mistakes, was not knowing our own people."

Some political scientists, such as Graham Allison in *Essence of Decision* (1971), emphasized a bureaucratic politics model to interpret events. They suggested that it is difficult to hold individuals accountable for decisions and "outcomes," because of the way the impersonal, oversized bureaucracy resists change, follows standard operating procedures, and becomes rutted in traditional channels. This bureaucracy had to be reformed to encourage more intragovernment dissent and debate, eschew fixed doctrines and knee-jerk anticommunism, and study the historical record to avoid making the same mistakes again and again. Critics of this analysis, however, blamed Vietnam on strong presidents such as Johnson, who actually controlled the bureaucracy through appointments, an overpowering personality, and a pervasive ideology. This viewpoint implied that a future change in presidents would bring about diplomatic reformation. A more assertive Congress, some argued, could rein in the "imperial presidency."

Was Vietnam, as some suggested, a prime example of American global expansionism and arrogance that continually required intervention abroad? Two post-Vietnam incidents in 1975 seemed to suggest as much. With polls in Europe indicating major declines in U.S. standing after the fall of Saigon, Cambodian patrol boats seized the U.S. merchant ship *Mayaguez* in May. "Let's look ferocious," said Kissinger, so as to refute charges that Washington had become a helpless giant after Vietnam. U.S. marines assaulted Koh Tang Island off the Cambodian coast, and U.S. warships and planes attacked Cambodian targets, nearly killing the *Mayaguez* crew in the process. Cambodians released the *Mayaguez* and its crew, but forty-one Americans died. Similarly, when the inhabitants of Portuguese East Timor tried to assert their independence in December 1975, Ford and Kissinger flashed a green light for the Indonesian military regime to annex the island, saying that "it is important that whatever you do succeeds quickly." A bloody invasion and civil war followed, leaving some 200,000 Timorese dead.

The Vietnam War, said other critics, revealed the shortcomings of the containment doctrine, which had failed to make distinctions between peripheral and vital areas and which applied military force to political problems. Ronald Steel, an eloquent critic of *Pax Americana,* likewise concluded: "Never confuse knights and bishops with pawns." The historian Henry Steele Commager commented that "some wars are so deeply immoral . . . that those who resist it are the truest patriots." To some, then, defeat became a victory for humane values. In contrast to those who blamed the antiwar activists for encouraging the enemy and weakening congressional resolve, historians of the peace movement have offered a more modest judgment. Antiwar opponents "produced an awareness of an alternative America that stripped away through dissent and resistance the rational, moral, and political legitimacy of Washington's war in Indochina." Thus: "The dissidents did not stop the war. But they made it stoppable."

By the late 1970s public discussion of the Vietnam experience and its consequences increased. Films such as *Coming Home* (1978), *The Deer Hunter* (1978), and *Apocalypse Now* (1979) heightened public attention. Depicting the soldiers' Vietnam were memoirs such as C. D. B. Bryan's *Friendly Fire* (1976), Ron Kovic's *Born on the Fourth of July* (1976), Philip Caputo's *A Rumor of War* (1977), and Michael Herr's *Dispatches* (1977); oral histories such as Al Santoli's *Everything We Had* (1981) and Mark Baker's *Nam* (1981); and novels such as James Webb's *Fields of Fire* (1978).

The dedication of the Vietnam Veterans Memorial in Washington in November 1982 gave the 2.8 million survivors of service in the war "a wailing wall" so that "by tracing the letters cut into the granite we could find what was left of ourselves." Early stereotypes of Vietnam veterans as emotional cripples unable to adjust to civilian life were soon replaced by "survivor-heroes," gritty, can-do, take-charge supermen, as portrayed by Sylvester Stallone and Chuck Norris in the back-to-Vietnam films of the Reagan era. Recent studies indicate that only 2 percent of 2.8 million Vietnam veterans suffered from posttraumatic stress disorder and that the reported high rates of suicides were comparable to those of the civilian population.

Most accounts of the war have emphasized the *American* experience in Vietnam, even as hundreds of thousands of Vietnamese, Cambodian, and Laotian refugees came to the United States and gained citizenship over the next two decades. Instead of a real country on the far side of the Pacific with its own history and culture, Vietnam had become, as one writer put it, "another word for mistakes or dishonesty or whatever." The only "Vietnamese words we learned were the cusswords," recalled a veteran.

Debate on the war came to center on whether the United States could have won. Many conservatives articulated a "stab-in-the-back" theory, namely, that the United States could have won had protesters not impeded the war effort and had civilian officials not restrained the military. President Ronald Reagan declared that American troops "were denied permission to win." Doubters have raised imposing questions about such thinking. Because the bombing of North Vietnam did not significantly impede the flow of matériel and soldiers to the South, perhaps only a U.S. invasion of the North would have sufficed to defeat the enemy. This strategy would have entailed heavy American casualties and a long occupation of a hostile population that had fought against foreigners for decades. Would Americans volunteer for a cause with such an uncertain end? Would they tolerate huge draft calls? An invasion of the North, moreover, would have risked war with both the Soviet Union and China. In fact, China sent substantial forces to North Vietnam between 1965 and 1969, credibly threatening intervention if the United States moved north with "dire consequences for the world." To say that Washington lacked the "will" to win

Vietnam Memorials. These statues, part of the memorial site in Washington, D.C., honor the men and women who served in the Vietnam War. On the left is the Vietnam Veterans Memorial by Frederick Hart, and on the right is the Vietnam Women's Memorial by Glenna Goodacre. Both stand near the long wall on which the names of Americans who died in Vietnam are etched. (National Park Service)

misses the real limits on U.S. power. "What distinguishes me from [Lyndon] Johnson," Nixon once said, "is that I have the *will* in spades." Yet Nixon wisely rejected tactical nuclear weapons or an invasion of the North because he recoiled from the domestic and international consequences.

To have won, suggested some, the United States would also have had to destroy what it was trying to save. What would remain after "victory"? Perhaps at best an internally divided, economically feeble nation needing huge infusions of U.S. aid but still vulnerable to collapse. Even with the military unleashed, it would still have faced intractable problems: an inhospitable terrain and climate; an elusive adversary deeply committed to its cause, battle-tested, and able to live off the land (*its* land); and a South Vietnamese people who often sheltered communist soldiers. As for allies sharing the burden, most European partners urged Washington to stop wasting its resources on a fruitless venture. Of America's forty allies by treaty, only Australia, New Zealand, South Korea, and Thailand sent combat troops.

The United States could not have won, others have argued, because of South Vietnam. Coups and attempted coups too often rocked the unpopular Saigon governments. ARVN troops were "armed farces," said one U.S. adviser, "very poor fighters" whose "timidity endangered American lives." ARVN forces suffered the same problems that afflicted their government: poor morale, corruption, and nepotism. The "war of attrition" alienated many South Vietnamese, as did the unsettling strategic hamlet program, disruptive "search and destroy" missions, leveling of villages, bombings of innocents, and spraying of Agent Orange. Cultural differences also separated Americans from Vietnamese. Bars and prostitution flourished in a rural Buddhist society made rapidly urban by fleeing refugees. High-tech computers hummed and giant war machines rumbled in a land of water buffalo, rice paddies, and traditional peasant folk.

Problems in the U.S. military itself reduced the chances for victory. To reassure superiors that they were turning back the enemy, some officers submitted false reports on the numbers killed. "If he's dead and Vietnamese, he's VC [Vietcong]" became the prevailing assumption in the field. The military also suffered from corruption and mismanagement—even a black market for equipment developed. By early 1971 some 40,000 GIs had become heroin addicts. "Fragging"—the murder of officers by enlisted soldiers by means of a hand grenade or other weapon—further reduced combat effectiveness. Educational deferments under the draft system meant that high school dropouts outnumbered college graduates in combat. The rotation system for officers—one year in Vietnam to "punch your ticket"—undermined military cohesion and the benefits of experience. Disgusted with the "groupthink pressure" and "pretense," General Colin Powell later wrote that many of "my generation . . . vowed that when our turn came to call the shots, we would not quietly acquiesce in half-hearted warfare for half-baked reasons that the American people could not understand or support."

The United States also faced tenacious adversaries who suffered remarkable losses but kept coming. Defending their nation against outsiders, the Vietnamese enemy seemed indomitable. "Everything we knew commanded us to fight," a Vietcong veteran remembered. "Our ancestors called us to war. Our myths and legends called us to war."

Whatever the answer to the Vietnam tragedy, succeeding administrations would have to operate in a domestic political setting of uncertainty about the direction of American foreign relations. Conservative defenders of the war stood ready to criticize any policy that smacked of retrenchment or "another Munich." Liberals and radicals stood alert to dispute any policy that seemed to offer "another Vietnam."

FURTHER READING FOR THE PERIOD 1969–1977

See works on the Cold War, the Third World, and other topics cited in earlier chapters.

For foreign relations during the Nixon and Ford presidencies, and for Richard M. Nixon the person, see Stephen E. Ambrose, *Nixon* (1989, 1991); James Cannon, *Time and Chance* (1994) (Ford); Mark Feeney, *Nixon at the Movies* (2004); John R. Greene, *The Presidency of Gerald R. Ford* (1994); Jussi Hanhimäki, *Flawed Architect* (2004); Joan Hoff, *Nixon Reconsidered* (1994); Walter LaFeber, *The Deadly Bet* (2005) (election of 1968); Roger Morris, *Richard Milhous Nixon* (1989); Richard Reeves, *President Nixon* (2001); and Melvin Small, *The Presidency of Richard Nixon* (1999).

For Henry A. Kissinger, see Christopher Hitchens, *The Trial of Henry Kissinger* (2001); Walter Isaacson, *Kissinger* (1992); Roger Morris, *Uncertain Greatness* (1977); and Robert D. Schulzinger, *Henry Kissinger* (1989).

For Congress see Loch K. Johnson, *A Season of Inquiry* (1985) and *Bombs, Bugs, Drugs, and Thugs* (2000), Robert G. Kaufman, *Henry M. Jackson* (2000); Kathryn S. Olmsted, *Challenging the Secret Government* (1997); and Keith W. Olson, *Watergate* (2003).

For Soviet-American relations, détente, and SALT, see Michael B. Froman, *The Development of the Idea of Détente* (1992); Raymond L. Garthoff, *Détente and Confrontation* (1995); Jonathan Haslam, *The Soviet Union and the Politics of Nuclear Weapons in Europe* (1990); David Holloway, *The Soviet Union and the Arms Race* (1983); Wilfred Loth, *Overcoming the Cold War* (2002); Keith L. Nelson, *The Making of Détente* (1995); John Newhouse, *Cold Dawn* (1973); Matthew J. Ouimet, *The Rise and Fall of the Brezhnev Doctrine in Soviet Foreign Policy* (2002); M. E. Sarotte, *Dealing with the Devil* (2001) (Ostpolitik); Richard W. Stevenson, *The Rise and Fall of Détente* (1985); Jeremi Suri, *Power and Protest* (2003); and Terry Terriff, *The Nixon Administration and the Making of U.S. Nuclear Strategy* (1995).

For China and Japan, see Rosemary Foot, *The Practice of Power* (1995); Evelyn Goh, *Constructing the U.S. Rapprochement with China, 1961–1974* (2004); Arnold Xiangze Jiang, *The United States and China* (1988); Ronald C. Keith, *The Diplomacy of Zhou Enlai* (1989); Walter LaFeber, *The Clash* (1997) (Japan); James Lilly, *China Hands* (2004); James Mann, *About Face* (1999) (China); Robert S. Ross, *Negotiating Cooperation* (1995); Robert S. Ross and Jiang Changbin, eds., *Re-Examining the Cold War* (2001); Michael Schaller, *Altered States* (1997) (Japan); Ross Terrill, *Mao* (1993); Nancy B. Tucker, *Taiwan, Hong Kong, and the United States* (1994) and *China Confidential* (2001); and Patrick Tyler, *A Great Wall* (2000).

The end and lessons of the Vietnam War are explored in Dale Andrade, *America's Last Vietnam Battle* (2001); Pierre Asselin, *A Bitter Peace* (2002); Michael R. Belknap, *The Vietnam War on Trial* (2003); Larry Berman, *No Peace, No Honor* (2001); Eric Dean Jr., *Shook Over Hell* (1997); Leslie H. Gelb and Richard K. Betts, *The Irony of Vietnam* (1979); Allan E. Goodman, *The Lost Peace* (1978); John Hellmann, *American Myth and the Legacy of Vietnam* (1986); Susan Jeffords, *The Remasculinization of America* (1989); Rhodri Jeffreys-Jones, *Peace Now!* (1999); Ben Kiernan, *The Pol Pot Regime* (2002); Jeffrey Kimball, *Nixon's Vietnam War* (1998); Michael Lind, *Vietnam: The Necessary War* (1999); John Prados, ed., *Inside the Pentagon Papers* (2004); William Shawcross, *Sideshow* (1979) (Cambodia); Wayne Thompson, *To Hanoi and Back* (2000); James Wilibanks, *Abandoning Vietnam* (2004); and Randall B. Woods, ed., *Vietnam and the American Political Tradition* (2003). See also works listed in Chapter 9.

International economic questions, including the North-South debate, are covered in David P. Calleo, *The Imperious Economy* (1982); Albert L. Danielson, *The Evolution of OPEC* (1982); I. M. Destler, *Making Foreign Economic Policy* (1980); Francis J. Gavin, *Gold, Dollars, and Power* (2004); Jeffrey A. Hart, *The New International Economic Order* (1983); Diane B. Kunz, *Butter and Guns* (1997); Allen J. Matusow, *Nixon's Economy* (1998); and Robert K. Olson, *U.S. Foreign Policy and the New International Economic Order* (1981).

Environmental issues, population, food, and their intersection with the international economy and world politics are examined in Scott Barrett, *Environment and Statecraft* (2003); Robert Boardman, *International Organization and the Conservation of Nature* (1981); Lynton K. Caldwell, *International Environmental Policy* (1984); Ann L. Hollick, *U.S. Foreign Policy and the Law of the Sea* (1981); Raymond F. Hopkins and Donald J. Puchala, *Global Food Interdependence* (1980); John McCormick, *Reclaiming Paradise* (1989); William Murdoch, *The Poverty of Nations* (1980); Clyde Sanger, *Ordering the Oceans* (1987); and Ross B. Talbott, *The Four World Food Agencies in Rome* (1990).

For Africa and some Third World issues, see Andrew DeRoche, *Black, White, and Chrome* (2001) (Zimbabwe); Piero Gleijeses, *Conflicting Missions* (2001); Fernando A. Guimarães, *The Origins of the Angolan Civil War* (1998); Gerald Horne, *From the Barrel of a Gun* (2001) (Zimbabwe); Robert J. McMahon, *The Limits of Empire* (1999); Whitney W. Schneidman, *Engaging Africa* (2004); and P. David Searles, *The Peace Corps Experience* (1997).

For the Middle East, oil, and the Arab-Israeli conflict, see Warren Bass, *Support Any Friend* (2003); James A. Bill, *The Eagle and the Lion* (1988) (Iran); George W. Breslauer, *Soviet Strategy in the Middle East* (1990); Avner Cohen, *Israel and the Bomb* (1998); James F. Goode, *The United States and Iran* (1997); Douglas Little, *American Orientalism* (2002); Melani McAlister, *Epic Encounters* (2001); William B. Quandt, *Decade of Decisions* (1977); Yezid Sayigh, *Armed Struggle and the Search for State* (1998) (Palestinians); David Schoenbaum, *The United States and the State of Israel* (1993); Kenneth W. Stein, *Heroic Diplomacy* (1999); and Daniel Yergin, *The Prize* (1991) (oil).

Latin America–U.S. relations, including Chile, are treated in Peter Kornbluh, *The Pinochet File* (2003); Morris H. Morley, *Washington, Somoza, and the Sandinistas* (1994); Stephen G. Rabe, *The Road to OPEC* (1982) (Venezuela); Paul E. Sigmund, *The United States and Democracy in Chile* (1993); and Peter H. Smith, *Talons of the Eagle* (1996).

See also Robert L. Beisner, ed., *Guide to American Foreign Relations Since 1600* (2003).

For comprehensive coverage of foreign-relations topics, see the articles in the four-volume *Encyclopedia of U.S. Foreign Relations* (1997), edited by Bruce W. Jentleson and Thomas G. Paterson.

CHAPTER 11

To Begin the World Over Again: Carter, Reagan, and Revivalism, 1977–1989

Diplomatic Crossroad

The Iranian Hostage Crisis, 1979–1981

"DEATH TO CARTER! Death to America!" chanted the radical Islamic student demonstrators outside the U.S. Embassy in Teheran, Iran, on November 4, 1979. Suddenly, hundreds stormed the embassy that their religious leader Ayatollah Ruhollah Khomeini had branded a "nest of spies." In the chancery, undercover CIA officers shredded classified documents. "Man, we're gonna have an Alamo," said one U.S. marine as the armed militants broke into rooms and seized frightened Americans. "We're paying you back for Vietnam," snarled one attacker.

All told, sixty-six Americans were captured. A few U.S. officials escaped, and Canadian diplomats later spirited them out of Iran. According to the jubilant students, American hostages would go free only after Shah Mohammad Reza Pahlavi returned to Iran for trial.

The admission of the Shah to a New York hospital two weeks earlier had provided the immediate catalyst for seizing the embassy. But Iranian hostility had been smoldering since the 1950s. Assuming the Peacock Throne in 1941, the young Shah increasingly relied on U.S. advice and assistance—a dependence demonstrated most vividly in 1953 after he left Iran, when nationalists, led by Prime Minister Mohammad Mossadegh, nationalized the Anglo-Iranian Oil Company. In Operation AJAX, the CIA plotted with royalist Iranians and British officials, restored the Shah to the throne, and drove Mossadegh from the country. The Shah soon became a staunch anticommunist ally of the United States. In 1957, with CIA assistance, he organized SAVAK, a secret police organization that suppressed dissent and terrorized the people.

In the 1970s popular discontent with the Shah swelled. Muslim clergy resented Western influences, including Hollywood movies and rights for women. Intellectuals and students protested the growing tyranny. Social democrats who had fled

American Hostage in Iran.
On November 8, 1979, this blindfolded, hand-tied American captive was paraded on the grounds of the U.S. Embassy in Teheran. A jeering crowd taunted the frightened American early in the Iranian hostage crisis. (AP/Wide World Photos)

with Mossadegh in the 1950s demanded a constitutional government. For different reasons, merchants, young workers, and feudal landholders felt aggrieved by the Shah's modernization of the economy, which brought inflation, unemployment, inadequate housing, and preferential jobs for skilled foreigners. SAVAK, symbol of the Shah's police state, committed untold brutalities that helped to unite disparate groups against the monarch and his sponsor, the United States.

Massive purchases of American arms also fueled unrest. In the period 1973–1978, the Shah spent $19 billion of the nation's oil wealth to buy U.S. helicopters, fighter aircraft, destroyers, and missiles, because, he argued, Iran had to fend off numerous enemies—the Soviet Union, Iraq, radical Arabs, domestic radicals— and had to police the Persian Gulf. Despite the mightiest military in the Middle East, many Iranians thought that the Shah squandered the nation's resources as a stooge of the United States.

President Jimmy Carter, visiting Teheran in late 1977, "dumbfounded" observers when he praised the Shah for making Iran "an island of stability in one of the more troubled areas of the world." The president, of course, was paying polite deference to an ally, and after Vietnam, American leaders looked to regional powers such as Iran to assist in preserving global interests. Reports of unrest in Iran elicited a standard Washington response: "It's not our country; the Shah is in control; we don't know enough about what could happen if he lost control—the communists might take over." Carter did not know that the Shah was dying of cancer—a condition perhaps making the monarch fatalistic and lethargic.

In 1978, demonstrations, riots, and strikes shook Iran. "Hang firm and . . . count on our backing," Carter told the Shah after the latter declared martial law. National Security Affairs adviser Zbigniew Brzezinski urged that the Iranian army smash the opposition and stage a coup. Secretary of State Cyrus Vance rebutted that the "iron fist" would not work because the largely conscript Iranian army would disintegrate. U.S. officials ignored advice to open direct communication with Khomeini, the evident leader of the revolution, then in exile in Paris. Not until senior "Wise Man" George Ball visited Iran in November did Washington fully understand "that the Shah was on the way to a great fall" and "like Humpty Dumpty, his regime could not be put together again."

The Shah appointed a puppet government and flew to Egypt on January 16, 1979. Making it clear that Islamic clerics intended to govern Iran, the Ayatollah rejected the new regime and soon installed his own. When he fueled rampant anti-Americanism in angry speeches, American citizens began to depart. After leaving Teheran, the Shah moved from Egypt to Morocco to the Bahamas to Mexico. Few nations wanted to give sanctuary to a repudiated despot. Even Carter rescinded an American offer of welcome to the Shah. With Republican critics lambasting Carter for treating the Shah like "a flying Dutchman" in search of a safe place to land, the president learned in October that the monarch would die of a malignant lymphoma unless a New York hospital admitted him. Despite warnings that such a move could ignite protest against Americans in Iran, Carter relented. The Shah arrived in New York on October 22; on November 4 militant students seized the embassy.

As stunned Americans watched "America Held Hostage" each night on television, it became clear that the hostage-takers wanted more than the Shah. First, the hostage-grabbing was Iran's way of preventing the Shah from launching a counterrevolution from the United States in a replay of 1953. Second, it helped Iran break diplomatic relations with the United States, which Khomeini called a "global Shah" never to be trusted. Finally, the hostage drama permitted the eighty-one-year-old Khomeini—whose dark, piercing eyes glared from posters throughout the country—to use anti-Americanism to overwhelm civilian moderates who competed for control of the revolution.

Spending sleepless nights, President Carter felt "the same kind of impotence that a powerful person feels when his child is kidnapped." Within the administration, Vance and Brzezinski differed bitterly. The latter advocated retaliatory action to preserve U.S. honor, even at the cost of lives, Vance urged "care and caution in trying to achieve a solution . . . without spilling blood." On November 14 the president froze Iranian assets in the United States valued at about $8 billion. Except for the release of thirteen hostages arranged by the Palestinian leader Yasir Arafat, all other negotiations through intermediaries came to naught.

As the diplomats struggled to communicate with an Iranian government that often seemed incapable of functioning, the hostages suffered through an ordeal lasting 444 days. At first blindfolded with their hands and feet tied, they thought that they would be either released quickly or killed. For a long time they could not speak or read newspapers. The hostages lost weight and became sick. They constantly fought boredom, melancholy, and fear. The worst terror they endured was a mock execution, preceded by abusive interrogation. Asked later if he would ever return to Iran, one freed hostage shot back: "Yeah, in a B-52."

On April 7, 1980, after another failed secret overture, the United States broke relations with Iran. With political advisers warning that "you can forget about a second term" if he did nothing, Carter ordered the Joint Chiefs of Staff to launch a rescue mission. "Stunned" that such a momentous decision had been "made in my absence," Vance made "volcanic" objections when he returned from a trip. The secretary stressed that the hostages faced no immediate physical danger. Even if the raid succeeded, numerous Americans would die. He warned that the Iranians might retaliate by seizing U.S. journalists and other Americans in Teheran, creating another hostage crisis. The whole Middle East might become inflamed with the Iranians pushed into the arms of the Soviets. None of Carter's advisers agreed with Vance. The president vowed to "stick with the decision I made." "America needs a win . . . real, real bad," remarked "Chargin' Charlie" Beckwith, the rescue mission's ground commander. Later he admitted that the odds of success were "about 50 percent."

On April 24, eight helicopters lifted off the supercarrier *Nimitz* in the Arabian Sea. Six C-130 Hercules transports took to the skies from Egypt. All headed for a rendezvous in the Iranian desert; from there rescue teams of Green Berets and Rangers planned to infiltrate Teheran and assault the U.S. Embassy to free the hostages. But the helicopters ran into dust storms; two malfunctioned before reaching Iran, and another lost a hydraulic line at the rendezvous point. The president accepted Colonel Beckwith's recommendation to abort the mission. In the hasty exit, a helicopter and a C-130 collided, killing eight crew members. The saddened president then told the nation the news. Vance quietly resigned. Critics pounded Carter for undertaking a project sure to cause the deaths of many hostages. "Thank God for the sandstorm," later remarked one hostage. Others asked if "the Three Stooges now directed foreign policy." After the rescue attempt, Americans seemed resigned to a prolonged crisis. Many citizens displayed yellow ribbons to symbolize their prayers, while radio stations belted out "Bomb Iran" to the tune of the Beach Boys' hit song "Barbara Ann."

Four events finally facilitated a resolution. First, the Shah died in Egypt in July 1980. So suspicious were the Iranian militants, one hostage recalled, that many would not believe the Shah was sick "until he actually died, and even then [they doubted it]." Second, Khomeini's Islamic clerics won control of the parliament and thus no longer needed the hostages for their political purposes. Third, in September, Iraq and Iran went to war, and Iran found that it had few friends or funds. And fourth, Ronald Reagan, who promised a tougher posture, was elected president.

Meanwhile, American and Iranian diplomats met with Algerian mediators. On the day before Reagan took office, an agreement was struck: release of the hostages in exchange for unfreezing Iranian assets in the United States. On January 20, 1981—shortly after Reagan's inauguration—the hostages gained their freedom. After 444 days they returned home to a relieved nation that celebrated briefly and then tried to forget.

Some second-guessing did occur. Should Carter have played up the hostage issue so much, thereby signaling to the Iranians that they had in fact stung and would continue to sting Americans? But with the Iranians jeering Washington day after day, with television cameras daily chronicling this gross violation of diplomatic immunity, with Carter's vaunted compassion for other human beings—could the president have done otherwise?

Washington had lost an ally with a large army, huge quantities of oil, intelligence posts next to the Soviet Union, and billions of dollars to spend on U.S.-made weapons. The long crisis had wounded American pride and helped bring down the Carter presidency. President Reagan drew a simple lesson: America had to build up its military to deter enemies. Others thought that the hostage travail reinforced a lesson of Vietnam: American aid and weaponry, such as had flowed to the Shah, cannot guarantee the survival of an unpopular regime. As the Iranian revolution descended into tyranny, executions of Khomeini foes, and disputes with other Muslims in the Middle East, some Americans prided themselves on once having supported the Shah. Some officials found solace because Iran remained ardently anti-Soviet. Very quickly Washington sought new security ties with other "regional influentials"—Pakistan, Turkey, Saudi Arabia, and Iraq.

The outpouring of emotional patriotism that greeted the returning hostages suggested another conclusion: The nation hungered for heroes who could rekindle American pride. From "temporary pacifists" after Vietnam, wrote one analyst, "the video images from Iran" turned Americans into a "pack of snarling wolves." An Oklahoma man who judged Carter too timid looked to the imperial past for inspiration: "I agree with Teddy Roosevelt. Walk softly and carry a big stick," the Oklahoman said. "And club the hell out of them if you need to."

Zbigs and Zags: Carter's Divided Administration

Teddy Roosevelt's "big stick" was exactly what Jimmy Carter had found wrong with American foreign policy when he came to office in 1977—too much bluster, too much military, and too much insensitivity toward Third World peoples. He promised to reduce military budgets, bring some of America's overseas forces home, trim arms sales abroad, and slow nuclear proliferation. He berated the Republicans for supporting dictatorial regimes. Yet at times Carter sounded like an inveterate Cold Warrior. Lamenting a decline of U.S. power, he criticized the White House for accepting Soviet domination of Eastern Europe and authorizing huge grain sales to the Soviet Union.

After the downbeat years of Watergate, Vietnam, CIA abuses, and soaring oil prices, the election of the wealthy peanut farmer with a toothy smile inspired hope. After graduating from the Naval Academy and serving on a nuclear submarine, Carter entered Georgia politics and became governor in 1970. After a four-year gubernatorial term, this relatively obscure Democrat set out to win the presidency and astounded the professionals by doing so. Carter cherished hard work, family responsibility, and religion. Energetic, ambitious, and self-confident, Carter seemed to some people sanctimonious and arrogant. A quick learner, he paid meticulous attention to details. Unwilling to prioritize, he tried to be "desk officer for everything." An "outsider" to Washington politics, Carter had little experience in foreign affairs. He did hold membership in the Trilateral Commission, which brought together business, political, and academic notables for discussions of global problems facing industrial nations. And Carter had followed the fractious debate over Vietnam and knew that a new national foreign-policy consensus had not yet taken form. "Deeply troubled by the lies our people had been told," he sensed a need for national redemption.

Carter selected Cyrus Vance as his secretary of state. A wealthy, West Virginia–born, Yale-educated lawyer, Vance held top posts in the Department of Defense in the 1960s, learning from Vietnam that Washington could not "prop up a series of regimes that lacked popular support." He favored quiet diplomacy to improve Soviet-American relations. When Vance resigned in April 1980, he did so not only to protest the hostage rescue mission, but also to reprove Carter for embracing the "visceral anti-Sovietism" of Zbigniew Brzezinski, the national security affairs adviser.

Outspoken, arrogant, and aggressive, Brzezinski blamed most of the world's troubles on the Soviets. He sought military superiority and worked to play China off against the Soviet Union. To counter Vance's argument that a military coup in Iran would produce bloodshed, Brzezinski coldly pronounced that "world politics was not a kindergarten." State Department officers often bristled over Brzezinski's strong-arm bureaucratic methods and his back-channel contacts with foreign leaders. "While Mr. Vance played by the Marquis of Queensberry rules," remarked one official, "Mr. Brzezinski was more of a street fighter." The president believed that Vance and Brzezinski would balance one another: "Zbig would be the thinker, Cy would be the doer, and Jimmy Carter would be the decider." But acrimonious infighting soon made the administration's foreign policy appear inconsistent, marked by zigs and zags.

The Carter administration pursued basically traditional goals. At the start Carter officials rejected the extreme options of Fortress America (isolationism) and Atlas America (global policeman) in favor of Participant America. That meant emphasizing preventive diplomacy: advancing the peace process in the Middle East; reducing nuclear arms; normalizing relations with China; stimulating improvements in human rights; and creating economic stability through talks on the law of the sea, energy, and clean air and water. The president wanted to avoid a reactive foreign policy enmeshed in short-term, day-to-day crises.

Cyrus R. Vance (1917–2002). "Cy" Vance brought extensive diplomatic experience to his post as secretary of state. Vance won plaudits for negotiating the Panama Canal treaties and SALT-II. His resignation in 1980 was the first such act made in protest by a secretary of state since that of William Jennings Bryan in 1915. (National Archives)

Makers of American Foreign Relations, 1977–1989

Presidents	Secretaries of State
Jimmy Carter, 1977–1981	Cyrus R. Vance, 1977–1980
	Edmund Muskie, 1980–1981
Ronald Reagan, 1981–1989	Alexander M. Haig, Jr., 1981–1982
	George P. Shultz, 1982–1989

Andrew Young (b. 1932).
A graduate of Howard University and the Hartford Theological Seminary, the Reverend Young had been Dr. Martin Luther King's right-hand man in the civil rights movement of the 1950s–1960s and a member of Congress from Georgia before Carter named him ambassador to the United Nations. Young was forced to resign in 1979 when he admitted meeting with representatives of the Palestine Liberation Organization, whose participation in negotiations he deemed essential to Middle East peace. (© CORBIS)

Carter especially sought to restore U.S. influence in the Third World. He preferred to emphasize North–South rather than East–West issues and to make concessions to nationalism, even to leftist regimes. Third World crises, he argued, sprang from deep-seated, indigenous economic, social, racial, and political problems. The appointment of Andrew Young as ambassador to the United Nations symbolized Carter's sympathetic approach. An African American veteran of the civil rights movement, Young gradually improved the U.S. dialogue with suspicious Third World diplomats. But in 1979 Carter had to fire him after Young made unauthorized contact with representatives of the Palestine Liberation Organization, a group that the United States refused to recognize.

The soul of American foreign policy, Carter insisted, should be the defense and expansion of human rights for foreign peoples. Drawing on his own religious commitment, Carter vowed to win for all peoples the freedom to work, vote, worship, travel, speak, assemble, and receive a fair trial. Slavery, genocide, torture, forced labor, arbitrary arrest, rigged elections, and suspensions of civil liberties all became anathema. Dictators must respect human rights or face cutbacks in American foreign aid.

While telling Americans to put their "inordinate fear of communism" behind them, he actually reinvigorated the containment doctrine by initiating new weapons systems, by encouraging nationalism in Eastern Europe, and by cultivating Third World governments. Improved Sino-American ties, continued strategic arms limitations talks, and public denunciations of Soviet violations of human rights also might check Moscow. By 1979 Carter, having moved closer to Brzezinski's views, sounded the familiar Cold War calls for "a more muscular foreign policy." The following year he proclaimed the Carter Doctrine, or containment in the Persian Gulf. Confrontation more than cooperation came to mark Soviet-American relations under Carter.

The Panama Canal and High-Voltage Nationalism in Latin America

At the outset Carter launched an active diplomacy toward Latin America, the Middle East, and Africa. In Latin America, Carter championed human rights and worked to accommodate nationalism. More than ever, Latin American governments claimed an independent role in world politics and shunned U.S. advice. They petitioned Washington for lower tariffs, higher commodity prices, and less diplomatic backing of North American corporations locked in disputes with their governments. The Carter administration saw high stakes: $59 billion in trade (1979); investments of $24.4 billion (1979); vital imports of petroleum, copper, and tin; and Latin America's thirty votes in the United Nations. Foreign aid ($726 million in 1977–1978) continued as one means of exerting influence.

Panama became the first testing ground. Panamanians had long resented the 1903 treaty granting the United States the Canal Zone, a ten-mile-wide, 500-square-mile slice of territory that cut their nation in half—"a foreign flag piercing its own heart." After bloody anti-American riots in 1964, President Lyndon B. Johnson had started talks, but they barely crawled forward.

Carter brought the negotiations to fruition. Two treaties were signed in 1977 and ratified the following year. One treaty, abrogating the 1903 document, provided for the integration of the Canal Zone into Panama and increased Panama's percentage of the canal's revenues. The other treaty granted the United States the right to defend the "neutrality" of the canal forever. In a national vote, Panamanians approved the treaties by a 2 to 1 margin, but nationalistic sentiment against a continued U.S. role in Panamanian affairs ran high. When General Omar Torrijos identified "lots of electric currents" in his country, the U.S. negotiator Ellsworth Bunker thanked him for "keeping the voltage down."

Conservative critics in the United States soon denounced the treaties as diabolical instruments of appeasement. Many Americans thought that the United States owned the canal. Ronald Reagan mangled the historical record: "We bought it, we paid for it, it's ours, and we're going to keep it." Giving up a key waterway would supposedly weaken U.S. defense and leave Panama vulnerable to Soviet or Cuban subversion. The Conservative Caucus flooded senatorial offices with claims that the treaty would turn the Caribbean into a "Red Lake."

The Carter administration countered with a full-court press. The Committee of Americans for the Canal Treaties enlisted veteran diplomat W. Averell Harriman, labor leader George Meany, and army general Maxwell Taylor, among others. The National Association of Manufacturers and multinational corporations holding large investments in Latin America endorsed the agreements. Treaty advocates stressed the goodwill that Washington would gain after terminating the imperialistic document of 1903. Nonratification could "poison" trade with Latin America and invite terrorist attacks on the canal. The canal's value had diminished because modern aircraft carriers and supertankers had too much beam to squeeze through the locks. Moreover, less than 10 percent of U.S. foreign trade went through it.

As the debate peaked in early 1978, the administration used arguments that alarmed Panamanians. A "memorandum of understanding," signed by Torrijos and Carter, provided for U.S. intervention after the year 2000 to thwart "any aggression or threat directed against the Canal or against the peaceful transit of vessels through the Canal." When asked what the United States would do after 2000 if the Panamanians closed the canal for repairs, Brzezinski shot back: "Close down the Panamanian government for repairs." On March 16, 1978, the Senate approved the neutrality treaty 68 to 32; the other treaty passed on April 18 by a similar count—in both cases with only one vote more than the two-thirds tally needed. Carter later acknowledged that "some fine members of Congress had to pay with their political careers for their votes."

The Carter administration also contended with nationalist stirrings in Nicaragua. Since 1936 the Somoza family had ruled that Central American state. Dictatorial, brutal, and corrupt, the Somoza dynasty nevertheless had gained grudging U.S. support as a reliable anticommunist ally and had received military aid, which it often used to suppress critics. Nicaragua had served as a staging area for CIA operations against Guatemala (1954) and Cuba (1961). All the while, Nicaraguans suffered high rates of poverty, malnutrition, and illiteracy, and the Somozas amassed great wealth. A long-smoldering popular rebellion exploded in 1978, led by the leftist Sandinista National Liberation Front (FSLN). Business executives, Catholic clergy, and intellectuals joined the crusade to unseat the Somozas and reduce U.S. influence. General Anastasio Somoza Debayle, a graduate of West Point (1946), answered with torture, executions, and bombings of civilians.

Carter tried to ease Somoza's departure and restrict the radical Sandinistas. Somoza balked and the effort failed. After the FSLN opened its final offensive in mid-1979, Washington encouraged the national guard—Somoza's hated personal army—to preserve order. When this tactic also misfired, Somoza fled the battle-scarred country in July 1979; he was later assassinated in Paraguay.

The new Nicaraguan government promised a mixed economy and pluralistic politics. But only after Mexico, Venezuela, and others offered loans did Carter ask Congress to appropriate $75 million in economic assistance. Not until July 1980 did Congress allocate funds, with conservatives calling the Sandinistas communists because they welcomed Cuban advisers and resented Washington's long-time ties with Somoza. Tension soon ran high, especially when Carter suspended economic aid in early 1981 after the Sandinistas aided rebels who were challenging the U.S.-backed government of El Salvador.

Cuba also remained high on the hemisphere's agenda. Carter initially sought to reduce tensions with Fidel Castro. In March 1977, U.S. and Cuban negotiators began to discuss normalization of relations. In September, Cuba and the United States established "interests sections" in each other's country (essentially embassies without full diplomatic recognition). Carter also lifted the ban on travel to Cuba. Castro in 1978 made gestures toward improved relations by releasing 3,600 political prisoners. Several irritants diminished these positive steps. The Soviet Union was pouring about $3 million a day into Cuba to sustain the island's fragile economy, weakened by the longstanding U.S. trade embargo and Castro's mismanagement. Washington still viewed Cuba as a Soviet puppet and charged that Cuban troops in Angola and Ethiopia acted as Soviet surrogates. Citing Cuba's commitment to revolutions in the Third World, Castro claimed Cuban troops had entered Angola as early as the 1960s, independently of the Soviets. Secret, high-level U.S.-Cuba talks in 1978–1980 failed to normalize relations or relax the trade embargo.

In spring 1980, Castro suddenly announced that Cubans wishing to leave the country could use Peruvian visas if they could get them. Thousands jammed into the Peruvian Embassy grounds in Havana. Carter thereupon announced that Cubans who wanted to join their families already in the United States would be welcome. Castro soon declared that Cubans who wanted to emigrate could do so by boat from the port of Mariel. A "freedom flotilla" began to shuttle between Cuba and Florida, as 100,000 Cubans entered U.S. processing centers. Castro emptied his jails of "undesirables" and cynically put them on boats to the United States. "Fidel has flushed his toilet on us," the mayor of Miami bitterly charged. Americans felt tricked, especially as evidence mounted that many *Marielitos* had criminal records.

Elsewhere in Latin America, right-wing governments resisted Carter's efforts to improve human rights, although Haiti, Argentina, and the Dominican Republic did release hundreds of political prisoners. In 1977 Carter suspended military aid to Guatemala when its regime sanctioned the murder and torture of political opponents; two years later he froze U.S. aid to Bolivia after that nation's military seized power. Military assistance to Latin America dropped from $210 million in 1977 to only $54 million in 1979, as Carter kept dictators at arm's length. The prime minister of Barbados remarked that Carter had done much "to correct the image of the United States as an unfeeling giant."

Carter's Activism in the Middle East and Africa

The Iranian revolution and hostage crisis, civil war in Lebanon, Arab-Israeli conflict, Iran-Iraq War, Soviet thrust into Afghanistan, and Western reliance on Persian Gulf oil put the Middle East in the headlines. Saudi Arabia served as America's largest supplier of imported oil. In 1980 Israel and Egypt together received about one-third of all U.S. foreign aid. During the period 1971–1981, the United States sold $47.7 billion worth of arms to Mideast countries. U.S. weapons became the instruments of war in the region: Israel used U.S. warplanes to attack Palestinian communities in Lebanon, and Iran used American arms to battle Iraq. Syrians and Iraqis brandished Soviet armaments.

Building on Kissinger's efforts, Carter concentrated on bringing Egypt and Israel to the peace table. President Anwar el-Sadat of Egypt personally advanced the process. In November 1977 he astonished the world by journeying to Jerusalem to offer peace and security to Israel in exchange for an Israeli withdrawal from lands occupied since 1967. When the Sadat initiative faltered, Carter interceded, inviting Sadat and Israeli prime minister Menachem Begin to Camp David. From September 5 to 17, 1978, the three leaders and their aides engaged in often heated discussion. Carter pressed Begin to withdraw to Israel's 1967 border so that the restored territories might provide a homeland for Palestinians. Israel could not have both peace and captured territories, Carter reasoned. He favored an agreement based on the 1967 United Nations Resolution 242, by which Arabs would recognize Israel's right to live in peace and security in exchange for Israeli withdrawal from seized territories. Acting as "draftsman, strategist, therapist, friend, adversary, and mediator," Carter wooed and cajoled. He persuaded Sadat to accept compromises since the Egyptian leader seemed to want an agreement more than did Begin. Carter promised both sides huge amounts of aid if they would settle their differences.

Egypt and Israel signed two Camp David Accords. The first stated goals: negotiations leading to self-government for the West Bank and Gaza and subsequent participation of Jordanians and Palestinians in the peace process. The second, a "framework" for peace, provided for Israeli withdrawal from the Sinai in exchange for Egyptian diplomatic recognition. Following further protracted negotiations (in which Carter flew to the Middle East to meet separately with Begin and Sadat), the Egyptian-Israeli Peace Treaty was signed on March 26, 1979. It provided for the phased withdrawal of Israel from the Sinai, to be completed in 1982; the stationing of UN forces along the Egyptian-Israeli boundary; full economic and diplomatic relations between Cairo and Tel Aviv; and the opening of negotiations on Palestinian rights in the occupied West Bank and Gaza. After thirty years of war, peace formally came to part of the Middle East. Other Arabs, especially the PLO, denounced the treaty as a "dead horse" for not recognizing the right of Palestinians to a homeland. By the end of Carter's administration, the troops of Israel and the PLO, the latter with Syrian help, were shooting at one another in Lebanon.

Although sub-Saharan African issues lacked the urgency of Middle Eastern problems, the Carter administration strove to identify the United States with black African nationalism and to end the "last vestiges of colonialism" in Zimbabwe/Rhodesia and Namibia. Ambassador Young became the president's chief adviser, with "African solutions for African problems" as his motto. He believed that support for a strong and stable black Africa, through aid and trade, would reduce Soviet influence on the continent. African nationalism, not U.S. intervention, would contain the USSR and protect U.S. interests.

Much seemed at stake in Africa. The continent had political clout—a third of the membership in the United Nations. Africa possessed a bulging storehouse of raw materials. For example, Zaire ranked as the United States' largest supplier of cobalt; Nigeria the second largest source of imported oil; Gabon supplied manganese; Namibia had the world's largest uranium mine; and South Africa shipped manganese, platinum, chromium, and antimony. By 1979 Americans had invested some $4 billion in black Africa and about $2 billion in South Africa. Total annual trade with Africa passed the $30 billion figure. Africa's ports and airfields also lay along strategic sea lanes. The region's political instability invited great-power competition. Because American blacks had descended from Africans, they kept national leaders alert to African issues and politically accountable.

The Carter administration worked especially hard to cultivate Nigerian friendship. Africa's most populous nation, Nigeria ranked seventh in world oil production and carried weight in African politics. Nigeria became independent in 1960 and in 1967 suffered a civil war in which victory over Biafran separatists cost half a million lives. World opinion, including that of the United States, grew hostile toward the military regime that had perpetrated this tragedy. But in the 1970s, when America suffered its energy crisis and Nigeria expanded its oil production, relations improved. Both Carter and Young visited Nigeria.

South Africa's riches, traditional ties to the United States, and white minority government ensured its continuing prominence on the U.S. diplomatic agenda. Carter chided white South African rulers for apartheid—an official system of segregating nonwhites and whites that included removals of blacks to designated homelands, discriminatory wages based on race, and denial of voting rights and civil liberties for blacks. Visiting South Africa, Vice President Walter Mondale angered whites by calling for a one-person, one-vote policy, because "perpetuating an unjust system is the surest incentive to increase Soviet influence and even racial war." Carter rejected economic sanctions as a means to foster change, because trade stood at $4 billion in 1979 and America's top corporations operated there, including General Motors, Mobil, Exxon, Ford, General Electric, and Firestone. Although critics argued for disinvestment, the most some American companies would consider was a voluntary pledge to follow nondiscriminatory employment practices in South Africa. By 1979 only 116 of the 300 American firms active there had taken the pledge.

Many black African leaders protested the sale of American aircraft to the regime. They criticized Carter's approval of Export-Import Bank loans (subsequently stopped by Congress). One Nigerian official condemned America's "outright collaboration with South Africa." Citing the flow of strategic minerals from South Africa, and claiming that disinvestment would hurt native blacks by causing unemployment, Carter officials argued that steady pressure, short of economic sanctions, would move South Africa to reform. The white regime's changes, however, amounted to little more than the "desegregation of the deck chairs on the *Titanic.*"

In Zimbabwe/Rhodesia, the civil war between whites and insurgent blacks finally ended. Ian Smith's white government, formed in 1965, had made token gestures to black majority rule, but Carter insisted on real change. The president persuaded Congress in 1977 to repeal the Byrd Amendment (1971), which had permitted U.S. trade with Zimbabwe/Rhodesia in chromium, despite the UN-declared economic boycott of Smith's regime. Carter in 1979 refused to endorse white-manipulated elections. Finally, British-led negotiations culminated in an all-races, nationwide election held in April 1980, which produced a new government for Zimbabwe led by the former black rebel Robert Mugabe.

By the end of Carter's term, U.S. influence in Africa stood higher than ever, and trade was improving. Washington gained access to military facilities in Somalia after that nation expelled the Soviets in 1977. Soviet and Cuban influence in Africa confined itself mainly to Ethiopia and Angola. Nigeria's President Obasanjo reflected widespread opinion when he warned Moscow and Havana that Africa would not welcome a "new imperial power."

The Red Thread: SALT-II, Afghanistan, and the Carter Record

Carter's efforts in the Third World were ultimately subsumed by conflicting interpretations of Soviet behavior. Some Carter officials believed that global problems did not always stem from Soviet intrigue and that the Soviet Union suffered domestic troubles, an unimaginative and aged leadership, and nationalist stirrings in Eastern Europe. But Brzezinski and his NSC staff countered that Soviet expansionism in the Middle East and Africa had to be faced down, not negotiated away. The president eventually leaned toward the hard-line Brzezinski.

When Carter urged respect for human rights, the Kremlin responded by harassing Soviet Jews who applied to emigrate to Israel and dissident intellectuals who criticized the communist regime. From the American perspective, too, the Soviets seemed bent on a military buildup: Cuban troops and Soviet advisers stayed in Angola; the Soviet navy and Warsaw Pact forces modernized; and greater numbers of missiles pointed at NATO countries. "We were enthusiastically arming ourselves, like binging drunks, without any apparent political need," one Soviet official later admitted. In this environment laced with suspicion and hostility, Secretary Vance journeyed to Moscow in March 1977 to reenergize SALT (Strategic Arms Limitation Talks) with a sudden, publicized proposal for deep cuts in ICBMs—precisely the category in which the Soviets were strongest. The Soviets thought Carter was saying: "Either you accept our position or we start an arms race and the Cold War again." Vance made no headway: "We got a wet rug in the face and were told to go home."

In March 1978 Carter denounced the Kremlin for conducting a proxy war in Ethiopia by using Cubans to battle Somalia, a newfound American friend that had futilely invaded Ethiopia to seize disputed land. The president's blunt speech, boasted Brzezinski, meant "we weren't soft." In May, Brzezinski traveled to China to remind the Soviets that they should worry about Sino-American "parallel interests." Hints of American arms sales to the People's Republic prompted one Soviet official to complain that the United States was "smuggling" weapons aimed against the USSR through the "back door" in Asia. As Soviet-American trade increased, Moscow understandably expressed puzzlement over "constant zigzags" in U.S. behavior.

In the SALT-II talks of 1977–1979, the Soviets tried but failed to block American development of the new MX (missile experimental), an improved ICBM designed to carry ten MIRVs; the Trident-II submarine-launched ballistic missile, capable of carrying fourteen warheads; and the cruise missile. The Americans failed to restrict the new Soviet supersonic "Backfire" bomber. Its range of 5,500 miles threatened Western Europe and China. Prolonged negotiations nonetheless culminated in the SALT-II treaty, signed at the Vienna summit in June 1979.

The agreement for the first time established numerical equality in total strategic nuclear delivery vehicles, each limited to 2,400. The treaty capped MIRVed launchers at 1,200 and limited the number of warheads per delivery vehicle. Whereas the treaty required the Soviets to dismantle more than 250 existing delivery vehicles, the Americans could expand from their current 2,060 to the ceiling of 2,250. Each nation could conduct technical verification of the other's compliance without interference.

SALT-II soon fell victim to the deteriorating Soviet-American relationship. In the Senate, opponents argued that progress on nuclear-arms control should be linked to Soviet behavior on other issues, such as human rights and Africa. Democratic senator Henry Jackson of Washington and other hawks also claimed that the Soviets, by the mid-1980s, could exploit a "window of vulnerability" and destroy America's land-based missiles in a first strike. SALT-II therefore endangered American security. Dovish critics, however, found SALT-II limitations too meager, permitting continued nuclear-weapons growth.

The Carter administration concentrated on rebutting conservative critics. Without SALT-II, the State Department explained, the Soviets would enlarge their nuclear forces at a brisker pace. Compelled to keep up, the United States would fuel an expensive arms race. As for the alleged vulnerability of American ICBMs, Carter officials explained that the Soviets would have to deposit two warheads squarely on every ICBM silo to ensure destruction—an unlikely scenario: The timing would have to be near-perfect so that one incoming warhead would not explode and destroy other warheads before they reached their targets ("fratricide"). Nor would the president stand by and let American ICBMs be destroyed in their silos. Even if a Soviet first strike somehow destroyed the land-based ICBMs (only 30 percent of U.S. nuclear forces), SLBMs and strategic bombers would remain to annihilate tens of millions of Soviet people. "They [Soviets] are not supermen; they are not fools either," remarked one official. With senatorial approval of the treaty in doubt, Carter tried to win votes from hawks by announcing an expensive five-year military expansion program and a plan to deploy 572 Pershing-II ballistic missiles and ground-launched cruise missiles in Western Europe to counter the Soviet medium-range SS-20 missiles aimed at America's allies.

The Soviet invasion of Afghanistan in late December 1979 killed the SALT-II treaty and elevated to orthodoxy Brzezinski's hard-line views about a malevolent Soviet Union. Some 50,000 Red Army troops marched into neighboring Afghanistan to sustain a Soviet client challenged by Islamic rebels. The Soviets also intervened because they wanted to maintain Afghanistan as a "buffer" against the spread of Islamic fundamentalism in central Asia. Moscow also feared that covert CIA assistance to the insurgents since July might cause the Afghans to "do a Sadat on us" by aligning with the United States. Was Afghanistan the first step in a Soviet master plan to take over the oil-rich Persian Gulf region? With an eye on domestic opinion, Carter hyperbolically proclaimed "the greatest threat to peace since the Second World War." "Putting 'a Red thread' through the complexities of the Gulf area seemed to us to be a desirable and justified simplification" to arouse the American people, Brzezinski later admitted.

In retaliation, Carter withdrew the SALT-II treaty from the Senate, stopped high-technology sales and grain shipments to the USSR, and pulled the United States out of the Summer Olympic Games scheduled for Moscow. Carter also outlined military measures: arms assistance for Pakistan; creation of U.S. naval facilities in Oman, Kenya, Somalia, and Egypt; formation of a rapid deployment force for use in the Middle East; positioning of two aircraft carrier groups in the region; and a much increased defense budget. And last, CIA assistance began to sustain Afghan resistance in a ten-year struggle that would become, as Brzezinski told Carter, the Soviet Union's "Vietnam War."

On January 24, 1980, the president proclaimed the Carter Doctrine: "An attempt by any outside force to gain control of the Persian Gulf region will be regarded as an assault on the vital interests of the United States" and "will be repelled by use of any means necessary, including military force." As a statement of containment, it sounded familiar themes. But serious problems impeded implementation. When Washington offered $400 million to Pakistan, its prime minister said "peanuts" and demanded more. The Saudis refused to let the U.S. military use their facilities. Most nations rejected Carter's call for an Olympics boycott.

As Soviet-American relations deteriorated, Sino-American ties improved. Both Beijing and Washington sought to use each other to contain the Soviet Union. Following U.S. diplomatic recognition in early 1979, China embarked on a three-week incursion against Vietnam to show it "had no fear of the Soviet Union." A U.S.-China trade agreement in 1980 enabled the Export-Import Bank to extend credits to the People's Republic. U.S. companies signed contracts to tap China's oil. In 1977–1980 China ranked fourth in the world as a buyer of U.S. agricultural exports, taking about half of the nation's cotton exports in 1979 alone. Mineral-short America eyed China's large deposits of tin, chrome, and tungsten. In 1980 American exports to China totaled $4 billion, up from $807 million in 1974. China replaced the Soviet Union as Washington's largest communist trading partner; in 1980 U.S. exports to the Soviet Union stood at a comparatively low $1.5 billion.

Taiwan's status, however, remained contentious. Washington severed formal diplomatic relations with the Republic of China on Taiwan, unilaterally terminated the 1954 mutual defense treaty, and withdrew all U.S. forces and military installations

MX Launch Test. The "missile experimental" carried ten warheads and was first deployed in 1986. President Reagan decided to place MX missiles in fixed ICBM silos, reversing President Carter's decision to deploy the missiles in a network of tracks and underground shelters, shuttling the MXs so that the Soviets could not target them. (U.S. Air Force)

from the island. But private Americans maintained strong economic links, and low-level official ties continued through an "Institute." Washington also kept up the flow of military aid. The People's Republic insisted on ultimately repossessing Taiwan, but threats of force subsided. U.S. cultural interactions with Taiwan remained strong, especially so when Taiwanese teams won world championships in Little League baseball during the 1970s.

During the Carter presidency, many Americans sensed that the nation's role as the world's sheriff, banker, business manager, and teacher had eroded. High OPEC prices, huge deficits in the balance of payments, haunting memories of Vietnam, revolution in Nicaragua, return of the Canal Zone to Panama, Castro's defiance, Soviet nuclear equivalence and the jilted SALT-II, the Iranian hostage crisis, and Afghanistan—all seemed to project an image of American weakness. Carter could not persuade Americans that a decline in U.S. power was inevitable in an interdependent, multipolar world of some 150 nations. When he urged energy conservation as "the moral equivalent of war," wags spelled out the acronym MEOW. Indeed, the American people suffered "a serious case of empire shock for the first time in their cultural history."

Carter left a mixed record. Too often, administration policy appeared erratic because of the constant feuding between the State Department and Brzezinski's National Security Council. Carter lacked FDR's charm, Eisenhower's popularity, JFK's television presence, LBJ's ability to handle Congress, and Nixon's talent for exploiting the spectacular. Carter also violated some of his stated goals. He promised to withdraw U.S. forces from South Korea but then reversed himself. Strongly advocating nuclear nonproliferation, he nonetheless agreed in 1980 to ship 38 metric tons of enriched uranium fuel to India, even though New Delhi had snubbed the nonproliferation treaty. He promised to reduce defense spending but actually increased the Pentagon's budget by 14.5 percent in his last year. Instead of reducing arms sales abroad, they climbed from $12.8 billion in 1977 to $17.1 billion in 1980.

Carter's human-rights policy also seemed selective. Carter chose *realpolitik* when Vietnamese armies overthrew the genocidal Pol Pot regime in Cambodia in late 1978. U.S. aid went to Khmer Rouge guerrillas to contain the perceived expansion of Soviet influence via Hanoi, even though Carter had called the Khmer Rouge "the worst violators of human rights in the world today." Amnesty International, founded in 1961 to monitor the worldwide status of human rights, cited the governments of Argentina, Brazil, Guatemala, Indonesia, Iran, Morocco, the Philippines, South Korea, Taiwan, and Thailand for condoning or practicing torture, political terrorism, or arbitrary arrest. In 1976–1980 Washington delivered $2.3 billion in military aid to those ten nations and sold them weapons worth $13.7 billion. Thousands of foreign officers and police also trained at U.S. military schools. Carter's human-rights efforts led to the freeing of hundreds of political prisoners abroad, but the president's detractors faulted his effort as either too little or too meddlesome.

Carter officials believed that the administration pursued noble goals, achieved diplomatic successes, and infused morality into American foreign policy to prove that U.S. power lay not simply in military capabilities but also in the nation's values. The administration candidly explained the limits of U.S. influence in a world of diffused power and stressed the need to deal with long-range issues, not just immediate crises. Pointing to the Egyptian-Israeli peace, Panama Canal treaties, normalization of relations with China, progress on the law of the sea, North-South dialogue, end to civil war in Zimbabwe, nuclear modernization of NATO, and an improved American status in Africa, Professor Brzezinski proudly filled out the administration's report card: A−/B+.

The 1980 Republican presidential candidate, Ronald Reagan, disputed that high grade. The former Hollywood actor and California governor slammed Carter for leading America into decline. In a display of raw anticommunism, Reagan declared that an expansionist Soviet Union "underlies all the unrest that is going on. If they weren't engaged in this game of dominoes, there wouldn't be any hot spots in the world." Rallying to Reagan's promise to "make America great again," the electorate turned Carter out by giving him only 41 percent of the popular vote. The Republicans also gained control of the Senate; liberal, dovish senators Birch Bayh of Indiana, Frank Church of Idaho, John Culver of Iowa, and George McGovern of South Dakota joined Carter in defeat.

Ronald Reagan's Mission to Revive Hegemony

Ronald Reagan had no experience in foreign affairs before he became president. He preferred movies and television to reading books, riding horses to roundtable discussions. Time and time again, he revealed an ignorance of fundamental information. After returning from his first trip to South America, he announced: "They're all individual countries." Reagan also became noted for reckless and exaggerated statements, factual inaccuracies, and right-wing sloganeering. He acted more on his instincts than on patient reasoning. His staff, fearing ill-thought utterances, carefully managed his public performances. Surrounded by communications specialists who tapped his natural talent, Reagan proved an effective communicator. "Being a good actor pays off," he told students at China's Fudan University.

Reagan became a very popular president, winning a landslide reelection in 1984 against former vice president Walter Mondale. Even when Reagan suffered setbacks, Americans applauded his poised, amiable, down-to-earth, speak-from-the-heart manner, his self-deprecating humor (especially about his age), and his dogged consistency in his convictions. This "warmly ruthless man," one aide wrote, made decisions like "a Turkish pasha, passively letting his subjects serve him, selecting only those morsels of public policy that were especially tasty."

Several beliefs rooted in the American past guided the Reagan administration. First, Reagan and his conservative allies believed in a devil theory: A malevolent Soviet Union instigated international insecurity, ignited civil wars, promoted terrorism, and built an "evil empire." Soviet leaders stood poised "to commit any crime, to lie, to cheat" to achieve a communist world. Such rhetoric overlooked the many successful Soviet-American agreements of the recent past. Reagan officials thought in terms of bipolarism, global containment, and confrontation—with one exception: They lifted the grain embargo so that U.S. farmers could sell billions of dollars of wheat and corn to the Soviet Union.

Second, because the Soviets had allegedly achieved "a definite margin of [military] superiority," Reagan vowed to surpass them. "Defense is not a budget item,"

Coke in China. In 1981 the Coca-Cola Company opened a plant in China, where the famous soft drink is known as "tasty happiness." The humorist Art Buchwald commented: "I don't mind 800 million Chinese drinking a bottle a day, but I don't want them to bring back the empties." (Courtesy The Coca-Cola Company, 1979)

he told the Pentagon. "Spend what you need." They did—and more. Running up huge federal deficits, he launched the largest peacetime arms buildup in American history, spending $2 trillion. Reagan pushed plans for the B-1 bomber; ordered the stockpiling of the neutron bomb; and resumed production of poison gas for chemical warfare. The administration, moreover, expanded the navy, beefed up special forces units for counterinsurgency warfare, and continued the Trident-II submarine, MX, cruise missile, Stealth bomber, and mobile Midgetman missile programs. Military appropriations increased by 50 percent, growing from $143.9 billion in 1980 to $294.7 billion in 1985. In 1985 the Pentagon was spending $28 million an hour, twenty-four hours a day, seven days a week.

Third, Reagan believed it essential to gain public support for a more militarized, interventionist foreign policy. He implored the American people to abandon their post-Vietnam "self-doubt" in favor of a "national reawakening." Whipping up emotional patriotism, Reagan reassured Americans that "we've closed the door on a long, dark period of failure."

The fourth driving force became known as the Reagan Doctrine. The president in 1985 pledged support for anticommunist "freedom fighters" who battled the Soviets or Soviet-backed governments. The CIA, with congressional approval, funneled aid to insurgents in Afghanistan, Nicaragua, Angola, Cambodia, and Ethiopia. Reagan made overt what had been covert: the attempted overthrow of governments deemed inimical to U.S. interests. The Reagan Doctrine emphasized military action through allies, proxies, and paramilitary assets so that fewer American soldiers would fight and die in foreign lands as elite forces organized others to do the dirty work of shadow wars.

Fifth, Reagan and his advisers believed that nations must embrace private capitalism and privatize managed economies. American leaders frequently lectured Third World nations on the "magic of the marketplace." The Reagan administration refused to sign the long-awaited Law of the Sea Treaty, protesting that the agreement did not adequately protect American deep-sea mining companies.

Sixth, citing the failure of the Carter administration to support friendly dictators in Iran and Nicaragua, the Reaganites accepted Ambassador to the United Nations Jeane Kirkpatrick's distinction between "authoritarian" and "totalitarian" regimes. Authoritarian regimes in countries such as the Philippines, Chile, South Korea, and South Africa sustained capitalist economies and would supposedly respond to U.S. suggestions for reform. Communist totalitarian regimes imposed managed economies and resisted change. Given such thinking, Reagan officials downgraded human-rights tests for friendly authoritarian governments.

Finally, Reagan envisioned the United States as a missionary model for other nations. "The United States is the economic miracle," bragged the president. "The world's hopes rest with America's future." This reformist zealotry found expression through institutions such as the National Endowment for Democracy, created in 1983 as a propaganda agency using federal and private funds to promote free enterprise and democratic politics. The endowment gave millions of dollars to foreign political parties, labor unions, and publishers, many with an antileft bias. Reagan could even quote Tom Paine and Thomas Jefferson: "we have it in our power to begin the world over again" and "to spread the sacred fire of liberty" everywhere.

"Give War a Chance." During his confirmation hearings in January 1981, Secretary of State–designate Alexander M. Haig Jr. said: "There are more important things than peace—there are things which we Americans must be willing to fight for." Some people thought him too eager to apply military solutions to political problems and too inclined toward confrontation with the Soviet Union and leftist Third World nations. (Bob Englehart, *Hartford Courant*)

Reagan named General Alexander M. Haig, Jr., secretary of state. A steely-eyed military professional famous for his mixed metaphors and his ambition, Haig feuded with just about everybody. The volatile secretary abruptly resigned in June 1982. George P. Shultz followed Haig. An economist and business executive, Shultz often clashed with Secretary of Defense Caspar W. ("Cap") Weinberger, especially after Weinberger announced in 1984 that the United States should use military force only under certain conditions: with long-term public and congressional support; for "clearly defined political and military objectives"; and with "the clear intention of winning." Shultz chastised Weinberger as a big spender who refused to use newly augmented U.S. forces. Shultz also battled hawkish CIA director William J. Casey, who once asserted that "the business of Congress is to stay out of my business."

Richard V. Allen, a business consultant, served as Reagan's assistant for national security affairs. After Allen departed in 1982 under suspicion of scandal, the office of national security adviser suffered instability and more scandal. Under William Clark, Reagan's political crony from California, NSC staffwork became so cumbersome that Shultz thought it "worse than a university." Then came Robert C. McFarlane, a former marine who never argued against misguided policies because "if I'd done that, Bill Casey, Jeane Kirkpatrick, and Cap Weinberger would have said I was some kind of commie." John M. Poindexter, an active-duty admiral with a Ph.D. in nuclear physics, succeeded McFarlane, but he had to resign in late 1986 when the Iran-contra affair erupted.

Despite strong opposition from Weinberger and Shultz, Reagan ordered the National Security Council to carry out a covert project to trade arms to Iran in return for the release of U.S. hostages held in Lebanon. Because he also empowered the NSC secretly to aid the Nicaraguan *contras,* the two operations eventually commingled. To ensure secrecy, McFarlane and Poindexter ran both schemes in total disregard of Congress and almost completely outside the purview of the Defense and State Departments. Relying on CIA connections, the action officer in charge of both operations, marine lieutenant colonel Oliver North, flaunted his contempt for

Reagan in Doubt. When the crisis over the arms sale to Iran and aid to the *contras* erupted in 1986–1987, Reagan could not remember the details of his decisions. Diagnosis of Alzheimer's disease in 1994 raised the question of whether Reagan had suffered any mental impairment during his presidency. Because doctors had apparently not tested him for Alzheimer's disease while president, it seemed impossible to judge whether Reagan's mental lapses were the result of dementia or simply the normal failings of an elderly president who remembered only the details that interested him. (Bill Schorr © United Features Syndicate)

"WHAT DO I KNOW...AND WHEN WILL I KNOW IT?"

Congress, professional diplomats, and traditional bureaucrats. When North diverted profits from the Iranian arms sales to the *contras,* Poindexter approved but did not tell Reagan because he wanted the president "to have some deniability so that he would be protected." Shultz later portrayed Reagan as an innocent dupe misled by his inner circle. Yet the record shows that at top-level meetings on Iran-Contra, President Reagan made the basic decisions, without monitoring every operational detail.

Reagan's appointment of Frank C. Carlucci, a seasoned diplomat, and then General Colin Powell, as his next NSC advisers did not quiet a national crisis that badly besmirched the Reagan presidency. In 1989 North was found guilty of three felonies, and in early 1990 Poindexter was convicted of five felony charges, including lying to Congress. A federal appeals court later overturned both convictions because Congress had granted immunity to the two men for testimony given to congressional committees. All told, some 190 Reagan officials were indicted or convicted of illegal activities.

Soviet-American Crises and Antinuclearism

Reagan assumed that the Soviet Union outspent the United States on armaments and outdistanced it in nuclear weapons. The United States had to close the "window of vulnerability"—the theoretical vulnerability of American land-based ICBMs to a Soviet first strike—by enlarging the American nuclear arsenal. The

Soviets outranked the United States in ICBMs and SLBMs but lagged behind in strategic bombers and nuclear warheads. And at least two-thirds of Soviet nuclear arms consisted of vulnerable ICBMs in fixed silos. Reagan failed to count on the American side the defense spending of NATO allies. As for the "window of vulnerability," in 1983 the president's own Commission on Strategic Forces reported that the window did not exist and that America's triad of air-, sea-, and land-based nuclear weapons provided sufficient deterrence.

Statements by Reagan officials about winning a nuclear war stimulated a transatlantic debate. The evangelist Billy Graham, World Council of Churches, and Union of Concerned Scientists urged restraint in the nuclear arms race. The American Medical Association declared that "there is no adequate medical response to a nuclear holocaust." The veteran Kremlinologist George F. Kennan recommended an immediate 50 percent cut in nuclear arsenals on both sides, the denuclearization of much of Europe, a complete ban on nuclear testing, and a freeze on new weapons. The House of Representatives in 1983 also passed a freeze resolution. Proponents argued that America's infrared satellites could verify a freeze on the testing and deployment of ballistic missiles.

George Shultz (b. 1920).
A graduate of Princeton University (he had a tiger tattoo on his buttocks) and the Massachusetts Institute of Technology (Ph.D., 1949), Shultz served as secretary of labor, director of the Office of Management and Budget, and secretary of the treasury in the Nixon administration. In 1982 he joined the Reagan cabinet as secretary of state. One pundit said Shultz had "the charisma of a drowsy clam." (Department of State)

In May 1983 the Roman Catholic Bishops of the United States issued a pastoral letter that called "the arms race one of the greatest curses on the human race." Feminists ridiculed the sexual nature of the discourse on nuclear strategy wherein "white men in ties" talked about "missile size, . . . vertical erector launchers, thrust-to-weight ratios, soft lay downs, [and] deep penetrations." Scientists postulated that even people who survived a nuclear war would face a devastating "nuclear winter": Clouds of debris, dust, and smoke from mass fires would block the sun's rays, cooling the earth's temperatures and killing plant and animal life.

In 1981, huge crowds in Bonn, London, Rome, and Amsterdam called for a ban on the installation of Pershing and cruise missiles. Activists demanded that both Washington and Moscow sit down to talk. Statements by U.S. officials evoked alarm. Reagan mentioned the possibility of a limited nuclear war in Europe, thus sparing the two great powers. He once misstated that cruise missiles were defensive weapons—in fact, they were designed to overcome Soviet defenses and to strike deep in the USSR. He even said that SLBMs could be recalled after firing.

To satisfy Western European leaders who welcomed U.S. missiles but wanted less domestic protest, and to quiet the American antinuclear movement, Reagan reluctantly agreed to talks in Geneva on intermediate-range nuclear forces (INF) in Europe. For these negotiations, which opened in November 1981, Washington proposed to stop planned deployment of the new Pershings and cruise missiles in NATO nations if Moscow would dismantle its SS-20, SS-4, and SS-5 missiles pointed at Western Europe. The Soviets initially rejected this "zero option," because it excluded British and French nuclear forces and U.S. weapons on submarines and aircraft. Moscow deployed more triple-warhead SS-20s, and in 1983 Pershing-IIs deployed first to Great Britain and then to West Germany. In November 1983, to express their displeasure over these new missiles, the Soviets suspended the INF talks. Meetings did not resume until early 1985, only to falter again.

Negotiations on strategic nuclear weapons fared no better. Reagan replaced SALT with START—Strategic Arms Reduction Talks. Negotiations began in

"Star Wars" in 1984. President Reagan made a passionate case for the Strategic Defense Initiative to prevent a "madman" with missiles from blackmailing "all of us." Some scientists assured him that they could create his "dream"—an effective ballistic missile defense system. In this artist's sketch, a space-based electromagnetic ray gun destroys a nuclear-armed reentry vehicle presumably launched from the Soviet Union. SDI development still limped along in the new century. (U.S. Army/Department of Defense, Still Media Records Center)

Geneva in 1982, but the U.S. proposal for deep cuts stalled. The reason became obvious: The American plan sought drastic reductions in those very weapons that constituted the bulk of Soviet deterrent power.

Then came President Reagan's announcement of the Strategic Defense Initiative in March 1983. Soon dubbed "Star Wars," SDI envisioned an anti-ballistic missile defense system in space—a laser or particle beam shield that could intercept Soviet ballistic missiles and destroy them in space. Even if such a weapon could destroy most incoming weapons, skeptical scientists noted that "the remaining 5 or 10 percent would be enough to totally destroy civilization." Others argued that if SDI ever did work, it would undermine deterrence itself by eliminating the danger of Soviet attack, thus freeing the United States to use nuclear weapons without fear of retaliation. The president, however, optimistically viewed it as the perfect defense, a way to "get rid of those atomic weapons. Every one," he said privately. As SDI research advanced, with some test results actually faked to keep congressional funds flowing, START sputtered.

Other events spoiled the negotiating environment. After months of strikes and protests by Poland's Solidarity labor movement, the Polish military cracked down in December 1981, imposing martial law and arresting Solidarity leaders. Washington reacted quickly. It suspended economic agreements with Poland's communist regime. Reagan cut back Soviet-American trade and banned Soviet airline flights to the United States. NATO countries reacted cautiously, in part because they wanted to continue their lucrative trade with the Soviets and Soviet clients.

Mikhail Gorbachev (b. 1932) and Ronald Reagan (1911–2004). In May 1988, at the Moscow summit meeting, the two leaders continued the warm personal relationship that helped end the Cold War. (Photo by Bill Fitz-Patrick, The White House, Courtesy Ronald Reagan Library)

On September 1, 1983, Korean Air Lines Flight 007, en route from Anchorage, Alaska, to Seoul, South Korea, strayed some 300 miles off course and crossed Soviet airspace near a strategic nuclear base. Soviet planes scrambled. When the Korean pilot did not acknowledge warning shots, a Soviet jet blasted the Boeing 747 with one missile, killing all 269 passengers aboard. Reagan lambasted this "act of barbarism." Soviet officials claimed KAL 007 was on a spy mission for the United States. Moscow later revealed that the shootdown had occurred in international airspace and that Soviet authorities had crudely covered up their error. Yet the "simplistic overreaction" in the United States so exacerbated tensions that NATO military exercises in November caused the frightened Kremlin leadership to fear a nuclear first strike. Informed about this nuclear "near-miss," Reagan recited to aides the biblical story of Armageddon and made his first public plea to banish nuclear weapons "from the face of the earth." Until tempers cooled, we "can't cook porridge together," said Ambassador Dobrynin.

Another obstacle to an arms-control agreement was the infirmity of Soviet leadership—until the arrival of Mikhail S. Gorbachev in 1985. Leonid Brezhnev died in 1982; his aging successors, Yuri Andropov and Konstantin Chernenko, died within three years. Gorbachev became the new general secretary of the Communist party, at age fifty-four one of the Soviet Union's youngest leaders, with a personality quite "different from the wooden ventriloquism of the average Soviet apparatchik." Determined to reform the sluggish Soviet economy through restructuring (*perestroika*) and to open the suffocating authoritarian political system through liberalization (*glasnost*), Gorbachev initiated stunning changes in his own nation and across the globe.

"Deeply affected" by the disastrous accident at the Chernobyl nuclear power station in 1986, the new general secretary altered the Soviet position on nuclear weapons. He unilaterally stopped further deployment of intermediate-range missiles. He halted nuclear-weapons tests. In November 1985 Gorbachev and Reagan met in Geneva. Although they could not agree on SDI or an extension of SALT-II, they established warm personal relations during their talks. Then in early 1986 Gorbachev called for an end to all nuclear weapons by the year 2000. At another summit meeting in Reykjavík, Iceland, in October 1986, the conferees made tremendous progress by agreeing to reduce warheads, missiles, and bombers and to remove all American and Soviet intermediate missiles from Europe. Reagan found the results "breathtaking." But when Gorbachev said that "this all depends, of course, on your giving up SDI," Reagan ended the meeting abruptly. Yet the atmosphere had clearly changed for the better.

The Washington summit meeting in December 1987 finally saw the signing of the Intermediate-Range Nuclear Forces (INF) Treaty, which provided for the elimination of all U.S. and Soviet INF missiles anywhere and verification of their destruction through on-site inspections. What had changed? Gorbachev had taken the initiative by accepting the "zero option" and giving Washington "120 percent of what it wanted" in negotiations. The warmth between Reagan and Gorbachev facilitated negotiations. "When I told him [Gorbachev] we should put our cards on the table, he took out his Visa and Mastercard," Reagan later joked. "We will leave Afghanistan," promised foreign minister Eduard Shevardnadze, a welcome change from the dour Andrei Gromyko. The antinuclear movement had produced strong antinuclear public opinion in Europe and America. Most obvious, the two superpowers saw the treaty as beneficial to their quite different national interests. Both faced economic troubles spawned by the long Cold War. "Our economy," said one Soviet official, "has been literally eviscerated by military spending." The Senate approved the INF Treaty by a 95 to 5 vote in May 1988, and the dismantling of missiles began that summer.

Gorbachev also boldly advanced other issues. In April 1988 he signed a UN-mediated accord providing for the withdrawal of all Soviet forces from Afghanistan. They departed early the next year, acknowledging a conspicuous defeat for the Soviet military, caused in part by the "Stinger" antiaircraft weapons that the United States had shipped to the Afghan *mujahedeen* ("holy warriors"). In December 1988 the Soviet leader announced a unilateral Soviet cut of 500,000 ground troops. Moscow reduced its support for the Sandinistas in Nicaragua and negotiated for the removal of Cuban troops from Angola. The Soviets also stopped jamming Voice of America broadcasts.

The "Backyard": Central America and the Caribbean

The Reagan administration read events in the Third World as related chapters in an East-West, Cold War book written by the two superpowers, not as independent short stories composed by distinct, indigenous sources. In the Third World U.S. in-

CENTRAL AMERICAN EYE CHART

P
OV
ERTY
HUNGER
INJUSTICE
CORRUPTION
REVOLUTION

DEMOCRATS

Sacramento Bee

'C - O - uh - M - M - uh - U - uh - N - uh - I - S - M!'

"Communism."   Critics of Reagan's interventionism in Central America believed that the president misread the sources of instability in the region. (Dennis Renault, *Sacramento Bee*)

fluence had to be restored to repel "beachheads of tyranny, subversion, and terror." Hegemony was at stake. Reagan quoted the Truman Doctrine, resuscitated the domino theory, and stressed military and covert means over negotiations. Central America, long in the United States' grip but restless under the burden of profound economic, political, and social divisions, figured prominently in Reagan's counter-revolutionary crusade.

The State Department claimed that Moscow used Cuba to propagandize revolution, train insurgents, and promote "Cuba-model states" that would "provide platforms for subversion" and pose a "direct military threat at or near our borders." President Reagan increasingly made a strategic case: As a major trade route, the Caribbean provided "our lifeline to the outside world," and "Soviet military theorists . . . want to tie down our attention and forces on our own southern border and so limit our capacity to act in more distant places such as Europe, the Persian Gulf, the Indian Ocean, the Sea of Japan." Fearing "another Cuba," Reagan officials determined to defeat leftist insurgents in El Salvador, topple the Sandinista government in Nicaragua, and draw Guatemala and Honduras into a tighter U.S.

military network. Through billions of dollars in aid, CIA operations, weapons and advisers, splashy military maneuvers, and support for the anti-Sandinista army known as the *contras,* Washington plunged more deeply into Central America.

Critics charged that Reagan exaggerated the Soviet-Cuban threat, underplayed the local causes of disorder, bypassed opportunities for negotiations, and shored up the right wing and military. Such policies helped invite what Washington wanted most to prevent: Soviet influence in the area. Senator Christopher Dodd (Democrat-Connecticut) decried the "ignorance" of the Reagan diplomats who "seem to know as little about Central America in 1983 as we knew about Indochina in 1963." Downplaying a Soviet threat, Dodd declared that "if Central America were not racked with poverty, there would be no revolution."

In El Salvador, the Reagan administration nevertheless found a textbook "case of armed aggression against a small country by Communist powers acting through Cuba." El Salvador was a poor country plagued by a high infant mortality rate, illiteracy, and violence. The army and a small landed elite had long ruled the nation. Two percent of the people owned half the land. In October 1979, however, reform-minded colonels seized power and organized a new government under José Napoleón Duarte, a Christian Democratic party leader. The elite responded by organizing "death squads" to assassinate moderates and radicals alike. Leftists formed the Farabundo Martí Front for National Liberation (FMLN). In 1980 national guard troops raped and killed four American churchwomen, but the Salvadoran government refused to prosecute the officers who ordered the murders. Even though Carter had extended economic and military aid to the Duarte government, the Reagan administration dramatically increased both programs. "They thought it was like rolling a drunk," former ambassador to El Salvador Robert E. White remarked. "El Salvador is Spanish for Vietnam" became a popular antiwar bumper sticker.

Congress insisted that the administration certify human-rights progress in the country. Every six months officials dutifully issued optimistic but disingenuous statements. "Everybody *knew,* Congress *knew,* what they [Salvadoran military forces] were doing," a U.S. embassy official recalled. "What's improvement, anyway? You kill eight hundred and it goes down to two hundred, that's improvement." The UN Truth Commission reported in 1993 that 85 percent of the 75,000 people killed in the Salvadoran civil war died at the hands of government forces and gun-for-hire death squads. Although U.S. military advisers trained some of the units responsible for murdering civilians, American diplomats did not exert "high-level pressure for change on Salvadoran military leaders." Despite spending 4.5 billion in El Salvador during the 1980s, victory in the bloody civil war still eluded Reagan when he left office. Only after four more years of killing on both sides did the combatants finally negotiate a United Nations–sponsored peace in January 1992.

The Reagan administration blamed much of the Salvadoran trouble on Cuba and Nicaragua, which sent small supplies of arms to the insurgents. Secretary Haig announced that the Soviets had a "hit list" of Central American states, with Nicaragua first, El Salvador second. The Sandinistas invited thousands of Cuban medical specialists and teachers into their poor country, used Cuban advisers and Soviet weapons to build a strong military, and limited free speech as they moved to a one-party government. As the United States had long treated Cuba, so it treated

Nicaragua in the 1980s: putting pressure on a small, proud, doggedly radical government to the point where it faced a choice between capitulation or seeking outside help for defense. Reagan first cut off all foreign aid. In November 1981, he ordered the CIA to train and arm the anti-Sandinista *contras*. "Let's make the bastards sweat," CIA director William Casey told his covert operators. A mercenary army of 15,000, including former supporters of Somoza, the *contras* were "a mixed bag," according to General Colin Powell. "We worked with what we had." From bases in Honduras and Costa Rica the *contras* raided Nicaragua, sabotaging bridges, oil facilities, and crops, and using CIA "coercive techniques" (including "direct physical brutality") against civilians.

Although in 1982 Congress had prohibited the use of funds to overthrow the Nicaraguan government, Reagan officials winked at the restriction. In early 1984 Congress discovered that the CIA had worked with *contra* commandos to mine three Nicaraguan ports. "I am pissed off," roared Senator Barry Goldwater at the CIA's Casey. When Nicaragua went to the World Court to charge a breach of international law, Washington refused to recognize the court's jurisdiction. In mid-1984, Congress banned aid to the *contras*. Meanwhile, Nicaraguan-American talks in Mexico produced no agreement. Aid to the *contras* did not stop. In 1985–1986, following Reagan's explicit instructions "to do whatever you have to do to help these people keep body and soul together," Colonel North of Reagan's NSC shifted to the *contras* profits from secret arms sales to Iran by using Israeli intermediaries and a Swiss bank account. North also coordinated a network of planes and ships (without "USG fingerprints") and funded the building of a large airstrip in Costa Rica—all without informing Congress. If the "story gets out, we'll all be hanging by our thumbs in front of the White House," said Reagan.

In early 1985 Reagan admitted publicly what he had long denied: Washington sought to topple the Sandinista government—he wanted it to say "uncle." In May he imposed an economic embargo and blocked loans to Nicaragua from the World Bank and the Inter-American Development Bank. Congress appropriated $27 million for "humanitarian" aid to the *contras*. Still, the *contra* war did not go well. The insurgents constantly feuded among themselves, generated little popular support, and could not seize and hold towns. But they forced the Sandinistas to shift funds from social programs to defense and to restrict civil liberties, thus slowing the revolution and arousing internal dissent. Hence Reagan officials treated negotiations as "nothing more than a necessary smokescreen to quiet opposition to the paramilitary program." Washington snubbed the Contadora group (Mexico, Venezuela, Panama, and Colombia), which in 1983 had persuaded the five Central American states to limit foreign advisers, reduce arms, and promote democracy. Reagan officials stiff-armed the 1987 peace plan by Costa Rican president Oscar Arias Sánchez but had to negotiate when the *contras* agreed to a cease-fire in March 1988. Hobbled by the Iran-Contra scandal, Reagan resisted appeals for more aid to the *contras*. When Reagan left office, the Sandinistas still governed. Under arrangements brokered by the Central American presidents, the Washington-backed candidate Violetta Barrios de Chamorro soundly defeated Sandinista President Daniel Ortega Saavedra in elections finally held in 1990. After nearly a decade of civil war, 30,000 Nicaraguans had died and the ravaged economy had sunk to the second poorest in the hemisphere.

Haig claimed that Cuba was "exporting revolution and bloodshed" to El Salvador and Nicaragua. "I'll make that island a fucking parking lot," he thundered. Reagan banned tourist and business visits to Cuba, denied Cuban officials visas for travel in the United States, and restricted importation of Cuban newspapers and magazines. Cuba actually endorsed the Contadora process and urged negotiations in order to obviate U.S. intervention. In December 1984 Washington did agree to return to Cuba about 2,700 criminals who had come by boat in the 1980 Mariel exodus, and Castro promised to let Cubans reunite with families in the United States. But when the United States, in mid-1985, started up Radio Martí to act as "an electronic Bay of Pigs" beaming propaganda into Cuba, Castro angrily abrogated the accord.

U.S. troops invaded the tiny Caribbean island of Grenada on October 25, 1983, thus sending "shivers up Castro's spine about whether or not they [the Cubans] might be next." More than 6,000 Americans went ashore to oust a Marxist regime that Reagan termed "a Soviet-Cuban colony, being readied as a major military bastion to export terror." More than 100 people died, including about 25 Cubans helping to build an airstrip. Reagan claimed that the airfield would serve the Cuban and Soviet militaries, but British engineers said it was to boost Grenada's tourist trade. The administration also justified the invasion as the rescue of 1,000 Americans, many of them medical students. By mid-December, having deported surviving Cubans from the island and closed the Soviet Embassy, U.S. forces evacuated Grenada. The mission had cost $75.5 million. World opinion disapproved this modern example of a "Gilbert-and-Sullivan war." North Americans celebrated victory, only days after a bomb killed 241 U.S. soldiers in Lebanon.

Hornets' Nests in the Middle East, Africa, and Asia

The Reagan administration failed to sustain Carter's initiatives in the Middle East. Reagan did seek to gain some sort of homeland for the Palestinians and to guarantee Israel's security through a new Arab-Israeli accord. But Lebanon descended into savage civil war and suffered a punishing Israeli invasion and Syrian occupation; the Iran-Iraq War disrupted oil shipments; Libya and the United States skirmished; Israel and the United States bickered bitterly; and terrorists victimized the innocent, including many Americans. Saudi Arabia and Jordan refused to relax tensions with Israel yet kept placing large orders for U.S. arms. Reaganites assumed that the Soviet Union coveted the region. But Israel considered the PLO and Arab nationalism the greater threats; and the Arabs designated Israel, not Moscow, as enemy number one.

In late 1981, in open defiance of the U.S. position, Israel suddenly announced its annexation of the Golan Heights. When Reagan suspended an Israeli-American military agreement, Prime Minister Menachem Begin exploded: "Are we a banana republic?" To American protests against Israeli bombing raids of PLO camps in Lebanon, Begin cited U.S. bombing in Vietnam. Then came the Egyptian radicals' assassination of President Sadat and Israel's invasion of Lebanon.

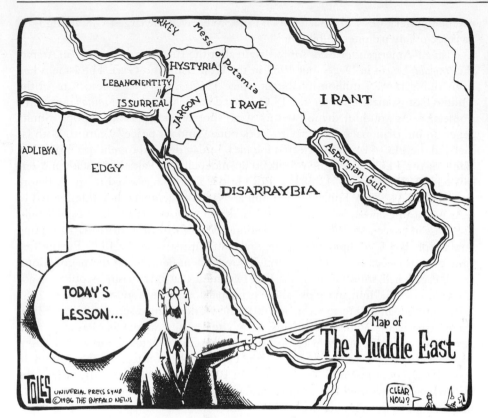

Lebanon had long suffered factionalism between Muslims and Christians. For decades, displaced Palestinians had moved into the country, and in 1970–1971 PLO fighters driven from Jordan joined them. When civil war erupted in the mid-1970s, Lebanon invited Syria to restore order; Syrian troops arrived and stayed. From bases in Lebanon the PLO harassed and murdered Israelis. Israel thereupon invaded Lebanon in June 1982 and captured Beirut, helping to destroy much of the capital city. U.S. officials then arranged the withdrawal of both the PLO and Israel from Beirut and created a peacekeeping force that included U.S. marines. Soon Muslims targeted Americans. In April 1983 bombs hit the U.S. Embassy in Beirut, killing 63 people. Then, in October, a terrorist drove a truck loaded with explosives into a building full of sleeping American troops, killing 241. Weinberger's aide, General Colin Powell, thought the United States had "stuck its hand into a thousand-year-old hornet's nest with the expectation that our presence might pacify the hornets." In February 1984, with public criticism rising, Reagan withdrew the marines.

After 533 days and scores of deaths, the marines could not quell Lebanon's multifaceted war. Critics chastised the administration for not penalizing Israel for its use of U.S. weapons in violation of contractual restrictions. When the veteran diplomat George Ball claimed that Israel's "rampaging Army" had "devastated a nation [Lebanon]," Cold War hawks accused him of anti-Semitism. Washington soon patched up relations with Israel, which in 1985 received the largest U.S. foreign-aid package of any nation—$3 billion.

Israeli-American relations soured again after the Palestinian uprising (in Arabic, the *intifada*) began in December 1987 in the West Bank and Gaza. The Israelis had been ruling the 1.5 million inhabitants since 1967. Like other Palestinians in the Middle East (some 5 million), the PLO-backed participants in the *intifada* wanted a homeland. As youthful demonstrators were shot down by Israeli troops, Shultz urged an international conference to work out a "land for peace" solution. Both Israel and the PLO adamantly rejected the idea. Jordan decided to relinquish the West Bank to the PLO, which then declared an independent Palestinian state and endorsed UN Resolution 242. When PLO leader Yasir Arafat asked to speak before the General Assembly, Shultz denied him a visa. UN members thereupon voted to hear Arafat in Geneva, Switzerland, where the PLO leader recognized Israel's right "to exist in peace and security" and renounced "all forms of terrorism." Accepting Arafat's pledge, U.S. diplomats opened talks in Tunisia with the PLO for the first time ever in December 1988. The Israeli government denounced the negotiations.

Reagan had announced in his first inaugural that "terrorism" would replace Carter's focus on "human rights" as the principal concern of foreign policy. In 1985 alone, more than 800 terrorist incidents in the world claimed some 900 lives, 23 of them Americans. Mideast terrorists drew the greatest attention. Passengers on American commercial jets became hijack and murder victims, and U.S. citizens were taken hostage. In one case in 1985, U.S. warplanes forced to the ground an Egyptian airliner known to be carrying four Palestinians who had earlier seized the Italian cruise ship *Achille Lauro* and murdered a wheelchair-bound American. "You can run but you can't hide," warned Reagan.

The Reagan administration especially blamed Libyan radical Muslim ruler Moammar Gadhafi for much of the terrorism. Diplomatic relations with Libya were severed in early 1981; the following year Washington imposed an embargo on oil imports from Libya; and in early 1986 Reagan banned all trade. After a series of terrorist attacks at busy European airports, Reagan officials fingered Libyan responsibility, sent U.S. warships into the Gulf of Sidra. When a terrorist explosion killed a GI in West Berlin in April, U.S. fighter-bombers demolished Gadhafi's Soviet-built air force and bombed his official residence, killing dozens, including the dictator's adopted daughter. That same year audiences cheered Hollywood heartthrob Tom Cruise as he went from "hot dog" to *Top Gun* (1986) in celluloid dogfights against Libyan MiGs.

Reagan also tilted toward Iraq in the Iran-Iraq War. Iraq had begun the bloody conflict in 1980 to seize Iranian oil lands and topple the Khomeini regime, which had incited Shi'ite Muslims in Iraq to rebel. Washington quietly supplied Iraq with military intelligence, a half-billion dollars in credits, and dual-use technology, even though "we knew [Iraqi dictator Saddam Hussein] was an S.O.B., but he was our S.O.B." In May 1987 two sea-skimming missiles fired by an Iraqi aircraft hit the U.S. frigate *Stark,* killing 37 crewmen. Iraq apologized. Reagan soon beefed up the U.S. naval presence in the Persian Gulf and "reflagged" Kuwaiti oil tankers as American vessels. The next year, in July, the U.S.S. *Vincennes,* thinking itself under attack, shot down a civilian Iranian airliner, killing all 290 aboard. Washington admitted error

Shaking Hands with Saddam Hussein. Iraqi President Saddam Hussein (b. 1937) greets Donald Rumsfeld (b. 1932), then special envoy of President Ronald Reagan, in Baghdad on December 20, 1983. The Reagan administration pragmatically extended aid to Iraq in its war with Iran, even though Saddam Hussein had invaded his neighbor, harbored known terrorists, abused the human rights of Iraqi citizens, used chemical weapons against Iranians, and pursued long-range nuclear aspirations that included an eventual nuclear weapons capability. As secretary of defense twenty years later, Rumsfeld directed more bellicose policies toward Saddam Hussein and Iraq. (CNN TV photo from National Security Archive, © Getty Images)

while covering up the fact that the *Vincennes* was inside Iranian territorial waters at the time of the shootdown. At last, in August 1988, Iran and Iraq agreed to end a conflict that had killed hundreds of thousands.

In Africa, too, Reagan had to deal with knotty, long-term issues. Death-dealing famine, as in Sudan in the mid-1980s; civil wars in Angola and Ethiopia, where Soviet and Cuban troops assisted ruling regimes and covert CIA aid helped insurgents; the unresolved status of South Africa–dominated Namibia; and the dehumanizing policy of apartheid in South Africa—all demanded attention. Toward white-ruled South Africa he at first launched "constructive engagement." South Africa endured Washington's official disapproval of apartheid and urgent requests for reforms, but no economic sanctions. The policy amounted to a "kid-glove, all carrot-and-no-stick approach," said critics.

Nonetheless, when the Pretoria government rejected serious reform, black South Africans marched, protested, and died, demanding that people around the world take sides. As violence spread across South Africa, Reagan worried that the opportunistic Soviets might exploit the turmoil. Protest in the United States, led by the Free South Africa Movement, a broad-based coalition, forced the issue onto the American political agenda. Claiming that "sanctions may hurt, but apartheid kills," members of Congress joined with church, labor, and intellectual leaders to picket the South African embassy in Washington, D.C. South African bishop Desmond M. Tutu, the 1984 Nobel Peace Prize recipient, toured the United States appealing for economic pressure against his government. Cities and states passed divestiture laws requiring the sale of stock they owned in U.S. companies operating in South Africa. Some companies pulled out; by 1986, U.S. investments had dropped to $1.3 billion from $2 billion in 1981. To head off congressional action, Reagan, in September 1985, added a few sanctions to the earlier (1962) embargo on arms sales to South

Africa. But in October 1986, with an unusual bipartisan consensus and over Reagan's veto, Congress passed stiffer economic sanctions, including a ban on new American investments in and oil exports to South Africa.

Good news did come from Namibia. South Africa had governed this former German colony since World War I, even defying the United Nations when it revoked Pretoria's mandate in 1966 and demanded independence. Since the early 1970s the radical South West African People's Organization (SWAPO), with Cuban and Soviet support, had battled South African armies from bases in Angola and Zambia. After twelve years of sporadic negotiations, however, Angola, Cuba, and South Africa signed a U.S.-mediated agreement in December 1988 for a Cuban troop withdrawal from Angola and black majority rule in Namibia. Formal independence came in March 1990.

In Asia, Ferdinand Marcos's Philippines became a troublesome ally. Elected president in 1965, Marcos had created a dictatorship marked by corruption, martial law, and personal enrichment. By the early 1980s his country groaned under a huge foreign debt of more than $20 billion, high unemployment, and economic stagnation. He jailed, tortured, and murdered critics. Business, Roman Catholic Church, civil libertarian, and professional leaders demanded reform. The accelerating discontent with Marcos came suddenly to a head in August 1983, after assassins gunned down the anti-Marcos leader Benigno S. Aquino. The evidence pointed to a successful military conspiracy.

Investments of $2 billion, trade sales of similar value, and outstanding debts owed to American banks seemed in jeopardy. So, too, did two major U.S. bases: Subic Bay Naval Station and Clark Air Base. The Reagan administration distanced itself from Marcos and pressed for reforms. When Marcos stole an election from Benigno Aquino's widow, Corazon Aquino, turmoil tore across the Philippines. Besieged by his own people and abandoned by Washington, Marcos, on February 25, 1986, went into exile in Hawai'i. U.S. aid soon flowed to the Aquino government.

An altogether different kind of issue stood at the center of Japanese-American relations: a huge trade deficit as Japan grew dramatically as an economic competitor. "We send Japan low-value soybeans, wheat, coal and cotton," one business leader remarked. "They send us high-value autos, motorcycles, TV sets, and oil-well casings. It's 1776 and we're a colony again." In 1985 the total U.S. trade deficit (more imports than exports) mounted to an all-time high of $148.5 billion—$50 billion of it with Japan. The overall deficit derived in large part from the strong dollar abroad (making American goods expensive in other countries) and the indebtedness of Third World nations, which forced them to buy fewer U.S. products. Japan's tariff barriers, cartels, and government subsidies also made it difficult for American goods to penetrate Japanese markets. Protectionists demanded retaliatory, higher tariffs on Japanese goods so that ailing American industry could better meet import competition and American workers could hold their jobs. In 1985 Japan voluntarily set quotas on automobile and carbon-steel shipments to the United States and promised trade liberalization at home, but Washington wanted more. The 1988 Omnibus Trade and Competitiveness Act "had Japan in its sights" when it authorized U.S. retaliation against nations that refused to negotiate reductions in trade barriers. As the Reagan era ended, Japan's foreign minister characterized the Japanese-American trade relationship as "at its worst since the war."

Triumphs and Hazards: The Reagan Legacy

Reagan claimed foreign-policy successes, especially in the twilight of his presidency: Namibia, the INF Treaty, the departure of dictators in Haiti (Jean-Claude Duvalier) and the Philippines (Ferdinand Marcos), termination of the Iran-Iraq War, talks with the PLO, and Cuban withdrawal from Angola. At the end, Reagan seemed less ideological, more adaptable. Improved relations with the Soviet Union suggested that the Cold War was winding down. The Soviets pulled out of Afghanistan and loosened their grip on Eastern Europe. Some analysts argued that the huge Reagan military spending forced the economically hobbled Soviets to make concessions. Others noted that the remarkable changes initiated by Gorbachev sprang less from U.S. pressure than from a new generation of Soviet leaders and courageous Eastern European dissidents. Reagan very well may have undercut American power and prestige in the long run by running up a tremendous debt and neglecting to repair the American economy or to improve American education to become more competitive in the international marketplace. The conservative columnist George F. Will wrote that Reagan "has been a great reassurer, a steadying captain who calmed the passengers and, to some extent, the sea." But, Will added, Reagan's "cheerfulness" was "a narcotic, numbing the nation's senses about hazards just over the horizon."

Reagan bequeathed to his successor, Republican Vice President George Bush, several failures and unresolved international issues. Reagan (and Bush) had paid little attention to global environmental questions. Soil erosion reduced food production at a time when the world's population was growing rapidly. Toxic wastes, acid rain, shortages of clean water, the overcutting of forests, and the overgrazing of fields hurried environmental decline, which in turn burdened governments. A warming of the earth's climate owing to the "greenhouse effect" of carbon dioxide and other gases building up in the atmosphere, scientists reported, might raise ocean levels, flooding farmlands and dislocating millions of people. Unless corrected, these problems would spawn political unrest. Some positive signs appeared: population-control programs in many Third World nations; public-health programs providing an effective vaccine against malaria; immunization programs against measles and polio; and India's attainment of self-sufficiency in food production. But the Reagan administration barely noticed.

Environmental questions also figured in Canadian-American relations. Canadians grew alarmed that polluted American air in the form of acid rain was destroying their forests and contaminating their water. Tension between Ottawa and Washington reached an awkward high. Although Reagan showed scant interest in acid rain, he did launch negotiations leading to the United States–Canada Free Trade Agreement of 1988. This accord created the world's largest free trade area. The two nations exchanged more goods and services each year, worth about $166 billion in 1989, than any other two countries.

Any accounting of the Reagan legacy includes the president's failure to energize the peace process in the Middle East. The Iran-Contra scandal and intervention in Lebanon rank as major foreign-policy blunders. In Central America, Reagan registered a large death count, continued civil wars, economic disarray, and a bankrupt attachment to the *contras*. On South Africa, Congress had to push Reagan to express serious disapproval of apartheid. The trade and budget deficits grew to huge proportions in the Reagan years, and the United States became a debtor nation. Trade conflict with Japan intensified as the United States struggled to compete with the trans–Pacific power.

In the 1980s, after Vietnam and the Iranian hostage crisis, Americans worked to reassert their international supremacy. They built up massive military and nuclear forces; they financed insurgencies; they reaffirmed their self-appointed mission to purify an imperfect world; they restated their belief in American exceptionalism. In his upbeat farewell address, Ronald Reagan declared that "America is respected again in the world, and looked to for leadership." Other voices suggested that he "may have left time bombs ticking away for the future."

FURTHER READING FOR THE PERIOD 1977–1989

For overviews and various topics, see William C. Berman, *America's Right Turn* (1994); John Ehrman, *The Rise of Neoconservatism* (1995); Raymond L. Garthoff, *Détente and Confrontation* (1985) and *The Great Transition* (1994); Ole R. Holsti and James N. Rosenau, *American Leadership in World Affairs* (1984); Wilfred Loth, *Overcoming the Cold War* (2002); Don Oberdorfer, *From the Cold War to a New Era* (1998); Odd Arne Westad, ed., *The Fall of Détente* (1995); and William C. Wohlforth, *Cold War Endgame* (2003).

For Jimmy Carter and his foreign relations (specific policies and regions are listed later), see Douglas Brinkley, *The Unfinished Presidency* (1998); John Drumbell, *The Carter Presidency* (1993); Gary M. Fink and Hugh Davis Graham, eds., *The Carter Presidency* (1998); Burton I. Kaufman, *The Presidency of James Earl Carter, Jr.* (1993); David S. McLellan, *Cyrus Vance* (1985); Kenneth E. Morris, *Jimmy Carter, American Moralist* (1996); A. Glenn Mower, *Human Rights and American Foreign Policy* (1987); Jerel A. Rosati, *The Carter Administration's Quest for Global Community* (1987); David Skidmore, *Reversing Course* (1996); Gaddis Smith, *Morality, Reason, & Power* (1986); and Robert A. Strong, *Working in the World* (2000).

Reagan policies are studied in Coral Bell, *The Reagan Paradox* (1989); Michael K. Bohn, *The Achille Lauro Hijacking* (2004); Lou Cannon, *President Reagan* (1991); Richard S. Conley, *Reassessing the Reagan Presidency* (2003); Robert Dallek, *Ronald Reagan* (1984); Theodore Draper, *A Very Thin Line* (1991) (Iran-Contra); Beth A. Fischer, *The Reagan Reversal* (1997); Frances FitzGerald, *Way Out There in the Blue* (2000); Allan Gerson, *The Kirkpatrick Mission* (1991) (UN); Susan Jeffords, *Hard Bodies* (1993); Haynes Johnson, *Sleepwalking Through History* (1991); Peter Kornbluh and Malcolm Byrne, eds., *The Iran-Contra Scandal* (1993); Mark P. Lagon, *The Reagan Doctrine* (1994); Paul Lettow, *Ronald Reagan and the Quest to Abolish Nuclear Weapons* (2005); Morris Morley, *Crisis and Confrontation* (1988); Edmund Morris, *Dutch* (1999); William E. Pemberton, *Exit with Honor* (1997); Michael Rogin, *Ronald Reagan* (1987); Michael Schaller, *Reckoning with Reagan* (1992); Peter Schweitzer, *Reagan's War* (2002); James M. Scott, *Deciding to Intervene* (1996) (Reagan Doctrine); Gil Troy, *Morning in America* (2005); and David C. Wills, *The First War on Terrorism* (2004). Specific topics and regions are listed below.

Economic and environmental issues can be explored in C. Fred Bergsten and William R. Cline, *The United States–Japan Economic Problem* (1987); Edward Goldsmith and Nicolas Hildyard, eds., *The Earth Report* (1988); Edward M. Graham and Paul R. Klugman, *Foreign Direct Investment in the United States* (1995); Anne G. Keatley, ed., *Technological Frontiers and Foreign Relations* (1985); John H. Makin, *The Global Debt Crisis* (1984); John McCormick, *Reclaiming Paradise* (1989); Jürgen Schmandt et al., eds., *Acid Rain and Friendly Neighbors* (1988); Jeffrey J. Schott, *The Uruguay Round* (1994); Spencer Weart, *The Discovery of Global Warming* (2004); Gilbert R. Winham, *International Trade and the Tokyo Round Negotiations* (1986); and Donald Worster, ed., *The Ends of the Earth* (1988).

For relations with the Soviet Union (except for the nuclear arms race, listed below), see Dana H. Allin, *Cold War Illusions* (1995); Archie Brown, *The Gorbachev Factor* (1996); Alexander Dallin, *Black Box* (1985) (KAL 007); Seymour M. Hersh, *"The Target Is Destroyed"* (1986); Bruce Jentleson, *Pipeline Politics* (1986) (East-West energy trade); Robert G. Kaiser, *How Gorbachev Happened* (1991); Jack Matlock, *Reagan and Gorbachev*

(2004); Michael McCgwire, *Perestroika and Soviet National Security* (1991); Matthew Ouimet, *The Rise and Fall of the Brezhnev Doctrine in Soviet Foreign Policy* (2003); Timothy W. Ryback, *Rock Around the Bloc: A History of Rock Music in Eastern Europe and the Soviet Union* (1990); Leon V. Sigal, *Hang Separately* (2000); and Helene Sjursen, *The United States, Western Europe and the Polish Crisis* (2003).

For the nuclear arms race, SALT-II, SDI, and the antinuclear movement, Donald C. Baucom, *The Origins of SDI* (1992); Dan Caldwell, *The Dynamics of Domestic Politics and Arms Control* (1991) (SALT-II); David Callahan, *Dangerous Capabilities* (1990) (Nitze); Matthew Evangelista, *Innovation and the Arms Race* (1988); Jonathan Haslam, *The Soviet Union and the Politics of Nuclear Weapons in Europe* (1990); Edward T. Linenthal, *Symbolic Defense* (1989) (SDI); David S. Meyer, *A Winter of Discontent* (1990) (freeze); John Newhouse, *War and Peace in the Nuclear Age* (1989); Jerome Price, *The Antinuclear Movement* (1989); Thomas R. Rochon, *Mobilizing for Peace* (1988); Scott D. Sagan, *Moving Targets* (1989); Steven K. Smith and Douglas A. Wertman, *U.S.-Western European Relations During the Reagan Years* (1992); Strobe Talbott, *Endgame* (1979) (SALT-II), *Deadly Gambits* (1984), and *The Master of the Game* (1988) (Nitze); Douglas C. Waller, *Congress and the Nuclear Freeze* (1987); and Daniel Wirls, *Buildup* (1992).

The CIA, U.S. covert operations, counterinsurgency, and counterrevolution are explored in Anne H. Cahn, *Killing Détente* (1998); Loch Johnson, *America's Secret Power* (1989); Michael T. Klare and Peter Kornbluh, eds., *Low-Intensity Warfare* (1988); Douglas MacEachn, *U.S. Intelligence and Confrontation in Poland, 1980–1981* (2002); Kathryn S. Olmsted, *Challenging the Secret Government* (1996) (investigations of CIA); Joseph E. Persico, *Casey* (1990); D. Michael Shafer, *Deadly Paradigms* (1988); and Gregory F. Treverton, *Covert Action* (1987).

For U.S. relations with the Third World, see Richard E. Feinberg, *The Intemperate Zone* (1983); Melvin Gurtov and Ray Maghroori, *Roots of Failure* (1984); Gabriel Kolko, *Confronting the Third World* (1988); Stephen D. Krasner, *Structural Conflict* (1985); Barry Rubin, *Modern Dictators* (1987); and Marshall D. Shulman, ed., *East-West Tensions in the Third World* (1986).

Middle East topics, Arab-Israeli conflict, and the peace process are examined in George W. Ball, *Error and Betrayal in Lebanon* (1984); Mahmoud G. El-Warfally, *Imagery and Ideology in U.S. Policy Toward Libya* (1988); Nicholas Lahan, *Selling AWACS to Saudi Arabia* (2002); George Lenczowski, *American Presidents and the Middle East* (1989), Zachary Lochman and Joel Beinin, eds., *Intifada* (1989); A. F. K. Organski, *The $36 Billion Bargain* (1990) (aid to Israel); Don Peretz, *Intifada* (1990); William B. Quandt, *The Peace Process* (1993); Yezid Sayad, *Armed Struggle and the Search for State* (1997); David Schoenbaum, *The United States and the State of Israel* (1993); Steven L. Spiegel, *The Other Arab-Israeli Conflict* (1985); Joseph T. Stanik, *El Dorado Canyon* (2002); and Daniel Yergin, *The Prize* (1991) (oil).

For U.S.-Iranian relations and the hostage crisis, see James A. Bill, *The Eagle and the Lion* (1988); Charles-Phillippe David et al., *Foreign Policy in the White House* (1993); David Farber, *Taken Hostage* (2004); Mark J. Gasiorowski, *U.S. Foreign Policy and the Shah* (1991); James E. Goode, *The United States and Iran* (1997); David Harris, *The Crisis* (2005); Daniel Patrick Houghton, *U.S. Foreign Policy and the Iran Hostage Crisis* (2001), Russell L. Moses, *Freeing the Hostages* (1996); R. K. Ramazani, *Revolutionary Iran* (1987); Paul Ryan, *The Iranian Rescue Mission* (1985); Ofira Seliktat, *Failing the Crystal Ball Test* (2000) (Carter and Iran); William Shawcross, *The Shah's Last Ride* (1988); Gary Sick, *All Fall Down* (1985) and *October Surprise* (1991) (hostages and Reagan election); and Marvin Zonis, *Majestic Failure* (1991).

For Asia, see David Bain, *Sitting in Darkness* (1984) (Philippines); C. Fred Bergsten and William R. Cline, *The United States–Japan Economic Problem* (1987); Raymond Bonner, *Waltzing with a Dictator* (1987) (Marcos); H. W. Brands, *Bound to Empire* (1992) (Philippines); Roger Buckley, *U.S.-Japan Alliance Diplomacy* (1992); William H. Gleysteen, Jr., *Massive Entanglement, Marginal Influence* (1999) (South Korea); Harry Harding, *A Fragile Relationship* (1992) (China); Richard J. Kessler, *Rebellion and Repression in the Philippines* (1989); Walter LaFeber, *The Clash* (1997); and Edith Terry, *How Asia Got Rich* (2002).

For Latin America and the Panama Canal treaties, see David W. Engstrom, *Presidential Decision Making Adrift* (1997) (Mariel boatlift); J. Michael Hogan, *The Panama Canal in American Politics* (1986); Eldon Kenworthy, *America/Américas* (1995); Walter LaFeber, *The Panama Canal* (1989); Gordon K. Lewis, *Grenada* (1987); Abraham F. Lowenthal, ed., *Exporting Democracy* (1991); John Major, *Prize Possession* (1993) (Panama); Louis A.

Pérez, Jr., *Cuba and the United States* (1997); and Lars Schoultz, *Human Rights and United States Policy Toward Latin America* (1981), *National Security and United States Policy Toward Latin America* (1987), and *Beneath the United States* (1998).

Mexican–American relations are the subject of George W. Grayson, *The Politics of Mexican Oil* (1980) and *Oil and Mexican Foreign Policy* (1988); Jacqueline Mazza, *Don't Disturb the Neighbors* (2001); Robert A. Pastor and Jorge G. Castañeda, *Limits of Friendship* (1988); W. Dirk Raat, *Mexico and the United States* (1996); and Stanley Weintraub, *Marriage of Convenience* (1989).

For Central America, especially Nicaragua and El Salvador, see Ariel C. Armony, *Argentina, the United States, and the Anti-Communist Crusade in Central America* (1997); Cynthia J. Arnson, *Crossroads* (1994); Morris J. Blachman et al., eds., *Confronting Revolution* (1986); Kenneth M. Coleman and George C. Herring, eds., *Understanding the Central American Crisis* (1991); Lesley Gill, *The School of the Americas* (2004); Martha Honey, *Hostile Acts* (1994) (Costa Rica); Stephen Kinzer, *Blood of Brothers* (1991) (Nicaragua); Peter Kornbluh, *Nicaragua* (1988); Walter LaFeber, *Inevitable Revolutions* (1993); Anthony Lake, *Somoza Falling* (1989); William M. LeoGrande, *Our Own Backyard* (1998); Morris H. Morley, *Washington, Somoza, and the Sandinistas* (1994); Holly Sklar, *Washington's War on Nicaragua* (1988); Christian Smith, *Resisting Reagan* (1996); Gaddis Smith, *The Last Years of the Monroe Doctrine, 1945–1993* (1994); and Thomas W. Walker, ed., *Revolution and Counterrevolution in Nicaragua* (1991).

South Africa and African questions are treated in Gerald J. Bender et al., eds., *African Crisis Areas and U.S. Foreign Policy* (1985); Donald R. Culverson, *Contesting Apartheid* (1999); Alexander deWaal, *Famine That Kills* (1989); Richard W. Hull, *American Enterprise in South Africa* (1990); Janice Love, *The U.S. Anti-Apartheid Movement* (1985); Robert K. Massie, *Loosing the Bonds* (1997) (South Africa); Martin Meredith, *In the Name of Apartheid* (1988); William Minter, *King Solomon's Mines Revisited* (1986); Francis N. Nesbitt, *Race for Sanctions: African Americans Against Apartheid, 1946–1994* (2004); and Jennifer S. Whitaker, *How Can Africa Survive?* (1987).

See also Robert L. Beisner, ed., *Guide to American Foreign Relations Since 1600* (2003).

For comprehensive coverage of foreign-relations topics, see the articles in the four-volume *Encyclopedia of U.S. Foreign Relations* (1997), edited by Bruce W. Jentleson and Thomas G. Paterson.

CHAPTER 12

Imperial America: The United States and the World Since 1989

✳ *9/11 and After*

A PRESIDENTIAL SPEECHWRITER called it "the worst crime ever recorded on video-tape." Early in the morning of September 11, 2001, fifteen Saudi Arabians and four Egyptians, secretly armed with box-cutters, boarded four commercial airliners. Two planes took off from Boston, the other two from Newark, New Jersey, and Washington, D.C. At 8:46 A.M. and 9:03 A.M., respectively, the two hijacked Boston aircraft exploded into the north and south towers of the World Trade Center in New York City. At 9:39 A.M., the Washington jetliner struck and destroyed a portion of the Pentagon. At 10:10 A.M., the Newark aircraft, possibly intended for the White House, plunged to a fiery demise in a field in western Pennsylvania after passengers overpowered the plane's hijackers. By midday both World Trade Center towers had collapsed and the death toll numbered 2,823 in New York City, 45 in Pennsylvania, and 189 in Washington, D.C. The victims came from more than eighty countries around the world.

Stunned Americans gaped in disbelief as television networks played and re-played the horrific montage. The novelist John Updike watched from a tenth-floor apartment in Brooklyn Heights as the south tower "fell straight down like an elevator, with a tinkling shiver and a groan of concussion distinct across the mile of air." New York mayor Rudy Giuliani, rushing to the World Trade Center, "looked up and saw a man jump out—above the fire, must have been at least [a] hundred stories—and my eye followed him, almost transfixed, all the way down." In Florida at the time of the attacks, President George W. Bush viewed replays of the second New York explosion and commented tersely: "We're at war." That evening, over national television, he announced what came to be known as the Bush Doctrine: "We will make no distinction between the terrorists who committed these acts and those who harbor them." Before going to bed he noted in his diary: "The Pearl Harbor of the twenty-first century took place today."

313

September 11, 2001. Billowing smoke over the Manhattan skyline marked the first hostile attacks on the American mainland since British forces burned Washington in 1814. The United States found itself at war with international terrorists. (© Reuters/CORBIS)

In the nation's capital, the intelligence community belatedly "connected the dots." Only minutes before the attacks, CIA Director George J. Tenet told a member of Congress that the Saudi exile Osama bin Laden and his terrorist network Al-Qaeda (Arabic for "the Base"), operating out of Afghanistan, were "going to do something big." Tenet proved prophetic. Federal investigators pieced together evidence that the nineteen hijackers—trained in Afghanistan and organized and financed in Germany, England, and Spain with money sent from around the world—had entered the United States on tourist or student visas. They adopted American lifestyles to avoid suspicion, in some cases living in quiet, middle-class communities for several years prior to the attacks. Some took rudimentary flight training in California and Florida, which enabled them to operate the jetliners after they had killed or intimidated pilots and crews. Communicating primarily through the Internet, the terrorists exploited "the very global transportation, communication, and economic system they protested" by attacking Wall Street and the Pentagon, the symbols of America's global predominance. Osama bin Laden himself soon appeared on videotape to praise the hijackers: "Here is America struck by God Almighty in one of its vital organs. . . . God has blessed a group of vanguard Muslims, the forefront of Islam, to destroy America!"

The events of 9/11 (soon a universally adopted shorthand) triggered what has been called "the most rapid and dramatic change in the history of U.S. foreign policy." Before the terrorist attacks, the Bush administration had espoused a realist foreign policy that designated China and Russia as Washington's competitors and rejected nation building in the developing world. Less than a year after 9/11, the administration acknowledged that "we are menaced less by fleets and armies than by catastrophic technologies falling into the hands of the embittered few." Instead of global rivalry, "today, the world's great powers find themselves . . . united by common dangers of terrorist violence and chaos." The new approach also stressed the need to use force preemptively against the "unknown, the uncertain, the unseen, and the unexpected."

Even as most of the world after 9/11 rallied behind Washington's demand that the Islamic fundamentalist Taliban government of Afghanistan hand over bin Laden and his followers, President Bush declared a global war against terrorism "to rid the world of evil." Notwithstanding a successful autumn military campaign that ousted the Taliban from Kabul and bloodied Al-Qaeda (but failed to find bin Laden), Bush raised the stakes in his State of the Union address in January 2002. He singled out Iraq, Iran, and North Korea "and their terrorist allies" as "an axis of evil, arming to threaten the peace of the world [with] weapons of mass destruction." Iraq especially posed a "grave and growing danger." Bush gave notice: "I will not stand by as peril grows closer and closer."

Bush officials told the British in July 2002 that "military action" against Iraq "was now seen as inevitable" and that "intelligence and facts were being fixed around that policy." Linkages between Saddam Hussein's regime and 9/11 proved elusive, despite claims that Washington had "bulletproof" evidence of Hussein's ties to Al-Qaeda. Administration hawks apparently saw an opportunity to build a new pillar of U.S. power in the Middle East, replacing Saudi Arabia with a democratic Iraq that was friendly to Israel, harbored no terrorists, and could pump oil for the world economy. Hard-liners led by Secretary of Defense Donald H. Rumsfeld, Deputy Secretary of Defense Paul Wolfowitz, and Vice President Richard Cheney increasingly argued for "regime change" in Baghdad because Hussein allegedly threatened "America and the world with horrible poisons and diseases and gases and atomic weapons." A September eleventh with weapons of mass destruction would kill "tens of thousands of innocent men, women, and children," warned Rumsfeld. It was "a slam dunk" that Iraq had the weapons, Tenet assured Bush, and another adviser warned that "we don't want the smoking gun to be a mushroom cloud." Bush admonished the United Nations on the first anniversary of 9/11: "If [other governments] do not act, America will." When ten million people in six hundred cities around the world marched on February 15, 2003, against the impending invasion of Iraq, the president claimed never to listen to "focus groups." When the UN Security Council debated a resolution for war against Iraq later that month, U.S. officials told allies that the decision "is ours, and we have made it. The only question now is whether the Council will go along with it or not." Calling Washington a "reckless," "naïve," "simplistic," and "unilateralist . . . cowboy," France, Germany, Russia, and China mustered a majority to defeat an explicit UN resolution. Backed by a congressional joint resolution authorizing military force, Bush went ahead and attacked Iraq anyway.

George W. Bush (b. 1946). Looking pensive, the president viewed the damaged Pentagon from a helicopter on September 14, 2001. Prior to the terrorist attacks, the Bush administration had pursued a "go-it-alone" foreign policy—rejecting the Kyoto Protocol on global warming, withdrawing from the Anti-Ballistic Missile Treaty, refusing to back the International Criminal Court, and showing little interest in negotiations with North Korea or between Israel and the Palestinians. In *Against All Enemies* (2004), the White House counterterrorism expert Richard Clarke claimed that Bush had done a "terrible job" by ignoring the threat from Al-Qaeda prior to 9/11. Nonetheless, Bush won reelection in 2004 by a narrow margin over Democratic senator John F. Kerry of Massachusetts. (AP/Wide World Photos)

WANTED DEAD OR ALIVE. Osama bin Laden (b. 1957). The mastermind behind 9/11 and Al-Qaeda's earlier attacks on the U.S. embassies in Kenya and Tanzania (1998) and the navy destroyer *Cole* (2000), bin Laden had declared a *jihad* (or holy war) against Americans. Distributed by the Rewards for Justice Program through the State Department, matchbook covers bearing the Al-Qaeda leader's likeness offered payments of up to $5 million for information leading to his capture. (Robert E. Goodrich)

Operation Iraqi Freedom began on March 20, 2003, and the ensuing twenty-six day military campaign proved spectacularly successful. At a cost of only 161 dead, the U.S.- and British-led coalition, numbering some 250,000 troops, conquered Iraq in "almost half the time, with one-third the casualties, and at one-fourth the cost" of the first Gulf War of 1991. Despite gloomy prognostications that Baghdad would become another Stalingrad, superior weapons and tactics turned the war into a rout. The toppling of Saddam Hussein's statue in the heart of Baghdad on April 9 signaled the end of his brutal regime. Coalition forces occupied the rest of battered Iraq within a week. On May 1, greeted by a huge banner spelling MISSION ACCOMPLISHED, Bush made a flashy tail-hook landing in a navy jet aboard the returning aircraft carrier *Abraham Lincoln* and pronounced the official end of major combat operations.

Military triumph brought gloating and grand expectations. Victory proved that virile Americans were "from Mars" and hesitant Europeans ("old Europe," in Rumsfeld's dismissive words) were "from Venus." Bush officials likened the coming democratization of Iraq to that of Germany or Japan after World War II, a "demonstration effect" for the Arab world so that "it will no longer produce ideologies of hatred that lead men to fly airplanes into buildings in New York and Washington."

Yet euphoria dissipated quickly. After months of futile searching, even after interviewing captured Iraqi scientists, the chief inspector of the 1,400-strong U.S. Iraq Survey Group admitted that "we were all wrong" about the weapons of mass destruction that had supposedly posed such an imminent threat; nor did the belated capture of Saddam Hussein in December 2003 ease the increasingly dangerous tasks of military occupation. From looting in the first weeks after the fall of Baghdad, to small hit-and-run attacks during June, to suicide truck bombings in August, to more coordinated assaults well into 2004, American Occupation forces faced an escalating "guerrilla-type campaign"—a "long, hard slog," in Rumsfeld's phrase. The Pentagon and State Department struggled to devise a scheme to transfer sovereignty to a provisional government, to train a professional army and police forces, and to plan economic reconstruction in a country where the unemployment rate reached as high as 60 percent. Instead of deterring terrorism, the chaos following victory seemed to attract extremists to Iraq, including members of Al-Qaeda, who "weren't there before." The number of U.S. soldiers killed soon surpassed the death toll (138) during the combat war, reaching more than 1,700 by August 2005. Faced with mounting occupation costs of $4 billion per month, Bush asked Congress on the second anniversary of 9/11 for an additional $87 billion in reconstruction funds, eventually increasing the federal deficit to a record $427 billion by 2005. The president pledged to do "whatever is necessary" to achieve "this central victory in the war against terror." Despite successful elections in early 2005 in which a Shi'ite coalition won a majority of seats in the new Iraqi parliament, substantial U.S. forces remained to combat the growing insurgency.

Thus did the United States persevere in "a world war" against "Islamic fundamentalism." This new Cold War for the "American Millennium" once again seemed to ensnare the nation in a protracted international conflict that invited possibly limitless commitments. Vice President Cheney predicted that the crusade against ter-

UDAY SADDAM HUSAYN
National Assembly Member/
Olympic Chairman/
Saddam Feyadeen Chief

QUSAY SADDAM HUSAYN
AL-TIKRITI
Special Security Organization
(SSO) Supervisor/Baêth Party
Military Bureau Deputy Chairman

Uday Hussein (1964–2003) and Qusay Hussein (1966–2003). These Pentagon "playing cards" with photographs of Saddam Hussein's sons (the Ace of Hearts and the Ace of Clubs) were part of an effort to identify leading Iraqi officials as "high-value targets" during and after the invasion of Iraq. Uday and Qusay were killed during a firefight in Mosul by soldiers of the U.S. 101st Airborne's Second Combat Team in July 2003. (Liberty Playing Cards)

rorism might require military action against "forty or fifty countries" and last more than fifty years. This time the doctrine of preemptive war, rather than containment, propelled decisionmaking. "A la carte multilateralism," as one State Department official called it, replaced collective security. States of the former Soviet bloc became America's new allies, while many former Western partners distanced themselves from Washington's increasingly imperial preeminence. The world had been considerably reshuffled in little more than a decade since George W. Bush's father, George H. W. Bush, presided over the end of the first Cold War and hailed a "new world order" of peace and prosperity.

The Earthquakes of 1989–1991

The post–Cold War era had started promisingly enough with the fall of the Berlin Wall in 1989. When East German officials unexpectedly announced on November 9, 1989, that citizens could leave the country through the infamous twenty-eight-mile-long Berlin Wall, a raucous, three-day celebration ensued. Thousands of Berliners cavorted atop the ten-foot Wall in front of the Brandenburg Gate. Down came sections of the concrete edifice, and workers dismantled the famous platform where John F. Kennedy and Ronald Reagan had hurled defiant speeches across the Wall. West German chancellor Helmut Kohl told President George H. W. Bush by phone: "Without the United States this day would not have been possible." The day after the Wall came down, moreover, a bloodless coup in Sofia, Bulgaria, ousted Todor Zhivkov, the hard-line Communist party boss for the past thirty-five years.

By the end of November, mass demonstrations were peacefully terminating communist rule in Czechoslovakia, and during Christmas week a bloody popular uprising toppled the tyrannical regime of Nicolae Ceausescu in Romania. It was "one of those rare times," according to *Time* magazine, "when the tectonic plates of history shift beneath men's feet, and nothing after is quite the same."

The seismic events of 1989 would not have occurred without major impetus from Soviet president Mikhail S. Gorbachev. Since his accession to leadership in the Kremlin in March 1985, Gorbachev's bold effort at reforming the Soviet Union had acquired a momentum of its own. To revive the sick Soviet economy, plagued by declining productivity and a demoralized work force, the Soviet leader warned that "everyone must change, from the worker to the minister to the secretary of the central committee." What started out as a fairly limited foreign-policy agenda—ending the war in Afghanistan, improving relations with China, and negotiating arms-control agreements with the United States—quickly mushroomed.

Gorbachev identified the huge drain on Soviet resources caused by the superpower competition as one area of potential savings. He decided on military cuts *despite* the Reagan military buildup, "wasteful expenditures that we were not going to match," he later insisted. Thus, in his "Fulton in reverse" speech of December 1988, Gorbachev astounded the world by announcing that over the next two years his country would unilaterally cut its military forces by 500,000 men and 10,000 tanks. In visits to Western Europe in spring and summer 1989, the charismatic Soviet leader called for a "common European home" that would eliminate "the probability of an armed clash." Gorbachev quietly passed the word to East European officials that Soviet troops would not intervene to put down uprisings.

The veteran communist oligarchs of Eastern Europe heard the message and lost their nerve. At year's end in Prague, a large sign tallied up the results: "Poland—10 Years / Hungary—10 Months / East Germany—10 Weeks / Czechoslovakia—10 Days / Romania—10 Hours." Not expecting Eastern Europe to self-destruct "like a beheaded Hydra," Gorbachev encouraged the process. "Life punishes harshly anyone who is left behind in politics," he said in advising East Germans to open the Wall to "avoid an explosion."

The toppling of communist regimes in Eastern Europe had repercussions inside the Soviet Union. During late August 1989, a million citizens of Estonia, Latvia, and Lithuania linked arms to form a human chain four hundred miles long in protest against the fiftieth anniversary of Stalin's annexation of the Baltic states. In March 1990 the Lithuanian Parliament declared formal independence from the Soviet Union, and Estonia's governing body renounced Soviet law. In May Latvia declared independence, and in July Ukraine proclaimed itself sovereign. Gorbachev tried to slow the surging separatist tide, but he promised not to use force.

Gorbachev soon went from confident master of events to bewildered victim of forces he had unleashed. He won the Nobel Peace Prize but lost his country. By the end of 1991 the economically hobbled Soviet Union had disintegrated into fifteen squabbling independent nations. The Communist party disbanded, and the weakened central government recognized the independence of the three Baltic states. Russia declared its independence and with many of the republics formed the Commonwealth of Independent States in December. Boris Yeltsin's Russian government

McDonald's in Moscow. A worldwide symbol of capitalist bounty came to Moscow in early 1990 when McDonald's opened in Pushkin Square. McDonald's Canadian subsidiary had spent fourteen years negotiating a contract with Soviet authorities. By 2003, 29,000 McDonald's in 120 countries were serving Big Macs to 16 billion customers per year. (Used with permission from McDonald's Corporation)

soon took over the Kremlin, the KGB, and the Soviet Foreign Ministry. Gorbachev stepped down. On Christmas day 1991, at 7:32 P.M. (Moscow time), the red hammer-and-sickle flag atop the Kremlin fluttered downward for the last time.

Indispensable Nation: Bush-Clinton-Bush and Post–Cold War Priorities

Studied nonchalance appeared to be the official U.S. reaction to the opening of the Berlin Wall. By then the Bush administration had made up its collective mind that Gorbachev was "for real" and that Washington would cooperate with Moscow in smoothing the transition to a post–Cold War world. The quiescent response to events in Berlin was deliberate—a signal that the United States did not seek to exploit the upheavals in Eastern Europe.

Prudence became the watchword. George H. W. Bush and his foreign-policy team were cautious about almost everything. Adaptable rather than ideologically zealous, conservative, fearful of doing the wrong thing, Bush prided himself on "my hyperadrenalin, political instincts." His conservatism had deep roots. Born in Massachusetts in 1924 to a wealthy, old Yankee family, Bush became a decorated navy pilot in World War II, attended Yale (B.A., 1948), and then moved to Texas, where he amassed greater wealth in the booming oil industry of the 1950s. After serving in Congress (1967–1971) and as ambassador to the United Nations (1971–1973), U.S. representative to China (1974–1975), and CIA director (1976–1977), he unsuccessfully challenged Ronald Reagan for the Republican presidential nomination in 1980 and then accepted second spot on the ticket. Always a loyalist, Bush supported Reagan's policies.

Bush selected a compatible secretary of state in James A. Baker III, a close friend from Texas who had skillfully managed his political campaigns. Like Bush, born

Makers of American Foreign Relations Since 1989

Presidents	Secretaries of State
George H. W. Bush, 1989–1993	James A. Baker III, 1989–1992
	Lawrence Eagleburger, 1992–1993
William J. Clinton, 1993–2001	Warren M. Christopher, 1993–1997
	Madelaine K. Albright, 1997–2001
George W. Bush, 2001–	Colin L. Powell, 2001–2005
	Condoleezza Rice, 2005–

(1930) to the elite, Baker had become a Texas corporate lawyer after graduation from Princeton University. "A man I can accomplish things with," said Soviet foreign minister Eduard Shevardnadze after their first meeting. National Security Adviser Brent Scowcroft worked easily with Baker and with Baker's successor, Lawrence Eagleburger, without the feuding of previous administrations. A former army general "with few edges and fewer enemies," Scowcroft acted as facilitator, broker, and coordinator, not as architect of policy.

The election of five-term Arkansas governor William J. Clinton in 1992 seemed to bring a different generational perspective to the White House. A graduate of Georgetown University and Yale Law School, Rhodes scholar, Vietnam War protester and draft avoider, and at age forty-six the second youngest elected president, Clinton pledged during the campaign to maintain America's global leadership. Yet he hoped to "keep foreign policy submerged" until he dealt with domestic priorities such as taxes, deficits, economic growth, health care, and welfare reform. His campaign slogan, "It's the economy, stupid," might also have applied to Russian relations, for Clinton later regretted that "we should have done more—*much* more" to underwrite Russia's transition to a market economy. Notwithstanding Clinton's election to a second term in 1996, Republican majorities in Congress after 1994 brought cuts in foreign aid, delays in ambassadorial appointments, and the Senate's rejection of the Comprehensive Nuclear Test Ban Treaty in 1999. Also bedeviling the president in 1998–1999 were unsuccessful impeachment proceedings started by Congress after Clinton's apparent perjury over a sex scandal.

Sixty-seven-year-old Warren M. Christopher became Clinton's first secretary of state. This alumnus of the University of Southern California and Stanford Law School had served as deputy secretary of state during the Carter years and had negotiated the release of American hostages from Iran in 1980–1981. Disciplined, dignified, and dour, Christopher proved an indefatigable negotiator. Replacing Christopher for the second term was UN ambassador Madeleine Albright, a former Georgetown University professor who resurrected Cold War certitudes. The blunt-speaking Albright quickly earned a hawkish reputation. "If we have to use force," she announced, "it is because we are America. We are the indispensable nation."

Christopher maintained collegial relations with Clinton's national security affairs adviser, Anthony Lake. This Harvard and Princeton graduate exhibited little of the egotism and manipulative qualities often found in White House advisers. Asked to define a new grand strategy for the post–Cold War era, Lake in 1993 proposed the "enlargement" of free markets and democracies as a substitute for containment. Lake's equally self-effacing successor, Samuel R. "Sandy" Berger, outlined more concrete goals for Clinton's second term—integrating Eastern and Western Europe without provoking Russia; liberal trade expansion; cooperation against "transnational threats" such as terrorism and drugs; and working toward a "strong, stable Asia Pacific Community."

As the U.S. economy improved in the 1990s, Clinton quickly recognized that the "new virility symbols are exports and productivity and growth rates" rather than nuclear missiles. He skillfully lobbied through Congress the North American Free Trade Agreement (NAFTA). In 1994, Washington signed the "Uruguay Round" of GATT accords liberalizing world trade. The agreement also created a new World Trade Organization, which Clinton hailed as promoting "a vision of economic renewal" for the United States and the world. In pushing as well for U.S. participation in both a future Free Trade Area of the Americas and the Asia Pacific Economic Cooperation forum, the president preached the new "gospel of geoeconomics." Worrisome, however, was the 1998 U.S. trade deficit of $233.4 billion—a record.

Nowhere was the primacy of geoeconomics more evident than in American initiatives, in conjunction with the International Monetary Fund (IMF), to act as the "drivewheel" of the international political economy. When the Mexican peso collapsed in 1994, Washington fashioned an international financial bailout that included a $50 billion credit, with the United States ($20 billion) and the IMF ($18 billion) the chief backers. The announcement of a $10.2 billion credit line to Russia during Boris Yeltsin's reelection campaign in 1996 clearly reflected Washington's policy preferences. The United States contributed $5 billion to an overall $41.5 billion loan to Brazil in fall 1998, provided that Brazil implement IMF-approved measures to balance its huge budget deficit.

During the Asian financial crisis of 1997–1998, U.S. Treasury officials, working through the IMF, orchestrated a financial package of $115 billion, in return for which Asian countries promised banking and budget reforms. With financial markets gyrating wildly in January 1998, Deputy Treasury Secretary Lawrence Summers jetted to China, Hong Kong, Thailand, Malaysia, Singapore, and South Korea to contain the "Asian economic flu." Despite leftist complaints that IMF requirements undercut social welfare reforms and increased unemployment, Summers contrasted Clinton's successful rescue with the Coolidge-Hoover failure to assist the war-stricken European economies in the 1920s and 1930s. Clinton's successor reaffirmed the "Washington consensus" in support of free trade and globalization by pledging after the World Trade Center attacks that "we will defeat [the terrorists] by expanding and encouraging world trade."

Fifty-four-year-old George W. Bush, eldest son of the ex-president, entered the White House in 2001. The younger Bush graduated from Yale University and Harvard Business School, drilled for oil in Texas, and briefly owned the Texas Rangers baseball team. An excessive drinker in his youth, Bush embraced religion at age forty and modeled himself on Sam Houston, another famous Texan, whose victory over alcohol had been "transformative." During the 2000 campaign, the self-described "gut player" and "clear-eyed realist" promised humility and "moral clarity."

Madeleine Korbel Albright (b. 1937). Born in Prague, the daughter of a Czech diplomat who defected to the United States in 1948, Albright was raised as a Roman Catholic and apparently did not learn until she became secretary that her parents had been born Jewish and three of her grandparents had died in the Holocaust. After attending Wellesley College (B.A. 1959) and earning a Ph.D. at Columbia University (1976), Albright served on the National Security Council staff during the Carter administration and later taught political science at Georgetown University. As Clinton's ambassador to the United Nations (1993–1996), she at first supported the UN's expanded role in international peacekeeping. In her memoir *Madame Secretary* (2003), she summed up Clinton's foreign policy as "determined to do the right thing but in a tough-minded way." (Bureau of Public Affairs, U.S. Department of State)

Bush chose two African Americans, Colin Powell and Condoleezza Rice, as secretary of state and national security adviser, respectively. Powell had already served as national security adviser under Reagan and as chair of the Joint Chiefs of Staff under the elder Bush and Clinton. A reluctant warrior, Powell often clashed with the hawkish defense secretary Rumsfeld, who once said that Powell's job "is to talk them to death, and mine is to hit them over the head." Despite "all the Texas, Alamo macho that made Powell uncomfortable," his soldierly code of obedience kept him in "my own lane," as he put it. Once, however, when told that his boss slept early and soundly, Powell retorted: "I sleep like a baby, too—every two hours I wake up screaming." Rice, a former Stanford University political scientist, tried to coordinate between contending factions, and eventually succeeded Powell as secretary of state in 2005. In her first year she regarded Iraq and terrorism as peripheral issues ("chump change") and wanted to "get on with the big issues: Russia, China, NATO expansion." Priorities changed after 9/11.

Russian Disintegration, German Reunification, NATO Expansion, Balkan Hell

The turning point in Soviet-American relations seems to have been Secretary Baker's visit to Moscow in early May 1989, when Gorbachev offered specific reductions for the Conventional Forces in Europe negotiations (CFE) that came close to NATO's proposals. A cordial meeting in September between Baker and Foreign Minister Shevardnadze in Jackson Hole, Wyoming, broke the impasse over Strategic Arms Reduction Talks (START) when the Soviets dropped their demand that the United States abandon its SDI research. Gorbachev prompted jubilation at the Malta summit in December by renouncing Soviet "bridgeheads in Cuba and Central America" and recognizing America's permanent role in Europe. At the Washington summit of June 1990, the senior Bush and Gorbachev signed agreements to improve trade, reduce chemical weapons, expand university undergraduate exchanges, and negotiate deeper cuts in strategic arms.

Bush continued his special relationship with Gorbachev over the next two years. During Germany's rapid reunification Bush helped to ensure Soviet acquiescence by emphasizing that only membership in NATO could keep the new Germany from ever moving aggressively eastward. When Iraq invaded Kuwait in early August 1990, Washington and Moscow jointly called for an "international cutoff of all arms supplies" to Iraq. Bush kept in telephone touch with Gorbachev throughout the Gulf crisis. The relationship also paid off in the START-I accord signed in Moscow in July 1991. The treaty limited each nuclear superpower to 1,600 delivery vehicles and 6,000 strategic nuclear devices. Only 4,900 such devices could be carried by intercontinental ballistic missiles (ICBMs) or submarine-launched ballistic missiles (SLBMs). The remaining 1,100 devices permitted under the treaty included warheads and bombs carried by cruise missiles and strategic bombers.

Then came the abortive coup against Gorbachev of August 18–21. With Russian president Boris Yeltsin and his top aides holed up in the Russian parliament building, Bush ordered the National Security Agency to help Yeltsin make "secure calls" to Soviet military commanders. When the revolt fizzled, legitimate authority shifted to Yeltsin and the Russian republic. Even though Bush saw a strong central government as essential for keeping control over the Soviet nuclear arsenal, he quickly adapted to a Yeltsin-led Russia, as evidenced by a $24-billion Western aid package to Russia. Just before Bush left office in January 1993, he and Yeltsin signed a START-II agreement in Moscow that provided for the cutting of nuclear warheads and bombs to 3,500 (U.S.) and 2,997 (Russia) and for eliminating all multiple warhead (MIRV) intercontinental missiles by the year 2003.

Clinton also pursued a "Russia first" policy. Viewing Yeltsin as "the personification of reform," Clinton's principal expert on Russian affairs, Strobe Talbott, urged "shock therapy" and tightfisted monetarism to create "the kind of Russia we want," despite high unemployment and the removal of safety nets for the Russian people. Clinton regularly wrote Yeltsin detailed letters and gave Yeltsin unconditional support when he dissolved the Russian Duma (parliament) in October 1993 and then turned army guns on recalcitrant legislators.

Critics claimed that by sticking to Yeltsin "like Krazy Glue," Clinton was repeating Bush's mistake with Gorbachev. Such criticism seemed valid, as Russia's gross national product fell by 20 percent during the first four years of reforms, as inflation ate up personal savings, as thousands of Russian troops failed to suppress a revolt in the breakaway republic of Chechnya in 1994–1996, and as a Russian Mafia exploited a growing black market in Russia's cities. Notwithstanding several summit meetings with "my friend Bill," Yeltsin's failing health and inability to cope with Russia's economic crisis made him an unreliable partner. Nor could more than $60 billion in Western loans after 1992 prevent the Russian economy from collapsing. Yeltsin's successor after 1999, former KGB officer Vladimir Putin, brought a modicum of stability to the Kremlin, and his immediate support for America's war against terrorism after 9/11 earned him the status of "soul brother" to President George W. Bush. Despite Washington's unilateral withdrawal from the ABM Treaty in November 2001, Bush and Putin signed a treaty in May 2002 wherein each country promised to reduce its strategic nuclear warheads to between 1,700 and 2,200 by the year 2012. Given its own "terrorist" threat from Chechen separatists, Russia's continued alignment with the West under Putin seemed far preferable to links "with the Iraqs and Irans, the North Koreas, and Cubas of the world."

As for the new Germany, Chancellor Kohl put forward a plan for confederation between East and West Germany, thus making reunification "a matter for Germans to decide." East Germany's citizens continued to migrate to the West at a high rate. Local government, public services, the economy, and civic morale in the GDR steadily eroded. In early 1990, West German politicians and parties built alliances in the East for an anticipated post-election unification. The Kohl-supported center-conservative coalition won a landslide victory in the March GDR elections. Kohl initiated currency union and economic merger in July 1990. Then, in September, the four powers agreed to end their postwar occupation. In October the two Germanies formally reunited. Bush's advisers believed that "an unattached Germany on the loose in Central Europe" looked more threatening to Moscow "than one embedded in NATO." Gorbachev soon dropped objections to a reunited Germany in NATO in exchange for a promise of Western economic aid and a smaller German army.

Kohl moved quickly to dispel fears of "hob-nailed boots and spike helmets" by limiting future troop strength and pledging never to build nuclear, chemical, or biological weapons. Germany became the dominant voice in the European Community (EC), pressed for aid to Eastern Europe and the former Soviet republics, and pledged billions of dollars (but not troops) to the Gulf War. Steadfast in their commitment to European integration and NATO, Germans later contributed to peace-keeping missions in the Persian Gulf, Somalia, Yugoslavia, and Afghanistan. Kohl's successor, Gerhard Schroeder, continued to cooperate by deploying troops and war-planes in the Kosovo conflict in 1999. Differences over Iraq in 2002–2003 temporarily "poisoned" relations, as Schroeder opposed Washington's unilateral "adventure" and his justice minister compared George W. Bush to the "Nazi Adolf."

The conversion of the Economic Community into the European Union (EU) through ratification of the Maastricht Treaty in fall 1993 advanced integration in the west, but European reluctance to intervene in Bosnia underscored the continent's continued disunity. In the Eastern European nations, Poland, Hungary, and Czechoslovakia (divided into Czech and Slovak republics in 1993) progressed most quickly in organizing market economies and democratic governments. The other former Soviet republics and clients faced smoldering ethnic and national rivalries long frozen by the Cold War. The EU Council decided in 1995 to establish a European Central Bank, issue a common currency (the "Euro"), and complete the European Monetary Union by July 2002. In 2002 the EU did invite Estonia, Latvia, Lithuania, Cyprus, the Czech Republic, Hungary, Malta, Poland, Slovenia, and Slovakia to join, with full integration achieved in May 2004.

President Clinton announced in 1994 that the question of NATO expansion eastward was no longer "whether" but "when and how." He publicly designated Poland, Hungary, and the Czech Republic as the first beneficiaries of NATO membership. European leaders proceeded to rubber-stamp Clinton's proposals, notwithstanding George F. Kennan's prediction that this "most fateful error" would "impel Russian foreign policy in directions decidedly not to our liking." The three new members officially joined NATO in March 1999, and in March 2004 seven more countries joined the alliance: Estonia, Latvia, Lithuania, Slovenia, Slovakia, Romania, and Bulgaria. Russia accepted partnership status.

NATO had already demonstrated its ineffectiveness in dealing with the Balkan crisis. Despite CIA predictions of bloody ethnic violence in Yugoslavia, the Bush administration deferred to European allies when they recognized an independent Croatia and Slovenia in summer 1991. Serbia proclaimed a new Federal Republic of Yugoslavia (including Montenegro) and incited Serbs living in the other republics—especially in Bosnia—to take up arms. Croats and Muslims living in Bosnia declared an independent state. After Bosnia-Herzegovina became independent in April 1992, Serbs began to shell Sarajevo, the city where a 1914 assassination had triggered World War I. Bosnian Serbs grabbed territory and displaced Bosnian Muslims through the horrors of "ethnic cleansing," which included the mass rape of Muslim women by Serbian soldiers. Serbian militia seized approximately 70 percent of the Bosnian hinterland. France and Britain dispatched "Blue Helmets" (UN troops) to safeguard relief supplies but rejected military intervention. By 1993 perhaps as many as 150,000 people had perished.

President William Jefferson Clinton (b. 1946) and Richard C. Holbrooke (b. 1941).   Photographed in 1997, President Clinton (right) was using crutches because of a knee injury. Clinton's presidency subsequently suffered a serious blow when a sex scandal caused him to become only the second president to be impeached. A former aide to Henry Kissinger, Holbrooke served in Jimmy Carter's State Department and later as ambassador to Germany, assistant secretary of state for Europe, and chief diplomatic troubleshooter in the Balkans for the Clinton administration. After successfully negotiating the 1995 Dayton agreement, which ended the war in Bosnia, Holbrooke in 1998 helped to broker a temporary cease-fire in the southern Yugoslavian province of Kosovo, where Muslim ethnic Albanians battled against their Serbian overlords. (White House Photo)

Clinton inherited this "problem from hell." Americans feared getting bogged down in age-old ethnic rivalries impervious to outside influence. The Pentagon took note of the rugged terrain and told Clinton: "We do deserts, we don't do mountains." Although Clinton issued warnings to the Serbs and proclaimed America's humane concern, he lacked foreign support and a domestic consensus. He proposed lifting the arms embargo against Bosnia and launching air strikes against the Bosnian Serbs, but NATO balked because of its own peacekeeping forces on the ground.

Starting in February 1994, NATO did carry out air strikes against Serbian planes in "no-fly" zones and against Serb artillery shelling Sarajevo. Bosnian Serbs nonetheless succeeded in displacing Muslims from much of Bosnia. When Bosnian Serbs in July seized the safe havens of Srebrenica and Zepa and massacred thousands of Muslims within sight of UN peacekeepers, Washington flashed a green light, whereupon the Croatian army overran Serb-held territory in northwest Bosnia and NATO intensified its air attacks. Yugoslav president Slobodan Milosevic asserted his authority over the Bosnian Serbs and agreed to a cease-fire in October 1995. A peace conference convened at Wright-Patterson Air Force Base in Ohio. The Dayton Accords of December 14, 1995, retained a Croat-Muslim Federation and a Serb Republic within a single Bosnian state, with Sarajevo to remain as a multiethnic capital. The United States agreed to contribute 20,000 personnel as part of a 60,000-member NATO implementation force that would separate the parties and assist in reconstruction.

In 1999, Kosovo became the next Balkan crisis to spark international consequences. In this largely ethnic Albanian, Muslim province of Yugoslavia, President Milosevic ordered further ethnic cleansing. When Milosovic rejected NATO's demands to halt the persecution and preserve Kosovo's autonomy, Clinton ruled out U.S. ground forces and chose air power. The NATO bombing campaign unleashed even more cruelties in Kosovo, as the Serbs systematically burned, looted, raped, and forced 800,000 Muslim refugees to flee to neighboring Albania and Macedonia. Pounded by air attacks, encircled by hostile nations, and suffering a NATO-imposed oil embargo, Milosevic relented in early June under an agreement to withdraw his forces from Kosovo, permit the return of refugees, accept a NATO security presence, and grant greater autonomy to Kosovo. The International War Crimes Tribunal at The Hague indicted and later tried Milosevic and his top aides for war crimes against the peoples of Kosovo and Bosnia.

Despite disagreements over Kosovo, America's NATO allies invoked Article V for collective defense after the terrorist attacks of September 2001, but the Bush administration declined offers of military assistance in Afghanistan. The subsequent recriminations over the invasion of Iraq raised questions about the future of the Atlantic alliance. With Condoleezza Rice reportedly proposing to "forgive Russia, ignore Germany, and punish France," could an expanded Europe forge a new partnership with the United States, or was divorce likely?

Hope and Tragedy in Africa

As communism collapsed in Eastern Europe, apartheid soon expired in South Africa. As with change in Europe, the main impetus for reversing decades of social, political, and economic discrimination came from within—in this case, from within a nation of 35 million blacks, people of mixed race, and Asians ruled by 6.7 million whites. Washington played a modest role in nurturing the process.

The Namibia-Angola agreement in 1988 prepared the way by withdrawing Cuban and South African troops from Angola. Antiapartheid organizations now found it increasingly difficult to obtain outside assistance and weapons to mount guerrilla campaigns inside South Africa. Harsh measures by Pretoria's security police also neutralized most armed black nationalist activity. Thus when South Africa's white leaders recommended negotiating an end to apartheid, beleaguered black activists responded positively.

The Bush administration pressed Pretoria to negotiate by maintaining economic sanctions. From 1986 to 1989, sanctions cost South Africa $32 billion to $40 billion. When F. W. de Klerk became president in September 1989, he lifted prohibitions against dissent, stopped executions, freed selected political prisoners, legalized banned organizations such as the African National Congress (ANC), and desegregated beaches and some housing areas. De Klerk also released the political prisoner and ANC leader Nelson Mandela in February 1990.

Twenty-six parties entered serious talks for a democratic South Africa in early 1993. Four straight years of zero economic growth helped spur compromises. Agreement finally came in September 1993, and South Africa's first all-race elections were held in April 1994. The ANC handily won, and the septuagenarian

Mandela became South Africa's first black president. After the parliament drew up a constitution, the U.S. Congress repealed sanctions. Mandela and de Klerk shared the Nobel Peace Prize in 1993. Mandela's regime welcomed U.S. aid and investment. Firms that had previously disinvested, such as Ford, Honeywell, General Electric, Sara Lee, and Citibank, quickly returned. By 1996 more than 500 U.S. companies were operating in South Africa, with a total asset value of $3.5 billion. A Truth and Reconciliation Commission attempted to heal the past.

Overshadowing much of sub-Saharan Africa, however, was the growing HIV/AIDS pandemic. In 2000, a U.S. National Intelligence Estimate predicted a "demographic catastrophe over the next twenty years" with possibly a quarter of southern Africa's population dying from the disease, thus raising the likelihood of "revolutionary wars, ethnic wars, genocides, and disruptive regime transitions." With the percentage of adults living with the virus surging from 2 to 20 percent in the first years of the new century, President George W. Bush pledged $15 billion in the global fight against AIDS. Because AIDS killed mainly adults between twenty and forty-five years old, Africa's children faced a grim future.

Ghastly television pictures of emaciated African children had helped spur U.S. intervention a decade earlier. In December 1992, George Bush senior ordered 28,150 U.S. troops to the Horn of Africa on a humanitarian mission to feed the starving population of civil-war-torn Somalia. Bush hoped that U.S. forces could restore order, move relief supplies to desperate Somalis, and then turn peacekeeping duties over to the United Nations. Operation Restore Hope succeeded at first. U.S. officials initiated cooperative relations with the most powerful Somali warlord, General Mohamed Farah Aidid, who controlled Mogadishu. Relief operations fed the hungry, and mediation efforts progressed, with clan leaders agreeing to negotiate national reconciliation. With starvation stopped, the United Nations tried to restore political stability to the country. President Clinton left 8,000 U.S. logistical troops in Somalia, along with a 1,000-person quick-reaction force. Such attempts at nation building, even under UN auspices, aroused nationalist resentment. In mid-1993 Aidid's forces attacked Pakistani peacekeeping troops, killing twenty-four. U.S. forces under UN command tried unsuccessfully to kill Aidid in a "decapitation mission."

In early October, nineteen U.S. Army Rangers died in a bloody firefight. A shocked Clinton watched television pictures of dead U.S. soldiers being dragged through the streets of Mogadishu by seemingly jubilant Somalis. Convinced that public opinion opposed the sacrifice of "one American life," he withdrew all U.S. forces by April 1994, leaving the mission to the UN. Critics identified a new syndrome— "Vietmalia, combining *Vietnam* and *Somalia*." Somalia remained tumultuous.

Just a month after U.S. personnel departed Somalia, mass killing erupted in the central African republic of Rwanda. A suspicious April 1994 plane crash that killed the presidents of Rwanda and Burundi, both members of the dominant Hutu majority, touched off massacres of the Tutsi minority that left more than 800,000 dead in eighty-nine days. With macabre television images reinforcing American stereotypes about "backward" and "savage" Africans, the Clinton administration resisted proposals for vigorous intervention, concentrated on evacuating U.S. citizens, and even instructed officials to avoid the term *genocide*. Not until the massacres had ended did Clinton order U.S. troops in July to secure the airport in Kigali so that

Nelson Mandela (b. 1918).
A founder of the African National Congress (ANC), this attorney and member of the Xhosa tribe was a young man when the white South African government jailed him in November 1962. Following his release from prison in February 1990, Mandela gave the black-nationalist salute. (Reuters/Bettmann)

relief supplies could flow directly to Rwanda and stem the flood of refugees into neighboring Burundi, Tanzania, and Zaire.

The Rwanda massacres embarrassed Washington. On visiting Africa in 1998, President Clinton apologized for not "calling these crimes by their rightful name: genocide." Washington helped create the African Crisis Response Initiative, designed to assist African countries to organize joint forces for rapid intervention in the future. Despite such plans, further fighting flared between Hutus and Tutsis in Burundi in 1996, and the next year a revolt, backed by Rwanda, Uganda, and Eritrea, toppled long-time U.S. client Mobutu Sese Seko in Zaire (renamed the Democratic Republic of Congo). The new government of Laurent Kabila promptly slaughtered thousands of Hutu *genocidaires* exiled in the eastern provinces. Over the next five years the Democratic Republic of the Congo suffered some 3.3 million "excess deaths" from combat and disease. The second Bush administration disingenuously blamed the United Nations for having "failed to act once again."

U.S. relations also fared badly with Sudan, whose Islamist regime temporarily sheltered Osama bin Laden during the mid-1990s. Washington fired cruise missiles at a Sudanese pharmaceutical plant in August 1998 in retaliation for deadly terrorist attacks by Al-Qaeda on U.S. embassies in Kenya and Tanzania. American missiles also struck targets in Afghanistan, apparently just missing bin Laden. Skeptics, however, suggested that Clinton, facing impeachment, was following a *"Wag the Dog"* strategy—so named for a contemporary movie in which a president foments a phony war to deflect attention from a sex scandal.

Elsewhere in Africa the U.S. record was mixed. Washington maintained close ties with General Sani Abacha's repressive military regime in Nigeria, which exported $6.3 billion in oil, gas, and other commodities to the United States in 1997, making it the fifth largest supplier of foreign oil. Abacha's death in 1998 began a turbulent transition to civilian rule. Although civil wars destabilized former Cold War clients such as Liberia, Sudan, Somalia, and Zaire (Congo), recent targets of U.S. assistance (South Africa, Ghana, Ethiopia, Mozambique, Uganda, and Mali) made significant political and economic progress in the 1990s. In 1996 American trade with the eleven countries of southern Africa totaled $9 billion, the equivalent of U.S. trade with Russia and former Soviet republics. During a six-nation visit in March 1998, President Clinton hailed the "beginning of a new African Renaissance," but Congress killed his proposed Africa Trade and Investment Act. Despite combined economic growth rates of 2.9 percent in 2002 (higher than the world average), Africa's future depended on solutions to the AIDS crisis and ending civil wars. Nelson Mandela's condemnation of the war against Iraq "in no uncertain terms" indicated that the Bush administration's obsession with terrorism risked a dangerous replay of Cold War disregard for African priorities.

Markets, Invasions, and Implosions in Latin America

The first Bush administration only slowly reversed past policies toward Latin America. The Western Hemisphere seemed to be advancing from military regimes to popularly elected governments (as in Argentina, Chile, and Brazil). Narcotics continued to flow into the profitable U.S. marketplace despite expensive antidrug operations; the Latin American debt, rampant inflation, and sluggish growth rates imperiled economies; a graying Fidel Castro still bedeviled Washington; an escalating crisis with Panama threatened further instability in the Caribbean. But after the Sandinistas lost elections in 1990 to U.S.-backed Violeta Barrios de Chamorro and her National Opposition Union, the civil war in Nicaragua finally ended. The civil war in El Salvador was stopped under a UN-brokered agreement in 1992, leaving Central America with staggering costs of reconstruction and reconciliation and tens of thousands dead. Latin America's economic linkage with the United States nonetheless remained strong: In 1990 40 percent of the region's exports flowed to the United States.

Bush's and Clinton's sponsorship of NAFTA, as well as the agreement to implement a Free Trade Area of the Americas (FTAA) by 2005, held the promise of a more prosperous Latin America. Disagreements over farm subsidies, as well as financial crises in Brazil and Argentina, slowed integration so that only a Central American Free Trade Agreement (CAFTA) was achieved by 2005. Debts also slowed progress. In 1990, Latin American countries owed more than $400 billion. Brazil, Mexico, and Argentina owed the most, and much of it to U.S. banks. The debt crisis hurt the United States. As debtors struggled to meet debt-service payments, they trimmed their imports; U.S. exports then slumped by billions of dollars, and North American jobs were lost. Latin migrants trying to escape grinding poverty pressed against U.S. immigration gates. The narcotics trade expanded as poor farmers turned to lucrative drug crops for income. Because health services and educational outlays had to be reduced and economic-development projects scuttled throughout Latin America, political unrest spread.

Secretary of the Treasury Nicholas F. Brady instituted a program in 1989 that provided for some debt relief and lower interest rates. Several agreements between commercial banks and Latin American governments, and backed by the IMF, cut debt burdens by about one-third. In return, Latin American debtors accepted market-opening requirements—controlling inflation, attracting foreign investment, and reducing trade restrictions. Brady's initiatives seemed to work. Spurred by NAFTA and planning for the Free Trade Area of the Americas, Latin American exports grew from an average 4.5 percent during the 1980s to 9.9 percent in the 1990s, while foreign investments leaped from $6.7 billion in 1990 to $22.4 billion in 1996. Political corruption and a growing fiscal crisis, however, triggered an "implosion" in Argentina in December 2001 when that country defaulted on its $140 billion foreign debt; the financial meltdown threatened to infect Uruguay, Paraguay, and even Brazil. Latin America in 2002 suffered its worst economic performance in two decades, with a negative growth rate of 1.1 percent. Not until the summer of 2003—after the war against Iraq that several Latin American countries opposed—did the Bush administration encourage the IMF to restructure Argentina's debt repayments.

When President Carlos Salinas of Mexico proposed a free trade agreement with Washington in 1990, he reversed more than a century of "building walls to keep out U.S. goods, investment, and influence." Embraced by the Bush administration, signed by Canada, Mexico, and the United States in 1992, approved by Congress in 1993, the resulting North American Free Trade Agreement created the world's

McDONALD
DIARIO EL HERALDO
San Pedro Sula
HONDURAS

THE AMERICAN
ADDICTION

The American Addiction.
This political cartoon from a
Honduran newspaper reflected the
Latin American perspective that
the drug crisis in the United States
stemmed not from the production
of cocaine in Latin America but
from the consumption of
dangerous drugs in North
America. Could the cartoonist also
be suggesting that the drug trade
was destroying Latin America?
(McDonald/Diario El Heraldo, San
Pedro Sula, Honduras)

largest free trade bloc, comprising 370 million people with a combined gross domestic product of $6.5 trillion. President Clinton subsequently negotiated side agreements with Mexico to protect workers' rights and environmental standards, and he mobilized an effective lobbying effort that included former presidents and secretaries of state. Bilateral trade rose by $17 billion annually between 1993 and 1996, with a $7 billion net surplus for U.S. exports. Statistics revealed 100,000 U.S. jobs lost due to NAFTA by 1997, but unemployment rates reached historic lows as the revived U.S. economy created 2.5 million new jobs per year in the mid-1990s. Despite continuing bilateral problems with drugs and illegal immigration, NAFTA promised to expand an already burgeoning "Mexamerica," the 2,000-mile border society where two cultures blended "like reluctant lovers in the night, embracing for fear that letting go could only be worse."

Many Americans believed that the flourishing drug trade endangered international stability and hence U.S. security. Between 1985 and 1995 the world production of opium and coca leaves roughly tripled, as drug prices dropped and U.S. prisons filled to capacity with people convicted of drug-related crimes. With 489 million people, 128 million passenger cars, 11.5 million trucks, and 2.2 million railroad cars passing through U.S. border inspections per year, actually finding drugs was "like trying to catch minnows at the base of Niagara Falls."

The United States spent upwards of $3 billion a year in a supply-side war against foreign sources and middlemen. Under Bush and Clinton, U.S. counternarcotics aid flowed to the Andean nations of Peru, Bolivia, and Colombia, but Washington also increasingly stressed the importance of staunching demand inside the United States itself. This apparent change stemmed in part from pressure from Latin Americans who contended that North Americans unfairly blamed them for the drug problem. "No one is forcing the gringos to snort coke, so let Washington deal with it," they seemed to say. For example, an estimated 72 million Americans (34 percent of the population) had used illegal drugs, while only 3.9 percent of Mexico's population had done the same.

Mexico had become a major source of marijuana and heroin and a major highway for South American cocaine shipments. From Bolivia, Peru, and Colombia came coca, which was processed into cocaine and crack. (Tons of opium/heroin also entered the United States from the "Golden Triangle" of Burma, Thailand, and Laos and the "Golden Crescent" of Iran, Afghanistan, and Pakistan.) Any nation that came into contact with the drug trade became exposed to corruption, drug addiction, violence, and death. Illegal drug money bribed politicians in some Latin American states. In Colombia the sharpshooters of the militarized drug cartels assassinated judges, journalists, police officers, and public officials. Leftist guerrillas called the *Sendero Luminoso* (Shining Path) used the drug trade to help finance their rebellion in Peru. Drug profits, not reinvested in long-term development, distorted regional economies; the "laundering" of "narcodollars" befouled banking systems. Colombia took courageous steps to defeat the drug lords of the Medellín and Cali cartels, only to produce the "hydra effect" of more dispersed operations and new drug fiefdoms in Mexico, Venezuela, and Brazil.

The arrest in 2002 of the principal Mexican drug lord Benjamin Arellano Felix did little to stem the traffic. Nor did Washington's direct participation in Plan

General Colin Powell's Briefing on Panama. Born in New York City in 1937, Powell earned a B.S. degree from the City University of New York before he began his military career. In 1987–1989 the army general served as assistant to the president for national security affairs, and in 1989 he was named chair, Joint Chiefs of Staff. Here he gives a briefing, on December 20, 1989, shortly after U.S. troops attacked Panama. He later served as secretary of state from 2001 to 2005. (Department of Defense)

Colombia reap much benefit. Despite $700 million per year in U.S. military aid after 1998, the Colombian government's war against narco-trafficking guerrillas had the reverse effect of increasing the production of coca and poppies (heroin). Farther south, the triborder region of Paraguay, Argentina, and Brazil had become by 2003 "the world's new Libya," where drug lords and terrorists with "widely disparate ideologies" met to "swap tradecraft." Narcotics had become "a shared tragedy for both halves of the hemisphere."

The drug issue became central to Panamanian–United States relations after General Manuel Antonio Noriega took power in 1983. As the intelligence chief of the Panama Defense Forces, he had come to know Panama's thriving world of drug trafficking. As Panamanian banks laundered drug money, Noriega became a millionaire by cutting deals with Colombia's cocaine barons. By the late 1980s his dictatorial rule and drug-running had stirred anger in North Americans eager to blame the swaggering Panamanian for U.S. drug problems.

Official Washington and Noriega had long been covert allies. As a young officer in the 1960s, Noriega received regular payments from the CIA; during the 1980s he helped train the *contras*. Thus Washington turned a blind eye to his drug trafficking until 1988, when two Florida grand juries indicted the dictator for shipping Colombian drugs to the United States. Washington froze Panamanian assets in the United States and offered Noriega a safe haven in Spain; the defiant Panamanian strongman stirred anti-*yanqui* rallies in the fall of 1989. General Powell called Noriega "a dope-sniffing, voodoo-loving thug."

In the early hours of December 20, 1989, President Bush launched Operation Just Cause. The invasion of Panama by 22,500 troops proved a violent success. A billion dollars' worth of property in Panama City was damaged and 516 Panamanians died. The resistance proved greater than anticipated. When U.S. troops finally located Noriega in the Vatican Embassy in Panama City, the psychological operations team resorted to rock-and-roll music boomed over loudspeakers to induce surrender. Among the musical messages played were "Born to Run," "Crying in the

Cuban Refrain. The cartoonist Mike Peters captures the words of nine U.S. presidents who thought they could overthrow Cuba's defiant leader. Forty years after his accession to power in 1959, an unrepentant Fidel Castro still vowed "Socialism or death" and accused Wall Street capitalists of playing "Russian roulette" with the world economy. The price of free markets, he claimed, is paid in human misery, child labor, prostitution, and drug traffic. (Mike Peters/ Dayton Daily News; © King Features Syndicate)

Chapel," "I Fought the Law and the Law Won," and "We Gotta Get Outta This Place." Foiled in his efforts to reveal CIA secrets and embarrass President Bush, Noriega was convicted of cocaine smuggling in April 1992 and went to prison.

Bush's popularity shot up after the military invasion of Panama. Democrats and Republicans alike cheered even though Bush had not consulted Congress. Critics, however, lambasted the administration for violating the UN Charter and the Organization of American States (OAS) Charter, which contain nonintervention provisions. The OAS censured the United States, and only a U.S. veto prevented a UN Security Council resolution condemning the invasion.

The U.S. military also intervened in poverty-stricken Haiti to restore a deposed president. Elected in 1990, the Reverend Jean-Bertrand Aristide fled nine months later when Haitian military leaders resisted his plans for demilitarization and social reform. A junta headed by General Raul Cedras terrorized and tortured political opponents, as Haitians tried to escape on makeshift boats. Clinton, fearing an immigration crisis, denounced the junta but ordered the U.S. Coast Guard to turn back refugees seeking asylum. "A total fuck-up," recalled Anthony Lake, as the Pentagon hesitated to use force so soon after the Somalia debacle. Not until late summer 1994 did Clinton act decisively. With a 20,000-strong invasion force set to land within thirty-six hours, a negotiating team headed by Jimmy Carter and Colin Powell persuaded the junta to step down to avert bloodshed. Operation Uphold Democracy disarmed the Haitian military, returned Aristide to power, then left on schedule in April 1995. Haiti's living standards remained the poorest in the hemisphere. Another coup in early 2004 deposed Aristide a second time, whereupon U.S. forces once again intervened temporarily to restore order.

As for Cuba, the end of the Cold War caused Castro's Cuba to retrench but not repent. Castro announced in 1992 that Cuba would no longer give military support to revolutionary movements, that Cuba was "desovietized forever." The end of Soviet subsidies produced tremendous economic hardship and thus increased the number of Cubans fleeing in makeshift rafts across the Florida Straits. After thirty-seven refugees drowned when Cuban authorities sank their hijacked boat in August 1994, rioting in Havana prompted Castro to denounce Washington for encouraging hijackers; henceforth Cuban police would not stop people from leaving so long as they did not hijack boats or planes. More than 35,000 departed in the next month. Clinton tried to "demagnetize" the United States by barring entry to the *balseros* (rafters). He then reached an agreement with Havana that increased to 20,000 the legal immigrants permitted into the United States annually, required Cuba to halt illegal immigration, and placed refugees under detention. To discourage a new exodus, Washington promised to return all future boat people to Cuba.

Bilateral efforts to resolve the refugee problem ended abruptly. Three civilian aircraft piloted by a Cuban-American group called Brothers to the Rescue flew toward Cuba in February 1996 in search of boat people. Because the Brothers organization had been warned about previous violations of Cuban air space, Cuban MiGs gave chase and shot down two of the planes, killing four crew members. "This is not *cojones* [testicles]," Madeleine Albright lectured Havana, "this is cowardice."

Congress quickly passed the Helms-Burton bill by large majorities. The legislation not only allowed U.S. citizens (including naturalized Cuban Americans) to sue foreign companies that did business using properties confiscated by the Castro regime, it also barred any relaxation of sanctions until a democratic government ruled in Cuba. When the EU claimed that Helms-Burton violated the rules of the new World Trade Organization, Clinton temporarily suspended suits against foreign firms while maintaining the punishing embargo. Castro continued to rail about North America's "canned culture" invasion that "transmits poisonous messages . . . to all families, to all homes, to all children."

Clinton instituted a modest thaw in early 1999 by authorizing U.S. citizens to send at least $1,200 a year to Cuban families and increasing passenger flights to and from Cuba. Additional Clinton reforms ran afoul of the legal-political controversies surrounding six-year-old refugee Elian Gonzalez, rescued off the Florida coast and eventually returned to his Cuban father in spring 2000 against the angry protests of Cuban Americans. Florida's decisive role in George W. Bush's disputed electoral victory that fall returned Cuban policy to Republican hard-liners. Washington spurned Castro's offer to cooperate after 9/11 in the war against terrorism and in the housing of Taliban and Al-Qaeda prisoners at the Guantánamo Bay naval base. In fall 2003, Bush tightened sanctions against Castro, prompting a Cuban diplomat to counter that Bush should "stop acting like a cowboy." The U.S. Chamber of Commerce and key corporations nonetheless continued to press Washington to end the embargo.

Mideast Quagmires

The invasion of Kuwait by Iraq on August 2, 1990, led to a significant exercise of U.S. power. Saddam Hussein cited old territorial claims to occupy Kuwait in the name of all "zealous Arabs who believe in one Arab nation." Washington feared that Hussein might next invade Saudi Arabia and thus control 40 percent of the world's oil. The senior Bush pledged: "This will not stand." He organized an international coalition of thirty countries to liberate Kuwait. By November the UN had imposed economic sanctions and demanded Iraqi withdrawal. Bush initially sent some

200,000 American troops as part of a multinational peacekeeping force to defend Saudi Arabia (Operation Desert Shield). In early November he increased the expeditionary force (including allied contingents) to 700,000. The Security Council commanded Iraq to evacuate Kuwait by January 15, 1991, or else face military attack. Bush did not announce the offensive buildup until after the November midterm elections. UN sanctions cut off 90 percent of Iraq's imports and 97 percent of its exports. Iraq replied that it would consider withdrawal from Kuwait only if Israel relinquished its occupied territories. When Bush asked for authorization to send U.S. troops into combat under a UN resolution, Congress debated for four days before a majority in both houses narrowly approved.

Operation Desert Storm began with a spectacular aerial bombardment of Iraq and Kuwait on January 16. For five weeks satellite television coverage via Cable News Network (CNN) enabled Americans to watch Tomahawk cruise missiles hit Iraqi targets and U.S. Patriot missiles intercept Iraqi Scud missiles. Bush and Baker masterfully kept the coalition intact, persuading Israel not to retaliate after Iraqi Scud attacks and keeping Gorbachev "steadfast" as allied bombs devastated Russia's erstwhile client. Finally, on February 23, hundreds of thousands of allied ground forces invaded Kuwait and eastern Iraq. Iraqi troops scrambled to leave Kuwait, blowing up 800 oil wells as they retreated. Allied aircraft flew hundreds of sorties along the "Highway of Death" from Kuwait City to Basra. After only one hundred hours of fighting on the ground, Iraq accepted a UN-imposed cease-fire. Bush exulted: "By God, we've kicked the Vietnam syndrome once and for all." Iraq's casualties numbered at least 25,000 military dead. U.S. forces suffered only 148 deaths and 458 wounded, but 140,000 service personnel were exposed to low levels of the nerve agent sarin; by 2002 more than half of Gulf War veterans had sought medical care or filed disability claims.

The elder Bush did not order troops to Baghdad to capture Saddam Hussein because he did not want to "rule Iraq" as an "occupying power in a bitterly hostile land." He hoped that the Iraqi military or disgruntled associates in the Ba'ath party would oust Saddam in a coup. Yet when Kurds in northern Iraq and Shi'ites in the south rebelled, Bush did little to help. Saddam Hussein crushed both rebellions. Public pressure persuaded Bush to send thousands of U.S. troops to northern Iraq, where the United Nations designated a "no-fly" zone prohibiting Iraqi aircraft from attacking Kurds. Hussein's survival left a sour taste for Americans who wanted a clear-cut victory.

Under Security Council Resolution 687, Iraq had to accept the inviolability of the boundary with Kuwait; tolerate the presence of UN peacekeepers on its borders; and fully disclose all chemical, biological, and nuclear weapons, including missiles, and cooperate in their destruction. What allied bombs had missed, UN inspectors tried to locate. Saddam Hussein's scientists and engineers had built nuclear facilities that were within months of producing nuclear weapons when the Gulf War began. Inspectors found and destroyed more than 100 Scud missiles, 70 tons of nerve gas, and 400 tons of mustard gas.

Saddam Hussein nonetheless continued to bedevil Washington. In retaliation for an apparent Iraqi assassination plot against former president Bush, Clinton ordered missile attacks on Baghdad in 1993. He sent 36,000 troops to Kuwait the following year to deter Iraqi military movements southward, and then bombed Iraq again in 1996 when Hussein crushed a Kurdish revolt in northern Iraq. UN sanctions to force removal of all weapons of mass destruction reportedly contributed to the deaths of many Iraqi civilians, including half a million children. Asked about the human costs, Secretary Albright replied that "the price is worth it." Baghdad played a six-year shell game by interfering with UN inspectors as they searched for chemical weapons and biological stores of anthrax, botulinum, and aflatoxin. The Iraqi government protested the UN inspection teams' sharing of intelligence data with U.S. officials—information later used to target sites for U.S. air strikes. In February and November 1998 the United States rushed forces to the Persian Gulf, each time deferring attack when Iraq promised complete access for inspectors.

When Saddam Hussein again stiff-armed UN inspectors on the eve of Clinton's impeachment in December 1998, the president launched a joint Anglo-American bombing campaign aimed at "degrading" Iraq's military capabilities. Several hundred Tomahawk missiles (more than in the Gulf War) fired over a period of four days targeted suspected weapons sites but also provoked criticism from China, Russia, and France. Clinton weighed options for "regime change" in Iraq, but the war in Kosovo and renewed violence between Israelis and Palestinians in autumn 2000 diverted his attention. Meanwhile, Saddam Hussein defied the new UN Monitoring, Verification, and Inspection Commission (UNMOVIC). The second Bush administration did little more than propose "smart sanctions" until the 9/11 attacks seemed to suggest links between terrorism and so-called rogue regimes. Planning for the invasion of Iraq quickly followed.

Not surprisingly, both wars against Iraq influenced the Arab-Israeli peace process. When the elder Bush took office in 1989, Secretary Baker pressed both sides but especially implored Israel: "Forswear annexation. Stop settlement activity." The end of the Cold War actually improved the diplomatic climate. No longer subsidized by the Soviet Union, Yasir Arafat also alienated oil-rich Saudi Arabia and the Gulf emirates by his ill-fated backing of Iraq during the 1991 war. When Israel showed restraint in the face of Iraqi missile attacks and Washington promised an expanded peace process after the war, Arafat reluctantly cooperated.

A breakthrough came after secret meetings between Israeli and PLO representatives in Norway. In September 1993, Israeli prime minister Yitzhak Rabin and Arafat signed in Washington a declaration of principles for eventual Palestinian self-rule in the Gaza Strip and in the Jericho area of the West Bank. Israel and Jordan signed a peace accord in July 1994 after the United States agreed to forgive Jordan's foreign debt, but Syria refused to make peace despite a visit by Clinton to Damascus.

Rabin's assassination in November 1995, Palestinian terrorist bombings, and the election of hard-line prime minister Benjamin Netanyahu in 1996 stalled the peace process. At a nine-day summit in Maryland in October 1998, Arafat and Netanyahu did agree to some Israeli pullbacks in return for changes in the PLO Charter calling for Israel's destruction. Secret Israeli–PLO negotiations in Stockholm set the stage for what was supposed to be a final peace agreement at Camp David in July 2000. Despite Israel's apparent willingness to cede much of the West Bank, the Camp David summit foundered over details. The Likud leader Ariel Sharon's visit in September to Jerusalem's Temple Mount, a disputed area, ignited Palestinian clashes that quickly escalated into a second *intifada*. The violence increased after Sharon became prime minister in early 2001. Viewing Sharon as an ally in the war against terrorism, George W. Bush did not personally intercede until after the successful invasion of Iraq, when he arranged in June 2003 a summit between Sharon and the new Palestinian prime minister Mahmoud Abbas. Despite Bush's promise, to "ride herd" on the resulting "road map," diplomacy foundered again in the face of Palestinian suicide bombings, Israeli assassinations of Palestinian leaders, and Sharon's insistence on retaining Jewish settlements in occupied territory. Not until Arafat's death and Abbas's election as Palestinian president in early 2005 did negotiations resume under a fragile truce.

Feuding and Trading with China, Vietnam, and Japan

Human rights and trade issues continued to dominate U.S. relations with Asia under the Bushes and Clinton. During the night of June 3–4, 1989, Chinese soldiers and tanks stormed into Beijing's Tiananmen Square. Hundreds—perhaps thousands—of demonstrators lay dead. For weeks unarmed students had been holding peaceful prodemocracy rallies and appealing for talks with government leaders. China's octogenarian rulers saw the students' call for political liberalization to match economic reforms as an attempt "to create chaos under the heavens." Deng Xiaoping thereupon crushed the prodemocracy movement and ordered the arrest and execution of protesters. With Tiananmen "a record-breaking world event on television," world opinion became outraged.

Prodemocracy Courage, Tiananmen Square, Beijing, China. In early 1989 university students and sympathizers camped in Beijing's great square. They made hopeful speeches about democracy and even built a towering replica of the Statue of Liberty. Drawing inspiration from Poland's Solidarity movement, the young prodemocracy activists pleaded with their nation's aged leaders to liberalize China's politics. In June the military swept into the square. After the massacre, one person—probably a student—braved tanks in a sobering example of the classic contest between the courageous individual and the powerful state. (AP/Wide World Photos)

Bush signaled China that he wanted to keep relations intact. He suspended weapons sales and deferred new World Bank loans to China but continued Beijing's most-favored-nation trade status. Convinced that global security required stable and friendly Sino-American ties, Bush sent Brent Scowcroft secretly to Beijing on June 30 with the message that "we can do a lot more for them when they aren't killing their own people." Critics charged that the United States was shortsightedly siding with China's elderly clique while alienating the nation's younger, progressive, future leaders. Bush cheered such leaders in Prague but snubbed them in Beijing.

Despite China's negative record on human rights, its economy boomed during the 1990s. U.S. trade with China reached $33.1 billion in 1992, with an $18.3 billion surplus in China's favor; by 1997 the figures climbed to $63 billion and $39.5 billion. The Clinton administration renewed China's most-favored-nation trading privileges in June 1993 after the Beijing government released several prominent dissidents. Beijing's establishment of diplomatic ties with South Korea in 1992, its growing trade with Seoul, and its pressure on North Korea to permit international nuclear inspection also pleased Washington. When Clinton again granted China most-favored-nation status in 1994, he frankly declared that human rights and trade issues were henceforth delinked.

Tensions nonetheless increased after a visit by Taiwan's president to his Cornell University alma mater in May 1995. Accusing Washington of a plot to "divide, weaken, and contain China," Beijing precipitated a crisis in March 1996 by firing three ballistic missiles close to Taiwan and conducting military exercises in the Taiwan Strait. Secretary of Defense William Perry warned of "grave consequences," as two U.S. carrier task forces steamed ostentatiously toward the region. Both sides soon backed off, as the United States reaffirmed its support of "one China," and the Chinese agreed not to sell nuclear technology to states that supported terrorism. A week-long state visit to the United States by Chinese president Jiang Zemin in October 1997 promised a "constructive strategic partnership."

The second Bush administration reignited tensions in early 2001 when a U.S. surveillance aircraft collided with a Chinese jet and crash-landed on Hainan Island. No sooner did Bush apologize than he announced arms sales and "whatever it takes to help Taiwan defend itself." Again 9/11 altered the landscape, as Bush made two fruitful trips to China and President Jiang Zemin visited Bush's Texas ranch in October 2002. With China becoming a full member of the World Trade Organization, Secretary Powell promised the "three Cs"—a "candid, constructive, and cooperative relationship." Despite its opposition to the war against Iraq, Beijing cooperated in containing North Korea's nuclear threat. The instant popularity of seven-foot-six-inch Yao Ming as a member of the Houston Rockets basketball team also enhanced China's image in the United States.

U.S. relations with Vietnam also improved. In fall 1992, President Bush announced the "last chapter of the Vietnam War" after a full accounting of the 2,265 U.S. military personnel still listed as missing in action (MIAs). The Clinton administration then lifted the nineteen-year-old trade embargo in February 1994. Within hours PepsiCo erected a giant, inflated can of soda in the middle of Ho Chi Minh City and gave away 40,000 cans of the international soft drink. General Electric set up offices two blocks from the infamous "Hanoi Hilton" prison. Despite a devastating war and two decades of isolation, many of the 71 million Vietnamese apparently retained a certain attraction to things American. Hanoi undoubtedly saw a strong U.S. economic presence as a possible counter to its giant neighbor China.

President Clinton established full diplomatic relations in July 1995, and his appointment as ambassador of Pete Peterson, a former prisoner of war in North Vietnam for seven years, defused much of the resentment against normalization. Ironically, the economic growth fueled by foreign investment ($8.6 billion in 1996) most benefited the south where Nike and other companies utilized infrastructure left by the Americans. Just as joint historical symposia on the Vietnam War helped to reconcile the past, so did Colin Powell's visit to Hanoi in 2001 wherein the former U.S. soldier wowed his hosts by singing the country classic "El Paso" during an off-the-record talent show.

Trade issues dominated the Japanese-American relationship as well. Anti-Americanism in Japan and "Japan bashing" *(Nihon tataki)* in the United States bedeviled the world's two major economies. In 1990 the world's ten largest banks had headquarters in Japan. Japan's biggest company, NTT, was more than twice the size of America's leading corporation, IBM. By 1990 the dollar-rich Japanese controlled 25 percent of California's banking assets and owned almost half of downtown Los Angeles. When Japanese firms acquired the MCA and Columbia movie studios in the early 1990s, it seemed that Godzilla was mounting a cultural invasion.

Predictions of Japan's global economic hegemony soon fizzled. The Japanese variant of capitalism, with close ties among corporate "families" of manufacturers, suppliers, exporters, and banks, proved ill-adapted to globalization. Japan's highly structured society encouraged high production and savings from its citizens but discouraged bold Japanese entrepreneurs equivalent to America's Ted Turner or Bill Gates. As the New York stock exchange soared in the mid-1990s, Tokyo's Nikkei average slumped to half the levels of the late 1980s. U.S. exports to Japan jumped from $27 billion in 1986 to $47.8 billion in 1992 to $66 billion in 1997, even though the trade deficit (in Japan's favor) still hovered around $50 billion in the mid-1990s. McDonald's ranked as Japan's largest restaurant chain by 1995 and Apple Computer became the second largest vendor of personal computers. After Japanese banking losses during the Asian financial crisis of 1997–1998, the $8 trillion U.S. economy stood roughly twice as large as Japan's. Nonetheless, Tokyo still maintained large trade surpluses, with every dollar earned adding to Japan's huge foreign investments.

Washington much valued Japan's close military alliance with the United States and its shouldering of more of the mutual defense costs. American officials praised Tokyo for providing economic assistance to developing nations such as the Philippines. North Korea's nuclear ambitions and China's potential menace to Taiwan reinforced Tokyo's desire for continuing military ties even in the absence of a Soviet enemy. Relations were temporarily strained by the rape of a twelve-year-old girl on Okinawa by three U.S. servicemen in 1995, and in 2001 when the nuclear submarine *Greenville* accidentally rammed a Japanese fishing boat and killed nine. Apologies for such incidents helped to maintain the U.S.-Japan security alliance, including Tokyo's $40-billion-per-year self-defense forces (plus paying 70 percent of burden sharing for U.S. troops in Japan). As the new millennium began, many Americans still held ambivalent attitudes about their erstwhile enemy and long-time ally—as "miracle and menace, docile and aggressive, fragile blossom and Tokyo Rose."

Global Bewilderments and Opportunities

"Gosh, I miss the Cold War," President Clinton half-joked after American soldiers were killed in Somalia. Indeed, the post–Cold War era seemed less manageable than the bipolar system it replaced—so full of "terrorists"; so rife with religious, tribal, and ethnic tensions; so overarmed; so wracked by economic catastrophes; so divided on the basis of gender; so plagued by illicit drugs, crime, and AIDS; so threatened by the proliferation of nuclear weapons and the deterioration of the natural environment; so burdened by overpopulation and famines.

Arms sales accelerated across the post–Cold War world. Showing up in the world arms market were U.S. Stinger missiles that the Reagan administration had given in the 1980s to radical Islamic rebels in Afghanistan. After the Soviet withdrawal, Reagan's Afghan "freedom fighters" used the weapons against their rivals, became traffickers in heroin, trained *jihad* terrorists and assassins, and suppressed the rights of indigenous Afghan women. The United States continued to export $15 billion in weapons each year as Third World governments lined up to buy with money better spent on health and education.

Other weapons posed deadly threats. The release of sarin gas into the Tokyo subway by a Japanese religious cult in 1995 and the mysterious deaths of five American anthrax victims after 9/11 raised the chilling specter of biological and chemical terrorism. With biological weapons banned since 1972, the 1993 Chemical Convention (ratified by Washington in 1997) required signatories to destroy all chemical weapons by the year 2005 and to submit to rigorous inspection. More than one hundred nations in 1997 signed a treaty banning antipersonnel land mines, but

A North Korean Nuclear Threat?
This cartoon depicts North Korean dictator Kim Jong Il "flashing" a nuclear threat against Uncle Sam in late 2002. Although President George W. Bush had publicly declared his loathing of Kim, a "pygmy" who was "starving his own people" in "a Gulag the size of Houston," Washington's ensuing war against Iraq kept the Korean crisis on the back burner for the next year. North Korea's 1-million-man army and potential nuclear capability also reinforced the scholar Leon Sigal's maxim that "you don't want to get into a pissing match when the other guy has a full bladder." (Dan Wasserman, Copyright © 2002, Tribune Media Services. Reprinted with permission.)

President Clinton refused to sign it because U.S. troops in Korea relied on mines to protect against a North Korean attack.

Nuclear proliferation remained a grave threat to all nations. Even though South Africa dismantled its nuclear weapons after 1993, Israel, Pakistan, and India had all joined the nuclear club, and others such as Iran, Iraq, and North Korea aspired to do so. Pakistan dismissed its chief scientist in early 2004 for illegally sharing nuclear technology with Iran and Libya, shortly after both countries agreed to curtail their weapons programs and accept UN inspections. As for the former Soviet republics, Congress provided nearly $1.5 billion to help Russia, Belarus, Ukraine, and Kazakhstan dismantle much of the former Soviet nuclear arsenal and safeguard the remaining nuclear materials inside Russia. In a "Megatons to Megawatts" arrangement, President Clinton promised to buy from Russia 500 metric tons of highly enriched uranium over a 20-year period for $12 billion. Calling nonproliferation "one of our nation's highest priorities," Clinton did what he could to prevent "nuclear yardsales" and to maintain nuclear security inside Russia.

The discovery that North Korea had accumulated enough plutonium to make several atomic bombs spawned a short-lived crisis in the early 1990s. Pyongyang threatened to withdraw from the Nuclear Proliferation Treaty (NPT), which North Korea had signed in 1985. A "private" visit by former president Jimmy Carter to North Korea in October 1994 brokered an agreement whereby North Korea agreed to halt its nuclear weapons program and submit to international inspection; in return Washington promised $4 billion in energy aid. The matter remained quiescent until autumn 2002, when North Korea admitted to cheating on nuclear weapons, withdrew from the NPT, and threatened to turn Seoul into a "sea of fire" unless the

United States signed a nonaggression pact. Protracted negotiations among the United States, China, Russia, Japan, and North and South Korea sought to achieve "multilateral security."

"Until now the cold war provided an alibi" to ignore many global issues, wrote a leading analyst. "No longer." The deterioration of the international environment and deteriorating public health threatened to undermine international stability. A sample of recent data revealed problems:

- In 2005 British Prime Minister Tony Blair identified global climate change as "the Number One threat on humanity in the 21st century."

- Every year, 8 million people die of AIDS, tuberculosis, and malaria, predominantly in poor countries.

- An earthquake near Sumatra in December 2004 triggered tidal waves (or tsunamis) that killed hundreds of thousands of victims around the Indian Ocean littoral.

- Plants worldwide are blooming an average 5.2 days earlier per decade, and animals are migrating toward cooler climates—further evidence of global warming.

- In 2002, 3.2 million people died of AIDS and about 42 million people were living with HIV/AIDS. Forty-five million more will become infected by 2010.

- "World food production will have to increase by more than 75% over the next thirty years to keep pace with population growth," a UN official has estimated.

- With an estimated 2.7 million children dying every year of infectious diseases preventable by vaccines, multibillionaire Bill Gates has committed $1.4 billion to support the Global Alliance for Vaccines and Immunizations.

As evidenced by "collapsing fisheries, falling water tables, shrinking forests, dying lakes, crop-withering heat waves, and disappearing species," the world faced a host of borderless issues. Continued growth in population meant a greater use of scarce resources, more pollution, more disease, and more famines such as those that wracked Africa in the 1980s and 1990s. Overgrazing and tree cutting in countries such as Bangladesh produced quick runoffs of rainfalls and flooding, washing away precious topsoil and killing many. In turn, these ecological/economic problems generated political instability and social disintegration. Yet the first Bush administration vetoed monies for the UN Population Fund in 1989 because the agency supported birth-control programs that allowed abortions. Because Washington did not want the 1982 Convention on the Law of the Sea to restrict private American business, not until fall 1997 did President Clinton transmit the treaty to the Senate, where it still remains pending.

If China became "rich in exactly the same way we got rich," President Clinton noted in 1996, "we won't be breathing very well" and will face "irreparable damage to the global environment." Yet less developed countries resented lectures from industrial nations that had perpetrated environmental wrongs for decades. At the 1992 Earth Summit in Rio de Janeiro, attended by 178 nations, Bush senior spoke against strong environmental protection rules, charging that they would cost jobs. He refused to sign the Biodiversity Treaty designed to slow the loss of endangered species. Clinton, however, signed the treaty in 1993 (it still remains pending in the Senate).

Deforestation of the Amazon.   The burning of tropical forests in order to open land to farming, grazing, and settlement has eliminated hundreds of plant and animal species. The clearing has also accelerated soil erosion and filled the atmosphere with carbon dioxide, one of the greenhouse gases causing global warming. In the years 1981–1990, more than 40 million acres of tropical forests were lost each year. The photograph on the left was taken by Skylab 2 in 1973 on a partly cloudy day in the Amazon basin. The photograph on the right, taken by the crew of the space shuttle *Discovery* in 1988, reveals the effects of burning as thick smoke covers the same area. (Courtesy of NASA)

"We do not have generations," noted the Worldwatch Institute's Lester R. Brown. "We only have years in which to turn things around." Entertainers regularly supported environmental causes, most notably the rock star Bono's tour in 2002 to publicize relief for debt-ridden, AIDS-stricken African nations. The Clean Air Act of 1990 took steps to reduce acid rain and toxic wastes in the air. Washington also began "debt-for-nature swaps" wherein Third World nations willing to undertake major programs to protect the environment enjoyed some debt reduction.

The UN Environmental Program kept "global commons" issues alive. Eighty-six nations agreed at Helsinki in mid-1989 to phase out the manufacture and use of ozone-destroying chemicals by the year 2000; by 1994 their efforts had reduced by half the *increase* in the concentration of CFCs in the atmosphere. Through the efforts of the World Health Organization (WHO), infectious diseases such as small-pox and malaria have nearly been eliminated. Combating the global spread of AIDS is the organization's next daunting task. Genetic-engineering programs funded by the World Bank hope to launch a "gene revolution" to improve farm productivity. A conference in Kyoto in 1997 attended by 166 countries agreed to a Global Warming Convention under which developed nations must reduce carbon dioxide, methane, and other greenhouse gas emissions by 6 to 8 percent below their 1990 levels. Despite approval by Clinton, the younger Bush withdrew from the pact in 2001 "because first things first are the people who live in America."

In early 1994 the State Department focused for the first time on the treatment of women in its annual human-rights report. Its grim findings included forced sterilizations and abortions in China; coerced prostitution in Thailand and Burma; husbands killing their wives because of insufficient dowries in India; laws making adultery illegal for women but not for men in Morocco. The United Nations reported in 2000 that two-thirds of the world's 876 million illiterate people are female. Worldwide, women held only 14 percent of top managerial jobs, 10 percent of seats in national legislatures, and 6 percent of cabinet-level posts. In 1996, the United States joined Canada in making genital mutilation (2 million victims per year) and other gender-based abuses grounds for asylum. With UN conventions on the rights of women still unratified by the United States, the State Department in November 2001 indicted Afghanistan's Taliban regime for "egregious acts of violence against women, including rape, abduction, and forced marriage."

Because "information, ideas, and money now pulse across the planet at light speed," international communications issues assumed new importance. Since the 1970s, developing nations had been calling for a "New Information Order" in which the powerful developed nations would have to report news accurately and fairly. Third World critics charged that the control of information by developed nations—especially the United States—created dependency and retarded economic growth. Because of its remote-sensing satellites, the United States allegedly could marshal greater information than weaker states in negotiations on tariffs and other issues. Through the International Telecommunications Satellite Consortium (INTELSAT), founded in 1964 to coordinate the use of satellites, the United States has also preserved control of the majority of the electromagnetic spectrum for itself and its allies. By 1999, Time Warner, the world's largest TV producer, was selling thousands of hours of programs to 175 countries. Such dominance helped, for example, to increase sales of sneakers to China through video images of Michael Jordan slam-dunking a basketball. An international agreement in 1997 opened the $600 billion global telephone market to greater competition, with U.S. companies poised to increase their one-third share. Although 90 percent of the 610 billion e-mail messages on the World Wide Web were in English by 2000, experts predicted that Internet traffic in other languages will soon predominate. Electronic commerce (or "e-business") totaled $145 billion in 1999 and was expected to reach $7.29 trillion worldwide by 2004.

Powerful governments were vulnerable to opponents with easy access to the new technology. In 1989 protesting Chinese students used fax machines to communicate with the outside world. International revulsion against the Chinese crackdown was so extensive largely because the ghastly events appeared on worldwide television. Nor could Islamic censorship in Iran suppress the "tide of godlessness" represented by bootleg videocassettes of "Baywatch" and *Titanic*. In 2000 a young hacker from the Philippines launched a virus that cost some $15 billion in damages in the United States alone. Computers seized after 9/11 revealed Al-Qaeda plans to destroy U.S. power grids by attacking the computer systems that controlled them—a form of "e-jihad," or holy war on-line.

Globalization (roughly defined as the process of integrating peoples politically, culturally, and economically into a larger community) made foreign relations less foreign. The impact of NAFTA on both St. Joseph, Missouri, and Racine, Wisconsin, for example, was the loss of manufacturing jobs when textiles and refrigeration plants relocated to Mexico and the addition of employees by high-tech firms eager to take advantage of the booming export market. Even college sports became globalized, as nearly three hundred student athletes from fifty-nine countries had accepted basketball scholarships at American universities by 1998. Street protests against the effects of globalization began with the "Battle in Seattle" in 1999 and were repeated at subsequent economic summits. Many critics saw globalization as "neoimperialism wearing Bill Gates's face and Mickey Mouse's ears," exploiting "women, minorities, the poor, and developing regions. It fouls ecosystems, displaces local cultures . . . and deepens the divide (digital and otherwise) between the global haves and have-nots." A French sheep farmer became a national hero in 1999 by destroying a McDonald's restaurant to "protect culinary sovereignty." Yet the widespread popularity of the Japanese game Pokemon suggested "true cultural globalization, not just Americanization." For good or ill, contemporary globalization grew "farther, faster, cheaper and deeper."

What the veteran analyst George F. Kennan called the global "bewilderments" of the new millennium were accompanied by pressing domestic problems. Americans ballyhooed victory in the Cold War, but "why doesn't it feel better?" asked one journalist. The United States in 1998 trailed twenty-two other leading industrialized nations in high school graduation rates. Even with a revived economy and balanced budget by 2000, America suffered an increasing division between rich and poor; millions unable to afford medical insurance and adequate health care; workers losing jobs as corporations "outsourced" abroad. Clinton warned that the "currency of national strength in this new era will be denominated not only in ships and tanks and planes, but in diplomas and patents and paychecks."

As demonstrated after 9/11, however, America's military might and global reach grew ever more predominant. Even during the Clinton years, the defense budget remained on "Cold War autopilot" ($270 billion in 1999) and the Pentagon developed new weapons systems and strategies for use against "rogue" states and terrorists. The air force emphasized "stealth" aircraft that could deliver "smart" bombs and missiles without alerting enemy radar. The navy reluctantly planned new generations of cruise-missile ships to replace its aging supercarriers. The army stressed hand-to-hand combat by small units of "Rangers" at some cost to historically preferred large-scale battles of maneuver by division and corps, and the Marine Corps rose to a new level of parity with the other services as the arm that could most readily attack from the sea. Dubbed Tomahawk Diplomacy after the American cruise missile of choice, the new strategy smacked of nineteenth-century "gunboat diplomacy"—the arbitrary application of military and naval force against less "civilized" people to teach them proper behavior. The military increasingly took on the roles of peacekeepers and nation builders in such faraway places as Somalia, Haiti, Afghanistan, and Iraq. Carrier task forces even brought humanitarian assistance to tsunami victims in the Indian Ocean in early 2005.

The second Bush administration added its own impetus to this "revolution in military affairs." Secretary Rumsfeld spurred the military bureaucracy to move faster and assume more risks. The younger Bush worried less about U.S. casualties and preferred "boots on the ground" to putting "a million-dollar missile on a five-dollar tent." Not only did the Bush team wage two victorious wars halfway around the world in two years, but it also forged military ties and base agreements with former Soviet clients from Eastern Europe to Central Asia. All told, some half million uniformed and civilian personnel served in 725 military installations abroad under Bush. "Homeland security" (including a new Cabinet-level department) became part of national security, as Congress passed the Patriot Act in autumn 2001 that expanded the federal government's power to conduct electronic surveillance, hold military trials for suspected terrorists, and other activities that arguably infringed on basic civil rights. Legal arguments that the Geneva Convention did not apply to terrorists led to abuses, including torture, reported desecration of the Koran, and sexual humiliation of Iraqi prisoners by U.S. military personnel at Abu Ghraib prison near Baghdad in 2004. Further, the new Bush Doctrine of military preemption, including the possible first use of nuclear weapons, against emergent threats "before they are fully formed" caused as much "shock and awe" as did the invasion of Iraq. The president pledged to maintain "military strengths beyond challenge." Indeed, with more than twice the resources of any two countries, U.S. military power overshadowed all potential rivals for the near term, perhaps prolonging what political scientists call a "unipolar moment" through "command of the commons" (seas, space, and air). Moreover, with American products from velcro to videos to Viagra popular everywhere, America's soft power matched its hard power.

Condoleezza Rice (b. 1954). President George W. Bush's former assistant for national security affairs became the nation's sixty-sixth secretary of state in January 2005. She thus became "America's face to the world," in Bush's words. (AFP/Getty Images)

Such extraordinary power prompted observers to ruminate, both positively and negatively, about an American global empire. One critic acknowledged an "informal" empire "richly equipped with imperial paraphernalia: troops, ships, planes, bases, proconsuls, local collaborators, all spread around the luckless planet." The second Bush administration's haughty, go-it-alone style led many, including allies, to see Uncle Sam as the playground bully; the French coined the pejorative label "hyperpower" and pinned it on Washington. Still others argued that Americans "don't really have what it takes to rule the world," that Americans are much better at conquering than "running a screwed-up sun-scorched sandpit like Iraq." Diplomacy receded as a method to resolve differences, and the Bush administration frequently ignored or bypassed the United Nations as that "chatterbox on the Hudson." When the occupation of Iraq became "untidy," Bush's appeal to the United Nations to help the "young democracy" met a "chilly" reception.

"We are the only country capable of projecting power globally and often the only one with impartial standing to mediate disputes," Clinton's national security adviser Sandy Berger had written prophetically in 2000. "If we fail to support our friends, . . . nations will increasingly coalesce against us." A British journalist wrote similarly of the "paradox" of American power—"too great to be challenged by any other state, yet not great enough to solve problems such as global terrorism and nuclear proliferation." After 9/11, nervous Americans pondered and debated such advice, mindful of both the good and bad consequences of their behavior—much as they had done throughout their history.

FURTHER READING FOR THE PERIOD SINCE 1989

Some works listed in Chapter 11 also cover topics in this period.

For studies of 9/11 and after, see Tariq Ali, *Bush in Babylon* (2003); Jon Lee Anderson, *The Fall of Baghdad* (2004); Anonymous, *Imperial Hubris* (2005); Andrew Bacevich, *American Empire* (2002) and *The New American*

Militarism (2005); Sara Beck and Malcolm Downing, eds., *The Battle for Iraq* (2003); Walter Brasch, *America's Unpatriotic Acts* (2004); Stephen Brill, *After* (2003); Matthew Brzezinski, *Fortress America* (2004); Jason Burke, *Al Qaeda* (2004); Richard Clarke, *Against All Enemies* (2004); John K. Cooley, *An Alliance Against Babylon* (2005); Steve Coll, *Ghost Wars* (2004); Anthony H. Cordesman, *Terrorism, Asymmetric Warfare, and Weapons of Mass Destruction* (2001) and *The Gulf War* (2003); Richard Crockett, *America Embattled* (2003); Mark Danner, *Torture and Truth* (2005); Mary L. Dudziak, ed., *September 11 in History* (2003); Jim Dwyer and Kevin Flynn, *102 Minutes* (2005); David Enders, *Baghdad Bulletin* (2005); Norman Friedman, *Terrorism, Afghanistan, and America's New Way of War* (2003); David Frum and Richard Perle, *An End to Evil* (2003); Karen J. Greenberg and Joshua Dratel, eds., *The Torture Papers* (2005); John Lewis Gaddis, *Surprise, Security, and the American Experience* (2004); Rohan Gunaratna, *Inside Al Qaeda* (2002); David Harvey, *The New Imperialism* (2003); Seymour Hersh, *Chain of Command* (2004); Dilip Hiro, *War Without End* (2002); Robert Kaplan, *Paradise and Power* (2004); Gilles Kepel, *Jihad* (2002) and *The War for Muslim Minds* (2004); Bruce Lincoln, *Holy Terrors* (2003); Sandra Mackey, *The Reckoning* (2002); Paul Murphy, *The Wolves of Islam* (2004); Williamson Murray and Robert H. Scoles Jr., *The Iraq War* (2003); Donal Neuchterein, *Defiant Superpower* (2005); Kenneth M. Pollock, *The Coming Storm* (2002); David S. New, *Holy War* (2002); Clyde Prestowitz, *Rogue Nation* (2003); Jonathan Randall, *Osama* (2004); Ahmed Rashid, *Jihad* (2002) and *Taliban* (2001); Paul Rutherford, *Weapons of Mass Persuasion* (2004); Peter Scarborough, *Rumsfeld's War* (2004); and Bob Woodward, *Bush at War* (2002) and *Plan of Attack* (2004).

Studies that emphasize the Bush-Clinton-Bush years and characteristics of the post–Cold War world include William C. Berman, *America's Right Turn* (1994) and *From the Center to the Edge* (2001) (Clinton); Michael Beschloss and Strobe Talbott, *At the Highest Levels* (1993); Meena Bose and Rosanna Perotti, eds., *From Cold War to World Order* (2002); Fraser Cameron, *US Foreign Policy After the Cold War* (2002); James E. Cronin, *The World the Cold War Made* (1996); Ivo H. Daalder and James M. Lindsay, *American Unbound* (2003); Michael Dobbs, *Madeleine Albright* (1999); Elizabeth Drew, *Fear and Loathing in George W. Bush's Washington* (2004); Craig R. Eisendrath and Melvin A. Goodman, *Bush League Diplomacy* (2004); H. Richard Frimen, *NarcoDiplomacy* (1996); Raymond Garthoff, *The Great Transition* (1994); John Robert Greene, *The Presidency of George Bush* (2000); Fred Greenstein, ed., *The George W. Bush Presidency* (2003); William Greider, *Fortress America* (1998); Stefan Halper and Jonathan Clarke, *America Alone* (2004); Mark Hertsgaard, *The Eagle's Shadow* (2002); Michael Hirsh, *At War with Ourselves* (2004); Stanley Hoffmann, *World Disorders* (1999); William G. Hyland, *Clinton's World* (1999); Chalmers Johnson, *The Sorrows of Empire* (2004); Haynes Johnson, *The Best of Times* (2001) (Clinton); John B. Judis, *The Folly of Empire* (2004); Lawrence Kaplan, *NATO United, NATO Divided* (2004); James Kitfield, *War and Destiny* (2005); Joe Klein, *The Natural* (2002) (Clinton); Paul Krugman, *The Great Unraveling* (2003); Charles Kupchan, *The End of the American Era* (2002); Lewis Lapham, *Theater of War* (2002); Robert J. Lieber, ed., *Eagle Adrift* (1997); Michael Mandelbaum, *The Dawn of Peace in Europe* (1997); Robert S. Litwak, *Rogue States and U.S. Foreign Policy* (2000); James Mann, *The Rise of the Vulcans* (2004); John Newhouse, *Imperial America* (2004); Anne Norton, *Leo Strauss and the Politics of American Empire* (2004); Joseph S. Nye, *The Paradox of American Power* (2002); Herbert S. Parmet, *George Bush* (1998); John G. Ruggie, *Winning the Peace* (1996); Stephen Schier, ed., *High Risk and Big Ambition* (2004); James M. Scott, *After the End* (1999); Todd G. Shields et al., *The Clinton Riddle* (2004); Peter Singer, *The President of Good & Evil* (2004) (George W. Bush); Paul B. Stares, *Global Habit* (1996) (drugs); Ronald Steel, *Temptations of a Superpower* (1995); Jessica Stern, *The Ultimate Terrorists* (1999); Ron Suskind, *The Price of Loyalty* (2004); Kenneth W. Thompson, ed., *The Bush Presidency* (1998); Emmanuel Todd, *After the Empire* (2004); and Robert W. Tucker and David C. Henrickson, *The Imperial Temptation* (1992).

For the dramatic changes in the Soviet Union and Eastern Europe, for why the Cold War ended, and for the consequences of these changes for U.S. foreign relations, see Timothy Garton Ash, *The Uses of Adversity* (1989), *The Magic Lantern* (1990), and *Free World* (2005); Anders Åslund, *Gorbachev's Struggle for Economic Reform* (1989); Ronald D. Asmus, *Opening NATO's Door* (2004); Archie Brown, *The Gorbachev Factor* (1996); Janusz Bugajski, *Cold Peace* (2005); Stephen F. Cohen, *Failed Crusade* (2000); Laurent Cohen-Tanugi, *An Alliance at Risk* (2003) (NATO); Dusko Doder and Louise Branson, *Gorbachev* (1990); Matthew Evangelista, *Unarmed Forces* (1999); Andrew Felkey, *Yeltsin's Russia and the West* (2002); John Lewis Gaddis, *The United States and the End of the Cold War* (1992); Carlotta Gall and Thomas de Waal, *Chechnya* (2002); Marc Garcelon, *Rev-*

olutionary Passage (2005); Michael Hogan, ed., *The End of the Cold War* (1992); Jerry F. Hough, *Democratization and Revolution in the U.S.S.R., 1985–1991* (1997); Andrew Jack, *Inside Putin's Russia* (2005); Robert G. Kaiser, *Why Gorbachev Happened* (1991); William W. Kaufmann, *Glasnost, Perestroika, and U.S. Defense Spending* (1990); Richard Lebow and Janice Gross Stein, *We All Lost the Cold War* (1993); Allen Lynch, *The Cold War Is Over— Again* (1992); Michael Mandelbaum, ed., *Central Asia and the World* (1994) (former Soviet republics); Michael McCgwire, *Perestroika and Soviet National Security* (1991); Thomas G. Paterson, *On Every Front* (1992); T. R. Reid, *The United States of Europe* (2004); David Remnick, *Lenin's Tomb* (1993); David Satter, *Darkness at Dawn* (2004); Robert Service, *Russia* (2003); Lilia Shevtsova, *Putin's Russia* (2005); William C. Wohlforth, *Cold War Endgame* (2003); Christopher I. Xenakis, *What Happened to the Soviet Union* (2002); and Ivan Zasoursky, *Media and Power in Post-Soviet Russia* (2002).

For Germany and reunification, see Timothy Garton Ash, *In Europe's Name* (1993); Dan Diner, *German Anti-Americanism* (1995); Michael A. Freney and Rebecca S. Hartley, *United Germany and the United States* (1991); Charles S. Maier, *Dissolution* (1997) (East Germany); and Stephen F. Szabo, *The Diplomacy of German Unification* (1992).

For the wars in the former Yugoslavia and the international response, see Michael E. Brown, ed., *The International Dimensions of Internal Conflict* (1996); Norman Cigar and Paul Williams, *Indictment at the Hague* (2002); Donald C. F. Daniel et al., *Coercive Inducement and the Containment of International Crises* (1999); James Gow, *The Triumph of the Lack of Will* (1997), John Hagan, *Justice in the Balkans* (2003); David Halberstam, *War in a Time of Peace* (2001); Kemal Kurspahic, *Prime Time Crime* (2003); Matthew McAllester, *Beyond the Mountains of the Damned* (2002) (Kosovo); Miron Rezan, *Europe's Nightmare* (2001) (Kosovo); Cees Wiebes, *Intelligence and War in Bosnia, 1992–1995* (2003); and Susan L. Woodward, *Balkan Tragedy* (1995).

The spread of nuclear weapons and efforts at nonproliferation are explored in Graham Allison, *Nuclear Terrorism* (2004); Ronald J. Bee, *Nuclear Proliferation* (1995); William E. Burrows and Robert Windrem, *Critical Mass* (1994); Nathan E. Busch, *No End in Sight* (2004); Jeane Gilleman, *Biological Weapons* (2004); Joseph Cirincione et al., *Deadly Arsenals* (2002) and *WMD in Iraq* (2004); Ronald E. Powaski, *Return to Armageddon* (2000); Stephen I. Schwartz, ed., *Atomic Audit* (1998); Leon V. Sigal, *Disarming Strangers* (1998) (North Korea); and Raju Thomas, *The Nuclear Nonproliferation Regime* (1997).

International economic issues are discussed in C. Fred Bergsten, *Dilemmas of the Dollar* (1996); Victoria DeGrazia, *Irrestistible Empire* (2005); Alfred E. Eckes Jr. and Thomas W. Zeiler, *Globalization and the American Century* (2003); Barry Eichengreen and Peter H. Lindert, eds., *The International Debt Crisis in Historical Perspective* (1990); Antoni Estevadeordal, *Integrating the Americas* (2004); George W. Grayson, *The North American Free Trade Agreement* (1995); Ricardo S. Grinspun and Maxwell A. Cameron, eds., *The Political Economy of North American Free Trade* (1993); Gary G. Hufbauer and Jeffrey J. Schott, *NAFTA* (1993); Kent Jones, *Who's Afraid of The WTO* (2003); Mary Cusimano Love, ed., *Beyond Sovereignty* (2003); Patrick Low, *Trading Free* (1993); John R. MacArthur, *The Selling of Free Trade* (2002); William A. Orme Jr., *Understanding NAFTA* (1996); Louis W. Pauly, *Who Elected the Bankers?* (1997); Stephen J. Randall and Herman W. Konrad, eds., *NAFTA in Transition* (1995); Maryse Robert, *Negotiating NAFTA* (2002); Peter Singer, *One World: The Ethics of Globalization* (2002); Robert Solomon, *Money on the Move* (1999); and Joseph E. Stiglitz, *Globalization and Its Discontents* (2002) and *The Roaring Nineties* (2003).

Environmental issues are explored in Richard E. Benedick, *Ozone Diplomacy* (1998); Lee-Anne Broadhead, *International Environmental Politics* (2002), David E. Fisher, *Fire and Ice* (1990); Laurie Garrett, *Microbes Versus Mankind* (1997); Thomas F. Homer-Dixon, *Environmental Scarcity and Global Security* (1993); Alexander King and Bertrand Schneider, *The First Global Revolution* (1991); Paul Klugman, *The Age of Diminished Expectations* (1990); Jeremy Leggett, *Carbon War* (2001) (global warming); Ralph B. Levering and Miriam L. Levering, *Citizen Action for Global Change* (1999); Jim MacNeill et al., *Beyond Interdependence* (1991); Jessica T. Mathews, *Preserving the Global Environment* (1990); George D. Moffett, *Global Population Growth* (1994); Spencer Weart, *The Discovery of Global Warming* (2004); and Donald Worster, ed., *The Ends of the Earth* (1989).

For refugees and relief and immigration policy, see Frank B. Bean et al., *At the Crossroads* (1998) (Mexico); John F. Hutchinson, *Champions of Charity* (1996) (Red Cross); Gil Loescher, *Beyond Charity* (1993);

Michael S. Teitelbaum and Myron Weiner, eds., *Threatened Peoples, Threatened Borders* (1995); and Reed Ueda, *Postwar Immigrant America* (1994).

For cultural relations, communications, and globalization see Royce J. Ammon, *Global Television and the Shaping of World Politics* (1999); Wilson Dizard Jr., *Digital Diplomacy* (2001); Thomas L. Friedman, *The Lexus and the Olive Tree* (1999); Richard F. Kuisel, *Seducing the French: The Dilemma of Americanization* (1993); Frank Ninkovich, *U.S. Information Policy and Cultural Diplomacy* (1996); Aviad E. Raz, *Riding the Black Ship: Japan and Tokyo Disneyland* (1999); James L. Watson, ed., *Golden Arches East* (1998); and Donald Wilhelm, *Global Communications and Political Power* (1990).

For Japan, China, and Asia, see Zachary Abuza, *Militant Islam in Southeast Asia* (2003); Victor Cha and David Kang, *Nuclear North Korea* (2004); Chu-yuan Cheng, *Behind the Tiananmen Massacre* (1990); Stephen D. Cohen, *Cowboys and Samurai* (1991); Warren I. Cohen, ed., *Pacific Passage* (1996); Bruce Cumings, *Divided Korea* (1995); Craig C. Garby and Mary Brown Bullock, eds., *Japan* (1994); Bruce Gilley, *China's Democratic Future* (2004); Peter Hays Gries, *China's New Nationalism* (2004); Sheila K. Johnson, *The Japanese Through American Eyes* (1990); Paul Klugman, ed., *Trade with Japan* (1992); Walter LaFeber, *The Clash* (1997) (Japan); David M. Lampton, *Same Bed, Different Dreams* (2000) (U.S.-China); Edward J. Lincoln, *Japan's Unequal Trade* (1990); Robert S. McMahon, *The Limits of Empire* (1999) (Southeast Asia); Andrew Nathan and Perry Link, eds., *The Tiananmen Papers* (2001); Michael O'Haulon and Mike Mochizuki, *Crisis on the Korean Peninsula* (2003); Charles Perry and Toshi Yoshihara, *US-Japan Alliance* (2003); Kenneth Pyle, *The Japanese Question* (1992); Michael Schaller, *Altered States* (1997) (Japan); Hazel Smith, *Hungry for Peace* (2005) (North Korea); Patrick Smith, *Japan* (1997); and Robert L. Suettinger, *Beyond Tiananmen* (2004).

For Africa, including intervention in Somalia, see the Brown and Daniel books cited above, and Michael Barnett, *Eyewitness to a Genocide* (2003) (Rwanda); Michael Clough, *Free at Last?* (1992); John L. Hirsch and Robert B. Oakley, *Somalia and Operation Restore Hope* (1995); Heidi Holland, *The Struggle* (1990) (ANC in South Africa); Douglas Johnson, *The Root Causes of Sudan's Civil Wars* (2004); Jeffrey A. Lefebvre, *Arms for the Horn* (1991) (Ethiopia and Somalia); Tom Lodge, *Politics in South Africa* (2004); Susan Collin Marks, *Watching the Wind* (2000) (South Africa); Robert K. Massie, *Loosing the Bonds* (1998) (South Africa); Fatima Meer, *Higher Than Hope* (1990) (Mandela); Larry Minear and Thomas G. Weiss, *Humanitarian Politics* (1995); Francis Njubi Nesbitt, *Race for Sanctions* (2004); Andrew Norman, *Robert Mugabe and the Betrayal of Zimbabwe* (2004); Samantha Power, *"A Problem from Hell"* (2002) (genocide); Sherene Razack, *Dark Threats and White Knights* (2004) (Somalia); Peter J. Schraeder, *United States Foreign Policy Toward Africa* (1994); and Jonathan Stevenson, *Losing Mogadishu* (1995).

The Palestinian question, Israel, and the Middle East are discussed in Irvine Anderson, *Biblical Interpretation of Middle East Policy* (2005); Richard J. Chasdi, *Tapestry of Terror* (2002); Deborah J. Gerner, *One Land, Two Peoples* (1990); F. Robert Hunter, *The Palestinian Uprising* (1991); Burton I. Kaufman, *The Arab Middle East and the United States* (1996); David McDowall, *Palestine and Israel* (1990); Tim Niblock, *"Pariah States" and Sanctions in the Middle East* (2002); Anne Marie Oliver and Paul Steinberg, *The Road to Martyrs' Square* (2005); Kenneth Pollock, *The Persian Puzzle* (2004); William B. Quandt, *Peace Process* (1993); Barry Rubin, *The Tragedy of the Middle East* (2004); Yezid Sayigh, *Armed Struggle and the Search for State* (1997); David Schoenbaum, *The United States and the State of Israel* (1993); Bernard Wasserman, *Israelis and Palestinians* (2003); and Eyal Zisser, *Assad's Legacy* (2002).

Iraqi-U.S. relations and the Persian Gulf War and its impact are the subject of Deborah Amos, *Lines in the Sand* (1992); Rick Atkinson, *Crusade* (1993); Lawrence Freedman and Efraim Karsh, *The Gulf Conflict* (1993); Stephen R. Graubard, *Mr. Bush's War* (1992); Khihir Hamza, *Saddam's Bombmaker* (2000); Efraim Karsh and Inari Rautsi, *Saddam Hussein* (1991); Jean E. Krasno and James D. Sutterlin, *The United Nations and Iraq* (2002); John R. MacArthur, *Second Front* (1992) (censorship); Ken Matthews, *The Gulf Conflict and International Relations* (1993); Judith Miller and Laurie Mylroie, *Saddam Hussein* (1990); Morris M. Mottale, *The Origins of the Gulf Wars* (2001); John Mueller, *Policy and Opinion in the Gulf War* (1994); Joseph S. Nye, Jr., and Roger K. Smith, eds., *After the Storm* (1992); Michael A. Palmer, *Guardians of the Gulf* (1992); Oliver Roy, *Globalized Islam* (2004); Geoff Simons, *Targeting Iraq* (2002); Jean Edward Smith, *George Bush's War* (1992); Kenneth R. Timmerman, *The Death Lobby* (1991); and Steve A. Yetiv, *Explaining Foreign Policy* (2004).

For U.S. relations with Latin America, see Jan S. Adams, *A Foreign Policy in Transition* (1992) (Central America); Sergio Aguayo, *Myths and (Mis)Perceptions* (1998) (Mexico); Peter Andreas, *Border Games* (2000) (Mexico); John Booth and Thomas Walker, *Understanding Latin America* (1993); Maxwell A. Cameron and Brian W. Tomlin, *The Making of NAFTA* (2001); Richard Crandall, *Driven by Drugs* (2002) (Colombia); Timothy J. Dunn, *The Militarization of the U.S.-Mexico Border* (1996); H. Michael Erisman, *Cuba's Foreign Relations in a Post-Soviet World* (2002); Guy Gugliotta and Jeff Leen, *Kings of Cocaine* (1989); Patrick J. Haney and Walt Vanderbush, *The Cuban Embargo* (2005); Susanne Jonas, *The Battle for Guatemala* (1991); Walter LaFeber, *Inevitable Revolutions* (1993); Juan J. Lopez, *Democracy Delayed* (2002) (Cuba); Abraham F. Lowenthal, *Partners in Conflict* (1990); Abraham F. Lowenthal and Katrina Burgess, eds., *The California-Mexico Connection* (1993); Donald J. Mabry, ed., *The Latin American Narcotics Trade and U.S. National Security* (1989); Christopher Mitchell, ed., *Western Hemisphere Immigration and United States Foreign Policy* (1992); Alfredo Molano, *Loyal Soldiers in the Cocaine Kingdom* (2004); Morris Morley and Christopher McGillion, *Unfinished Business* (2002) (Cuba); Robert A. Pastor, *Whirlpool* (1992), *Integration with Mexico* (1993), *Exiting the Whirlpool* (2001), and *Cuba, the United States, and the Post-Cold War World* (2005); Leigh A. Payne, *Uncivil Movements: The Armed Right Wing and Democracy in Latin America* (2000); Joaquin Roy, *Cuba, the United States, and the Helms-Burton Doctrine* (2000); Bert Ruiz, *The Colombian Civil War* (2002); Lars Schoultz, *Beneath the United States* (1998); Peter D. Scott and Jonathan Marshall, *Cocaine Politics* (1991); Peter H. Smith, *Talons of the Eagle* (1996); Sidney Weintraub et al., eds., *U.S.-Mexican Industrial Integration* (1991); and Howard J. Wiarda, *American Foreign Policy Toward Latin America in the 80s and 90s* (1992).

For Panama and the war against Noriega, consult Kevin Buckley, *Panama* (1991); John Dinges, *Our Man in Panama* (1990); Frederick Kempe, *Divorcing the Dictator* (1990); R. M. Koster and Guillermo Sanchez, *In The Time of the Tyrants* (1990); Walter LaFeber, *The Panama Canal* (1989); John Lindsey-Poland, *Emperors in the Jungle* (2003); and Margaret E. Scranton, *The Noriega Years* (1991).

See also Robert L. Beisner, ed., *Guide to American Foreign Relations Since 1600* (2003).

For a comprehensive survey of foreign-relations topics, see the articles in the four-volume *Encyclopedia of U.S. Foreign Relations* (1997), edited by Bruce W. Jentleson and Thomas G. Paterson.

Index

Italic page numbers indicate maps, photos, illustrations, or captions.

American Asiatic Association, 18

American Century, 130

American Committee for Outlawry of War, 85

American culture: Cuba and, 228, 333; cultural relations, 43; Soviet Union and, 194; spread of, 82, 174, 190, 207; U.S. sense of superiority about, 58; Vietnam War and, 275. *See also* Culture

American Expeditionary Force, 59

American Federation of Labor, 137

American Medical Association, 297

American Military Observers Mission, 135

American National Exhibition (1959), *193*

American Peace Commission, 62

"American peril," 19

American Relief Administration, 87

American Union Against Militarism, 59

Amnesty International, 292

Amtorg Trading Corporation, 87

Anaconda Corp., 82, 261

ANC (African National Congress), 326–27

Andropov, Yuri, 299

Anglo-American Oil Company, 278

Anglo-American relations, *40;* Alaska boundary crisis and, 40; Cold War and, 163; naval cooperation, World War II, 123; Panama Canal and, 24; prior to World War II, 75; rapprochement, 8, 39–44; Venezuelan boundary dispute and, 6–7; World War I and, 51; World War II and, 119–26, 129. *See also* Great Britain

Anglo-Japanese Alliance, 36–37

Angola: CIA and, 294; Cuba and, 261, 262, 289, 307, 308, 309; independence of, 262; Namibia and, 326; Soviet Union and, 289, 300

Anthrax, 335

Anti-American feeling: in Dominican Republic, 32; in Iran, 280; in Japan, 338; in Latin America, 106, 116, 206–7, 260–61; in Panama, 284, 331; prior to World War I, 42; propaganda, 169; in Third World, 208; in Uruguay, 206–7; in Venezuela, 29

Anti-ballistic missiles (ABMs), 255, 257, 298

Anti-Ballistic Missile (ABM) treaty (1972), 256, 323

Anticolonial revolution, 200–201

Anti-Comintern Pact, 89

Anti-communist sentiments, 283, 289–91, 293, 294

Antihijacking treaty, with Cuba (1973), 261

Anti-imperialism, *97;* Cuba and, 3; Latin America and, 106; progressives and, 27;

Roosevelt, F., and, 130; Spanish-American-Cuban-Filipino War and, 14–16; waning of, 8

Anti-Imperialist League, 15–16

Antimony, 288

Antinuclear movement, 300

Antipersonnel land mines, 339–40

Anti-Semitism, 93, 136, 137

Antitrust laws, foreign trade and, 82

Antiwar movements: Nixon and, 249–50, 268; Vietnam War, 242–43, 268–69, 273; World War II, 85–87, 92. *See also* Pacifists

ANZUS Pact, 188

AP (Associated Press), 82

Apartheid, 175, 288, 307, 326

Appeasement policy, 89, 91–92, 93, 100

Apple Computer, 339

Aquino, Benigno S., 308

Aquino, Corazon, 308

Arabian-American Oil Company (Aramco), 147

Arabs: gendered language about, 202; Soviet Union and, 203; U.S. Middle East policy and, 166, 204–5. *See also* Middle East

Arafat, Yasir, 280, 306, 336

Arbitration, of international disputes, 86

Arellano Felix, Benjamin, 330

Argentia, Newfoundland, conference (1914), 119–22, 124, *133*

Argentina: anti-imperialism in, 106; drug traffic and, 331; Great Depression and, 116; human rights in, 286, 292; Mexico and, 35; military aid to, 175; Pan Americanism and, 116; United Nations and, 141

Arias Sánchez, Oscar, 303

Aristide, Jean-Bertrand, 332

Armour Corp., 71

Arms buildup, Roosevelt, F., and, 120

Arms embargo: against Spain, 92; World War II, 77

Arms sales: arms manufacturers and, 92; to belligerent nations, 74–78, 92, 93; Carter and, 292; to China, 93; to Middle East, 287; in post-Cold War period, 339; to South Africa, 307–8

Armstrong, Anne, 252

Army, 58; Air Corp, 74–78; Air Service, 58; Rangers, 327

Army League, 58

Army of the Republic of Vietnam (ARVN), 238; casualties, 216; cease-fire and, 271; problems of, 274–75; Tet offensive and, 214–16; U.S. military aid to, 234–35,

Cold War and, 195; Eastern Europe and, 324; establishment of, 170; Korean Air Lines Flight 007 crash and, 299; military arsenal, 225; Poland and, 298; Soviet Union and, 289; West Germany and, 192

North Korea: boundaries, 186; Japan and, 339; Korean War, 181–83; nuclear weapons, *340,* 340–41; as part of "axis of evil," 315; Soviet Union and, 182; Vietnam War and, 215–16

North Vietnam: China and, 249, 267, 268; communism and, 221; peace negotiations with, 268, 269–70; Soviet Union and, 267, 268; Tet offensive and, 214–17; U.S. air strikes against, 239, 242; U.S. espionage mission in, 239. *See also* Vietnam War

Novikov, Nikolai, 164

NSC-68, 170–71

NTT (company), 338

Nuclear energy, 190

Nuclear freeze, 257

Nuclear Nonproliferation Treaty (1968), 237

Nuclear Proliferation Treaty (NPT), 340

Nuclear weapons: arms limitations, 164, 193–94, 289–91, 292, 297–98, 300, 322–23; arms race, 225, 255–57; atomic bomb, 153–57, 162, 171, 176–77, 185, 186; Baruch Plan, 164; Cold War strategy, 255; Cuba and, 230–33, 261; deployment of, 257; Eisenhower and, 209; freeze, 297; glossary, 257; hydrogen bomb, 170, 200; Iraq, 335; Israel, 258; Kennedy and, 225; limited nuclear war, 297; neutron bomb, 257, 294; Nixon and, 255–56; North Korea, *340,* 340–41; parity, 255; People's Republic of China, 199; proliferation of, 176–77, 190, 191, 208, 340; Reagan and, 296–300; Soviet Union and, 170, 193–94, 230–33, 255–56, 296–300; strategic, 297–98; Taiwan Strait crisis and, 199; test ban treaties, 225, 233, 294, 320–21; testing, 171, 200; thermonuclear bombs, 170, 188, 190; uranium imports and, 175; Vietnam and, 240, 274 "window of vulnerability," 296, 297; "zero option," 297, 300

"Nuclear winter," 297

Nuremberg Laws (1935), 136

Nutrition, 266

Nye, Gerald P., 74, 77, 92

Nye Committee, 92

Nyerere, Julius K., 265

OAS (Organization of American States), 205, 206, 261, 332

Obasanjo, Olusegun, 289

Obregón, Alváro, 114

Oder-Neisse line, 256

Office of Strategic Services (OSS), 150

Office of War Information (OWI), *155*

Offshore oil drilling, 267

Ohio (ship), *25*

Oil industry and trade: Cold War and, 163; Latin America, 107, 108, 260; Mexico, 114–16; Middle East, 203; Nigeria, 288; offshore oil drilling, 267; OPEC, 254, 261; prices, 261; U.S. sales to Japan, 127

Okinawa, 171, 172

Olney, Richard, 4–6, *7,* 10

Olympia (warship), 13

Olympic Games (1904), 43

Olympic Games (1972), 259

Olympic Games (1980), 291

Omnibus Trade and Competitiveness Act (1988), 308

OPEC (Organization of Petroleum Exporting Countries), 254, 261

Open Door Policy, 18–19, 28, 36, 38, 39, 42, 97, *98,* 99, 101, 102, 106, 132; Cold War period, 176; in Eastern Europe, 160, 162; interwar period, 83; postwar period, 172

"Open Skies" proposal, 194

Operation Ajax, 278

Operation Castration, 229

Operation Desert Shield, 334

Operation Desert Storm, 334

Operation Iraqi Freedom, 316

Operation Just Cause, 331

Operation Magic, 127, 129

Operation Mongoose, 230

Operation Northwoods, 230

Operation Overlord, 130–32, *133*

Operation Restore Hope, 327

Operation Rolling Thunder, 239

Operation Torch, 130

Operation Uphold Democracy, 332

Opium, 330

Oregon (ship), 27

Organization of American States (OAS), 205, 206, 261, 332

Organization of Petroleum Exporting Countries (OPEC), 254, 261

Orlando, Vittorio, 63

Orozco, José Clemente, 114

Ortega, Daniel, 303

SS-5 missiles, 297

SS-20 missiles, 290, 297

"Stab-in-the-back" theory, 273

Stalin, Joseph: Balkans and, 318; character of, 88, *158;* China and, 104, 174, *182;* Cold War and, 158–59; death of, 186, 190, 191, 192; de-Stalinization, 194; early Cold War crises, 162–65; Eastern Europe and, 160–61; Hitler and, 88–89; Korean War and, 184–85; Molotov and, 88, *168;* NATO and, 171; on Open Door policy, 176; percentage agreement and, 145; postwar Japan and, 172; Potsdam Conference and, 148–49; Roosevelt and, 131–32; Soviet boundaries and, 130; Truman Doctrine and, 166–67; Yalta Conference and, 142–45

Standard Oil Company, 28, 92, 108, 114

Standing army, 58

"Standstill diplomacy," 259

Stark (frigate), 306

Stark, Harold R., 123

START (Strategic Arms Reduction Talks), 297–98, 322–23

"Star Wars," 298, *298,* 300

State Department: Angola and, 262; Cold War and, 197; growth of, 150; Latin America and, *227;* McCarthyism and, 192; Peace Corps and, *227;* role of, 80

Stealth bombers, 294

Steel, Ronald, 272–73

Steffens, Lincoln, 70

Stettinius, Edward R., *123,* 140–41, *158*

Stevenson, Adlai, 189, *189,* 232

Stilwell, Joseph W., 133–34

Stimson, Henry L., *79, 100,* 162; atomic bomb and, 162; China policy, *97,* 97–99, 106; Communist party and, 87; Geneva disarmament conference and, 85; Nicaragua and, 110; postwar planning and, 141; as secretary of state, 80; as secretary of war, 43, 123; World War II and, 123

Stimson Doctrine (1932), 98 100, 103

Stinger missiles, 300, 339

St. Louis Olympic Games (1904), 43

St. Louis World's Fair (1904), 17

Stockdale, James B., 239

Straight, Willard, 38, 43

Strategic Air Command (SAC), 188, 195

Strategic Arms Limitation Talks: SALT-I, 255–56; SALT II, 256, 289–92

Strategic Arms Limitation Treaty (1972), 254, 255

Strategic Arms Reduction Talks (START), 297–98, 322–23; START-I, 322; START-II, 323

Strategic Defense Initiative (SDI), 257, 298, *298,* 300

Strategic hamlet program (South Vietnam), *235,* 238

Strategic nuclear weapons, 257, 297–98

Stuart, J. Leighton, 174

Subic Bay Naval Station, Philippines, 308

Submarine-launched ballistic missiles (SLBMs), 255, 256, 297, 322; defined, 257; Trident-II, 290, 294

Submarine warfare, 46–50, 53–57, 59; Lend-Lease Act and, 124; U.S. defense against, 120–21

Sudan, 307, 328

Suez Canal: Egypt's seizure of, 204; Great Britain and, 203, 204

Sugar trade, 9, 30, 107, 111, 112, 113, 260

Summers, Lawrence, 321

Sunday, Billy, 57

SUNFLOWER (peace initiative), 244

Sun Zhongshan (Sun Yat-Sen), 71, 101–2

Surface-to-air missiles (SAM), 257, 258

Sussex (ship), 56

SWAPO (South West Africa People's Organization), 308

Swift (company), 71

Syria: communism and, 205; Egypt and, 204; mandate system and, 63; occupation of Lebanon by, 304, 305; Soviet Union and, 287; U.S. intervention in, 205

Tacna-Arica dispute, 107

Tactical nuclear weapons, 257

Taft, Robert A., 170, 183

Taft, William Howard, *17, 26;* Anglo-American relations and, 41; Caribbean region and, 42; China and, 28; Cuba and, 30; imperialism and, 27, 28; Japan and, 36, 38; Mexican Revolution and, 34; Philippines and, 16–17

Taiwan (Formosa), 134, 292; Carter and, 291–92; Chinese hostilities toward, 337; Eisenhower and, 209; Korean War and, 182, 183, 186–88; Nationalist China, 173; Nixon's China trip and, 250, 251; U.S. defense of, 198–99. *See also* Nationalist China

Taiwan Strait crises, 198–99, 337–38

Takahira, Kogoro, 36–37, 38

Talbott, Strobe, 323

Taliban government, Afghanistan, 315, 343; prisoners, 333

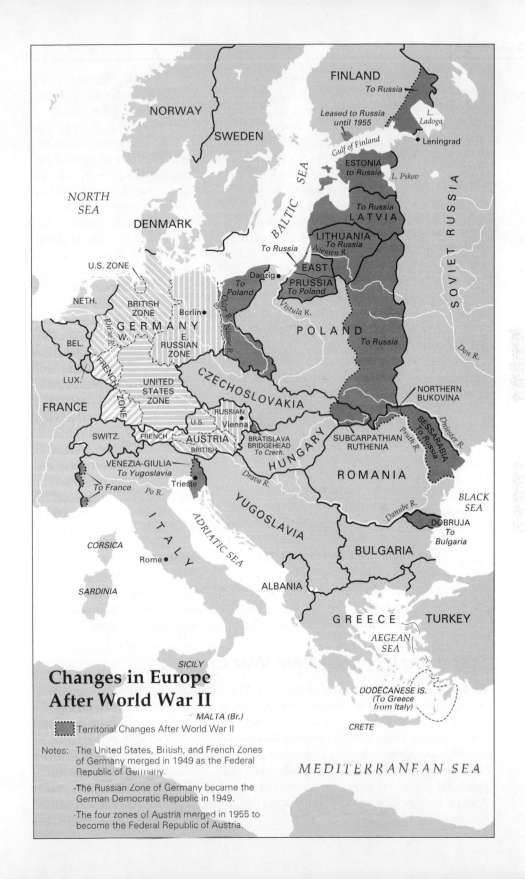

FINLAND
To Russia

Leased to Russia until 1955

L. Ladoga

NORWAY

SWEDEN

• Leningrad

Gulf of Finland

BALTIC SEA

ESTONIA
to Russia

L. Pskov

NORTH SEA

DENMARK

To Russia
LATVIA

LITHUANIA
To Russia

Niemen R.

U.S. ZONE

NETH.

GERMANY
BRITISH ZONE

Berlin •

W.

E.
RUSSIAN
ZONE

To Russia

SOVIET RUSSIA

Oder R.

Danzig •
To Poland

EAST
PRUSSIA
To Poland

Vistula R.

POLAND

To Russia

BEL.

Rhine R.

FRENCH ZONE

LUX.

UNITED
STATES
ZONE

CZECHOSLOVAKIA

FRANCE

SWITZ.

FRENCH

U.S.

RUSSIAN

Vienna •

AUSTRIA

BRITISH

BRATISLAVA
BRIDGEHEAD
To Czech.

HUNGARY

SUBCARPATHIAN
RUTHENIA

NORTHERN
BUKOVINA

BESSARABIA
To Russia

Dniester R.

Pruth R.

VENEZIA-GIULIA
To Yugoslavia

To France

Po R.

Trieste •

ITALY

ADRIATIC SEA

Drava R.

YUGOSLAVIA

ROMANIA

Danube R.

BLACK
SEA

DOBRUJA
To Bulgaria

CORSICA

Rome •

BULGARIA

SARDINIA

ALBANIA

GREECE

TURKEY

AEGEAN
SEA

SICILY

DODECANESE IS.
(To Greece from Italy)

CRETE

Don R.

Changes in Europe After World War II

MALTA (Br.)

Territorial Changes After World War II

Notes: The United States, British, and French Zones of Germany merged in 1949 as the Federal Republic of Germany.

-The Russian Zone of Germany became the German Democratic Republic in 1949.

-The four zones of Austria merged in 1955 to become the Federal Republic of Austria.

MEDITERRANEAN SEA

161

The Soviets charged the United States with a double standard. "Poland—a big deal!" Molotov complained after Yalta. "But how governments are being organized in Belgium, France, Germany, etc., we do not know. We have not been asked, . . . We have not interfered." Molotov contended that an Open Door in Eastern Europe would mean ultimate American economic domination of war-weakened nations.

Throughout 1945 and 1946 the United States sought influence in Eastern Europe to counter the Soviets. Washington tried nonrecognition of the pro-Soviet governments but abandoned that tactic when Stalin agreed to allocate a few "insignificant ministries" to noncommunists. Perhaps the atomic bomb would act as a compellent. At the London Conference in October 1945, Molotov actually asked Byrnes if he had "an atomic bomb in his side pocket." "If you don't cut out all this stalling and let us get down to work," Byrnes joked, "I am going to pull an atomic bomb out of my hip pocket and let you have it." Still, monopoly over the bomb did not budge the Soviets from Eastern Europe, and Washington never practiced a blatant "atomic diplomacy" of direct threat.

Secretary of War Henry L. Stimson rejected the bomb as a diplomatic weapon when he told Truman in September 1945 that the United States should share atomic data to spur postwar cooperation. Merely negotiating with "this weapon rather ostentatiously on our hip" would only increase Soviet suspicion and distrust, said Stimson, then seventy-eight. Commerce Secretary Henry Wallace supported Stimson, but Secretary of the Navy James V. Forrestal argued against any effort to "buy [Soviet] understanding and sympathy. We tried that once with Hitler." Truman sided with Forrestal.

The United States also used foreign aid as a diplomatic weapon in Eastern Europe. Byrnes stated the policy in 1946: "We must help our friends in every way and refrain from assisting those who . . . are opposing the principles for which we stand." In short, no loans or aid for Eastern Europe. This policy backfired, for it left those countries dependent on Soviet aid and drove them deeper into the Soviet orbit. In Czechoslovakia, for example, the United States abruptly severed an Export-Import Bank loan. Noncommunist foreign trade minister Hubert Ripka complained bitterly when U.S. officials offered 500,000 tons of wheat if they would "throw the Communists out of the Czechoslovak Government." Instead, "these idiots in Washington have driven us straight into the Stalinist camp." Truman's pressure tactics thus helped intensify the Cold War—that is, Moscow leaders read American policies as threats to their security and so tightened their grip.

Stiffening Up: Early Cold War Crises

At the London Conference of Foreign Ministers (September–October 1945), Byrnes demanded representative governments in Bulgaria and Romania before he would sign any peace treaties with the former German satellites. Molotov countered with questions about British-dominated Greece and American-dominated Japan. At the Moscow Conference in December 1945, however, Stalin permitted a token broadening of the Romanian and Bulgarian regimes and also accepted Byrnes's proposals for a general peace conference to be held in Paris and a United Nations Atomic Energy Commission to prepare plans for international control.